To Tim —

Great meeting you at Capstone —

cheering for you!

Jeff Myers

1 Chron 12:32

UNDERSTANDING
THE TIMES

A SURVEY OF
COMPETING
WORLDVIEWS

JEFF MYERS &
DAVID A. NOEBEL

UNDERSTANDING THE TIMES
Published by Summit Ministries
P.O. Box 207
Manitou Springs, CO 80829

In cooperation with
David C Cook
4050 Lee Vance Drive
Colorado Springs, CO 80918 U.S.A.

David C Cook U.K., Kingsway Communications
Eastbourne, East Sussex BN23 6NT, England

The graphic circle C logo is a registered trademark of David C Cook.

The website addresses recommended throughout this book are offered as a resource to you. These websites are not intended in any way to be or imply an endorsement on the part of David C Cook, nor do we vouch for their content.

Unless otherwise noted, all Scripture quotations are taken from the ESV® Bible (The Holy Bible, English Standard Version®), copyright © 2001 by Crossway, a publishing ministry of Good News Publishers. Used by permission. All rights reserved. Scripture quotations marked KJV are taken from the King James Version of the Bible. (Public domain.); NIV 1984 are taken from the Holy Bible, New International Version®, NIV®. Copyright © 1973, 1984 by Biblica, Inc.™ Used by permission of Zondervan. All rights reserved worldwide. www.zondervan.com; NIV are taken from the Holy Bible, NEW INTERNA-TIONAL VERSION®, NIV®. Copyright © 1973, 2011 by Biblica, Inc.® Used by permission. All rights reserved worldwide. NEW INTERNATIONAL VERSION® and NIV® are registered trademarks of Biblica, Inc. Use of either trademark for the offering of goods or services requires the prior written consent of Biblica, Inc.

LCCN 2014932409
ISBN 978-1-4347-0958-5
eISBN 978-0-7814-1378-7

© 2016 Summit Ministries

Printed in the United States of America
First Edition 2015
Second Edition 2016

2 3 4 5 6 7 8 9 10 11

051817

CONTENTS

FOREWORD

The book you are holding has a very long story. It began when I was a junior in college and was asked to lead a study group on communism. From that day until now, my interest in the subject has led me to the conclusion that Marxism is a religious worldview. And like other worldviews, it competes for allegiance. This got me wondering: How does Christianity measure up to other competing worldviews? The answer took years to sort out. The first edition of *Understanding the Times* was the finished product of that sorting-out process.

It's been over twenty-five years since those early copies of *Understanding the Times* embarked on their maiden voyages to the bookshelves and consciousness of faithful Christian readers all over the country. The original nine-hundred-page tome was a labor of love by the generous hearts of the Summit family. Shortly thereafter, partnerships were formed with Harvest House and the Association of Christian Schools International (ACSI), with hundreds of thousands of copies reaching laypeople and Christian students alike.

The impact and reception was far greater than anything we could have imagined.

In light of that history, I am deeply pleased with this revised and updated edition. Jeff and his team have completed a marvelous achievement that will take its rightful place in the long legacy of this book. Their efforts have ensured that there will be still more generations that understand the times (1 Chron. 12:32).

David A. Noebel, Founder
Summit Ministries

ACKNOWLEDGMENTS

This book began as a work of trepidation: How do you take a classic work—and one of the most popular texts on biblical worldview—and update it?

Thanks to the wisdom of teams, though, it turned into something that transformed those who were part of it. From the Verdoorn family, who helped make it financially possible, to Joey Amadee, whose tireless genius conceived and wrote every line of code for its brilliant digital delivery system, I find myself humbled and inspired.

A "who's who" of subject matter experts checked various chapters for accuracy and logic. These included Dr. Nabeel Qureshi, Dr. Hunter Baker, Dr. Paul Kengor, Dr. Douglas Groothuis, Dr. Scott Smith, Dr. Francis J. Beckwith, Dr. W. Gary Phillips, Dr. Scott Rae, Atty. Casey Luskin, Dr. Clark Rose, Prof. Ernest "Skip" Burzumato, Atty. Jeffrey Ventrella, Dr. Eric Patterson, Dr. Jay W. Richards, and Dr. Richard Shumack. Their helpful comments and insights were thoughtful and impassioned.

David Knopp was our project manager, keeping the trains running on time with the aid of the impeccably organized Amanda Bridger. My executive assistant, Tosha Payne, looked over just about every chapter and gave comments that erased errors and doubts about whether the thing was actually interesting to read.

Our editors and proofreaders, Carlos Antonio Delgado, Robert Hand, Jason Graham, Trudy Friesema, and Dr. Paul Copan read every word and made just the right suggestions in just the right places.

The entire team has dedicated hours upon hours to help me craft the best edition of *Understanding the Times*. Nevertheless, wherever this volume may be found deficient, that responsibility lies solely with me.

Our curriculum director, Roy Faletti, developed the relationships with schools that tested the whole project with their students.

I would also like to thank our Vice President of Programs, Eric Smith, who kept the Summit boat moving smoothly through the water while I wrote six hours a day for nearly a year.

My long-time friend John Stonestreet participated in brainstorming sessions and high-level edits and helped me chart a course of accuracy while avoiding theological landmines.

Finally, I would like to thank the Myers children, who patiently listened to me read from newly written chapters and then asked questions. May the understanding of what is within these pages be part of your generation's legacy.

Jeff Myers, President
Summit Ministries

PREFACE

How to Use the Understanding the Times Series

Noted Christian writer and teacher Del Tackett has said that the Understanding the Times (UTT) series needs to be the core in every high school, college, and seminary today. Colson Center president, John Stonestreet, has said that Understanding the Times should have a place in every Christian's home library. Why is this series so important for Christian students and adults in all walks of life to use often in today's complex world?

- *Understanding the Faith: A Survey of Christian Apologetics*—**the first book in the series. Christians can use the UTT series to better understand theology and apologetics.** The knowledge of a solid Christian worldview is a vital starting place for understanding God. And learning to defend the Christian worldview is critical for those who want to share their faith with an unbelieving world. Theology and apologetics aren't just academic exercises for pastors and church leaders; they are worthy endeavors for every believer.

- *Understanding the Times: A Survey of Competing Worldviews*—**the second book in the series. Christians can use the UTT series to gain biblical worldview insight.** *Understanding the Times* helps Christians understand the six major worldviews that drive today's major global events. When issues occur, *UTT* should be one of the books that Christians access to help them form a biblical response. Researchers have cited that only a minority of believers possess a proper biblical worldview. And the faithful would be well advised to know the precepts of the other five major worldviews at odds with Christianity.

- *Understanding the Culture: A Survey of Contemporary Issues*—**the third book in the series. Christians can use the UTT series to transform culture.** Once a believer is steeped in biblical theology, apologetics, and worldview, he or she can communicate biblical truth to friends, loved ones, and associates. The gospel affirms the requirement for sharing God's Word on timely topics, as well as developing strong relationships from which to influence and change cultural structures and values. UTT helps believers engage biblical faith in life areas where God has placed them today.

As a result, the UTT series is eminently useful for students, teachers, pastors, businesspeople, public leaders, and others who want their faith to make an impact on twenty-first-century society.

	SECULARISM	MARXISM	POSTMODERNISM
THEOLOGY	Atheism	Atheism	Theological Suspicion
PHILOSOPHY	Materialism & Naturalism	Dialectical Materialism	Anti-Realism
ETHICS	Moral Relativism or Utilitarianism	Proletariat Morality	Cultural Relativism
BIOLOGY	Neo-Darwinism	Punctuated Equilibrium	Anti-Essentialism
PSYCHOLOGY	Mind/Body Monism (Self-Actualization)	Mind/Body Monism (Classical Conditioning)	Decentered Self
SOCIOLOGY	Personal Autonomy	Proletariat Society	Social Constructionism
LAW	Legal Positivism	Proletariat Law	Critical Legal Studies
POLITICS	Progessivism	Statism	Political Pessimism or Liberalism
ECONOMICS	Economic Interventionism	Socialism	Economic Interventionism
HISTORY	Social Progress	Historical Materialism	Historical Revisionism

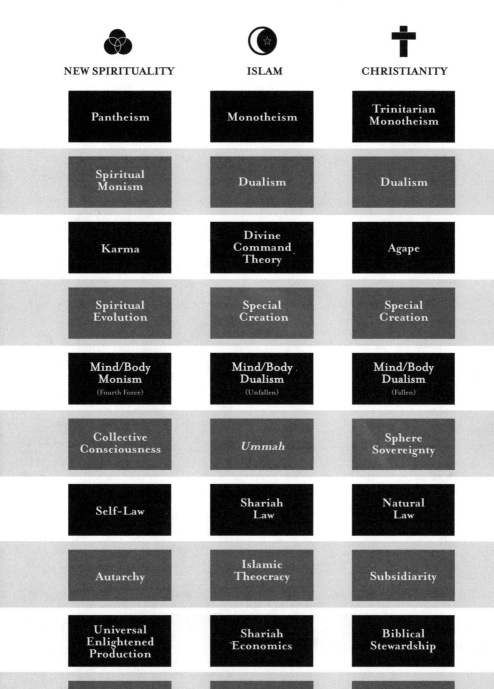

NEW SPIRITUALITY	ISLAM	CHRISTIANITY
Pantheism	Monotheism	Trinitarian Monotheism
Spiritual Monism	Dualism	Dualism
Karma	Divine Command Theory	Agape
Spiritual Evolution	Special Creation	Special Creation
Mind/Body Monism (Fourth Force)	Mind/Body Dualism (Unfallen)	Mind/Body Dualism (Fallen)
Collective Consciousness	Ummah	Sphere Sovereignty
Self-Law	Shariah Law	Natural Law
Autarchy	Islamic Theocracy	Subsidiarity
Universal Enlightened Production	Shariah Economics	Biblical Stewardship
Evolutionary Godhood	Pan-Islam	Redemptive Narrative

CHAPTER

1

THE BATTLE
OF IDEAS

1. THE SECRET TO UNDERSTANDING THE WORLD OF IDEAS

To understand the world of ideas, we must figure out how tennis champs return opponents' blazing fast serves and how chess masters memorize the position of every piece on the board.

If you've ever been on a tennis team, your coach probably told you to "keep your eye on the ball." But that's not good enough if you have to return a 150-mile-per-hour serve from former world-champion tennis player Andy Roddick. By the time you react to the serve, the ball is already past you. Yet those who played Roddick regularly returned such serves. How could they possibly do this?

> **To understand the world of ideas, we must figure out how tennis champs return opponents' blazing fast serves and how chess masters memorize the position of every piece on the board.**

Now think about how chess grand masters read the chess board. After just briefly seeing the board of a partially played chess game, they are able to remember the exact placement of the pieces. Do they have photographic memories?

Maybe tennis and chess champions are just made differently from the rest of us. Maybe they're more gifted. It would be somewhat of a relief if this were true, because we'd be off the hook for having to figure out their secrets and apply them to our own lives. But it's not that simple.

2. CHAMPIONS SUCCEED BY MASTERING THE WORLD'S PATTERNS

Champions have learned to see things differently. This gives them a level of success the rest of us find amazing. Understanding how they do it is the key to successfully navigating our complicated, confusing, and contentious world. There are two keys to unlocking the mystery.

Key No. 1: We live in a rule-governed universe. Andy Roddick can't serve the ball anywhere he likes. He has to make it land in a certain square on the court, or it doesn't count. Similarly, pieces on a chess board cannot be moved wherever the player wishes. There are rules about what each piece can do. Life is like that too. There are rules. If we can understand and live by them, we can find purpose and learn how to make the world a better place.

Key No. 2: When the rules are followed or ignored, patterns emerge. Our friend David Wheaton played against Andy Roddick a few times and described his serve as "unbelievably enormous." David said, "If Roddick hits a 150 mile-per-hour serve in the corner, there's no way to touch it unless you've accurately guessed where it is going to hit." Most of us would just stand there while the ball whizzed past. Experienced players don't do this, obviously. They study the patterns of tennis serves. David told us,

> Good returners "absorb" several things about a big server so they can learn or get a sense of where the serve might be going: they notice where the ball toss is, they notice where the server likes to serve on big points and where he's been going on previous points, and maybe they even notice where the server looks before he serves.... Just a lot of little things that give the returner an idea of where the ball might go.[1]

In other words, tennis serves reveal patterns. If you can observe and respond to those patterns, you have a shot at winning, or at least not getting completely crushed.

But what about the chess players? The myth of the photographic memory of chess grand masters evaporated when researchers ran a test in which they *randomly* placed the pieces on the board in a way they would never appear during an actual game. Under these conditions, the memories of the baffled grand masters were almost as poor as the control group of non-chess players.[2]

It turns out that chess experts use their experience regarding how chess pieces move to make sense of the patterns of play. They divide the board into chunks and remember the position of the pieces in each chunk, which enables them to reproduce with incredible accuracy the position of all the pieces on the board. But they can do this only when the pieces are placed as they would be during an actual game. These chess grand masters aren't memorizing the entire board; they are making sense of the patterns that emerge when the game is played according to the rules.

Of course, it takes a lot of practice to recognize patterns, whether in tennis or chess or anything else. Malcolm Gladwell refers to what he calls the "10,000-hour rule," the number of hours of intensive concentration and practice it takes to master a subject. If you worked at it eight hours a day, it would take you three and a half years to get that kind of experience.[3] There is no real shortcut to this rule, at least individually. However, if you have a wise mentor, someone who guides you, builds on your successes, and coaches you in avoiding mistakes, you can become an expert more quickly than other people, though it will still take concentrated effort.[4]

Rules. Patterns. It doesn't matter whether we're playing a sport or a board game or shopping or just navigating through the streets to a friend's house. We are constantly trying our hand at pattern recognition on the assumption that the world is a rule-based place.

Here's a big question, though: Are there patterns that extend to life's big questions? If so, is it possible to discern patterns that reveal where we come from, what the good life looks like, how we should treat others, and what happens when we die? If there are patterns for such things, is it possible to figure out which patterns are good or bad, true or false, just or unjust?

Here's an even bigger question if all of the above is possible: Given the sheer volume of ideas in the world today, is it even possible to accomplish such a massive feat as figuring out the rules and patterns that answer life's ultimate questions? This volume is designed to set you on the course to finding answers to these questions.

This chapter introduces a way of thinking about the world we think you will find compelling and helpful. We'll discuss how ideas become persuasive and how to identify patterns of ideas so you can understand the world around you. We'll also examine six worldviews that influence just about everyone in the world today, and we'll see how that influence manifests itself in the key academic disciplines operating in America's institutions of higher learning.

So now that you know where we're coming from, let's look at the history of the ideas on which this book is based.

3. Where *Understanding the Times* Comes From

The book you are reading has a history stretching back more than fifty years. As a student at Hope College in Holland, Michigan, David Noebel attended a chapel service addressing the topic of communism. The speaker, an Australian medical doctor named Fred Schwarz, said communism was fast growing and persuasive because it was *religious*. It answered life's ultimate questions, inspired ardor and devotion, and gave meaning to people's lives. It had a means of winning and discipling converts, as well as a vision of spreading to the whole world.

Something clicked for Noebel. Maybe the battles of our age are not first and foremost military battles but battles of *ideas*. And these ideas are compelling because they are religious. As a Christian preparing for ministry, Noebel thought Christians ought to understand the world of ideas in order to not be taken captive by deceptive philosophies (Col. 2:8).[5] With these thoughts in mind, Noebel approached the speaker to ask a few questions. The college president noted Noebel's interest and invited him to form a study group about communism.

Noebel took up this challenge and came to see communism as a direct competitor to Christianity. Millions were being misled, and millions of lives hung in the balance. And communism wasn't the only counterfeit worldview, he realized; many ideas were battling for the hearts and minds of people, nations, and cultures.

Years later, in 1991, Noebel compiled his extensive knowledge about worldviews into a nine-hundred-page book called *Understanding the Times*, one of the bestselling worldview texts of all time. All together, there are more than six hundred thousand copies in print. If you've heard the term *worldview*, you've likely been influenced by Noebel or someone he influenced.

Soon after the publication of *Understanding the Times*, Noebel asked Jeff Myers to develop an accompanying curriculum featuring videos of Christian thinkers and in-depth reading. More than one hundred thousand people have studied this curriculum. *Understanding the Times* has been periodically revised and expanded to keep up with the emergence of new ideas and the repackaging of old ones. You are holding the latest version, which updates the language, examples, sources, and organization of the original while maintaining its core structure.[6]

But let's go back to the concept of patterns. Do ideas, as well as tennis serves and chess moves, flow in patterns? If so, is it possible to tell whether they are consistent with or different from God's pattern?

4. IDEAS FLOW IN COMPLEX PATTERNS

Imagine walking around a crowded room and then being asked to describe whom and what you saw. You might remember a few details, but a trained investigator or spy would remember much more. He could describe the room with astounding detail. Why? Because he's trained in a *way of seeing*. He knows what to pay attention to and what to ignore. In the movies and on television, such a person always looks like a genius who possesses a supernatural awareness. In reality, understanding comes from discipline and training. In his book *Cold-Case Christianity*, J. Warner Wallace, a highly regarded cold-case detective, demonstrates how detectives identify the details they see and go through a mental checklist to figure out which details are clues and which are background noise.[7]

The *Oxford English Dictionary* defines an *idea* as "a thought or suggestion as to a possible course of action."[8] What we conceive, what we believe, and our general impressions about the world are always based on *something*. If they are not based on an accurate understanding of truth, we'll always be disoriented, unable to distinguish between genuine clues and background noise. This is why it is important, as the sixteenth-century scientist Johannes Kepler phrased it, to "[think] God's thoughts after him." God made the rules. To bear his image well, we should try to understand them, discern the patterns they create, and live differently as a result.

But it's harder to pick out patterns when we have lots of information as opposed to when our choices are simple. Let's say you open the cupboard and find nothing to eat except a packet of seafood-flavored noodles and a packet of chicken-flavored noodles. *Noodles are noodles*, you tell yourself. *Just pick one.* If you're at the Public Market in Emeryville, California, though, there are seventeen different food stalls offering cuisine from all over the world. Each of these restaurants offers about ten choices. It takes more thoughtfulness to decide when you have 170 choices as opposed to 2.

The same is true with religion. Today, largely because of the Internet, people have more information about religion—and everything else—than ever before. In 2011, according to Domo, a company that helps other companies make sense of the Internet, *every passing minute* 204,166,667 email messages were sent, YouTube users uploaded forty-eight hours of new video, Twitter users sent more than one hundred thousand tweets, and Instagram users shared thirty-six hundred new photos.[9] By the time you read this, the numbers will be even higher.[10] There is literally so much information on the Internet that it distracts people from doing what they ought to do. The *New York Times* reports that the cost of interruptions to people's workdays—looking at the latest video they've been forwarded or checking out someone's Twitter feed—is around $650 billion dollars a year in lost productivity.[11]

> Today, largely because of the Internet, people have more information about religion—and everything else—than ever before.

Some people try to manage the accelerating growth of information by multitasking. Ironically, those who constantly switch between tasks are actually less productive because each activity has its own rules, and it takes time for the mind to switch from one set of rules to another.[12] In the case of driving and texting, this literally kills people. The more than three thousand texting-while-driving deaths each year prove that our capacity is not fast enough to switch between tasks.[13]

In this world of ballooning information, if you are curious about some obscure religion, you can get answers in two or three mouse clicks. No matter how remote the area in which they live, people from all over the world can access all of the world's ideas and do it with their smartphones while walking down the street. The problem is, of course, that the more information we have, the harder it is to figure out what to do with it all. Even utterly wrong ideas can boast a cool website, making them appear credible. Information growth is exponential; wisdom's demise is precipitous.

> In this world of ballooning information, if you are curious about some obscure religion, you can get answers in two or three mouse clicks.

So who can make their way in a world like this? Those capable of quickly figuring out the rules and recognizing the patterns of ideas. It's true with tennis and chess, and it's true with life's ultimate questions. People with discernment can see the relationship between all of the pieces of information they are trying to process at any given moment. If they are thoughtful about spiritual things, this capacity will enable them to better understand God, the world, and their relationship to God and the world.

5. The World's Patterns Are Different from God's Pattern

What we understand about God and the world affects what we believe about everything else, including what kinds of arguments we find persuasive and how we justify our intended actions. That's why the apostle Paul said in Romans 12:2, "Do not be conformed to this world, but be transformed by the renewal of your mind, that by testing you may discern what is the will of God, what is good and acceptable and perfect." To understand what God wants from us, we must identify the world's patterns, refuse to conform to them, and be transformed to embrace a God-pleasing pattern of living.

We call a pattern of ideas a **worldview**. A worldview answers such fundamental questions as *Why are we here? What is the meaning and purpose of life? Is there a difference between right and wrong? Is there a God?* We all develop ideas in our attempt to answer these questions, and our ideas naturally give rise to a system of belief that becomes the basis for our decisions and actions. Our worldview is like a map. It helps us know where we are, where we need to go, and the best route to get there.

> *Worldview:* **a pattern of ideas, beliefs, convictions, and habits that help us make sense of God, the world, and our relationship to God and the world.**

Our worldview does not merely reflect what we think the world *is* like; it directs what we think the world *should be* like. In other words, our worldview not only *describes* reality; it *prescribes* how we how we should act and respond to every aspect of life. Because our ideas *do* determine how we behave, the bottom line is that our ideas *do* have consequences.

This doesn't mean that everyone is aware of his or her deeply held ideas. If we were to ask a person on the street about her philosophy of life, we would probably get a blank stare. But if we asked how life began, she would probably offer some sort of answer, even if the answer was not completely coherent. Still, her belief would impact the way she lives her life. It's also often the case that people are unaware of where their deeply held beliefs come from. If we were to continue our street conversation by asking *why* this woman believes what she claims to believe, she might shrug and reply, "I don't know; I just believe it." Often people pick up their beliefs like they catch colds—by being around other people! And since ideas are everywhere—on television, in books and magazines, at the movies, and in conversation with friends and family—it's easy to pick them up without considering whether they're worth believing.

> **Often people pick up their beliefs like they catch colds—by being around other people!**

Regardless of where they come from, the ideas we embrace about the nature of reality lead to a set of core beliefs, which in turn form convictions about how we should live meaningfully. This beefs up our definition of *worldview*. A worldview is a "pattern of ideas," but it's also a "pattern of beliefs, convictions, and habits that help us make sense of God, the world, and our relationship to God and the world."

Of course, some Christians don't act Christianly. There are also Muslims and Secularists whose lifestyles are inconsistent with what they believe. The Christian idea of the sinful nature predicts this. Human *actions* fall short of human *aspirations*. For example, if a person embraces the idea of sexuality as an expression of love between a married man and woman, he or she will probably believe in abstaining from sexual activity outside of marriage, which reflects a value of sexual purity and a conviction to safeguard it. This does not mean, however, that the person will never indulge in pornography in a moment of weakness. Such indulgence does not invalidate the person's ideas, beliefs, convictions, and habits, but it will produce guilt because the person knows pornography is harmful. On the other hand, a person with no existing beliefs about love and marriage will still feel guilty but may not understand why. People who continue to indulge in pornography may end up in a habitual pattern shaped by the culture's permissive stance rather than what God wants.

Ideas have consequences. They form our beliefs, shape our convictions, and solidify into habits.

There are hundreds of different worldviews. Is it possible to know which of them, if any, is actually true? If you look in the religion section of a bookstore, you'll see books not only on Christianity and Islam, of course, but also on Confucianism, Buddhism, Taoism, Hinduism, Vedantism, Jainism, Shintoism, and many other religions. Each **religion** attempts to explain what the world is like and how we should live. You'll also notice books on Secularism and atheism in the religion section. This might seem odd, but when you think about it, even atheists have a set of beliefs about the cause, nature, and purpose of the universe. They're religious.[14] Even people who don't care about any of this are religious; their religion says the ultimate questions don't matter. All worldviews are religious.

> *Religion:* a system of belief that attempts to define the nature of God and how human beings can understand and interact with the divine; any system of belief that prescribes certain responses to the existence (or nonexistence) of the divine.

> Ideas have consequences. They form our beliefs, shape our convictions, and solidify into habits.

If everyone is religious we would expect their beliefs to lead to certain actions. C. S. Lewis put it this way:

> We are now getting to the point at which different beliefs about the universe lead to different behavior.... Religion involves a series of statements about facts, which must be either true or false. If they are true, one set of conclusions will follow about the right sailing of the human fleet[;] if they are false, quite another set.[15]

Here's where we are so far. All people try to make sense of the rules of the world by developing ideas. These ideas flow in patterns, which we call worldviews. People's worldviews lead them to value certain things, which leads to particular convictions governing their behavior. These convictions solidify into habits that affect the way people live.

6. Why Should We Care?

As people try to figure out the rules and patterns of the world, they diagnose what is wrong with the world and suggest prescriptions. As in medicine, a wrong diagnosis could lead to mistreating a disease or leave a serious illness untreated. If everyone lived in isolated caves, the consequences of our actions wouldn't affect others. But we aren't isolated. We live in families, communities, cities, and countries. The consequences of bad beliefs can cause serious pain. Some ideas in history have led to death for millions. Nazism systematically exterminated approximately 21 million people, not counting the tens of millions who died in battles initiated by the Nazi regime.[16] Communist regimes slaughtered well over 100 million people in the twentieth century. As we will see in the chapter on Marxism in this volume, the slaughter continues to this day.

Every one of these deaths was in the service of an idea. Ideas have consequences, sometimes unspeakably tragic ones. Like a wildfire, these ideas began with a single flame and rapidly spread before a stunned and unprepared populace, engulfing millions. People thought Adolf Hitler was a pompous fool early in his career. Who could have predicted he would actually amass enough power to slaughter millions? Similarly, who could have imagined that a radical writer named Karl Marx, a man deeply unpopular even with his friends, would be capable of unleashing an idea—communism—that would destroy more people than any other idea in history?

Is it possible to understand ideas and their consequences? More important, is it possible to identify bad ideas in time to stop them before they can lay waste to the lives, hopes, and dreams of countless people? Fortunately, the answer is yes. To grasp the world of ideas, we don't need to know everything about everything. In the following pages, we'll take an in-depth look at the pattern of ideas, beliefs, convictions, and habits that makes up the Christian worldview. We'll suggest that understanding Christianity as a worldview will help us make sense of the world. Understanding other worldviews—other patterns—will confirm the essential truths of Christianity.

Here's a sports analogy: Let's say you play against a team that has sixty completely different plays. It would be hard to prepare for such a complex strategy. But if you know the team actually has six basic plays, each with ten variations, then by figuring out the six plays, you can make better guesses about each variation and know how to counteract it.

In this book we'll discover the six plays and the ten variations that worldview "teams" are running these days. Based on this information, we'll form a mental model from which we can make more accurate guesses about how people all over the world see things. We will examine six dominant worldviews: Christianity, Islam, Secularism, Marxism, New Spirituality, and Postmodernism. Each of these six worldviews claims to present the truth. Then we'll examine each worldview as expressed in ten key academic disciplines to see whether they are, in fact, true.

7. But First, a Warning

Before we analyze the six dominant worldviews, though, a warning is in order: Proponents of many worldviews don't like it when you start poking their nests. This is especially true of academics. Questioning professors and authorities can anger them and make them want to attack. At Summit, we've been called every name in the book: "intolerant," "bigoted," "idiotic," "fanatical," "conspiracy minded," and, our favorite, "bloviating motormouths."

Not all professors have chips on their shoulders. Still, if you embrace a Christian worldview, you should understand that you might be in someone's gun sights. For example, atheist philosopher Richard Rorty, one of the most famous professors of the twentieth century, once proclaimed,

> The fundamentalist [by which he meant Christian] parents of our fundamentalist students think that the entire "American liberal Establishment" is engaged in a conspiracy.... These parents have a point.... When we American college teachers encounter religious fundamentalists, we do not consider the possibility of reformulating our own practices of justification so as to give more weight to the authority of the Christian

scriptures. Instead, we do our best to convince these students of the benefits of sec-ularization.... Rather, I think those students are lucky to find themselves under the benevolent *Herrschaft* [teaching] of people like me, and to have escaped the grip of their frightening, vicious, dangerous parents.[17]

Rorty was not condemning abusive parents; he was condemning *Christian* parents who, by raising their kids according to a Christian worldview, are "frightening, vicious, [and] dangerous."

Nowhere are the attacks more vicious than in the sciences. Several years ago Richard Sternberg, a Smithsonian scientist with two PhDs in evolutionary biology, was fired as editor of a Smithsonian science journal for publishing an article written by Cambridge-educated scientist Stephen Meyer. The reason? Meyer's article defended *intelligent design*, a scientific movement that suggests natural processes cannot in and of themselves explain the great complexity we encounter in the universe.

"[The senior Smithsonian scientists] were saying I accepted money under the table, that I was a crypto-priest, that I was a sleeper cell operative for the creationists," said Sternberg, who at the time was a Smithsonian research associate. "I was basically run out of there."[18]

A *Washington Post* investigation revealed that Sternberg, who is *not* a creationist, was dismissed because of an orchestrated campaign by the National Center for Science Education (NCSE), a lobbying group fighting to keep criticism of naturalistic evolution out of public schools. In other words, the article Sternberg published was not attacked because its argu-ments were poor but because these scientific elites had already decided that *no questioning of naturalistic evolution was to be allowed*.[19]

Apparently, refusing to believe that everything that exists evolved through random-chance processes, as naturalistic evolutionists believe and teach in schools, is like refusing to wear clothes; it automatically disqualifies a person from appearing in public. Sternberg's firing led to a chilling, and even a freezing, of free speech among scientists. We have spoken with dozens of scientists who keep their reservations about evolution to themselves because speaking out might damage their careers.

If you live as we are suggesting in this book, you will probably come under attack as well. We're going to pre-pare you to respond, not with name calling or sarcasm, but with reasonable arguments. People who make their livings mocking Christianity are actually barring access to a skeleton-filled closet of disastrous ideas. But if you crack that closet door, they're going to be ticked. Why? Because they have become so accustomed to the ideas they've picked up that they cannot imagine the world being any other way. Ideas persist in the thought stream just as viruses enter the bloodstream. When we said ear-lier that people pick up ideas the way they catch colds, the research shows that this is not far from the truth.

> Apparently, refusing to believe that everything that exists evolved through random-chance processes, as naturalistic evolutionists believe and teach in schools, is like refusing to wear clothes; it automatically disqualifies a person from appearing in public.

8. IDEAS SPREAD LIKE VIRUSES

In the 1950s a professor at Yale University named William McGuire developed a theory about how people come to embrace the ideas they find compelling. His insights can help us understand how we might come to adopt good ideas and oppose bad ones.

McGuire theorized that ideas are actually very much like viruses, spreading from person to person. In our fallen and increasingly indiscriminate culture, bad ideas lamentably take root more easily than good ones. Thus, effective leaders must play a dangerous game: they must engage not only in building up good ideas but also in rooting out bad ones. How is it possible to do this without being incurably infected by the very ideas they hope to stand against?

Medical research in the mid-twentieth century demonstrated that a human body can develop immunity to a disease through the process of inoculation, which introduces to the body a weakened form of a disease to give the body's natural defense mechanism time to develop immunity to it.

Professor McGuire wondered whether the same theory would hold true for resisting bad ideas.[20] To test his inoculation theory, McGuire exposed subjects to widely accepted claims, such as "People should brush their teeth daily." He then exposed them to counter-claims (e.g., "Brushing your teeth is bad for you") after preparing test groups with varying levels of defense:

- **No preparation** ("Here's an argument—see what you think.")
- **Reinforcement of previous preparation** ("You know that brushing your teeth is good, right?")
- **Warning of attack** ("You will be exposed to a persuasive argument that brushing your teeth is bad.")
- **Inoculation** ("You will hear an argument stating that brushing your teeth wipes away saliva, which is the tooth's natural protective agent.")
- **Inoculation plus refutation** ("When you hear the argument that brushing your teeth is bad because it wipes away saliva, keep in mind that saliva cannot dislodge prepared foods from the teeth—only a brush can consistently do that.")
- **Inoculation plus refutation plus preparation** ("You now know one argument you'll hear to persuade you that brushing your teeth is bad, but you'll be presented with several arguments, and it will be up to you to think them through and refute them.")[21]

In the end, the most effective strategy for resisting counterpersuasion, as you might guess, was the last one: inoculation plus refutation plus preparation. The *least* effective strategy was reinforcement of previous preparation. In fact, more people in this test condition believed the false argument than those in the "no preparation" condition.

That people who have been equipped with the truth could so easily fall for falsehoods is a stunning result. To the extent this research applies to social and political beliefs, we can conclude the following: For people to believe a claim, they must be prepared to defend it against its challengers. Merely repeating a message over and over again—even with increasing fervency, emotion, and clever staging—is actually *counterproductive*, worse than no preparation at all.

The antidote to indoctrination is to tell the truth, expose people to the lies that would deceive them, show them how to refute those lies, and prepare them with the thinking skills necessary to continue resisting falsehoods. This begins by understanding the worldviews—the patterns of ideas, beliefs, convictions, and habits—that rule the world today. Again, there are six: Christianity, Islam, Secularism, Marxism, New Spirituality, and Postmodernism. Let's dig in.

> **The antidote to indoctrination is to tell the truth, expose people to the lies that would deceive them, show them how to refute those lies, and prepare them with the thinking skills necessary to continue resisting falsehoods.**

9. The Six Worldviews

As we noted earlier, a *worldview* is a "pattern of ideas, beliefs, convictions, and habits that help us make sense of God, the world, and our relationship to God and the world." If you know a worldview's assumptions, you can more accurately guess what its adherents believe and why.

There may be hundreds of worldviews operating today. Even some well-known ones, such as Judaism, have relatively few (around thirteen million) followers worldwide. But many bizarre and even humorous worldviews have attracted followers. As the London *Telegraph* reported, 176,632 people in a 2012 national census of England and Wales considered their religious affiliation to be the "Jedi Knights."[22] Another 6,242 said they worshipped heavy-metal music.[23] Obviously we can't cover every worldview that has attracted followers, so we're going to look at the six worldviews that make up the vast majority of the world's population and are evangelistic (inviting everyone else to join them).

1. Christianity. More than 2 billion people in the world claim to be Christians, nearly one-third of the world's population. What they mean by "Christian," of course, varies widely—some people claim to be Christians because their parents were Christian or because they live in a predominantly Christian country. Still, no one doubts that Christianity is a dominant influence in the world. Christianity goes back to the teachings of Jesus Christ, the Messiah prophesied for centuries among the Israelites in the Old Testament. Christians believe that God has revealed himself in the Bible as well as in nature, but especially in the person of Jesus Christ. Because Jesus Christ was God incarnate (as a human being), his life is at the center of the human story.

> **The Christian worldview offers a narrative of all history. This narrative starts with God's special creation of human beings, delves into the consequences of their fall from grace, and promises redemption through the sacrificial death of Jesus on the cross and his subsequent resurrection.**

Christianity has had a profound influence on the world. French philosopher Luc Ferry, a nonbeliever, claims that Christianity alone established the idea that because we are made in the image of the Creator, all human persons have rights.[24] Famed British atheist Bertrand Russell said something similar: "What the world needs is Christian love, or compassion."[25] Whether or not Russell acknowledged it, such love and compassion result directly from following in the footsteps of Christ himself, the epitome of love and compassion.

The Christian worldview offers a narrative of all history. This narrative starts with God's special creation of human beings, delves into the consequences of their fall from grace, and promises redemption through the sacrificial death of Jesus on the cross and his subsequent resurrection.

2. Islam. Islam began September 24 in AD 622, when seventy *muhajirun* pledged loyalty to an Arabian trader from Mecca who had fled to Medina and began receiving special revelations from Allah. The trader's name: Muhammad. His submission to God gave his religion its name; *Islam* means "submission." Those who submit to Allah and his prophet Muhammad are called Muslims. Islam is based on a creed prayed aloud five times a day: "There is no God but Allah, and Muhammad is his prophet."

Muslims believe that their holy book, the Quran, is God's full and final revelation. The Quran specifies five things a person must do to become a Muslim:

1. Repeat "There is no God but Allah, and Muhammad is his prophet."
2. Pray the salat (ritual prayer)[26] five times a day.
3. Fast during the month of Ramadan.
4. Give one-fortieth of one's income to the needy.
5. If able, make a pilgrimage to Mecca.[27]

According to Serge Trifkovic, "Islam is not a 'mere' religion; it is a complete way of life, an all-embracing social, political, and legal system that breeds a worldview peculiar to itself."[28] Islam has grown rapidly in the last few decades; 1.6 billion people in the world now claim to be adherents.

3. New Spirituality. What we term New Spirituality is perhaps the most difficult worldview to precisely define. You don't have to sign, recite, or proclaim anything in particular to join, nor must you attend a church. While unofficial in its dogma, the New Age culture contains an extensive set of beliefs that, once understood, predict what people with those beliefs will value and how they will act.

New Spirituality is a free-flowing combination of Eastern religions, paganism, and pseudoscience that pops up in odd places. Some of the bestselling books of all time—by authors such as Deepak Chopra, Rhonda Byrne, Marilyn Ferguson, and Shakti Gawain—describe a world spiritual in nature but not governed by a personal, all-powerful God. Rather, the spirituality in the world is "consciousness," an energy in which we all participate and can even learn to control. Talk-show host Oprah Winfrey has admitted to holding many of these beliefs.

> New Spirituality is a free-flowing combination of Eastern religions, paganism, and pseudoscience that pops up in odd places.

We will study New Spirituality not because it is deeply philosophical or consistent but because some of its associated beliefs—karma, Gaia, being "one" with the environment, reincarnation, meditation, holistic health, and so forth—are a daily part of life for millions of Americans and have influenced such academic areas as psychology and medicine.

4. **Secularism.** Secularism comes from the Latin word *saecularis*, roughly meaning "of men," "of this world," or "of this time." Secularists believe humans are the center of reality. They disdain the influence of those who believe in ideas of gods, an afterlife, or anything beyond what we can sense. The primary identifying characteristic of Secularism is its *nonbelief* in other worldviews. Ironically, though, Secularists do generally have an agreed-upon set of beliefs about the cause, nature, and purpose of the universe. So even though they view their beliefs as the *opposite* of religion, they are actually quite religious.

Interestingly, in the twentieth century, several fairly well-known philosophers, such as John Dewey and Julian Huxley, and later Paul Kurtz and Corliss Lamont, combined the term *secular* ("we are for the world") and the term *humanism* ("we are for humans") and developed a philosophy of Secular Humanism. Their manifesto, published in 1933 and updated in 1973 and 2000, led thousands of like-minded individuals to form a club called the American Humanist Association (AHA), whose motto is "Good without a god." With no apparent sense of irony, the AHA operates as a tax-exempt organization based on the IRS section 501(c)(3) *religious* nonprofit exemption. Though its founders have passed away, the AHA still recruits members. Their dues support a publishing company and a monthly publication.

We'll discuss Secularism and the Secular Humanist movement more in coming chapters, but it is sufficient for now to recognize Secularism as an umbrella term for a set of beliefs the vast majority of academics today accept unquestioningly. We use the term *Secularism* as a prediction, not a label: if someone accepts a Secularist viewpoint on such disciplines as theology, philosophy, and ethics, we can predict fairly accurately what they believe about biology, psychology, and so forth.

5. **Marxism.** Some religious worldviews develop over hundreds or thousands of years, but others are made up whole cloth in a very short period of time. Such is the case with Marxism and its offshoots Leninism, Maoism, Trotskyism, Fabian socialism, and the various socialist organizations that operate in the United States and around the world. Marxism was invented by Karl Marx, a scholar determined to demonstrate that ownership of private property, the basis for capitalism, was the root of the world's evils.

To Marx, history could be defined as a struggle between the haves (the owners) and the have-nots (the workers). If only the workers would rise up to overthrow the owners, they could form a workers' paradise in which all wrongs are righted, all possessions are shared, and all injustices are brought to an end. The utopian state at the end of this long and bloody struggle is called *communism*. People who strive to bring about this state are called *communists*, and their Bible is *The Communist Manifesto*, Marx's most famous and enduring work. Other such manifestos are still in print today, including the teachings

> Some say it's pointless to include Marxism as a dominant worldview in this volume, but we disagree. Despite the collapse of the Union of Soviet Socialist Republics (USSR), which dominated what is now called Russia, around 20 percent of the world's population still lives under the rule of communists.

of Chinese communist leader Mao Tse-tung and a book published by Harvard University Press called *Empire*.

Some say it's pointless to include Marxism as a dominant worldview in this volume, but we disagree. Despite the collapse of the Union of Soviet Socialist Republics (USSR), which dominated what is now called Russia, around 20 percent of the world's population still lives under the rule of communists. The largest communist country in the world today is China. In spite of its growing industry, China's communist rulers are still very much in control. And when we also consider countries operating on the principles Marx taught but not using the label *communist*, we are talking about a *majority* of the world's population living every day with the consequences of Marx's philosophies. As we will see, despite its clearly atheistic philosophy, Marxism has also made many inroads into the church. Some evangelicals involved in the so-called Christian Left have embraced key tenets of Marxism.

6. **Postmodernism.**[29] People talk about postmodern art, postmodern architecture, and even postmodern ways of doing church, and yet they don't realize that Postmodernism is a well-thought-out and deep philosophical worldview. The father of Postmodernism, German philosopher Friedrich Nietzsche, had many disciples, including Jacques Derrida, Michel Foucault, Martin Heidegger, Jean-François Lyotard, and Richard Rorty. All are now dead, but their teachings strongly influence higher education to this day.

We will learn more about the complexities of Postmodernism throughout this volume. In short, though, we can say Postmodernism began as a reaction against modernism, the idea that science and human reason can solve humankind's most pressing problems. While science can be used for great good, Postmodernists understand it to be hopelessly corrupted by the quest for power. It was scientific "progress," for example, that enabled the creation of weapons of mass destruction.

According to Postmodernists, the modern story of science and technology is one of many attempts to formulate what's called a *metanarrative*, or grand story of reality that claims universally valid, "God's-eye"-view, pristine knowledge of the world. Postmodernists say metanarratives become so compelling that people stop questioning them, and it's precisely then that they become destructive and oppressive. Postmodernists are generally suspicious of all modern metanarratives because they are so often used as tools of oppression. Many Postmodernists engage in a process of examining exactly what causes people to fall under the spell of various metanarratives. This is called *deconstruction*. The way deconstruction works on metanarratives is similar to someone revealing how a magic trick is done: in the revealing, people stop being deceived. Postmodernists believe "deconstructing" dominant metanarratives causes them to lose their stranglehold on people's minds.

We'll see, though, that Postmodernists have been carried away by their own ideas, calling everything into question—even the idea that we can know reality itself!

So there you have it. **Christianity, Islam, New Spirituality, Secularism, Marxism,** and **Postmodernism.** By understanding these six worldviews, we'll see how people come to grips with the rules of the world and form patterns they hope will answer life's ultimate questions.

10. Ten Ways of Looking at the World

"What do you want to major in?" is probably the first question asked of any student on his or her way to college. For some, this strikes fear into the heart: "Am I supposed to know that already?" For others, it doesn't matter—they just want a diploma so they can more easily qualify for a job. But one thing most people never consider is this: The various academic departments aren't just places where professors stash what they know. They're actually different ways of thinking about the ultimate questions of life.

In an ideal world, the academic departments—philosophy, psychology, law, and so forth—would combine their insights to form a *uni* (meaning "whole") *versity* (meaning "body") in which the parts come together to closely resemble the truth. In reality, though, various academic departments usually keep to themselves, using introductory and general education courses to persuade potential "majors" to study with their faculty for the remainder of their academic careers.

Some academic departments—the *applied* sciences, for example—focus on what you can do with the knowledge developed by the *pure* sciences. Applied sciences include engineering, medicine, business, and education. Many people say the applied sciences are most important because they're most needed in society, and hence most likely to lead to a paying job. Certainly we want young adults to be gainfully employed and to work hard toward the greater good. But it is unwise to rush into a career without first trying to understand the various ways of knowing; before you learn how to do, it's wise to learn how to know! Otherwise you might be stuck making a living without any sense of how to make a life.

In this study we will focus on ten basic disciplines, the seeds from which most things in academia grow: theology, philosophy, ethics, biology, psychology, sociology, law, politics, economics, and history. Here's a brief overview of each:

1. Theology. An *-ology* means "study of." *Theos* means "God." Theology is the study of God. Theology seeks to answer the question, "How did I and everything else *get* here?" When people see something beautiful and are asked, "How do you *know* it is beautiful?" they might point out a few details, but often they will say, "I don't know. It just is." How is it that they really know? The theologian says knowing about God's nature and character is the key to figuring out what is most important in life.

2. Philosophy. *Philo* means "love"—that has to do with the nature of companionship. It is the root word for the name of the city of Philadelphia, which is nicknamed "the city of brotherly love." *Sophia* is the Greek word for "wisdom," so when you put *philo* and *sophia* together, you get "love of wisdom." The philosopher seeks to be wisdom's companion by answering questions like "What is real?" and "How do I *know* anything?" To the philosopher, the good life consists of figuring out what the nature of reality is, how we know what we know, and how to accurately know about reality and knowledge.

3. Ethics. *Ethos* is the Greek word for "goodness." Ethicists are not merely searching for a life that *feels* good but searching for "the good life"—a life that actually *is* good. So ethics is the study that seeks to answer questions like "How should I live?" "What does it mean to live a good life?" and "If *everyone* lived the way I'm living, would it be good for us all?" Ethicists seek to understand the various ways people act based on what they believe, and then how those actions enable them to pursue the good life.

4. Biology. *Bios* means "life." Biology is the study of life. Biology seeks to answer the question "What does it *mean* to be alive?" When we see something alive, we know it is alive. But *how* do we know? Ask a group of children sometime, "If you had a robot, what would you have to change to bring it to life?" They might say, "It would have to have a heart." If you asked why, they might respond, "To pump blood." To which you might say, "But there are lots of creatures that are alive that don't have hearts." Pressing the issue further with the children would probably be cruel, but you get the point. Biologists study living things to assist us in understanding the natural world and making predictions about it. If we see our predictions coming true, we can claim to know true things about the world. Biology is at the heart of the sciences because if we can figure out what makes something alive, then we can perhaps better understand our own aliveness.

5. Psychology. *Psyche* is the Greek word for "soul." Psychology seeks to answer the question "What makes me *human*?" Most people see human beings as different from other creatures, but what makes us unique? From observation we know most creatures are unreflective; that is, they don't contemplate or communicate about their plans for the future, nor do they appear to feel regret or shame over their past actions. Human beings do all these things and more. Is it possible to understand why people do what they do? Psychologists study the way animals and humans act in order to see if they can figure out something about human nature to help struggling people find a path to a better life.

6. Sociology. *Socios* is the Greek word from which we get our word *society*. Whereas psychologists study the individual self and its relationship to other selves, sociologists suspect life will be better if we can answer the question "How do we live in community with one another?" The differences between people, after all, are vast. To really understand how we can live together in community, we ought to have some insight into our various cultures, languages, religious beliefs, and historical challenges. These differences are complex and go back generations, sometimes even millennia. At the end of the day, sociologists hope that by understanding how societies develop, grow, and relate to one another, we might learn to live in greater harmony.

7. Law. The word *law* comes from an Old English word *lagu*, which refers to the rules or ordinances by which we are governed.[30] It's the same word from which we get our words *legislate* and *legislature*. The study of law revolves around the question "What constitutes *just* and *orderly* governance?" In order to live together in an orderly way, we need laws we all agree to follow. If even a few people were to decide not to stop at red lights, it would create uncertainty and chaos for everyone. To keep society from breaking down, then, we must have rules and a means of making people obey them. A society's philosophy of law determines its level of thriving. Lawmakers and legal scholars must consider whether the law is punishing evildoing sufficiently while not harming the freedoms of the just and hardworking. And how, they must ask, does the law ensure fairness without being

> What is liberty without wisdom, and without virtue? It is the greatest of all possible evils; for it is folly, vice, and madness, without tuition or restraint.
>
> — Edmund Burke

unfair to one group or another? Figure out the answers to these questions, legal scholars say, and we'll all be better off.

8. Politics. *Polis* means "city." *Politics* means "the rule of a city." When people think of politics, political commercials or people with big, fake smiles wearing suits and kissing babies often come to mind, and they dismiss politics as being silly or pompous. But the study of politics really does matter. Politics answers the question "What is the best way to *organize* community?" Everyone in the world lives in multiple political jurisdictions: neighborhoods, cities, counties, states, nations. By living where you live, you agree to abide by the rules governing those jurisdictions. But who makes these rules? Who gets to pick the rule makers? Properly conceived, politics offers a platform from which to encourage virtue, and virtue is at the heart of good government. To those who think it is *only* about liberty, the great British statesman Edmund Burke said, "What is liberty without wisdom, and without virtue? It is the greatest of all possible evils; for it is folly, vice, and madness, without tuition or restraint."[31]

9. Economics. In Latin, the word for "economics" means "the art of running a household." Economics answers the question "How can individuals and the community be optimally *productive*?" Let's say you have a lawnmower, some gas, and a willingness to mow other people's lawns. One of your customers might say, "If you mow my lawn, I'll give you some fresh eggs from my chickens." That's fine, but what if you don't *want* eggs? To make it possible for your customer to get what she wants while giving you what you want, you can use a means of exchange called money, based on people's agreement about the relative value of things compared to other things. Economics becomes infinitely more complex, though, when people want to *borrow* money to acquire very expensive things, or to capitalize a large enterprise. How are these loans made? What rules govern complex transactions such as these? What, if anything, should the various levels of government have to say about all this? Economists try to make sense of this complexity so people can get what they want, which will help them live better lives.

10. History. The study of history seeks to answer the question "How did people in the past think and act on theology, philosophy, ethics, biology, psychology, sociology, politics, law, and economics? What happened in the past could help us understand what we should do now. How can we repeat the good decisions and avoid repeating the bad ones? What *counts* as a good or bad decision? But the historian's task actually goes beyond these questions, because there are too many facts to write about, and someone must decide which facts are important and which ones aren't, as well as which facts are included in the account and which facts are left out. People who think America's founders were bad people who mistreated others will tend to choose confirming facts—such as the fact that some founders' owned slaves—in order to persuade others that America ought to abandon its founding principles. Should our agendas drive our study of history? Is it possible to select and interpret facts objectively? These are important questions, because if history is told inaccurately, it might lead people to make bad decisions—which in turn could hinder human flourishing.

As you can see, each academic discipline approaches knowledge differently, but with the same goal: to understand how to live meaningful lives, both individually and together. Many more academic disciplines exist, of course, but we believe these ten to be properly basic. By understanding something about these ten, we'll be able to figure out what to do with the rest.

Before we go any further, though, we need to make an admission, without which the rest of this book will not make any sense: we are biased.

11. Our Bias: The Christian Worldview Explains Things Best

In this book we hope to show a multitude of ways the Christian worldview best explains the existence of the universe and all things related to it. In a systematic analysis of how each worldview approaches the ten disciplines presented in the previous section, Christianity claims that an acknowledgment of God's nature and character, and the life and work of Christ, will reveal capital *T* Truth (as opposed to isolated cultural or personal truths). As we will see, a robust Christian perspective of each of the disciplines is clear and compelling.

1. Theology. The evidence compels us to believe in the existence of a personal and holy God, a designed universe, and an earth prepared for human life. This evidence together outweighs any argument for atheism (belief in no god), polytheism (belief in many gods), or pantheism (belief in god *as* the universe). Theology begins with verse one of the Bible: "In the beginning, God created the heavens and the earth" (Gen. 1:1). According to John 1, God's creation was through the person of Jesus Christ, whom the apostle Paul referred to as "the fulness of the Godhead" (Col. 2:9 kjv).

2. Philosophy. We will present evidence that the notion of mind (*logos*) preceding matter is superior to the atheistic stance of matter preceding mind. From the very first book of the Bible, we understand that God created not only the world but the entire universe. Further, he made it possible for us to observe something of his revelation and to know that our observations are meaningful. Other creatures know things in a manner of speaking, but humans *know that we know*. We have a capacity to contemplate what our knowing revealer shows us. Christianity says we can know things because they have been ordered in such a way that our senses can perceive them, and this is because of Jesus Christ, who is the Logos [revealed knowledge] of God (John 1:1).

3. Ethics. The concept that right and wrong can be objectively known based on the nature and character of a personal, loving God is, we believe, superior both theoretically and practically to any concept of moral relativism or pragmatism. The gospel of John says that Jesus Christ is "the true light" (John 1:9; see also 3:19–20). That is, he is the source of what is truly good. In his light we can see what spiritual darkness previously hid from our view.

4. Biology. We argue that the concept of a living God creating life fits the evidence better than spontaneous generation and macroevolution. We see the scientific side of God in the beginning when he organized every creature "according to their kinds" (Gen. 1:21). Interestingly, Jesus Christ is described throughout the New Testament of the Bible as "the life" (John 1:4; 11:25; see also Col. 1:16).[32] When it comes to understanding life—physical as well as spiritual—we believe the Christian worldview offers superior insight.

5. Psychology. Understanding human beings as possessing both bodies and souls, even though we are sinful, imperfect, and in need of a savior, far outweighs expecting humans, as many contemporary psychologists argue, to be guilt free and in control of their behavior. Human life is different from other forms of life (Gen. 2:7).[33] We intuitively understand that something is wrong with us. What will make it right? A savior. And who, according to Christianity, is that savior? Jesus Christ (Luke 1:46–47; Titus 2:13).[34]

6. Sociology. The evidence demonstrates that society functions best when the institutions of family, church, and state exercise their proper authority within their God-ordained spheres. At its most basic level, society flourishes when it is built on strong families composed of a father, mother, and children. Sociology is hinted at in Genesis 1. God said to Adam and Eve, "Be fruitful and multiply and fill the earth" (v. 28)[35] and in Genesis 2, when the man and woman became "one flesh" (v. 24). Of all the ways God could have revealed himself to the world, he chose to do it through the one means all human beings could understand: he sent his Son, Jesus Christ (Isa. 9:6; Luke 1:30–31).[36]

7. Law. God hates the perversion of justice. This truth provides a firmer foundation than legal theories that prey on the innocent and let the guilty go free. In Genesis, God laid down rules to form the optimal conditions for human flourishing. When God rescued a culture of slaves even before he provided a permanent home for them, he gave them a law—the laws of Moses, the Torah. This fledgling nation came to be with *law*, not with *land*. Throughout Scripture, the Messiah, whom Christians believe is Jesus Christ, is characterized as a lawgiver (Gen. 49:10; Isa. 9:7).[37]

8. Politics. Christians believe the idea that rights are a gift from God secured by government is more logically persuasive, morally appealing, and politically sound than any atheistic theory that maintains human rights are derived from the state. We see the beginning of political authority several places in Genesis, notably in Genesis 9:6,[38] when cities were formed around the principle of preventing human bloodshed. Interestingly, among the names given to Jesus Christ throughout the Bible was a political title King of Kings and Lord of Lords (Isa. 9:6; Luke 1:33; 1 Tim. 6:15; Rev. 19:16).[39]

9. Economics. We will show that the concept of private property and using resources responsibly to glorify God is nobler than coercive government policies that destroy individual responsibility and incentives to work. God put Adam in the garden to work it and keep it. That's economics. Throughout all of Scripture, the Messiah, Jesus Christ, is described as the owner of all things (Ps. 24:1; 50:10–12; 1 Cor. 10:26),[40] which says something about the principles of stewardship that undergird economic reality.

10. History. The Bible's promise of a future kingdom ushered in by Jesus Christ is far more hopeful than utopian schemes dreamed up by sinful, mortal humans. Genesis 3:15[41] describes an ongoing battle between good and evil, a battle won when the offspring of the woman (often thought of as the coming Messiah) crushes the work of the Evil One. Correspondingly, Jesus is described as the "the Alpha and the Omega" (Rev. 1:8), the beginning and the end of history. History has a direction and a goal.

Christians view these ten disciplines as sacred, not secular. They are imprinted in the created order. All ten disciplines are addressed in just the first few chapters of the Bible; they manifest and accent certain aspects of the

> In every discipline, we think the Christian worldview shines brighter than any other worldview. It better explains our place in the universe and is more realistic, more scientific, more intellectually satisfying, and more defensible. Best of all, it is faithful to the one person with the greatest influence in heaven and on earth— Jesus Christ.

---

created order. Further, God shows himself in the person of Jesus Christ in such a way as to underline the significance of each discipline. The integration of these various categories into society has come to be known as Western civilization.[42]

In every discipline, we think the Christian worldview shines brighter than any other worldview. It better explains our place in the universe and is more realistic, more scientific, more intellectually satisfying, and more defensible. Best of all, it is faithful to the one person with the greatest influence in heaven and on earth—Jesus Christ. But can we actually know Christianity is true?

12. How Can We Understand What Is Actually True?

We think the Christian worldview is true, but to make this claim, we must have some concept of truth. Truth has two parts: understanding what is true with our *minds* (Rom. 12:2)[43] as well as our *hearts* (Heb. 4:12).[44] The authors of *Making Sense of Your World* suggest four tests for evaluating whether or not a worldview is true at a mind and heart level:

1. **The test of reason**: Is it reasonable? Can it be logically stated and defended?
2. **The test of the outer world**: Is there some external, corroborating evidence to support it?
3. **The test of the inner world**: Does it adequately address the "victories, disappointments, blessings, crises, and relationships of our everyday world"?
4. **The test of the real world**: Are its consequences good or bad when applied in any given cultural context?[45]

To say the Christian worldview is true is to say that it best describes the contours of the world *as it actually exists*. We're not asking you to take our word for it: follow *God*, not *us*. If at any point you are confused, prayerfully search God's Word under the guidance of wise counselors with a determination to understand and obey every good thing you need to do God's will.

Understanding the truth, though, is only the first step. We must also learn to communicate truth, "always being prepared to make a defense to anyone who asks you for a reason for the hope that is in you ... with gentleness and respect" (1 Pet. 3:15). Critics say Christianity is irrational, unhistorical, and unscientific. Christianity is more than equal to these criticisms, but we must be trained to articulate how and why.

13. Can't We All Just Get Along?

In questioning the truth or falsehood of various worldviews, we risk a great deal. Whether we accept Christianity, Islam, Secularism, Marxism, New Spirituality, or Postmodernism, we accept a worldview that describes the others as hopelessly distorted. They cannot all depict things as they really are; their competing claims cannot all be true.

Some people in history have tried to get around the differences between worldviews by telling a parable. Perhaps you've heard it: Six blind men come into contact with an elephant. One handles the tail and exclaims that an elephant is like a rope. Another grasps a leg and describes the elephant as a tree trunk. A third feels the tusk and says the animal is similar to a spear, and so on. Since each feels only a small portion of the whole elephant, all six men give correspondingly different descriptions of their experience.

So no one is really right or wrong, you see. We're all correct in our own way, with our limited knowledge—or so it seems at first glance. *But how do we know the blind men are all touching the same elephant?* The parable assumes that (1) each man can discern only part of the truth about the nature of the elephant, and (2) *we* know something the blind men don't—everyone is touching a real elephant.

The first assumption says no one possesses complete knowledge; the second assumption says we *know* no one possesses complete knowledge because *we* know what the elephant (or reality) is *really* like. But there's a contradiction here. On the one hand, the story claims that we—the blind men—have only limited knowledge. But if everyone is blind, no one can know the ultimate shape of the elephant. We need someone who is not blind, someone who knows all truth and communicates it accurately to us.

We will not claim in this book that non-Christian worldviews are completely false. We can find grains of truth in each. Secularism, for example, does not deny the existence of the physical universe and our ability to know it. Marxism accepts the significance and relevance of science. Post-modernism acknowledges the importance of texts and words. Islam acknowledges a created universe. New Spiritualists teach there is more to reality than matter. And all five non-Christian worldviews, to one extent or another, understand the importance of "saving" the human race.

> A major dividing line separates non-Christian worldviews from Christianity: What do you do with Jesus Christ?

However, a major dividing line separates non-Christian worldviews from Christianity: What do you do with Jesus Christ? Christianity views Jesus Christ as the true and living way.[46] He is the key to reality itself.[47] Early Christians were known as members of the Way.[48] All other major worldviews reject Jesus Christ as savior, lord, and king. Some deny that he ever existed.

This is too big of a difference to overlook. Who is Jesus? Did he live on this earth two thousand years ago? Was he God in the flesh (God incarnate)? Did he come to the earth to reveal God's will for us and save the human race from sin? These are important questions. As the apostle Paul pointed out, Christianity lives or dies on the answers: "If Christ has not been raised, then our preaching is in vain and your faith is in vain" (1 Cor. 15:14).

14. IRRECONCILABLE DIFFERENCES

If Postmodernists, for example, are correct in their belief that no metanarrative can describe reality, then Christianity is doomed. Christianity depends on understanding real universal truths, such as all people have sinned and fallen short of God's glory (Rom. 3:23);[49] God loves the whole human race (John 3:16);[50] and Christ died for our sins (1 John 2:2).[51] If these universal claims are false, then Christianity is implausible.

> According to a George Barna survey, 63 percent of teenagers agreed that "Muslims, Buddhists, Christians, Jews, and all other people pray to the same god, even though they use different names for their god."

If the assumptions of Secularism and Marxism are correct, anyone proclaiming the existence of the supernatural is potentially dangerous. Secularists and Marxists understand this quite clearly. For instance, Marx viewed all religion as a drug that deluded its adherents—an "opiate of the masses." Some Secularists even portray Christians as mentally imbalanced. James J. D. Luce, the assistant executive director of Fundamentalists Anonymous, said, "The fundamentalist experience can be a serious mental health hazard to perhaps millions of people."[52] His organization works to "heal" Christians of their "mental disorder"—their Christian worldview. Harvard's Edward O. Wilson takes this a step further, contrasting liberal theology with aggressive "fundamentalist religion," which he describes as "one of the unmitigated evils of the world."[53]

On the other end of the spectrum, New Spiritualists reject the personal God of the Bible as a dangerous myth separating people into religious factions. They seek instead a "higher consciousness." Bestselling New Spiritualist author Neale Donald Walsch claims that God revealed to him personally that "no path to God is more direct than any other path. No religion is the 'one true religion.'"[54] In an interview with Bill Moyers, filmmaker George Lucas said, "The conclusion I've come to is that all the religions are true."[55] Lucas's and Walsch's convictions are shared in the wider population, even among many Christians. According to a George Barna survey, 63 percent of teenagers agreed that "Muslims, Buddhists, Christians, Jews, and all other people pray to the same god, even though they use different names for their god."[56] So, the claim continues, if we don't have peace on Earth yet, it is only because some wrongly persist in their exclusionist beliefs.

Either Christians correctly describe reality when they speak of a loving, wise, just, personal, creative God, or they are talking nonsense. The basic tenets of the Bible cannot blend well with the non-Christian claim that we are good enough to save ourselves. We say only one view fits the facts: Christianity. God, the creator of the universe, saw its importance, loved it, loved *us*, so he sent his Son to redeem it—and *us*.

Clearly, adherents of other worldviews strongly disagree with our conclusion that only Christianity fits the facts. Some of them are prepared to attempt to dismantle our arguments. So the battle for truth is on. What case can each worldview make for itself? That's what we'll discover next.

ENDNOTES

1. Personal email correspondence between David Wheaton and Jeff Myers, January 14–15, 2013.
2. K. Anders Ericsson and Neil Charness, "Expert Performance: Its Structure and Acquisition," *American Psychologist* 49, no. 8 (August 1994): 725–47.
3. For more information see Malcolm Gladwell, *Outliers* (New York: Little, Brown, and Company, 2008).
4. See, for example, Dorothy Leonard and Walter Swap, "Expertise: Developing and Expressing Deep Smarts" and "Recreating Deep Smarts through Guided Experience," in *Deep Smarts: How to Cultivate and Transfer Enduring Business Wisdom* (Boston: Harvard Business School, 2005), chaps. 3 and 8.
5. Colossians 2:8: "See to it that no one takes you captive by philosophy and empty deceit, according to human tradition, according to the elemental spirits of the world, and not according to Christ."
6. First published in 1991, *Understanding the Times* covered the biblical Christian worldview, the Marxist-Leninist worldview, and the Secular Humanist worldview. An appendix briefly surveyed an emerging worldview called Cosmic Humanism. A later edition added Postmodernism and Islam to its consideration. The current edition

examines the same six worldviews with the names slightly altered in some cases (such as with Secularism) to reflect the changes in terminology used by the proponents of those views. The biggest change is from Cosmic Humanism to New Spirituality. The term *Cosmic Humanism* was intended to be a more academic approach to what was then called the New Age movement. The term never really gained traction. We use the term *New Spirituality* in this edition because we feel it better reflects both the content and the methods people use who are searching for "higher consciousness" today, especially in the ways they incorporate insights from Eastern religions, such as Buddhism and Hinduism.

7. J. Warner Wallace, *Cold-Case Christianity* (Colorado Springs: David C. Cook, 2013).

8. *Oxford English Dictionary*, s.v. "idea," www.oxforddictionaries.com.

9. For more statistics and references, see the info-graph compiled from multiple sources at "Data Never Sleeps," Domo, 2010–2011, accessed January 29, 2016, http://visual.ly/data-never-sleeps.

10. How big is the Internet? If each byte of data (the size of one letter or number) were the size of the largest bacteria (0.5 mm), the amount of data YouTube users upload each day would be about twenty-one terabytes, enough to wrap around the sun three times. See "How Much Data Is on the Internet?," Doug Camplejohn, *Fliptop* (blog), accessed January 29, 2016, http://blog.fliptop.com/blog/2011/05/18/how-much-data-is-on-the-internet/.

11. Cited in Steve Lohr, "Is Information Overload a $650 Billion Drag on the Economy?," *Bits* (blog), *New York Times*, December 20, 2007.

12. Joshua Rubinstein, David E. Meyer, and Jeffrey E. Evans, "Executive Control of Cognitive Processes in Task Switching," *Journal of Experimental Psychology: Human Perception and Performance* 27, no. 4 (2001): 763–97.

13. Cited in James R. Healey, "Feds: Phoning, Texting Killed 3,092 in Car Crashes Last Year," *USA Today*, December 8, 2011, http://content.usatoday.com/communities/driveon/post/2011/12/nhtsa-cell-phones-killed-3092-car-crashes-/1#.UUsnoldnF8E.

14. John Dewey, the father of modern education, helped organize a group of philosophies into what he hoped would be a new worldview that replaced Christianity. He called it *Secular Humanism*. The word *secular* means "that which pertains to worldly things rather than religious things." And yet Dewey was forthright about the fact that his new philosophy was, in fact, religious: "Here are all of the elements for a religious faith…. Such a faith has always been implicitly the common faith of mankind." John Dewey, *A Common Faith* (1934; repr., New Haven, CT: Yale University Press, 1962), 87.

15. C. S. Lewis, *Mere Christianity* (New York: Macmillan, 1972), 58.

16. R. J. Rummel, "Democide: Nazi Genocide and Mass Murder" (New Brunswick, NJ: Transaction Publishers, 1992), chap. 1.

17. Quoted in Robert B. Brandom, ed., *Rorty and His Critics* (Malden, MA: Blackwell, 2000), 21–22.

18. Quoted in Michael Powell, "Editor Explains Reasons for 'Intelligent Design' Article," *Washington Post*, August 19, 2005, www.washingtonpost.com/wp-dyn/content/article/2005/08/18/AR2005081801680.html.

19. Naturalistic evolution, as we will see in the "Biology" chapter of this volume, says nature is all there is, and the complexity of all of life evolved through random-chance processes starting from nothing. In the view of George Gaylord Simpson, a respected paleontologist, "Man is the result of a purposeless and natural process that did not have him in mind. He was not planned. He is a state of matter, a form of life, a sort of animal, and a species of the Order Primates, akin nearly or remotely to all of life and indeed to all that is material." George Gaylord Simpson, *The Meaning of Evolution* (New Haven, CT: Yale University Press, 1971), 345.

20. See, for example, William J. McGuire and Demetrios Papageorgis, "Effectiveness of Forewarning in Developing Resistance to Persuasion," *Public Opinion Quarterly* 26, no. 1 (Spring 1962): 24–34.

21. Cited in Em Griffin, *The Mind Changers: The Art of Christian Persuasion* (Wheaton, IL: Tyndale, 1982).

22. Cited in Henry Taylor, "'Jedi' Religion Most Popular Alternative Faith," *Telegraph*, December 11, 2012, www.telegraph.co.uk/news/religion/9737886/Jedi-religion-most-popular-alternative-faith.html.

23. Taylor, "Alternative Faith."

24. Luc Ferry, *A Brief History of Thought* (New York: Harper Perennial, 2011), 60.

25. Bertrand Russell, *Human Society in Ethics and Politics* (New York: Mentor, 1962), viii.

26. The call to prayer, the *shahada*, is an integral part of the salat: *"Allahu Akbar; Ashadu anna la ilaha illa Allah; Ashadu anna Muhammadan rasul Allah; Haiya 'ala al-salat; Haiya 'ala al-falah; Al-salat khayrun min al-nawm; Allahu Akbar; La ilaha illa Allah."* The English translation is "God is most great; I bear witness there is no God but God; I bear witness Muhammad is the prophet of God; Come to prayer; Come to well-being; Prayer is better than sleep; God is most great; There is no God but God." See more at "Salat: Muslim Prayer," ReligionFacts.com, November 10, 2015, accessed March 26, 2016, www.religionfacts.com/islam/practices/salat-prayer.htm#sthash.U8xtC709.dpuf.

27. Norman L. Geisler, *Baker Encyclopedia of Christian Apologetics* (Grand Rapids: Baker, 1999), 368–69.

28. Serge Trifkovic, *The Sword of the Prophet* (Boston: Regina Orthodox, 2002), 55.

29. Since we will be speaking of Postmodernism as an identifiable pattern of ideas, we will capitalize all references to the term as a worldview.

30. The online etymology website www.etymonline.com says this about the word *law*: law (n.), Old English *lagu* (plural *laga*, comb. form *lah-*) "law, ordinance, rule, regulation; district governed by the same laws," from Old Norse **lagu* "law," collective plural of *lag* "layer, measure, stroke," literally "something laid down or fixed," from Proto-Germanic **lagan* "put, lay" (see lay [v.]). Replaced Old English æ and *gesetnes*, which had the same sense development as *law*. Cf. also *statute*, from Latin *statuere*; German *Gesetz* "law," from Old High German *gisatzida*; Lithuanian *istatymas*, from *istatyti* "set up, establish." In physics, from 1660s. *Law and order* have been coupled since 1796.

31. Edmund Burke, *Reflections on the Revolution in France* (New York: Library of Liberal Arts, 1955), 288.

32. John 1:4: "In [Christ] was life, and the life was the light of men"; John 11:25: "Jesus said ..., 'I am the resurrection and the life. Whoever believes in me, though he die, yet shall he live' "; Colossians 1:16: "By [Christ] all things were created, in heaven and on earth, visible and invisible, whether thrones or dominions or rulers or authorities—all things were created through him and for him."

33. Genesis 2:7: "The LORD God formed the man of dust from the ground and breathed into his nostrils the breath of life, and the man became a living creature."

34. Luke 1:46–47: "Mary said, 'My soul magnifies the Lord, and my spirit rejoices in God my Savior' "; Titus 2:13: "[We are] waiting for our blessed hope, the appearing of the glory of our great God and Savior Jesus Christ."

35. Genesis 1:28: "God blessed [Adam and Eve]. And God said to them, 'Be fruitful and multiply and fill the earth and subdue it, and have dominion over the fish of the sea and over the birds of the heavens and over every living thing that moves on the earth.' "

36. Isaiah 9:6: "To us a child is born, to us a son is given; and the government shall be upon his shoulder, and his name shall be called Wonderful Counselor, Mighty God, Everlasting Father, Prince of Peace;" Luke 1:30–31: "The angel said to her, 'Do not be afraid, Mary, for you have found favor with God. And behold, you will conceive in your womb and bear a son, and you shall call his name Jesus.' "

37. Genesis 49:10: "The scepter shall not depart from Judah, nor the ruler's staff from between his feet, until tribute comes to him; and to him shall be the obedience of the peoples"; Isaiah 9:7: "Of the increase of his government and of peace there will be no end, on the throne of David and over his kingdom, to establish it and to uphold it with justice and with righteousness from this time forth and forevermore. The zeal of the LORD of hosts will do this."

38. Genesis 9:6: "Whoever sheds the blood of man, by man shall his blood be shed, for God made man in his own image."

39. Isaiah 9:6: "To us a child is born, to us a son is given; and the government shall be upon his shoulder, and his name shall be called Wonderful Counselor, Mighty God, Everlasting Father, Prince of Peace"; Luke 1:33: "He will reign over the house of Jacob forever, and of his kingdom there will be no end"; 1 Timothy 6:15: "[God]will display [Christ's appearance] at the proper time—he who is the blessed and only Sovereign, the King of kings and Lord of lords"; Revelation 19:16: "On his robe and on his thigh he has a name written, King of kings and Lord of lords."

40. Psalm 24:1: "The earth is the LORD's and the fullness thereof, the world and those who dwell therein"; Psalm 50:10–12: "Every beast of the forest is mine, the cattle on a thousand hills. I know all the birds of the hills, and all that moves in the field is mine. If I were hungry, I would not tell you, for the world and its fullness are mine"; 1 Corinthians 10:26: "The earth is the Lord's, and the fullness thereof."

41. Genesis 3:15: "I will put enmity between you and the woman, and between your offspring and her offspring; he shall bruise your head, and you shall bruise his heel."

42. See Alvin J. Schmidt, *How Christianity Changed the World* (Grand Rapids: Zondervan, 2004).

43. Romans 12:2: "Do not be conformed to this world, but be transformed by the renewal of your mind, that by testing you may discern what is the will of God, what is good and acceptable and perfect."

44. Hebrews 4:12: "The word of God is living and active, sharper than any two-edged sword, piercing to the division of soul and of spirit, of joints and of marrow, and discerning the thoughts and intentions of the heart."

45. W. Gary Phillips, William E. Brown, and John Stonestreet, *Making Sense of Your World: A Biblical Worldview* (Salem, WI: Sheffield, 2008), chap. 3.

46. John 14:6: "Jesus said to [Thomas], 'I am the way, and the truth, and the life. No one comes to the Father except through me.' "

47. Colossians 1:16: "By [Christ] all things were created, in heaven and on earth, visible and invisible, whether thrones or dominions or rulers or authorities—all things were created through him and for him"; Hebrews 1:1–3: "Long ago, at many times and in many ways, God spoke to our fathers by the prophets, but in these last days he has spoken to us by his Son, whom he appointed the heir of all things, through whom also he created the world. He is the radiance of the glory of God and the exact imprint of his nature, and he upholds the universe by the word of his power. After making purification for sins, he sat down at the right hand of the Majesty on high"; John 1:1–3: "In the beginning was the Word, and the Word was with God, and the Word was God. He was in the beginning with God. All things were made through him, and without him was not any thing made that was made."

48. Acts 9:2: "[Saul] asked [the high priest] for letters to the synagogues at Damascus, so that if he found any belonging to the Way, men or women, he might bring them bound to Jerusalem."

49. Romans 3:23: "All have sinned and fall short of the glory of God."

50. John 3:16: "God so loved the world, that he gave his only Son, that whoever believes in him should not perish but have eternal life."

51. First John 2:2: "He is the propitiation for our sins [turning away God's wrath], and not for ours only but also for the sins of the whole world."

52. James J. D. Luce, "The Fundamentalists Anonymous Movement," *Humanist* 46, no. 1 (January/February 1986).

53. Edward O. Wilson, "The Relation of Science to Theology," *Zygon* 15, no. 4 (December 1980); 433.

54. Neale Donald Walsch, *The New Revelations: A Conversation with God* (New York: Atria Books, 2002), 97.

55. Quoted in Bill Moyers, "Of Myth and Men: A Conversation between Bill Moyers and George Lucas on the Meaning of the Force and the True Theology of *Star Wars*," *Time*, April 26, 1999, 92.

56. George Barna, *Third Millennium Teens* (Ventura, CA: Barna Research Group, 1999), 48. It should be noted that of the teenagers surveyed, 70 percent were active in a church youth group, and 82 percent identified themselves as Christians.

CHAPTER **2**

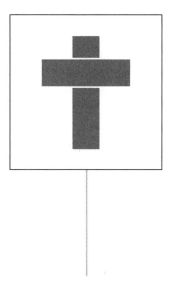

CHRISTIANITY

1. C. E. M. JOAD AND *THE RECOVERY OF BELIEF*

It's easy to imagine C. S. Lewis turning on the radio after an intense morning of writing *The Lion, The Witch and the Wardrobe* and hearing the voice of C. E. M. Joad on the British Broadcasting Company. Joad was a popular philosopher with a cheery, red face and a bristly beard who, for a time, was Britain's most popular radio personality.

His program revolved around answering questions listeners sent in, some serious ("What is the meaning of life?") and others not so serious ("How can a fly land upside down on the ceiling?"). His answers often included subtle jabs at Christians. People loved it. Joad was a big deal.

Bizarrely, Joad was later caught trying to ride on trains without paying and was fired. Soon thereafter he was diagnosed with cancer. These devastating events led Joad back to the faith of his childhood, and shortly before his death, he penned a stunning book called *The Recovery of Belief*. "It is because ... the religious view of the universe seems to me to cover more of the facts of experience than any other that I have been gradually led to embrace it," Joed said.[1] "I now believe that the balance of reasonable considerations tells heavily in favor of the religious, even of the Christian view of the world."[2]

While we don't know every factor involved in Joad's return to faith, we do know that he had read C. S. Lewis's writings. Perhaps Joad found himself entranced with a mythical lion named Aslan, creator of an imaginary land called Narnia, who shed his own innocent blood to triumph over the White Witch and ransom the treacherous Edmund. Perhaps Joad saw something of Edmund in himself and something of Christ in Aslan. It's just a story, but it rings true: we know ourselves as betrayers in need of saving.

2. CHRISTIANITY: THE GREAT MYTH THAT TURNED OUT TO BE TRUE

The basics of the Christian worldview to which C. E. M. Joad returned are quite simple: there is a God; through Jesus Christ, God created the world (Col. 1:16);[3] human beings were made in God's image but fell into sin; the fall of humanity brought sin and brokenness to the rest of creation; and God's Son, Jesus Christ, paid for sin and bought redemption with his own life (Rom. 5:8).[4] It is, as J. R. R. Tolkien once persuaded a reluctant C. S. Lewis, the great myth that became fact!

The Christian worldview is based squarely on the person of Jesus Christ. As John Stott said, "Christ is the centre of Christianity; all else is circumference."[5] Jesus declared, "God so loved the world, that he gave his only Son, that whoever believes in him should not perish but have eternal life" (John 3:16). Other religions may offer advice on how to search for God, but **Christianity** turns that search on its head: God is the one who gets in touch with us. He walked in the garden with Adam and Eve, dwelled in the temple, and revealed himself in Jesus Christ. He is called Immanuel, "God with us." He is the shepherd who searches for his lost sheep (Matt. 18:12).[6] He is the master who came to earth "not to be served but to serve" and give his life to ransom us from our captivity to sin (Mark 10:45).[7]

Christianity: a theistic worldview centered on the person of Jesus Christ that derives it understanding of the world through the teachings of the Holy Bible.

Nonbelievers find this story fantastical. Some think it's too simplistic; others think it's too complicated. Some find claims of miracles absurd, while others bristle at the very idea of supernatural authority. Those who have been hurt by people claiming to be Christians may carry emotional objections. If Christianity is true, though, those who live in unbelief have much to lose: not only do they misunderstand the world we live in, but they sit under God's judgment (John 3:36).[8] Doubtless many find this an unpopular teaching of Christianity, even unreasonable and out of touch.

But disliking parts of a worldview is not the same as disproving it; an idea's complexity, simplicity, or unpopularity is not evidence that it is unreasonable. In this chapter we'll dig for the truth in the mysteries of theology, philosophy, science, and ethics in order to see whether Christianity fulfills its claim as the consummate answer to life's ultimate questions.

Christians believe God makes himself known in nature and in the Bible. These two forms of revelation establish a worldview—a pattern of ideas, beliefs, convictions, and habits—that leads us and others to flourish.

Many people think they know what Christianity is all about; some have even attended church all their lives and never grasped its essence. Christianity isn't just a set of commands and inspirational sayings; it is a story that God is telling, a story that makes sense of all other stories.

> Christians believe God makes himself known in nature and in the Bible. These two forms of revelation establish a worldview—a pattern of ideas, beliefs, convictions, and habits—that leads us and others to flourish.

3. The Christian Story

God is not only the beginning of the Christian story; his existence is the prelude. In philosophical terms, he's the necessary condition for everything else. A story needs a storyteller who is outside the story, capable of telling it. No storyteller, no story.

The argument that demonstrates the universe was caused, and that the cause is sufficient for its effect, is called the *cosmological argument* for God's existence. Some claim energy by itself was sufficient to cause our universe. But while the universe is full of energy, energy itself has never been shown to create information like the ordered information we see in human DNA. Also, energy doesn't have a *plan*, and yet the universe seems ordered and purposeful. It's reasonable, then, to conclude that whatever caused the universe must, according to a predetermined purpose, be capable of producing order. This is suspiciously close to how the Bible describes God.

But the Bible's description of God goes beyond his necessary existence as designer. The Bible claims God is personal and has made himself known to his creation. Further, the Bible describes God as active in his creation, specifically in overcoming humanity's fall into sin and bringing about the subsequent rescue, or redemption, of what he made. Let's take a look at these claims.

God is personal. Pure energy does not create; it explodes. The harnessing of energy for purposeful ends indicates the presence of someone with a plan who is doing the harnessing. The Genesis creation account describes God as this kind of designer. A God who desires purpose rather than randomness and who enacts his authority rather than permitting chaos—such a God has the characteristics of a person.

The existence of humanity also suggests that God is personal. Natural causes and forces cannot explain why the world is populated with *persons* rather than mere entities. Whatever—or *whoever*—caused the universe must also be capable of causing persons. The existence of personhood in the universe suggests that the first cause must be personal as well.

To summarize where this brings us so far, the universe we experience suggests an intelligent, purposeful, personal designer brought it into existence.

Further, the way humans are created reveals something about the character of the God who created us. The biblical God creates humans "in his own image" (Gen. 1:27) and charges us with the task of stewarding his creation. The significant role of humanity in the world is unique to the biblical account.

In contrast to the biblical account, New Spirituality claims god is pure energy, or consciousness. In this view, god has no personality or will. God is a tool to be used, not a person to be known. As William E. Brown points out, in the movie *Star Wars*, Obi-Wan Kenobi doesn't tell Luke Skywalker, "The force loves you" or "The force died for your sins." He tells him to "*use* the force." The metaphor is significant: we *use* things; we *relate* to persons.

The Bible says God's characteristics are fully independent of our understanding or use of them. "Be still, and know that I am God" (Ps. 46:10); "How unsearchable are his judgments and how inscrutable his ways!" (Rom. 11:33); "The God who made the world and everything in it, being Lord of heaven and earth, does not live in temples made by man, nor is he served by human hands, as though he needed anything, since he himself gives to all mankind life and breath and everything" (Acts 17:24–25).

We cannot bend God to our expectations. We cannot program him to be predictable. In C. S. Lewis's *The Lion, the Witch and the Wardrobe*, Mr. Beaver tried to describe Aslan, the Christ figure, to Lucy, who expressed trepidation that Aslan was a lion: "He isn't safe?" Lucy asked. "'Course he isn't safe," said Mr. Beaver. "But he's good. He's the King, I tell you."

God has made himself known. The word *revelation* ("to reveal") is from the Greek word *apokaluptō*, which means "to uncover, to unveil, or to lay bare."[9] God doesn't just reveal his plan; he reveals *himself*. He is *transcendent* (beyond and separate from the world) as well as *immanent* (in the world). When God expressed his thoughts, the universe came into being (Gen. 1:1; John 1:1).[10] His presence sustains the world (Col. 1:16–17).[11] The universe speaks of God's creativity and presence; it speaks the language of God.[12]

That God expresses himself communicatively tells us he is relational. Relationship is not something God *does* but something he *is*. God is triune, one God made manifest in three persons: God the Father,[13] God the Son,[14] and God the Holy Spirit.[15] This relationship in the Godhead is closely tied to what God would have *us* do. Matthew 28:19 says, "Go therefore and make disciples of all nations, baptizing them in the name of the *Father* and of the *Son* and of the *Holy Spirit*." All three persons are critical to our mission in the world.

When people say they can't believe in God because he has not shown himself, they are overlooking a critical fact: this is exactly what he has done. The problem is not a lack of visible evidence but an unwillingness to see. As Elizabeth Barrett Browning wrote in her poem *Aurora Leigh*,

> Earth's crammed with heaven,
> And every common bush afire with God;
> But only he who sees, takes off his shoes,
> The rest sit round it, and pluck blackberries,
> And daub their natural faces unaware
> More and more, from the first similitude.[16]

Like an artist, God is visible in his works, and especially in the person of Christ. Yet he is visible only if we have eyes to see (John 10:30; 14:7–8).[17]

God has created. God created through *fiat*, a Latin word meaning "let it be." What God wants happens. What God says goes. Even *nothing* became *something* when God told it to.

Many skeptics doubt whether human life has any special meaning. For a depressing example, attend Samuel Beckett's play *Breath*. The curtain opens to a stage littered with trash. The audience hears a birth cry, then the sound of breathing, and then another cry. Twenty-five seconds after it opens, the curtain closes. The message: life begins with crying and ends with crying, and everything in between is garbage. Lest you think this is a prank, as of last count *Breath* has been performed 1,314 times, with eighty-five million people in attendance, making it Beckett's most viewed play.[18]

Life is more than an "episode between two oblivions,"[19] as Ernest Nagel memorably phrased it. We are more than "dust in the wind," as an old song describes it.[20] The biblical creation account uses the word *good* to describe creation's value. Our English word *good* simply does not convey the goodness of this kind of good. The Hebrew word *tob* means "good in every way possible: in potential, in beauty, in convenience, in joy, in fruitfulness, in economics, in wisdom, in sensuality, in happiness, and even in morality."[21] God was pleased with creation's goodness and called for it to flourish. To Adam and Eve he said, "Be fruitful and multiply and fill the earth" (Gen. 1:28). It was not a micromanaged event; God unleashed creation with an express desire to see it *teem* with life.[22]

Humanity's appearance receives special attention in the biblical creation narrative. Each step along the way God said, "Let there be ...," and it was as he said. In Genesis 1:26, with human creation, the language abruptly changed. Instead of *"Let there be,"* the text says, *"Let us make."* After creating humans and imbuing them with purpose, God said it was *"very* good" (v. 31). In Hebrew, the phrase is *meod tob.* It is almost impossible to exaggerate the resonant awesomeness this phrase is meant to convey. It literally means "exceedingly, heartbreakingly, abundantly, richly, loudly, immeasurably good in a festive, generous, happy, intelligent, charming, splendid way." Those who view humans as a plague are not, from God's perspective, wise and brave but stingy, small minded, and bitter—Scrooges on a cosmic level.[23]

It was not only the individual creation of Adam and Eve that was good; their relationships with God, with each other, and with creation itself were also good. Christians themselves often miss the true significance of God's design. Lesslie Newbigin, who invested his life as a missionary and theologian in India, once related a conversation with a Hindu friend, who said,

> I can't understand why you missionaries present the Bible to us in India as a book of religion. It is not a book of religion—and anyway we have plenty of books of religion in India. We don't need any more! I find in your Bible a unique interpretation of universal history, the history of the whole of creation and the history of the human race. And therefore a unique interpretation of the human person as a responsible actor in history. That is unique. There is nothing else in the whole religious literature of the world to put alongside it.[24]

Part of our responsibility as human actors is to work. Genesis 2:15 says, "The LORD God took the man and put him in the garden of Eden to work it and keep it." Work is not a product of the fall; it is very much woven into the fabric of God's very good plan for us. We should work for the love of the work itself, "for the sake of doing well a thing that is well worth doing," as Dorothy Sayers put it.[25]

Companionship is also part of God's design. "It is not good that the man should be alone; I will make him a helper fit for him" (Gen. 2:18). Relationship and work go together. "Two are better than one, because they have a good reward for their toil" (Eccles. 4:9). Spreading order across the chaos is a task so large and so joyful that it is a pity for it to be done alone. But mere companionship is not all that's described in Genesis. It is also about a marriage between a man and woman who delight in each other's company, work side by side, and fulfill God's commands to flourish. Their names were Adam and Woman. (Woman's name was subsequently changed to Eve, but that came later.)

The Christian story of creation is this: a relational creator made human beings in his image, releasing them to relate and create. This is the foundation of everything—of human rights, social order, marriage. It is, in short, the framework for the good life—for the individual and for all of civil society.

> The Christian story of creation is this: a relational creator made human beings in his image, releasing them to relate and create. This is the foundation of everything—of human rights, social order, marriage. It is, in short, the framework for the good life—for the individual and for all of civil society.

So what went wrong?

Human beings are fallen. Things function best according to their design. If we ignore God's design for eating, our bodies function poorly. If we ignore creation's delicate balance, we overharvest and choke the life out of the earth. Ignoring design breaks faith with the Designer. The theological term for this is *sin*. Cornelius Plantinga Jr. defines *sin* as "not only the breaking of law but also the breaking of covenant with one's savior. Sin is the smearing of a relationship, the grieving of one's divine parent and benefactor, a betrayal of the partner to whom one is joined by a holy bond."[26]

Genesis 3:6 narrates the horrifying way our first parents ate of the forbidden Tree of Knowledge of Good and Evil, intentionally breaking their relationship with God in order to pursue their *own* good, their *own* delight, and their *own* wisdom.[27] Disobedience broke all of the key relationships in their lives. In shame they hid from the God with whom they had previously communed. Their unity with each other dissolved into squabbling and blame. The fruitfulness of nature at their touch was replaced with pain, frustration, deceit, and toil.

In the midst of this misery, it was an act of God's mercy not to prolong their lives forever. Death finally came to Adam and Eve, but not before long life gave them a front-row seat to the shriveling consequences wrought by their misuse of the Tree of Knowledge of Good and Evil, and sin's consequent vandalism of the world. Saint Augustine used the Latin phrase *incurvatus in se* to describe the grisly way sin curves in on itself. Martin Luther explained:

> Our nature, by the corruption of the first sin being so deeply curved in on itself *(incurvatus in se)* that it not only bends the best gifts of God towards itself and enjoys them, as is plain in the works-righteous and hypocrites, or rather even uses God himself in order to attain these gifts, but it also fails to realize that it so wickedly, curvedly, and viciously seeks all things, even God, for its own sake.[28]

As we pursue everything for our own sakes, our perception of reality grows ever more at odds with what actually exists. We imagine ourselves to be free and beautiful, but in actuality we grow more hunched, pinched, and sickly with each passing day. Try as we might to ignore the effects of sin in our lives, reality has a way of knocking on the back door when we refuse to meet it at the front door.

One of the most embarrassing aspects of sin is the tendency to *blame* others rather than repent. The man blamed God for creating the woman and blamed the woman for giving him the fruit. The woman blamed the serpent for tempting her (Gen. 3:12–13).[29] When we see sin as something others do to us, when we judge ourselves by our good intentions and impute bad motives to others, when we treat as evil that which prevents us from getting our way, we are witnessing the metastasizing of sin in our lives. Only one outcome is possible: "Sin when it is fully grown brings forth death" (James 1:15).

> Sin is not just *out there*; it is *in here*. It affects structures as well as persons. Whole communities, indeed whole nations, fall in its wake.

Sin is not just *out there*; it is *in here*. It affects structures as well as persons. Whole communities, indeed whole nations, fall in its wake. Sin never heals; it only corrupts. Sin attacks our humanity—frenzied, we cannibalize the humanity of others. The spiral is downward, always, and endless. We tremble at the destination but refuse to change course; we are addicts, dressing up like gods, wrecking relationships, sadistically bruising that which is fragile. The morning light finds us bloated and bleary, tearfully swearing, "Never again." But self-destruction is our bent. Some bleed out through disastrous lifestyle choices; others suffocate on haughtiness and contempt. But no matter the means, we all die.

In the midst of this tragedy, still we hold certain graces in common. We bear God's image even yet. We help people and people help us. Crops grow. Sunsets remain beautiful. But we are *thoroughly* fallen; nothing is unaffected by our fallenness. Worse, we are *absolutely* fallen; nothing we can do for ourselves will fix our fallenness.

If the Christian story is true, we are badly in need of rescue. Who will help us?

God redeems. Some see God as a judge who, after a couple of millennia of contemplation, decided to punish his own Son for the sin of humanity. This picture falls far short of the full truth. In Scripture God reveals himself as the redeemer buying back his wayward creation. We see his redemptive nature in the garden when he told the serpent, "I will put enmity between you and the woman, and between your offspring and her offspring; he shall bruise your head, and you shall bruise his heel" (Gen. 3:15). God took a basic human kinesthetic act—standing on our feet—and transformed it, metaphorically, into a weapon to destroy slithering evil. The one who deceived at the beginning will be crushed at the end (Rom. 16:20; Rev. 12:9).[30]

> At the end of all things, according to Christianity, the serpent who said "Take, eat" in the garden will be defeated by the Savior who said "Take, eat" in the upper room.

Consider, too, the Passover, God's redemption of the Israelites from Egyptian slavery. The centerpiece of the Passover celebration was a meal of preparation (Exod. 12), again a basic act, which Jesus repeated with his disciples (Mark 14). At the end of all things, according to Christianity, the serpent who said "Take, eat" in the garden will be defeated by the Savior who said "Take, eat" in the upper room. And to put an exclamation point on it, Christ's victory will be commemorated with the meal of meals: a wedding feast (Rev. 19:9).[31]

The redemptive language in Scripture indicates that God cares about everydayness. We stand, walk, run, chew, swallow, and digest. These are not just temporal activities; at the end of all things lays the promise of a new earth as well as a new heaven. Eternity is not about escaping the physical but about redeeming it. All things will be made new (Rev. 21:1–5).[32]

The Christian story, then, is of a personal, relational God who created optimal conditions for human flourishing, against whom humanity has rebelled and continues to rebel. It's a story of buying back the rebels in order to set things right again. As you can imagine, those who do not wish this story to be true view it with immense suspicion. So we must be prepared to answer the question, "How do we know it's true?"

4. GENERAL AND SPECIAL REVELATION: HOW GOD MAKES HIMSELF KNOWN

Let's review for a moment. Every one of us is on a journey. To complete this journey, we need a map, a reliable guide showing where we are, where we are going, and the route between the two. If, for example, you are searching for a good school to attend, you might identify successful people and inquire about where they got their training. When it comes to life's ultimate questions, though, we need more than just quick advice. We need someone to bring the dark things to light. This is called *revelation*, a term we discussed earlier in some detail.

So what has been revealed? The famed American scientist Carl Sagan asserted that "the cosmos is all that is or ever was or ever will be."[33] In his television series *Cosmos*, he rhapsodized, "It makes good sense to worship the sun and the stars because we are their children."[34] Compelling prose, to be sure, but terrible theology and even worse science. The evidence that life arose from nothing through random-chance processes is not as clear cut as secular evangelists like Sagan would have us believe. There are, rather, very good reasons to believe in a God who makes himself known.

Christians believe God has revealed himself in a *general* way through creation and in a *personal* way through his divine words and acts recorded in the Bible, especially in the person of Jesus Christ. Millard Erickson defines the two forms of revelation this way: "On the one hand, *general revelation* is God's communication of Himself to all persons at all times and in all places. *Special revelation*, on the other hand, involves God's particular communications and manifestations which are available now only by consultation of certain sacred writings."[35] Let's examine the Christian view of both, starting with general revelation.

5. GENERAL REVELATION: NATURE SPEAKS OF GOD'S DESIGN

The late Dallas Willard, one-time department chair and professor of philosophy at the University of Southern California, identified the great philosophers—Plato, Aristotle, Saint Augustine, Saint Thomas Aquinas, William of Ockham, René Descartes, Baruch Spinoza, Gottfried Wilhelm Leibniz, John Locke, George Berkeley, Immanuel Kant, and Georg W. F. Hegel—as theists, in one form or another, even though their particular theistic beliefs differed from one another. Even David Hume, whom Secularists embrace as one of their own, declared, "The whole frame of nature bespeaks an intelligent author; and no rational enquirer can, after serious reflection, suspend his belief a moment with regard to the primary principles of genuine Theism and Religion."[36]

> *General Revelation:* God's universal revelation about himself (Ps. 19:1–6; Rom. 1:18–20) and morality (Rom. 2:14–15) that can be obtained through nature.

Although it takes special revelation to show us the ultimate truths set down in Scripture and embodied in Jesus Christ, general revelation can bring us to a general knowledge of God because it gives insight into *how* he has communicated his nature and character in creation. Most times, the questions surrounding general revelation are phrased something like this: Did life come from a living, intelligent God who loves order and beauty, or did it arise randomly from inert matter?

People tend to believe in the most likely solution to a problem, so it is unsurprising to find most agreeing that "In the beginning, God created the heavens and the earth" and "all things therein" (Gen. 1:1; Acts 17:24 KJV). Justin Barrett, a senior researcher at the University of Oxford's Centre for Anthropology and Mind, found in his research that children instinctively believe the world was created with purpose. They are predisposed to believe in a creator-God.[37]

If you find it difficult to believe in random particles assembling themselves into a fine-tuned universe, you are not alone. The English astronomer and mathematician Fred Hoyle, who coined the term *big bang* and served for years as a leading atheist spokesman, said there is a better chance of producing a Boeing 747 via a junkyard explosion than there is of arriving at life by accident.[38] Further, Hoyle expressed skepticism about the chance development of DNA, noting that merely lining up the necessary enzymes by chance would consume twenty billion years. Three respected scientists—Charles Thaxton, Walter Bradley, and Roger Olsen—wrote in *The Mystery of Life's Origin* that "the undirected flow of energy through a primordial atmosphere and ocean is at present a woefully inadequate explanation for the incredible complexity associated with even simple living systems, and is probably wrong."[39]

Christianity says a creator-God, not a sequence of random cosmic accidents, is responsible for an orderly, beautiful, meaningful cosmos. The Bible says, "The heavens declare the glory of God, and the sky above proclaims his handiwork" (Ps. 19:1). Evolutionist Paul Amos Moody affirmed, "The more I study science the more I am impressed with the thought that this world and universe have a definite design—and a design suggests a designer. It may be possible to have design without a designer, a picture without an artist, but my mind is unable to conceive of such a situation."[40]

> Christianity says a creator-God, not a sequence of random cosmic accidents, is responsible for an orderly, beautiful, meaningful cosmos.

The universe is a product of design, Christianity says, and everyone can observe this whether or not other arguments suppress that truth.

6. Can General Revelation Lead People to God?

Of course, there are disagreements among Christians about origin issues. But when top scientists contradict atheists' claims, it catches our attention. Robert Jastrow is one person whom atheists wish would have just kept quiet. After completing a PhD in theoretical physics at Columbia University, Jastrow became one of the first employees of NASA, chairing the committee that outlined the scientific goals of moon exploration. It was because of Jastrow's extraordinary credentials and stellar career that the scientific community was so startled when he concluded,

> At this moment it seems as though science will never be able to raise the curtain on the mystery of creation. For the scientist who has lived by his faith in the power of reason, the story ends like a bad dream. He has scaled the mountains of ignorance; he is about to conquer the highest peak; as he pulls himself over the final rock, he is greeted by a band of theologians who have been sitting there for centuries.[41]

Sometimes insight about general revelation leads people to a personal relationship with God through Christ. Many discover God through the evidence of a structured universe or the purposeful nature of reality. As with renowned philosopher C. E. M. Joad, some come to believe in a personal God and in Jesus Christ as his appointed means of redemption. But general revelation does not necessarily lead people to faith. Biblically speaking, one divine purpose of general revelation is to remove people's excuses for *not* believing in God. Recall Romans 1:19–20:

> What can be known about God is plain to [people], because God has shown it to them. For his invisible attributes, namely, his eternal power and divine nature, have been clearly perceived, ever since the creation of the world, in the things that have been made. So they are without excuse.

C. S. Lewis framed this "excuse removal" like this:

> Suppose there were no intelligence behind the universe. In that case nobody designed my brain for the purpose of thinking. Thought is merely the by-product of some atoms within my skull. But if so, how can I trust my own thinking to be true? But if I can't trust my own thinking, of course, I can't trust the arguments leading to atheism, and therefore have no reason to be an atheist, or anything else. Unless I believe in God, I can't believe in thought; so I can never use thought to disbelieve in God.[42]

Once the excuses are removed, we enter the domain of special revelation.

7. Special Revelation: Divine Communication through Inspired Scripture

General revelation is a necessary but insufficient means for revealing the Creator. The character of creation tells us *what* exists but not *why*: Why am I here? Why is there something wrong with us? Why can't we fix ourselves? Christianity turns to the Bible as the opening of heaven's door, showing us what God is like, what he wants us to do, and how we might be saved from our distress.

Christians view Scripture as the way God revealed himself over the course of sixteen hundred years in the recorded words of leaders, prophets, and sages. These writings are not ordinary; they express precisely what God wants to communicate. They are set apart. The biblical word for "set apart" is *holy*. We even call God's revelation "the Holy Bible." Christians also call the Bible "God's Word" because it is, in a real sense, his "speech" (Matt. 4:4; John 17:17–20).[43] The teachings and events recorded there are the most reliable basis for understanding all reality.

We use the term *divine inspiration* to describe the doctrine of how God's words ended up in Scripture. This addresses how a mighty and intelligent God could have communicated his written message to us, which his chosen human vessels rendered just so. It's a vitally important question. Those who claim to be Christians and yet deny the Bible's divine inspiration are ignoring the Scripture's own claim to be God breathed (2 Tim. 3:16–17).[44]

> *Special Revelation:* God's unique revelation about himself through the Scriptures (Ps. 19:7–11; 2 Tim. 3:14–17), miraculous events (e.g., dreams, visions, prophets, prophecy, etc.), and Jesus Christ (John 1:1–18).

In 2009, a minister named Marilyn Sewell interviewed the acerbic atheist Christopher Hitchens. Trying to exempt herself from Hitchens's criticisms of Christianity, Sewell said, "I'm a liberal Christian, and I don't take the stories from the scripture literally. I don't believe in the doctrine of atonement (that Jesus died for our sins, for example). Do you make a distinction between fundamentalist faith and liberal religion?"

Hitchens replied, "I would say that if you don't believe that Jesus of Nazareth was the Christ and Messiah, and that he rose again from the dead and by his sacrifice our sins are forgiven, you're really not in any meaningful sense a Christian."[45]

How interesting: an avowed atheist could see this simple truth, and a self-proclaimed minister could not. One would expect self-identified Christians to affirm the integrity of their holy book. But some find the Bible's extraordinary claims embarrassing and think they can soften Secularists' criticisms by expressing skepticism or disbelief. As Christopher Hitchens showed, though, the effect is the opposite: Secularists already see Christians as typically soft headed. When Christians cave in to criticism, Secularists just shrug and add one more descriptor: cowardly.

> I would say that if you don't believe that Jesus of Nazareth was the Christ and Messiah, and that he rose again from the dead and by his sacrifice our sins are forgiven, you're really not in any meaningful sense a Christian.
>
> —Christopher Hitchens

Christians need not feel embarrassed about the Bible. There is intriguing evidence justifying the Christian's belief in the divine inspiration of the Bible. For example, given that different men in very different circumstances authored its books over many centuries, the unity of teaching in the Bible is *startling*. The Bible has changed billions of lives, and even nonbelievers accept the genius of its moral teachings. This cannot be claimed, truthfully, of any other book. British broadcaster Melvyn Bragg put it this way: "The Bible is one of the fundamental makers of the modern world. It has set free not only its readers and its preachers but those who have used it as a springboard to achieve gains and enrichment in our world never before enjoyed by so many."[46]

In studying the Bible, the reader meets God's most direct form of special revelation: the person of Jesus Christ. "In Jesus of Nazareth," wrote Carl F. H. Henry, "the divine source of revelation and the divine content of that revelation converge and coincide."[47] Christ's teachings, actions, and, most significantly, his resurrection provide the cornerstone for special revelation and a solid foundation for Christian theism. The Holy Spirit, too, plays an important role in this dialogue. Henry explained, "Scripture itself is given so that the Holy Spirit may etch God's Word upon the hearts of his followers in ongoing sanctification that anticipates the believer's final, unerring conformity to the image of Jesus Christ, God's incarnate Word."[48]

Our need to be conformed to the character of Christ is why Christians don't just read the Bible once and set it aside but study it as the living Word of God and seek constantly to apply its teachings. It's a project from which a person never graduates until finally arriving in God's presence and knowing the whole and complete truth (1 Cor. 13:12).[49]

For all of these reasons, we need to understand what special revelation is all about. We'll examine it by seeking to answer five questions:

1. How are we to understand the Bible?
2. What does the Bible say about humanity?
3. What does the Bible say is wrong with us?
4. What does the Bible say about how we should live?
5. How are we to understand other worldviews based on the Bible?

1. How are we to understand the Bible? What Scripture means depends on God's intention, not our interpretation. The apostle Peter was clear: "No prophecy of Scripture comes from someone's own interpretation. For no prophecy was ever produced by the will of man, but men spoke from God as they were carried along by the Holy Spirit" (2 Pet. 1:20–21).

What resources do we have to understand the Bible? The answers include careful study, listening to the Holy Spirit, and participation in the body of Christ. As Paul told Timothy, "Do your best to present yourself to God as one approved, a worker who has no need to be ashamed, rightly handling the word of truth" (2 Tim. 2:15). The analogy of craftsmanship is powerful. Take music, for example. There are many ways for an orchestra conductor to interpret the opening sequence of Beethoven's Fifth Symphony. By directing the orchestra to play the notes at a different pace or volume, the conductor brings out new understandings of the piece. But if the orchestra plays other notes, it is no longer performing Beethoven's work. Similarly, if the musicians are poorly trained, the screeching violins and burping brass will destroy any credibility the conductor's interpretation might otherwise have had.

Craftsmen know that long before the work of interpretation has any meaning, the strenuous work of understanding must be carried out. Interpretation (what the text *means*) precedes application (what the text means *to me*). The next time you're in a Bible study and someone says, "Here's what the text means to me," consider whether that person has thoroughly understood God's intended meaning before you pay attention to his or her application.

2. What does the Bible say about humanity? The Christian worldview ascribes meaning to human existence right from the start, based on God's declaration, "Let us make man in our image, after our likeness" (Gen. 1:26). Naturalistic worldviews rely on chance and time to explain birds capable of aerial navigation and bees that communicate through dance. Christians credit an all-knowing God who ordered the universe in a beautiful symphony of light, life, sound, and color.

Saying "God did it" isn't a cop-out. C. E. M. Joad's conversion came about through recognizing that the Christian explanation of human nature better fits the facts of experience and allows a more comprehensible view of the world. He said his "changed view of the nature of man ... led to a changed view of the nature of the world."[50] Why would a philosopher like Joad, and so many others through the ages, draw this conclusion? Because they understand the nature of thinking. The mind is not merely the random chemical firings of synapses in the brain. If we understand, it's because we were meant to.

> With me, the horrid doubt always arises whether the convictions of man's mind, which has been developed from the mind of the lower animals, are of any value or at all trustworthy. Would any one trust in the convictions of a monkey's mind, if there are any convictions in such a mind?
>
> —Charles Darwin

Even Charles Darwin recognized the problem adherents of atheistic, naturalistic explanations of the mind encounter: "With me, the horrid doubt always arises whether the convictions of man's mind, which has been developed from the mind of the lower animals, are of any value or at all trustworthy. Would any one trust in the convictions of a monkey's mind, if there are any convictions in such a mind?"[51]

3. What does the Bible say is wrong with us? Embedded in Marxism are stunning examples of humanity's inhumanity. The record stretches from Karl Marx's consistent dishonesty and misrepresentation of facts in his writings to the slaughter of millions of innocent citizens at the hands of Marxist-Leninist dictators.[52] Even a *Moscow News* article referred to the "horrors" of Stalinism, noting that Joseph Stalin was responsible for mass murder. Robert Conquest documented Stalin's systematic annihilation of millions of Ukrainians, and Jung Chang and Jon Halliday wrote of China that "Mao Tse-tung, who for decades held absolute power over the lives of one-quarter of the world's population, was responsible for well over 70 million deaths in peacetime, more than any other twentieth-century leader."[53] R. J. Rummel and Stéphane Courtois documented the slaughter of millions more.[54]

> The Bible never waxes romantic about human nature. Stories of revenge, genocide, false imprisonment, greed, lust, and murder, among many other forms of evil, fill its pages, putting the inhumanity of humans toward one another fully on display.

The Bible never waxes romantic about human nature. Stories of revenge, genocide, false imprisonment, greed, lust, and murder, among many other forms of evil, fill its pages, putting the inhumanity of humans toward one another fully on display. As C. E. M. Joad said,

> Is it not obvious that human arrogance and love of power, that human brutality and cruelty, that, in a

word, man's inhumanity to man, are responsible for ... [tragic events such as the Holocaust]; obvious, too, that it is precisely these characteristics that have written their melancholy record upon every page of human history?[55]

But here's the hard news: if the moral code given in the Bible is a *window* through which we can discern evil and corruption in the world, it is also a *mirror* in which we see every detail of our own utter sinfulness (Jer. 17:9; Rom. 3:10–23).[56]

R. C. Sproul is fond of saying we are a lot more like Adolf Hitler than we are like Jesus Christ.[57] When we ask ourselves whether our inclinations are good or evil and whether it is fair to blame society for our urges to steal, lust, or lie, we must face our own bent toward sin. G. K. Chesterton was right: our penchant for vice is ubiquitous. And the Bible is certainly right: our hearts are "deceitful [and] desperately sick" (Jer. 17:9).[58] Even "our righteous deeds are like a polluted garment" (Isa. 64:6) because we perform them out of a prideful belief in our own saving power. "Know thyself," the ancient Greeks said. We do—and it's not pretty.

The distance between God and us is vast, and the implications for our lives are staggering. Carl F. H. Henry said,

> Christianity declares that God is more than the ground and goal of the moral order. Unequivocally it lays stress on the reality of God's judgment of history. It affirms, that is, the stark fact of moral disorder and rebellion: "the whole world lieth in wickedness" (1 John 5:19). By emphasizing the fact of sin and the shattered moral law of God, the dread significance of death, the wiles of Satan and the hosts of darkness, Christian ethics sheds light on the treacherous realities of making moral choices.[59]

The reality of which Henry speaks, that "all have sinned and fall short of the glory of God" (Rom. 3:23), is a unique aspect of the Christian ethical system. D. James Kennedy wrote,

> When a person makes up his own ethical code he always makes up an ethical system which he thinks he has kept. In the law of God, we find a law which smashes our self-righteousness, eliminates all trust in our own goodness, and convinces us that we are sinners. The law of God leaves us with our hands over our mouths and our faces in the dust. We are humbled before God and convinced that we are guilty transgressors of his law.[60]

Once we truly grapple with how corrupt we are, it is easier to see how hopeless we are without divine intervention. The vehicle carrying our hopes and dreams hasn't just been in a fender bender. It is wrecked. We must first wallow in our deadness in Adam before we glory in our aliveness in Christ (Rom. 5:12–21; Eph. 2:1–10).[61]

The Christian ethical code points to our sinful nature and introduces the only one who can save us, the man who has not transgressed, Jesus Christ. Put simply, "the law is given to convince us that we fail to keep it."[62] When we realize this truth, we are driven for salvation to the One who has not failed.

4. What does the Bible say about how we should live? We cannot simply rely on Christ to save us while continuing in our sinful ways. Rather, once we embrace the ultimate sacrifice God made for us, we gain power through the Holy Spirit to adhere to his moral order. This does not mean it is easy to do what is morally right. As C. S. Lewis said, "There is nowhere this side of heaven where one can safely lay the reins on the horse's neck. It will never be lawful simply to 'be ourselves' until 'ourselves' have become sons of God."[63]

In the power of the Holy Spirit, we have the capacity to live as the apostle Paul instructed Christians: "Let love be genuine. Abhor what is evil; hold fast to what is good" (Rom. 12:9). Christian morality is founded on the conviction of an absolute moral order outside of, and yet somehow inscribed on, our very being. It flows like a river

> It will never be lawful simply to "be ourselves" until "ourselves" have become sons of God.
>
> — C. S. Lewis

from the nature of the Creator through the nature of created things and into our minds and hearts. We cannot make it up. To quote Lewis again, "The human mind has no more power of inventing a new value than of imagining a new primary colour, or, indeed, of creating a new sun and a new sky for it to move in."[64]

According to a good number of secular philosophies, we should treat all morals as relative to the situation or to the culture in which we were raised. In practice, even Secularists treat some abstract values (such as justice, love, and courage) as absolute. They cringe at the Nazi Holocaust, the abuse of child soldiers, and sex trafficking. The Christian worldview explains how we intuitively know these things are wrong: not because we've been raised in certain cultures or have had a certain kind of training but because moral truth actually exists for all people in all cultures at all times.

This moral understanding, according to the apostle John, is "the true light, which gives light to everyone … coming into the world" (John 1:9). The apostle Paul called it "the work of the law … written on their hearts, while their conscience also bears witness" (Rom. 2:15). This insight gives light to our ethical eyes, as we will see in the "Ethics" chapter, so we can "take every thought captive to obey Christ" (2 Cor. 10:5).

Many who finally begin to reflect on the deeper things of life—"How did I get here? Why am I here? Where am I going?"—discover the Christian answers to these questions are more complete, more robust. Even today the vast majority of people (an average of 92 percent[65]) believe in God, a fact Paul also found to be true in the Athens of his day (Acts 17:23).[66]

When we understand God's nature and character, and when we acknowledge Christ's atoning sacrifice, the Christian worldview gains tremendous explanatory and transformative power:

- Putting Christian economics into practice results in prosperity for the greatest number of people, even while the interventionist welfare state seems to secure generational poverty.
- Putting Christian sociology into practice encourages strong families and guards against widespread drug use, crime, unemployment, poverty, and disease; whereas secular views of sexuality destroy the family, which holds society together.
- Putting Christian law into practice guarantees human rights as God ordained, while its denial—in France for two centuries, in the Soviet Union for seventy years, and in the United States for the last half century—has resulted in a history of carnage.[67]
- Putting Christian theology and philosophy into practice results in salvation of the soul (Matt. 16:26),[68] enlightenment of the mind, and purpose in life.

5. How are we to understand other worldviews based on the Bible? Often the children's game of tag features a "home base" to which one can cling for safety; resting in this neutral zone frees one from making decisions, from taking risks. But there is no neutral zone in the war of ideas. To reject one worldview is to automatically go over to another side. C. S. Lewis expressed it starkly in *The Abolition of Man*: "Either we are rational spirit obliged for ever to obey the absolute values of the *Tao* [moral order], or else we are mere nature to be kneaded and cut into new shapes for the pleasures of masters who must, by hypothesis, have no motive but their own "natural" impulses."[69]

The other five worldviews we will consider in this book—Islam, Secularism, Marxism, New Spirituality, and Postmodernism—all came about long after Christianity, so we can't expect the Bible to address them specifically. But the other worldviews present in Bible times, some of which were much more popular than Christianity itself, were similar enough to give insight into modern perspectives. Christianity views non-Christian worldviews as based on "the basic principles of this world" and not on Christ (Col. 2:8).[70] In a word, they are foolish. It is foolish to say, "There is no God" (Ps. 14:1).[71] It is foolish to scan the heavens and argue for chance and accident. It is foolish to examine the human body without an eye to design. It is foolish to experience the seasons of life and never sense the witness of God. It is foolish to listen to Handel's *Messiah* and picture evolving monkeys making music.

> **It is foolish to listen to Handel's *Messiah* and picture evolving monkeys making music.**

As we draw this chapter to a close, let's briefly examine the other five worldviews and see how the Christian worldview interacts with each.

Islam. As the number of adherents of Islam grows rapidly, Christians are faced with having to understand and grapple with the implications of a worldview that only a few short years ago, most Americans saw as an exotic and distasteful set of beliefs held by people we don't understand in parts of the world we don't think much about. But with rapid immigration and a global economy, every Christian will encounter Islam as both a religion and a political ideology.

For Christians especially, Islam presents a confusing dilemma. Muslims believe in one God. They acknowledge Jesus as a prophet. They believe in moral absolutes. And yet Muslims see Christians as blasphemers because they believe in the Trinity, a doctrine they say has led to secularization and corruption. In countries like Nigeria, where the Christian-Muslim divide is especially intense, some have embraced Chrislam, a synthetic religion combining elements of Christianity and Islam. But while Christians and Muslims must learn to live together, their beliefs are incompatible. Islam cannot answer the ultimate questions of life in a way that satisfies the tests of truth.

> **Muslims believe in one God. They acknowledge Jesus as a prophet. They believe in moral absolutes. And yet Muslims see Christians as blasphemers.**

Secularism and Marxism are cousins. To both, it is seen as misguided and possibly dangerous to stake much on a belief in God as revealed in the Bible. Divine action is not needed to explain life's existence, they insist. This *naturalism* reduces both Secularism and Marxism to one reliable way of knowing: *scientism*, the notion that reliable knowledge comes only from scientific inquiry and method. But explaining all of reality is a burden far too heavy for science to carry. Even Julian Huxley, one of the twentieth century's leading evolutionists, recognized the limited nature of the scientific method:

> Science has removed the obscuring veil of mystery from many phenomena, much to the benefit of the human race: but it confronts us with a basic and universal mystery— the mystery of existence in general, and of the existence of mind in particular. Why does the world exist? Why is the world-stuff what it is? Why does it have mental or subjective aspects as well as material or objective ones? We do not know.[72]

Even if science could go beyond *how* and reveal to us *why* we exist as we do, it has very little to say about things that make life worth living: we ponder, we laugh, we sing, we are capable of doing good, we feel guilt and sadness over our own wrongdoing and that of others, we create things, we reason our way to conclusions, and experiences of beauty and craftsmanship deeply move us.

Naturalists cannot account for these things, but they depend on them for meaning in life, just as you and I do. To describe them as secondary, derivative, or mere reflections of material reality is inadequate. As C. S. Lewis pointed out, we ascribe meaning to our things, which is not a reasonable assumption if they proceed from a random universe. For casting such a wide net, worldviews based on naturalism catch very little.

New Spirituality. New Spirituality's view of God as impersonal consciousness is irreconcilable with the biblical concept of God as a personal, relational being who reveals himself generally in nature and specially through Scripture. When it comes to the nature of God and reality, the Christian worldview offers a confidence not found in New Spirituality. Hebrews 11:1[73] explains that biblical faith is based on confidence and assurance, not wishes or guesses. Based on the historical eyewitness accounts of Jesus's life, death, and resurrection, Christians are confident of his claim that he is "the way, and the truth, and the life" (John 14:6). In contrast to the all-roads-lead-to-God notion, the map of Christianity shows only *one* road leading to God : the road passing through the life, teachings, death, and resurrection of Jesus Christ (John 8:31–32; 14:6; Col. 2:2; 2 Pet. 1:16–18; 1 John 5:20).[74]

Postmodernism. Postmodernism considers truth to be particular to a person's language, community of origin, and socially constructed self. The Christian worldview, by contrast, claims the existence of an objective truth that can be known. This truth is universal in its scope and application—nearly everything about Christianity is. God created the *whole universe*, and sin is a *universal* condition affecting every human being. Christ died to redeem the *whole world*. Christians are to love God with *all* their hearts and minds and their fellow human beings around the *whole world* (Matt. 22:37–37). Christians may join Postmodernists in critiquing *scientific materialism*, the idea that only matter exists and that only science can reveal its nature, but they will find Postmodernism's assertion that "all worldviews are local" unpersuasive.

> Postmodernism considers truth to be particular to a person's language, community of origin, and socially constructed self.

8. Where Does Faith Come In?

Unfortunately, some Christians see faith as indefensible. Belief by its very nature is "beyond reason," they say. These Christians point to Colossians 2:8 (NIV 1984), where the apostle Paul wrote, "See to it that no one takes you captive through hollow and deceptive philosophy." People who use this verse as an anti-philosophical proof text do so by omitting its ending, in which Paul described the kind of philosophy he was warning Christians against—philosophy "which depends on human tradition and the basic principles of this world rather than on Christ."

Paul did not see Christianity as beyond reason or inaccessible to those unfamiliar with localized Jewish traditions. In Acts 17, he confronted the vain and deceitful philosophies of the atheistic Epicureans and pantheistic Stoics—the professional Secularists and New Spiritualists of his day. He countered their ideas with Christian ideas, he reasoned with them, he preached to them, and he accented three truths many Christians would like to soft-pedal: the resurrection of Jesus Christ (Acts 17:18), God's creation of the universe (v. 24), and the judgment to come (v. 31).[75]

Of course, while Paul's hearers understood creation and suspected him to be correct about judgment, they thought he was crazy to argue for the resurrection of the dead. Even here Paul gave arguments that scholars like N. T. Wright and Gary Habermas have expanded upon in our own day. Josh McDowell says, "After more than seven hundred hours of studying this subject and thoroughly investigating its foundation, I have come to the conclusion that the resurrection of Jesus Christ is one of the most wicked, vicious, heartless hoaxes ever foisted upon the minds of men, or it is the most fantastic fact of history."[76] McDowell's conclusion: this improbable and thrilling event actually happened. You can follow these arguments in McDowell's book *The New Evidence That Demands a Verdict*,[77] N. T. Wright's book *The Resurrection of the Son of God*, and Gary Habermas's book *The Case for the Resurrection of Jesus*.

Once we have captured every idea and made it obedient to Christ, we should use these thoughts to

- "destroy arguments and every lofty opinion raised against the knowledge of God" (2 Cor. 10:5);
- "walk in [Christ], rooted and built up in him and established in the faith, just as [we] were taught, abounding in thanksgiving" (Col. 2:6–7);
- "see to it" that we are not taken captive "by philosophy and empty deceit, according to human tradition, according to the elemental spirits of the world, and not according to Christ" (v. 8); and
- be "zealous for what is good" without fear, "always being prepared to make a defense to anyone who asks" for the reason for our hope, and to do so "with gentleness and respect, having a good conscience" that puts slanderers to shame. Along with this, we must be willing to "suffer for doing good, if that should be God's will, than for doing evil" (1 Pet. 3:13–17).[78]

We encourage you to consider these passages a magnifying glass through which to examine every area of your life: the way you daily invest your time, energy, giftings, relationships, and creativity. If Christianity is so reasonable, though, why do so many people resist believing it?

9. If Christianity Is True, Why Doesn't Everyone See It?

Either a supreme mind has always existed and at specific points in time created matter and the universe, or matter is eternal and formed the universe by itself. There really aren't any other viable options on the table at this point. Christian arguments are reasonable when it comes to seeing the universe as the product of design (general revelation) and the Bible as the most accurate description of the Designer and how we might come to know him through Jesus Christ (special revelation).

But why do so many people not see what Christians believe to be self-evidently true? The key may be found in John 1:1–2, 10–11:

> In the beginning was the Word, and the Word was with God, and the Word was God. He was in the beginning with God.... He was in the world, and the world was made through him, yet the world did not know him. He came to his own, and his own people did not receive him.

We humans have two problems: the world is dark and we are blind. In the sense of general revelation, what is true about God is plainly seen. Regarding special revelation, though, the Christian worldview must be believed to be understood. So how do we come to this belief? Christian interpretations vary, but an old hymn weaves together what most can agree on: "I sought the Lord, and afterward I knew / He moved my soul to seek Him, seeking me. / It was not I that found, O Savior true; / No, I was found of Thee."[79]

Without revelation to light the way, people cannot comprehend truth. They'll invent counterfeit worldviews in an attempt to shed light on their own paths. We'll take a look at each of these worldviews in turn, starting with one many people see as a close cousin of Christianity: Islam.

ENDNOTES

1. C. E. M. Joad, *The Recovery of Belief* (London: Faber and Faber, 1952), 16.
2. Joad, *Recovery of Belief*, 22.
3. Colossians 1:16: "By him [Christ] all things were created, in heaven and on earth, visible and invisible, whether thrones or dominions or rulers or authorities—all things were created through him and for him."
4. Romans 5:8: "God shows his love for us in that while we were still sinners, Christ died for us."
5. John R. W. Stott, *Basic Christianity* (Grand Rapids: Eerdmans, 1958), 21.
6. Matthew 18:12: "What do you think? If a man has a hundred sheep, and one of them has gone astray, does he not leave the ninety-nine on the mountains and go in search of the one that went astray?"
7. Mark 10:45: "Even the Son of Man came not to be served but to serve, and to give his life as a ransom for many."
8. John 3:36: "Whoever believes in the Son has eternal life; whoever does not obey the Son shall not see life, but the wrath of God remains on him."
9. Dr. Bruce Ware, "Doctrine of Scripture," *Biblical Training*, accessed March 12, 2014, www.biblicaltraining.org /library/doctrine-scripture/systematic-theology-i/bruce-ware.
10. Genesis 1:1: "In the beginning, God created the heavens and the earth"; John 1:1: "In the beginning was the Word, and the Word was with God, and the Word was God."
11. Colossians 1:16–17: "By him [Christ] all things were created, in heaven and on earth, visible and invisible, whether thrones or dominions or rulers or authorities—all things were created through him and for him. And he is before all things, and in him all things hold together."
12. For more information, see Francis Collins, *The Language of God* (New York: Free Press, 2007).

13. Malachi 2:10: "Have we not all one Father? Has not one God created us? Why then are we faithless to one another, profaning the covenant of our fathers?"; Matthew 23:9: "Call no man your father on earth, for you have one Father, who is in heaven"; John 14:9–10: "Jesus said ..., 'Have I been with you so long, and you still do not know me, Philip? Whoever has seen me has seen the Father. How can you say, 'Show us the Father'? Do you not believe that I am in the Father and the Father is in me? The words that I say to you I do not speak on my own authority, but the Father who dwells in me does his works"; 1 Corinthians 8:6: "For us there is one God, the Father, from whom are all things and for whom we exist, and one Lord, Jesus Christ, through whom are all things and through whom we exist"; Ephesians 1:3: "Blessed be the God and Father of our Lord Jesus Christ, who has blessed us in Christ with every spiritual blessing in the heavenly places"; Ephesians 4:6: "[There is] one God and Father of all, who is over all and through all and in all"; Hebrews 1:3: "[Christ] is the radiance of the glory of God and the exact imprint of his nature, and he upholds the universe by the word of his power. After making purification for sins, he sat down at the right hand of the Majesty on high."

14. John 1:1: "In the beginning was the Word, and the Word was with God, and the Word was God"; John 1:14: "The Word became flesh and dwelt among us, and we have seen his glory, glory as of the only Son from the Father, full of grace and truth"; John 5:18: "This was why the Jews were seeking all the more to kill him, because not only was he breaking the Sabbath, but he was even calling God his own Father, making himself equal with God"; John 8:58: "Jesus said ..., 'Truly, truly, I say to you, before Abraham was, I am'"; John 10:30–33: "'I and the Father are one.' The Jews picked up stones again to stone him. Jesus answered them, 'I have shown you many good works from the Father; for which of them are you going to stone me?' The Jews answered him, 'It is not for a good work that we are going to stone you but for blasphemy, because you, being a man, make yourself God'"; Philippians 2:5–8: "Have this mind among yourselves, which is yours in Christ Jesus, who, though he was in the form of God, did not count equality with God a thing to be grasped, but made himself nothing, taking the form of a servant, being born in the likeness of men. And being found in human form, he humbled himself by becoming obedient to the point of death, even death on a cross"; Colossians 2:9: "In [Christ] the whole fullness of deity dwells bodily"; Hebrews 1:8: "Of the Son [God] says, 'Your throne, O God, is forever and ever, the scepter of uprightness is the scepter of your kingdom.'"

15. Matthew 28:19: "Go therefore and make disciples of all nations, baptizing them in the name of the Father and of the Son and of the Holy Spirit"; 2 Corinthians 3:16–18: "When one turns to the Lord, the veil is removed. Now the Lord is the Spirit, and where the Spirit of the Lord is, there is freedom. And we all, with unveiled face, beholding the glory of the Lord, are being transformed into the same image from one degree of glory to another. For this comes from the Lord who is the Spirit"; 2 Corinthians 13:14: "The grace of the Lord Jesus Christ and the love of God and the fellowship of the Holy Spirit be with you all"; Ephesians 4:4–6: "There is one body and one Spirit—just as you were called to the one hope that belongs to your call—one Lord, one faith, one baptism, one God and Father of all, who is over all and through all and in all."

16. Elizabeth Barrett Browning, *Aurora Leigh*, 3rd ed. (London: Chapman and Hall, 1857), 304.

17. John 10:30: "I and the Father are one"; John 14:7–8: "[Jesus said,] 'If you had known me, you would have known my Father also. From now on you do know him and have seen him.' Philip said to him, 'Lord, show us the Father, and it is enough for us.'"

18. C. J. Ackerley and S. E. Gontarski, eds., *The Faber Companion to Samuel Beckett* (London: Faber and Faber, 2006), 73.

19. Ernest Nagel, *Logic without Metaphysics: And Other Essays in the Philosophy of Science* (New York: Free Press, 1956), 17.

20. Kerry Livgren, "Dust in the Wind," recorded by Kansas, © 1978 Kirshner.

21. Based on definition in Spiros Zodhiates, ed., *Hebrew-Greek Key Word Study Bible: King James Version* (Chattanooga: AMG, 2008), s.v. *"tob."*

22. See Andy Crouch's thought-provoking book *Culture Making: Recovering Our Creative Calling* (Downers Grove, IL: InterVarsity, 2008).

23. See, for example, E. Calvin Beisner, "The Competing World Views of Environmentalism and Christianity," Cornwall Alliance for the Stewardship of Creation, accessed March 26, 2014, www.cornwallalliance.org/docs / THECOM~1.PDF. In this essay, Beisner noted a statement from Britain's Prince Phillip that if he were to be reincarnated, he would want to come back as a killer virus to decrease the human population to manageable levels.

24. Lesslie Newbigin, *A Walk through the Bible* (Louisville, KY: Westminster John Knox, 1999), 4, quoted in John W. Miller, *How the Bible Came to Be: Exploring the Narrative and Message* (Mahwah, NJ: Paulist, 2004), 113.

25. Dorothy L. Sayers, *Letters to a Diminished Church* (Nashville: W Publishing Group, 2004), 118.

26. Cornelius Plantinga Jr., *Not the Way It's Supposed to Be: A Breviary of Sin* (Grand Rapids: Eerdmans, 1995), 12.

27. Genesis 3:6: "When the woman saw that the tree was good for food, and that it was a delight to the eyes, and that the tree was to be desired to make one wise, she took of its fruit and ate, and she also gave some to her husband who was with her, and he ate."

28. Martin Luther, *Lectures on Romans*, 515–16, quoted in Mark Johnston, *Saving God: Religion after Idolatry* (Princeton, NJ: Princeton University Press, 2009), 88.

29. Genesis 3:12–13: "The man said, 'The woman whom you gave to be with me, she gave me fruit of the tree, and I ate.' Then the LORD God said to the woman, 'What is this that you have done?' The woman said, 'The serpent deceived me, and I ate.'"

30. Romans 16:20: "The God of peace will soon crush Satan under your feet"; Revelation 12:9: "The great dragon was thrown down, that ancient serpent, who is called the devil and Satan, the deceiver of the whole world—he was thrown down to the earth, and his angels were thrown down with him."

31. Revelation 19:9: "The angel said to [John], 'Write this: Blessed are those who are invited to the marriage supper of the Lamb.' And he said to me, 'These are the true words of God.'"

32. Revelation 21:1–5: "Then I [John] saw a new heaven and a new earth, for the first heaven and the first earth had passed away, and the sea was no more. And I saw the holy city, new Jerusalem, coming down out of heaven from God, prepared as a bride adorned for her husband. And I heard a loud voice from the throne saying, 'Behold, the dwelling place of God is with man. He will dwell with them, and they will be his people, and God himself will be with them as their God. He will wipe away every tear from their eyes, and death shall be no more, neither shall there be mourning, nor crying, nor pain anymore, for the former things have passed away.' And he who was seated on the throne said, 'Behold, I am making all things new.' Also he said, 'Write this down, for these words are trustworthy and true.'"

33. Carl Sagan, *Cosmos* (New York: Random House, 1980), 4.

34. Carl Sagan, *Cosmos*, directed by Adrian Malone (Australian Broadcasting Corporation, Carl Sagan Productions, and KCET, 1980).

35. Millard J. Erickson, *Christian Theology*, 3 vols. (Grand Rapids: Baker, 1983), 1:153.

36. Quoted in J. P. Moreland and Kai Nielsen, *Does God Exist? The Great Debate* (Nashville: Thomas Nelson, 1990), 211. What can a naturalist do with mind, soul, altruism, creativity, rationality, conscience, song, and laughter?

37. Martin Beckford, "Children Are Born Believers in God, Academic Claims," *Telegraph*, November 24, 2008, www.telegraph.co.uk/news/religion/3512686/Children-are-born-believers-in-God-academic-claims.html.

38. Fred Hoyle, *The Intelligent Universe* (London: Michael Joseph, 1983), 18–19.

39. Charles Thaxton, Walter Bradley, and Roger Olsen, *The Mystery of Life's Origin: Reassessing Current Theories* (New York: Philosophical Library, 1984), 186. Students particularly interested in biological origins should also read Percival Davis and Dean Kenyon, *Of Pandas and People*, 2nd ed. (Richardson, TX: Foundation for Thought and Ethics, 1993).

40. Paul Amos Moody, *Introduction to Evolution* (New York: Harper and Row, 1962), 497.

41. Robert Jastrow, *God and the Astronomers* (New York: Norton, 1978), 116.

42. C. S. Lewis, *Broadcast Talks* (London: Geoffrey Bles, 1944), 37–38.

43. Matthew 4:4: "[Jesus] answered, 'It is written, "Man shall not live by bread alone, but by every word that comes from the mouth of God"'"; John 17:17–20: "Sanctify them in the truth; your word is truth. As you sent me into the world, so I have sent them into the world. And for their sake I consecrate myself, that they also may be sanctified in truth. I do not ask for these only, but also for those who will believe in me through their word."

44. Second Timothy 3:16–17: "All Scripture is breathed out by God and profitable for teaching, for reproof, for correction, and for training in righteousness, that the man of God may be complete, equipped for every good work."

45. "The Hitchens Transcript," *Portland Monthly*, December 17, 2009, www.pdxmonthly.com/articles/2009/12/17/christopher-hitchens.

46. Melvyn Bragg, *The Book of Books* (Berkeley, CA: Counterpoint, 2011), 5.

47. Carl F. H. Henry, *God, Revelation, and Authority*, vol. 2, *God Who Speaks and Shows* (Waco, TX: Word Books, 1976), 11.

48. Henry, *God Who Speaks and Shows*, 2:15.

49. First Corinthians 13:12: "Now we see in a mirror dimly, but then face to face. Now I know in part; then I shall know fully, even as I have been fully known."

50. Joad, *Recovery of Belief*, 46.

51. Charles Darwin, *The Life and Letters of Charles Darwin*, 2 vols., ed. Francis Darwin (London: John Murray, 1887), 1:316.

52. See Paul Johnson, *Intellectuals* (New York: Harper and Row, 1988), 52.

53. Jung Chang and Jon Halliday, *Mao: The Unknown Story* (New York: Alfred A. Knopf, 2005), 3.

54. R. J. Rummel, *Death by Government* (New Brunswick, NJ: Transaction Publishers, 1994); Stéphane Courtois et al., *The Black Book of Communism: Crimes, Terror, Repression* (Cambridge, MA: Harvard University Press, 1999).

55. Joad, *Recovery of Belief*, 46.

56. Jeremiah 17:9: "The heart is deceitful above all things, and desperately sick; who can understand it?"; Romans 3:10–23: "'None is righteous, no, not one; no one understands; no one seeks for God. All have turned aside; together they have become worthless; no one does good, not even one. Their throat is an open grave; they use their tongues to deceive. The venom of asps is under their lips. Their mouth is full of curses and bitterness. Their feet are swift to

shed blood; in their paths are ruin and misery, and the way of peace they have not known. There is no fear of God before their eyes.' Now we know that whatever the law says it speaks to those who are under the law, so that every mouth may be stopped, and the whole world may be held accountable to God. For by works of the law no human being will be justified in his sight, since through the law comes knowledge of sin. But now the righteousness of God has been manifested apart from the law, although the Law and the Prophets bear witness to it—the righteousness of God through faith in Jesus Christ for all who believe. For there is no distinction: for all have sinned and fall short of the glory of God."

57. R. C. Sproul, *Before the Face of God*, vol. 2 (Grand Rapids: Baker, 1993).

58. Jeremiah 17:9: "The heart is deceitful above all things, and desperately sick; who can understand it?"

59. Carl F. H. Henry, *Christian Personal Ethics* (Grand Rapids: Eerdmans, 1957), 209.

60. D. James Kennedy, *Why I Believe* (Waco, TX: Word Books, 1980), 91.

61. Romans 5:12–21: "Just as sin came into the world through one man, and death through sin, and so death spread to all men because all sinned—for sin indeed was in the world before the law was given, but sin is not counted where there is no law. Yet death reigned from Adam to Moses, even over those whose sinning was not like the transgression of Adam, who was a type of the one who was to come. But the free gift is not like the trespass. For if many died through one man's trespass, much more have the grace of God and the free gift by the grace of that one man Jesus Christ abounded for many. And the free gift is not like the result of that one man's sin. For the judgment following one trespass brought condemnation, but the free gift following many trespasses brought justification. For if, because of one man's trespass, death reigned through that one man, much more will those who receive the abundance of grace and the free gift of righteousness reign in life through the one man Jesus Christ. Therefore, as one trespass led to condemnation for all men, so one act of righteousness leads to justification and life for all men. For as by the one man's disobedience the many were made sinners, so by the one man's obedience the many will be made righteous. Now the law came in to increase the trespass, but where sin increased, grace abounded all the more, so that, as sin reigned in death, grace also might reign through righteousness leading to eternal life through Jesus Christ our Lord"; Ephesians 2:1–10: "You were dead in the trespasses and sins in which you once walked, following the course of this world, following the prince of the power of the air, the spirit that is now at work in the sons of disobedience—among whom we all once lived in the passions of our flesh, carrying out the desires of the body and the mind, and were by nature children of wrath, like the rest of mankind. But God, being rich in mercy, because of the great love with which he loved us, even when we were dead in our trespasses, made us alive together with Christ—by grace you have been saved—and raised us up with him and seated us with him in the heavenly places in Christ Jesus, so that in the coming ages he might show the immeasurable riches of his grace in kindness toward us in Christ Jesus. For by grace you have been saved through faith. And this is not your own doing; it is the gift of God, not a result of works, so that no one may boast. For we are his workmanship, created in Christ Jesus for good works, which God prepared beforehand, that we should walk in them."

62. Kennedy, *Why I Believe*, 90.

63. C. S. Lewis, *God in the Dock* (Grand Rapids: Eerdmans, 1970), 286.

64. C. S. Lewis, *The Abolition of Man* (New York: MacMillan, 1955), 56–57.

65. Luis Lugo et al., *U.S. Religious Landscape Survey* (Washington, DC: Pew Research Center, 2008), 162, http://religions .pewforum.org/pdf/report-religious-landscape-study-full.pdf.

66. Acts 17:23: "As I [Paul] passed along and observed the objects of your worship, I found also an altar with this inscription, 'To the unknown god.' What therefore you worship as unknown, this I proclaim to you."

67. Yes, carnage in the United States: abortion kills 1.2 million unborn babies every year.

68. Matthew 16:26: "What will it profit a man if he gains the whole world and forfeits his soul? Or what shall a man give in return for his soul?"

69. Lewis, *Abolition of Man,* 84.

70. Colossians 2:8: "See to it that no one takes you captive by philosophy and empty deceit, according to human tradition, according to the elemental spirits of the world, and not according to Christ."

71. Psalm 14:1: "The fool says in his heart, 'There is no God.' They are corrupt, they do abominable deeds, there is none who does good."

72. Julian Huxley, *Essays of a Humanist* (New York: Harper and Row, 1964), 107.

73. Hebrews 11:1: "Now faith is the assurance of things hoped for, the conviction of things not seen."

74. John 8:31–32: "Jesus said to the Jews who had believed him, 'If you abide in my word, you are truly my disciples, and you will know the truth, and the truth will set you free'"; John 14:6: "Jesus said ..., 'I am the way, and the truth, and the life. No one comes to the Father except through me'"; Colossians 2:2: "[May] their hearts ... be encouraged, being knit together in love, to reach all the riches of full assurance of understanding and the knowledge of God's mystery, which is Christ"; 2 Peter 1:16–18: "We did not follow cleverly devised myths when we made known to you the power and coming of our Lord Jesus Christ, but we were eyewitnesses of his majesty. For when he received honor and glory from God the Father, and the voice was borne to him by the Majestic Glory, 'This is my beloved Son, with

whom I am well pleased,' we ourselves heard this very voice borne from heaven, for we were with him on the holy mountain"; 1 John 5:20: "We know that the Son of God has come and has given us understanding, so that we may know him who is true; and we are in him who is true, in his Son Jesus Christ. He is the true God and eternal life."

75. Acts 17:18: "Some of the Epicurean and Stoic philosophers also conversed with him. And some said, 'What does this babbler wish to say?' Others said, 'He seems to be a preacher of foreign divinities'—because he was preaching Jesus and the resurrection"; Acts 17:24: "The God who made the world and everything in it, being Lord of heaven and earth, does not live in temples made by man"; Acts 17:31: "[God] has fixed a day on which he will judge the world in righteousness by a man whom he has appointed; and of this he has given assurance to all by raising him from the dead."

76. Josh McDowell, *The New Evidence That Demands a Verdict* (Nashville: Thomas Nelson, 1999), 203.

77. McDowell, *New Evidence*.

78. First Peter 3:13–17: "Now who is there to harm you if you are zealous for what is good? But even if you should suffer for righteousness' sake, you will be blessed. Have no fear of them, nor be troubled, but in your hearts honor Christ the Lord as holy, always being prepared to make a defense to anyone who asks you for a reason for the hope that is in you; yet do it with gentleness and respect, having a good conscience, so that, when you are slandered, those who revile your good behavior in Christ may be put to shame. For it is better to suffer for doing good, if that should be God's will, than for doing evil."

79. "I Sought the Lord," music by George W. Chadwick, circa 1880, public domain.

CHAPTER 3

*I*SLAM

1. SEPTEMBER 11, 2001

September 11, 2001: Exactly 316 years to the day after Muslim invaders were turned away at the gates of Vienna, Austria.[1] The world watched in horror as four commercial airliners were mutated into flying missiles in the service of radical Islamist ideology. On each flight, hijackers used knives or box cutters, mace, and pepper spray to keep passengers at bay, threatening to detonate bombs if anyone tried to fight back. Little did the passengers suspect the planes themselves would become the bombs. At 8:14 a.m., American Airlines Flight 11, a nonstop flight from Boston to Los Angeles, was the first to be hijacked. Five armed men murdered several people on the flight before ramming the plane into the North Tower of the World Trade Center in New York City thirty-two minutes later.

United Airlines Flight 175, also bound for Los Angeles, was similarly hijacked at approximately 8:45 a.m. Fifteen minutes later one brave passenger, Peter, risked a call to his father:

> It's getting bad, Dad—A stewardess was stabbed—They seem to have knives and Mace—They said they have a bomb—It's getting very bad on the plane—Passengers are throwing up and getting sick—The plane is making jerky movements—I don't think the pilot is flying the plane—I think we are going down—I think they intend to go to Chicago or someplace and fly into a building—Don't worry, Dad—If it happens, it'll be very fast—My God, my God.[2]

As the phone connection abruptly ended at 9:03 a.m., Peter's father witnessed Flight 175 crash into the World Trade Center's South Tower, instantly immolating all on board and untold numbers in the building.

American Airlines Flight 77, departing from Washington, DC, and also intended for Los Angeles, was hijacked minutes before 9:00 a.m., and thirty minutes later crashed into the Pentagon. United Airlines Flight 93, departing Newark, New Jersey, for San Francisco, left twenty-five minutes behind schedule, and approximately forty-six minutes into the flight, the hijackers gained control of the cockpit. Some of the passengers phoned loved ones and heard of the other attacks. Recognizing the likely intentions of their own aircraft's hijackers, they stormed the cockpit. Their efforts were in vain, however. United Flight 93 "plowed into an empty field in Shanksville, Pennsylvania, at 580 miles per hour, about 20 minutes' flying time from Washington, D.C."[3]

> In the course of one day, Americans became tragically aware that they had been asleep while a very powerful worldview emerged from a centuries-long slumber in a bid for global power.

In the course of one day, Americans became tragically aware that they had been asleep while a very powerful worldview emerged from a centuries-long slumber in a bid for global power. Shocked and angered, the nation was asking, "What kind of people would sacrifice their lives to kill as many as possible?" The answer was discovered almost immediately: the hijackers were all Saudi and Egyptian Muslim men. If all the terrorists were Muslim, Americans wondered, might any Muslim be a terrorist? Muslim Americans wondered if their neighbors would seek revenge on all Muslims, including those not prone to violence.

2. RADICAL VERSUS MODERATE ISLAM

Those who observed the events of September 11, 2001, especially those who lost loved ones, find it difficult to view **Islam** outside the prism of their experience. If we are to understand the worldview of Islam on its own terms, though, we need to seek to understand what Islam says about itself and not just rely on our visceral reactions.

Violent, radical Muslims who dream of establishing a global Islamic state and are willing to use violence to achieve this end do exist. Most Muslims, though, simply want to engage in Muslim practices and raise their families according to Muslim traditions. They hope more people will convert to Islam, but they have little interest in establishing a global Islamic state if it is going to involve violence or tearing down the structures of democracy from which they have obtained personal benefit. Such Muslims are often called *moderates*. This is not to imply that they are less devout, but rather that they welcome building economic ties with the West instead of destroying it.[4]

In any event, distinguishing between moderate and radical Muslims is not easy. In the respected *Foreign Policy* magazine, John L. Esposito and Dalia Mogahed summarized research conducted by the Gallup corporation. The research revealed substantive errors in what Americans think about radical Islam. Radicals, in fact, are *not* more likely to attend religious services than moderates. They earn more money and stay in school longer than moderates, and they express more satisfaction with their financial situations. They are also as likely as moderates to express admiration of the West's technology, democracy, and freedom of speech.

> *Islam:* a theistic worldview centered on the life of the prophet Muhammad that derives its understanding of the world through the teachings of the Quran, Hadith, and *Sunnah*.

The researchers wrote, "We find that Muslim radicals have more in common with their moderate brethren than is often assumed. If the West wants to reach the extremists, and empower the moderate Muslim majority, it must first recognize who it's up against."[5] This astounding statement would be rejected out of hand were it not for the researchers' credentials: Esposito is a respected professor of Islamic studies at Georgetown University, and Mogahed is one of the most influential Muslim women in the world.

The key difference between moderate and radical Muslims is this: radicals are more likely to believe that the West "threatens and attempts to control their way of life."[6] So how can we tell the difference between moderates and radicals? Gallup asked Muslims in several countries whether they thought the 9/11 attacks were justified (on a scale of 1 to 5, where 1 was "totally unjustified" and 5 was "completely justified"). Those who answered "4" or "5" were defined as radical. Only 7 percent of Muslims fit this designation, but with more than 1.6 billion Muslims in the world today, this means there could be at least 112 million radical Muslims.[7]

3. SHOULD WE BE AFRAID?

At 7:15 p.m. on November 4, 2004, armed guards wearing bulletproof vests and carrying machine guns surrounded Geert Wilders and announced, "You will have to leave at once." Shoving him into an armored car, the men told him he was in extreme danger of being assassinated and would have to stay in a safe house until further notice. Since that day, Wilders, a high-level political leader, hasn't been home. He cannot go out in public without a bulletproof vest and a contingent of armed guards.

Word of these death threats against Wilders and a colleague, Ayaan Hirsi Ali, immediately reached the news media, which reported that "anti-Muslim politicians" had "gone into hiding." Wilder's crime: in a speech he stated that "the existence of peaceful Muslims should not blind us to the fact that Islam is a violent ideology that should be rejected by Muslims and non-Muslims alike."[8]

Wilders was not in Afghanistan, or even Iraq, but in the Netherlands.[9] His experience is discomforting because it points to a substantial problem Westerners face: As Islam grows,

---

more and more people are discovering Islam as an ideology—a worldview—that by its nature demands political control at the expense of democracy, freedom, and constitutional government. And yet we're conflicted: we have Muslim neighbors who work hard, get along with others, and are peaceful, law-abiding citizens.

So which is it? Is Islam, as Wilders describes it, a "violent ideology" waiting to subvert the West or a peaceful religion with more than a billion adherents? We think the question can only be answered by viewing Islam as a worldview, a pattern of ideas, beliefs, convictions, and habits. More than that, though, we need to understand that Islam is a system of practices by which Muslims believe they demonstrate submission to Allah. By understanding Islam's founding principles, sources of revelation, and key teachings as a complete worldview, we will perceive Islam more clearly and know how to respond biblically.

Islamist: a Muslim who embraces the full application of shariah law and who views jihad as a call to conquer nonbelieving nations.

According to M. Zuhdi Jasser, a Muslim medical doctor and a US Navy veteran, it is helpful to distinguish between two groups: Muslims and **Islamists**.[10] Muslims are people who are "culturally" Islamic. They were born into Muslim families or converted to Islam and identify with Islamic culture and try to follow its practices. Muslims take Islam seriously, but they can get along with non-Muslims and can live comfortably in societies that are not Islamic in nature.

Shariah Law: Derived primarily from the Quran and *Sunnah*, shariah law is the moral and legal code that governs the lives of Muslims. Shariah addresses a wide variety of subjects, such as diet, hygiene, prayer, contracts, business, crime, and punishment.

Islamists, sometimes called *Islamic fundamentalists*, are radicals who believe in the literal application of the teachings of Muhammad and the full application of **shariah law**, the moral code of Islam outlined in the Quran and other teachings and rulings Muslims consider authoritative.[11] Shariah law governs everything from diet and sexual practices to the punishment of crime. Many of its aspects are shockingly harsh, legitimizing slavery, advocating physical abuse of wives, demanding heavy taxation of Christians and Jews living in Muslim lands, and calling for the killing of Muslims who convert to another faith.[12]

Jihad: from the Arabic word translated as "struggle," jihad is both the inner spiritual battle of every Muslim to fulfill his or her religious duties and the outer, physical struggle against the enemies of Islam.

Muslims and Islamists seem to differ in their understanding of **jihad**. *Jihad* means "to fight against non-Muslims," and it is clearly commanded of all Muslims in the Quran.[13] Muslims see jihad as a battle to discipline themselves, or perhaps a call to defend themselves against those who attack Islam. Islamists, on the other hand, see jihad as it was historically seen, as a conquest of nonbelieving nations.[14] To the Muslim way of thinking, the world was originally Islamic, and every person was born a Muslim. Those who are not now Muslims are in rebellion.

To Islamists, the use of force is justified against such rebellion. Usually this takes the form of a strict application of shariah law and strident education campaigns to win converts and inspire nominal Muslims to be more Islamist.

Some think there is a third category of Muslims: **jihadis**. According to Nabeel Qureshi, a convert from Islam to Christianity who upon graduation from medical school became an evangelist rather than a physician, jihadis are Islamists who have crossed the line into weaponizing their beliefs. By committing themselves to physical violence, jihadis have made themselves into a sort of army dedicated to destroying the West.[15]

Jihadi: an Islamist who embraces the use of terrorism in pursuit of jihad.

While Western Muslims say jihad is only for defensive purposes, jihadis include as legitimate "defense" anything that conquers the world's resistance to Islam becoming a global civilization. They believe the use of physical force and terror in the pursuit of jihad is entirely called for, and "peace" with Islam will occur only when nonbelievers submit. While Islamists might not participate in overt violence, many tacitly approve of these techniques.[16]

One difficulty in the Islamic faith is that jihad is required of all Muslims and is always described in a warlike fashion. Would-be moderate Muslims are presented with a serious dilemma: Do they participate in jihad by warring against their neighbors, ignore it, or explain it as a form of personal self-discipline that has nothing to do with warfare?[17] Those in the group we've called *Muslim*, as opposed to Islamists and jihadis, mostly try to reinterpret the meaning of jihad as a form of personal discipline, or they just ignore the concept altogether. In fact, as strongly as many Muslims feel about their Islamic identity, they simply do not follow through with Muslim practices. As Abdu Murray, a former Muslim and leader of Aletheia International, says, most Muslims simply do not adhere to many of the commands of Islamic scripture. "I can't tell you how many Muslims are nominal at best," he notes. "They are [only] cultural Muslims. If it were a crime to be an orthodox Muslim, they couldn't be convicted of it.... They hold their worldview with a varying degree of tightness."[18]

Because of the explicit aims of Islamists, many people dread Islam's growth. Many Christians hold this view, as do adherents of other worldviews. Many Muslims are afraid as well; they disagree with radicalism but refuse to vocalize their true beliefs so as not to dishonor their families or undermine their religious leaders. Salman Rushdie, a Muslim novelist who has lived under threat of death for decades because he spoke out against radical Islam, said, "The trouble with fear is that it's not susceptible to reason. You can say to people, 'Here are seventy-two reasons not to be afraid' and they'll say, 'Yeah, but I'm still scared.'"[19]

Fear is one thing we must never give in to, and only one thing makes it go away: love. "Perfect loves casts out fear" (1 John 4:18).[20] When we are filled with love, even tough love, we gain fortitude. Love can transform fear into moral courage; reason alone cannot.

From the standpoint of love, we can see Islam as a worldview as diverse as Christianity, Judaism, Buddhism, or Hinduism, with factions, differing convictions, and varying levels of commitment. We engage it with the gospel just as we engage other worldviews.

4. THE HISTORY OF ISLAM

Islam means "submission." A Muslim is "one who submits" to Allah and the principles of Islam as embodied in the **ummah**, the worldwide community of Muslims. The *ummah* is a very strong force for Muslims, binding together religious commands, ideology, and cultural practices, providing both a comforting sense of belonging and a reassuring hierarchy: children are subject to adults, women to men, the individual family to community leaders, and community leaders to the Islamic state. Individual identity and interests are subordinated.[21] The

Ummah: from the Arabic word for "nation," *ummah* is the collective community of Muslims around the world.

ummah, though not a formal structure, exerts enormous power; it is something Muslims do not want to upset or disagree with or offend. To break away from it is to be alienated and lost.

Today Islam is a major world religion, boasting a membership of nearly one-fourth of the world's population. The majority of Muslims are not Arabs. The largest Muslim populations in the world reside in Indonesia, followed by Pakistan, India, and Bangladesh. Nearly half of the world's Muslim population lives in these four countries.

The founder of Islam was Muhammad. According to the Islamic narrative, he was born around AD 570 in Mecca, or modern-day Saudi Arabia. The city's culture at that time was characterized by polytheism, the belief in many deities, and animism, the belief that various spirits inhabit plants, animals, and other objects in the world. As a merchant, Muhammad also regularly encountered the monotheism of Jews and Christians.

When he was around forty years of age, Muhammad became troubled by a series of visions he thought were demonic. One of his wives, Khadija, persuaded him to think that the

Quran: the central holy book of Islam that Muslims believe to be the literal word of God, recited verbatim from God to Muhammad through the angel Gabriel.

visions were from God. In AD 610, according to Muslim tradition, Muhammad claimed the angel Gabriel visited him and commissioned him as a prophet of God. He spent the next several years transmitting the message orally into what Muslims consider the most pure understanding of God, the holy **Quran.**

The message Muhammad said God gave him was simple and elegant: there is one God who made all things, to whom all people must submit, and there will be a day of judgment in which all humans will be judged according to their deeds, both good and evil. Muhammad believed Islam to be the final, all-encompassing religion God was giving humankind. The dictation of the Quran continued for twenty-three years until Muhammad's death in AD 632.

By the early seventh century, Mecca was a trading center of great religious, economic, and political power on the Arabian Peninsula. It boasted the Kaaba (a large, black, box-like building) that contained 360 tribal deities, including statues of Mary and Jesus, which various tribes placed there on their regular pilgrimages to the city. According to Muslim tradition, Muhammad proclaimed these tribal gods to be an offense to God, igniting a controversy that threatened the wealthy city's stability. At first Muhammad expressed reluctance to confront Mecca's leaders, but he overcame his bashfulness through subsequent visions. Inevitably, Muhammad's teaching led to a clash with Meccan leaders. In AD 622, Muhammad fled to Medina (then called *Yathrib*), an event known to Muslims as *hegira*, the migration that began the Muslim era and the Islamic calendar.

From Medina, Muhammad's followers, known today as Muslims, began raiding merchant caravans to gain wealth. Early victories like the one at the Battle of Badr in AD 624, in which 324 Muslims were said to have defeated a Meccan force three times their number, added to the perception that Islam was indeed God's will. Two years later, Muslims repelled a Meccan attack on Medina in the Battle of al-Ahzab. The following year Muhammad agreed to a treaty with Meccan leaders permitting him to enter the city as a pilgrim. On January 11 of AD 629, Muhammad and about ten thousand warriors captured Mecca and cleansed the Kaaba of its idols. Today Mecca is Islam's most holy place.

Muhammad and his followers continued to spread Islam by conquering the surrounding areas. Within one hundred years of its founding, Islam had subjugated parts of Europe, the Middle East, and North Africa through military conquest. Literally tens of millions, including Christians, were taken into slavery or killed. American president Teddy Roosevelt, in his 1916 book *Fear God and Take Your Own Part*, wrote, "Wherever the Mohammedans have had a complete sway, wherever the Christians have been unable to resist them by the sword, Christianity has ultimately disappeared."[22]

When Muhammad died in AD 632, three caliphs ("successors") took his place. Later, Ali ibn Abi Talib, Muhammad's cousin and son-in-law, took power. The murder of Ali in AD 661 is the root of a conflict that rages still. Those who insisted the successor should be elected by popular vote became the Sunni Muslims. Currently about 80 percent of Muslims worldwide hold to **Sunni Islam**. The Shiite ("faction") Muslims, however, believed the successor should be someone from the bloodline of Muhammad, a family member or descendant.

Shiite Islam, or **Shia Islam**, is a powerful force among Muslims, especially following the 1979 revolution when the Ayatollah ("sign of Allah") Khomeini gained control of the country of Iran. Shiites remain a majority in Iran, and significant communities of Shiites persist in Iraq and other countries. While they agree that no prophets can succeed Muhammad, Shiites have leaders called *imams*, whom they believe God has gifted to guide Muslims. (Sunnis also have imams, but they are more lay leaders.) Sunnis and Shiites agree on the importance of the Quran but acknowledge differing collections of Muhammad's sayings and teachings.

> *Sunni Islam:* the largest branch of Islam, this faction believes that Muhammad's successor should be chosen by a consensus of Muslims.

> *Shiite Islam (aka Shia Islam):* the second largest branch of Islam, this faction believes that Muhammad's successor should be someone from his bloodline.

Sufi Islam: a branch of Islam that arose as a protest to the worldliness invading the Muslim faith, this faction believes that Allah has a personal and mystical nature.

Sufi Islam arose in protest to the worldliness overtaking Islam in its early days, when the wealth and power gained through military conquest seemed to compromise religious commitment. Sufism gradually gained attention through the writings of the famous Sufi scholar al-Ghazali, who spread spiritual renewal among the Muslim people. In contrast to the majority Muslim belief that Allah reveals only his will but not his personal nature, Sufism advocates a personal experience and oneness with Allah that sometimes borders on pantheism. The result is a lively, less legalistic form of Islam. Sufism has been and continues to be fascinating to many Westerners. This is especially true of the writings of its famous poets, such as Jalal al-Din Rumi (d. 1273).

Islam also has many smaller offshoots. While orthodox Islam holds that Muhammad was the final prophet in a long succession of prophets, some groups claim that other prophets since Muhammad have come. The Baha'i World Faith was established in 1844 and boasts the prophet Baha Allah. The Nation of Islam (aka the Black Muslims) is a racially motivated offshoot of Islam founded by Elijah Muhammad (d. 1975), whom his followers considered to be a modern-day prophet. Mainstream Islam rejects both the Nation of Islam and Baha'i.

5. ISLAM IS A WORLDVIEW

Irshad Manji is one of a kind. A Canadian woman and lesbian activist who was raised Muslim and still claims an Islamic faith, Manji is the object of scorn among Muslims and a curiosity to everyone else. Sassy and vulnerable in her writing and speaking, Manji readily admits her weaknesses and inconsistencies and vigorously expresses the weaknesses and inconsistencies of Islam itself. For Manji, the problem of Islam is its limits on individual freedom—the only force, she believes, that would move the world beyond the religious conflict of our age. She identifies three problems preventing Islam from coexisting peacefully with Christianity and Secularism:

1. **Uniformity.** To maintain unity, Muslim leaders demand uniformity. "Thinking differently instigates the crumbling of empire."
2. **Suppression of disagreement.** Discussing problems openly is seen as a display of weakness. "Debate brings out fissures. Fissures divide. Thus, debate amounts to division."
3. **Elimination of critical thought**. Thinking differently is dangerous in Islam, says Manji. When leaders settled on particular interpretations of Muhammad's teachings, "the very idea of innovation became criminalized."[23]

Manji insists she is not advocating the diminishment of Islamic community. "I'm arguing for individuality—not individualism,"[24] she says. Most Muslims, though, see that as a distinction without a difference. They have refused to rally to her point of view.

Manji and those who agree with her are right about at least one thing: unthinking allegiance is the temptation of every worldview, even those that claim to value free thought. When people allow others to think for them, they essentially set up those others as idols. The Bible, on the other hand, repeatedly emphasizes loving God with one's *mind*, being prepared to give an *answer*, and not being deceived by wrong philosophies (Matt. 22:37; 1 Pet. 3:15; Col. 2:8).

While Muslim scholars may debate about whether there is room for different interpretations of Muhammad's teachings, Islam is nevertheless best understood as a comprehensive worldview. Salem Azzam, the secretary general of the Islamic Council of Europe, explains:

> Islam does not divide life into domains of the spiritual and the secular. It spiritualizes the entire existence of man and produces a social movement to reconstruct human life in the light of principles revealed by God. Prayer and worship in Islam are means to prepare man to fulfill this mission. Islam aims at changing life and producing a new man and a new society, both committed to God and to the welfare of mankind. That is why Islam is not a religion in the limited sense of the word; rather it is a complete code of life and a culture-producing factor.[25]

Urban Vermeulen, former president of the European Union of Arabists and Islamicists, states simply, "In Islam you can't eat à la carte, you have to take the whole menu."[26] So what is the whole menu? Let's have a look at what Islam teaches about God, the Bible, Jesus, salvation, and judgment.

6. BASIC ASPECTS OF THE ISLAMIC WORLDVIEW

Islam, like Christianity, has an overarching story explaining all of life and the world. Islam's story is very different from Christianity's, however. On the surface are many commonalities between Islam, Christianity, and Old Testament Judaism: one sovereign creator-God who is maximally powerful, who interacts with his creation, who has spoken to humanity through messengers, and who has "inscripturated" his message in holy books. Despite these initial similarities, however, the worldview Islam proposes is very different from Christianity and Judaism.

What Islam teaches about the nature of God. Many think Islam's God is named Allah, while the God of Christianity is Yawheh. However, *Allah* is the Arabic word for God, not the name of God. Arabic-speaking Christians also use the word *Allah* to refer to God. Still, this does not mean that Christians and Muslims worship the same God. As we shall see, the attributes of Allah and the nature of his revelation differ significantly from the witness of the Old and New Testaments. If the biblical witness is accurate, then Muslims either worship the one true God falsely or they worship another god altogether. There is much debate in the Christian community about this, and it is not our goal to settle the debate in this text. For the sake of clarity in this chapter, we'll refer to "God" and distinguish between Muslim and Christian understandings.

> If the biblical witness is accurate, then Muslims either worship the one true God falsely or they worship another god altogether.

According to Islam, God is eternal and self-existent. He created everything and set the universe in order. When God spoke, the Quran says, the world was created. "To Him is due the primal origin of the heavens and the earth: when He decreeth a matter, He saith to it: 'Be,' and it is" (Quran 2:117). God is viewed as sovereign over humans and history. Like

Christians, Muslims ponder how God can be all powerful while allowing humans to have a will and exercise responsibility. Aside from the Sufis, however, Muslims traditionally view God as utterly transcendent. He relates to people only through the prophets and authoritative teachings. Unlike Christianity, Islam does not see humans as made in God's image. God does not share his attributes or nature with anyone or anything else.

Muslims strongly reject the Christian doctrine of the Trinity and deny the deity of Jesus Christ. The idea of one God in three persons is viewed as **shirk** (the sin of polytheism, or the worship of many gods). The Quran denounces the Trinity in no uncertain terms: "They do blaspheme who say 'God is one of three in a Trinity,' for there is no god except One God. If they desist not from their word (of blasphemy), verily a grievous penalty will befall the blasphemers among them" (Quran 5:73). As we will see in the "Theology" chapter, the denial of this doctrine makes a big difference in the Islamic understanding of how God relates to his creation, especially humanity.

> *Shirk*: the unforgivable sin of idolatry or polytheism in Islam; in Arabic it means to "partner" another with God; i.e., worship anyone or anything besides Allah.

What Islam teaches about the Bible. Muslims believe God communicated his will to human beings primarily through a series of prophets, twenty-five of whom are named in the Quran. These include biblical prophets of the Old and New Testaments who originally taught Islam, Muslims say, a fact they believe is lost today because of the corruption of Scripture over time. While God gave special books to Moses, David, Jesus, and Muhammad, Muslims believe the Quran, God's communication with Muhammad, is the only authoritative and uncorrupted scripture preserved without error.

Muslims believe that Islam not only supersedes Christianity, but it is, in fact, the *fulfillment* of Christianity. Christian scholars obviously reject this claim. If one religion is to fulfill another, they say, there must be significant *continuity* between the two. But the path of Islam differs substantially from the trajectory of the Christian message. In response, Islam rejects the reliability of the Old and New Testaments on which Christian scholars base their conclusions.

What Islam teaches about Jesus. Muslims acknowledge the virgin birth of Jesus and his miraculous acts but deny his claim to be God incarnate, his death on a cross as an atoning sacrifice for sin, and his resurrection on the third day. While the following passage contains some ambiguities (i.e., whether it denies that the Jews were those who killed Jesus or that Jesus *did not die* on the cross), most Muslims interpret it to say that Jesus was not crucified at all:

> They that said (in boast), "We killed Christ Jesus the son of Mary, the Apostle of God"; but they killed him not, nor crucified him, but so it was made to appear to them, and those who differ therein are full of doubts, with no (certain) knowledge, but only conjecture to follow, for a surety they killed him not: nay, God raised him up unto Himself; and God is Exalted in Power, Wise. (Quran 4:157–58)

This denial, of course, makes any claim of Islam being a continuation of the Christian faith impossible. The center of the Christian message is the atoning work of Jesus Christ in his life, death, and especially, according to the apostle Paul (whom Muslims view as the great corrupter of Christianity), his resurrection:

> Being found in human form, he humbled himself by becoming obedient to the point of death, even death on a cross. (Phil. 2:8)

> I delivered to you as of first importance what I also received: that Christ died for our sins in accordance with the Scriptures, that he was buried, that he was raised on the third day in accordance with the Scriptures. (1 Cor. 15:3–4)

> If Christ has not been raised, then our preaching is in vain and your faith is in vain. We are even found to be misrepresenting God, because we testified about God that he raised Christ, whom he did not raise if it is true that the dead are not raised. For if the dead are not raised, not even Christ has been raised. And if Christ has not been raised, your faith is futile and you are still in your sins. (vv. 14–17)

Clearly, to deny Jesus's death on the cross is to renounce the gospel of Jesus Christ. In this sense, Islam does not *fulfill* the Christian faith. Rather, it attempts to *replace* it.

What Islam teaches about salvation. Because Islam rejects the claim of Jesus's death on the cross, Muslims understand salvation very differently. As the late Syracuse University sociology professor Hammudah Abdalati asserts, "The Muslim cannot entertain the dramatic story of Jesus's death upon the cross just to do away with all human sins once and for all." Abdalati explains why Muslims cannot accept the truth of Jesus's sacrifice:

> The Muslim does not believe in the crucifixion of Jesus by his enemies because the basis of this doctrine of crucifixion is contrary to Divine mercy and justice as much as it is to human reason and dignity. Such a disbelief in the doctrine does not in any way lessen … the Muslim's belief in Jesus as a distinguished prophet of God. On the contrary, by rejecting this doctrine the Muslim accepts Jesus but only with more esteem and higher respect, and looks upon his original message as an essential part of Islam.[27]

> **Muslims argue for the superiority of their view of Jesus, but in so doing they deny Jesus's death on the cross—which is at the core of the Christian faith—and thus renounce the gospel of Jesus Christ.**

Muslims argue for the superiority of their view of Jesus, but in so doing they deny Jesus's death on the cross—which is at the core of the Christian faith—and thus renounce the gospel of Jesus Christ. Clearly, there is no reconciling these two views.

What Islam teaches about judgment. Muslims embrace the creation account in Genesis but deny the significance of the fall. This puts Islam on an entirely different theological trajectory. The biblical understanding is that Adam's and Eve's rebellion put all of creation under a curse. The ground is cursed (Gen. 3:17)[28] and has been "groaning" ever since (Rom. 8:19–23).[29] Muslims reject "the Christian view that God in fact 'cursed' the ground (Gen. 3:14–24)," wrote Badru Kateregga. "All that God tells man in relation to the ground after the descent of Adam to earth is as quoted: 'Therein Ye shall live and therein Ye shall die, and therein Ye shall be brought forth [in the resurrection]' (Quran 7:25)."[30]

To reject the doctrine of the fall means that Muslims also reject the biblical teaching of a humanity captive to evil and destined, without a redeemer, to behave corruptly in all their actions. To become a Muslim does not require redemption in the sense of being made new, as Christianity teaches (2 Cor. 5:17, for example). It is not about what is in your heart, Muslims say, but what is in your actions; change comes from the outside in, not the inside out.

Denying the fall carries many implications, including political ones. Due to their understanding of the fall of humanity, Christians distrust the ability of political authority to further God's will—since politicians, like everyone else, are fallen. Muslims disagree. They see political authority, when under the control of Islam, as capable of advancing God's agenda.

Muslims also have a very different view of who will be saved and who will perish in the final judgment. According to the Quran, each person's good deeds will be weighed in the balance to determine who goes to paradise and who goes to hell:

> The weighing on that day [Day of Resurrection] will be the true [weighing]. So as for those whose scale [of good deeds] will be heavy, they will be the successful [by entering paradise]. And as for those whose scale will be light, they are those who will lose their own selves [by entering hell] because they denied and rejected Our *Ayat* [proofs, evidences, verses, lessons, signs, revelations]. (Quran 7:8–9)

Although this passage refers to the balance of righteous deeds, Muslims still see God's mercy as central to salvation. Muhammad reportedly said, "None of you would get into Paradise because of his good deeds alone, and he would not be rescued from Fire, not even I, but because of the Mercy of Allah."[31]

In the end, it comes down to whether Jesus is the savior. He is not, Hammudah Abdalati said: "Each person must bear his/her own burden and be responsible for his/her own actions, because no one can expiate for another's sin."[32] There is no assurance of salvation in Islam, save one thing: being martyred in the cause of jihad.[33] We'll deal with this provision shortly, and its effect on the world today.

Meanwhile, let's take a look at how Islam grapples with general and special revelation. What are its sources of revelation, and what do these sources tell us about humanity, what's wrong with humanity, and what course of action should govern our lives?

7. General Revelation: The Law Known to All

Khurshid Ahmad says, "The basic Islamic concept is that the entire universe was created by God, whom Islam calls Allah and who is the Lord and the Sovereign of the Universe. He is the Lord of the universe which He alone sustains."[34] Muslims, like Christians, believe creation belongs to God; we humans are stewards of it. Hammudah Abdalati explained: "The actual and real owner of things is God alone, of Whom any proprietor is simply an appointed agent, a mere trustee."[35] In the "Economics" chapter, we will term this *stewardship* of one's property and resources.

By proclaiming the existence of a supernatural God, however, Muslims find themselves in the same place as Christians, having to explain how to know something about the supernatural when our tools of understanding seem to work only inside of nature. Muslims wrestle, as Christians do, with questions such as these: Did the universe have a beginning, or has it always existed? Was the beginning caused or uncaused? Is the agent of cause personal or impersonal?

Islamic philosophers developed the *kalam cosmological argument* for the existence of God to answer these questions. Christian philosophers not only commend but employ this argument today. *Kalam* is the Arabic word for "discourse," and *cosmology* is "the study of the order, structure, and design of the universe." Today, the most popular form of the kalam cosmological argument is this:

> Everything that begins has a cause
> The universe began
> The universe was caused

Norman Geisler says, "The *kalam* ... argument is a horizontal (linear) form of the cosmological argument. The universe is not eternal, so it must have had a Cause. That Cause must be considered God. This argument has a long and venerable history among such Islamic philosophers as Alfarabi, Al Ghazali, and Avicenna."[36]

As is true with the Christian worldview, philosophical arguments about God can take us only so far; they demonstrate the reasonableness of a first cause or prime mover, but they do not tell us *specifically* what God is like. For that we need special revelation.

8. SPECIAL REVELATION: WHERE MUSLIMS TURN FOR DIRECTION

Like other worldviews, Islam proposes answers to life's ultimate questions, and it claims sources of knowledge in support of its answers. Let's apply to Islam essentially the same five questions we applied to Christianity to see if we can figure out how Islam grapples with the nature of what really exists and how we should live:

1. On what sources of revelation does Islam draw?
2. What does Islam say about humanity?
3. What does Islam say is wrong with us?
4. What does Islam say about how we should live?
5. How are we to understand other worldviews based on Islam?

1. On what sources of revelation does Islam draw? Muslims believe God graciously sent messengers to every nation to teach submission and warn people against false religious teachings and practices (Quran 16:36; 35:24). Moses and Jesus are considered prophets of Islam, as well as Ishmael, Isaac, and Jacob (3:67; 61:6; 2:136). Muslims are expected to honor these prophets and their respective books (4:136). As we noted earlier, Muslims understand religions predating Muhammad as having been originally Islamic, and their prophets Muslims (15:10).

Muhammad is seen as the successor of the prophets of old (61:6). Many Muslims even believe the Bible contains prophecies about him, most significantly Deuteronomy 18:15–18 and John 14:16.[37] While other prophets were for a certain time and place, Muhammad is considered to be *the one prophet for all humankind* (Quran 7:158; 34:28) as well as the final prophet (33:40). A well-known hadith says, "Allah's Apostle said, 'My similitude in comparison with the other prophets before me, is that of a man who has built a house nicely and beautifully, except for a place of one brick in a corner. The people go about it and wonder at its beauty, but say: "Would that this brick be put in its place!" So I am that brick, and I am the last of the Prophets.' "[38]

As the seal of the prophets, Muhammad's teachings, embodied in the Quran (from the verb *qara'a*, "to read" or "to recite"), are viewed as the incomparable, infallible, and final revelation from God (Quran 17:88–89), confirming all previous revelations (10:37; 46:12).

Muslims believe the words of the Quran are the literal words of God, which were dictated word for word to the prophet Muhammad over a period of twenty-three years through the angel Jibril (Gabriel). Muslims believe the previous revelations were textually corrupted. The Quran is the culmination of God's revelation to humanity, which God kept incorruptible and inscribed on a tablet in heaven (Quran 85:21–22): "We have, without doubt, sent down the Message [the Quran]; and We will assuredly guard it (from corruption)" (15:9).

Khurshid Ahmad claims the following about the Quran:

> The Qur'an is the revealed book of God which has been in existence for the last fourteen hundred years and the Word of God is available in its original form. Detailed accounts of the life of the Prophet of Islam and his teachings are available in their pristine purity. There has not been an iota of change in this unique historic record.[39]

When you think of the Quran, keep in mind that Muslims believe it to be the best and most beautiful book on earth. There is no equal, and nothing surpasses it in content or quality.[40] To disrespect the Quran is a grave insult to Muslims, the most heinous act a person could commit.

The other major source for Islamic theology today is the **Hadith**. The Hadith is composed of traditions of the teachings, rulings, and actions of Muhammad and his early and chief companions. These traditions include the *Sunnah*, descriptions of Muhammad's exemplary actions.[41]

Hadith: The oral history of Muhammad's teachings, rulings, and the actions of his early companions.

Muslims believe these two sources are authoritative, providing lenses through which Muslims apply God's revelation to all of life.

2. What does Islam say about humanity? The biblical message is that we are created in the image of God (Gen. 1:26–27),[42] and that despite the fall, we continue to bear that image (James 3:9).[43] Being made in God's image distinguishes humans from all other creatures, including angels. The Islamic perspective is radically different. Badru Kateregga says,

> The Christian witness, that man is created in the "image and likeness of God," is not the same as the Muslim witness. Although God breathed into man his spirit, as both Christians and Muslims believe, for Islam the only divine qualities entrusted to humans as a result of God's breath were those of knowledge, will, and power of action. If people use these divine qualities rightly in understanding God and following his law strictly, then he has nothing to fear in the present or the future, and no sorrow for the past.[44]

Muslims acknowledge humans as God's "vice regents" on Earth but reject the *imago Dei* ("image of God"). Muslims see humans as slaves of God, not his sons and daughters.

3. What does Islam say is wrong with us? When Allah created the world, Muslims say, Adam and Eve were actually Muslim. Adam was even a prophet of Islam. Although Adam and Eve disobeyed Allah's original prohibition and ate from the forbidden tree, their mistake (not sin) was quickly forgiven. And though their actions resulted in the world not being as it should be (with humans rebelling against God), Allah has sent Islam to offer humanity a way back to its pristine state.

Muslims believe every human being is born a Muslim in a state of submission to Allah. But from very young ages, we are led astray to worship false gods or to deny God altogether. It was up to the prophets of Allah to speak to the nations and correct these errors of belief and practice.

Because the world was created in submission to Allah and every human being is born a Muslim, to refuse to become a Muslim is rebellion against Allah. It is the obligation of Muslims to battle rebellion against God through jihad. Jihad has two facets. First, it is the battle against temptation and sin for the sake of developing virtue and self-control. In other words, it can imply battling one's own rebellion. The second facet is the battle against any and all who oppose Islam.

Some call this second aspect of jihad *holy war*. As the famous Arab historian Ibn Khaldun (1333–1406) said, "In the Muslim community, the holy war is a religious duty, because of the universalism of the Muslim mission and the obligation to convert everybody to Islam either by persuasion or by force."[45] Fighting against non-Muslims is viewed not as an act of *aggression* but as an act of *restoration*—the offering of Allah's mercy to those willing to end their rebellious ways.

To the more radical Muslims, the Islamists, *peace* occurs when non-Muslims cease rebelling. The vision of Islamists, then, is that one day Islam will establish peace by quashing such rebellion at a global level. If Islamists seem dismissive when accused of aggression, it is because they view jihad as merely a *response* to aggressive *unbelief*. They think, "*You* are the ones in rebellion against Allah. We are *helping* you be restored to him, as he commands, and as is best for you." Western Muslims take pains to assure Westerners that Islam is a religion of peace, but we must be careful to recognize that Islamists do not hold this view, nor do the extremist Islamists we have called *jihadis*, who are eager to use physical violence to complete Muhammad's mission.

To the Islamist mind, any nation that refuses to permit Muslims to live as they please and to adopt and propagate Islam must be forced into submission for its own good and for the glory of God. Islam is *Dar al-Islam* ("house of peace"), and those nations that refuse Islam are considered *Dar al-Harb* ("house of war"). Because there is no official leader to issue a call to jihad, jihadis often take it upon themselves to fight the West when and how they can. To these Islamists, the refusal to allow shariah law is a great offense that must be fought against.

In areas dominated by Islam, there is a provision called ***dhimmitude*** in which Christians and Jews ("people of the Book") may live in peace without converting to Islam. As *dhimmis*, though, Christians and Jews are officially second-class citizens and are often harassed, persecuted, oppressed, and sometimes killed.

Dhimmitude: a provision in shariah law that allows *dhimmis* (i.e., non-Muslims) to live in Islamic states in exchange for paying the *jizya* (i.e., tax).

Dhimmis: non-Muslims living in Islamic states.

Jizya: a tax imposed on *dhimmis* (i.e., non-Muslims) living in Islamic states.

Shahada: the first pillar of Islam, *shahada* is the confession of faith: "There is no God but Allah, and Muhammad is his prophet."

Salat: the second pillar of Islam, *salat* is praying five times per day facing Mecca.

Zakat: the third pillar of Islam, *zakat* is the donation of 2.5 percent of a Muslim's annual income.

Dhimmis must pay the *jizya* (the tax upon unbelievers), a burden so onerous that sometimes non-Muslims can do little more than live as slaves.

4. What does Islam say about how we should live? According to Islam, more important than what you *believe* is what you *do*. Adherents have only five basic requirements, possibly six, to which they must conform. As they do so, their individual actions are subsumed into the community, creating a collective mind-set and generating a way of life unique from all other religions in the world.

The first pillar of Islam is the *shahada*, the confession of faith: *There is no God but Allah, and Muhammad is his prophet.* If a person recites this confession with sincerity of mind and heart, then he or she is a Muslim. Under this pillar, all other obligations are subsumed, for to believe in God and Muhammad as his prophet is to obey the Quran and follow the example of Muhammad's life.

The second pillar is *salat*, or prayer. Muslims are expected to engage in prayer five times a day facing Mecca. On Friday, Muslim men (and, in some cases, women) are expected to meet at a mosque to engage in noon prayer. Prayer provides a daily rhythm to Muslim life. Muslims hope to please God by remembering him constantly with regulated prayer. Muslims also hope that systematic praying will help them avoid temptations to immorality. The mosque is central to Islamic life. Recep Tayyip Erdogan, the president of Turkey, described their purposes in military terms, reciting an Islamic poem: "The mosques are our barracks, the domes our helmets, the minarets our bayonets and the faithful our soldiers."[46]

The third pillar is *zakat*, almsgiving. Muslims are expected to give 2.5 percent of their annual capital to the poor, either directly or through Muslim charitable organizations. Giving to the poor is intended to achieve a generous lifestyle and a sense of caring for the Muslim community, especially those lacking physical and financial means.

The fourth pillar is *sawm*, fasting during Ramadan. This involves refraining from food, smoking, and sexual relations during daylight hours, though these may be enjoyed after sundown. These periods of fasting are to encourage and enable Muslims to develop self-control, to discourage bad habits, and to refocus their minds on personal spiritual progress.

The fifth pillar is a pilgrimage called *hajj*. All Muslims are expected to make a pilgrimage to Mecca at least once in their lifetimes if their finances and health permit. During their pilgrimages, Muslims don white garments and remove all indicators of status or class. This practice is intended to help Muslims recognize that before God they are all equal. Racial, gender, and economic differences are muted as masses of Muslims from many nations bow together to worship Allah.

> *Sawm:* the fourth pillar of Islam, *sawm* is a special time set aside for fasting during the month of Ramadan.

Those Muslims we are referring to as Islamists would add jihad, the principle of compelling non-Muslims to cease their rebellion against God, as the sixth pillar.[47] Jihad is seen as the most self-sacrificing action Islamists can undertake. Indeed, Islamists who die in jihad are guaranteed entrance into Paradise, where men have access to scores of perpetual virgins. Women, however, are not told what awaits them.

> *Hajj:* the fifth pillar of Islam, *hajj* is the mandatory pilgrimage to Mecca for all Muslims with the ability and means to make the journey.

These pillars encompass the basic moral obligations for Muslims. Obey them and you are considered to be faithfully submitted to Allah. But there is also the matter of law. The Quran specifies "prohibitions on certain foods (pork, carrion, wine, animals slaughtered in pagan ceremonies), a number of legal rules concerning family law (marriage, divorce, and inheritance), criminal law (the *hudud* crimes, including penalties of highway robbery, illicit sexual activity, slander, and wine-drinking), rules about witnesses, and commercial regulations including the ban on *riba* (interest) and forms of contracts."[48] This law is called *shariah*.

Because the Quran does not address all questions of law, Muslim legal scholars also turn to a second source, the *Sunnah*, to discern the shape of shariah. This body of material contains many more legal rulings and examples than the Quran. A fundamental difficulty is that many of the hadith present conflicting or contradictory rulings arising from different places and times. Because much of the historical context is unrecorded, examples and rulings are left open to debate.[49]

> *Sunnah:* part of the Hadith describing Muhammad's exemplary actions.

In addition to the Quran and the *Sunnah*, a third source for shariah is the communal consensus, called *ijma'*, expressed among Muslim jurists of the first three centuries of Islam. An example of shariah arising from this source is male circumcision, a practice not commanded in the Quran. In some areas, the practice of female "circumcision" (really, female genital mutilation, often including a removal of the clitoris, either partially or in its entirety) is seen as demanded by shariah as well. This illustrates how local customs sometimes rise to the level of shariah in Muslim communities.

The fourth source for shariah arises from legal reasoning needed to address situations otherwise unaddressed in the Quran and the Hadith. But not all Muslims support this approach to legal rulings, which has given rise to various legal traditions. One of the more pronounced differences regards the consumption of alcohol. Malise Ruthven notes, "While some jurists would argue that only fermented products of the date-palm and vine are prohibited, others, basing their judgments on the *qiyas*, would insist that all alcoholic drinks are forbidden, since the effective cause or common denominator (*'illa)* behind the prohibition was the same in each case."[50]

The greatest headache for Muslim legal scholars concerning life in the modern world is the *principle of abrogation*, which states that later passages in the Quran overrule (thus abrogate) earlier passages.[51] It is a significant question because the peaceful, merciful nature of Allah presented in the first part of the Quran disappears in the second part, replaced by a version of Allah with a noticeable sense of revenge and bloodlust. If later passages supersede earlier ones, we can expect adherents to become more aggressive and violent the more doctrinally sensitive they become.

The greatest source of disagreement among Muslim sects is their respective interpretations of shariah law. Muslims themselves disagree about its application because the Quran does not speak to *all* (or even many) legal issues.[52] In addition, many of its statements are ambiguous and addressed to specific historical situations. Ruthven comments, "As for the specific injunctions about the Muslims' struggles against and relationship with the non-Muslims, these varied according to situations and were too specific to be termed 'laws' in the strict sense."[53]

While Ruthven seems to downplay the grip shariah law has on Muslims, throughout Islamic history, many Muslims have read such commands as normative, especially as they are applied to help non-Muslims cease their rebellion against God. Modern Muslims, especially those educated in the West, see the difficulty but, perhaps out of fear or a desire not to disturb Muslim unity, often remain silent.

To illustrate the threatening nature of shariah law, consider the case of Youcef Nadarkhani, an Iranian Christian pastor who, first in 2006 and then again in 2009, was arrested for converting to Christianity. He faced possible execution but was freed only through international pressure sparked by extensive media coverage. His attorney, Mohammed Ali Dadkhah, jailed in a brutal prison for advocating Nadarkhani's case and other human-rights cases, was not released.[54]

5. How are we to understand other worldviews based on Islam? In contrast to a biblical Christian view of the nature of humanity, the Muslim community cannot, within its religion, find a sound basis for individual freedom. Adherence is demanded; those who leave Islam are in danger of losing their lives, those who choose not to belong are in danger of subjugation or death, and basic human rights are violated as a matter of course.[55]

On the one hand, there is a tradition of tolerance in Islam. Abul Ala Mawdudi, a prominent Pakistani Muslim scholar, states, "[A]ll non-Muslims will have the freedom of conscience, opinion, expression, and association as the one enjoyed by Muslims themselves, subject to the same limitations as are imposed by law on Muslims."[56] On the other hand, Samuel Shahid writes,

> Mawdudi's views are not accepted by most Islamic schools of law, especially in regard to freedom of expression like criticism of Islam and the government. Even in a country like Pakistan, the homeland of Mawdudi, it is illegal to criticize the government or the head of state. Many political prisoners are confined to jails in Pakistan and most

other Islamic countries. Through the course of history, except in rare cases, not even Muslims have been given freedom to criticize Islam without being persecuted or sentenced to death. It is far less likely for a *Zimmi* [*dhimmi* Christian or Jew living in Muslim-dominated lands] to get away with criticizing Islam.[57]

> **In contrast to a biblical Christian view of the nature of humanity, the Muslim community cannot, within its religion, find a sound basis for individual freedom**

The oppression of *dhimmis* commanded by the Quran is a severe tax, or *jizya*. "All taxes on trade and transport paid by Muslims were generally doubled for *dhimmis*," observes Bat Ye'or. "In addition, the population—but particularly the *dhimmi* communities—was subject to ruinous extortions designed to cover the financing of incessant wars."[58] Because Muslims have often been at war, non-Muslims who dare to remain in Muslim lands are fleeced to finance Muslim aggression (or, more rarely, defense). Most troubling is how these non-Muslims are treated when they cannot pay the *jizya*. Churches have been destroyed, people have been dispossessed from their houses, and children have been taken and sold into slavery, not to mention personal atrocities, such as dismemberment, torture, and death.[59]

There was a time when Muslims embraced adherents of other monotheistic faiths (such as Jews and Christians), but this came to an end with the finished work of Muhammad and the full revelation of the Quran. Now God accepts only Muslims: "Should anyone desire a religion other than Islam, it will not be accepted and in the Hereafter he will be among the lost" (Quran 3:85).[60]

Except in the Ahmadiyyah tradition and possibly in Baha'i, there is no Muslim tradition of a state of peace in which Muslims leave everyone else alone. Non-Muslims must be made to submit, and even Jews and Christians are considered to be in rebellion until they do so. Muhammad Sayyid Tantawi, the grand sheikh of Al-Azhar University in Cairo, said, "All Jews are not the same. The good ones become Muslims, the bad ones do not."[61]

> **There was a time when Muslims embraced adherents of other monotheistic faiths (such as Jews and Christians), but this came to an end with the finished work of Muhammad and the full revelation of the Quran.**

Several Muslim legal scholars have explored the possibility of adjusting the Quran to fit more with modern times, but most Muslim authorities view these efforts with disdain. Because Muhammad was the final prophet and the Quran God's final revelation, Muslims reject all claims to new divine revelation or inspired prophets. Thus, they are highly critical of groups branching off of Islam, such as the Baha'i,[62] the Ahmadiyyah,[63] and the Nation of Islam (i.e., Black Muslims),[64] which assert prophetic continuation past Muhammad.

The conflict between Islam and other worldviews, then, will likely persist as long as Islam continues to grow as a force in the modern world. And given that Muslim families typically have significantly more children per family than non-Muslim families, this is practically guaranteed. This alarming reality concerns many people in the world. One worldview, Secularism, sees both Islam and Christianity as dangerous because they aim to take over the world. If they do, any hope of building a society based on science and reason will be dashed. As we will see in the next chapter, the notion that all deity-based worldviews must be put in their place is the motivating force of the Secularist worldview.

ENDNOTES

1. Muslim Ottoman Turks had, for almost two hundred years, attempted to conquer the city of Vienna, Austria. The success of Muslim armies continued nearly unabated from the time of Muhammad until AD 1529, when Suleiman the Magnificent failed to breach the city with his massive army. Subsequent Muslim armies continued attempting to attack the city until 1683, when the king of Poland, John III Sobieski, and his massive cavalry, decisively defeated the Ottoman army.

2. Thomas H. Kean et al., *The 9/11 Commission Report* (Washington, DC: National Commission on Terrorist Attacks upon the United States, 2004), 8, www.9-11commission.gov/report/911Report.pdf.

3. Kean et al., *9/11 Commission Report*, 14.

4. Gallup World Poll, 2001–2007, cited in John L. Esposito and Dalia Mogahed, "What Makes a Muslim Radical?," *Foreign Policy* (November 2006): 3, http://media.gallup.com/WorldPoll/PDF/MWSRRadical022207.pdf.

5. Esposito and Mogahed, "What Makes a Muslim Radical?," 1.

6. Esposito and Mogahed, "What Makes a Muslim Radical?," 3.

7. Esposito and Mogahed, "What Makes a Muslim Radical?"; Gallup Poll, cited in John L. Esposito and Dalia Mogahed, *Who Speaks for Islam?* (New York: Gallup, 2007), 69–70; Global Muslim population as of 2010, cited in "The Future of the Global Muslim Population," Pew Research Center, January 27, 2011, www.pewforum.org/2011/01/27/the-future-of-the-global-muslim-population/.

8. Geert Wilders, *Marked for Death* (Washington, DC: Regnery, 2012), 191.

9. Wilders is labeled a far-right-wing politician, his enemies threaten him publicly, a popular rap song fantasized about killing him, and in a supreme irony, he has been put on trial for hate crimes. Holocaust survivor Elie Wiesel said he learned from the Nazis that when people say they want to kill you, believe them. Wilders takes that message seriously, he says. As a result, he is, in essence, a prisoner in his own land.

10. See M. Zuhdi Jasser, *A Battle for the Soul of Islam* (New York: Threshold Editions, 2012).

11. When we quote from the Quran in this book, we use primarily the translation of Abdullah Yusuf Ali. It is an older translation (sounding much like the King James Version of the Bible), but it is well respected and widely known. See Abdullah Yusuf Ali, trans., *The Holy Qur'an: Text, Translation, and Commentary* (Washington, DC: American International Printing Company, 1946). In some quotations from Ali's translation, we have taken the liberty of smoothing out the text, removing unnecessary punctuation and poetic capitalization of letters.

12. The authoritative source on shariah is Ahmad ibn Naqib al-Misri, *Reliance of the Traveller: A Classic Manual of Islamic Sacred Law*, rev. ed., trans. Nuh Ha Mim Keller (Beltsville, MD: Amana Publications, 1994). For a detailed critique of shariah from a Secularist perspective, refer to Andrew G. Bostom, *Sharia versus Freedom: The Legacy of Islamic Totalitarianism* (Amherst, NY: Prometheus, 2012). Also worth noting: the charter of Hamas, the ruling party of the Palestinian Territories, proclaims the legitimacy of slavery in its charter by calling on slaves to fight the enemy even without their masters' permission. Hamas Charter, 1988, in Jerusalem Fund, www.thejerusalemfund.org/carryover/documents/charter.html.

13. For a detailed list of the 164 references in the Quran, see Yoel Natan, comp., "164 Jihad Holy War Verses in the Koran," accessed March 26, 2014, www.answering-islam.org/Quran/Themes/jihad_passages.html. Also refer to al-Misri, *Reliance of the Traveller*, 599–605.

14. A detailed history of Islamic conquest is available in William J. Federer, *What Every American Needs to Know about the Qur'an: A History of Islam and the United States* (St. Louis: Amerisearch, 2011).

15. From personal conversations with Dr. Nabeel Qureshi, May 2013.

16. Ahmad ibn Naqib al-Misri points out that "it is offensive to conduct a military expedition against hostile non-Muslims without the caliph's permission." But he further notes that "if there is no caliph (Muslim head of a country) …, no permission is required." Muslims may then wage war as they see fit. al-Misri, *Reliance of the Traveller*, 602.

17. Mark Gabriel, who grew up as a devout Muslim in Egypt, earned a doctorate in Islamic studies, and even taught at Al-Azhar University in Cairo, Egypt, the most prestigious Islamic university in the world, devotes chapter 13 of his book *Jesus and Muhammad* (Lake Mary, FL: FrontLine, 2004) to interpreting the Quranic references to *jihad* and explaining how it is impossible to logically describe it as merely a spiritual struggle. See especially pages 126–27.

18. "What Do We Make of Radical Islamicism?," *Summit Journal* 13, no. 1 (January 2013): 1, 3, www.summit.org/media/journal/2013-01_Summit_Journal-WEB.pdf.

19. Quoted in Irshad Manji, *Allah, Liberty, and Love* (New York: Free Press, 2011), 232.

20. First John 4:18: "There is no fear in love, but perfect love casts out fear. For fear has to do with punishment, and whoever fears has not been perfected in love."

21. Wilders, *Marked for Death*, 113.

22. Theodore Roosevelt, *Fear God and Take Your Own Part* (New York: George H. Doran, 1916), 197.

23. Manji, *Allah, Liberty, and Love*, 46.

24. Manji, *Allah, Liberty, and Love*, 49.

---

25. Salem Azzam, in Khurshid Ahmad, ed., *Islam: Its Meaning and Message*, 3rd ed. (Leicestershire, UK: Islamic Foundation, 2010).

26. Urbain Vermeulen, "Urbain Vermeulen over de Islamisering van Onze Samenleving," *Het Laatste Nieuws*, October 27, 2004.

27. Hammudah Abdalati, *Islam in Focus* (Indianapolis: Amana, 1975), 17.

28. Genesis 3:17: "To Adam [God] said, 'Because you have listened to the voice of your wife and have eaten of the tree of which I commanded you, "You shall not eat of it," cursed is the ground because of you; in pain you shall eat of it all the days of your life.'"

29. Romans 8:19–23: "The creation waits with eager longing for the revealing of the sons of God. For the creation was subjected to futility, not willingly, but because of him who subjected it, in hope that the creation itself will be set free from its bondage to corruption and obtain the freedom of the glory of the children of God. For we know that the whole creation has been groaning together in the pains of childbirth until now. And not only the creation, but we ourselves, who have the firstfruits of the Spirit, groan inwardly as we wait eagerly for adoption as sons, the redemption of our bodies."

30. Badru D. Kateregga and David W. Shenk, *Islam and Christianity: A Muslim and a Christian in Dialogue* (Grand Rapids: Eerdmans, 1981), available on *The World of Islam: Resources for Understanding*, 2.0 (Colorado Springs: Global Mapping International, 2009), CD-ROM, 5350.

31. Abdul Hamid Siddiqui, trans., Sahih Muslim, bk. 39, hadith 6769, www.nur.org/en/nurcenter/islamicsources /Sahih_Muslim_Hadith_No_6769_77861.

32. Abdalati, *Islam in Focus*, 17.

33. In folk Islam, the faithful who die during the pilgrimage to Mecca, the hajj, also attain a guarantee of paradise.

34. Ahmad, *Islam*, 29.

35. Abdalati, *Islam in Focus*, 125.

36. Norman L. Geisler, *Baker Encyclopedia of Christian Apologetics* (Grand Rapids: Baker, 1999), 399.

37. Deuteronomy 18:15–18: "The LORD your God will raise up for you a prophet like me from among you, from your brothers—it is to him you shall listen—just as you desired of the LORD your God at Horeb on the day of the assembly, when you said, 'Let me not hear again the voice of the LORD my God or see this great fire any more, lest I die.' And the LORD said to me, 'They are right in what they have spoken. I will raise up for them a prophet like you from among their brothers. And I will put my words in his mouth, and he shall speak to them all that I command him'"; John 14:16: "I [Jesus] will ask the Father, and he will give you another Helper.

38. Sahih al-Bukhari, vol. 4, bk. 56, hadith 735, www.usc.edu/org/cmje/religious-texts/hadith/bukhari/056-sbt.php.

39. Ahmad, *Islam*, 43.

40. These assertions are addressed in some detail in chapter 9 "An Evaluation of the Qur'an," in Norman L. Geisler and Abdul Saleeb, *Answering Islam: The Crescent in Light of the Cross*, rev. ed. (Grand Rapids: Baker, 2002), 183–210.

41. Faslur Rahman, *Islam*, 2nd ed. (Chicago: University of Chicago Press, 1979): "The difference between the two is that whereas a Hadith as such is a mere report … the Sunna is the very same report when it acquires a normative quality and becomes a practical principle for the Muslim" (45); "This authority of Muhammad refers to the verbal and performative behavior of the Prophet outside the Quran" (50); and "To his Companions his life was a religious paradigm and as such normative" (52).

42. Genesis 1:26–27: "Then God said, 'Let us make man in our image, after our likeness. And let them have dominion over the fish of the sea and over the birds of the heavens and over the livestock and over all the earth and over every creeping thing that creeps on the earth.' So God created man in his own image, in the image of God he created him; male and female he created them."

43. James 3:9: "With [the tongue] we bless our Lord and Father, and with it we curse people who are made in the likeness of God."

44. Kateregga and Shenk, *Islam and Christianity; The World of Islam: Resources for Understanding* CD-ROM, 5350.

45. Ibn Khaldun, *The Muqaddimah: An Introduction to History*, trans. Franz Rosenthal (Princeton: Princeton University Press, 1967), 183.

46. Quoted in "Turkey's Charismatic Pro-Islamic Leader," BBC News, November 4, 2002, http://news.bbc.co.uk/2 /hi/europe/2270642.stm.

47. The notion of *opposition* varies among Muslims. Some attempt to limit it to actual aggression, primarily of a military variety, and thus view jihad as exclusively defensive in posture. The history of Islam relegates this perspective to a minority view—in its early years, Islam spread through conquest. Many contemporary Muslims understand "defense" as the response needed against anything or anyone who would seek to inhibit Islam from becoming a global civilization. Additionally, since Muslims believe that the world originally was Islamic, and that every person is born a Muslim, they can easily move toward holding any and all non-Muslims as inherently in opposition to Islam.

48. Malise Ruthven, *Islam: A Very Short Introduction* (Oxford, UK: Oxford University Press, 1997), 75.

49. Ruthven, *Islam*, 76.

50. Ruthven, *Islam*, 79.

51. "But, further, it had to be set out as to which specific command was earlier in time and which later." Ruthven, *Islam*. This briefly describes the Islamic teaching on abrogation; i.e., the more recent commands or rulings supersede those earlier and remain obligatory.

52. "But still the strictly legislative portion of the Quran is relatively quite small. Besides the detailed pronouncement on the law of inheritance and laying down punishments for crimes such as theft and adultery, which are not defined legally, there is little in it that is, properly speaking, legislative." Ruthven, *Islam*, 69.

53. Ruthven, *Islam*.

54. Perry Chiaramonte, "American Pastor Imprisoned in Iran to Go on Trial Next Week," Fox News, January 14, 2013, www.foxnews.com/world/2013/01/14/trial-date-set-for-american-pastor-imprisoned-in-iran/.

55. Wilders, *Marked for Death*, 68.

56. Quoted in Samuel Shahid, "Rights of Non-Muslims in an Islamic State," accessed February 4, 2016, www.answering-islam.org/NonMuslims/rights.htm.

57. Shahid, "Rights of Non-Muslims."

58. Bat Ye'or, *Islam and Dhimmitude: Where Civilizations Collide*, trans. Miriam Kochan and David Littman (Madison, NJ: Fairleigh Dickinson University Press, 2002), 71.

59. See the discussion in Stuart Robinson, *Mosques and Miracles: Revealing Islam and God's Grace*, 2nd ed. (Upper Mt. Gravatt, Australia: City Harvest, 2004), 202. Robinson records that even as recent as 1997, almost fifty Christians were killed, several in a Sunday school class, apparently because they failed to pay *jizya*.

60. Quoted in Jane Dammen McAuliffe, *Qur'anic Christians: An Analysis of Classical and Modern Exegesis* (Cambridge, UK: Cambridge University Press, 1991), 118. Important note: many English translations of the Quran include a parenthetical notation (submission to God) in this quotation to soften its impact, but such a notation is not made in the Arabic original.

61. Quoted in Andrew G. Bostom, *The Legacy of Islamic Antisemitism* (Amherst, NY: Prometheus Books, 2008), 33.

62. See "The Baha'i Faith," www.bahai.org; and Baha'i Faith, www.us.bahai.org. For Christian interactions with the Baha'i Faith, see Francis J. Beckwith, *Baha'i: A Christian Response to Baha'ism* (Minneapolis: Bethany House, 1985); and William M. Miller, *The Baha'i Faith: Its History and Teachings* (South Pasadena, CA: William Carey Library, 1984).

63. "Muslim Movements and Schisms: A Study of the Ahmadiyyah Movement," in John Gilchrist, *Jesus to the Muslims*, vol. 1 (South Africa: Benoni, 1986), www.answering-islam.org/Gilchrist/Vol1/9c.html.

64. C. Eric Lincoln, *The Black Muslims in America*, 3rd ed. (Grand Rapids: Eerdmans, 1994); Steven Tsoukalas, *The Nation of Islam: Understanding the "Black Muslims"* (Phillipsburg, NJ: P&R, 2001).

CHAPTER 4

SECULARISM

1. THE BATTLE OF IDEAS: THE BATTLE OF STORIES

If you want to beat a sports opponent, study his playing style, develop a strategy, and compete with all your heart. When the clock runs out, you'll know whether it was enough. But what if the competition is not in sports but in the world of ideas? Judging by the way advocates of Secularism promote their worldview, the answer is to defeat your opponent by turning his audience against him. *Tell a story in which your opponent is the bad guy, so people will discount him from the start.* Stories have tremendous power—for good or for ill.

True stories helped William Wilberforce turn the British public against slavery, saving thousands of lives and setting millions free. False stories helped Nazi Germany and communist leaders in Russia slaughter tens of millions of people and enslave hundreds of millions more.

The greatest worldview conflicts in Western civilization today result from the collision of stories. The story of Western civilization taught until fairly recently was this: the best aspects of the West resulted from its grounding in the Christian worldview, particularly the Christian understanding of morality, human value, and economic freedom. Secularism challenges this narrative and tells another story, claiming credit for the best aspects of the Western world while laying the blame for the worst aspects at Christianity's feet.

> *Secularism:* an atheistic and materialistic worldview that advocates a public society free from the influence of religion.

To understand **Secularism** as a worldview, we'll look at the Secularist narrative, as well as the rise of Secularism as a pattern of ideas, beliefs, convictions, behaviors, and habits, and then dig into what Secularists believe—and try to persuade others to believe—about the world.

2. SECULARISM: REWRITING THE STORY OF CIVILIZATION

The term *propaganda* refers to "mass 'suggestion' or 'influence' through the manipulation of symbols and the psychology of the individual … with the ultimate goal of having the recipient of the appeal come to 'voluntarily' accept this position as if it were his or her own."[1] Propaganda campaigns typically portray opponents as possessing evil character qualities and motives in order to incite feelings of indignation and revulsion toward them, such that any harm directed their way is viewed as an act of just retribution.[2]

Many worldview battles in our day are examples of propaganda, in which the most extreme language possible is used to caricature those on the other side. For example, in 2011, when a majority of North Carolinians voted for a constitutional amendment establishing marriage between a man and woman as the only valid or recognized legal domestic union in the state, the diatribes rapidly multiplied:

- "North Carolina—keeping hate alive."[3]
- "Really brings out the human garbage side of our species."[4]
- "NC's electorate is dumb as trash."[5]

Even mainstream-media outlets ran with this theme. One op-ed piece in the *Los Angeles Times* featured this headline: "Obama, Gay Marriage, and a Win for Bigotry in NC."[6] This kind of rhetoric entirely ignores the arguments about whether gay marriage is a good idea or not. It seeks instead to portray opponents as hateful, bigoted, dumb human garbage. This is propaganda. It's a rewriting of history to turn public opinion against traditional-marriage advocates without making—or employing watered down versions of—actual arguments.

It's no secret that Americans disagree with one another about many things. These disagreements occasionally lead to sharp words.[7] But the issue below the surface, the one almost no one talks about, is the way history is rewritten to justify a particular worldview, and not just on a single issue like gay marriage. For instance, you've probably heard the following narrative (exaggerated to make a point):

> The followers of Jesus were evil liars whose goal was to establish a macho, misogynistic cult. The good people of Rome tried to stop them, but the wicked emperor Constantine managed to establish Christianity as Rome's official religion anyway. Once in power, Christians intentionally undermined Rome's strength until this once-great civilization collapsed. The church blindly pressed forward in its obsession with control, plunging Europe into the Dark Ages. It took a few hundred years, but Europe was eventually rescued by scientists and philosophers who bravely risked their lives to challenge the church's teaching that the earth was flat and the center of the universe. Occasionally, Christians gained power long enough to burn tens of thousands of witches, massacre millions of natives, and launch cruel crusades against innocent, civilized Muslims. Fortunately, due to the brilliance of those who rejected the church's teachings, the Enlightenment saw the triumph of science and reason over religion. However, we must not let down our guard, because greedy, ignorant Christians resent the progress made by clever, reasonable Secularists, and they will do everything they can to manipulate their way into power to prevent decent folk from having a good time and living their lives in freedom.

There isn't a single "fact" in this story, yet many consider it to be accurate history.[8] The most popular college history text in print today, *A People's History of the United States*, is a 768-page diatribe—bereft of a single footnote—offering precisely this point of view.

If people believe this story, they'll not only view Secularism as the key to human flourishing; they'll insist on locking Christians out of positions of influence. Is it working? To find out, let's dive into an examination of what the worldview of Secularism is all about, assess its level of influence, and delve into the particular ways it seeks to answer life's ultimate questions.

3. The Secularist Narrative

Based on an exhaustive review of Secularist writings, it is important to Secularists to present themselves as unbiased and neutral, whereas Christians—and presumably other theists—are biased and extremist. David Niose, as an example, considers Secularism to be a "post-theological worldview."[9]

Secularism is derived from the word *saeculum*, which is a Latin term for a span of time, typically a generation. As José Casanova phrased it, "Secular then stands for self-sufficient and exclusive secularity, when people are not simply religiously 'unmusical' but are actually closed to any form of transcendence beyond the purely secular immanent frame."[10] In other words, Secularists' concern is for the current age (as opposed to eternity) and human beings (as opposed to God).

Regardless of their personal theological commitments, Secularists seem to believe that all public considerations—education and government, primarily—must be based on *materialism*, the idea that only the physical world exists. Georgetown University professor Jacques Berlinerblau says, "The secularish are here-and-now people. They live for this world, not for the next."[11] If materialism is true, any concern about nonmaterial things such as God, spirituality, or an afterlife is at best misguided and at worst dangerously deluded.

Berlinerblau defines *Secularism* narrowly as "a political philosophy concerned with the best way to govern complex, religiously pluralistic societies."[12] Is Secularism truly just a narrow political stance, something that affects how people view religion and politics, or is it something more? We think there is enough evidence to prove that Secularism is a worldview: a coherent pattern of ideas, beliefs, convictions, and habits. Understanding Secularism as a worldview helps us see where it conflicts with Christianity so we are not taken captive by its false teachings, and so we can articulately respond to areas in which Secularist teachings threaten human flourishing.

Proponents of Secularism have engaged in a century-long project to develop scientific, historical, and even theological credibility in order to ensure Secularism's place as the dominant narrative of culture. Whether they have succeeded with this project is a point of contention, but understanding the ways Secularism asserts itself as a worldview will help unlock how practically every university class is taught today. It also helps demystify much of what happens in politics, government, and the media.

> Proponents of Secularism have engaged in a century-long project to develop scientific, historical, and even theological credibility in order to ensure Secularism's place as the dominant narrative of culture.

Secularism's opposition to Christianity does not mean the two worldviews have nothing in common. Secularists share a concern with thinking Christians about the direction America is headed. Self-described atheist and humanist Susan Jacoby says, "During the past four decades, America's endemic anti-intellectual tendencies have been grievously exacerbated by a new species of semiconscious anti-rationalism, feeding on and fed by an ignorant popular culture of video images and unremitting noise that leaves no room for contemplation or logic."[13]

Thoughtful Christians would agree. In fact, in 2008 Prometheus Books, a publishing company founded by atheist philosophy professor Paul Kurtz for the express purpose of promoting Secularism, published *Distracted*, a book voicing deep concern with the direction of popular culture. The author, Maggie Jackson, asks, "Are we heading into a dark age? To ask this question is first to wonder whether we at present have much of a collective appetite for wrestling meaningfully with uncertainties, and whether we have the will to carve out havens of deep thinking amid the tempests of time."[14] Thoughtful Christians wonder this too.

While Secularists and Christians are both concerned about America's direction, when it comes to understanding why we're off course and what should be done about it, their answers could not be more different. To unlock the differences, we'll look at the history of Secularism, examine whether it is truly a coherent worldview, and expose its aims and methods.

4. THE HISTORY OF SECULARISM IN AMERICA

Modern-day American Secularists are intellectual descendants of Thomas Jefferson and Benjamin Franklin, deists who endorsed the basic morality of the Christian God but did not believe in his miraculous, direct involvement in the world. Doctrines considered divisive, such as the Trinity, were done away with. These American founders, Secularists claim, were searching for a civic religion, not a saving faith, which they say is why specific references to God were omitted from the Constitution.[15]

The seeds of deism planted in the eighteenth and nineteenth centuries came to full bloom in the twentieth century, first in America's universities and then in popular culture. Quoting noted sociologist Christian Smith, Hunter Baker observes that Smith sees today's Secularism as a very purposeful movement with clear aims:

> The secularization of the public order was the result of an intentional program by secular activists. These activists "were largely skeptical, freethinking, agnostic, atheist, or theologically liberal" well educated persons "located mainly in knowledge-production occupations ... who generally espoused materialism, naturalism, positivism, and the privatization or extinction of religion." This group successfully changed the dominant understandings of science, higher education, primary and secondary education, public philosophy, church-state doctrine, the model of personhood (from the soul to a psychologized self), and journalism.[16]

If, as Smith claims, the growth of Secularism was intentional, we'd expect it to propose answers to life's ultimate questions. It does indeed. Among those advancing Secularism, none were so bold and clear about their views and aims as a uniquely twentieth-century group of professors and theologians who called themselves Secular Humanists.

5. The Rise of Secularism

In the 1930s, a group of atheist and agnostic professors—including University of Michigan professor Roy Wood Sellars and John Dewey, widely considered to be the father of American public education—wrote and signed a document called the *Humanist Manifesto*. The manifesto's goal was to develop a new religious movement based on science, an inspirational faith to replace the dogmatic "old attitudes" promoted by theistic religions. The authors wrote,

> Today man's larger understanding of the universe, his scientific achievements, and deeper appreciation of brotherhood, have created a situation which requires a new statement of the means and purposes of religion. Such a vital, fearless, and frank religion capable of furnishing adequate social goals and personal satisfactions ... must be shaped for the needs of this age.[17]

The original manifesto was updated forty years later, in 1973, and signed by hundreds of prominent scholars, including Francis Crick, early pioneer in DNA research, famed psychologist B. F. Skinner, and dozens of secular "ministers." A third version, subtitled *A Call for a New Planetary Humanism*, was released in the year 2000.

The central theme of all three manifestos is the elaboration of a philosophy and value system that excludes belief in God and traditional religion.[18]

The signers of the various humanist manifestos agreed to focus their work on the "needs of this age" (Secularism) and on advancing humanity rather than concern with God

---

> **Secular Humanism:** a religious and philosophical worldview that makes humankind the ultimate norm by which truth and values are to be determined; a worldview that reveres human reason, evolution, naturalism, and secular theories of ethics while rejecting every form of supernatural religion.

(humanism). They described themselves, therefore, as Secular Humanists. Today, **Secular Humanism** is probably the most concise expression of what Secularists believe, whether or not they embrace that title.

As you can imagine, the humanist manifestos received a lot of attention for their ebullient claims regarding both the secular nature of reality and the capacity of science to solve humanity's problems. Alarmed by the bold anti-Christian stance of the *Humanist Manifesto*, Christian pastors and professors saw Secular Humanism as a secret force designed to carry Secularist ideas deep into the institutions of power, particularly the courts and universities. Today, Secularists are quick to deflect such criticism by downplaying the authority of these controversial statements. The manifestos, they claim, are not "permanent or authoritative dogmas" but "subject to ongoing critique." Twenty-first-century Secularists like the light Secular Humanism has provided, but they fear being burned by its heat.

Some Secularists go further and deny having any influence at all. Jacques Berlinerblau, for example, writes,

> Where exactly was the empire of American Secularism? Where was its army? its impassioned hordes? its war chest? There was none of that. Though there were elite units, so to speak. Secularism's defenders were stationed in print and television newsrooms. They worked in cinema and the domains of high art. Down on campus you had entire platoons of bespectacled secularists who sympathized with the cause. But those elites were either too unfocused, or too poorly led, or too weakly aligned with the movement, or too few, to repel the onslaught of the Revivalists.[19]

It is more than a little ironic to find a leading Secularist expressing defenselessness because his empire "only" controls print and television news, the popular culture, and "entire platoons" of college professors. As we will see, by the time Berlinerblau began downplaying Secularism's influence, its triumph was complete, with its ideas deeply embedded in nearly every channel of influence.

6. Where Secularism Is Influential Today

In 1976, a professor from California named Peter Angeles edited a boisterous volume titled *Critiques of God* in which he predicted that supernatural religions would soon disappear from the earth. Science, according to Angeles, displaced God from heaven because no such place exists, and it has displaced him from earth because a creator was no longer necessary. Angeles insisted, "It is not that God is being relegated to a remote region. It is not that God has become a bodiless abstraction (a sexless It). It is the realization that there is no God left to which to relate. Without God, what is left? Man and the universe. That should be enough. That has to be enough because that is all there is."[20]

Things didn't turn out as Angeles expected. Susan Jacoby concedes, "As we now know, the conclusion that American fundamentalists were a dying breed was a misjudgment of historical (dare one call it biblical?) proportions."[21]

Today, though, Secularists can find hope in the Pew Research Center's new research: among those eighteen to twenty-nine years of age, one-third claim no religious affiliation.[22] While some of these young people merely have commitment issues, many are probably Secularists. David Niose, president of the American Humanist Association, notes that 12 to 18 percent of Americans are Secularists.[23]

This 12 to 18 percent includes only those who claim the Secularism title. The larger issue may be those claiming the Christian mantle but living as if Secularism were true. Author Craig M. Gay names the problem "practical atheism." "Under modern conditions," he says, "the question of God is simply irrelevant to so much of what we do on a daily basis that it eventually drops out of mind and heart. God is simply forgotten."[24] One common approach among Christian thought leaders to the rise of Secularism is to grant Secularism's assumptions but sentimentally labor to make the Christian peg fit in the Secularist hole. "Christians are people too," they plead. According to Gay, these efforts, while well intended, only serve in replacing biblical truth with a counterfeit gospel: "It seems that once truly Christian faith and hope are lost, they have quite often, under modern conditions, only been transmuted into faith and hope in a humanly constructed future."[25]

Secularists can be viewed in their natural habitat at nearly any of America's more than three thousand colleges and universities. Here Secularists have found success, capturing impressionable young adults as they are released into the wild. Many Secularists see themselves as liberators, lifting students out of religious superstition and other nonsense holding back society's progress.[26] According to a report by the National Bureau of Economic Research (NBER), whose president is a professor at MIT, Secularists embrace a "Science Drives out Superstition Hypothesis," which says, "if religion reflects primarily ignorance, irrational fears, and superstition, then increased education could reduce religiosity by reducing ignorance and inculcating science."[27]

> Interestingly, given Secularists' preoccupation with science, researchers who have examined the presence of religion on college campuses have found that the greatest influence of Secularism is in the humanities and social sciences, not in the biological or physical sciences.

Interestingly, given Secularists' preoccupation with science, researchers who have examined the presence of religion on college campuses have found that the greatest influence of Secularism is in the humanities and social sciences, not in the biological or physical sciences.[28] According to the NBER study, being a physical- or biological-sciences major had a negligible impact on students' faith, but

> being a Humanities or Social Science major has a statistically significant negative effect on religious attendance and self-assessed importance of religion in one's life. Social Science seems to have slightly stronger effects. All of the negative effects of both of these majors appear to become more negative over time, with the effect of being a Social Science major on religious importance almost doubling.[29]

Given that religious students are attracted to humanities majors in high numbers, the damaging effect of the humanities and social sciences should be of special note for those concerned about Christian students losing their faith on campus.[30]

How many professors claim a Secularist worldview? Of the 1,417 professors queried in a 2006 study called "Politics of the American Professoriate Survey," 22.9 percent said they either didn't believe in God (atheist) or didn't know whether there is a God (agnostic). By contrast, 34.9 percent said they knew God exists and had no doubts about it. Interestingly, the levels of belief in God among professors were highest in accounting and elementary education but lowest in psychology and mechanical engineering. If these study results hold true, your chances of having an atheist or agnostic professor in the humanities, social sciences, computer science, and engineering are about one in three. In the physical and biological sciences, your chances of having an atheist or agnostic professor are one in two, but as we saw earlier, students in these majors aren't as negatively affected in their faith. The only places in the university not controlled by Secularists, according to this survey, are in the health or agriculture departments.

"Still," some people say, "that's not too bad. The percentages of atheists and agnostics on campus are higher than in the general population, but they're not the majority." True on the surface, but let's scratch deeper. Your chances of running into a professor who believes in God are two in three. But only half of those express any kind of Christian belief. And among professors who claim to be Protestant or Catholic, the chances that the person will be religiously conservative—that he or she will actually believe the Bible is true, for example—are about one in twenty.

For example, if the national statistics hold true at, say, Princeton University, we would expect to find only 21 professors who are Christian and oriented toward traditional values (for example, against abortion and in favor of marriage being defined as between one woman and one man) out of more than 1,100 full-time and visiting professors. On the other hand, we would expect, on average, 262 professors who are Secularist. In the end, you're ten times more likely to run into a Secularist professor than a Christian professor who is oriented toward traditional values.[31]

Some critics have taken issue with the pervasiveness of Secularism on campus, pointing to a finding from the Spirituality in Higher Education project at UCLA that 81 percent of professors consider themselves spiritual. But the definition of *spiritual* employed in the survey was whether a person is actively searching for meaning and purpose in life, is becoming a more self-aware and enlightened person, and is finding answers to life's mysteries and "big questions." This is so broad a definition, we're astounded the researchers found 19 percent of professors who disagreed with it.

The UCLA view of *spirituality* as a vague search for meaning and purpose stands in opposition to any meaningful definition of *religion*. To be *spiritual* means that a person is "interested in different religious traditions, seeks to understand other countries and cultures, feels a strong connection to all humanity, believes in the goodness of all people, accepts others as they are, and believes that all life is interconnected and that love is at the root of all the great religions."[32] Religions, on the other hand, make claims to exclusivity: they can't all be equally correct in their assessment of what is real, what is wrong with us, and what ought to be done about it. Thoughtful adherents of Christianity, Islam, Buddhism, Hinduism, or any one of dozens of other major religions would, in all likelihood, find themselves disagreeing with UCLA's definition of *spirituality*.

So a student heading off to college is practically guaranteed to encounter Secularism and will find it a very rare species of professor who will share the student's desire to maintain a faith in God, in Jesus, in the truth of the Bible, and in the application of these beliefs to the culture.

Still, just because Secularism is pervasive does not mean it is coherent. So we must ask: Is it actually fair to claim that Secularism is a discernible pattern of ideas, beliefs, convictions, and habits?

> A student heading off to college is practically guaranteed to encounter Secularism and will find it a very rare species of professor who will share the student's desire to maintain a faith in God, in Jesus, in the truth of the Bible, and in the application of these beliefs to the culture.

7. IS SECULARISM ACTUALLY A WORLDVIEW?

Recall the definition of a *worldview*: "a pattern of ideas, beliefs, convictions, and habits that help us make sense of God, the world, and our relationship to God and the world." When they see this definition, some Secularists dismiss it. "I don't believe in God; therefore I do not have a religious worldview by your definition."

Let's take this criticism in two parts. First, does Secularism offer a comprehensive view of reality? Charles Taylor, the widely acknowledged leading expert on Secularism, thinks so. Taylor finds inadequate the common notion that Secularism is merely a means of secularizing public spaces; neither is Secularism only a description of the general decline of belief and practice. Rather, he says, Secularism "consists of new conditions of belief; it consists in a new shape to the experience which prompts to and is defined by belief; in a new context in which all search and questioning about the moral and spiritual must proceed."[33] In other words, Secularism is more than *disbelief* in God. It is *belief* in ways of seeing life and the world that do not involve God or religion.

Hunter Baker agrees. Secularization theory may have begun as a political theory, he says, but as it expanded in the twentieth century, it came to "affect 'the totality of cultural life and ideation' … in a variety of areas such as the arts, philosophy, and literature."[34] It is hardly possible for it to be otherwise. When one rejects the idea of divine creation, the range of possible theories about human purpose narrows considerably. A Secularist must, almost by definition, be a materialist (believing that only the material world exists), and if a materialist, then a determinist (since by believing that human behavior is determined by evolutionary heritage, no free will exists).

We see, then, that Secularism passes the first test of being a pattern of ideas, beliefs, convictions, and habits. Now let's look at the second part of the criticism—Secularism's denial of being religious. "We don't believe in God," Secularists claim, "therefore we are not religious. After all, what is *secular* if not the rejection of religion?"

Not so fast. *Secular* certainly implies the rejection of *supernatural* religion, but not all religion is supernatural. If we accept the dictionary definition of *religion* as "any set of beliefs about the cause, nature, and purpose of the universe," then the very fact that Secularism is consistent—and in that consistency attempts to answer life's ultimate questions—does make it religious.

The late anthropologist Clifford Geertz, for many years a professor at Princeton University, referred to both Secularism and religion as "cultural systems."[35] Mark Juergensmeyer, perhaps the world's foremost expert on global religion and religious violence, claims that Secular Nationalism is a "strange religion" that spreads with missionary zeal and is, like religion, "an ideology of order."[36]

Emile Durkheim, the founder of the field of sociology and perhaps the principal architect of what we now call the social sciences,[37] considered religions to be, as paraphrased in a recent report, "functional organizations that use striking ideas to foster collective action and the interests of the religious community as a community, including influence over both daily interactions among members and relationships with those outside."[38] For Durkheim, a worldview need not be supernatural to count as religious. It just needs to focus on the sacred, the "collective ideals that have fixed themselves on material objects.... They are only collective forces hypostasized, that is to say, moral forces; they are made up of the ideas and sentiments awakened in us by the spectacle of society, and not of sensations coming from the physical world."[39]

Secularism is clearly a cultural system using striking ideas to foster collective action and influence its members to focus on collective ideals with missionary zeal. By this criterion, Secularism is a religion, just one that denies the relevance of the supernatural.

If Secularism is indeed a religious worldview, we can compare its views on general and special revelation to other worldviews to see if they sufficiently answer life's ultimate questions. Let's start with the idea of general revelation—that there is something revealed to all people that explains the universe as we know it.

8. HOW WE GOT HERE: A SECULARIST VIEW OF GENERAL REVELATION

One reason Secularists are offended at being called religious is their embrace of the narrative that religion and science are opposed to each other. Religion is based on superstition and ignorance, they say; whereas science is the systematic, impartial application of reason and intelligence. Science has rescued the modern world from the religiously backward.

It's not like that. According to Hunter Baker, "What happened in the matter of science and religion was the creation of a legend."[40] Part of this legend is that evolution explains the existence of all things. This, for Carl Sagan, "is a fact, not a theory."[41] Even though Charles Darwin felt the need to postulate a supernatural force to explain the initial appearance of life, the Secularist cannot afford such a concession. Harvard paleontologist Richard Lewontin admitted this bias when he said, "Materialism is absolute, for we cannot allow a Divine Foot in the door."[42] The famed E. O. Wilson concurred: "A scientific humanist ... is someone who suggests that everything in the universe has a material basis. And that means everything, including the mind and all its spiritual products."[43]

To Secularists, science isn't just one way of knowing. It is the *only reliable way* of knowing. A true definition of *science*, to their way of thinking, excludes supernatural

> To Secularists, science isn't just one way of knowing. It is the only reliable way of knowing.

explanations for any event, including the origin of life. For Secularists, naturalism explains everything. Julian Huxley summed it up: "Modern science must rule out special creation or divine guidance."[44]

Why must science rule out creation? As we have noted, science cannot observe or measure the supernatural and therefore cannot "know" anything about it. Of course, by this definition science cannot render judgment on the theory of evolution either. One-time-only historical events, such as the origin of life, fall outside the parameters of the scientific method. They cannot be repeated, observed, tested, or falsified.[45] Accordingly, neither creationism nor an evolutionary account of origins is strictly "scientific."

Secularism relies on evolution for much more than a theory about the origin of life. The theory of evolution has significant implications for ethics, sociology, law, and politics. Secularists believe that evolutionary theory provides the grounds for a proper understanding of the world.

For this reason, Secularists encourage teaching evolution as "fact" throughout our educational system—thereby relegating the supernatural, especially God, to the world of literary mythology. And this is in every class, not just biology. In the words of Julian Huxley, "It is essential for evolution to become the central core of any educational system, because it is evolution, in the broad sense, that links inorganic nature with life, and the stars with earth, and matter with mind, and animals with man. Human history is a continuation of biological evolution in a different form."[46]

Since Huxley's time, however, many in the scientific community have challenged the idea that Darwin's theory of evolution can explain the existence of all things.[47] To the Secularist mind, though, this is a distressing turn of events. Secularists are fond of labeling Christians as dogmatic, but they neglect to mention that believing life to have arisen from nonlife is as sacred a doctrine to Secularists as the doctrine of the incarnation is to Christians. Secularist Keith Parsons, for example, asserts, "With the environment operating to remove nonviable variations, the appearance of life on earth becomes a certainty rather than an extreme improbability."[48] This is a statement of faith, and since it is not based on evidence, even a blind faith.

> Secularists are fond of labeling Christians as dogmatic, but they neglect to mention that believing life to have arisen from nonlife is as sacred a doctrine to Secularists as the doctrine of the incarnation is to Christians.

Darwin's embarrassment over his theory's conflict with the fossil record is evidenced by the fact that in *The Descent of Man*, "Darwin did not cite a single reference to fossils in support of his belief in human evolution."[49] Despite Darwin's own reservations, however, atheists wrested the theory from his hands and proclaimed evolution to be fact. Julian Huxley declared that Darwin "rendered evolution inescapable as a fact … [and] all-embracing as a concept."[50]

Perhaps in 1960 Huxley could get away with such a rash claim. But today, as we demonstrate in this text, faith in evolution as the grand explanation of all things has become a counterrational religious dogma. "Evolution is a religion," says evolutionist Michael Ruse. "This was true of evolution in the beginning, and it is true of evolution still today." Ruse further says, "Evolution, therefore, came into being as a kind of secular ideology[,] an explicit substitute for Christianity. It stressed laws against miracles and, by analogy, it promoted progress against providence."[51]

So where are we? General revelation, from the Secularist standpoint, bets the farm on science as the only means of knowing. It's a more risky bet than Secularists admit. In the introduction to the 1971 edition of Darwin's *The Origin of Species*, L. H. Matthews admitted, "The fact of evolution is the backbone of biology, and biology is thus in the peculiar position of being a science founded on an unproved theory—is it then a science or a faith? Belief in the theory of evolution is thus exactly parallel to belief in special creation—both are concepts which believers know to be true but neither, up to the present, has been capable of proof."[52]

The sort of faith Matthews described is dissatisfying when it comes to the questions humanity is really asking. The philosopher C. E. M. Joad, whom we met in the chapter on Christianity, offered a devastating critique: "A religion which is in constant process of revision to square with science's ever-changing picture of the world might well be easier to believe, but it is hard to believe it would be worth believing." It seems, though, that Secularists believe it nonetheless. What this belief looks like in its particulars is the topic to which we will next turn.

9. Special Revelation: Where Secularists Turn for Direction

Like Christianity and Islam, Secularism proposes answers to life's ultimate questions, and it claims sources of knowledge that reliably support the legitimacy of these answers. As in the chapters on other worldviews, let's see if we can understand Secularism better by posing five questions:

1. On what sources of revelation do Secularists draw?
2. What does Secularism say about humanity?
3. What does Secularism say is wrong with us?
4. What does Secularism say about how we should live?
5. How are we to understand other worldviews based on Secularism?

1. On what sources of revelation do Secularists draw? If you ask enough Secularists which books have influenced them most, you'll often hear the following:

- Thomas Paine, *The Age of Reason*
- Charles Darwin, *The Origin of Species*
- Friedrich Nietzsche, *On the Genealogy of Morals*
- Sigmund Freud, *Civilization and Its Discontents*
- John Dewey, *Democracy and Education*
- Bertrand Russell, *Why I Am Not a Christian*
- Simone de Beauvoir, *The Second Sex*
- Abraham Maslow, *Toward a Psychology of Being*

Within the last few years, a canon of New Atheism has developed, in the popular culture at least, with the writings of Richard Dawkins, Sam Harris, Daniel Dennett, and the late Christopher Hitchens, who are referred to in a wry apocalyptic reference as the "four horsemen of atheism" because they seem to take glee in attacking religion with every thought weapon they can find. In Dawkins's lectures, for instance, he often wins standing ovations among Secularist students and professors with an artful ad hominem:

> The God of the Old Testament is arguably the most unpleasant character in all fiction: jealous and proud of it; a petty, unjust, unforgiving control-freak; a vindictive, bloodthirsty ethnic cleanser; a misogynistic, homophobic, racist, infanticidal, genocidal, filicidal, pestilential, megalomaniacal, sadomasochistic, capriciously malevolent bully.[53]

The various humanist manifestos also serve as a source of Secularist revelation. As the author of the 1973 manifesto, philosophy professor Paul Kurtz tried pitching a tent big enough to hold more than just atheists. "Secular Humanists may be agnostics, atheists, rationalists, or skeptics, but they find insufficient evidence for the claim that some divine purpose exists for the universe," he wrote. "They reject the idea that God has intervened miraculously in history or revealed himself to a chosen few, or that he can save or redeem sinners."[54]

If a clearer statement of secular belief has been written, we haven't found it, except for this oft-quoted line from the 1973 manifesto: "If no deity will save us, we must save ourselves."[55] Hundreds of people, indicating agreement, affixed their signatures to the document.[56] The subsequent *Humanist Manifesto 2000* included hundreds more signatures.

> If a clearer statement of secular belief has been written, we haven't found it, except for this oft-quoted line from the 1973 manifesto: "If no deity will save us, we must save ourselves."

As mentioned earlier, Kurtz also began a publishing company called Prometheus Books, now located in Amherst, New York. The Prometheus catalog serves as a pretty clear canon of Secularist belief, though some of it is disturbing, including a book attempting to normalize adult-child sex. And on the chance that "the hand that rocks the cradle [truly] rules the world," Prometheus even publishes children's books, including one by Chris Brockman called *What about Gods?*, which reads in part,

> Many people say they believe in a god. Do you know what a god is? Do you know what it means to believe in a god? A god is a mythical character. Mythical characters are imaginary, they're not real. People make them up. Dragons and fairies are two of many mythical characters people have made up. They're not real.[57]

Good-bye Santa. Good-bye tooth fairy. Good-bye ... Jesus.

In spite of the substantial agreement among Secularists about embracing science and rejecting Christianity, many have questioned whether Secularism is truly a coherent enough worldview to attract the masses. That a lot of people have signed the *Humanist Manifesto* may or may not mean anything. Some people are quite promiscuous with their signatures, especially on college campuses. Plus, organizations like the American Humanist Association are relatively small, operating on about the same budget as a church with twenty staff members (of which there are several hundred in the United States). The AHA's founders and chief promoters are all dead. It is also possible that most Secularists have never even heard of AHA's manifesto and would never sign it even if they had.

But it would be wrong to confuse the issues of whether someone believes something and whether he or she is willing to affix a signature to it. When we talk about worldviews, we're talking about the ideas people hold and their subsequent commitment to certain beliefs, convictions, and resulting habits, not about the organizations to which they pay dues. If we can understand someone's theology, philosophy, and ethics, we can probably make fairly accurate guesses about his or her views in other disciplines as well. Probabilities, not certainties, are sufficient to help us understand the patterns of ideas.

2. What does Secularism say about humanity? As we've seen, most Secularists believe the theory of evolution is the basis for explaining everything we need to know about how we got here and what we should do now. In the Secularist worldview, we are evolving animals, continually progressing onward and upward toward some form of biological and social perfection. Julian Huxley believed that "all reality is a single process of evolution."[58] Secularists believe we are capable of controlling our own evolutionary development. Huxley wrote, "Today, in twentieth-century man, the evolutionary process is at last becoming conscious of itself and is beginning to study itself with a view to directing its future course."[59]

> In the Secularist worldview, we are evolving animals, continually progressing onward and upward toward some form of biological and social perfection.

But what is it that makes someone human? Christians and Muslims believe God made human beings. Christians further believe God made human beings as his own image bearers. But if Secularists are correct that evolution explains everything, what is it that makes humans unique? Nothing, really. Most Secularists embrace some form of mind/body monism , which says that human beings are made of one substance, merely matter in motion. We have no spirits or souls, and our minds are only projections of brain activity.

At first glance, this sounds absurd. No *minds*? How can we think if we have no minds? But Secularists are not saying we do not think; they view the mind and the brain as essentially the same thing. Corliss Lamont, one-time "humanist chaplain" at Harvard, explained: "If … the monistic theory of psychology is true, as Naturalism, Materialism, and Humanism claim, then there is no possibility that the human consciousness, with its memory and awareness of self-identity intact, can survive the shock and disintegration of death. According to this view, the body and personality live together; they grow together; and they die together."[60]

Therefore, consistent Secularists go beyond viewing the eternal realm as irrelevant; they deny its existence altogether. Lamont went further, rejecting a belief in immortality is the first step to becoming a Secularist: "The issue of mortality versus immortality is crucial in the argument of Humanism against supernaturalism. For if men realize that their careers are limited to this world, that this earthly existence is all that they will ever have, then they are already more than half-way on the path toward becoming functioning Humanists."[61]

The second implication of the monistic view of the mind arises from the belief that the mind is physical, and that it arose through evolutionary processes. If this is so, is the mind still evolving? Some Secularists believe a more efficient mind is arising today in the form of computer technology. Victor J. Stenger, author of *Not by Design*, claimed, "Future computers will not only be superior to people in every task, mental or physical, but will also be immortal." He believed it will become possible to save human "thoughts which constitute consciousness" in "computer memory banks," as well as program computers in such a way as to give them the full range of human thought. He said, "If the computer is 'just a machine,' so is the human brain."

Stenger also foresaw the possibility of computers becoming the next step in the evolutionary chain—the new higher consciousness. He concluded, "Perhaps, as part of this new consciousness, we will become God."[62] This isn't just fringe sentiment from a science-fiction blogger writing from his or her parents' basement. Stenger was widely cited as one of the top New Atheists of our day. Some have taken to calling this *transhumanism* and anticipate that technology will develop to the point of overcoming human limitations and making human ethical dilemmas a thing of the past. Nick Bostrom, a member of the faculty of philosophy at Oxford University, says we will get to the point where we can rightly be described as "posthuman."[63]

> *Transhumanism:* a humanistic movement that hopes to advance humanity beyond its physical and mental limitations through the application and integration of biotechnology.

Why is it so important for Secularists to believe that thinking is nothing more than bits and bytes of brain activity? C. S. Lewis saw the implication long before the dawn of the computer age:

> The Naturalists have been engaged in thinking about Nature. They have not attended to the fact that they were thinking. The moment one attends to this it is obvious that one's own thinking cannot be merely a natural event, and that therefore something other than Nature exists. The Supernatural is not remote and abstruse: it is a matter of daily and hourly experience, as intimate as breathing.[64]

3. What does Secularism say is wrong with us? The problem with humanity, according to Secularists, is that we are not sufficiently disenchanted with spiritual things. Charles Taylor notes,

> Unbelief for great numbers of contemporary unbelievers, is understood as an achievement of rationality. It cannot have this without a continuing historical awareness. It is a condition which can't only be described in the present tense, but which also needs the perfect tense: a condition of "having overcome" the irrationality of belief. It is this perfect-tensed consciousness which underlies unbelievers' use of "disenchantment" today.[65]

But *why* Secularists believe we aren't sufficiently disenchanted—*that* takes some explaining. Remember, Secularists are by definition committed to some version of evolution as the explanation for all that is. The belief that all life evolved from nonlife, that it has been evolving upward and onward for 3.6 billion years,[66] colors Secularists' attitudes toward all reality,

> If, as Secularists believe, all reality is an evolutionary pattern that moves upward step by step to create rational thought and morality in the most advanced species, then our history also must be a progressive march toward a better world.

especially history. It's a simple case of a new story giving rise to new meaning: That is, if, as Secularists believe, all reality is an evolutionary pattern that moves upward step by step to create rational thought and morality in the most advanced species, then our history also must be a progressive march toward a better world. As the evolutionary process continues, so must progress continue. History is the story of development from nonlife to life, simple to complex, unintelligent to intelligent, animal to human, amoral to moral. With each successive generation we become more fit for survival. Julian Huxley said, "Man's destiny is to be the sole agent for the future evolution of this planet."[67]

This is not to say that Secularists are buoyant in their hopes for humanity. Some, like the late science-fiction writer Isaac Asimov, saw the problem clearly: "In the first place, the phrase 'the survival of the fittest' is not an illuminating one. It implies that those who survive are the 'fittest,' but what is meant by 'fittest'? Why, those are 'fittest' who survive. This is an argument in a circle."[68] Perhaps the squeamishness comes from the thought that the survival-of-the-fittest principle might function among humans the way it functions in nature: "red in tooth and claw" as Alfred Lord Tennyson suggested, with no concern for the weak or poor.[69] Even Secularists find themselves repulsed by the way the survival-of-the-fittest doctrine was the explicit justification Marxists gave for their genocide and Hitler gave for his Aryan policies.[70]

Still, when they must choose between the survival of the fittest and the idea that humanity fell from an innocent state, they choose the former. To John Dietrich, it wasn't about rising and falling. It was only about rising: "There never has been any Garden of Eden or perfect condition in the past, there never has been any fall, and there has been a constant rise. Man has been climbing slowly up the ages from the most primitive condition to the present civilization."[71] Julian Huxley was even more explicit, insisting that the "rise and fall of empires and cultures is a natural phenomenon, just as much as the succession of dominant groups in biological evolution."[72]

What keeps humanity from progressing to its full potential is that people not sufficiently enlightened about the inevitability of human progress along Secularist lines of reasoning. Such people, they say, take us backward when we should be moving forward. The American Humanist Association's president, David Niose, says in *Nonbeliever Nation* (a book Richard Dawkins calls "excellent"),

> It's no secret that a major cause of this regression is the Religious Right, the loose-knit but powerful movement that has been changing the dynamics of American politics for over three decades. Guised as representing "traditional family values," the Religious Right is driven by a small minority that is extreme in its views, well funded, organized, and fueled by a fear of modernity that unfortunately resonates on a mass level.[73]

Reading *Nonbeliever Nation* leaves one with the clear impression that religious people, especially evangelical Christians, are bad and Secularists are good. It's a new version of the old story: everything negative in America is the fault of religion, particularly Christianity. Secularism, say its advocates, has led to lower crime, better education, and greater prosperity.[74] These arguments have often been refuted, but they persist nonetheless.

Why do so many Americans not see Secularism's supposed superiority? To Niose it is a kind of conspiracy:

> When the media and others refer to a "militant atheist," the object of that slander is usually a nonbeliever who had the nerve to openly question religious authority or vocally express his or her views about religion. This reflects a double standard that nonbelievers endure. Religious individuals and groups frequently declare, sometimes subtly and sometimes not, that you are a sinner and that you will suffer in hell for eternity if you do not adopt their beliefs, but they will almost never be labeled "militant" by the media or the public. Instead, such individuals are typically called "devout" or perhaps "evangelical." No doubt this double standard stems from the predominant notion that tells us that Americans are "a religious people." The lesson is clear: if you're not a fervent believer, shut up about it.[75]

Niose is right about one thing. There is bias in the media. But it is probably in the opposite direction of what he suspects. The media's suspicion of Christianity, especially of conservative Christianity, is legendary.[76]

4. What does Secularism say about how we should live? By denying the existence of God, Secularists also deny the existence of an absolute moral code that must be obeyed. They view God's commands (traditionally understood to be the absolute moral order) as harmful fiction. According to Paul Kurtz, "The traditional supernaturalistic moral commandments are especially repressive of our human needs. They are immoral insofar as they foster illusions about human destiny and suppress vital inclinations [i.e., in the sexual arena]."[77]

What we must do, according to Secularists, is acknowledge that morality is biological, not theological. V. M. Tarkunde, the father of India's civil rights movement, explained: "Moral behavior of a rudimentary type is found in the higher animals and can be traced even to lower forms of life. This fact is enough to establish that the source of morality is biological and not theological."[78] As we evolve biologically, we need to adjust our ethical principles to evolve as well. It is eminently doable, according to Fred Edwords, president of the United Coalition of Reason: "It should be obvious from the most casual observation that human beings are quite capable of setting up systems and then operating within them."[79] To Edwords, what is ethical and moral is obvious to all thinking people (except those, presumably, whose religious commitments cloud their judgment). Julian Wadleigh called this "natural law" and said, "It is not a set of precise rules but a guide that must be followed using plain common sense."[80]

Christians respond to Secularist ethical claims by saying that we would not be able to know these ethical laws had God not planted them on our hearts to begin with. Wadleigh, though, asserted that evolution is just as good an explanation for natural law as a creator:

> The Declaration [of Independence] speaks of natural law as an endowment by a creator, whereas I speak of it as the result of humankind's evolution as a social animal.

There is a difference, but that difference concerns the questions of how and why we have natural law—not whether or not natural law exists. Regardless of its origin, it is the same natural law.[81]

5. How are we to understand other worldviews based on Secularism? As is now clear, Secularism makes claims about the nature of reality and the duties of humanity that are at odds with the claims of other worldviews. Let's take a look at the Secularist response to each of the other worldviews we are considering.

New Spirituality. To Secularists, any reference to the supernatural is ignorant, super-stitious, or both. Secularists have developed a substantial body of research attempting to demystify supernatural experiences. These include books debunking paranormal experiences to books dismissing claims of after-death experiences. The idea that there are supernatural principles at work in the world is absurd to Secularists, and they will stand in opposition to those who claim otherwise, whether Billy Graham, the Dalai Lama, Eckhart Tolle, Deepak Chopra, or Oprah Winfrey.

Marxism. Secularism and Marxism are the pilot and copilot of the airship of materialism.[82] They share the basic belief that the physical, or material, world is all that exists. Thus, they share nearly identical assumptions about the nature of nature and the nature of humanity, as well as identical critiques of supernatural religion. Where they diverge is on the principle of freedom.

Secularists tend to believe that a secular state will lead to the greatest freedom for the greatest number of people. Marxists believe the principle of freedom is a tool used by those in power to keep the workers from rising up and seizing control of wealth. Secularists wish religion would go away, and they would use their own influence to restrict its expression. But they recoil at the crude way Marxists have tried to destroy it. That said, we will see in the "Ethics" chapter that Secularist ethical arguments are insufficiently robust to rein in Marxist atrocities. After all, if the fittest survive, who's to say that the Marxists are not merely doing what comes naturally? Secularism may consider Marxist cruelty to be bad manners, but they lack the ethical foundation on which to correct it.

Christianity and Islam. Christianity and Islam insist that there is a creator-God. For Secularists, that fact alone is enough to destroy them as credible worldviews. To quote Isaac Asimov, "To those who are trained in science, creationism seems like a bad dream, a sudden reliving of a nightmare, a renewed march of an army of the night risen to challenge free thought and enlightenment."[83] Still, Secularists realize that some Christians and Muslims are more secular than religious, and they want these people in their camp. As long as they're willing to give up being guided by the supernatural in their public actions, they can be in the club. Otherwise, they're dangerous. Georgetown professor Jacques Berlinerblau says,

> Secularism's this-worldly tincture has a policy implication. Secularism cannot tolerate religious groups that are otherworldly in radical ways. The most dangerous proponents of faith are those who abhor the saeculum, who view it as incorrigibly corrupt, sinful, and carnal. Their hatred of the present world leads them to hasten their (and our) promotion to the next. A leading and troubling indicator of an anti-secular worldview is an exaggerated concern with one's fate after death.[84]

Berlinerblau makes it clear that he believes a person with "otherworldy" beliefs is no different psychologically from a suicide bomber.

Postmodernism. Postmodernism questions Secularism's legitimacy where it hurts the most; that is, whether science and reason can reveal truth. Secularism maintains faith in science and reason while rejecting supernatural faiths. Postmodernism rejects *all* narratives that claim to access the truth. Secularists believe this amounts to nihilism. Paul Kurtz wrote, "Science does offer reasonably objective standards for judging its truth claims. Indeed, science has become a universal language, speaking to all men and women no matter what their cultural backgrounds."[85] So whereas Secularists believe science can bring us objective truth, Postmodernists see scientific statements as containing cultural and personal agendas that prevent their audience from truly knowing reality. Thus Postmodernism serves, as sociologist David Martin memorably phrased it, as the "secularization of Secularism."[86]

10. WHERE DOES FAITH COME IN?

As we have mentioned already, Secularists are people of faith. They have a thorough faith in the scientific method, the theory of naturalistic evolution, and materialism. They have faith in what they consider to be reasoned arguments that are self-evident to all who are not deluded by other faiths. Above all, they have faith in their own human capacities. Based on these expressions of faith, Secularists over the years have developed coherent views in all ten disciplines we will consider later, including theology and ethics.

Many Secularists today, though, have begun to rethink their belief in the inevitable rise of Secularism. The world is becoming more religious, not less. For example, noted sociologist Peter Berger has recanted his earlier prediction of Secularism's supplanting of religion in American society. In *Mind and Cosmos*, Thomas Nagel stunned the academic world by rejecting materialist explanations altogether: "It is prima facie highly implausible that life as we know it is the result of a sequence of physical accidents together with the mechanism of natural selection."[87] He also calls into question the Secularist explanation for mind and thinking: "If evolutionary biology is a physical theory—as it is generally taken to be—then it cannot account for the appearance of consciousness and of other phenomena that are not physically reducible."[88]

Since Nagel is an atheist and one of the most respected philosophers in the world, his work—published by the prestigious Oxford University Press—is hard to dismiss. Also hard to dismiss is an anthology of essays from leading experts called *Rethinking Secularism*, which questions the validity of Secularism's core assumptions. In the popular sphere, Eben Alexander's account of his after-death experience draws on his training as a neurosurgeon and responds to Secularist arguments about the existence of the supernatural.[89]

Taken together, the evidences of growing doubt about Secularism could irreparably damage its foundations. Christians and others may find Secularism's arguments intimidating but do not have sufficient reason to concede to them.

When it comes to a worldview attempting to intimidate Christians into setting aside their convictions, though, Secularism is nowhere as intimidating a worldview as Marxism. How this is so is what we will examine carefully in the next chapter.

ENDNOTES

1. Anthony R. Pratkanis and Elliot Aronson, *Propaganda: The Everyday Use and Abuse of Persuasion* (New York: W. H. Freeman, 2001), 11.

2. Adolf Hitler's campaign to annihilate Jewish people is the most famous example of the uses of propaganda. It wasn't so much that Hitler expected the German people to rise up and kill the Jews; he merely needed them to avert their eyes as his minions did so. Indeed, Hitler's propaganda was so effective, the German people began to see the Jews as aggressors against whom extreme action was warranted. At the time most Germans did not know the import of their words and attitudes. When the fog of war cleared, though, more than six million European Jews had lost their lives. In *Dehumanizing the Vulnerable: When Word Games Take Lives,* William Brennan parallels the word games of Hitler and abortion advocates. He demonstrates that propaganda is not a thing of the past: it is a current reality; we must always be on guard. See William Brennan, *Dehumanizing the Vulnerable: When Word Games Take Lives* (Fort Collins, CO: Life Cycle Books, 2000).

3. Mike Schwandt, Facebook post, quoted in Paul Stanley, "Gay Rights Activists, Christian Leaders React to NC Ban on Gay Marriage," *Christian Post,* May 10, 2012, www.christianpost.com/news/gay-rights-activists-christian-leaders-react-to-nc-ban-on-gay-marriage-74733/.

4. Whidbey, May 11, 2012 comment on "North Carolina Passes Amendment Banning Same Sex Marriage," Fark.com, www.fark.com/comments/7100902/76813019#c76813019.

5. Ari Ezra Waldman, "Three Lessons from North Carolina's Amendment One," *Towleroad* (blog), May 9, 2012, www.towleroad.com/2012/05/waldmanamendmentone.ht.

6. Dan Turner, "Obama, Gay Marriage, and a Win for Bigotry in NC," *Los Angeles Times,* May 9, 2012, http://articles.latimes.com/2012/may/09/news/la-ol-north-carolina-marriage-20120509. What observers may not have realized is that accusations of "bigotry" and "hate" are a political strategy, encouraged in this instance by gay activists Marshall K. Kirk and Erastes Pill in a 1987 article called "The Overhauling of Straight America."

7. Peter Schweizer illustrates this battle of language in one particular manifestation, political battles between liberals and conservatives. In his book *Makers and Takers* (New York: Doubleday, 2008), Schweizer documents the way in which liberals attack conservatives as mean, evil, hypocritical, greedy, arrogant, dumb, and emotionally crippled. Schweizer says, "Liberals are certainly entitled to their opinions. But they are not entitled to their own set of facts." Schweizer's research convinced him that these characterizations were untrue, and that, in fact, liberals in the aggregate were more selfish, more focused on money, less hardworking, less emotionally satisfied, less honest, and less knowledgeable about civics and economics. Conservatives, on the other hand, Schweizer argued, were happier and better adjusted, more successful as parents, more generous, and less angry. Below the surface, though, the battles between "conservatives" and "liberals" may actually be proxy wars between two religious worldviews, Christianity and Secularism.

8. See the acclaimed book by Rodney Stark, *The Triumph of Christianity* (New York: HarperOne, 2011), for a balanced view from a respected historian and sociologist.

9. David Niose, *Nonbeliever Nation: The Rise of Secular America* (New York: Palgrave Macmillan, 2012), 92.

10. José Casanova, "The Secular, Secularizations, Secularisms," in Craig Calhoun, Mark Juergensmeyer, and Jonathan VanAntwerpen, eds., *Rethinking Secularism* (New York: Oxford University Press, 2011), 67.

11 Jacques Berlinerblau, *How to Be Secular: A Call to Arms for Religious Freedom* (New York: Houghton Mifflin Harcourt, 2012), 180.

12. Berlinerblau, *How to Be Secular,* 5.

13. Susan Jacoby, *The Age of American Unreason* (New York: Vintage Books, 2008), xi–xii.

14. Maggie Jackson, *Distracted: The Erosion of Attention and the Coming Dark Age* (Amherst, NY: Prometheus Books, 2008), 213–14.

15. Hunter Baker, *The End of Secularism* (Wheaton, IL: Crossway Books, 2009), 68.

16. Christian Smith, *The Secular Revolution: Power, Interests, and Conflict in the Secularization of American Public Life* (Berkeley, CA: University of California Press, 2003), 1, quoted in Baker, *End of Secularism,* 122.

17. "Humanist Manifesto I," *New Humanist,* 1933, www.americanhumanist.org/Humanism/Humanist_Manifesto_I.

18. Unfortunately for Secular Humanists, their optimistic assessments of humanity have been tragically timed. The signing of the first *Humanist Manifesto,* for example, took place in full view of the rise of totalitarian communism in Russia and the emergence of the Third Reich. The second manifesto was much more subdued, appropriately so, at the height of the Cold War and the threat of the nuclear holocaust. The third manifesto was optimistic once again. One year later: September 11 and the opening of a new chapter in the centuries-long war between Islamicism and the West.

19. Berlinerblau, *How to Be Secular,* 118.

20. Peter Angeles, ed., *Critiques of God* (Buffalo, NY: Prometheus Books, 1976), xiii.

21. Jacoby, *Age of American Unreason,* 185.

22. Cary Funk et al., *"Nones" on the Rise,* (Washington, DC: Pew Research Center, 2012), 10, www.pewforum.org/Unaffiliated/nones-on-the-rise.aspx.

23. Data from the American Religious Identification Survey, in Niose, *Nonbeliever Nation*, 14.

24. Craig M. Gay, *The Way of the (Modern) World* (Grand Rapids: Eerdmans, 1998), 239.

25. Gay, *Way of the (Modern) World*, 259.

26. Neil Gross and Solon Simmons, "The Religiosity of American College and University Professors," *Sociology of Religion* 70, no. 2 (2009): 102; see also Smith, *Secular Revolution*.

27. Miles S. Kimball et al., "Empirics on the Origins of Preferences: The Case of College Major and Religiosity" NBER Working Paper Series (Cambridge, MA: National Bureau of Economic Research, 2009), 7.

28. Kimball, "Empirics on the Origins," 18.

29. Kimball, "Empirics on the Origins."

30. Kimball, "Empirics on the Origins," 22.

31. Cited in Gross and Simmons, "Religiosity of American College and University Professors," 114–18.

32. Alexander W. Astin et al., *Spirituality and the Professoriate: A National Study of Faculty Beliefs, Attitudes, and Behaviors* (Los Angeles, CA: Higher Education Research Institute, 2005).

33. Charles Taylor, *A Secular Age* (Cambridge, MA: Belknap, 2007), 20.

34. Baker, *End of Secularism*, 99, quoting in part Peter L. Berger, *The Sacred Canopy* (New York: Anchor, 1990), 107.

35. Quoted in Calhoun, *Rethinking Secularism*, 25.

36. See Mark Juergensmeyer, "Rethinking the Secular and Religious Aspects of Violence," in Calhoun, *Rethinking Secularism*, 185–203.

37. See Craig J. Calhoun, *Classical Sociological Theory* (London: Wiley-Blackwell, 2002), 106.

38. Kimball, "Empirics on the Origins," 4.

39. Quoted in Steven Lukes, *Emile Durkheim, His Life and Work: A Historical and Critical Study* (Palo Alto, CA: Stanford University Press, 2005), 25.

40. Baker, *End of Secularism*, 153.

41. Carl Sagan, *Cosmos* (New York: Random House, 1980), 27.

42. Richard Lewontin, "Billions and Billions of Demons," *New York Review of Books*, January 9, 1997.

43. Edward O. Wilson, "Biology's Spiritual Products," *Free Inquiry* (1987): 14.

44. Julian Huxley, *Evolution: The Modern Synthesis* (New York: Harper and Brothers, 1942), 457.

45. However, Secularists accept both the big bang, a one-time event, and spontaneous generation as science.

46. Julian Huxley, "At Random," television interview, November 21, 1959.

47. Stephen C. Meyer, "Intelligent Design: The Origin of Biological Information and the Higher Taxonomic Categories," *Proceedings of the Biological Society of Washington* 117, no. 2 (November 30, 2005): 213–39. Available online at www.discovery.org/scripts/viewDB/index.php?command=view&id=2177.

48. Quoted in J. P. Moreland and Kai Nielsen, *Does God Exist?: The Great Debate* (Nashville: Thomas Nelson, 1990), 185.

49. Percival Davis and Dean H. Kenyon, *Of Pandas and People*, 2nd ed. (Richardson, TX: Foundation for Thought and Ethics, 1993), 107.

50. Julian Huxley, *Essays of a Humanist* (London: Chatto and Windus, 1964), 9.

51. Michael Ruse, "How Evolution Became a Religion," *National Post*, May 13, 2000, B1.

52. L. H. Matthews, introduction to Charles Darwin, *The Origin of Species* (London: J. M. Dent and Sons, 1971), x–xi, quoted in Luther D. Sunderland, *Darwin's Enigma* (San Diego, CA: Master Books, 1984), 30–31.

53. Richard Dawkins, *The God Delusion* (New York: Mariner Books, 2008), 51.

54. Paul Kurtz, "A Secular Humanist Declaration," *Free Inquiry* 1 (Winter 1980/81): 5.

55. Paul Kurtz, ed. *Humanist Manifestos I and II* (Amherst, NY: Prometheus Books, 1973), 4.

56. Kurtz, "Secular Humanist Declaration."

57. Chris Brockman, *What about Gods?* (Buffalo, NY: Prometheus Books, 1978), 1–2.

58. Julian Huxley, *The Humanist Frame* (New York: Harper and Brothers, 1961), 15.

59. Huxley, *Humanist Frame*, 7.

60. Corliss Lamont, *The Philosophy of Humanism* (New York: Frederick Ungar, 1982), 81–82.

61. Lamont, *Philosophy of Humanism*, 82.

62. Victor J. Stenger, *Not by Design* (Buffalo, NY: Prometheus Books, 1988), 188–89.

63. See Nick Bostrom, "A History of Transhumanist Thought," *Journal of Evolution and Technology* 14, no. 1 (April 2005), www.nickbostrom.com/papers/history.pdf.

64. C. S. Lewis, *A Mind Awake: An Anthology of C. S. Lewis*, ed. Clyde S. Kilby (New York: Harcourt, 1968), 205.

65. Taylor, *Secular Age*, 269.

66. There is absolutely no scientific support for the theory of spontaneous generation.

67. Huxley, *Essays*, 77.

68. Isaac Asimov, *The Wellsprings of Life* (London: Abelard-Schuman, 1960), 57.

69. Alfred Lord Tennyson, *In Memoriam A. H. H.* (London: Bankside, 1900), 60.

70. See Richard Weikart, *From Darwin to Hitler: Evolutionary Ethics, Eugenics, and Racism in Germany* (New York: Palgrave Macmillan, 2004).

71. John Dietrich, *The Fathers of Evolution and Other Addresses* (First Unitarian Society, 1927), 245.

72. Huxley, *Essays*, 33.

73. Niose, *Nonbeliever Nation*, 4.

74. For a refutation of Niose's arguments on the crime issue, see John R. Lott, *Freedomnomics* (Washington, DC: Regnery, 2007), especially chap. 4, "Crime and Punishment." Lott shows that liberal policies, such as legalized abortion and affirmative action, were correlated with higher levels of crime, and conservative policies, such as the death penalty, law enforcement, and right-to-carry laws, were correlated with lower levels.

75. Niose, *Nonbeliever Nation*, 46.

76. *World Magazine* editor Marvin Olasky documents this bias in his book *Prodigal Press* (Wheaton, IL: Crossway Books, 1988).

77. Paul Kurtz, ed., *The Humanist Alternative* (Buffalo, NY: Prometheus Books, 1973), 50.

78. Quoted in Morris B. Storer, ed., *Humanist Ethics* (Buffalo, NY: Prometheus Books, 1980), 156.

79. Frederick Edwords, "The Human Basis of Law and Ethics," *Humanist* (May/June 1985): 11.

80. Julian Wadleigh, "What Is Conservatism?" *Humanist* (November/December 1989): 21.

81. Wadleigh, "What Is Conservatism?"

82. In his evaluation of this chapter, Hunter Baker, whose book *The End of Secularism* we quoted earlier, said he believes the issue today is not Marxism but "social leveling." He states, "Liberal secularists tend to embrace a form of equality which demands economic leveling *and* religious leveling. The economic leveling occurs through democratic socialism. Religious leveling occurs via secularism." Email correspondence, June 18, 2013. See also www.acton.org/pub/religion-liberty/volume-21-number-1/social-leveling-socialism-secularism.

83. Isaac Asimov, "The 'Threat' of Creationism," in Ashley Montagu, ed., *Science and Creationism* (Oxford, UK: Oxford University Press, 1984), 183. For an in-depth study on the politicization of science and how humanists use science to stifle dissent, see Tom Bethell, *The Politically Incorrect Guide to Science* (Washington, DC: Regnery, 2005).

84. Berlinerblau, *How to Be Secular*, 183.

85. Paul Kurtz, *Humanist Manifesto 2000: A Call for a New Planetary Humanism* (Amherst, NY: Prometheus Books, 2000), 22.

86. Quoted in Baker, *End of Secularism*, 108.

87. Thomas Nagel, *Mind and Cosmos* (New York: Oxford University Press, 2012), 6.

88. Nagel, *Mind and Cosmos*, 14–15.

89. Eben Alexander, *Proof of Heaven: A Neurosurgeon's Journey into the Afterlife* (New York: Simon and Schuster, 2012).

CHAPTER 5

MARXISM

1. A ZOMBIE WORLDVIEW BACK FROM THE DEAD

It's not a movie we'd recommend, but the opening sequence of *Shaun of the Dead*, a cult-classic zombie flick, is pretty revealing. Set to an upbeat carnival tune, each brief scene features people shuffling along, blankly staring ahead, checking their cell phones—just going through the motions. The filmmaker's argument is whimsically clear: If zombies invaded today, we'd have a hard time picking them out. Just about *everyone* seems disconnected, unthinking, and apathetic.

In human history, ideas can be like zombies; when you think they're dead, they are revived, now more dangerous than before. Such is the case with Marxism and its political offshoot, communism: they're back from the dead and once again among us.

Most people have a vague sense of Marxism's destructive nature. "It's a good idea on paper, but it never worked in reality," they say. Very few take Marxism seriously as a worldview; the words *Marxism* or *communism* conjure images not of fearsome military power or a hundred million dead bodies but of silly propaganda posters, ridiculous dictators who have no clue how out of step they are with the rest of the world, and clueless hippies wearing Che Guevara T-shirts. Many believe that if you can laugh at it, you don't have to think about it. That's a mistake.

So what are these ideas, Marxism and communism? Very simply, **Marxism** is the philosophy of Karl Marx. A Marxist is someone who embraces this philosophy. *Communism* is the word Marx used to describe the ideal state achieved when his views are put into practice, so a communist is a person who applies Marx's ideas to the government and the economy. **Communism** stands in contrast to **capitalism**, an economic system in which private citizens own the means of production rather than the government, and in which competition and the market forces of supply and demand determine prices rather than government decree. **Socialism** is another key term you'll see a lot in Marxist writings and just about everywhere in society today. Marx defined *socialism* as "the abolition of private property."

Karl Marx did most of his work in the British Museum in London, where he fled when his revolutionary activities elsewhere caused whole nations to dislike him. There was a lot to dislike. Marx was a famously rude person whose unwillingness to bathe or get a haircut was legendary, as was his inattentiveness as a husband and father.[1] And though he claimed to understand the working man, Marx never set foot in an actual factory that we know of or made a living by physical labor.[2]

On February 21, 1848, Marx published *The Communist Manifesto* with the assistance of Friedrich Engels, a young revolutionary who subsidized Marx's prodigious financial appetite with money earned, ironically, from his father's factory. After reciting the evils of factory owners, the manifesto states,

The Communists disdain to conceal their views and aims. They openly declare that their ends can be attained only by the forcible overthrow of all existing social conditions. Let the ruling classes tremble at a

Marxism: an atheistic and materialistic worldview based on the ideas of Karl Marx that promotes the abolition of private property, public ownership of the means of production (i.e., socialism), and the utopian dream of a future communistic state.

Communism: the Marxist ideal of a classless and stateless utopian society in which all property is commonly owned and each person is paid according to his or her abilities and needs.

Capitalism: an economic system in which capital assets are privately owned, and the prices, production, and distribution of goods and services are determined by competition within a free market.

Socialism: an economic system based upon governmental or communal ownership of the means of production and distribution of goods and services.

Communistic revolution. The proletarians [working class] have nothing to lose but their chains. They have a world to win. [Proletarians] of all countries, unite![3]

The manifesto is vivid, even prosaic. Its call to violent force is chilling, especially since its fans have taken its admonitions literally for more than 150 years now, marching Marx's bloodthirsty ideas across the pages of history as surely as Alexander the Great's armies marched across Asia.

When the Berlin Wall finally fell in 1989, many thought communism itself would crumble too. In quick succession, the Soviet Union and its satellite states bit the Marxist hand that promised (and claimed) to feed them. Yet many nations today still put their faith in communism, among them China, Cuba, and North Korea.

And yet, very few in the West have truly come to grips with what has happened in history when Marxists get their way. We all know about the horrors of Nazi Germany, but the slaughter of well over one hundred million people by communist regimes in the twentieth century seems not to have registered. Specifically, historians now estimate, only as a starting point, anywhere from 20 to 60 million deaths in the Soviet Union,[4] 40 to 70 million in China,[5] 2 million in Cambodia (by the Khmer Rouge), 1.6 million in North Korea, and 1.2 million in Yugoslavia.[6] And the slaughter continues to this day. China's one-child policy, instituted in 1971, led to 336 million abortions, many performed against the will of the parents.[7] We know a lot about Hitler—who his girlfriend was, what kind of music he listened to—but virtually nothing about Lenin, Stalin, Mao Tse-tung, Pol Pot, or the others in communism's panoply. Remarkably, communism in the twentieth century killed twice the combined dead from World Wars I and II.

Why the indifference? Maybe it's because, as Joseph Stalin is reported to have said, "One death is a tragedy; a million is just a statistic." But these were people like you and me, with hopes and dreams and memories and families who loved them. It is too late to stand up for them, but we can and must honor their memory by proclaiming, "Never again." Up against the silence surrounding communism's atrocities, the first act of healing is to speak. *Qui tacet consentit*—"silence equals consent." There are many reasons we should care, not the least of which is George Santayana's admonition: "Those who cannot remember the past are condemned to repeat it."[8] We should also care because Marxism's evil was one of supposed virtue: Marxists reconciled themselves with evil because they believed it served an ultimate good. In history when leaders are willing to use any means to achieve what they consider to be the ultimate good, it invariably leads to atrocity. Such is the case with Marxism. It's up to us today to see that it never happens again. As the British statesman Edmund Burke said, "When bad men combine, the good must associate; else they will fall, one by one, an unpitied sacrifice in a contemptible struggle."[9]

Marxists doubtless will see our analysis as unfair and will reel off a laundry list of uncontrollable historical circumstances and the unfortunate rise of a few bad actors who they claim are truly to blame. To find out if they're right, we'll dig into the influence of Marxism today, examine its basic principles, discern what kind of worldview it is, and explore its answers to life's ultimate questions. For the most part, we'll use the words of the Marxists themselves, not their critics, to move the discussion along. First, we'll answer the question "Is this even something we should still care about?"

2. Is Marxism Still Influential Today?

> Remarkably, communism in the twentieth century killed twice the combined dead from World Wars I and II.

Nazism is a relic of the past. Sure, there are self-proclaimed Nazis out there, a handful of social misfits who favor swastikas as an angry fashion accessory. But their line of actual influence is thin, and being "anti-them" has in general become a rather weak cause. While we want to be alert to the rise of fascism, we need not waste time scouring the Internet to see if Hitler moustaches are a growing fashion trend. Maybe Marxism and communism are like that: unpleasant but not a threat. If so, being anti-communist is a cause for embarrassment, like having a crazy uncle who sits on the front porch and hurls insults at passersby.

Many see Marxism and communism as nonthreatening. Some even think it's a little cool. The image of Marxist revolutionary Che Guevara, Fidel Castro's most ruthless lieutenant and overseer of Cuba's first prison camp, La Cabaña, is one of the most famous icons in the world. Hollywood has even made a movie about his private journals, *The Motorcycle Diaries*, to romanticize Guevara's lust for violent overthrow.[10]

But Marxism and oppression go together like *peanut* and *butter*. By its very nature, Marxism requires a radical remaking of society—wresting capital out of the hands of citizens and dismantling laws protecting private property. In far too many cases, Marxists came in as liberators, ruled as tyrants, and are remembered as criminals. Stalin's gulags, Pol Pot's killing fields , North Korea's famines, East Berlin's wall, and China's one-child policy and its millions of missing girls are only exhibits 1 through 5. Sometimes atrocities like these take decades to unfold, but the line of cause and effect eventually becomes apparent to those with eyes to see.

But this still does not answer the question, Are Marxism and communism relics of the past, or should we still be concerned?

Let's look at two aspects of Marxism's influence: Marxism around the world and Marxism in the university.

Marxism around the world. The world's five communist countries (China, Vietnam, Laos, North Korea, and Cuba) account for approximately one of every five people on the planet. They are not, however, the only ones dealing with Marxism's implications. Socialism is the official policy of many other nations (Bangladesh, India, Sri Lanka, Portugal, Tanzania, Guyana).[11] If we add to that list the countries with powerful socialist parties (France, Greece, Venezuela, Sweden, Zambia, Syria, Norway, Libya, Algeria, among others), those that pursue socialist policies as a matter of practice, such as Zimbabwe, or those that are bent on destroying private property, it's easy to see that Karl Marx still wields power from the grave.

The Communist Manifesto outlined ten ideas, a sort of "Ten Commandments," that serve in some ways as a series of steps by which a society can be transitioned to communism. Read the list carefully; one or more of these ten items makes the news just about every day, and some of them have been accepted in America and the West:

1. Abolition of property in land and application of all rents of land to public purposes
2. A heavy progressive or graduated income tax
3. Abolition of all rights of inheritance

4. Confiscation of the property of all immigrants and rebels
5. Centralization of credit in the banks of the state, by means of a national bank with state capital and an exclusive monopoly
6. Centralization of the means of communication and transport in the hands of the state
7. Extension of factories and instruments of production owned by the state; bringing waste lands into cultivation and improving the soil generally in accordance with a common plan
8. Equal obligation of all to work. Establishment of industrial armies, especially for agriculture
9. Combination of agriculture with manufacturing industries; gradual abolition of all distinctions between town and country through a more equable distribution of the populace over the country
10. Free education for all children in public schools; abolition of children's factory labor in its present form; combination of education with industrial production, and so on.

Marxists are convinced these steps are not only best but will inevitably occur as more and more nations evolve to a higher state of centralized planning. The reality, of course, is much more complex. Historian Bill Federer reviewed the historical records and found that state control of the economy goes back more than two thousand years.[12] As Federer sees it, the development of the United States of America was an enlightened move *away* from the principles of protocommunism and toward greater justice and equality of opportunity.

Today, since *communism* is still a bad word, those who want to achieve its goals but not claim its name have developed a new approach, which was identified as "state capitalism" in a special report by the *Economist* in 2012.[13] In a nutshell, state capitalism is the practice of federal governments taking ownership and management control of otherwise private businesses. Though the companies still operate in the private marketplace, they do so with the inequitable backing of state capital and power.[14]

The idea behind state capitalism is inherently socialistic, in spite of the use of the word *capitalism*. The state rules by force. Tax revenues are given under compulsion, foreclosing all other possible economic choices. At present, Russia, China, and other nations are committed to state capitalism, but so are many American leaders. Recently, for example, the US federal government has made aggressive moves in the health-care, energy, and banking sectors of the economy.

> *State Capitalism:* the practice of federal governments taking ownership and management control of private businesses.

Government control of the economy creates a significant justice issue because the government is so vulnerable to corruption. History professor Burton Folsom says the greatest corruption in American history came from government intervention in the economy, not from the free market.[15] The Hoover Institution's Arnold Beichman pointed out that socialism in the former Soviet Union, rather than distributing goods equally, actually created a class known as the *nomenklatura*, whose members "own everything, the auto factories, the dachas, the food markets, the pharmacies, the transport system, the department stores. Everything."[16] In practice, Soviet-created communism used government force to take from the powerless to give to the powerful.

Instead of achieving its stated goal of destroying class distinctions, socialism tends to remove competition and deposit cronyism in its place. Milovan Djilas said, "The Communist revolution, conducted in the name of doing away with classes, has resulted in the most complete authority of any single new class."[17] In Soviet times this elite class ran the economy into the ground. Will it do the same in our country?

Marxism in the university. Several decades ago, *U.S. News and World Report* revealed an alarming increase in the number of Marxist professors on university campuses.[18] In affirmation of the claim that ten thousand Marxist professors roam America's college campuses, Herbert London said, "Every discipline has been affected by its preachment, and almost every faculty now counts among its members a resident Marxist scholar."[19]

> Instead of achieving its stated goal of destroying class distinctions, socialism tends to remove competition and deposit cronyism in its place.

Interest in Marxism waned in the late 1980s as the world grappled with the fallout from Europe's and Asia's disastrous applications of the Marxist worldview. But a few stubborn Marxists hung on, among them Duke University's Fredric Jameson and Lancaster University's Terry Eagleton. Eagleton, whose books reviewers invariably see as "witty," recently published *Why Marx Was Right*. Frank Barry, a reviewer for the *Irish Times*, called the book a "short, witty, and highly accessible jaunt through Marx's thought in preparation for the second coming."[20] In 2012, the *Guardian*, a British newspaper, chronicled the return of Marxism noting the rise in interest in Marxism as the economy falters and people cast about for explanations.[21]

Martha Gimenez, a sociology professor at the University of Colorado and an influential academic, argues that Marxism is the proper framework through which to understand everything that happens in society today:

> We are, in Marx's terms, "an ensemble of social relations" ... and we live our lives at the core of the intersection of a number of unequal social relations based on hierarchically interrelated structures which, together, define the historical specificity of the capitalist modes of production and reproduction and underlay their observable manifestations.[22]

Author bell hooks (intentionally uncapitalized), whom *Essence* magazine called a "visionary feminist,"[23] weaves Marxist angst into virtually every line of her jarring prose. In a college commencement speech, hooks blamed the West's focus on future planning for violence and pain in the world: "Every imperialist, white supremacist, capitalist, patriarchal nation on the planet teaches its citizens to care more for tomorrow than today.... And the moment we do this, we are seduced by the lure of death.... To live fixated on the future is to engage in psychological denial. It is a form of psychic violence that prepares us to accept the violence needed to ensure the maintenance of imperialist, future-oriented society."[24]

What kind of person thinks it is evil to defer gratification and plan for the future? Perhaps a person who suspects that her well-assembled dish of ideas for this evening's party will be rancid by morning.

At any major university you'll find some professors overtly evangelistic about Marxism and many others sympathetic to Marx's aims. The *Socialist Worker* newspaper will probably be distributed on campus, and various leftist groups will compete for attention and funding. The same is likely true in your state capital and in Washington, DC.

How is it possible for Marxist ideas to still be attractive to so many for so many years after they presumably lost public favor? It only makes sense when one considers the two central doctrines Marxists use to make sense of everything else: dialectical materialism and economic determinism.

3. WHAT MARXISM TEACHES

The overarching Marxist narrative culminates in class equality through economic revolution. The exploiters—those who control the means of production (i.e., those who own businesses and employ people) lord it over the exploited (i.e., those who do manual labor, who do not have an ownership stake in their workplaces, or who do work but do not own their workplaces). Overthrowing the exploiters will free the exploited; we'll all be happier if we are all the same. Every so often there are protests clamoring for "people before profits," demanding a leveling of the economic playing field. While Wall Street corruption is well documented, protesters demanding the dismantling of the capitalistic system are merely repeating talking points, even if unwittingly, of Marxist agitators from a century ago.[25]

Those talking points consist of more than the seizure of private property. To understand Marxism, you need to grasp two ideas: (1) Everything is about economics, and (2) history is a struggle in which the move toward a state of communism is inevitable. The first idea is called *dialectical materialism*. The second is *economic determinism*. Let's look at each.

Dialectical materialism. The *Hegelian dialectic* was a view of history conceived by the German philosopher Georg Wilhelm Friedrich Hegel.[26] In his view, the way people see the world and act on it at any given time in history (the *thesis*) spawns a reaction, whose goal is the negation of the way things are done (the *antithesis*). The antithesis then becomes the norm and in turn is opposed in what is called the "negation of the negation." When the smoke clears from the conflict of the thesis and antithesis, a *synthesis* of the two ideas forms from a merging of the thesis and antithesis. The synthesis becomes, in turn, a new, more advanced thesis. For example, the differences between Greco-Roman democracy's democrat (thesis) and slave (antithesis) were lessened somewhat in the difference between feudalism's (synthesis) aristocrat and serf. Inevitably, though, the conflict process begins again, leading to yet another synthesis—now making a thesis of the feudalistic aristocrat and an antithesis of the serf—at an even more advanced level. For Marxists, the

> *Dialectical materialism:* the belief that only the material world exists and that class struggles are the mechanism behind social and economic progress (e.g., the current economic clash between the proletariat and bourgeoisie will eventually give way to socialism and the end of capitalism).

dialectical process is *the* means of progress. The conflict is always a spiral upward toward a better way of thinking.

Materialism in philosophy does not mean coveting luxury goods. Materialism says that only the world of matter exists. There is nothing outside of nature. No God or gods exist.

To Marxists, materialism and atheism are nonnegotiable. "In our evolutionary conception of the universe," Engels said, "there is absolutely no room for either a creator or a ruler."[27] As Fyodor Dostoyevsky said, the "problem of Communism is not an economic problem. The problem of Communism is the problem of atheism."[28] Even though evidence for materialism has not yet materialized, Marxists are confident it will. The Marxist scientist A. I. Oparin stated, "We have every reason to believe that sooner or later, we shall be able practically to demonstrate that life is nothing else but a special form of existence of matter."

Marx and Engels adapted Hegel's ideas about what happens in the mental realm to explain what happens in the material world.[29] This hybrid philosophy is called *dialectical materialism*. The world, according to Engels, is always changing, always evolving.[30] The goal is to always move forward, to be progressive. Nothing lasts forever. In this "endless maze of relations and interactions,"[31] things are always clashing and changing. Conflict is inevitable. You might think of conflict as bad. The Marxist, however, wants conflict. It is the only way society will advance. The main place this conflict takes place, Marxists say, is in the production of goods and the distribution of wealth. In short, it's all about economics.

Economic Determinism: the belief that economics determines the entire course of human history, ultimately and inevitability leading to a communist future.

Bourgeoisie: a term used in Marxist theory to describe those who own the means of production.

Proletariat: a term used in Marxist theory to describe the working-class wage earners who do not own the means of production.

Economic determinism. The view that economics is the foundation for the whole social superstructure is called **economic determinism**. Engels wrote, "In every historical epoch the prevailing mode of economic production and exchange, and the social organization necessarily following from it, form the basis upon which is built up, and from which alone can be explained, the political and intellectual history of that epoch."[32]

To the Marxist, the economic struggle between the **bourgeoisie** (the property owners) and the **proletariat** (the property-less workers) explains everything in history—politics, religion, law, and culture.

Today, Marxists apply this analysis by looking at all kinds of conflicts—between the haves and have-nots, the religious and nonreligious, blacks and whites, men and women, heterosexuals and homosexuals—as evidence of the dialectic process at work. Such conflicts are proxies for the true struggle. Scratch any conflict, and it will bleed economics.

Socialism and communism are both part of the Marxist's economic vocabulary, but they are not interchangeable terms. To the Marxist, socialism is the first phase or first step in the transition to the perfect economic system, which is communism.[33] Socialism begins with heavy taxation, government takeover of businesses, and the elimination of laws protecting private property. Eventually the government, which previously existed to keep the exploiters in power, will cease to exist. Government won't be needed anymore because economic classes will cease to exist and the means of production will be owned in common. This state of existence is called *communism*, which means "working in common."[34]

Some think they can date socialism without having to marry communism. Marxists, however, don't see it that way. Socialism inevitably *becomes* communism, they say. As for "fellow-traveling" liberals and progressives who do not recognize this and whom communists easily mislead and manipulate, they are—according to Lenin—"dupes" and "useful idiots."[35]

Let's review for a moment. Dialectical materialism says that only nature exists and that through the conflict of opposites (thesis and antithesis), society will evolve (synthesis). Economic determinism says this evolution is an economic process in which society moves to a more enlightened state of common ownership of the means of production, no one is exploited, and everyone works together. Christianity—and all religions, for that matter—will be overthrown because people will see religion as a trick used to keep them from standing up against injustice. Capitalism, democracy, and the free exchange of goods and services will also be overthrown by newer, better ideas. To Marxists, this is the course of history. It cannot be stopped.

> Some think they can date socialism without having to marry communism. Marxists, however, don't see it that way.

4. MARXISM AS A WORLDVIEW

According to Marxists, not a single aspect of society is untouched by the inevitable conflict between the reigning economic class and the oppressed economic class. The evolutionary compulsion to eliminate economic injustice drives and explains all of human history. Therefore, people who embrace dialectical materialism and economic determinism have something to say about everything else.

Marxism prides itself on being a thinking-person's worldview. All good philosophers, Marxists believe, will be good Marxists. Marx said, "The head of the emancipation is philosophy, its heart is the proletariat."[36] The author of a prominent philosophy book published in the USSR in the 1980s said, "One cannot become a fully conscious, convinced communist without studying Marxist philosophy. This is what Lenin taught."[37] Marxist philosophy isn't just pie-in-the-sky theory, though. "The philosophers have only interpreted the world in various ways," Marx stated. "The point, however, is to change it."[38]

To the Marxist, then, there is no such thing as pure philosophy—or pure anything else. As we will see later in this volume, Marxists want to capture every academic discipline and put it to work fomenting revolution. And we need to pay careful attention. We will start by peering beyond the Marxist idea of *revolution* into the Marxist idea of *revelation*—both general and special—to see what sources Marxists turn to in forming their plans for the world.

5. GENERAL REVELATION: WHAT MARXISTS SEE WHEN THEY LOOK AT THE WORLD

Marxists believe there are laws of nature we can actually discover.[39] One definite law, according to Marx, was the law of evolution. Marx loved Darwin's *Origin of Species* because it dealt a "death-blow ... to 'teleology [design in nature].' "[40] F. V. Konstantinov, in *The Fundamentals of Marxist-Leninist Philosophy*, echoes Marx: "Darwin put an end to the notion of the species of animals and plants as 'divine creations,' not connected with anything else, providential and immutable, and thus laid the foundation of theoretical biology."[41]

As Marx studied Darwin's work, he became convinced that evolution could explain human progress as well as the survival of the fittest in nature. In other words, evolution wasn't just biological; it was sociological. Lenin put it this way: "Just as Darwin put an end to the view of animal and plant species being unconnected, fortuitous, 'created by God' and immutable, and was the first to put biology on an absolutely scientific basis ... so Marx ... was the first to put sociology on a scientific basis."[42]

The application of evolution to society as well as biology is a central tenet of Marxism. Today, the belief in progress is often called *progressivism*, though we must be clear that not all progressives are Marxists. To embrace a belief in constant progress, people must give up their belief in a rational, purposeful, powerful God whose plans and purposes do not involve economic overthrow. Any "god" who would frown on economic overthrow must not, to Marxists, be allowed to exist. Marx and Engels considered evolution to be an important companion belief to Marxism. If evolution sneezes, Marxism will catch a cold. On the other hand, if evolution goes into cardiac arrest, Marxism's brain waves cease.

> As Marx studied Darwin's work, he became convinced that evolution could explain human progress as well as the survival of the fittest in nature.

Further, Marxists are forced to embrace spontaneous generation—the idea of life arising from nonliving matter. Marx boasted, "The idea of the creation of the earth has received a severe blow ... from the science which portrays the ... development of the earth as a process of spontaneous generation.... *Generatio aequivoca* [spontaneous generation] is the only practical refutation of the theory of creation."[43]

Engels held firm his belief in spontaneous generation when new scientific discovery placed it in doubt. Louis Pasteur (1822–1895) dealt the deathblow to spontaneous generation, but Engels was unconvinced: "Pasteur's attempts in this direction are useless; for those who believe in this possibility [of spontaneous generation] he will never be able to prove their impossibility by these experiments alone."[44] This, of course, is a statement of faith, not science. It may not be *blind* faith exactly, but surely it is visible only to those who would believe it regardless of the evidence.

What does the Marxist say about special revelation, about the things we cannot know by observation but must be revealed to us? With each worldview, we've sought to answer five questions:

1. On what sources of revelation does Marxism draw on?
2. What does this worldview say about humanity?
3. What does this worldview say is wrong with us?
4. What does this worldview say about how we should live?
5. How are we to understand other worldviews based on Marxism?

6. Special Revelation: How Marxists Answer the Ultimate Questions

1. On what sources of revelation does Marxism draw? As we've already noted, Marxists put their faith in the evolution of society through economic conflict. Like Snow White, the workers of the world are in a deathly stupor, victims of a spell cast by their oppressors: business owners, religious leaders, and politicians. This spell is broken when workers discover their true plight, throw off their chains, and form a workers' paradise in which everyone works according to their ability and takes only what they need. To those who have felt the lash of oppression, this narrative is deeply compelling. But why would Marxists believe it is true? What sort of revelation convinces them?

The Communist Manifesto is, according to one of its modern-day publishers, a work of "great prescience and power."[45] Commissioned by the Communist League and written by Marx and Engels, the manifesto laid out the league's purposes and program. It suggested a course of action for a proletarian revolution to overthrow capitalism and, eventually, to bring about a classless society.

Since the time of *The Communist Manifesto*, communists have formed various schools of intellectual thought (such as the Frankfurt School of Theodor Adorno and Herbert Marcuse), terrorist groups (such as the Red Brigades), and even interest groups (such as the Communist Party USA and International ANSWER). Prominent Marxist thinkers from the last hundred years include Herbert Aptheker, William Z. Foster, Paul Robeson, Gerda Lerner, Eric Foner, Howard Zinn, Antonio Gramsci, Gyorgy Lukacs, Walter Benjamin, and Eric Hobsbawn.

At the dawn of the twenty-first century, Michael Hardt and Antonio Negri audaciously set out to update *The Communist Manifesto* for today's global situation. Their book, *Empire*, was published in 2000. The *National Review* referred to *Empire* as "the Communist 'hot, smart book of the moment' "[46] and *Foreign Affairs* magazine called it a "sweeping neo-Marxist vision of the coming world order."[47] Hardt is a professor at Duke University who, according to Duke's website, teaches a couple of classes each semester and spends three hours in the office each week. Negri's career, on the other hand, is much more colorful. His association with the Red Brigades terrorist organization in Italy landed him in prison several decades ago. While behind bars, Negri won election to the Italian Parliament. Consequently, he claimed parliamentary immunity, was released from prison, and escaped to France, where he lived and taught for fourteen years. Eventually Negri returned to Italy to serve a reduced sentence of six years.

Harvard University Press described *Empire*, published in the middle of Negri's prison term, as "an unabashedly utopian work of political philosophy, a new *Communist Manifesto*." Hardt and Negri blame the United States, and specifically the US Constitution, for reengineering imperialism into a brutal, world-dominating ideology.[48] Four years after publishing *Empire*, they published the follow-up work *Multitude*, which called for people to rise up and attack capitalism. In 2009, the authors published *Commonwealth* to articulate specific ideas about how they would "govern the revolution" by holding wealth in common. This, the authors say, involves reimagining the opposition between the ideas of "public" and "private." It's a ruse, of course; reimagining the difference between public and private is the justification robbers give for reappropriating your wealth. Marx and Engels would probably be somewhat awed by the audacity of this project, and certainly proud.

2. What does Marxism say about humanity? Engels believed thought and consciousness were "products of the human brain and that man himself is a product of nature, which has been developed in and along with its environment."[49] He further stated, "All nature, from the smallest thing to the biggest, from a grain of sand to the sun, from the Protista [the primary living cell] to man, is in a constant state of coming into being and going out of being, in a constant flux, in a ceaseless state of movement and change."[50]

Class Consciousness: the belief that the working class is becoming increasingly aware of their position in society and their oppression by the bourgeoisie.

So everything is material. Humans are really nothing more than matter in motion, but they are always evolving and hopefully growing in their **class consciousness**, their awareness of their oppressed state.[51] This, in turn, will motivate a new ethic, a **proletariat morality**, to justify whatever actions Marxists take to overthrow our existing social conditions. According to *Scientific Communism: A Glossary,*

Devotion to the cause of the working class, collectivism, mutual aid, comradery, solidarity, hatred toward the bourgeoisie and toward traitors to the common cause, internationalism, and stoicism in struggle are traits which not only define the content of proletarian ethics, but also characterize the moral image of the typical representatives of the working class.[52]

Proletariat Morality: the belief that whatever advances the proletariat and communism is morally good, and whatever hinders the proletariat and communism is morally evil.

Based on proletariat morality, hard-core Marxists openly admit that killing the bourgeoisie was a basic duty. "We are exterminating the bourgeoisie as a class," said Martin Y. Latsis, a top official of Lenin's secret police.[53] Latsis and his comrades were quite candid. They saw their actions as moral, as necessary to creating their "better" world. Nikita Khrushchev, president of the USSR after Stalin, explained:

Our cause is sacred. He whose hand will tremble, who will stop midway, whose knees will shake before he destroys tens and hundreds of enemies, he will lead the revolution into danger. Whoever will spare a few lives of enemies, will pay for it with hundreds and thousands of lives of the better sons of our fathers.[54]

The evolved person's class consciousness leads to a new form of morality, one which erases his sense of mercy toward his former oppressors. In this heightened state he can control his destiny and eliminate those whose backward ways slow society's advance toward true communism.

3. What does Marxism say is wrong with us? The problem with society is an economic one to the Marxist. Marx said that in a capitalist society, the bourgeoisie equate personal worth with exchange value, leading to "naked, shameless, direct, brutal exploitation."[55] Marxism rejects the Christian view of the sin nature, that we are all corrupt and in need of a savior. The exploiters alone are guilty, and there is no salvation apart from their overthrow, which will lead to rapid societal transformation.[56]

William Z. Foster was one of those who believed the principles that built the Soviet Union could transform America as well. His 1932 book, *Toward Soviet America*, breathlessly proposed an ambitious vision for education in a future communist America. Foster wrote,

> Among the elementary measures the American Soviet government will adopt to further the cultural revolution are the following: the schools, colleges and universities will be coordinated and grouped under the National Department of Education and its state and local branches. The studies will be revolutionized, being cleansed of religious, patriotic and other features of the bourgeois ideology. The students will be taught on the basis of Marxian dialectical materialism, internationalism and the general ethics of the new Socialist society.[57]

Foster continued, "Science will become materialistic, hence truly scientific; God will be banished from the laboratories as well as from the schools."[58]

This must have sounded laughably ridiculous to his readers at the time. But go back and read Foster's statements once more. How much of his vision has already taken place?

If Foster were ever to achieve his vision for education, he had a chilling plan for the next step: dismantling the influence of the church. "The churches will remain free to continue their services," Foster stated, "but … other privileges will be liquidated. Their buildings will revert to the State. Religious schools will be abolished and organized religious training for minors prohibited. Freedom will be established for anti-religious propaganda."[59]

Foster wasn't just some nut with a typewriter. He was a true believer, a prominent union organizer, one of the earliest board members and top officials at the American Civil Liberties Union (ACLU), and a would-be dictator who honestly believed the United States could atone for its sins by forfeiting its capitalistic interests and submitting to the Soviet Union. Foster's enthusiastic support of the murderous Stalin made him such a complete ally of the Soviet Union that upon his death he was given a state funeral in Moscow's Red Square, complete with an honor guard headed by Soviet president Nikita Khrushchev.

At every step along the way, Marxists see the human problem as someone else's problem—property owners are devilish, and the property-less workers are saintly.

Before we move on, an important side note is in order about a word game being played in our modern society concerning the freedom-of-religion question. The Soviet Union and many other communist countries included the freedom of worship in their constitutions. This was mere windowdressing, propaganda to try to deflect criticism of the severe religious repression that everyone knew communists pursued relentlessly. At best, phony pledges of freedom of *worship* mean the freedom to *assemble for worship services*, which is very different from the freedom to live out one's religious convictions in a lawful manner. If you hear someone use the expression "freedom of worship" in place of "freedom of religion" in referring to the US Constitution, you should be very suspicious. Either that person is truly misinformed or is

> **At best, phony pledges of freedom of *worship* mean the freedom to *assemble for worship services*, which is very different from the freedom to live out one's religious convictions in a lawful manner.**

playing word games to try to change what the freedom of religion means.[60]

4. What does Marxism say about how we should live? Marxists see the march toward socialism and eventually communism as a historical inevitability. This is where social evolution will take us; resistance is futile. Those who march alongside will become *free*; and to those who resist, the Marxist says, "We know who you are and where you live; we will not be able to protect you when the revolution comes."

So how do Marxists say we should live, specifically? Those with a budding class consciousness will establish socialism, abolishing private property and eliminating class divisions. Since government exists only to protect the oppressors, once there are no more oppressors, government will no longer be needed. According to Lenin, "Only in Communist society when the resistance of the capitalists has been completely broken, when the capitalists have disappeared, when there are no classes ... only then the State ceases to exist."[61]

The revolt of the workers brings oppression to an end and establishes socialism. As socialism becomes established, oppression will cease, government will become unnecessary, and we will have true communism. Or will we? If humans continue to evolve, who's to say that communism is the final state? Marxists spend little time worrying about this contradiction. They're convinced that if they can just spark the revolution, everything else will take care of itself.

5. How are we to understand other worldviews based on Marxism? As you can imagine, Marxists strongly disagree with the other worldviews we are considering, but for different reasons than we do. Let's take a look at Marxism's views of them.

Christianity. Of all of the worldviews we've considered in this book, Karl Marx would probably consider Christianity the most insidious. His statement "Religion is the sigh of the oppressed creature, the heart of a heartless world, and the soul of soulless conditions. It is the opium of the people" was most likely directed at Christianity.[62] Christianity, he wrote, justified slavery, defended oppression, and taught Christians to seek their reward in heaven rather than on Earth. It preaches "self-contempt, abasement, submissiveness and humbleness, in short, all the qualities of the rabble, and the proletariat, which will not permit itself to be treated as rabble, needs its courage, its self-confidence, its pride and its sense of independence even more than its bread."[63]

The hatred is not mutual. Some Christians sympathetic to the plight of the poor regularly scour Scripture to find evidence justifying Marxism. Marxists think this is silly and naive. In their minds, the two worldviews are fundamentally at odds. Christian leftists may open their arms, but Marxists reject the embrace. We'll examine this issue more thoroughly in the chapter on economics.

Secularism. In the United States, claims *New York Times* columnist Ross Douthat, communism remained a "tribal phenomenon" that was "never a *mass* phenomenon in the way that the new secularism seems to be, or seems capable of becoming. It was an intellectual tribe, but not a political demographic."[64] It was not for want of trying. Secularist leader John

Dewey, prominent in forming America's system of public education and a former leader of the socialistic League for Industrial Democracy, believed socialism was the best economic system.[65] He claimed that "social control of economic forces is ... necessary if anything approaching economic equality and liberty is to be realized."[66] Dewey's worldview coincided with that of Karl Marx: we must embrace socialism to be truly free.

Dewey believed society would fail if it did not embrace socialism: "The cause of liberalism will be lost for a considerable period if it is not prepared to go further and socialize the forces of production, now at hand, so that the liberty of individuals will be supported by the very structure of economic organization."[67] He even believed socialism was the key to freedom, stating that a "socialized economy is the means of free individual development as the end."[68]

The Soviet Union saw John Dewey's writings on education as the means of fulfilling the demand of *The Communist Manifesto* for "free education for all children in public schools." Dewey traveled to the Soviet Union and upon his return wrote a glowing tribute in a special series of articles for one of the top journals of the American progressive left. Only years later, in response to Stalin's persecution of Leon Trotsky, did Dewey waver in his affinity for the Soviet regime.[69] John Dewey's student Corliss Lamont (one of the founders of Secular Humanism) was even more enamored of the Soviet Union than Dewey. He even headed up Friends of the Soviet Union, which historian Paul Kengor calls an "odious front group."[70]

New Spirituality. It is difficult to tell whether there is any convergence between New Spirituality and Marxism in practice, but in theory the two worldviews are radically different. Marxism strongly critiques all religion because it draws energy away from anti-capitalist fervor. Marxism's denial of any transcendent reality would draw protests from New Spiritualists, and they see Marxism's brutal way of pursuing its aims as a manifestation of negative energy and ego. In their comments on economics, however infrequent, New Spiritualists tend to focus on individualistic pursuits rather than rejection of capitalist structures.

Still, Marxism and New Spirituality do have a common grandfather. Georg Hegel, the philosopher whose "dialectic" approach is so fundamental to Marxist thinking, wrote frequently of the "over-soul," the "Soul of Nature," which bears more than a passing resemblance to the New Spirituality belief in a higher consciousness. Philosopher and mystic Ken Wilber has incorporated Hegel's thinking into New Spiritualist teachings. To speculate any further, though, would be to stretch the connections beyond where either Marxists or New Spiritualists have been willing to go. It is probably safest to say that Marxists would view New Spiritualists as muddle headed and unscientific, and New Spiritualists would view Marxists as well meaning but egoistic.

> Hegel, the philosopher whose "dialectic" approach is so fundamental to Marxist thinking, wrote frequently of the "over-soul," the "Soul of Nature," which bears more than a passing resemblance to the New Spirituality belief in a higher consciousness.

Islam. Muslims see their economic approach as a middle way between capitalism and socialism. Muslim economist Syed Nawab Haider Naqvi defines *socialism* as "the abolition of private property." This is also Karl Marx's definition in *The Communist Manifesto*.[71] In turn, Naqvi refers to capitalism as the unlimited freedom of private property, which divorces ethics from economics. To Muslims, economic justice requires economic well-being for all believers. To accomplish this, instituted within Islam are *zakat* (almsgiving for the sake of the poor), *jizya* (taxes levied against unbelievers within the Islamic community), and laws regarding inheritance.

On the issue of private property, Naqvi contends that Islamic economics rejects socialism's negation of private property but also rejects capitalism's alleged absolute view of private property. "Within the framework of a set of ground rules, individual (economic) freedom should be guaranteed, but the state should be allowed to regulate it in cases where the exercise of individual freedom becomes inconsistent with social welfare."[72] Naqvi also insists, "As to the ownership of private property[,] especially of land ownership, it has been restricted in various ways. For instance, individuals cannot own uncultivated lands, forests, grazing grounds, mines, etc. All these must be owned by the public authority for public welfare."[73] In the end, while Marxists maintain a critique of all religion, Islam is probably not as threatening to Marxism as Christianity. Islam is suspicious of private property, which, as far as Marxists are concerned, is at least a move in the right direction.

> In the end, while Marxists maintain a critique of all religion, Islam is probably not as threatening to Marxism as Christianity. Islam is suspicious of private property, which, as far as Marxists are concerned, is at least a move in the right direction.

Postmodernism. One might think that since both Marxists and Postmodernists take a critical stance toward dominant narratives, especially religious ones, they might be in agreement on many points. As the "Postmodernism" chapter in this book will show, many Postmodernists came out of the Marxist tradition. In fact, some of them viewed their project as making Marxism respectable. The postmodern obsession with the language of oppression, according to literature professor Gene Edward Veith, comes directly from Marxist thought.[74]

In another sense, though, Postmodernism is as post-Marxist as it is post-everything-else. A Marxist website, League for the Fifth International, which proclaims as its objective "fighting for the formation of a new world party of socialist revolution," identifies seven aspects of Postmodernism that it says Marxists must reject. It focuses primarily on Postmodernism's suspicion of scientific thought and the inevitability of communism based on social evolution.[75] Fredric Jameson, a professor at Duke University and an openly enthusiastic champion of Marxism, took a dialectic view of Postmodernism, pitting it against commercial capitalism's "colonization" of the culture. Though his argument is nuanced, the title of his book on the subject, *Postmodernism, or, the Cultural Logic of Late Capitalism*, seems to imply that Postmodernism was just another form of opposition rising against capitalism. This, he argued, is a good thing, but it too shall pass.[76]

7. CONCLUSION

If you were to imply in polite company that communism is still a relevant concern, you'd likely endure a lot of smirking and eye rolling. It has been said that the fear of being laughed at makes cowards of us all. Unfortunately it's often true. Most choose to be quiet rather than compel the mockers and scorners to define their terms and provide actual arguments justifying their views. With other worldviews we have honest disagreements. With Marxism it is hard to find common ground with the most violent, oppressive, and murderous system of thought ever constructed, a system many hundreds of times worse than the injustices it was supposed to rectify.

Some rationalize that while violent overthrows, labor camps, and systematic genocide are bad, communism and socialism are, in theory, harmless. This is breathtakingly naive. Whenever humans plant seeds of a massive centralized overhaul of society, the noxious weeds of corruption, violence, and oppression inevitably spring forth from the parched soil.

You do not need to take our word for it; Marxism's proponents could hardly be clearer. As we quoted earlier from *The Communist Manifesto*, Marx said, "The Communists disdain to conceal their views and aims. They openly declare that their ends can be attained only by the forcible overthrow of all existing social conditions."[77] *The Communist Manifesto* is a prescription for despotism. As Marx himself conceded, prefacing his ten points: "Of course, in the beginning, this cannot be effected except by means of despotic inroads." Marxism wasn't hijacked by despots; Marxism *demanded* despots.

How did this work out in practice? In 1918, Marxists attempted to rapidly institute socialism in Russia by seizing land from its owners. The Soviet constitution proclaimed "all private property in land is abolished, and the entire land is declared to be national property and is to be apportioned among agriculturists without any compensation to the former owners, in the measure of each one's ability to till it."[78]

The head revolutionary, V. I. Lenin, quickly realized that the Russian economy would never survive such a rapid move to socialism. In 1921 he declared,

> We are no longer attempting to break up the old social economic order, with its trade, its small-scale economy and private initiative, its capitalism, but we are now trying to revive trade, private enterprise and capitalism, at the same time gradually and cautiously subjecting them to state regulation just as far as they revive.[79]

During the transition period, Lenin experimented with a number of social methods to hasten the arrival of socialism and communism. Frustrated at how people lost their motivation to work when they could not personally benefit, Lenin demanded imprisonment, forced labor, and executions: "One out of every ten idlers will be shot on the spot."[80]

Lenin's easy resort to violence and force should cause any rational person to wonder what kind of system he was creating. Isn't this immoral? In order to answer that question we must understand that Marxism proposes an entirely different definition of *morality* than the definition Christianity proposes. Nikita Khrushchev stated,

> So long as classes exist on the earth, there will be no such thing in life as something good in the absolute sense. What is good for the bourgeoisie, for the imperialists, is disastrous for the working class, and, on the contrary, what is good for the working people is not admitted by the imperialists, by the bourgeoisie.[81]

This, then, is the whole problem with the old morality as Marxists perceive it—the old morality is simply a tool oppressors use to maintain their power. Lenin himself explicitly rejected Christian ethics as a tool of the exploiters:

Is there such a thing as communist morality? Of course there is. It is often suggested that we have no ethics of our own; very often the bourgeoisie accuse us Communists of rejecting all morality. This is a method of confusing the issue, of throwing dust in the eyes of the workers and peasants. In what sense do we reject ethics, reject morality? In the sense given to it by the bourgeoisie, who based ethics on God's commandments. On this point we, of course, say that we do not believe in God, and that we know perfectly well that the clergy, the landowners and the bourgeoisie invoked the name of God so as to further their own interests as exploiters.[82]

This is not to say that all Marxists are evil atheists hell bent on violence. But about this there can be no question: every time Marxism has been tried at a national level, terror and violence were chief among the methods used.

Marxism in the twentieth century openly justified mistreating its opponents by claiming it would serve the "higher good" in the long run. A good example of how this occurred is Lenin's—and subsequently Stalin's—extermination of the Ukrainian farmers who did not want to cooperate with the Communist Party's aims. When he recognized that his efforts to rapidly move toward socialism were failing, Lenin wrote that he would be willing to work with the "petty bourgeois proprietors" as long as their work furthered the Marxist cause, but "after that our roads part. Then we shall have to engage in the most decisive, ruthless struggle against them."[83]

Ultimately, Lenin declared that these farmers, which he called *kulaks*, needed to be eliminated as a class. They were not "human beings,"[84] he said, and thus he viewed them as legitimate objects of "economic terror."[85] Stalin took Lenin's philosophy to heart, stating, "To put it briefly: the dictatorship of the proletariat is the domination of the proletariat over the bourgeoisie, untrammeled by the law and based on violence and enjoying the sympathy and support of the toiling and exploited masses."[86] Consistent with his rhetoric, Stalin announced on December 27, 1929, "the liquidation of the kulaks as a class."[87]

> **The unmarked graves of tens of millions testify to the horrifying consequences of Marx's grand vision.**

Ivan Bahryany, a Ukrainian citizen who estimates that the Soviets killed ten million of his countrymen between 1927 and 1939, concluded, "The party clique which follows the slogan expressed by the saying 'the end justifies the means' is actually always ready to use any means."[88]

Clearly, then, Marxism views violence as temporarily necessary and not morally questionable. Marx, Lenin, Stalin, and a host of other Marxist heroes saw it as a *moral duty* to overthrow the exploiters by any means necessary. It was well worth the price paid, said Lenin, "even if for every hundred correct things we committed 10,000 mistakes, our revolution would still be—and it will be in the judgment of history—great and invincible."[89]

That Lenin and those who followed him were becoming exploiters of an even more brutal sort either did not register with (or was ignored by) the leaders who had the power to stop it. The unmarked graves of tens of millions testify to the horrifying consequences of Marx's grand vision. It is in many ways a reaction to Marxism's totalitarianism that many other worldviews began to forsake the idea of ruling by force and began to turn inward, toward spiritual enlightenment rather than societal change. Such is the case with the worldview of New Spirituality, which we will examine next.

ENDNOTES

1. Paul Johnson, *Intellectuals* (New York: Harper Perennial, 1988), 71–81.

2. Johnson, *Intellectuals*, 60.

3. Karl Marx and Friedrich Engels, *The Communist Manifesto*, trans. Samuel Moore (New York: Penguin Books, 2002), 258.

4. Alexander Yakovlev, in his important work *A Century of Violence in Soviet Russia* (New Haven, CT: Yale University Press, 2002), estimated that Stalin's regime alone killed more than 60 million.

5. Jung Chang and Jon Halliday record the latest figures of 70-million-plus killed under China's Mao Tse-tung in their seminal work, *Mao: The Unknown Story* (New York: Anchor, 2006).

6. Political scientist R. J. Rummel estimates that communism killed about 110 million people in the twentieth century (R. J. Rummel, "How Many Did Communist Regimes Murder?," November 1993, posted at University of Hawaii, accessed April 2, 2014, www.hawaii.edu/powerkills/COM.ART.HTM), while Stéphane Courtois, in *The Black Book of Communism: Crimes, Terror, Repression* (Cambridge, MA: Harvard University Press, 1999), estimates that communist regimes killed nearly 100 million in the twentieth century.

7. Sutirtho Patranobis, "China to Ease One-Child Policy: State Media," *Hindustan Times*, November 16, 2013, www .hindustantimes.com/world/china-to-ease-one-child-policy-state-media/story-Y7DluFOURVx5au7EGCyA7L .html.

8. George Santayana, *The Life of Reason* (Middlesex, UK: Echo Library, 2006), 131. The original publication was titled *The Life of Reason: Or the Phases of Human Progress* (New York: Charles Scribner's Sons, 1906). The quotation in this earlier volume was on page 284.

9. Edmund Burke, *The Works of Edmund Burke* (New York: George Dearborn, 1834), 1:187.

10. Alvaro Vargas Llosa, "The Killing Machine: Che Guevara, from Communist Firebrand to Capitalist Brand," *New Republic*, July 11, 2005, www.independent.org/newsroom/article.asp?id=1535.

11. These countries, at the time of writing, have constitutional references to socialism as their official policies.

12. See William J. Federer, *Change to Chains* (St. Louis, MO: Amerisearch, 2011), 81. Federer says, "In Sumeria about 2100 BC, the economy was organized by the State. Most of the arable land was the property of the crown; laborers received rations from the crops delivered to the royal storehouses ... [and] records were kept of all deliveries and distributions of nations. Tens of thousands of clay tablets inscribed with such records were found in the capital Ur. In Babylonia (c. 1750 BC)[,] the law code of Hammurabi fixed wages for the herdsmen and artisans, and the charges to be made by physicians for operations. In Egypt under the Ptolemies (323–30 BC)[,] the state owned the soil and managed the agriculture; the peasant was told what land to till, what crops to grow[;] his harvest was measured and registered by government scribes, was threshed on royal threshing floors, and was conveyed by a living chain of *fellaheen* into the granaries of the king. The government owned the mines and appropriated the ore. It nationalized the production and sale of oil, salt, papyrus, and textiles. All commerce was controlled and regulated by the State[;]... banking was a government monopoly. Taxes were laid upon every person, industry, process, product, sale, and legal document. Roman Emperor Diocletian brought nearly all major industries and guilds under detailed control ... taxation rose to such heights that men lost incentive to work or earn.... Thousands of Romans, to escape the tax gatherer, fled over the frontiers to seek refuge among the barbarians. Chinese Szuma Ch'ien (c. 146 BC) informs us that to prevent individuals from 'reserving to their sole use the riches of the mountains and the sea in order to gain a fortune, and from putting the lower class into subjection to themselves,' the Emperor Wu Ti of the Han Dynasty (reigning 140–87 BC) nationalized the resources of the soil, extended government direction over transport and trade, laid a tax upon incomes, and established public works, including canals that bound the rivers together and irrigated the fields. These stories, recounted by Will and Ariel Durant [*The Lessons of History*], underscore the continual drive for States to control citizens' lives, and highlight the truly unusual alignment of circumstances and beliefs which allowed for the formation of the United States of America."

13. "The Rise of State Capitalism," *Economist*, January 21, 2012, www.economist.com/node/21543160.

14. The development of state capitalism is illustrated specifically in Russia, China, and Brazil, where state governments have taken ownership of oil companies, telecom companies, and mining operations, respectively. For 2011, 80 percent of the Chinese companies in the MSCI stock index were government-run companies. Sixty-two percent of the Russian companies in the MSCI were government run, as were 38 percent of Brazilian companies listed. In 2010, four of the ten top revenue-earning companies in the world were state run: Sinopec Group ($273 billion, China), China National Petroleum Corporation ($240 billion, China), State Grid ($226 billion, China), and Japan Post Holdings ($204 billion, Japan). In China, the government is the biggest shareholder for the country's biggest 150 companies.

15. If you are interested, you can follow Folsom's line of thinking at Burt Folsom, *Where History, Money and Politics Collide*, (blog), www.burtfolsom.com/.

16. Arnold Beichman, "Immune from the Shortages," *Washington Times*, December 31, 1990, G3.

17. Quoted in Beichman, "Immune from the Shortages."

18. "Marxism in U.S. Classrooms," *U.S. News and World Report*, January 8, 1982, quoted in Ira Shor, *Culture Wars: School and Society in the Conservative Restoration 1969–1984* (London: Routledge, 1986).

19. Herbert London, "Marxism Thriving on American Campuses," The World and I, January 1987, www .worldandischool.com/public/1987/january/school-resource12337.asp.

20. Terry Eagleton, "Why Marx Was Right," Yale University Press, April 24, 2012, http://yalepress.yale.edu/yupbooks /reviews.asp?isbn=9780300181531 (content moved as of February 8, 2016).

21. Stuart Jeffries, "Why Marxism Is on the Rise Again," *Guardian*, July 4, 2012, www.guardian.co.uk/world/2012 /jul/04/the-return-of-marxism.

22. Martha E. Gimenez, "Marxism and Class, Gender, and Race: Rethinking the Trilogy," *Race, Gender, and Class* 8, no. 2 (2001): 23–33.

23. *Essence* magazine, bell hooks's review of *Remembered Rapture* (Henry Holt, 1999), Macmillan Publishers, accessed March 18, 2014, http://us.macmillan.com/rememberedrapture/bellhooks. Adopted as a pen name, *bell hooks* is the name of hooks's grandmother and is set in lowercase because "[hooks] believes that what is most important is the 'substance of books, not who I am.'" Heather Williams, "bell hooks Speaks Up," *Sandspur*, February 10, 2006, http:// archive.is/K5Yxn#selection-553.297-553.380.

24. Quoted in Jamie Glazov, "bell hooks and the Politics of Hate," frontpagemag.com, June 12, 2002, accessed February 8, 2016, http://archive.frontpagemag.com/readArticle.aspx?ARTID=25297.

25. In one such rally, covered by the national media, the keynote speaker was a New York University professor and devout Marxist Slavoj Žižek, who once wrote, "One should shamelessly repeat the lesson of Lenin's *State and Revolution*." Quoted in Alan Johnson, "The New Communism: Resurrecting the Utopian Delusion," *World Affairs Journal* (May/June 2012).

26. See Gustav A. Wetter, *Dialectical Materialism* (Westport, CT: Greenwood, 1977), 4. Wetter stated, "In Hegel's sense of the term, dialectic is a process in which a starting-point [a thesis, e.g., Being] is negated [the antithesis, e.g., Non-Being], thereby setting up a second position opposed to it. This second position is in turn negated i.e., by negation of the negation, so as to reach a third position representing a synthesis [e.g., Becoming] of the two preceding, in which both are 'transcended,' i.e., abolished and at the same time preserved on a higher level of being. This third phase then figures in turn as the first step in a new dialectical process [i.e., a new thesis], leading to a new synthesis, and so on."

27. Frederick Engels, *Socialism: Utopian and Scientific* (New York: International Publishers, 1935), 21.

28. Quoted in Whittaker Chambers, *Witness* (New York: Random House, 1952), 712.

29. V. I. Lenin, *Collected Works*, 45 vols. (Moscow: Progress Publishers, 1977), 7:409. Lenin wrote of the "great Hegelian dialectics which Marxism made its own, having first turned it right side up."

30. Frederick Engels, *Ludwig Feuerbach* (New York: International Publishers, 1974), 44.

31. V. I. Lenin, *The Teachings of Karl Marx* (New York: International Publishers, 1976), 27.

32. Marx and Engels, *Communist Manifesto*, 202–3.

33. See Raymond Sleeper, ed., *A Lexicon of Marxist-Leninist Semantics* (Alexandria, VA: Western Goals, 1983), 249. According to Sleeper, *The Political Dictionary* defines "socialism [as] the first phase of communism. The principle of socialism is: from each according to his abilities, to each according to his work.... Under communism the basic principle of society will be: from each according to his abilities, to each according to his needs."

34. V. I. Lenin, *Selected Works*, 38 vols. (New York: International Publishers, 1938), 9:479.

35. Paul Kengor, *Dupes* (Wilmington, DE: ISI Books, 2010).

36. Quoted in Johnson, *Intellectuals*, 58–59.

37. F. V. Konstantinov, ed., *The Fundamentals of Marxist-Leninist Philosophy* (Moscow: Progress Publishers, 1982), 78.

38. Karl Marx and Frederick Engels, *Collected Works*, 40 vols. (New York: International Publishers, 1976), 5:8.

39. Karl Marx, Frederick Engels, and V. I. Lenin, *On Historical Materialism* (New York: International Publishers, 1974), 461.

40. Karl Marx and Frederick Engels, *Selected Correspondence* (New York: International Publishers, 1942), 125.

41. Konstantinov, *Fundamentals of Marxist-Leninist Philosophy*, 42.

42. Lenin, *Collected Works*, 1:142.

43. Quoted in Francis Nigel Lee, *Communism versus Creation* (Nutley, NJ: Craig Press, 1969), 68. For a scientific look at the major issues involved in the theory of spontaneous generation, see David Berlinski's "On the Origins of Life," *Commentary*, February 1, 2006.

44. Frederick Engels, *Dialectics of Nature* (New York: International Publishers, 1976), 189.

45. From the Verso Books website, publisher of the most recent version of *The Communist Manifesto*. See www
.versobooks.com/books/1109-the-communist-manifesto.

46. David Pryce-Jones, "Evil Empire," *National Review Online*, September 17, 2001, 28.

47. "Capsule Review: Empire," *Foreign Affairs* (July/August 2000), https://www.foreignaffairs.com/reviews/capsule-review
/2000-07-01/empire.

48. Hardt and Negri, *Empire*. On page 207 the authors say, "Our pilgrimage on earth, however, in contrast to
Augustine's, has no transcendent telos beyond [purpose beyond this world]; it is and remains absolutely immanent
[here and now]. Its continuous movement, gathering aliens in community, making this world its home, is both
means and end, or rather a means without [an] end."

49. Lenin, *Teachings of Karl Marx*, 14.

50. Engels, *Dialectics of Nature*, 13.

51. Karl Marx, *A Contribution to the Critique of Political Economy* (New York: International Publishers, 1904), 11–12. Marx
said, "It is not the consciousness of men that determines their existence, but, on the contrary, their social existence
determines their consciousness." This view is identical to that of existentialists, who insist that existence precedes
essence, and thus attractive to both Marxists and Postmodernists.

52. Quoted in Sleeper, *Lexicon of Marxist-Leninist Semantics*, 106.

53. Quoted in Courtois, *Black Book of Communism*, 8.

54. Nikita Khrushchev, *Ukrainian Bulletin* (August 1960): 12, quoted in James D. Bales, *Communism and the Reality of
Moral Law* (Nutley, NJ: Craig Press, 1969), 121.

55. Marx and Engels, *Collected Works*, 6:487.

56. Marx said, "With the change of the economic foundation the entire immense superstructure is more or less
rapidly transformed." Marx, *Contributions to the Critique of Political Economy*, 12.

57. William Z. Foster, *Toward Soviet America* (New York: International Publishers, 1932), 316.

58. Foster, *Toward Soviet America*, 317.

59. Foster, *Toward Soviet America*, 316.

60. It is easy to search for this on the Internet using the search term "freedom of religion versus freedom of worship."
Here is one thoughtful article: Randy Sly, "Obama Moves Away from 'Freedom of Religion' toward 'Freedom
of Worship'?," *Catholic Online*, July 19, 2010, accessed March 26, 2014, www.catholic.org/national/national_story
.php?id=37390.

61. V. I. Lenin, *The State and Revolution* (New York: International Publishers, 1932), 73.

62. Karl Marx, *Critique of Hegel's Philosophy of Right*, trans. Annette Jolin and Joseph O'Malley (Cambridge, UK:
Cambridge University Press, 1970), 131; originally published in *Deutsch-Französische Jahrbücher*.

63. Marx and Engels, *Collected Works*, 6:231.

64. Ross Douthat, "Secularism and Marxism," *Atlantic*, June 15, 2007, www.theatlantic.com/personal/archive/2007/06
/secularism-and-marxism/54482/.

65. For an in-depth study of the British Fabian Society, see Sister M. Margaret Patricia McCarran, *Fabianism in the
Political Life of Britain, 1919–1931* (Chicago: Heritage Foundation, 1954). For an in-depth look at John Dewey's role
in bringing his brand of socialism into America's public schools, see B. K. Eakman, *Cloning of the American Mind:
Eradicating Morality through Education* (Lafayette, LA: Huntington House, 1998).

66. John Dewey, *Liberalism and Social Action* (New York: G. P. Putnam's Sons, 1935), 356–57.

67. Dewey, *Liberalism*, 88.

68. Dewey, *Liberalism*, 90.

69. See chapters 4–6 in Kengor, *Dupes*.

70. Kengor, *Dupes*, 108.

71. Marx and Engels, *Collected Works*, 6:498.

72. Syed Nawab Haider Naqvi, *Islam, Economics, and Society* (London: Kegan Paul International, 1994), 55.

73. Naqvi, *Islam*, 91.

74. Gene Edward Veith, *Postmodern Times* (Wheaton, IL: Crossway Books, 1994).

75. "Marxism versus Postmodernism," League for the Fifth International, January 30, 1997, www.fifthinternational
.org/content/marxism-versus-postmodernism. The complete list is as follows: (1) "There is no objective truth to
be comprehended by scientific thought; (2) there is no pre-given human subject; the human individual is only
a complex of interrelated outside influences and determinants; (3) language cannot represent reality; therefore,
the concept of ideology, where false ideas mask reality, is meaningless; (4) the idea of historical progression and
necessity is meaningless: social formations in history, sociology and anthropology must be 'mapped'—not judged
or categorised; (5) all social movements or societies based on the possibility of scientific knowledge and objective
truth rely on 'grand narratives' rather than inner logic to legitimise them; these 'meta-narratives' inevitably lead
to the legitimising of oppression; (6) the class struggle and socialism are precise examples of such meta-narratives;
in any case they have become outmoded by developments in the modern world; (7) the only form of resistance to

oppression that does not lead to another form of oppression is limited, local, piecemeal resistance; the surest form of resistance is to change ourselves, aspiring ultimately to turn our own lives into a 'work of art.'"

76. Fredric Jameson, *Postmodernism, or, the Cultural Logic of Late Capitalism* (Durham, NC: Duke University Press, 1990).

77. Marx and Engels, *Collected Works*, 6:519.

78. Harry W. Laidler, *History of Socialism* (New York: Thomas Y. Crowell, 1968), 384.

79. V. I. Lenin, written for special Pravda anniversary, November 7, 1921, quoted in Abraham Aaron Heller, *The Industrial Revival in Soviet Russia* (New York: Thomas Seltzer, 1922), 105.

80. Lenin, *Collected Works*, 26:414–15.

81. Nikita Khrushchev, "The Great Strength of Soviet Literature and Art," *Soviet Booklet* 108 (London: Farleigh Press, 1963), 30, quoted in James D. Bales, *Communism and the Reality of Moral Law* (Nutley, NJ: Craig Press, 1969), 5.

82. Lenin, *Collected Works*, 31:291.

83. Lenin, *Collected Works*, 36:255, 265.

84. Lenin, *Collected Works*, 36:129.

85. Lenin, *Collected Works*, 36:60.

86. Joseph Stalin, *J. Stalin Works* (Moscow: Foreign Languages, 1953), 6:118.

87. Quoted in Robert Conquest, *The Harvest of Sorrow* (Oxford, UK: Oxford University Press, 1986), 117.

88. Quoted in S. O. Pidhainy, ed., *The Black Deeds of the Kremlin* (Toronto: Basilian Press, 1953), 14. Robert Conquest (*Harvest of Sorrow*, 305) places the figure at 14.5 million.

89. Lenin, *Collected Works*, 28:72.

CHAPTER **6**

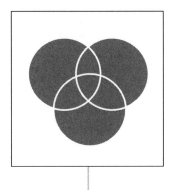

NEW SPIRITUALITY

1. BHAGAVAD GITA

Arjuna's heart pounded with anxiety as the chariot clattered onto the battlefield of Kuru. The horses snorted and tried to bolt, held back only by the expert guidance of Arjuna's chariot driver, Krishna.

"Stop here," commanded Arjuna uncertainly. There, in the middle of the battlefield, he could see what was about to unfold. On one side, the Pandavas, Arjuna's kin and followers, prepared their weapons for slaughter. On the other side, the troops of the Kaurava clan moved into formation. The Kauravas were his cousins, but today they were the enemy. As soon as the battle began, Arjuna knew he would destroy them without mercy. Or would he?

His heart pounding, his breath coming in gasps, a thousand thoughts filled Arjuna's head. He felt pity for those he would kill and dread that the battle might turn and his life might end today. I cannot fight, *he thought.* I have no will.

Arjuna watched as Krishna spoke reassuringly to the nervous steeds shivering in the rising light. At last he spoke. "I am weighed down by pity, Krishna; my mind is utterly confused," he confessed. "Tell me where my duty lies, which path I should take."

Krishna sighed and turned his gaze away from the enemy formations directly toward Arjuna's eyes. "Wise men do not grieve for the dead or for the living," he said simply.

"What ... are you ... saying?" asked Arjuna, startled.

Krishna replied matter-of-factly, "These bodies come to an end; but that vast embodied Self is ageless, fathomless, eternal."

Arjuna stared at Krishna, and suddenly he knew. This was no chariot driver; he was peering into the eyes of a god who had come down to steady Arjuna's nerves for what he must do. All the secrets of the universe were in the mind of this God-man holding the reins. It was a battle for a kingdom. It was also a battle for the warrior's tormented mind.

Tentatively, Arjuna broke away from Krishna's gaze and surveyed the enemy lines. "The mind is restless, unsteady, turbulent, wild, stubborn," he said slowly, choosing words as carefully as he knew how. "Truly, it seems to me as hard to master as the wind."

Krishna did not reply for a long time. "You are right, Arjuna," he said at last. "The mind is restless and hard to master, but by constant practice and detachment it can be mastered in the end."[1]

2. NEW SPIRITUALITY: THE MODERN SEARCH FOR MYSTERY

Arjuna and Krishna's conversation comprises an epic poem: the Bhagavad Gita, "The Song of the Blessed One," written perhaps more than two thousand years ago and to this day a treasured stanza of the Mahabharata, India's national epic poem. Like many famous poems, the Bhagavad Gita is more than metered verse. It is a code, a set of carefully chosen words placed thoughtfully on the page so as to jar loose the reader's imagination and communicate what those who believe in it consider to be a deep, persuasive reality.

For thousands of years Hindus have studied the narrative of Arjuna and Krishna as a source of truth not only about the unseen universe but also about the duty of man. It is a vision of what actually exists, an eternal, nonpersonal, encompassing *all*, the *Self*, standing in stark contrast to the individualistic, autonomous self at the heart of the secular vision of the world.[2]

But the message of the Bhagavad Gita is not just a Hindu vision. Today its description of reality weaves loosely a pattern of ideas, beliefs, values, and convictions held by millions of Americans, most of whom have no historical connection to the long-held religious traditions undergirding their own playfully held creeds.

Whether frivolously or seriously, almost everyone searches for meaning. Unfortunately, the answers religion and science offer often seem unsatisfactory. In this chapter we will explore an ancient worldview masquerading as a new path for meaning on which the human race can travel to achieve true enlightenment. We call this worldview **New Spirituality**.

On the one hand, New Spirituality is hard to define because it lacks a definitive core of belief. Christians believe in the death and resurrection of Jesus.[3] Secularists trust the scientific method. Marxists think feeding resentment about capitalism will lead to the truth. Muslims consider the creed of Islam worth living and dying for. Postmodernists, who pride themselves on rejecting all other metanarratives, seem to think suspicion is a sufficiently large frame in which to hang other beliefs.

So what do New Spiritualists believe is a sufficient source of hope that both explains the world and forms the basis of the good life?

> *New Spirituality:* a pantheistic worldview that teaches everything and everyone are connected through divine consciousness.

3. EVERYTHING IS SPIRITUAL

Deepak Chopra, a self-proclaimed spiritual teacher, thinks the problems we face in our world are primarily spiritual. On this point Christians would agree. Second Corinthians 10:4 says, "The weapons of our warfare are not of the flesh but have divine power to destroy strongholds." In fact, Christians might even find Chopra's framing of our spiritual problems compelling:

> All around us people ache with emptiness and yearning; there's a vacuum to be filled, and it's a spiritual vacuum. What other word really fits? Only when people are given hope that this ache can be healed will we truly know what the future holds. Let science join in the cure, because otherwise, we may wind up with marvels of technology serving empty hearts and abandoned souls.[4]

What is the healing hope of which Chopra speaks? For a growing number of spiritual teachers, business consultants, bestselling authors, and television hosts, hope springs from rejecting traditional religion and embracing our divinity, power, and godlikeness. Only this will give us meaning. Only this will enable us to change the world. As Rhonda Byrne claimed in her mega-bestseller *The Secret*, "The Secret means that we are creators of our Universe, and that every wish that we want to create will manifest in our lives."[5]

> For a growing number of spiritual teachers, business consultants, bestselling authors, and television hosts, hope springs from rejecting traditional religion and embracing our divinity, power, and godlikeness.

What we call *New Spirituality* is often referred to as the New Age movement, transcendentalism, neo-paganism, new consciousness, or just "spirituality." Previous editions of *Understanding the Times* used the term *Cosmic Humanism.* Ken Wilber, a prolific author in the field, uses the term "the integral vision" to describe his efforts to create a "composite map" of understanding based on insights from all of the world's cultures and traditions.[6] As this particular worldview has changed in the last twenty years, though, we think the term *New Spirituality* best explains the way its answers to life's ultimate questions have captured the imaginations of tens of millions of Americans.

New Spirituality is based on a radically different vision of the world, of the nature and character of God, and of the purpose of human beings in this world and the next from the vision of traditional religions. Yet it often confuses Christians because of frequent positive references to God and Jesus Christ.[7] The growth of New Spirituality in the last several decades has resulted in many people being taken captive by its ideas. As thinking Christians, we must understand where it comes from, what answers it proposes to the mysteries of life, and how it frames a view of the world unique from the other worldviews considered in this book. Proverbs 15:28 says, "The heart of the righteous ponders how to answer." So let's get started doing just that.

4. WHERE DOES NEW SPIRITUALITY COME FROM, AND WHY SHOULD WE CARE?

Fans of the science-fiction film *The Matrix* will recall a memorable scene of Neo watching a boy in Buddhist robes sitting cross-legged on the floor, bending metal spoons simply by staring at them. The boy explains to Neo, "Don't try to bend the spoon. That's impossible. Instead, only try to realize the truth.... There is no spoon."

The boy's statement reflects a view of reality utterly at odds with Western thought: the physical world we perceive is an illusion where nothing is objective except our own mental states. "Larry" and Andy Wachowski wanted to play on this view of the world while writing and directing *The Matrix*: "One of the things that we had talked about when we first had the idea of *The Matrix* was an idea that [we] believe philosophy and religion and mathematics all try to answer ... a reconciling between a natural world and another world that is perceived by our intellect."[8]

These thoughts are not new, of course. Among the forefathers of contemporary New Spirituality are poets and writers from the 1800s, such as Ralph Waldo Emerson and Henry David Thoreau. These men rejected the God of the Bible and instead wrote at length about a transcendent quality of spirituality experienced purely through personal introspection. This idea, known as **transcendentalism**, saw human beings and nature as inherently good but corrupted by society. Institutions, such as organized religion and politics, for example, participated in this corruption (this idea will be explored more fully in the "Sociology" chapter of this volume). Transcendentalism gained more traction through the writings of Emily Dickinson and Walt Whitman, as well as the self-help teachings of Mary Baker Eddy, Wallace Wattles, and Napoleon Hill. In the 1960s, this "new thought" morphed into a *syncretistic* worldview, a merging of Eastern religion with pop psychology, self-help teaching, meditation, and health-and-wealth doctrines designed to answer life's most pressing questions.

Transcendentalism: a religious and philosophical movement that arose in the early 1800s as a reaction against rationalism and organized religion, it teaches that human beings are inherently good and that nature is fundamentally divine.

One of the early chroniclers of New Spirituality's development was Marilyn Ferguson, author of a 1980s volume called *The Aquarian Conspiracy*. Ferguson detailed the unexpected confluence of Eastern spiritual influences and fringe science that launched the careers of a thousand spiritual teachers, including Deepak Chopra. The book is said to have deeply inspired politician and futurist Al Gore.[9] Translated into sixteen languages and spawning dozens of copycat books, *The Aquarian Conspiracy* was clearly onto something.

New Spirituality exploded in the 1990s and found wide dissemination through movies, television, and book sales. *The Celestine Prophecy*, published in 1993, sold over eight million copies in more than thirty-two countries, achieving distinction as the bestselling American hardcover book for two consecutive years. Author James Redfield wrote in the 1997 afterword, "We are manifesting nothing less than a new world view that will flourish in the next millennium." Another "modern-day spiritual messenger" was Neale Donald Walsch, the author of fifteen books on spirituality and everyday life. His first five books in the Conversations with God series all made the *New York Times* bestseller list, with the first book remaining on the list for more than two years. His books have been translated into twenty-seven languages, selling more than seven million copies worldwide.

But the popularity of New Spirituality had not yet reached its apex. Rhonda Byrne's *The Secret* became an international sensation after its release in 2006, selling nineteen million copies and being translated into forty-six languages. *The Secret* offered its worldview to a popular audience on the scale of *The Purpose Driven Life* by Christian pastor and author Rick Warren.[10]

New Spirituality feeds off popular dissatisfaction with organized religion. Deepak Chopra, whose books and television appearances have made him a household name to hundreds of millions of people around the world, claims that science has advanced to the point where religion has been revealed as nothing more than primitive superstition. "Religion cannot resolve this dilemma [of the human condition]; it has had its chances already. But spirituality can," he claims. "We need to go back to the source of religion. That source isn't God. It's consciousness."[11]

However, even a worldview that shuns identifiable religious traditions might itself be religious. Remember, a religion is a set of beliefs about the cause, nature, and purpose of the universe. Advocates of New Spirituality, therefore, are—without question—religious.

Weary of religious conflict and dogmatism, more and more people find a spirituality stripped of religious dogma attractive. And *spirituality* sounds freeing and accepting; *religion*, on the other hand, seems judgmental and boring. It's common to hear, "I'm spiritual but not religious." To those raised in religious households, this sounds like a distinction without a difference. However, to Robert C. Fuller, professor of religious studies at Bradley University, the difference is very real. Most people loosely define *spirituality* as "a private realm of thought and expression," says Fuller, whereas religion focuses on the "public realm" of institutions, rituals, and doctrines. Around 20 percent of Americans claim the "spiritual, but not religious" designation and show "higher levels of interest in mysticism" while holding "negative feelings toward both clergy and churches."[12]

Spirituality enables people to be interested in what lies beyond without having to grasp finely textured doctrines or apologize for the historical abuses people associated with their tradition have carried out. Even among would-be Secularists, spirituality is cool. When

> Spirituality enables people to be interested in what lies beyond without having to grasp finely textured doctrines or apologize for the historical abuses people associated with their tradition have carried out. Even among would-be Secularists, spirituality is cool.

spirituality is considered an active search for meaning and purpose in life or as an inter-est in self-awareness and enlightenment, even 81 percent of college professors considered themselves spiritual, according to a study by UCLA.[13] Is this growing interest a scattershot phenomenon, with each adherent developing his or her own beliefs? Or is New Spirituality a truly identifiable and widespread worldview? Let's see if we can answer these questions by taking a look at New Spirituality's teachings.

5. WHAT DOES NEW SPIRITUALITY TEACH?

No worldview exists in which adherents agree on everything. However, their shared agreement on fundamental issues provides ways we can predict what advocates would believe and teach in such disciplines as theology, philosophy, and ethics. While there are minor differences in the teachings of New Spirituality advocates such as Deepak Chopra, Eckhart Tolle, Rhonda Byrne, the Dalai Lama, and others, they seem to adhere to four basic beliefs.

1. Everything is consciousness. Eckhart Tolle is one of the world's most popular spiritual teachers. His books have sold tens of millions of copies. In a 2011 list of the top one hundred spiritual teachers in the world, Tolle was listed as number one.[14] "The whole is made up of existence and Being, the manifested and the unmanifested, the whole and God," says Tolle. "So when you become aligned with the whole, you become a conscious part of the interconnectedness of the whole and its purpose: the emergence of consciousness into this world."[15]

Those accustomed to thinking of the world as being populated with objects and people, and people as identifiable individuals who think in personal pronouns of "I" or "me," have a difficult time understanding where New Spirituality advocates are coming from.

For many, the introduction to the idea of consciousness, energy, Being, and related concepts was not through self-help books but through George Lucas's now classic film series *Star Wars*. "With *Star Wars*, I consciously set about to re-create myths and the classic mythological motifs," said Lucas. "I wanted to use those motifs to deal with issues that exist today.... I see *Star Wars* as taking all the issues that religion represents and trying to distill them down into a more modern and easily accessible construct.... I'm telling an old myth in a new way."[16]

> For many, the introduction to the idea of consciousness, energy, Being, and related concepts was not through self-help books but through George Lucas's now classic film series *Star Wars*.

When Lucas's characters "feel the force," they're not sensing the power of the Holy Spirit. In describing the force to Luke Skywalker, Obi-Wan Kenobi said, "Well, the Force is what gives a Jedi his power. It's an energy field created by all living things. It surrounds us and penetrates us. It binds the galaxy together." This could also serve as a good description of the idea of consciousness Tolle and others embrace, and it seems Lucas was mindful of this connection and interested in promoting it. "I've always tried to be aware of what I say in my films, because all of us who make motion pictures are teachers," Lucas says, "teachers with very loud voices."[17]

Consciousness is usually defined in vague terms. Deepak Chopra, however, lists the fol-lowing qualities of "pure consciousness": silent and peaceful, self-sufficient, awake, possessing infinite potential, self-organizing, spontaneous, dynamic, blissful, knowing, and whole.[18] How Chopra knows this is unclear; it leads to as many questions as it answers.

For example, many of the qualities Chopra lists are personal—the sorts of attributes a person, rather than a mindless force, would possess. If consciousness is personal, it would actually describe a sort of God. In the end, though, Chopra and others see consciousness as an *impersonal* force. What makes an impersonal force personal? According to New Spirituality advocates, the answer is you and me. To New Spiritualists, "God" is personal only in that our God experiences are subjective and personal.

The Bible teaches something entirely different about God's nature and character. In Exodus 3:14, God said to Moses, "I Am who I Am." In other words, "I am complete in and of myself." It's a clear statement of self-determination. The apostle Paul further affirmed God's self-existence in his speech to a religious society in Athens: "The God who made the world and everything in it, being Lord of heaven and earth, does not live in temples made by man, nor is he served by human hands, as though he needed anything, since he himself gives to all mankind life and breath and everything" (Acts 17:24–25). God is, as Christian philosopher Francis Schaeffer phrased it, "infinite-personal." This teaching has no part in New Spiritualist thinking.[19] If everything is **collective consciousness**, then ultimately everything is God. This brings us to the second core of New Spiritualist belief.

2. Every person is God. According to New Spiritualists, all is consciousness. Human beings, like all things, are part of this consciousness. We are not individuals in the normal Western sense of the term.

This aspect of New Spirituality has a long tradition among a particular group of Buddhists called Middle Way Consequentialists. Middle Way Consequentialists, who include the revered Tibetan Buddhist Dalai Lama, reject the existence of objective reality. What about a chair, for example, actually constitutes "chairness"? If we look at its individual parts, no chair is there. The chair isn't in the wood or in the varnish or even in the shape. The quality of chairness is a mental construction. This particular school of Buddhism applies this way of thinking to human beings. The Dalai Lama says, "Just as there is no chair to be found among its parts and no rose to be found among its petals, so there is no person to be found among its constituent aspects of body and mind."[20] He continues,

> Each of the physical and mental parts of which I am composed is similarly empty of any identifiable existence.... Our initial reaction to recognizing that things do not possess objective or inherent existence is understandably one of surprise. We are discovering that the actual way things exist is so very contrary to how we naturally relate to them.[21]

This way of thinking only makes sense if we view consciousness as what is actually real, and objects and people as separate and distinct things only because we are unable to view them in their "energy" state.

As you can imagine, scientists who make their living identifying, classifying, and measuring objects in the physical world disagree. Deepak Chopra, however, warns, "It is shortsighted

> *Consciousness:* the belief in a divine interconnected essence of reality.

to believe that because science today cannot explain consciousness, consciousness must lie beyond science's reach. But even if the origin of consciousness is too complex to be fully grasped by the human mind, that is not evidence that consciousness resides in a supernatural realm. In fact, though the question of how consciousness arises remains a puzzle, we have plenty of evidence that consciousness functions according to physical law."[22] To Chopra, even God is not necessary: "All we need is a universe that contains consciousness as an inseparable aspect of itself."[23]

But if everything is consciousness, and we call this consciousness "God," then God is not a separate person with identifiable attributes, as Christianity claims. The New Spiritualist "God" is actually a "god"—a force, a principle, a vibration, light and sound—not a thinking, willing, feeling being. God is consciousness, New Spiritualists say, and the better we understand consciousness, the clearer our godlikeness will be to us. "Each of us has access to a supra-conscious, creative, integrative, self-organizing, intuitive mind whose capabilities are apparently unlimited," said John Bradshaw. "This is the part of our consciousness that constitutes our God-likeness."[24] One New Spiritualist, Ruth Montgomery, supposedly channeled a spirit that spoke through her, claiming, "We are as much God as God is a part of us.... If each of us is God, then ... together we are God.... This all-for-one-and-one-for-all ... makes us the whole of ... God."[25] New Spirituality theologian John White states that "sooner or later every human being will feel a call from the cosmos to ascend to godhood."[26]

> **I am god. You are god Every person is god. This is what New Spirituality claims.**

I am god. You are god. Every person is god. This is what New Spirituality claims. Meher Baba declared, "There is only one question. And once you know the answer to that question there are no more to ask.... Who am I? [A]nd to that Question there is only one Answer—I am God!"[27] Shirley MacLaine, a movie actress and spiritual teacher, recommends beginning each day by affirming one's own godhood. "You can use I am God or I am that I am as Christ often did, or you can extend the affirmation to fit your own needs."[28]

Today, theologians and philosophers use the word *pantheism* to describe this belief. *Pan* means "all" and *theos* means "God." Pantheists believe "all is God." It's an accurate description of the theology of New Spirituality, as we will see in the "Theology" chapter of this volume.

> **Pantheism: the belief that everything in the universe is ultimately divine.**

3. Consciousness can be harnessed to achieve perfection. Eckhart Tolle's book *A New Earth* soared to prominence as one of Oprah Winfrey's book club recommendations. Hundreds of thousands of people bought it and recommended it to others. According to Tolle, the biblical prophecy of a new heaven and a new earth will be fulfilled as more people harness the power of consciousness. "The new earth arises as more and more people discover that their main purpose in life is to bring the light of consciousness into this world and so use whatever they do as a vehicle for consciousness," he says.[29]

One popular way of describing the power of consciousness is the "law of attraction." Remember that for New Spirituality advocates, "everything is energy."[30] Things are energy.

Thoughts are energy. Good thoughts produce good energy and bad thoughts inhibit it. As Rhonda Byrne says in *The Secret*, "Your thoughts become the things in your life,"[31] and "Your transmission creates your life and it creates the world."[32]

New Spirituality advocates often point to Jesus as an example of how to tap into the energy field called consciousness. As John White asserted, "The Son of God … is not Jesus but our combined Christ consciousness."[33] Jesus is looked on as one of a select company, having achieved Christ consciousness. Every person is encouraged to acquire this same level of consciousness.

New Spirituality sees Christ's life as important because it showed humanity how to achieve perfection, even godhood. John White states, "The significance of incarnation and resurrection is not that Jesus was a human like us but rather that we are gods like him—or at least have the potential to be."[34] If Jesus is just an example, not a savior, then the Bible's description of his life, death, and resurrection, and indeed his entire purpose as savior, is either wrong or irrelevant.

4. The purpose of life is overcoming "self." Although Secularism and New Spirituality both use the term *self*, they mean something entirely different. To the Secularist, the "self," or the self-aware individual, is the basic unit of human life.[35] To New Spiritualists from a Buddhist tradition, we must be rid of any sense of the self. The self does not exist. To New Spiritualists from some Hindu traditions, the "self" must be lost in the Universal Self (called *Brahman*) in order to have meaning. In the Bhagavad Gita, Krishna says, "He who has let go of hatred, who treats all beings with kindness and compassion, who is always serene, unmoved by pain or pleasure, free of the 'I' and 'mine,' self-controlled, firm and patient, his whole mind is focused on me—that man is the one I love best."[36]

> If Jesus is just an example, not a savior, then the Bible's description of his life, death, and resurrection, and indeed entire purpose as savior, is either wrong or irrelevant.

But how do we free ourselves from "I" and "me" and from selfishness and ego? The answer, from the perspective of New Spirituality, is twofold. First, people can free themselves daily and temporarily through such practices as yoga and meditation. Second, New Spiritualists believe people can be free forever through *reincarnation*: living their lives, dying, and being reborn until they gradually become more enlightened. The Dalai Lama says, "The root cause of our unenlightened existence within this cycle of rebirths—*samsara* in Sanskrit—is said to be our fundamental ignorance: our grasping at a sense of self."[37]

Between Buddhism and Hinduism, and even within various traditions in Buddhism, there are differences in understanding and defining reincarnation. For the purposes of this chapter, it is enough to understand reincarnation as the process by which the body passes away but the soul continues its quest for enlightenment in other forms. It can be a very confusing thing to understand, even for those who firmly believe it. The actress Shirley MacLaine, recalling the birth of her daughter, mused, "When the doctor brought her to me in the hospital bed on that afternoon in 1956, had she already lived many, many times before, with other mothers? Had she, in fact, been one herself? Had she, in fact, ever been my mother? Was her one-hour-old face housing a soul perhaps millions of years old?"[38]

An additional question MacLaine should have asked is, "How would my *daughter* know the answers to these questions?" Because if her birth was actually a rebirth, and she did not know this, how could she ever live her life differently so as to move toward greater enlightenment? To answer this question rather than believe in a God who sets the rules and judges people accordingly, believers in reincarnation place their faith in **karma**, which is a law of causality that says, very basically, good is returned to those who do good, and evil is returned to those who do evil.[39] In each successive lifetime, then, a person must pay off his or her past karmic failings, suffering for and learning from past evils. Chief among these failings is seeing ourselves as individuals. This separates us from the consciousness of the universe.

> *Karma:* a concept found in Eastern religions, karma is the belief that good is returned to those who do good, and evil is returned to those who do evil (either in this life or the next).

In order to understand themselves (and their paths to godhood), people must be cognizant of at least some of their past lives. Gary Zukav explains: "If your soul was a Roman centurion, an Indian beggar, a Mexican mother, a nomad boy, and a medieval nun, among other incarnations, for example, ... you will not be able to understand your proclivities, or interests, or ways of responding to different situations without an awareness of the experiences of those lifetimes."[40] Reincarnation can serve little purpose unless people can know about and learn from their past lives.

It is unclear, however, how if at all this awareness of previous lives takes place. It is also unclear how we became separated from the oneness of the universe in the first place. Unless our individual souls are somehow eternal, there must have been a *first* incarnation. But in this first life, there could not have been any previous lives in which to collect karmic debts. How, then, did we fall into individualism? New Spiritualists rarely address these questions, except to suggest that we ask them because we are not sufficiently enlightened not to.

> *Nirvana:* a concept found in Indian religions, nirvana is the transcendent state of ultimate peace and highest happiness achieved through one's release from the bondages of karma, suffering, worldly desire, and individual consciousness.

In any event, the end goal of reincarnation is to be completely cleansed of karmic debt, thereby losing individuality altogether in order to melt into the stream of consciousness. In Buddhism, the word *dukkha* means "suffering." The actual state of the final cessation of suffering is called **nirvana**. The Dalai Lama says, "Our pursuit of this peaceful state of nirvana is a quest for protection from the misery of samsara [cycle of rebirths], and particularly from the afflictions such as attachment and aversion that bind us within the vicious cycle of rebirths."[41]

6. NEW SPIRITUALITY AS A WORLDVIEW

As we can see so far, New Spirituality proposes answers to many of life's questions, though not necessarily coherent ones. New Spirituality proposes a theology ("God" is not a person but a force), a philosophy (we can gain wisdom by getting in touch with our God nature), an ethic (we can live best by avoiding those actions that would condemn us to more miserable future lives), a biology (a view of what "life" is—consciousness, the universal mind, and so forth), and a psychology (we can live in greater mental health if we are cleansed of ego).[42] As we will see throughout this book, from these starting points New Spiritualists propose what kind of society we should have, how laws should be structured, which political system is ideal, which economic system will produce wealth, how the flow of history has led us to this place, and where we should go next.

As with the other worldviews we've explored, let's see if we can get a sense of New Spirituality's understanding of both (1) general revelation, or what can be known and is obvious to all, and (2) special revelation, or what must be specially revealed to us, since it cannot be figured out.

7. GENERAL REVELATION: SCIENCE AND NEW SPIRITUALITY

Science is focused on observing and explaining the physical universe. Christians see the scientific method as a way of discovering God's design of the universe. Secularists view science as a means for understanding the mechanics of the natural world. New Spiritualists, however, have an odd relationship with science. In their view, science has been primarily an attempt to control nature for the benefit of human beings and has therefore been a destructive enterprise. A proper view of science, they argue, would lead to a better understanding of consciousness and a more harmonious relationship between human beings and planet Earth.

To begin with, New Spiritualists dispense with the need for a first cause (God) by claiming the universe was uncaused. As the Dalai Lama expresses it,

> From a Buddhist point of view, the continuum of substantial causes preceding our conception can be traced back to before the Big Bang, to when the universe was a void. Actually, if we follow the line of reasoning by which we trace our continuum back to before the Big Bang, we would have to acknowledge that there could not be a first moment to the continuum of substantial causes of any conditioned phenomenon.[43]

In other words, the universe is eternal. It has no cause or beginning. There is no point in looking for either.

The search for a cause of nature or the beginning of the universe has been fruitless, say New Spiritualists, because it has proceeded from wrong assumptions. Based on a Christian conception of God, says Marilyn Ferguson, early scientists like Isaac Newton saw the universe as a finely tuned machine and hoped to "finally explain everything in terms of trajectories, gravity, force. It would close in on the final secrets of a 'clockwork universe.' "[44]

But, say New Spiritualists, the idea of a mechanistic universe failed to explain the universe as we now know it. Quantum physics stepped into the gap, though. The father of quantum theory, Max Planck, proposed that "matter absorbed heat energy and emitted light energy discontinuously" in energy packets, which Albert Einstein called "quanta."[45] The behavior of matter, according to quantum theory, cannot be neatly predicted or slotted into mechanistic categories. The universe is more mysterious than we imagined, and this, to

New Spiritualists, affirms the power of human consciousness to shape the universe rather than merely obey its laws. As the physics professor in James Redfield's novel *The Celestine Prophecy* phrases it,

> The whole of Einstein's life's work was to show that what we perceive as hard matter is mostly empty space with a pattern of energy running through it. This includes ourselves. And what quantum physics has shown is that ... when you break apart small aspects of this energy ... the act of observation itself alters the results—as if these elementary particles are influenced by what the experimenter expects.... In other words, the basic stuff of the universe, at its core, is looking like a kind of pure energy that is malleable to human intention and expectation in a way that defies our old mechanistic model of the universe.[46]

Humans can shape the universe? This would indeed upset the apple cart of science. With these discoveries, says Marilyn Ferguson, "Our understanding of nature shifted from a clockwork paradigm to an uncertainty paradigm, from the absolute to the relative."[47] In other words, Ferguson believes, the latest scientific discoveries support New Spirituality beliefs.

The shift to this questionable new view of science is imperative, according to New Spirituality advocates, because the desire to control nature has placed our planet in deep peril. According to William Thompson, "The emergence of a scientific culture stimulates the destruction of nature, of the biosphere of relationships among plants, animals, and humans that we have called 'Nature.'"[48]

In 1979, scientist James Lovelock's book *Gaia: A New Look at Life on Earth* breathed life into New Spirituality's fringe approach to science. Lovelock said, "Taken as a whole, the planet behaves not as an inanimate sphere of rock and soil ... but more as a biological superorganism—a planetary body—that adjusts and regulates itself."[49] Lovelock drew the name *Gaia* from the ancient Greek goddess of the earth. Although he considers himself a "positive agnostic" and has tried to distance his theory from any religious connotations, New Spiritualists immediately promoted Lovelock's theory as scientific support for their worldview.

Gaia Hypothesis: postulated by James Lovelock, the Gaia hypothesis is the theory that all living organisms form a collective, self-regulating living entity.

The idea that a symbiotic global network of consciousness, which all living things and planetary systems share, departs radically from the idea that evolution occurs through random-chance processes and the survival of the fittest. The **Gaia hypothesis** emphasizes the cooperative spirit of the entire biosphere. The earth is not a "dead" habitat that happens to support life, Lovelock asserts, but a living, integrated system of soil, oceans, wind, and living things working together in harmony for the good of the whole.

The Gaia hypothesis visualizes the planet as a self-regulating system, implying purpose behind it all. While this may sound like intelligent design, an idea of great interest to Christians, New Spiritualists deny an intelligent, personal *designer*. To them, consciousness was a feature of the universe before the universe itself even existed. There is no "who" behind the "what."

Lovelock's vivid description of Gaia provided a spiritual basis for the modern ecological movement as well as the more radical offshoots of **ecofeminism** (the linking of feminism and ecology to fight male domination, which proponents say oppresses women and exploits the planet's resources) and **deep ecology** (the call for a radical restructuring of society based on the idea that all living things, not just human beings, should have legal rights).[50] Many ecologists, pointing to signs of ecological imbalance, say we should be paying closer attention to our mother—Mother Earth—or Gaia. Saving the planet is more than a moral imperative. It is our destiny.

8. Special Revelation: How New Spiritualists Answer the Ultimate Questions

Many have asked, "How do we know our assertions about the nature of reality are actually true?" But few New Spirituality teachers attempt to prove anything at all. True, some refer to quantum physics and the mysteries of the universe, but usually by way of creating room for the possibility of their beliefs as opposed to positively grounding them in truth. It is enough for many New Spiritualists that they are in touch with a higher consciousness; they believe their inner soul searching is the only proof their arguments need.

In light of this, let's answer the five questions we've focused on with each of the worldviews we've considered:

> *Ecofeminism:* a political philosophy that links the oppression of women and the exploitation of the environment with the values inherent in what advocates refer to as Western patriarchal society.

> *Deep Ecology:* an environmental philosophy based on the idea that all living beings form a spiritual and ecologically interconnected system, which is presently threatened by the harmful impact of human beings; a philosophy that advocates a radical restructuring of society toward environmental preservation, simple living, legal rights for all living creatures, and a reduction in the human population.

1. On what sources of revelation does New Spirituality draw?
2. What does New Spirituality say about humanity?
3. What does New Spirituality say is wrong with us?
4. What does New Spirituality say about how we should live?
5. How are we to understand other worldviews based on New Spirituality?

1. On what sources of revelation does New Spirituality draw? New Spirituality begins by denying the preeminence of any purported special revelation over any other. That is, New Spiritualists believe the Bible is no more a word from God than the Quran or the teachings of Confucius. This is not to say they are held in equally high regard. New Age advocate David Spangler says, "We can take all the scriptures, and all the teachings, and all the tablets, and all the laws, and all the marshmallows and have a jolly good bonfire and marshmallow roast, because that is all they are worth."[51]

So if there are no scriptures, what should we trust? Rhonda Byrne says simply, "Trust the Universe. Trust and believe and have faith."[52] She continues, "The truth is that the Universe has been answering you all of your life, but you cannot receive the answers unless you are aware."[53] The need is not for scripture but for awareness. But how do we achieve this awareness?

> *Meditation:* the art of focusing one's mind to induce a higher state of consciousness.

Meditation, sometimes with crystals or mantras, is often the method used to achieve a higher consciousness. A writer in *Life Times* magazine states emphatically, "My message to everyone now is to learn to meditate. It was through meditation that many other blessings came about."[54]

> *Channeling:* the practice of communicating with disembodied spirits through a medium.

Another method is **channeling**, which refers to the controversial New Spiritualist belief that disembodied spirits presumably speak to and through a gifted person engaged in meditation. These spirits, it's assumed, have greater awareness of consciousness because they are not limited by an attachment to a finite body. Elena, a spirit John Randolph Price allegedly channeled, describes beings like herself as "angels of light—whether from earth or other worlds. They search, select and guide those men and women who may be suitable subjects."[55] While all New Spiritualists embrace meditation as an important tool for attaining higher consciousness, not all New Spiritualists embrace channeling.[56]

Many New Spiritualists also point to near-death or out-of-body experiences as evidence that their understanding of the true nature of reality is correct. Raymond Moody, Kenneth Ring, and Melvin Morse are among the writers who claim that such experiences not only verify the existence of consciousness beyond the grave but more specifically the nature of spiritual experiences as described in other New Spiritualist writings.[57]

Other practices New Spiritualists use include astrology, fire walking, Ouija boards, crystal therapy, and aura readings. From a Christian viewpoint, these are occult practices condemned in Scripture (Deut. 18:9–14 and Rev. 22:15),[58] but to New Spiritualists, such practices provide useful insight into the nature of consciousness.

2. What does New Spirituality say about humanity? For Gary Zukav, consciousness, not individual existence, is our ultimate nature as human beings:

> All that is can form itself into individual droplets of consciousness. Because you are part of All that is, you have literally always been, yet there was the instant when that individual energy current that is you was formed. Consider that the ocean is God. It has always been. Now reach in and grab a cup full of water. In that instant, the cup becomes individual, but it has always been, has it not? This is the case with your soul. There was the instant when you became a cup of energy, but it was of an immortal original Being. You have always been because what it is that you are is God, or Divine Intelligence, but God takes on individual forms, droplets, reducing its power to small particles of individual consciousness.[59]

Eckhart Tolle affirms this view when he refers to the consciousness of the universe as "Presence" (capital *P*). All life forms, Tolle says, are "temporary manifestations of the underlying one Life, one Consciousness."[60] All spiritual forces are "preparing the ground for a more profound shift in planetary consciousness that is destined to take place in the human species. This is the spiritual awakening that we are beginning to witness now."[61]

For New Spiritualists, all knowledge exists in the godlikeness within us. If we connect with a higher consciousness, we transcend the limitations our physical existence imposes on us. Jack Underhill explained what would happen if everyone in the world were to connect with his or her godhood:

> For New Spiritualists, all knowledge exists in the godlikeness within us. If we connect with a higher consciousness, we transcend the limitations our physical existence imposes on us.

> They can turn off the sun and turn it back on. They can freeze oceans into ice, turn the air into gold, talk as one with no movement or sound. They can fly without wings and love without pain, cure with no more than a thought or a smile. They can make the earth go backwards or bounce up and down, crack it in half or shift it around.... There is nothing they cannot do.[62]

This very high view of human potential is a consistent feature in New Spirituality writings. Rhonda Byrne says,

> You are God in a physical body. You are Spirit in the flesh. You are Eternal Life expressing itself as You. You are a cosmic being. You are all power. You are all wisdom. You are all intelligence. You are perfection. You are magnificence. You are the creator, and you are creating the creation of You on this planet.[63]

3. What does New Spirituality say is wrong with us? The very high view New Spiritualists have of human potential is at odds with the traditional idea of human sinfulness expressed in Romans 3:23: "All have sinned and fall short of the glory of God." To Deepak Chopra, one benefit of the theory of evolution is to serve as "a blow against sin, the 'human stain' that could be atoned for but would always return. Evolution opened a way to escape the trap of sin by offering hope for progress in all aspects of life, although it took a long time for such a humane implication to strike home."[64] Chopra's understanding of evolution is at extreme odds with the common view among scientists (that evolution is mindless and material, and not intentionally moving in any particular direction), but what it means scientifically does not seem to be as important to him as how useful it appears in counteracting the Christian conception of the sin nature.

The real "sin" in New Spirituality, if there is such a thing, is failing to understand the true nature of consciousness. Eckhart Tolle says human beings have an "inherited dysfunction," a collective mental illness that creates suffering.[65] "You do not become good by trying to be good, but by finding the goodness that is already within you, and allowing that goodness to

> The real "sin" in New Spirituality, if there is such a thing, is failing to understand the true nature of consciousness.

emerge," he says. "But it can only emerge if something fundamental changes in your state of consciousness."[66] .

Tolle refers to this inherited dysfunction as "ego." It is a negative inner state that makes us miserable and prevents our spiritual growth from producing true health and understanding. It is possible to rid ourselves of it, Tolle writes: "To end the misery that has afflicted the human condition for thousands of years, you have to start with yourself and take responsibility for your inner state at any given moment. That means now. Ask yourself, 'Is there negativity in me at this moment?' "[67]

But if the individual's problem is negativity, and if society's problem is also negativity, how might society change? New Spirituality advocates say we need mass consciousness. Beverly Galyean says,

> Once we begin to see that we are all God, that we all have the attributes of God, then I think the whole purpose of human life is to reown the Godlikeness within us; the perfect love, the perfect wisdom, the perfect understanding, the perfect intelligence, and when we do that, we create back to that old, that essential oneness which is consciousness.[68]

Robert Muller says, "Only the unity of all can bring the well-being of all."[69] The founder of Transcendental Meditation (TM), Maharishi Mahesh Yogi, believed in gathering large groups for meditation for the purpose of decreasing violent crime, warfare, and terrorism. His followers call it the *Maharishi Effect* or *Super Radiance*.[70]

4. What does New Spirituality say about how we should live? The ideas of consciousness and godlikeness radically change how people live. As we saw in the Bhagavad Gita, and as is common in New Spiritualist writings, indifference to suffering is the basis of a good life. Love and compassion actually make the problem worse; they bind us to pain and suffering, prolonging negativity, individualism, and ego.

In contrast, Christianity teaches that we are obligated to help people in need. Proverbs 24:11–12 says, "Rescue those who are being taken away to death; hold back those who are stumbling to the slaughter. If you say, 'Behold, we did not know this,' does not he who weighs the heart perceive it? Does not he who keeps watch over your soul know it, and will he not repay man according to his work?" James 4:17 affirms, "Whoever knows the right thing to do and fails to do it, for him it is sin."

The law of karma, though, produces a very different response from the biblical injunction. If a person's misery helps cleanse him or her of negative karma, should we help alleviate his or her suffering? Wouldn't this stop short the cleansing process? The traditional Hindu resistance to interfering with someone else's karma kept Hindus from helping the sick or improving the lives of the downtrodden. Jesus, on the other hand, illustrated the idea of loving one's neighbor through the parable of the good Samaritan, and he even denied that sin is the sole cause of sickness (John 9:1–5).

> The traditional Hindu resistance to interfering with someone else's karma kept Hindus from helping the sick or improving the lives of the downtrodden.

Combined with a vision of human beings as God's image bearers, these beliefs led Christians to show compassion for the sick, the poor, and the needy.

These biblical teachings are in part what pricked the conscience of the revered Mahatma Gandhi, a Hindu and humanitarian who was concerned with the needs of the poor. Gandhi said it was Christian missionaries—not fellow Hindus—who "awakened in him a revulsion for the caste system and for the maltreatment of outcastes."[71] He acted *inconsistently* with his Hindu presuppositions and instead incorporated a biblical system of ethics.

According to New Spirituality, then, if something is wrong, it is because you will it so; if you're sick, it is because you want to be sick; if you're poor, it's because you want to be poor; if you get in an accident, it is because you wanted to be hurt. The way forward is to rid yourself of negativity, individualism, and ego. Rhonda Byrne states it emphatically: "You cannot 'catch' anything unless you think you can, and thinking you can is inviting it to you with your thought."[72] Aloofness to the human plight, not compassion or salvation, is the New Spiritualist approach.

5. How are we to understand other worldviews based on New Spirituality? New Spiritualists teach that all religions are alike in what really matters.[73] This wishful thinking is popular today. Perhaps you've heard, "We're really all saying the same thing; what is all the fighting about?"

Many people are unaware that in expressing this belief, they have been influenced by the compelling work of professor and writer Joseph Campbell, who rose to popularity through a film series and a book titled *The Power of Myth*. In *The Hero with a Thousand Faces* (1949), Campbell discussed the **monomyth** cycle of the hero's journey, a pattern, he claims, found in many cultures. The monomyth involves the hero receiving a "call to adventure" and passing "threshold guardians" (often with the aid of a wise mentor or spirit guide) before entering a dream-like world. There, after a series of trials, the hero achieves the object of his quest—often an atonement with the father, a sacred marriage, or an apotheosis (elevation to divine status). He then returns home.[74]

> *Monomyth:* **popularized by Joseph Campbell, a monomyth is the theory that cultures throughout time have shared a common theme within their popular stories— the "hero's journey," which unfolds in three distinct acts: the hero's departure, initiation, and triumphant return.**

For Campbell, almost all hero myths—religious and secular, throughout history and across cultures—contained at least a subset of these patterns. Thus, all religions told the same story. As you can imagine, Campbell's work has been profoundly influential in Hollywood among those who want to tap in to filmgoers' deep beliefs in order to give the stories true staying power.

Still, despite the commitment to radical pluralism, New Spiritualists can be quite critical of religion, especially those beliefs that focus on sin and salvation. Any such approach is "utopian," according to Eckhart Tolle, and it just makes the problem worse: "At the core of all utopian visions lies one of the main structural dysfunctions of the old consciousness: looking to the future for salvation. The only existence the future actually has is as a thought form in your mind, so when you look to the future for salvation, you are unconsciously looking to your own mind for salvation. You are trapped in form, and that is ego."[75]

In the end, in spite of its attempts at transcending differences in order to pursue mass consciousness, New Spirituality does try to argue the shortcomings of other worldviews. We've already covered New Spirituality's criticism of Christianity's emphasis on sin and salvation. What are its criticisms of other worldviews?

Secularism. According to the Bhagavad Gita, Secularism is demonic. One refrain addresses it specifically:

> They say that life is an accident caused by sexual desire,
> that the universe has no moral order, no truth, no God.
>
> Clinging to this stupid belief, drawn into cruelty and malice,
> they become lost souls and, at last, enemies of the whole world.
>
> Driven by insatiable lusts, drunk on the arrogance of power,
> hypocritical, deluded, their actions foul with self-seeking.
>
> Tormented by a vast anxiety that continues until their death,
> convinced that the gratification of desire is life's sole aim,
>
> Bound by a hundred shackles of hope, enslaved by their greed,
> they squander their time dishonestly piling up mountains of wealth.[76]

As you might expect, people who believe in consciousness as ultimate reality reject the idea that the human brain is, in the words of artificial-intelligence pioneer Marvin Minsky, "just a computer that happens to be made out of meat."[77] Deepak Chopra considers such blatant Secularism to be no better than the religious systems he rejects: "I am less concerned with attacks on God than I am with a far more insidious danger: the superstition of materialism."[78] He's right to be concerned. If, as the Secularist claims, materialism (only matter exists) and naturalism (everything has a natural explanation) are correct, then New Spirituality is untrue by definition.

Marxism. As we discussed earlier, Eckhart Tolle sees humans as cursed with an "inherited dysfunction," a collective mental illness that creates suffering.[79] When people try to change the world without first changing their state of consciousness, it always ends in disaster:

> The history of Communism, originally inspired by noble ideals, clearly illustrates what happens when people attempt to change external reality—create a new earth—without any prior change in their inner reality, their state of consciousness. They make plans without taking into account the blueprint for dysfunction that every human being carries within: the ego.[80]

Utopian visions will always fail, according to New Spirituality, if they attempt to succeed by changing physical structures. Remember, New Spirituality's ultimate reality is consciousness. Ignore this and you'll be wrong about everything else.

Islam. Although New Spiritualists claim to be aloof to both pain and pleasure, some spiritual teachers cannot help but notice that very old cultures, such as Islam, seem to thrive by inflicting pain on others. Tolle's explanation for this is as follows: "Because of the human tendency to perpetuate old emotion, almost everyone carries in his or her energy field an accumulation of old emotional pain, which I call 'the pain-body.' "[81] Tolle says, "In some nations, for example, in the Middle East, the collective pain-body is so acute that a significant part of the population finds itself forced to act it out in an endless and insane cycle of perpetration and retribution through which the pain-body renews itself continuously."[82]

Until Islam releases its need to be right, to proclaim absolute truth, and to attempt to cause others to fall in line with its presuppositions, New Spiritualists think it will be part of the problem rather than part of the solution. Some New Spiritualists committed to finding the common core in all religions turn to a twelfth-century Islamic teacher named Averroes (also called Ibn Rushd), whose teachings are carried on today in the writing and speaking of followers of Sufism, a mystical cult of Islam. But such thinking is confined to a tiny percentage of Muslims, and the Muslim community at large generally disdains its adherents.

9. CONCLUSION

New Spirituality is an identifiable pattern of ideas, beliefs, values, and convictions. Despite New Spirituality's shaky science, unwillingness to provide evidence for its claims, indifference to the human condition, and an often muddled and insubstantial basis for belief, tens of millions of people in America and hundreds of millions around the world embrace this worldview and its answers to life's ultimate questions. New Spirituality can be found all around us: in movies and music, on television, in our neighborhoods, and in our schools.

Although it stands in direct contrast to the Christian worldview in many ways, New Spirituality catches many Christians off guard through its constant references to God and Jesus Christ as a teacher of consciousness and an example of what we all have the potential to become. Christianity, in contrast, is not about needing a teacher or example. It is about our need, as sinners guilty before God, for a savior. The gospel of John records a conversation in which Jesus told his disciples, "I am the way, and the truth, and the life. No one comes to the Father except through me" (14:6). Confused, one of Jesus's disciples, Philip, replied, "Lord, show us the Father." In response, Jesus said, "Truly, truly, I say to you, whoever believes in me will also do the works that I do; and greater works than these will he do, because I am going to the Father. Whatever you ask in my name, this I will do, that the Father may be glorified in the Son" (vv. 12–13). Only when we acknowledge Jesus as savior will we find our true calling as ambassadors of truth, grace, love, and compassion in a hurting world.

> Although it stands in direct contrast to the Christian worldview in many ways, New Spirituality catches many Christians off guard through its constant references to God and Jesus Christ as a teacher of consciousness and an example of what we all have the potential to become.

ENDNOTES

1. Adapted from *Bhagavad Gita*, trans. Stephen Mitchell (New York: Three Rivers, 2000).

2. Hinduism is actually a religious culture that, according to Taylor University professor of philosophy and religion Winfried Corduan, "has moved back and forth through various phases of monotheism, henotheism, polytheism and animism, with each stage retaining at least a vestigial presence in the ensuing one. There is no set of core beliefs that remain constant throughout. The name itself, actually a label devised by Westerners, simply means 'the religion of India.'" Winfried Corduan, *Neighboring Faiths: A Christian Introduction to World Religions* (Downers Grove, IL: IVP Academic, 2012), 267. See also R. C. Zaehner, *Hinduism* (New York: Oxford University Press, 1983). Hinduism is primarily spread today through the practice of yoga, a meditational exercise. Whether this is harmful or not is the subject of much debate in the Christian community. For more information, see Albert Mohler's podcast "The Meaning of Yoga: A Conversation with Stephanie Syman and Doug Groothuis," "Thinking in Public," September 20, 2010, www.albertmohler.com/2010/09/20/the-meaning-of-yoga-a-conversation-with-stephanie-syman-and-doug-groothuis/.

3. First Corinthians 15:3–4: "I delivered to you as of first importance what I also received: that Christ died for our sins in accordance with the Scriptures, that he was buried, that he was raised on the third day in accordance with the Scriptures"; 1 Corinthians 15:14: "If Christ has not been raised, then our preaching is in vain and your faith is in vain"; 1 Corinthians 15:17–19: "If Christ has not been raised, your faith is futile and you are still in your sins. Then those also who have fallen asleep in Christ have perished. If in Christ we have hope in this life only, we are of all people most to be pitied."

4. Deepak Chopra and Leonard Mlodinow, *War of the Worldviews: Where Science and Spirituality Meet—and Do Not* (New York: Three Rivers, 2011), 304.

5. Rhonda Byrne, *The Secret* (New York: Atria Books, 2006), 113.

6. See Ken Wilber, *The Integral Vision: A Very Short Introduction to the Revolutionary Integral Approach to Life, God, the Universe, and Everything* (Boston: Shambhala, 2007).

7. New Spiritualist writers often refer to Jesus in a very positive but unbiblical way. Most see Jesus as a good man who managed to transcend ego and thus serves as an example worth following. Others refer to "Christ consciousness" as what made Jesus unique and as something we may also attain through various New Spiritualist practices. For more information see Douglas Groothuis, *Jesus in an Age of Controversy* (Eugene, OR: Wipf and Stock, 2002).

8. Fan interview with Larry and Andy Wachowski, "Wachowski Brothers Chat Transcript," MatrixFans.net, November 6, 1999, www.matrixfans.net/miscellaneous/wachowski-brothers-chat-transcript/#sthash.q4ohMZGm.dpbs.

9. The extent of Marilyn Ferguson's influence on Al Gore is unclear, but it is widely known that he was a fan of the book and invited Ferguson to visit the White House while he was vice president.

10. Rick Warren is a pastor and author in California whose book *The Purpose Driven Life* became a sensation, selling approximately thirty million copies and becoming one of the bestselling nonfiction books of all time.

11. Chopra and Mlodinow, *War of the Worldviews*, 6.

12. Robert C. Fuller, *Spiritual, but Not Religious* (New York: Oxford University Press, 2001), 5–6.

13. Alexander W. Astin et al., *Spirituality and the Professoriate: A National Study of Faculty Beliefs, Attitudes, and Behaviors* (Los Angeles, CA: Higher Education Research Institute, 2005).

14. "The Watkins Review Announces Its Spiritual 100 List," Market Wired, March 29, 2011, accessed February 10, 2016, www.marketwire.com/press-release/The-Watkins-Review-Announces-Its-Spiritual-100-List-1418721.htm.

15. Eckhart Tolle, *A New Earth: Awakening to Your Life's Purpose* (New York: Plume, 2005), 277.

16. Bill Moyers, "Cinema: Of Myth and Men; A Conversation between Bill Moyers and George Lucas," *Time*, April 26, 1999, 92.

17. Quote attributed to George Lucas, in "George Lucas: Heroes, Myths, and Magic," American Masters, January 13, 2004, www.pbs.org/wnet/americanmasters/database/lucas_g.html.

18. Chopra and Mlodinow, *War of the Worldviews*, 264–65.

19. For more on Schaeffer's thoughts on God's nature, see *He Is There and He Is Not Silent*, one of the books in The Francis A. Schaeffer Trilogy (Wheaton, IL: Crossway Books, 1990), 290.

20. The Dalai Lama, *A Profound Mind* (New York: Three Rivers, 2011), 93–94.

21. Dalai Lama, *A Profound Mind*.

22. Chopra and Mlodinow, *War of the Worldviews*, 17.

23. Chopra and Mlodinow, *War of the Worldviews*, 43.

24. John Bradshaw, *Bradshaw on the Family* (Deerfield Beach, FL: Health Communications, 1988), 230.

25. Ruth Montgomery, *A World Beyond* (New York: Fawcett Crest, 1971), 8–9.

26. John White, ed., *What Is Enlightenment?* (Los Angeles: J. P. Tarcher, 1984), 126.

27. Meher Baba, *The Mastery of Consciousness*, comp. and ed. Allan Y. Cohen (New York: Harper and Row, 1977), 23.

28. Quoted in F. LaGard Smith, *Out on a Broken Limb* (Eugene, OR: Harvest House, 1986), 181.

29. Tolle, *New Earth*, 299–300.

30. Byrne, *Secret*, 155.

31. Byrne, *Secret*, 9.

32. Byrne, *Secret*, 11.

33. John White, "A Course in Miracles: Spiritual Wisdom for the New Age," *Science of Mind* 10 (1986).

34. John White, *The Meeting of Science and Spirit* (New York: Paragon House, 1990), 217.

35. For a discussion of the history and research on "the self," see Paul C. Vitz, "The Embodied Self: Evidence from Cognitive Psychology and Neuropsychology," in Paul C. Vitz and Susan M. Felch, eds., *The Self: Beyond the Postmodern Crisis* (Wilmington, DE: ISI Books, 2006), 113–27.

36. *Bhagavad Gita*, 147.

37. Dalai Lama, *Profound Mind*, 22.

38. Quoted in Smith, *Out On a Broken Limb*, 12.

39. The Dalai Lama (*Profound Mind*, 16) calls karma a "law of causality." In the Hindu tradition, the law is called *dharma*, and the word *karma* is used to refer to a set of actions one undertakes to comply with *dharma*.

40. Gary Zukav, *The Seat of the Soul* (New York: Simon and Schuster, 1999), 29.

41. Dalai Lama, *Profound Mind*, 45.

42. Strictly speaking, most New Spiritualist viewpoints deny the reality of the world of space, time, and matter. For example, in some Hindu traditions, the idea that there are natural processes is part of the illusion called *maya*. Although maya is used in many different ways in Hindu writings, it often refers to the idea that ultimate reality is incomprehensible through human plans, categories, and concepts.

43. Dalai Lama, *Profound Mind*, 69.

44. Marilyn Ferguson, *The Aquarian Conspiracy* (Los Angeles: J. P. Tarcher, 1980), 26–27.

45. For an explanation of how New Spiritualists claim quantum theory in support of their views, see Douglas Groothuis, *Unmasking the New Age* (Downers Grove, IL: InterVarsity, 1986), 94–105.

46. James Redfield, *The Celestine Prophecy* (New York: Warner Books, 1993), 41–42.

47. Ferguson, *Aquarian Conspiracy*, 27.

48. William Irwin Thompson, "Nine Theses for a Gaia Politique," *In Context* 14 (Autumn 1986): 58, www.context.org/ICLIB/IC14/Thompson.htm.

49. Quoted in John P. Newport, *The New Age Movement and the Biblical Worldview* (Grand Rapids: Eerdmans, 1998), 287.

50. For more information, see E. Calvin Beisner, "The Competing World Views of Environmentalism and Christianity," Cornwall Alliance, accessed March 26, 2014, www.cornwallalliance.org/docs/THECOM~1.PDF.

51. David Spangler, *Reflections on the Christ* (Forres, Scotland: Findhorn, 1982), 73.

52. Byrne, *Secret*, 57.

53. Byrne, *Secret*, 172.

54. "The Joys and Frustrations of Being a Healer," *Life Times* 1, no. 3 (n.d.): 61.

55. John Randolph Price, *The Superbeings* (Austin, TX: Quartus Books, 1981), 51–52.

56. Not all who embrace meditation embrace channeling, but all who embrace channeling seem to begin with meditation. Kathleen Vande Kieft says, "Almost without exception, those who channel effectively meditate regularly. The process of channeling itself is an extension of the state of meditation.... The best way to prepare, then, for channeling is by meditation." Kathleen Vande Kieft, *Innersource: Channeling Your Unlimited Self* (New York: Ballantine Books, 1988), 114.

57. For more information, see J. Isamu Yamamoto (a Christian researcher on cults and world religions), "The Near Death Experience [Parts 1 and 2]," Christian Research Institute, June 10, 2009, accessed March 26, 2014, www.equip.org/articles/the-near-death-experience-part-one/ and www.equip.org/articles/the-near-death-experience-part-two/.

58. Deuteronomy 18:9–14: "When you come into the land that the Lord your God is giving you, you shall not learn to follow the abominable practices of those nations. There shall not be found among you anyone who burns his son or his daughter as an offering, anyone who practices divination or tells fortunes or interprets omens, or a sorcerer or a charmer or a medium or a necromancer or one who inquires of the dead, for whoever does these things is an abomination to the Lord. And because of these abominations the Lord your God is driving them out before you. You shall be blameless before the Lord your God, for these nations, which you are about to dispossess, listen to fortune-tellers and to diviners. But as for you, the Lord your God has not allowed you to do this"; Revelation 22:15: "Outside are the dogs and sorcerers and the sexually immoral and murderers and idolaters, and everyone who loves and practices falsehood."

59. Zukav, *Seat of the Soul*, 85–86.

60. Tolle, *New Earth*, 4.

61. Tolle, *New Earth*, 5.

62. Jack Underhill, "My Goal in Life," *Life Times* (Winter 1986/1987): 90.

63. Byrne, *Secret*, 164.

64. Chopra and Mlodinow, *War of the Worldviews*, 152.

65. Tolle, *New Earth*, 8–9.

66. Tolle, *New Earth*, 13.

67. Tolle, *New Earth*, 116.

68. Quoted in Francis Adeney, "Educators Look East," *SCP Journal* (Winter 1981): 29. *SCP Journal* is published by Spiritual Counterfeits Project, PO Box 4308, Berkeley, CA 94704.

69. Quoted in Benjamin B. Ferencz and Ken Keyes Jr., *PlanetHood* (Coos Bay, OR: Vision Books, 1988), 92.

70. Robert M. Oates, *Permanent Peace* (Fairfield, IA: Institute of Science, Technology, and Public Policy, 2002), 5, 12.

71. John Warwick Montgomery, *Human Rights and Human Dignity* (Grand Rapids: Zondervan, 1986), 113.

72. Byrne, *Secret*, 132.

73. Philosophers use the terms *esotericism* or *perennialism* in reference to the claim that all religions teach the same thing. It is an essential teaching of New Spirituality, as is evident particularly in the writings of Ken Wilber. See, for example, *Integral Vision*.

74. Joseph Campbell, *The Hero with a Thousand Faces* (Novato, CA: New World Library, 2008).

75. Tolle, *New Earth*, 308.

76. *Bhagavad Gita*, 171.

77. Quoted in Brad Darrach, "Meet Shaky, the First Electronic Person," *Life*, November 20, 1970, 68.

78. Chopra and Mlodinow, *War of the Worldviews*, 9.

79. Tolle, *New Earth*, 8–9.

80. Tolle, *New Earth*, 13.

81. Tolle, *New Earth*, 140.

82. Tolle, *New Earth*, 158.

CHAPTER **7**

POSTMODERNISM

1. WHAT IS TRUTH?

It was in 1979, I remember, that my younger brother died, the first person in my family to be tortured. He was sixteen years old....

The officer opened the meeting. I remember he started by saying that a group of guerrillas they'd caught were about to arrive and that they were going to suffer a little punishment.... You'll see the punishment they get. And that's for being communists ... for being subversives! And if you get mixed up with communists and subversives, you'll get the same treatment.... Their faces were monstrously disfigured, unrecognizable.

My mother went closer to the lorry [cart] to see if she could recognize her son. Each of the tortured had different wounds on the face. I mean, their faces all looked different. But my mother recognized her son, my little brother, among them.... My brother was very badly tortured, he could hardly stand up. All the tortured had no nails and they had cut off part of the soles of their feet....

Anyway, they lined up the tortured and poured petrol on them; and then the soldiers set fire to each one of them. Many of them begged for mercy. They looked half dead when they were lined up there, but when the bodies began to burn they began to plead for mercy. Some of them screamed, many of them leapt but uttered no sound.[1]

Thus reads the sickening account of the death of Petrocinio Menchu Tum, Rigoberta Menchu's brother, as Menchu recounted in her autobiography *I, Rigoberta Menchu: An Indian Woman in Guatemala*. Menchu's compelling narrative won her the 1992 Nobel Peace Prize and made her a hero on college campuses, where professors used her story to create sympathy for the Marxist guerrillas fighting the US-backed Guatemalan government.

When doctoral student David Stoll went to Guatemala to verify Menchu's story, however, he found much of it to be embellished far beyond what the facts would support. No villager had any memory of the Guatemalan army carrying out such a slaughter as Menchu described.[2] Menchu later admitted that she had not witnessed such an act. Stoll found many other inaccuracies and untruths, the most serious of which was Menchu's description of how the Guatemalan government's repressive actions led to support of the Marxist guerrillas. Local villagers told Stoll the guerrillas were not viewed as liberators; the people were terrified of them.

No one disputes the brutality of the Guatemalan government or its killing of Menchu's family members. But as Kevin J. Kelley commented, "U.S. leftists who give his [Stoll's] arguments a full hearing—and who have not been deafened by their own dogma—will find Stoll's analysis difficult to dismiss."[3]

The response from university professors was at once unexpected and utterly predictable. College instructors ordinarily insist on detailed documentation of student papers, and they exact severe penalties for falsehood. But in this case, professors who assigned Menchu's book to their students seemed indifferent or even defensive. Professor Marjorie Agosin of Wellesley College stated bluntly, "Whether her book is true or not, I don't care. We should teach our students about the brutality of the Guatemalan military and the U.S. financing of it."[4] Timothy Brook, a Stanford history professor, said, "The best teaching devices are those which are gently flawed. The ambiguities and nuances are great teaching tools."[5]

Beyond the question of whether Menchu's claims have merit lies an enormous question: Is the basis for truth itself being challenged? Are we to the point where something is seen as true not if it is factually correct but if it communicates powerfully about things [people] believe?

Welcome to **Postmodernism**. Where other worldviews try to orient themselves to what actually exists, Postmodernism plays by different rules. Postmodern philosopher Richard Rorty said, "We ... [should] give

> *Postmodernism*: a skeptical worldview, founded as a reaction to modernism, that is suspicious of metanarratives and teaches that ultimate reality is inaccessible, knowledge is a social construct, and truth claims are political power plays.

up the correspondence theory of truth, and start treating moral and scientific beliefs as tools for achieving greater human happiness, rather than as representations of the intrinsic nature of reality."[6]

Christians have two contradictory impulses when confronting Postmodernism. Some dismiss it as a ridiculous denial of what is obviously true. Others are strangely attracted to it: If truth is just a collection of artifacts giving the impression of truth, then who cares what others say about what we believe? If it seems true to us, then it is true regardless of how valid other people's criticisms might seem.

Myron B. Penner urges Christians not to dismiss the West's cultural and philosophical infatuation with Postmodernism: "Christians must come to terms with and work through the postmodern turn and its implications for faith, not ignore or retreat from it," he says.[7] At the same time, Penner warns those Christians flirting with Postmodernism to be careful not to get caught up in it to the point where words become emptied of all truth.[8]

Let's take both Penner's challenge and his warning seriously by examining Postmodernism, peering into the history of its development, grasping its central arguments, discerning whether it is, in fact, a worldview, and discussing what it says about general and special revelation.

2. WHAT IS POSTMODERNISM?

Postmodernism means "after modernism." But what, then, is modernism? **Modernism** is the common name given to the period of time from the 1700s through the 1900s in which assumptions about Christianity in the West—belief in the supernatural, a trust in biblical revelation, and the authority of the church—gave way to skepticism about religion, an embrace of scientific investigation and technological progress, a trust in human reason, and empiricism (the idea that we can only know what our senses can perceive). Postmodernism is suspicious of science and technology's ability, and religion's ability for that matter, to satisfactorily answer life's ultimate questions.

Modernism: **A broad term used to describe a range of arts, attitudes, philosophies, and cultural moods that emerged following the eighteenth-century Enlightenment. It is characterized by a strong belief in rationalism, empiricism, science, and technological progress, as well as skepticism toward the supernatural, special revelation, and the authority of religion.**

In the end, Postmodernism is a worldview that denies all worldviews. Not only does Postmodernism strongly critique the Secularist idea that science is the most comprehensive way of knowing about the world; it also critiques Christianity, New Spirituality, Islam, and Marxism. The problem, according to Postmodernism, is each worldview's claim to offer unbiased truth about the world. Since biased people always communicate

The problem, according to Postmodernism, is each worldview's claim to offer unbiased truth about the world.

worldviews, they say, they are incapable of telling the truth in a way that corresponds to the world as it actually is. Rather, they trick people into looking for universal truths where none can be found.

Theologian Kevin Vanhoozer points out that C. S. Lewis foresaw the shift toward Postmodernist thinking. Lewis's term was *bulverism*, after its imaginary inventor Ezekiel Bulver. Vanhoozer explains:

> Lewis imagines the moment that bulverism was born, when five-year-old Ezekiel heard his mother say to his father, "Oh, you say that because you are a man." Bulver intuitively grasped the stunning implication: arguments need not be refuted, only situated. One rebuts a thought simply by calling attention to the genealogy or location of its thinker.[9]

Having foreseen this way of forming arguments, probably nothing of what we see in Postmodernism today would surprise Lewis.

When Postmodernists say truth is "situated" or "embedded," they mean that it is impossible to see any issue objectively because we are limited by our experiences in the world. As James K. A. Smith puts it, "All of our experience is always already an interpretation."[10] A charitable understanding of this claim, according to R. Scott Smith, is to say "that we have the ability to compare our concepts with things as they truly are ... and adjust our concepts as needed to better fit with reality." If you have a general concept of a sports car, by learning more about such cars, you can fine-tune your concept to the point where you can tell the difference, say, between a Ferrari and a Porsche. But Postmodernists usually take it one step further: our concepts themselves are not objective because our very thoughts about them are affected by thinking them. Some even go so far as to deny that we ever have any direct access to reality at all—that we are only commenting on our comments and thinking about our thinking.

Postmodernism is difficult to grasp, but you can understand its basics by contemplating what Vanhoozer says are the seven assumptions on which Postmodernism rests (paraphrased here):

1. Postmodernists reject the idea that universal truth can be known; all people can know is whether their individual experiences are true for them.[11]
2. Postmodernists reject "reason" that applies everywhere at all times; reasonableness rests on whatever narratives, traditions, institutions, and practices various groups find reasonable.
3. Postmodernists reject that we can be objective in our knowledge—we are all situated in our experiences.
4. Postmodernists reject modernist narratives that try to explain everything in the world and claim universally valid, neutral, objective knowledge; the world is too fragmented and complex to say that any one worldview explains everything.
5. Postmodernists reject the idea of "God," or at least our ability to gain a God's-eye view of the world; we have to draw meaning out of the world for ourselves.
6. Postmodernists reject the idea that we can design institutions in society that would make objective decisions based on reason; knowledge about the social order is constructed through the language we use to describe reality to ourselves and is biased by its very nature.[12]

POSTMODERNISM

7. Postmodernists reject the notion that any person can be "neutral"; our cultures, languages, histories, and genders all color how we see the world.

In the end, due to our situatedness, Postmodernism says no one can have unmediated, direct, or immediate access to reality. You don't see that Ferrari as it actually is—you are only seeing what you interpret of its existence. If you say, "Wow, that's a cool car," all you're doing is talking about your idea of cool. If you say, "Wow, that's a Ferrari F12 Berlinetta," you're not so much identifying the car's essence as placing it in a mental category distinct from all other kinds of cars, and such categories are mainly a commentary on what you think, not what actually exists. Postmodernism has no use for the idea that anything has an identifiable "essence." We just see what we see.[13]

If Postmodernism sounds complicated to you, you're not alone. As we examine previously held ideas about truth, identity, and knowledge, we may be able to see why some people find it so compelling at this point in time.

For most of Western history, people not only assumed truth exists but that those disciplined enough to think well could find it. The postmodern turn, as Myron Penner describes it, says truth is not "out there" waiting to be discovered. Rather, truth is "socially constructed" through our interactions with one another, as filtered through our gender identity, where we grow up, and our life experiences. We don't so much find truth as construct it. Truth (with a capital *T*) about reality (the Truth) is replaced by our own collective "truths."

There's more. If truth can't be known because we have no way to think objectively about it, then attempts to guide people to truth do not actually help us; instead, they oppress us. Postmodern author Walter Truett Anderson even hesitates to use words like *abnormal* and *deviant* in any definitive way because, as he says, "those categorizations are under fire now, the boundary between normal and abnormal is as questionable now as are all the other boundaries that once defined social reality."

How did we come to the place where we deny capital *T* Truth and boundaries between truth and lies, good and evil? To answer this question, we need to understand a little of Postmodernism's history.

3. THE HISTORY OF POSTMODERNISM

Gorgias taught rhetoric in ancient Greece, making a living by teaching people to be persuasive on behalf of whatever cause they deemed important. What they used persuasion for wasn't important to Gorgias; effectiveness, not truth, was his aim. Gorgias explained his approach in a book called *On Nature or the Non-Existent*. While we no longer have the original text, we know the core argument of Gorgias's book went as follows:

> Nothing exists.
> Even if something exists, nothing can be known about it.
> Even if something can be known about it, knowledge about it can't be communicated to others.
> Even if it can be communicated, it cannot be understood.

If Gorgias was right, then both philosophy and communication were pointless. As you can imagine, he was accused of being a nihilist, someone who believes in nothing.

But Gorgias did not hold to **nihilism**. He wasn't saying that the rock you stubbed your toe on didn't actually exist. Nor was he saying you couldn't have known it existed, or that communicating to someone about it was impossible. Rather, he was pointing out the confusion between what exists and our thoughts about what exists. People only know and communicate about things because they themselves think. So when they tell others what they are thinking, are they communicating what exists or what they are thinking about what exists?

> *Nihilism:* the view that the world and human existence are without meaning, purpose, comprehensible truth, or essential value.

> *Sophism:* a pre-Socratic school of philosophy that taught the art of rhetoric and held skeptical views of truth, knowledge, and morality; a derogatory term used to describe a specious argument intended to manipulate, trick, or deceive.

The uncertain boundary between thought and existence enabled Gorgias to justify teaching people to present themselves as virtuous even if they were not. After all, if our thoughts about virtue don't describe anything real, why should virtuous people have a corner on the virtue market? Historians call Gorgias and his like-minded teachers *sophists. Sophia* is the Greek word for "wisdom." Sophists thought of themselves as wise. Today **sophism** carries a negative connotation; it's the root word for *sophistry*, by which we mean tricky, manipulative argument.

We know about the sophists mostly because of Plato, who wrote a series of dialogues, or conversations, in which his mentor Socrates encountered foolish people and disabused them of their silly philosophies. The Sophists always came out looking bad in Plato's dialogues, and his critique of them—put in the mouth of Socrates—made sense to most people for millennia. Truth was objective and knowable. Anyone who disagreed, who said truth was subjective and dependent on the perspective of the person looking at it, was in the minority.

In the 1800s German philosopher Friedrich Nietzsche helped resurrect sophism. He considered sophism superior to other views about knowledge and communication. According to Nietzsche, "Every advance in epistemological and moral knowledge has reinstated the Sophists."[14]

Nietzsche rejected the idea that objective truth can be known, which probably shocked those who knew him in his younger years. His nickname as a boy, after all, had been "the little pastor," since, according to his sister, Elisabeth, "he could recite biblical texts and hymns with such feeling that he almost made one cry." Nietzsche himself wrote of his commitment to Christ: "I have firmly resolved within me to dedicate myself forever to His service. May the dear Lord give me strength and power to carry out my intentions and protect me on my life's way."[15]

But by age eighteen, Nietzsche began changing his mind. He wrote, "If we could examine Christian doctrine and Church history with a free, unconstrained eye, we would be compelled to arrive at many conclusions which contradict generally accepted ideas."[16]

Before long, under the influence of the writings of Ludwig Feuerbach, Nietzsche began seeing "gods" as human creations. They were nothing more than a projection of our ideas of what is perfect. In his biography of Nietzsche, Julian Young summarized Feuerbach's—and Nietzsche's—view: "Rightly understood Jesus is not a gateway to another life but a role model for this one."[17]

Many people today sympathize with Nietzsche's shift in thinking: If Jesus was a good teacher but not God, we can embrace the parts of the Bible we like without having to explain or defend the uncomfortable parts. After all, if our claims about reality don't need to be true—just important to us—then a rejection of Christianity as capital *T* Truth is the nicest, most enlightened thing we can do!

If Nietzsche's thinking seems radical today, imagine how it appeared to the people of his time. By the time of Nietzsche's writing, modernism was well underway. People believed science would ultimately explain everything. Philosophers thought human reason could be developed to the point where we would no longer need to rely on special revelation to understand the world. But Nietzsche saw past this pretention to a time when anything we relied on for certainty would break down. Are we brave enough to face such a world?

Eventually, Nietzsche abandoned any notion of Christianity's value, though he knew chaos would result if people tried to live according to what he said. The most famous passage of his writing, in which a madman confronts his fellow citizens about God's death, is both honest and tragic:

> Whither is God? I will tell you. We have killed him—you and I. All of us are his murderers. But how did we do this? How could we drink up the sea? Who gave us the sponge to wipe away the entire horizon? What were we doing when we unchained this earth from its sun? Whither is it moving now? Whither are we moving? Away from all suns? Are we not plunging continually? Backward, sideward, forward, in all directions? Is there still any up or down? Are we not straying, as through an infinite nothing? Do we not feel the breath of empty space? Has it not become colder? Is not night continually closing in on us? Do we not need to light lanterns in the morning? Do we hear nothing as yet of the noise of the gravediggers who are burying God? Do we smell nothing as yet of the divine decomposition? Gods, too, decompose. God is dead. God remains dead. And we have killed him.[18]

By this statement Nietzsche did not mean to imply God was once alive and had died. He was assuming belief in God to be unnecessary—and that only our belief in God kept him alive—while encouraging the reader to get busy dealing with the implications of this fact.

If it had not been for people's growing cynicism about the ability of science and technology to solve all of our problems, Nietzsche's ideas might not have emerged as so important. As it was, his thinking profoundly influenced an entire generation of philosophers, among them Michel Foucault, a famous, influential, if personally troubled twentieth-century intellect. In 1948, as a young university student, Foucault attempted suicide. The resident doctor at the elite Parisian university where he was studying, L'École normale supérieure, concluded that Foucault was racked with guilt over his frequent nocturnal visits to the illegal gay bars of the French capital. Foucault's father, a strict disciplinarian who had previously sent his son to the most regimented Catholic school he could find, arranged for him to be admitted to a psychiatric hospital for evaluation. After his release, Foucault remained obsessed with death. He often joked about hanging himself and made further attempts to end his own life.

Foucault's youthful experiences with homosexuality, attempted suicide, and mental imbalance proved decisive for his intellectual development. His philosophy became a way of coping with his own rejection of absolute truth as well as a crusade to liberate humanity from labeling, marginalization, and suppression.[19] Before his death from AIDS, which he contracted through anonymous gay sex, Foucault turned the world of philosophy upside down with books like *Madness and Civilization* (1961), *The Birth of the Clinic* (1963), *Discipline and Punish* (1975), and *The History of Sexuality* (in three volumes, 1976–1984).

Apparently, Foucault saw himself as trapped in a cycle of the death of societal truths, a cycle first revealed by his hero, Nietzsche:

> Nietzsche indicated the turning-point from a long way off; it is not so much the absence or the death of God that is affirmed as the end of Man.... It becomes apparent, then, that the death of God and the last man are engaged in a contest with more than one round: is it not the last man who announces that he has killed God, thus situating his language, his thought, his laughter in the space of that already dead God, yet positing himself also as he who has killed God and whose existence includes the freedom and the decision of that murder? Thus, the last man is at the same time older and yet younger than the death of God; since he has killed God, it is he himself who must answer for his own finitude; but since it is in the death of God that he speaks, thinks, and exists, his murder itself is doomed to die; new gods, the same gods, are already swelling the future Ocean; Man will disappear.[20]

Foucault placed his finger on the carotid artery of modernism and found it to be as cold a corpse as Nietzsche's God. God was dead. Modernism attempted to enthrone humanity in his place, but everything important was slaughtered along with God. No one was left to be crowned.

> Modernism attempted to enthrone humanity in his place, but everything important was slaughtered along with God. No one was left to be crowned.

This sounds morbid, to be sure, and it is admittedly difficult to condense two thousand years of philosophical history into a few sentences. But the key takeaway remains: philosophy today operates on what Paul Ricoeur called a "hermeneutic of suspicion"—our interpretation of everything in society should express doubt about all truth claims.[21] Postmodernism cannot allow for thoughts and things to have any firmly knowable meaning aside from our interpretation. As Daniel Dennett understands, "If things had real, intrinsic essences, they could have real, intrinsic meanings." And that is simply unacceptable.[22]

4. WHAT ARE THE KEY CHARACTERISTICS OF POSTMODERNISM?

Most worldviews state and defend their basic assumptions about reality. Postmodernists, though, try to position their thinking as a way to see through other worldviews, not as a worldview itself. Postmodernism dismisses the truth claims of other worldviews by focusing on how language is used to create and maintain the structures of society. Some Postmodernists— such as Jacques Derrida—focus on "deconstructing" language to diminish its ability to persuade us that dominant truth claims actually represent truth. Others—Ludwig Wittgenstein and J. L. Austin, for example—analyze "speech acts" to show that there is no necessary relationship between a description and what is being described. In other words, a thought about a Ferrari and the Ferrari itself are related only incidentally. Thoughts are thoughts and things are things. Other philosophers, like Edmund Husserl, have responded to this way of thinking by pointing out that thoughts are not just random; they are about things, and they are intended to be about things. The thought has certain properties, and so does the object of the thought. These properties are part of the nature of the thought and of the thing. How Husserl communicates this sounds complicated, but it is important:

> **Postmodernism dismisses the truth claims of other worldviews by focusing on how language is used to create and maintain the structures of society.**

> That a representation refers to a certain object in a certain manner, is not due to its acting on some external, independent object, "directing" itself to it in some literal sense, or doing something to it or with it, as a hand writes with a pen. It is due to nothing that stays outside of the presentation, but to its own inner peculiarity alone.... A given presentation presents this object in this manner in view of its peculiarly differentiated presentational characteristics.[23]

> **If someone says A and you hear B, it is not because A has no essence but because you either aren't paying attention or are being ornery.**

In other words, objects and thoughts have qualities that present themselves consistently no matter who is thinking about them. If someone says A and you hear B, it is not because A has no essence but because you either aren't paying attention or are being ornery.

We recognize that this is an introductory text and that we're already wading in some pretty deep waters, so let's look at each piece of Postmodernist philosophy one at a time.

Language. Not everyone thinks in the same way or about the same things, but everyone uses language. Edward Sapir wrote in 1921,

> There is no more striking general fact about language than its universality. One may argue as to whether a particular tribe engages in activities that are worthy of the name of religion or of art, but we know of no people that is not possessed of a fully developed language. The lowliest South African Bushman speaks in the forms of a rich symbolic system that is in essence perfectly comparable to the speech of the cultivated Frenchman.[24]

To the Postmodernist, language is the best starting point, then, for trying to describe human experience. No matter where you live, language shapes the way you think. And those who have a greater command of the language are able to think more accurately. For example, a computer-programming expert with a larger vocabulary of technical words is able to think more precisely about computer programming than a novice.

But, according to Sapir, language does more than just shape our thoughts. It actually shapes our approach to life:

Peculiar modes of pronunciation, characteristic turns of phrase, slangy forms of speech, occupational terminologies of all sorts—these are so many symbols of the manifold ways in which society arranges itself and are of crucial importance for the understanding of the development of individual and social attitudes.[25]

Structuralism:
an intellectual movement that believes human knowledge is not based on an accurate understanding of reality but is the product of linguistically constructed forms or grammars that societies have developed over time.

Given the central role of language, one group of philosophers in the early 1900s argued that we should build our philosophy around language and relationships rather than around the nature of physical existence itself. This movement was called **structuralism**. Instead of focusing on scientific facts, structuralists look at how the way we use language causes us to view facts differently based on our experiences. So, for example, people who live in a rain-forest climate probably have words allowing them to more clearly describe different kinds of rain, whereas Eskimos presumably have more terms to describe snow. Structuralists aren't as interested in learning about rain or snow as they are interested in learning about how we talk about rain and snow based on our experiences.

Poststructuralism:
an intellectual movement that agrees with structuralism—it is more important to study language and relationship because it is impossible to have knowledge of objective reality—but progresses further by contending that human communication is not really about things but about the views and motivations of those involved in the conversation.

Poststructuralism. While structuralism was the starting point for many Postmodernists, Postmodernism itself is generally regarded as *poststructuralist* because Postmodernists see their thoughts about language as moving beyond how it functions to its use. Postmodernists think we cannot know the world directly. We only know it as we interpret it. Since our language structures our relationships, our talk about the objects in the world isn't really about those objects at all; it's really about ourselves. So, to use the previous example, when the rain-forest natives talk about rain and Eskimos talk about snow, they aren't really talking about rain or snow but about themselves—what they think is important about the weather and why. When your friend says, "There is a chair," he is not so much commenting on the chairness of the chair as he is making a statement about his own understanding of objects like chairs, about how he himself is not the chair, and how he thinks you should view the world similarly. As the German philosopher Martin Heidegger famously said,

The unitary fourfold sky and earth, mortals and divinities, which is stayed in the thinging of things, we call—the world. In the naming, the things named are called into their thinging. Thinging, they unfold world, in which things abide, and so are the abiding ones. By thinging, things carry out world.[26]

POSTMODERNISM

What … does … this … *mean?* Is Heidegger suggesting that things don't actually exist until we name them? No. He is implying that things only take on meaning as they become subject to our understanding through communication. It's a similar point to the one the sophist Gorgias made centuries ago.

We will critique this view later in this chapter and throughout this book, but you can imagine how exciting this way of thinking seemed to philosophers. It gave birth to whole new sets of questions crying out to be answered: How exactly do we use communication to structure our world? How do different communities and language groups understand the world differently? How is it possible that people's way of thinking in one culture makes complete sense to them but to no one else? And perhaps the trickiest question of all: How do people use language to get others to do what they want?

George Orwell's concern about the use and misuse of language to create dictatorial power led him to write *1984*, in which he chillingly described Newspeak, a way of changing language to limit the range of expression, and thus to limit thought. In one scene, Syme is lecturing her coworker Winston, the main character, about Newspeak's virtues:

> You haven't a real appreciation of Newspeak, Winston. Even when you write it you're still thinking in Oldspeak. I've read some of those pieces that you write in the *Times* occasionally. They're good enough, but they're translations. In your heart you'd prefer to stick to Oldspeak, with all its vagueness and its useless shades of meaning. You don't grasp the beauty of the destruction of words. Do you know that Newspeak is the only language in the world whose vocabulary gets smaller every year?[27] … Don't you see that the whole aim of Newspeak is to narrow the range of thought? In the end we shall make thought-crime literally impossible, because there will be no words in which to express it.[28]

> George Orwell's concern about the use and misuse of language to create dictatorial power led him to write *1984*, in which he chillingly described Newspeak, a way of changing language to limit the range of expression, and thus to limit thought.

If language structures how people think about things, then by eliminating certain words from usage and promoting other words, we can change the way people think. Now that's power! And this power is precisely what the poststructuralists were reacting against.

Poststructuralists have moved beyond structuralism (i.e., the consideration of how language structures our interactions), agreeing instead that language is primarily a tool of oppression, which the powerful use to impose ideas on everyone else.

Deconstruction. In the 1950s the world was still reeling from the ways brutal dictators manipulated language to create "cultural hegemony" (i.e., the way the ruling class dominates society by shaping its values and beliefs), commit violence, and exclude the views of those with whom they disagreed. Philosophers like Michel Foucault, Jean Baudrillard, Jacques Derrida, and

> *Deconstruction:* a method of literary analysis that questions the ability of language to represent reality adequately and seeks to discern and expose the purported underlying ideologies of a text.

Jean-François Lyotard began looking for clues as to how dictators pulled it off, and they found themselves dismayed at the way modernism—supposedly rational and objective—had become an element of control in the hands of those with ill intent.

As we have already mentioned briefly, Jacques Derrida, in particular, tried to show through his writings how texts of all kinds could be "deconstructed" to reveal their underlying assumptions and ideologies. Literature professors across the world had fun showing students how to ferret out a text's hidden or multiple meanings (*polysemy*). In the end, the reader's interpretation of the text became more important than the meaning the author intended to communicate, since, strictly speaking, there was no meaning in the text itself.[29] There couldn't be—thoughts and things did not have "essences" that were consistently identifiable. Your experience with something in the world cannot be generalized so that others' experiences of it can be said to be the same.

In 1968, Roland Barthes wrote a short essay titled "The Death of the Author." In this essay he argued that the origin of the text is not the important thing; rather, it is the destination—the reader. By allowing the reader to invent new meanings, the text is freed from the tyranny of the author's single intended meaning. For example, there is no reason to assume "that a Shakespearean play means exactly the same thing today as it did when first performed."[30] Each author (or artist) is the product of her own cultural setting and uses language to describe her interpretation of her own situation. Our situation is different, so our interpretation will obviously be different, as will the language we use to describe it. Thus, postmodern literary criticism claims that words cannot be known to accurately describe objects in the world. Words are about words, not about things. No matter how a writer constructs a sentence, it can never tell us about the real world, only about the world as the reader understands it. This concept is summed up in the phrase "That's just your interpretation."

Subjectivity. One of the ways Postmodernists think language functions as a tool of power in the modern world is by establishing metanarratives. A **metanarrative** is a unifying story about the world that aspires to explain everything as if from a God's-eye viewpoint. Metanarratives become so powerful that people who embrace them literally cannot imagine the world being any other way. Understanding the persuasive power of metanarratives, Postmodernists say, is the key to uncovering their secret power and freeing ourselves from their grip.

> *Metanarrative:* a single overarching interpretation, or grand story, of reality.

It's easy to imagine how this way of thinking leads to a denial of universal, objective truth. Let's say you lived in a country where every time people gained freedom, they used it to do horrible things to others. If someone arrived on your shores proclaiming, "Freedom is good. Support more freedom!" you would probably be suspicious: "This person wants freedom because he intends to do horrible things to us." If you then traveled to another country where freedom was cherished as the basis of a good society, you'd probably be conflicted. How would you resolve this conflict? Most people resolve it not by recognizing that freedom is a good thing when properly understood but by viewing freedom as neither good nor bad except when the situation makes it so. This is called *subjectivity*.

Subjectivity is what Jean-François Lyotard had in mind in his famous statement about "incredulity towards metanarrative."[31] To Lyotard, broad explanations are arrogant; they deserve suspicion because people's experiences are so varied, and people's experiences, not general statements about the world, are what we should be paying attention to.

Even as you read this book, Postmodernists would say, you are not really learning to understand the world as it actually is; you are merging the concepts you're learning about into both your experiences and your culture's influence on you. We cannot know whatever "real world" is out there, they say. Strictly speaking, there are seven billion interpretations of the world because each person on the planet sees the world based on his or her own subjective experiences and culture. Occasionally you'll hear Postmodernists use the term **anti-realism** to describe this suspicious approach to the so-called real world.[32]

> *Anti-realism:* the denial of the existence or accessibility of an objective reality.

So, for Postmodernists, capital *T* Truth cannot be known directly. There are only "truths" (small *t*) that are particular to a society or group of people and are limited to individual perception. Written or verbal statements can reflect only a particular localized culture or individual point of view. A catchphrase we often hear is "That may be true for you but not for me."

Yet by making the universal statement that there are no metanarratives, haven't Postmodernists actually created a metanarrative of their own? The story that all universal truths are false, that there are only local stories told by various cultures, is itself a story of the world. In some ways, Postmodernism is the anti-worldview worldview. But can we understand it well enough to predict how Postmodernists will view any given situation or academic discipline? This is the question we will tackle next.

5. THE WORLDVIEW OF POSTMODERNISM

We define a *worldview* as "a pattern of ideas, beliefs, convictions, and habits."[33] A worldview shapes what we pay attention to and what we ignore. What we believe and what we pay attention to can cause us to interpret the world in a certain way. Postmodernism claims to point out these things; it is an analyzer of these interpretations, not a generator making truth claims of its own. Is it even fair to call Postmodernism a worldview? Honest Postmodernists say yes because they realize that the tools used to "interpret the interpretations" of others come from someplace—they too are situated in any given Postmodernist's ideas, beliefs, convictions, and habits. Postmodernist author Walter Truett Anderson is one who acknowledges this and says that Postmodernism is one of four worldviews operating in the West today.[34]

Some worldviews begin with claims about reality—reality is God and his creation, or reality is consciousness, or reality is the primacy of the individual self. Other worldviews form as critical stances, reactions to other dominant worldviews. Marxism, for example, formed as a reaction against a biblical view of God, the duty of man, and stewardship of property. In this way Postmodernism is like Marxism. In the beginning Postmodernism was primarily a critical stance, a rejection of dominant worldviews. But, like Marxism, Postmodernism couldn't sustain itself as a mere reaction; it had to build something and answer important questions. The principles of Postmodernism, then, have been applied to everything from literature to political science to architecture and music.

Over time, as Daniel A. Farber and Suzanna Sherry argue, Postmodernism has become a robust way of thinking about everything:

> [Postmodernism] is a powerful and coherent mindset. It provides a philosophical outlook (social constructionism), a legal reform program, and a set of governing metaphors, all in one convenient package. This package has the added benefit of resonating with ideas that are popular in other parts of the academy. If one has doubts about the social construction of truth or merit, one can rest assured that the matter has been settled in the impenetrable prose of some esteemed French philosophers.[35]

So Postmodernism is more than a critical stance, and later in this book, we will discern identifiable postmodern patterns of thought in each of the ten disciplines we'll consider: theology, philosophy, ethics, biology, psychology, sociology, law, politics, economics, and history. These patterns are clear enough that we can predict with a fair degree of accuracy what Postmodernists will say or do about new things that come along. Let's look at Postmodernism's patterns next, starting with its understanding of general revelation.

6. General Revelation: Postmodernism and the World That Actually Exists

Christian author Nancy Pearcey relates the following firsthand experience:

> I witnessed a fascinating altercation at a conference at Boston University on science and postmodernism several years ago. Postmodernist philosophers led off by arguing that "there are no metanarratives," meaning no overarching, universal truths. Responding on behalf of the scientists was Nobel Prize-winning physicist Steven Weinberg, who replied: But of course there are metanarratives. After all, there's evolution—a vast metanarrative from the Big Bang to the origin of the solar system to the origin of human life. And since evolution is true, that proves there is at least one metanarrative.... To which the postmodernist philosophers responded, ever so politely: That's just your metanarrative. Evolution is merely a social construct, they said, like every other intellectual schema—a creation of the human mind.[36]

Some evolutionists agree with this. Daniel Dennett, for example, says that if naturalism (only nature exists) is true, then things do not have their own "essence"—any idea of essence is just what we make up to describe the world to ourselves. To Dennett, we cannot directly access the world as it actually is, so all we can hope for is to interpret what we observe as accurately as possible.[37]

It sounds bizarre to say that we can't know or even observe actual truth. Aren't there some truths we can all agree on, such as one plus one equals two, or stepping on the highway in front of a tractor trailer moving at sixty-five miles per hour will get you flattened? If Postmodernists don't see it this way, can we actually say that they have a view of general revelation, of things known to be true regardless of culture or life experiences?

Some Postmodernists see science as a form of coping rather than a reliable means of gaining knowledge. For example, Paul Feyerabend, former philosophy professor at the University of California, Berkeley, wrote,

To those who look at the rich material provided by history, and who are not intent on impoverishing it in order to please their lower instincts—their craving for intellectual security in the form of clarity, precision, "objectivity," [or] "truth"—it will become clear that there is only one principle that can be defended under all circumstances and in all stages of human development. It is the principle: anything goes.[38]

Here is Feyerabend's view of science in a nutshell: In the history of science, many theories have arisen, been accepted as established, promoted as the truth, and then eventually discarded. When a scientist promotes scientific data in support of a theory, that bit of data is anything but neutral because the scientist is biased. He can't see it any other way, even if his perception of the data fails to correspond to the characteristics of the data itself. If he's a powerful person and refuses to acknowledge that he is wrong, then it becomes a power play, and his agenda is no longer the pursuit of truth but gathering support for his biased views. In all fields of science, questions remain open as scientific theories are regularly tweaked. And to top it off, the scientific establishment is very much politicized.[39] Scientists are just as messed up as the rest of us.

> Some Postmodernists see science as a form of coping rather than a reliable means of gaining knowledge.

Doubts about the objectivity and neutrality of science arose in the mid-1900s from Michael Polanyi's *Personal Knowledge*[40] and Thomas Kuhn's *The Structure of Scientific Revolutions.*[41] Kuhn, for example, pointed out that science is not merely a progressive and incremental discipline for the study and recording of facts. So-called facts can be understood and interpreted in a variety of ways depending on the worldview assumptions of the scientist.[42]

In addition, Kuhn asserted that scientific theories, or paradigms, do not often fall out of favor because they are proven wrong. Rather, older theories tend to die out along with their proponents, while new and creative theories attract the attention of younger scientists who, in turn, promote their theories over the older ones.[43] A current scientific theory is just that: a current theory, which will be replaced by another current theory in the future. This is why science cannot tell us what is real, only what scientists believe to be the case at a particular time in history. Everyone, including the scientist, is locked into their particular cultures and languages and thus cannot claim to have an objective picture of the world.

Even mathematics is not immune from postmodern analysis. Doubts about the objectivity of math were brought to light with Douglas R. Hofstadter's Pulitzer Prize–winning book *Gödel, Escher, Bach: An Eternal Golden Braid,* published in 1979.[44] The author of another text, *Ethnomathematics: A Multicultural View of Mathematical Ideas*, Marcia Ascher, asserted that much of mathematics education depends upon assumptions of Western culture. For example, she wrote that no other culture "need share the categories triangle, right triangle, hypotenuse of a right triangle." Ascher wondered, "Is a square something that has external reality or is it something only in our minds?"[45]

In our chapters on Christianity and Secularism, we critiqued science for its unwarranted claim of providing certain answers to life's questions. But the Postmodernist critique goes far beyond this, claiming that because our observations are culturally and linguistically situated, the knowledge we gain from science does not ultimately help us understand the

> Whereas Christians might point to the sin nature to explain how our careful attempts at scientific knowledge can go wrong, Postmodernists don't think theories go wrong because they're flawed. They go wrong because true theories are impossible.

world as it actually is. Whereas Christians might point to the sin nature to explain how our careful attempts at scientific knowledge can go wrong, Postmodernists don't think theories go wrong because they're flawed. They go wrong because true theories are impossible. Reality is not accessible to us. When we try to access it, we're just interpreting it, and our efforts to nail down truth are just interpretations of our interpretations.

Of course, though, no one can really live as if nothing can be known, including Postmodernists. They quarrel with one another when they think their arguments have been interpreted incorrectly. They still drive across bridges constructed through principles of science in cars engineered for safety and efficiency. If muggers attack them, they'll complain if the police don't come to their rescue. At the end of the day, we might ask whether Postmodernism is something we should really be paying attention to, or whether Postmodernists are just ungrateful whiners who should be ignored. Knowing what you already know about Postmodernism, though, you probably suspect that it isn't that simple. Postmodernists do believe they have insight that enables them to approach life's ultimate questions. It is to these presumed answers—Postmodernism's version of special revelation—that we will now turn.

7. SPECIAL REVELATION: POSTMODERNISM'S ANSWERS TO THE ULTIMATE QUESTIONS

In our chapters on each of the six worldviews, we have focused on how proponents of those worldviews answer life's ultimate questions. How do they know their answers are actually true? General revelation says some things can be known because they present themselves to us directly through observation. Postmodernists may say all ways of knowing are tainted, but don't they still make actual claims about the world? On what basis do they make them? If they make them from their particular standpoint but act as if they should be generally applied, then they are being inconsistent. Anytime Postmodernists speak to the issue of government debt or traditional marriage or the rightness of a particular military action, they are being hypocritical in assuming that their particular viewpoints should affect our perceptions. Our question should be (politely), "Why should we assume that your particular viewpoint has any meaning for anyone else?" If they answer that question, write down the answer: it is the expression of what they believe to be an absolute truth.

1. On what sources of revelation does Postmodernism draw? Postmodernism is, in many ways, the height of hypocrisy. If it were true, we could never know it to be true. Its sources of revelation are mostly whip-smart professors: Michel Foucault, Jacques Derrida, Richard Rorty, and Martin Heidegger (philosophy), Jean-François Lyotard (philosophy and sociology), Jean Baudrillard (sociology), Jacques Lacan (psychology), Stanley Fish (literature and law), Ludwig Wittgenstein (language), and others. Most of these men had an extensive working knowledge of philosophy, literature, and even religion. But should their ideas be trusted? If "all ideas about human reality are social constructions," as Walter

Truett Anderson claims,[46] then why would we, or even Anderson, believe Anderson's own claim? Such a statement—which incidentally is a propositionally framed statement of absolute knowledge—would make no sense to someone whose cultural background and life experiences were different from Anderson's. But every one of these authors wrote and published books and articles on the assumption that people would understand them. Why would they do this? It contradicted everything they taught.[47]

Jacques Derrida, at least, clearly understood the kind of world Postmodernism was ushering in and declared his intention not to be among those who let their queasiness get the better of them. Postmodernists, Derrida claimed, "turn their eyes away" when faced with the prospect that ours is "the species of the nonspecies, in the formless, mute, infant, and terrifying form of monstrosity."[48] Social construction is like an onion—when you're done peeling, there is nothing left: no truth that we can perceive, no enduring conception of what it means to be human, no access to what is real. Postmodernists have trespassed into territory Gorgias might have feared to tread and Nietzsche saw only as he wavered back and forth across the boundary of what we now know to have been syphilis-induced insanity. A world devoid of ultimate meaning or purpose does not make itself easily accessible to a coherent worldview, and anyway there would be no point.[49]

2. What does Postmodernism say about humanity? In their book about postmodern economics, David Ruccio and Jack Amariglio make a startling statement: there is "no singular and unique 'I.' "[50] In other words, there is no self-identity and no permanent soul or mind. Postmodernists refer to human beings not as persons but as subjects, bodies, or units. "Person" suggests the existence of a singular and unique I who possesses a personality or human nature.[51] To Postmodernists there is no human nature. There is only an ever-evolving, highly sexual social animal with multiple subjective interests crying out for recognition and acceptance.[52]

> To Postmodernists there is no human nature. There is only an ever-evolving, highly sexual social animal with multiple subjective interests crying out for recognition and acceptance.

So when Anderson says all ideas about human reality are social constructions, he's not just proclaiming the social construction of thought. He's saying we are socially constructed. We don't exist as persons; we don't have souls but are "a collage of social constructs."[53] Mitchell Stephens builds on this stunning implication: "It's not just that we each have different sides to our personality; it's that we have no central personality in relation to which all our varied behaviors might be seen as just 'sides.' We are, in other words, not absolutely anything."[54]

But there is more. Postmodern psychologists are now asserting there is no one "self" but a multiplicity of "selves." Kenneth Gergen is a psychology professor at Swarthmore College. His book *The Saturated Self: Dilemmas of Identity in Contemporary Life* is considered one of the best introductions to postmodern psychology. Gergen states, "In place of an enduring core of deep and indelible character, there is a chorus of invitations. Each invitation 'to be' also casts doubt on the wisdom and authenticity of the others. Further, the postmodern person senses the constructed character of all attempts at being—on the part of both self and others."[55]

3. What does Postmodernism say is wrong with us? If "we" don't really exist, if we have no soul or, indeed, any identifiable self, why do we sense that there is something wrong with us and with the world? What is the nature of that wrong? Richard Rorty, one of the most well-known philosophers of the twentieth century, believed the problem is adherence to metanarratives such as Christianity. For Rorty, there was "no room for obedience to a nonhuman authority [i.e., God]." In fact, creating the new conception of what it means to be human was "a matter of forgetting about eternity."[56]

Postmodernists have difficulty living with the rejection of universal truths. The statement, for example, "The train is coming!" may convey a multitude of interpretations to different people—as good news perhaps, or bad news, or a metaphor. But we contend that if people fail to get off the tracks, the result of their interpretation may prove fatal. Real life is not open to infinite interpretations. There are, as even atheist philosopher Daniel Dennett acknowledges, "brute facts" in the real world.[57] There are essences. There are boundaries. There are categories of meaning that exist independent of our ability to perceive them. At any particular moment in time, either a train is coming down the tracks or not. This real-world fact is not a matter of our personal interpretation. Regardless of the word games, Postmodernists have a hard time escaping the demand that our ideas correspond to what actually exists.

4. What does Postmodernism say about how we should live? Richard Rorty advocated abandoning the search for objective truth in favor of **pragmatism**, the idea that truth is not "out there" to be discerned. Rather our experiences will enable us to generate a theory about living, which we can use to understand our experiences.

> *Pragmatism:* the belief that propositions do not mirror reality and should therefore be treated as tools and judged only by their practical consequences.

Rather than a quest for truth, Rorty suggested that the pragmatist strive for "hermeneutic conversation." Rorty invited his opponents to dialogue with him to see if they could reach agreement, or at least a fruitful disagreement. He said that the "hope of agreement is never lost as long as the conversation lasts."[58]

For Rorty, this use of language and dialogue was "edifying philosophy"—a chance to create some type of reality with the realization that we can never discover true or objective reality outside the boundaries of language, culture, and locality. Since there is no objective, universal Truth, Rorty suggested that perhaps we can reach some type of agreeable truths (small *t*) in order to get along with others.

But does truth result from such a conversation? Not really. Rorty's insistence on give-and-take and final agreement only sets the stage for another round of conversation where give-and-take results in further agreement or disagreement. Truth is never the result of continuing conversation, because the conversation will never be finished.[59]

5. How are we to understand other worldviews based on Postmodernism? If Postmodernism is accepted, the other worldviews we have considered must be discarded. Let's consider for a moment how Postmodernists are likely to view each of these worldviews.

Christianity. In *The Twilight of Atheism*, Alister McGrath says, "The very idea of deconstruction seems to suggest that the idea of God ought to be eliminated from Western culture as a power play on the part of churches and others with vested interests in its survival."[60] The insistence on absolute biblical truth is what leads to violence and oppression. Presumably, then, freedom from these absolutes would restore peace and balance. This is far off base. The three "-isms" (communism, Nazism, and fascism) of the twentieth century responsible for the slaughter of tens of millions were not exactly bastions of theism and Christianity.[61] As a matter of fact, all three were grounded in atheism, evolution, and socialism—three perspectives Postmodernists carry around in the backseat, though they may not turn to look at them very often.

Of course, there are self-proclaimed Christian Postmodernists, such as James K. A. Smith, Brian McLaren, Merold Westphal, Nancey Murphy, Stanley Hauerwas, and Alasdair MacIntyre, who reject the idea that deconstructionism entails the elimination of God. But even these individuals seem to consider biblical authors, like all authors, to be situated in their own cultures, experiences, and languages; what they wrote described their own subjective experiences as much as objective or eternal truths about God and humanity. These Christian Postmodernists would surely recoil at the way postmodern ideas about objective truth created room for evil to flourish. But what do they have to say about our actual nature as humans? Are we merely bundles of relations and not souls? There are enormous doctrinal implications to this. For one, sin becomes redefined as the disruption of relationships. Our primary problem is not being spiritually dead because of our sin against God but our incompetence in living in relationship with others. If this is so, the solution to sin is therapeutic: what we need is not to be rescued from the penalty of sin and the threat of eternal punishment but to follow Jesus's moral example of how to live well with others.

Christian Postmodernism often begins with what some have called the "hermeneutics of finitude," the notion that we are finite and limited in our humanness, so we must be humble or chastened in our claims to reality. That humans are fallen is certainly consistent with biblical teaching. But does it follow that we cannot understand reality? If we take this view too far, we might end up saying we cannot understand things Scripture clearly commands us to understand, in which case we make an idol out of our reluctance. This is not humility—it is stubborn sinfulness.

Perhaps a better perspective is to say that we can know reality truly, though not exhaustively. Like a jigsaw puzzle, we can see the picture emerging even if all of the pieces are not in place.[62] Imagine someone who is lost because he cannot match up what he sees in his

Christian Postmodernism: a hybrid worldview that incorporates elements of postmodern philosophy and Christian theology.

surroundings with the description of the area he sees on the map. We might conclude that he is lost because his perspective is limited by his physical nature (he can't fly up to get a bird's-eye view). But his lostness might also manifest in anger that leads to irrational thinking, embarrassment that leads to self-justification, frustration that leads to a stubborn refusal to stop and ask for directions. None of this, though, would mean that the proper route cannot be known or even that there is no possibility of an accurate map.

Ironically, by claiming that we do not have access to reality as it is in itself but only as we interpret it, we set our interpretations—what we think Scripture means—and what we experience of God over who God has actually revealed himself to be in his Word and in the world. This is far from a humble thing. It can in fact be spiritually dangerous.

Islam. Islam comprises a metanarrative purporting to explain all of reality. Postmodernism, while interested in how Islamic ideas developed and sustained themselves over time, has nonetheless rejected Islam's claim to objectively describe reality as it actually exists. This said, some Muslim philosophers have developed postmodern and anti-realist lines on the assumption that ultimate reality cannot be reduced to a series of statements we can know to be true or false. As more and more "facts" about Islam are called into question, such a line of thinking may allow Muslim thinkers to continue to assert the ongoing relevance of Islam as a rich source of cultural capital.[63]

New Spirituality. The New Spiritualists' claims that consciousness is the ground of reality, and that all life is merging toward unity, comprise a metanarrative that, like all others, Postmodernists reject. At the same time, however, some aspects of New Spirituality bear a striking resemblance to postmodern thought. What Buddhists call "the Middle Way," a school of thought initiated by a teacher named Nagarjuna who lived around one hundred to two hundred years after the birth of Christ, suggests that things do not exist independently of our apprehending them.[64] "Things" are empty of the qualities we consider to be existence, and as the Dalai Lama claims, "Emptiness is the ultimate truth."[65] Middle Way Buddhism and Postmodernism have a lot in common.

Secularism. Secularism makes claims to absolute truth based in science and rationality. Paul Kurtz, in *Humanist Manifesto 2000*, described Postmodernism as nihilistic in its claim that nothing can be known or communicated. Objective truth is knowable, Kurtz declared, and science offers "reasonably objective standards for judging its truth claims." Kurtz saw science as a true metanarrative: "Science has become a universal language, speaking to all men and women no matter what their cultural backgrounds."[66] As you might expect, Postmodernism rejects Secularism's claims. The metanarrative Secularism holds to be true, that objective reason based on scientific knowledge is possible, is the very claim against which Postmodernism reacted in the first place.

Marxism. According to Glenn Ward, the vast majority of mainstream Postmodernists emerged from the Marxist atheistic tradition.[67] Michel Foucault, for example, was at one time a member of the French Communist Party and at another time with a Maoist organization.[68] Jean Baudrillard wrote "within a loosely Marxist framework," thinking it was his responsibility to "bring Marx up to date."[69] During its early years, Marxism promised a this-worldly salvation for the enlightened irreligious. However, the passage of time and countless body bags led postmodernists to reject the Marxist metanarrative while maintaining a similar understanding of class oppression. Postmodernism, as a "wayward stepchild of Marxism," is now orphaned from its parent.[70]

8. CONCLUSION

Postmodernist Melville Herskovits wrote, "Even the facts of the physical world are discerned through the enculturative screen, so that the perception of time, distance, weight, size, and other 'realities' is mediated by the conventions of any group."[71] To which Hadley Arkes responded,

Happily for us all, this argument is fatally vulnerable to the recognition, accessible to the educated, the uneducated—and even, at times, to the overeducated—that there is a material world out there. That world happens to be filled with facts [truths] that do not depend for their existence as facts on the "experience" or the subjective "perceptions" of individuals. Even if the "enculturative screen" of Jersey City affected its natives with fanciful "perceptions" of "distance," the actual distance between Jersey City and Paris is very likely to remain the same.[72]

Arkes, a well-respected professor of political science at Amherst College, was onto something. Postmodernism isn't so much incorrect as it is fanciful at turns, pompous at others, and melodramatic on the whole.

As this chapter draws to a close, let's take a moment to shed light on Postmodernism's flaws so those who find their pulse quickened by its self-portrait can bring their thoughts and feelings into balance.

Postmodernism highlights important concerns but takes them too far. Yes, we can acknowledge differences between people groups, but these differences do not make it impossible to communicate even with people whose life experiences and cultural backgrounds are very different from our own. We can recognize that our experiences are a large part of who we are and yet make reasonable decisions about how to judge between competing viewpoints. Yes, we are shaped by our cultures, but this does not mean we cannot perceive reality as it actually is. The Ferrari we talked about earlier does exist in physical space and time, and our perceptions of it can match the perceptions of others; maybe we think it's cool because it actually is shaped in what can be generally acknowledged as an aesthetically pleasing manner. Yes, we ought to study the way language is used to manipulate people, and there are many instances of this kind of manipulation, but this does not mean all language use is therefore manipulation. Yes, it is interesting to trace the cultural roots of language and study how different traditions describe the world differently, but this does not mean the gulf between cultures is impassable. Postmodernism is not harmless; it will bite. But it can also be tamed.

Postmodernism is blind to the true power struggle language brings about. If each community, through its use of language, determines what is true, then who decides between rival communities in conflict (such as arose with suttee, the Hindu practice of burning a widow on her deceased husband's pyre; or with exterminating the Jewish people through systematic genocide; or with socialism's goal to abolish private ownership of property)? Since no community can claim to know what is objectively "right" in these situations, we have no real resources to draw on in opposing a person or group of people (such as Adolf Hitler and the Nazis) who decide to dispense with our cultural preferences and do whatever they want. Even today we are witnesses to this kind of escalation between warring factions, from the college campus to the political arena to the international scene.

Postmodernists contradict themselves. Take, for example, the phrase "True for you but not for me" or (more consistent with postmodern thinking) "You aren't in a position to know what is true for me." Either way, the Postmodernist has made a statement her philosophy cannot uphold. If the person making this statement means to apply it to you, then you might properly respond, "I get the impression that you think I should believe what you just said. If that is the case, why are you imposing your concept of truth on me?" Some of

> **Deconstructionists believe in authorial intent when they are the authors but deny that intent when it comes to anyone else's works.**

Postmodernism's self-contradictory nature can be seen in deconstructionists' approach to their own writings. D. A. Carson says he has never met a deconstructionist who would be pleased if a reviewer misinterpreted his work. He notes, "In practice deconstructionists implicitly link their own texts with their own intentions."[73] In other words, deconstructionists believe in authorial intent when they are the authors but deny that intent when it comes to anyone else's works.

Postmodernism's view of personhood is unsettling. Jürgen Habermas is a respected German Secularist philosopher who is concerned about Postmodernism's rejection of what makes us human. Glenn Ward explains:

> Habermas sees Postmodernism's apparent embrace of irrationality as morally bankrupt and believes ... that some sort of universally agreed-upon framework is both possible and necessary in order to ensure that freedom and justice are achieved. Habermas disputes the claims of some Postmodern thinkers that human identity is unstable, fragmented, or "in process": for him we all, deep down, share eternal human needs and desires. The failure of the Postmodernists is that they refuse to propose a route towards the fulfillment of these.[74]

The idea of the "self" as nothing more than a collage of social constructions is at odds with what we know of ourselves and others. Is it possible we act as if human nature exists because it actually does?

Postmodernism, when applied, can lead to grotesque results. For a telling example, look at the results of applying deconstructionism to law in the 1973 *Roe v. Wade* decision legalizing abortion on demand. In handing down their decision, the majority of the Supreme Court justices chose to look at the Constitution as a "living document"—that is, open to many interpretations (polysemy). As a result, they invented new meanings from the original text—meanings that were not openly stated—and came up with a novel interpretation regarding a woman's reproductive rights previously unnoticed for almost two hundred years. Since then, more than fifty million unborn children have been murdered at the request of their mothers. Babies have no "essential" nature, and therefore it is impossible to know what exactly it is we should be protecting.

Misunderstanding the relationship between words and meaning casts us adrift in the often turbulent sea of human relationships. Confucius said, "When words lose their meanings, people lose their freedom."[75] But there is a more serious consequence. As Michael Bauman points out, and as the slaughter of hundreds of millions of innocents in the twentieth century amply demonstrates, when words lose their meaning, people lose their lives.[76]

> **Misunderstanding the relationship between words and meaning casts us adrift in the often turbulent sea of human relationships.**

Postmodernism can push us to hone our ability to communicate accurately so as to account for the textures and nuances and shades of meaning that make up human interaction. From the Christian perspective, though, this task is important not because it is academically amusing but because our understanding of God's nature and character blossoms through the exercise. How so? The Bible's answer is clear: "In the beginning was the Word, and the Word was with God, and the Word was God" (John 1:1). God is a communicative God, and he desires for us to communicate with precision and grace. This is exactly what he himself has done in nature and in Scripture, which is why early philosophers deemed theology—the study of God—to be the "queen of the sciences." It is to the sometimes puzzling but always relevant discipline of theology that we now turn our attention.

ENDNOTES

1. Rigoberta Menchu, *I, Rigoberta Menchu: An Indian Woman in Guatemala*, ed. Elisabeth Burgos-Debray, trans. Ann Wright (Brooklyn, NY: Verso Books, 1984), 172–79.

2. David Stoll, *Rigoberta Menchu and the Story of All Poor Guatemalans* (Oxford, UK: Westview, 1999).

3. Quoted in Stoll, *Rigoberta Menchu*, back cover.

4. Quoted in Robin Wilson, "Anthropologist Challenges Veracity of Multicultural Icon," *Chronicle of Higher Education*, January 15, 1999, http://chronicle.com/article/Anthropologist-Challenges/5194/.

5. Quoted in Robert Strauss, "Truth and Consequences," *Alumni*, May/June 1999, accessed March 18, 2014, http://alumni.stanford.edu/get/page/magazine/article/?article_id=40702.

6. Richard Rorty, *Achieving Our Country: Leftist Thought in Twentieth-Century America* (Cambridge, MA: Harvard University Press, 1998), 96. The correspondence theory of truth says a proposition is true or false depending on how it matches up with, or corresponds to, the real world.

7. Myron B. Penner, ed., *Christianity and the Postmodern Turn* (Grand Rapids: Brazos, 2005), 30.

8. Penner, *Christianity and the Postmodern Turn*.

9. Kevin J. Vanhoozer, ed., *Postmodern Theology* (Cambridge, UK: Cambridge University Press), 76.

10. James K. A. Smith, "Who's Afraid of Postmodernism?," in Penner, *Christianity and the Postmodern Turn*, 225. See also R. Scott Smith, "Is Man the Measure? Truth and Postmodernism in Perspective," unpublished manuscript.

11. Postmodernists were not the first to offer such a view of knowledge. Bertrand Russell held a similar view—"all truths are particular truths." See Mary Midgley, *Evolution as a Religion* (London: Routledge, 2002), 127. Midgley offers a classic critique of this position, quoting Ludwig Wittgenstein that "particular propositions cannot always be prior to general ones. Both are elements in language, which is itself an element in our whole system of behaviour. In a crucial sense, the whole is always prior to its parts. And unquestionably this kind of belief in a law-abiding universe … is a precondition of any possible physical science."

12. Vanhoozer, *Postmodern Theology*, 10–13.

13. R. Scott Smith says that "on a naturalistic, evolutionary account of human nature, there are no essences" ("Is Man the Measure?," 142). To Postmodernists, it is possible to *describe* what you think people agree on, but you cannot say that anything is actually "true" or "false" or "good" or "evil." Smith deals with this in his book *In Search of Moral Knowledge: Overcoming the Fact-Value Dichotomy* (Downers Grove, IL: InterVarsity, 2014).

14. Quoted in Scott Consigny, "Nietzsche's Reading of the Sophists," *Rhetoric Review* 13, no. 1 (1994): 7.

15. Quoted in Julian Young, *A Philosophical Biography of Friedrich Nietzsche* (New York: Cambridge University Press, 2010), 18.

16. Quoted in Young, *Philosophical Biography of Friedrich Nietzsche*, 34.

17. Quoted in Young, *Philosophical Biography of Friedrich Nietzsche*, 36.

18. Friedrich Nietzsche, *The Gay Science*, trans. Walter Kaufmann (New York: Random House, 1974), 181. For a clear and understandable analysis of Nietzsche's anti-God and anti-Christ positions, see Will Durant, *The Story of Philosophy* (New York: Simon and Schuster, 1983), chap. 9.

19. John Coffey, "Life after Death of God? Michel Foucault and Postmodern Atheism," *Cambridge Papers*, December 1996, www.jubilee-centre.org/document.php?id=15.

20. Michel Foucault, *The Order of Things: An Archaeology of the Human Sciences* (New York: Vintage Books, 1994), 385. Students reading Foucault need to keep in mind his own admission, "I am fully aware that I have never written anything other than fictions." Quoted in Hubert Dreyfus and Paul Rabinow, *Michel Foucault: Beyond Structuralism and Hermeneutics*, 2nd ed. (Chicago: University of Chicago Press, 1983), 204; also in Penner, *Christianity and the Postmodern Turn*, 30.

21. Postmodernists who identify with the Christian tradition, of which there are a few who proceed through academic arguments rather than popular ones, also posit a "hermeneutics of finitude"—that we are finite and limited in our humanness, so we must be humble or chastened in our claims. We must be careful in saying this, though. If we take this view too far, we might end up saying we cannot understand things Scripture clearly commands us to understand—in which case we make an idol out of our reluctance. This is not humility—it is stubborn sinfulness.

22. Daniel Dennett, *The Intentional Stance* (Cambridge, MA: MIT Press, 1989), 319n8.

23. Edmund Husserl, *Logical Investigations*, trans. J. N. Findlay (London: Routledge and Kegan Paul, 1970), 2:603.

24. Quoted in Charles F. Hockett, "The Origins of Speech," *Scientific American* 203, no. 3 (1960): 89.

25 Quoted in Basil Bernstein, *Class, Codes and Control: Theoretical Studies towards a Sociology of Language* (New York: Schocken, 1971), 26.

26. Martin Heidegger, *Poetry, Language, Thought* (New York: Harper, 2001), 197.

27. George Orwell, *Nineteen Eighty-Four* (New York: Signet, 1949), 46.

28. Orwell, *Nineteen Eighty-Four*.

29. Kevin J. Vanhoozer, *Is There a Meaning in This Text?* (Grand Rapids: Zondervan, 1998), 158.

30. Glenn Ward, *Teach Yourself Postmodernism*, 2nd ed. (Chicago: McGraw-Hill, 2003), 162.

31. Jean-François Lyotard, *The Postmodern Condition: A Report on Knowledge* (Minneapolis: University of Minnesota Press, 1984), xxiv.

32. For a more complete definition of *anti-realism*, see Robert Audi, ed., *The Cambridge Dictionary of Philosophy*, 2nd ed. (Cambridge, UK: Cambridge University Press, 1999), 33, which reads in part, "rejection, in one form or another form or area of inquiry, of realism, the view that there are knowable mind-independent facts, objects, or properties."

33. It is important to note that a worldview also includes what we pay attention to (or ignore) and the habits formed by this attention or lack thereof. What we pay attention to or refuse to acknowledge forms our hopes and fears, and results in patterns of behavior. We are grateful to R. Scott Smith for explaining this, and to J. P. Moreland for recognizing it as a subtle but important nuance. For more information see J. P. Moreland, "Two Areas of Reflection and Dialogue with John Franke," *Philosophia Christi* 8 (2006): 307–8; R. Scott Smith, "Is Man the Measure? Truth and Postmodernism in Perspective," unpublished manuscript available from scott.smith@biola.edu; and "Religiously Based Moral Knowledge—and Final Issues," in Smith, *In Search of Moral Knowledge*, chap. 13.

34. Those four worldviews are (1) Postmodern-ironist: truth is socially constructed; (2) Scientific-rational: truth is found through disciplined inquiry (similar to what we call Secularism in this book); (3) Social-traditional: truth is found in the principles of Western civilization; and (4) Neo-romantic: truth is found through harmony with nature (similar to what we call New Spirituality in this book). Walter Truett Anderson, *Fontana Postmodernism Reader* (Waukegan, IL: Fontana, 1996).

35. Daniel A. Farber and Suzanna Sherry, *Beyond All Reason: The Radical Assault on Truth in American Law* (Oxford, UK: Oxford University Press, 1997), 124.

36. Nancy Pearcey, *Total Truth: Liberating Christianity from Its Cultural Captivity* (Wheaton, IL: Crossway Books, 2004), 114.

37. See R. Scott Smith, *Naturalism and Our Knowledge of Reality* (Burlington, VT: Ashgate, 2012), chap. 5.

38. Paul Feyerabend, "Anything Goes," quoted in Walter Truett Anderson, ed., *The Truth about the Truth* (New York: Tarcher, 1995), 199–200.

39. To understand how much of science has become politicized, see Tom Bethell's *The Politically Incorrect Guide to Science* (Washington, DC: Regnery, 2005).

40. Michael Polanyi, *Personal Knowledge: Towards a Post-Critical Philosophy* (Chicago: University of Chicago Press, 1974).

41. Thomas S. Kuhn, *The Structure of Scientific Revolutions*, 3rd ed. (1962; Chicago: University of Chicago Press, 1996).

42. Millard J. Erickson, *Truth or Consequences: The Promise and Perils of Postmodernism* (Downers Grove, IL: InterVarsity, 2001), 106–7.

43. Kuhn, *Structure of Scientific Revolutions*, 16–19.

44. Douglas R. Hofstadter, *Gödel, Escher, Bach: An Eternal Golden Braid*, 20th anniv. ed. (1979; New York: Basic Books, 1999).

45. Marcia Ascher, *Ethnomathematics: A Multicultural View of Mathematical Ideas* (Belmont, CA: Wadsworth, 1991), 193.

46. Walter Truett Anderson, *Reality Isn't What It Used to Be: Theatrical Politics, Ready-to-Wear Religion, Global Myths, Primitive Chic, and Other Wonders of the Postmodern World* (New York: HarperCollins, 1990), 3.

47. Alasdair MacIntyre attempts to respond to this argument by saying that there is a way to understand another form of life's language, and that is by becoming an insider and learning their language. From this new standpoint you can evaluate which way of life has the rationally superior resources. Rationality is tradition dependent, he says, but we can still adjudicate between rivals. But is this even possible? R. Scott Smith writes, "If all experience is interpreted, then even our experience of ourselves, as well as of the language, culture, and rational resources of that second way of life (even from within it) would be interpreted. It seems, therefore, that we would interpret this alien way of life according to our primary way of life, which could well involve translation (and mistranslation, for that matter)." See "Assessing MacIntyre's and Hauerwas's Projects," *In Search of Moral Knowledge*, chap. 10.

48. Jacques Derrida, *Writing and Difference* (London: Routledge, 2001), 370.

49. See Elizabeth A. Clark, *History, Theory, Text: Historians and the Linguistic Turn* (Cambridge, MA: Harvard University Press, 2004), 42–43, for a discussion of early Postmodern theories and Marxist historical teleology.

50. David F. Ruccio and Jack Amariglio, *Postmodern Moments in Modern Economics* (Princeton, NJ: Princeton University Press, 2003), 167.

51. Christian Postmodernists such as James K. A. Smith, Merold Westphal, Nancey Murphy, Stanley Hauerwas, and Alasdair MacIntyre, would disagree strongly with this claim, but we would press them to identify a philosophical or theological basis for such a nature that transcends culture or interpretation.

52. Ruccio and Amariglio, *Postmodern Moments*, 134.

53. Anderson, *Reality Isn't What It Used to Be*, 3.

54. Mitchell Stephens, "To Thine Own Selves Be True," *Los Angeles Times Magazine*, August 23, 1992, accessed February 11, 2016, www.nyu.edu/classes/stephens/Postmodern%20psych%20page.htm.

55. Kenneth J. Gergen, *The Saturated Self: Dilemmas of Identity in Contemporary Life* (New York: Basic Books, 2000), 174.

56. Rorty, *Achieving Our Country*, 18.

57. R. Scott Smith's definition of brute fact is something that does not have an explanation but is the kind of thing we could and should expect to have. See Smith, *Naturalism and Our Knowledge of Reality*, chap. 5.

58. Richard Rorty, *Philosophy and the Mirror of Nature* (Princeton, NJ: Princeton University Press, 1980), 318.

59. This is reminiscent of the Marxist dialectic (thesis, antithesis, and synthesis) in which the synthesis of agreement becomes a new thesis, disagreement is the antithesis, and the process is never ending.

60. Alister McGrath, *The Twilight of Atheism* (New York: Doubleday, 2004), 227.

61. R. J. Rummel, *Death by Government* (New Brunswick, NJ: Transaction, 1994).

62. Thanks to Alex McLellan for this helpful analogy, which he explores in his book *A Jigsaw Guide to Making Sense of the World* (Downers Grove, IL: InterVarsity, 2012).

63. This particular philosophical tradition was developed among Iranian scholars and is articulated in philosophical journals, such as *Falsafeh: The Iranian Journal of Philosophy* and *Hekmat va Falsafeh*.

64. The Dalai Lama, *A Profound Mind* (New York: Three Rivers, 2011), 87.

65. Dalai Lama, *Profound Mind*, 90.

66. Paul Kurtz, *Humanist Manifesto 2000: A Call for a New Planetary Humanism* (Amherst, NY: Prometheus Books, 2000), 22.

67. Ward, *Teach Yourself Postmodernism*, 78.

68. Mark Lilla, *The Reckless Mind: Intellectuals in Politics* (New York: New York Review of Books, 2001), 150.

69. Ward, *Teach Yourself Postmodernism*, 78.

70. Lawrence E. Cahoone, ed., *From Modernism to Postmodernism: An Anthology*, 2nd ed. (Malden, MA: Blackwell, 2003), 4–5. Also see Gene Edward Veith, *Postmodern Times: A Christian Guide to Contemporary Thought and Culture* (Wheaton, IL: Crossway Books, 1994), 75–76.

71. Melville Herskovits, *Cultural Relativism* (New York: Vintage Books, 1972), 15.

72. Hadley Arkes, *First Things: An Inquiry into the First Principles of Morals and Justice* (Princeton, NJ: Princeton University Press, 1986), 145.

73. D. A. Carson, *The Gagging of God: Christianity Confronts Pluralism* (Grand Rapids: Zondervan, 1996), 103.

74. Ward, *Teaching Yourself Postmodernism*, 179.

75. Quoted in F. A. Hayek, *The Fatal Conceit: The Errors of Socialism* (Chicago: University of Chicago Press, 1989), 106.

76. Michael Bauman makes this statement in a lecture titled "The Meaning of Meaning" given frequently at Summit Ministries' twelve-day conferences. To view the lecture go to www.summit.org/resources/summit-lecture-series/the-meaning-of-meaning/.

CHAPTER **8**

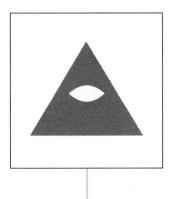

THEOLOGY

1. THREE POSSIBILITIES ABOUT GOD

You might think theology is only for pastors, seminarians, and theologians, but it's not. As we said in chapter 1, **theology** is the study of God and seeks to answer the question, "How did I and everything else get here?" Whether or not we've ever explored arcane theological terms such as *penal substitution* or *soteriology*, and because everyone asks this question, we are all, in a sense, theologians.

Thomas Aquinas was a highly regarded theologian and philosopher born almost eight hundred years ago. Though he died before age fifty, he is called the "Angelic Doctor" because of his fascinating insights and prodigious body of work.

In fact, Aquinas is still so famous that theologians refer to him simply as "Thomas," and their theologian friends all know whom they are talking about. Though brilliant in areas as diverse as ethics, psychology, and just-war theory, Aquinas considered theology to be the queen of the sciences and philosophy merely its handmaiden, because our understanding of God enables us to understand everything else.[1]

Theology: the study of God.

In the modern academy, however, philosophy is seen as a replacement for theology. After all, people who receive advanced research degrees are called doctors of philosophy, not doctors of theology. There is serious doubt about whether theology is worth our time.

Furthermore, many see theology as a matter of preference, like choosing music on a playlist. Don't like Christianity? Click the next selection. Actress Kristanna Loken once said, "I've investigated a number of religions. I was into Zen Buddhism for a while. But voodoo-ism is the one that stuck more. It's very interesting. Not that I practice it or anything."[2] Loken's attitude is common: religion is interesting as long as you don't actually believe it.

If God does not exist, theology is a waste of time. If God does exist, though, everything else is a waste of time if it does not take theology into account. What if, instead of skipping theology in the playlist of ideas, we sought to understand its unique rhythms and its particular structure? We might find ourselves at least appreciating, and possibly enjoying, its study. We might even find truth.

According to C. S. Lewis, there are only three basic possibilities about God. **Theism** is the assertion that a personal God exists independent of the universe. **Pantheism** asserts that god is impersonal and identical to the universe. **Atheism** rejects the existence of any god or gods. Most theological views, including those held by the six worldviews we examine in this book, are variations on one of these basic beliefs.[3]

Theism: the belief in the existence of a God or gods.

Pantheism: the belief that everything in the universe is ultimately divine.

Atheism: the belief that God does not exist.

In this chapter we'll examine the theological views of each of the six worldviews under consideration: Secularism, Marxism, Postmodernism, New Spirituality, Islam, and finally Christianity. Since the ultimate goal of this book is to show the truth of the Christian worldview over and above its competitors, the description of Christianity in this chapter—and in all the following chapters—is more detailed than the description of the other worldviews. As much as possible, though, we've let each of the other worldviews tell its own story in its own words. Having said all this, let's take a look at the theology of each of the six worldviews.

2. SECULARISM

Secular Humanist leader Paul Kurtz was one of those who saw Secularism and Christianity as completely incompatible. He declared,

Humanism cannot in any fair sense of the word apply to one who still believes in God as the source and creator of the universe. Christian Humanism would be possible only for those who are willing to admit that they are atheistic Humanists. It surely does not apply to God-intoxicated believers.[4]

Why would this be so? For Kurtz, "God himself is man deified."[5] To be secular means to admit to nothing higher than human life. It is, as the American philosopher Harold H. Titus said, a "religion without God"[6] that has "abandoned all conceptions of a supernatural and all forms of cosmic support."[7]

> **To be secular means to admit to nothing higher than human life.**

If Kurtz is to be believed, the denial of God's existence is Secularism's dominant theological view. So-called New Atheists like Richard Dawkins, Sam Harris, Daniel Dennett, and the late Christopher Hitchens are among the more prominent Secularist voices today. Their daunting efforts to make atheism respectable and put religion on the defensive seem to be having an effect.

> *New Atheism:* a contemporary form of atheism that not only denies the existence of God but also contends that religion should be vehemently criticized, condemned, and opposed.

There is little new about **New Atheism** except this: it is quite brash. Dawkins, a former professor at Oxford University, once admonished his audience to "Mock them [Christians], ridicule them in public. Don't fall for the convention that we're all too polite to talk about religion."[8]

Earlier atheists wrestled privately with their doubts and only reluctantly went public. The late science-fiction writer Isaac Asimov admitted,

> I am an atheist, out and out. It took me a long time to say it. I've been an atheist for years and years, but somehow I felt it was intellectually unrespectable to say one was an atheist, because it assumed knowledge that one didn't have. Somehow it was better to say one was a humanist or an agnostic. I finally decided that I'm a creature of emotion as well as reason. Emotionally I am an atheist. I don't have the evidence to prove that God doesn't exist, but I so strongly suspect he doesn't that I don't want to waste my time.[9]

The noted philosopher Bertrand Russell popularized his atheism in personal terms with a 1957 book titled *Why I Am Not a Christian*. Russell, who believed in God until age eighteen, wrote, "I am not a Christian.... I do not believe in God and in immortality; and ... I do not think that Christ was the best and wisest of men, although I grant Him a very high degree of moral goodness."[10]

The public admission of atheism is often, its converts claim, accompanied by a sense of freedom. British biologist and author Julian Huxley said, "I disbelieve in a personal God in any sense in which that phrase is ordinarily used." He went on to say, "For my own part, the sense of spiritual relief which comes from rejecting the idea of God as a supernatural being is enormous."[11]

Many Secularists bristle at the atheist label. They aren't telling anyone else what to do, they say; they just do not take God into account. But as Asimov, Huxley, and Russell understood, it's not enough to say, "I have no God beliefs." Evangelism is the logical copilot of belief: if there is no God, people ought to be notified of this. The New Atheists are simply being consistent. If they're right, then those who disagree are uninformed, irrational (for embracing wrong beliefs), or evil (for perpetuating "wrongness"). Tens of millions of books sold testify to the interest aggressive atheism has generated.

The most influential atheist of the twentieth century, though, was not the one who sold the most books but the one who most thoroughly influenced the American education system: John Dewey. Supernatural Christianity was un-American, Dewey thought. "I cannot understand," he said, "how any realization of the democratic ideal as a vital moral and spiritual ideal in human affairs is possible without surrender of the conception of the basic division to which supernatural Christianity is committed."[12] In this sense, Dewey presented a milder version of what Jean-Jacques Rousseau believed: that "theological intolerance," which claims salvation only through the church, is "pernicious" in any place other than a "Theocratic Government." People who make such claims must be "driven out of the State."[13] Dewey joined Rousseau in the belief that salvation from above promotes a "spiritual aristocracy" contrary to the ideals of democracy.

Dewey based his atheism on his understanding of scientific discoveries. "Geological discoveries," he said, "have displaced Creation myths which once bulked large."[14] Biology, said Dewey, has "revolutionized conceptions of soul and mind which once occupied a central place in religious beliefs and ideas."[15] He also said that biology has made a "profound impression" on the ideas of sin, redemption, and immortality. Anthropology, history, and literary criticism have furnished a "radically different version of the historic events and personages upon which Christian religions have built."[16] Psychology, too, has opened up "natural explanations of phenomena so extraordinary that once their supernatural origin was, so to say, the natural explanation."[17] For Dewey, science and the scientific method successfully swept God into the dustbin of history.

> For Dewey, science and the scientific method successfully swept God into the dustbin of history.

While Dewey, along with Huxley and Russell, popularized atheism in the twentieth century, their writing was largely matter-of-fact and polite. Today's New Atheists seem to treat Christianity as a personal offense. Whereas Dewey and company entertained a dialogue, the New Atheists seem intent on ending it. Some Secularists are embarrassed by the New Atheists. Georgetown professor Jacques Berlinerblau, for example, blames New Atheism for Secularism's image problem:

> Instead of honing their powers of critique on anti-secular revivalists [Berlinerblau's term for evangelical Christians], the New Atheists advanced a mixed-martial-arts assault on religion in general. They gleefully (and catastrophically) set about pitting nonbelievers against all believers. They thus included in their onslaught the one constituency in whose hands the future of secularism lies: religious moderates.[18]

It's hard not to see this as a cynical point. If the New Atheist arguments are true, as Berlinerblau believes, then his efforts to recruit moderates is not an attempt to let truth have its day; it's an effort to seduce less-discerning people into accepting an agenda contrary to their beliefs and interests.[19]

THEOLOGY

Ultimately it matters little whether Secularists aim to dethrone God or deify humanity. Secularism is irretrievably atheistic in the meaning of "no God": Either God doesn't exist or he is irrelevant to what is important. Both views put humanity in the place of God. Atheists certainly have the right to express their views, but they ought to be honest about the implications. Atheism, the outspoken atheist Ernest Nagel admitted, "can offer no hope of personal immortality, no threats of divine chastisement, no promise of eternal recompense for injustices suffered, no blueprints to sure salvation.... A tragic view of life is thus [an undeniable] ... ingredient in atheistic thought."[20]

3. MARXISM

Chou En-lai, the first premier of the People's Republic of China, declared flatly, "We Communists are atheists."[21] Marxism does not follow Secularism in attempting to soften atheism's image. From the university days of Karl Marx to the present, official spokespeople for Marxism have been consistent about the content of their theology—that God, whether known as a supreme being, creator, or divine ruler, does not, cannot, and must not exist.[22]

Marxists insist on atheism for ideological reasons: God is an impediment, even an enemy, to a scientific, materialistic, socialistic outlook. The idea of God, insisted Lenin, encourages the working class (the proletariat) to drown its terrible economic plight in the "spiritual booze" of some mythical heaven.[23] The God intoxicated make poor revolutionaries, and the working class (proletariat) must hold no beliefs that cause it to forfeit its only chance of creating a truly human-centered heaven on earth.

> The idea of God, insisted Lenin, encourages the working class (the proletariat) to drown its terrible economic plight in the "spiritual booze" of some mythical heaven.

Atheistic theology was at the heart of everything for Karl Marx. When Marx became an atheist at the University of Berlin, he was not thinking about surplus value or the dictatorship of the proletariat. He was thinking about the philosophies of Georg W. F. Hegel, Bruno Bauer, David Strauss, and Ludwig Feuerbach. "Philosophy makes no secret of it," Marx said. "Prometheus's admission: 'In sooth all gods I hate' is its own admission, its own motto against all gods, heavenly and earthly, who do not acknowledge the consciousness of man as the supreme divinity. There must be no god on a level with it."[24] Marx accepted Feuerbach's conclusion that God is a projection of humanity's own making.

For Marx, humanity is God, creating God in its own image and forming religions for the purpose of self-worship. "The criticism of religion ends with the teaching that man is the highest being for man," he said.[25] Man "looked for a superhuman being in the fantastic reality of heaven and found nothing there but the reflection of himself."[26]

Marx did part ways with his atheistic idols of philosophy by arguing that they were too passive. Thinking, theorizing, and writing can never, in themselves, lead to revolution. We should instead seize control of our destiny and shape it to our specifications. "The philosophers have only interpreted the world, in various ways," said Marx; "the point, however, is to change it."[27]

As Marx looked around society, he saw theism everywhere in charge. To his way of thinking, theism was a squatter needing to be evicted before humanity could settle into its true home. This may explain why *The Communist Manifesto* called for the "forcible overthrow" of not just economic structures but of *all* existing social conditions. Marx's economic theories—and indeed his entire worldview—were tailored to fit his theology. "Religion," said Marx, "is the sigh of the oppressed creature, the sentiment of a heartless world, as it is the spirit of spiritless conditions. It is the opium of the people."[28]

The marriage between atheism and Marxism comes as unwelcome news to those who believe Marx's economic program is basically Christian, as though they have been wooed by an unavailable suitor. An entire subset of Marxism called **liberation theology** was designed to win the hearts of Christians to the Marxist viewpoint.[29] Even so, the dialectical view of history is that once the working class is freed from its chains, religion will cease to exist. Any alliance between Marxism and Christianity would have been, by definition, temporary.

> *Liberation Theology:* **a political movement that interprets the teachings of Jesus Christ as a call to liberate the poor from the materialistic conditions of social, economic, and political oppression.**

The war against capitalism is also a war against religion. Marx put it this way:

> We want to sweep away everything that claims to be supernatural and superhuman, for the root of all untruth and lying is the pretension of the human and the natural to be superhuman and supernatural. For that reason we have once and for all declared war on religion and religious ideas and care little whether we are called atheists or anything else.[30]

Marxism demands adherence to atheism. To be a good Marxist entails being a propagator of atheism. To be the *best* Marxist is to see atheism as part of the scientific, materialistic, socialistic outlook and to strive to eradicate all religious sentiment.

4. POSTMODERNISM

Atheism is the theological belief that there is no God, no supernatural creator, no divine moral lawgiver, and no ultimate judge of humanity's actions. Secularists and Marxists are atheist by conviction. They think belief in God prevents people from doing what they ought. Classic Postmodernism, on the other hand, is atheistic by consequence: belief in God is a socially constructed story of the world, one of many oppressive narratives. Since no such story is true, it follows that no God exists.

> *Theological Suspicion:* **a general distrust toward any religion claiming to know absolute truth about reality.**

Because Postmodernists are not atheist by conviction, we have a hard time summarizing postmodern theology as atheism. Rather, we describe it as **theological suspicion**. Why? Because if you took the pulse of Postmodernism's heart, you'd find that suspicion is its basic rhythm:

- On whether absolute truth exists, Postmodernists are suspicious.
- On whether there is a discernible foundation for knowledge, Postmodernists are suspicious.
- On whether any metanarratives (any overarching stories that define reality) are true, Postmodernists are really suspicious.[31]

The postmodern reflex is to deny that religious truth claims can be known to accurately describe reality.[32]

Kevin J. Vanhoozer says, "Postmodernists agree with Nietzsche that 'God'—which is to say, the supreme being of classical theism—has become unbelievable, as have the autonomous self and finding true meaning in history."[33] In fact, most major postmodern theorists seem to have been atheists: Foucault and Derrida, but also Jean-François Lyotard, Georges Bataille, Roland Barthes, Jean Baudrillard, Pierre Macherey, Gilles Deleuze, Felix Guattari, and Jacques Lacan.[34]

Or not. Postmodernists famously reject labels, which makes their actual views hard to pin down. Are they militant atheists? Soft atheists? Village atheists? Speaking before a convention of the American Academy of Religion in 2002, Jacques Derrida commented, "I rightly pass for an atheist."[35] When asked why he would not say more plainly "I am an atheist," he replied, "Maybe I'm not an atheist."[36] How could Derrida claim to be and not be an atheist? The existence or nonexistence of God both require a universal statement about reality, a statement Derrida was unwilling to make. Mark Goldblatt says, "The only way to read Derrida on his own terms is mentally to insert the phrase 'or not' after every one of his statements."[37] In theology, as in everything else, Derrida preferred ambiguity to certainty.[38]

Likewise, Richard Rorty at one time admitted he was an atheist,[39] but in a subsequent work, *The Future of Religion*, he agreed with Gianni Vattimo's claim: "Atheism (objective evidence for the nonexistence of God) is just as untenable as theism (objective evidence for the existence of God)."[40] Rorty honestly wrestled with spiritual issues, trying to find something in theology and philosophy he thought made sense of the soul. In the end, he said,

> I came to realize that the search of the philosophers for a grand scheme that would encompass everything was illusory. Only a theism that combined a God with equal measures of truth, love, and justice, could do the trick. But since I could not imagine myself being religious, and had indeed become more raucously secular, I did not consider that an option for me.[41]

Rorty considered Christian truth and rejected it not because it was false but because he had a prior commitment to Secularism. Yet atheism, Rorty insisted, is also insufficient and must be abandoned in favor of something he labeled "anticlericalism." Local congregations are innocuous; the real danger lies in ecclesiastical institutions, such as the Roman Catholic Church. "Religion," he said, "is unobjectionable as long as it is privatized."[42]

Religious pluralism is the term we use to describe the recognition that many religions exist and that people disagree about what is true.[43]

Religious pluralism comes in two forms, *descriptive* and *prescriptive*. **Descriptive pluralism** simply acknowledges the obvious: many different religions exist, and their competing definitions of reality cannot all be true, so we must learn to tolerate one another. Tolerance, in this

Religious Pluralism: the acknowledgment that many different religions exist in today's diverse society.

Descriptive Pluralism: the belief that we should be tolerant of competing religions in order to get along with one another.

Prescriptive Pluralism: the belief that we should be tolerant of other religions because no single religion can be universally true for everyone.

case, means learning to live with people you think are wrong. **Prescriptive pluralism** goes one step further: there are many different religions, and none of them can make a claim to be the truth. All views are equally valid. It is this second kind of pluralism, prescriptive pluralism, that Rorty seemed to embrace.

In the premodern and modern eras, religious claims were judged to be either true or false. You may think a person's religious claims are unreasonable, but as long as she doesn't impose them on you, you agree to tolerate them. The new form of religious pluralism embraces the postmodern view of reality and says all religious claims are based on *preference* rather than on objective standards. With ice cream, you just like the flavor you like. No need to explain why. Postmodernism holds the same to be true about religion.

RELIGIOUS PLURALISM	
DESCRIPTIVE PLURALISM	PRESCRIPTIVE PLURALISM
Either God is or is not; we agree to disagree and tolerate one another's views.	*Either you prefer the notion of the existence of God or you do not. No one's claims are actually true for everyone.*
Either Jesus is savior or he is not; we agree to disagree and tolerate one another's views.	*Either you like the idea of Jesus being savior or you do not. No one's claims are actually true for everyone.*
Either miracles happen or they do not; we agree to disagree and tolerate one another's views.	*Either miracles appeal to you or they do not. No one's claims are actually true for everyone.*

To claim that your "truth" is universally true for everyone and not just for you will be seen as a desire on your part to oppress others. Of course, regardless of what we call them, everyone makes truth claims. They do not say, "This is true, but only if you like it." They say, "This is true, I am quite sure." Christianity makes such claims. So do Islam, Secularism, and Marxism. Even Postmodernism's claim that truth cannot be objectively known is itself a claim to truth. Why should such a claim be privileged over the claims of, say, Christianity? Why should the absence of the Ten Commandments at the local courthouse be privileged over their presence? Why should the absence of prayer in public schools trump its presence?

Postmodernism's claim that truth cannot be objectively known is itself a claim to truth.

These questions were difficult already; in some ways Postmodernism makes them more so.

Some people become atheists because they think Darwin solved the question of life's ultimate origins. Others become atheists because they look upon God's moral order as too restrictive. Still others convert to atheism because they agree with Sigmund Freud that "God [is] a projection. When children have problems, they run to their father for protection. When adults have problems, they project their earthly father into the skies, and they run to this entity for comfort."[44] Some look at the evil in the world and decide that no loving God could allow such a situation.[45] In the end, because of its intentional ambiguity, Postmodernism adds little to theological discussions.

5. NEW SPIRITUALITY

The theology of New Spirituality differs drastically from the other worldviews. As we mentioned earlier, New Spirituality rejects theism and atheism and embraces pantheism, which says everything is God. Pantheists have been around for a long time, but in its more sophisticated form, New Spirituality's pantheism goes further by linking spirituality to science. James Arthur Ray, a bestselling New Spirituality celebrity, says,

> Most people define themselves by this finite body, but you're not a finite body. Even under a microscope you're an energy field. What we know about energy is this: You go to a quantum physicist and you say, "What creates the world?" And he or she will say, "Energy." Well, describe energy. "OK, it can never be created or destroyed, it always was, always has been everything that ever existed always exists, it's moving into form, through form and out of form." You go to a theologian and ask the question, "What created the Universe?" And he or she will say, "God." OK, describe God. "Always was and always has been, never can be created or destroyed, all that ever was, always will be, always moving into form, through form and out of form." You see, it's the same description, just different terminology. So if you think you're this "meat suit" running around, think again. You're a spiritual being! You're an energy field, operating in a larger energy field.[46]

God, then, is not a person. God is a word used to describe the spiritual energy of which the universe is composed. To New Spiritualists, this is an exciting way to look at reality, a new fusion of religion and science.

While Secularists, Marxists, and Postmodernists agree that the physical universe is fundamentally energy, so New Spirituality is unique in ascribing divine characteristics to the energy at the source of all things. "Everything has divine power in it," says Matthew Fox, who refers to himself oxymoronically as a Roman Catholic New Ager. This divine force is what gives the planet its "sacredness."[47]

One of the best explanations of pantheism, and one of the most poetic, comes from a children's book titled *What Is God?*

> There are many ways to talk about God. Does that mean that everything that everybody ever says about God is right? Does that mean that God is everything? Yes! God is everything great and small! God is everything far away and near! God is everything bright and dark! And God is everything in between! If everything is God, God is the last leaf on a tree, if everything is God, God is an elephant crashing through the jungle.[48]

There you have it. Stars are God, water is God, plants are God, trees are God, the earth is God, whales and dolphins are God, everything is God. New Spiritualists worship the creation and the Creator at the same time. For them, there is no difference in essence.

So if everything is energy, and this energy is sacred, and we can call it God, what are we? We're part of the everything as well. We are, as Ralph Waldo Emerson put it, "part or particle of God."[49] Kevin Ryerson says, "What is God? God is the interlinking of yourself with the whole."[50] Eckhart Tolle offers a similar perspective:

> When forms around you die or death approaches, your sense of Beingness, of I Am, is freed from its entanglement with form: Spirit is released from its imprisonment in matter. You realize your essential identity as formless, as an all-pervasive Presence, of Being prior to all forms, all identifications. You realize your true identity as consciousness itself, rather than what consciousness had identified with. That's the peace of God. The ultimate truth of who you are is not I am this or I am that, but I Am.[51]

Unlike materialist (only nature exists) and naturalist (natural processes explain everything that exists) worldviews, New Spirituality asserts a transcendent realm consisting of spiritual relationships. This seems similar to Christianity, but it isn't. While the Christian believes in a creator-God who created us and all that exists and whose will can be known through general revelation in nature and special revelation in the Bible, for the New Spiritualist, there is no transcendent God "out there" apart from his creation. God is the creation. Marilyn Ferguson stated,

> New Spiritual theology, like fairy tales, guarantees a happy ending.

> In the emergent spiritual tradition God is not the personage of our Sunday School mentality.... God is experienced as flow, wholeness ... the ground of being.... God is the consciousness that manifests as Lila, the play of the universe. God is the organizing matrix we can experience but not tell, that which enlivens matter."[52]

Reincarnation: the belief that after biological death, the soul is reborn in a new body—either animal, human, or spirit—to continue its quest for enlightenment.

Many New Spiritualists believe that upon death a person's spirit rejoins the energy of the universe and will be reembodied through **reincarnation**. It's an important New Spiritualist belief: in subsequent lifetimes people can come to a fuller understanding of the nature of consciousness and how to be unified with it. New Spiritual theology, like fairy tales, guarantees a happy ending.

6. ISLAM

Like Christianity, Islam holds to **monotheism**. Like Christians, Muslims believe in one God who exists, who created the world, and who will one day hold humans to account. Unlike Christianity, Muslims reject the doctrine of the Trinity, the idea that God eternally exists as three distinct persons—the Father, the Son, and the Holy Spirit. Therefore, Muslims also reject the idea that Jesus Christ was God in the flesh. To believe in the deity of Christ, or the Trinity, is heretical.

Monotheism: the belief in a single deity.

God has ninety-nine names in the Quran (see surah 59:22–24 for some examples), but every Muslim affirms this God as One. This is encased in the creed, "*La ilaha illa Allah, Muhammadu Rasool Allah,*" or "There is no God but Allah, and Muhammad is his prophet." The 112th surah (chapter) of the Quran, though only four verses long, summarizes the Islamic understanding of the unity and nature of God: "In the name of God, the Most Gracious, Most Merciful. Say: He is God, the One and Only; God, the Eternal, Absolute; He begetteth not, nor is He begotten; and there is none like unto Him."[53]

Muslims affirm God as creator. The Quran often appeals to general revelation, the grandeur and order of the world as evidence of God's existence and his creative intelligence. But the Quran itself is held as special revelation, as the most important proof of God's existence. Surah 2:22 says,

> People, worship your Lord, who created you and those before you, so that you may be mindful [of him] who spread out the earth for you and built the sky; who sent water down from it and with that water produced things for your sustenance. Do not, knowing this, set up rivals to God.

The passage continues in verse 23 with a challenge to anyone who doubts the Quran:

> And if ye are in doubt as to what We have revealed from time to time to Our servant [Muhammad], then produce a Sura like thereunto; and call your witnesses or helpers (if there are any) besides God, if your (doubts) are true.

In the mind of the Muslim, the refusal of Jews and Christians to acknowledge the authority of the Quran is proof of their false worship. The term for this is *blasphemy*, and the penalties for it are very serious, including fines, prison, flogging, or even beheading.[54]

In an effort to seek peace, Western political leaders will commonly say things like "Christians, Jews, and Muslims worship the same God." This is misleading. Even if it were true that all three theistic religions worshipped the same God, and this is a matter of much controversy, Islam defines the nature and character of God very differently from Christianity or Judaism.

First, Muslims hold the Quran, not the Old and New Testaments, to be the true Word of God.[55] Some Muslims say the Quran is to Christianity what the New Testament is to the Old Testament—a new and superior revelation. The comparison is inaccurate. Christian theology does not claim the New Testament to be a replacement for the Old Testament; rather, the New Testament appeals to, is dependent upon, explains, and develops the themes of the Old Testament. Christians should have a high regard for the whole Bible—both Old and New Testaments.

Second, as we saw in the chapter on the Christian worldview, the Bible teaches a **Trinitarian monotheism**: only one God exists, and he has revealed himself as three persons—Father, Son, and Holy Spirit.[56] Jews reject this doctrine. Muslims consider the doctrine of the Trinity to be **polytheism** (the idea that many gods exist), which is blasphemy.[57] The Quran repeatedly

> ***Trinitarian Monotheism:***
> the belief in one God recognized as three separate and distinct persons: Father, Son, and Spirit.

> ***Polytheism:*** the belief in a multitude of deities.

warns against claims of Jesus being the Son of God (e.g., surah 4:171 and 5:73) and specifies eternal punishment for those who refuse to repent of this belief. Because the Quran says the doctrine of the Trinity is polytheistic, and because the Quran has absolute authority to Muslims, saying things like "Jesus is God" and "Jesus is the Son of God" constitutes an open-and-shut case of blasphemy.

Third, regarding Jesus's death on a cross, Muslims find repugnant the idea of God allowing one of his holy prophets to die such an ignominious death. Christians disagree. Both the Bible (e.g., 2 Chron. 36:16; Matt. 5:12; 23:31; Acts 7:52)[58] and the Quran (4:155)[59] testify to persecution and martyrdom among the prophets. In addition, the Bible presents the crucifixion not as an illustration of the weakness of God or Christ but rather as an expression of his power (1 Cor. 1:18).[60] Indeed, death by crucifixion came by Jesus's desire to lay down his life (John 10:14–18)[61] in fulfillment of God's promises (Isa. 53; Matt. 26:53–54).[62] Without this submission of Jesus's will, no one could have killed him (Matt. 26:54; John 10:18).[63] Jesus's resurrection from the dead illustrates that he is the Son of God (Rom. 1:4)[64] and has power over death (1 Cor. 15:23–26).[65]

7. Christianity

How we understand the nature and character of God will determine our understanding of everything else. Stephen D. Schwarz says,

> Theism, the belief that God is, and atheism, the belief that God is not, are not simply two beliefs.... They are two fundamental ways of seeing the whole of existence. The one, theism, sees existence as ultimately meaningful, as having a meaning beyond itself; the other sees existence as having no meaning beyond itself.[66]

Christian theology is theistic from verse one of the Bible: "In the beginning God created the heavens and the earth" (Gen. 1:1). That one sentence proclaims a God who is active in and yet separate from his creation, a designed universe, and an intentional life-sustaining earth. If Genesis 1:1 is true, atheism and pantheism are not.

> Christians see evidence of God everywhere; history, theology, philosophy, science, mathematics, and logic all point to the existence of a creator.

Further, the doctrine of the Trinity is one of God in three coexistent, coeternal persons. This is not polytheism, as Islam suggests. Christianity is unwaveringly monotheistic. The Christian case for theism rests on general revelation (the created order) and special revelation (the Bible). Let's take a look at each in turn.

8. General Revelation

The "whole workmanship of the universe," according to John Calvin, reveals and discloses God day after day. The psalmist said, "The heavens declare the glory of God" (Ps. 19:1).[67] Theism is established not by any single clue or evidence, says James Orr, but by "the concurrent forces of many, starting from different and independent standpoints."[68] Christians see evidence of God everywhere; history, theology, philosophy, science, mathematics, and logic all point to the existence of a creator. To the atheistic question, "Can you show me where God is?" the Christian responds, "Can you show me where God is *not?*"

If the universe were disorderly or chaotic, we couldn't expect it to behave in meaningful ways under controlled conditions. Newton's apple might not always fall down. It could hit a pocket of chaos and fall up, or travel sideways through a neighbor's plate-glass window. God's orderly nature led to modern science, according to C. S. Lewis; people expected law in nature, and "they expected Law in Nature because they believed in a Legislator."[69] That is, we see design because there actually is design, and thus there is a designer. One need not have read the Bible to see this. It is generally revealed to all.

Science is not the only way, or even the best way, of knowing truth, but it can reveal something about God to us. Stephen D. Schwarz cites four particular scientific discoveries that support the conclusion that God exists.

1. Second law of thermodynamics. The second law of thermodynamics states, "Although the total energy in the cosmos remains constant, the amount of energy available to do useful work is always getting smaller."[70] The second law of thermodynamics assumes that the universe is a closed system because there is nothing outside of it. The amount of useful energy is decreasing; therefore there must have been a time when the energy clock began ticking.[71]

> ***Second law of thermodynamics:*** a scientific law that states that the amount of usable energy in a closed system will decrease over time.

Walter Brown holds a PhD in mechanical engineering from MIT and for many years was a professor at the US Air Force Academy. "If the entire universe is an isolated system, then, according to the Second Law of Thermodynamics, the energy in the universe that is available for useful work has always been decreasing," he says. "However, as one goes back in time, the amount of energy available for useful work would eventually exceed the total energy in the universe, which, according to the First Law of Thermodynamics, remains constant. This is an impossible condition, implying that the universe had a beginning."[72] Moreover, in our experience, everything that begins to exist has a cause. Since a causal chain cannot be infinitely long, there must have been a first cause. We call this uncaused cause God.

2. Spontaneous generation. The alternative to special creation is that somehow life was generated spontaneously through chance circumstances and that it managed to survive. Through mutations and natural selection, it organized itself and became more complex over time, resulting in all of the variety of life we see today, including the diversity among human beings. According to one of today's most popular biology textbooks, though, after the experiments of Francesco Redi and Louis Pasteur in the mid-1800s unequivocally

> ***Spontaneous Generation:*** the belief that nonliving matter produced living matter through purely natural processes.

disproved the idea, "those who had believed in the spontaneous generation of microorganisms gave up their fight."[73] Four pages later, however, this same text suggests that research by Alexander Oparin and others makes it possible to believe once more that life can arise from nonlife.[74]

Modern experiments do not prove spontaneous generation. Because of the lack of evidence, many biology textbooks cover their tracks with a short section on **panspermia,** the idea that life arrived from outer space. But how did it get into outer space to begin with? It is odd that Secularists are so smug in claiming that life mysteriously arose from an extraterrestrial source when this is precisely the point on which they criticize Christians as "unscientific." Not even Charles Darwin was willing to make this leap. He wrote, "Probably all the organic beings which have ever lived on this earth have descended from some one primordial form, into which life was first breathed."[75] This assumes some sort of uncaused cause doing the breathing.

3. Genetic information theory. When Francis Crick and James Watson discovered the structure of DNA, they trumpeted it as a condemnation of the "god hypothesis" and a debunking of religious myths. More recent research in genetics, however, indicates the presence of information—and not merely of information but of *design.* Francis Collins says, "DNA can be thought of metaphorically as the language of God."[76] This is an astounding thing for Collins to say, given that he directs the National Institutes of Health (NIH) and is the man who led the Human Genome Project to "solve the mysteries of DNA," as *Time* magazine phrased it.[77]

In fact, DNA research is what led Antony Flew, the legendary British philosopher and champion of atheism, to renounce his atheism in a book titled *There Is a God:* "The most impressive arguments for God's existence are those that are supported by recent scientific discoveries." Flew came to this conclusion because "the findings of more than fifty years of DNA research have provided materials for a new and enormously powerful argument to design."[78]

4. Anthropic principle. Robert Jastrow, an astrophysicist instrumental in NASA's development, wrote, "The anthropic principle is the most interesting development next to the proof of the creation, and it is even more interesting because it seems to say that science itself has proven, as a hard fact, that this universe was made, was designed, for man to live in. It is a very theistic result."[79]

What is this anthropic principle to which Jastrow refers? *Anthro* means "pertaining to man." The **anthropic principle** says we can observe the universe only because it exists in a way that allows us as observers to exist. In other words, the universe must have properties that make the existence of intelligent life inevitable. As Albert Einstein affirmed, this requires intelligence: "The harmony of natural law ... reveals an intelligence of such superiority that, compared with it, all the systematic thinking and acting of human beings is an utterly insignificant reflection."[80]

Ongoing discoveries in physics and molecular biology continue to nudge scientists toward theism (see the "Biology" chapter for new research in intelligent design). Perhaps John Dewey's confident assertion that science was sweeping the supernatural into history's dustbin was a bit premature.[81]

9. SPECIAL REVELATION

Through Scripture we come to understand God as redeemer as well as creator. It is through the Bible we discover who this redeemer is: Jesus Christ, "the whole fullness of deity dwells" in human form (Col. 2:9).[82] While the twentieth-century Secular Humanists declared in the *Humanist Manifesto II* that "no deity will save us; we must save ourselves," Christian theism echoes the disciple Thomas, who referred to Jesus as "my Lord and my God" (John 20:28), and Peter, who said to Jesus, "You are the Christ, the Son of the living God" (Matt. 16:16) and later, "You have the words of eternal life" (John 6:68).[83]

Because of special revelation in the Bible, Christians understand God to be a knowable, relatable, self-aware person. In Isaiah 44:6, God said, "I am the first and I am the last, beside me there is no god." In Exodus 3:14, God said to Moses, "I Am who I Am." Besides possessing self-awareness, the God of the Bible expresses emotion, at times portrayed as sorrowful (Gen. 6:6),[84] angry (Deut. 1:37),[85] compassionate (Ps. 111:4),[86] jealous (Exod. 20:5),[87] and gratified with his work (Gen. 1:4).[88] This shows us God's willingness to reveal himself in ways we humans can understand.[89]

> Because of special revelation in the Bible, Christians understand God to be a knowable, relatable, self-aware person.

A careful reading of the Old and New Testaments reveals five characteristics among those central to our understanding of God.

1. God is powerful. Hebrews 1:10 declares, "You, Lord, laid the foundation of the earth in the beginning, and the heavens are the work of your hands." God is the source of all things, and he created the cosmos out of his own mind, according to his plan. But he also is the redeemer of what he created, said C. S. Lewis:

> Christianity thinks God made the world—that space and time, heat and cold, and all the colors and tastes, and all the animals and vegetables, are things that God "made up out of his head" as a man makes up a story. But it also thinks that a great many things have gone wrong with the world that God made and that God insists, and insists very loudly, on our putting them right again.[90]

God also demonstrates his power by moving his world to its purposeful end. The prophet Isaiah wrote (God speaking),

> Remember this and stand firm,
>   recall it to mind, you transgressors,
>   remember the former things of old;
> for I am God, and there is no other;

I am God, and there is none like me,
declaring the end from the beginning
    and from ancient times things not yet done,
saying, "My counsel shall stand,
    and I will accomplish all my purpose,"
calling a bird of prey from the east,
    the man of my counsel from a far country.
I have spoken, and I will bring it to pass;
    I have purposed, and I will do it. (Isa. 46:8–11)

Each created thing has an appointed destiny. God has a plan for his world. Nothing takes him by surprise. The Bible is emphatic on this point. The apostle Paul in his letter to the Romans said, "We know that for those who love God all things work together for good, for those who are called according to his purpose" (8:28). Scripture shows a God manifesting his power by a plan in which human choice and human responsibility are key components.[91]

2. God is self-determining. Christians believe God is self-determining in the expression of his power. What he wills happens. He is sovereign regarding his will, which means he is in charge—he has all authority. The book of Daniel records an instance of an ancient Babylonian king, Nebuchadnezzar, whose power was so great, he saw himself as having all authority: "Is not this great Babylon, which I have built by my mighty power as a royal residence and for the glory of my majesty?" (Dan. 4:30). Pride comes before a fall, and Nebuchadnezzar's fall was horrifying. Scripture says he was "driven from among men and ate grass like an ox, and his body was wet with the dew of heaven till his hair grew as long as eagles' feathers, and his nails were like birds' claws" (v. 33). Once he acknowledged God, Nebuchadnezzar's reason returned, and he regained authority. This time, though, he held it in proper perspective, praising God:

> God has a plan for his world. Nothing takes him by surprise.

His dominion is an everlasting dominion,
    and his kingdom endures from generation to generation;
all the inhabitants of the earth are accounted as nothing,
    and he does according to his will among the host of heaven
    and among the inhabitants of the earth;
and none can stay his hand
    or say to him, "What have you done?" (vv. 34–35)

This acknowledgment of God's sovereignty, coming from the mouth of a pagan ruler, serves as an extraordinary illustration of God's self-determination.

3. God is holy. God commanded his people to "be holy, for I am holy" (Lev. 11:44).[92] The word *holy* is from a Hebrew word that means "sacred, set apart, consecrated."[93] God is not to be taken lightly, thought of in a vain fashion, or referred to with a shrug. Because God is holy, Christianity says, he is fair and always right. He is truly interested in good winning over evil, and he knows exactly what the truly good is.

Today we might say God's nature is the source of goodness itself—pure and free from evil. The Bible assumes good and evil are knowable; rightness and "oughtness" are clear to us all, even when we are incapable of achieving them. As Proverbs 15:3 warns, God distinguishes between good and evil and is concerned with how we live (see also 5:21).[94] Since God's nature is rightness, and since he is knowable, now we too can understand rightness. God's absolute purity shines on our contamination; one look at ourselves and we know we need a redeemer.

> **If God is holy and his will is sovereign, then his very existence serves as judgment of all contrary wills.**

If God is holy and his will is sovereign, then his very existence serves as judgment of all contrary wills. We see what is right, and we know we've gone wrong. We suspect, rightly so, that we cannot continue this path without some sort of reckoning. This "going wrong" is called *sin*. God is the judge of people because all have sinned and fallen short of his glory (Rom. 3:23).[95] God does not take pleasure in the judgment of the wicked (Ezek. 33:11),[96] but judge he must (Jude v.15),[97] because he is holy.

Acts in the Bible, such as the great flood (Gen. 6:17–7:24), the destruction of Sodom and Gomorrah (Gen. 19), the deaths of Nadab and Abihu (Lev. 10:1–7), the fall of the Canaanites (Lev. 18–20), and indeed the fall of Israel (2 Kings 17) and Judah (2 Chron. 36), are all demonstrations of what happens when human behavior departs from God's nature. The judgment of God is not a popular subject, even among Christians. A great majority of people abhor the thought that the "God of love" could also be the "God of wrath." One cannot read the Bible, however, without encountering the judgment of God.[98]

4. God is patient. When we consider God's holiness, we must also remember this: he has revealed himself as patient. In Genesis 5 we meet a man named Methuselah, whose name literally means "When he is dead it shall be sent" (i.e., the deluge, or flood).[99] Methuselah lived longer than anyone else, and God withheld his judgment on the human race for nearly a thousand years.

Scripture is full of instances of God's patience. God withheld judgment on a people group called the Amorites because their sin had not yet reached its full measure (Gen. 15:16).[100] In fact, the phrase "full measure," which most people attribute to Abraham Lincoln's Gettysburg Address, is actually a biblical allusion to the way God weighs his judgment. Later in Scripture, God delayed his judgment upon the Israelites when they worshipped the golden calf (Exod. 32:11–14).[101] In the New Testament, God promises to save believers from eternal judgment (John 10:28).[102] God is holy, but he also knows that we are not holy, so he is patient with us.

5. God is love. Most people who know anything about God will tell you of his loving nature. This leads to a conflict, though. If God is holy, he must judge. To our way of thinking, judging is an unloving thing to do. Therefore, God cannot be both holy and loving. Some resolve this by saying God changed his mind: he used to be judging, but now he is loving. The biblical view is more robust: it is *because* of God's complete goodness that his love is meaningful. We are loved best by the One who is absolutely good, who knows what love truly is and what it costs, and who chooses to love anyway.

---

10. CONCLUSION

Because God is holy, he is completely in character as judge. Because God is love, he is also completely in character as redeemer. God's love is the central theme of redemption. John 3:16 tells us, "God so loved the world that he gave his only Son, that whoever believes in him should not perish but have eternal life." In love God provided an advocate for every individual—a righteous advocate who washes away the sin that should condemn us. God as the redeemer, in the person of Christ, saves humanity from his wrath.

Using John 3:16 as a text for portraying God's love, Christian writer Floyd Barackman points out the following characteristics of this love:[103]

- **God's love is universal.** God loves equally every nation, tribe, race, class, and sex. There were no social prejudices when God offered his Son. Christ died for the rich and for the poor; for the free and for the enslaved; for the old and for the young; for the beautiful and the plain.

- **God's love is gracious.** God loves sinners even when they hate him. Romans 5:8 says, "God demonstrates his own love toward us, in that while we were yet sinners, Christ died for us." The Christian doctrine of grace (from the Greek word from which we get our word *charity*) refers to the kindness of God. God is powerful enough to love the sinner while hating the sin. He expects his children to do likewise (Jude vv.22–23).[104]

- **God's love is sacrificial.** God did not send his only Son to Earth as a role model but as a perfect and atoning sacrifice for humanity's sin. Christ substituted himself for us. His substitutionary death was sacrificial and closely resembles the Old Testament concept of atonement. But there is a difference: atonement in the Old Testament was temporary; Christ's atonement was once and for all (1 John 2:2).[105] Through the death of Christ, God has made a way of reconciliation without compromising his holiness (Col. 1:20).[106] As restored and reconciled image bearers, Christians deliver this message to the world: be likewise reconciled to God (2 Cor. 5:11–21).[107]

> God as the Redeemer, in the person of Christ, saves humanity from his wrath.

- **God's love is beneficial.** For all those who receive Christ (John 1:12),[108] for all those who are born from above (3:3),[109] for all those who believe (v. 16),[110] there await certain eternal benefits given by God. Scripture declares that through God's grace, the believer will not be condemned (Rom. 8:1)[111] and will not be captive to sin (6:11).[112] Further, the believer is a new creation (2 Cor. 5:17)[113] who has been declared righteous (2 Cor. 5:21),[114] redeemed (1 Pet. 1:18–19),[115] forgiven (Eph. 1:7),[116] and is the recipient of the gift of eternal life (John 3:16).[117]

Based on this understanding of God's nature and his plan, Christians see other worldviews as falling short of the complete truth.

- If God exists, Secularism and Marxism fall short. They cannot explain the "why" behind the "what" of life. Like someone who might hop behind the wheel of a beautifully designed car without understanding its design or purpose, the Marxist and Secularist understandings of reality are stunted, lacking fullness and grace.

- By denying God's personal nature, New Spiritualists strip humanity of purpose. If nothing exists but an impersonal force, human existence is no more meaningful than the existence of rocks and trees, stars and oceans. In this view, God is not a personal being who has relationships; "he" becomes an "it." And "it" cannot love you; "it" cannot help you rise to your true potential; "it" cannot restore you to your original design.

- If God is triune, if he is truly three coexistent, coeternal persons in one, equal in purpose and in essence but different in function, then Islam cannot account for God's love or his sacrifice for our sins. There is no security, just severity.

- If God exists and is personal and triune, Postmodernism's understanding of reality as socially constructed fails to explain the world as it is. Neither our perspectives nor our preferences can dictate reality. If God is holy, we will be judged; our preferences are irrelevant.[118]

In the end, as the English moral philosopher Mary Midgley says, "It may simply not be within our capacity—except of course by just avoiding thought—to think of [the universe] as having no sort of purpose or direction whatever."[119] Christian theology begins with this and goes further: it is not that the truth is *unknowable* or that we are confused; it is that truth is *knowable* and we have *rebelled*. Because God clothes our rebellion in robes of redemption, we can do more than wonder whether the universe is purposeful. We can live as if it actually is.

Speaking of what is knowable, though, brings several philosophical questions into play: How do we know what we know? What is actually real? Who are "we" anyway? These are questions philosophers deal with every day. Is philosophy something Christians should care about? Is such a thing as Christian philosophy even possible? These are the questions we will tackle in the next chapter on the discipline of philosophy.

ENDNOTES

1. In *God, Revelation, and Authority,* Carl F. H. Henry explains the demise of theology this way: "The dethronement of theology as queen of the sciences was unwittingly abetted and made almost inevitable by the very scholar who had sponsored its coronation, namely, Thomas Aquinas. Theology as 'queen' implied in Thomism a distinctive relationship between philosophy and theology; philosophy was to prepare the way in the role of natural theology for revealed truth expressed in authoritative church dogmas and papal pronouncements. This approach promised free investigation at the basic level. Its secret commitment to the so-called *philosophia perennis* or fundamental principles of Thomism as the only intelligible philosophy, however, limited the disposition to question all presuppositions. When speculative empiricism countered rather than commended transcendent revelation and Thomism finally ran an unimpressive course, Karl Barth reacted to the opposite extreme: theology, said he, was neither queen of sciences nor even a theoretical science at all. Moreover, Barth dooms philosophy in toto, at least in his earliest writings, to ignorance of ultimate reality. The philosophic quest for cognitive knowledge of the transcendent Barth dismissed as arbitrary and misguided; God, he insists, is to be known not cognitively, but in personal faith-response to a dialectical divine disclosure. To know God, the philosopher must in effect cease to philosophize and become a theologian. No possibility exists, even on revelational grounds, of a Christian philosophy or world view. This negative neo-orthodox view of philosophy grew largely out of Kant's and Hegel's radical erosion of biblical faith. Neo-orthodox theology rejected the liberal Protestant synthesis that had sought by rational reflection on religious experience to harmonize modern science, philosophy and theology. Barth not only rejected the theory that authentic theology makes its

assertions on the basis of an inductive examination of religious experience, but he also insisted that theology is not a rational, scientific study. For him the role of philosophy in the service of theology is purely negative, being limited to exposure of the inadequacies and inconsistencies of speculative alternatives to revelation." Carl F. H. Henry, *God, Revelation, and Authority* (Wheaton, IL: Crossway Books, 1999), 1:203.

2. Kristanna Loken, quoted in *Rolling Stone*, July 24, 2003, 46.

3. Other views of God have been proposed, including *polytheism* (many gods, as in Hinduism) and *panentheism* (god is *in* everything, as in Wicca).

4. Paul Kurtz, ed., *The Humanist Alternative* (Buffalo, NY: Prometheus Books, 1973), 178.

5. Paul Kurtz, *The Fullness of Life* (New York: Horizon, 1974), 35–36.

6. Harold H. Titus, "Humanistic Naturalism," *Humanist* 1 (1954): 33.

7. Titus, "Humanistic Naturalism," 30.

8. Richard Dawkins, quoted in Lillian Kwon, "Atheists Rally for Reason; Urged to Mock the Religious," *Christian Post*, March 24, 2012, www.christianpost.com/news/atheists-rally-for-reason-urged-to-mock-the-religious-72033/.

9. Isaac Asimov, interview by Paul Kurtz, in "An Interview with Isaac Asimov," *Free Inquiry* 2 (Spring 1982): 9.

10. Bertrand Russell, *Why I Am Not a Christian and Other Essays on Religion and Related Subjects* (New York: Simon and Schuster, 1967), 5.

11. Julian Huxley, *Religion without Revelation* (New York: Mentor, 1957), 32.

12. John Dewey, *A Common Faith* (1934; New Haven, CT: Yale University Press, 1962), 84.

13. Jean-Jacques Rousseau, *Rousseau: The Social Contract and Other Later Political Writings*, ed. Victor Gourevitch (New York: Cambridge University Press, 1997), 151.

14. Dewey, *Common Faith*, 31.

15. Dewey, *Common Faith*.

16. Dewey, *Common Faith*.

17. Dewey, *Common Faith*.

18. Jacques Berlinerblau, *How to Be Secular* (New York: Houghton Mifflin Harcourt, 2012), 55.

19. Berlinerblau, *How to Be Secular*.

20. Quoted in Peter Angeles, ed., *Critiques of God* (Buffalo, NY: Prometheus Books, 1976), 17.

21. Quoted in James D. Bales, *Communism: Its Faith and Fallacies* (Grand Rapids: Baker, 1962), 37.

22. See David B. T. Aikman's PhD dissertation "The Role of Atheism in the Marxist Tradition," UMI Dissertation Services, 1979. Aikman covers all aspects of Marxist atheism in his five-hundred-plus-page dissertation.

23. V. I. Lenin, *Collected Works*, 45 vols. (Moscow: Progress Publishers, 1978), 10:83.

24. Karl Marx and Friedrich Engels, *On Religion* (New York: Schocken Books, 1974), 15.

25. Karl Marx and Frederick Engels, *Collected Works*, 40 vols. (New York: International Publishers, 1976), 3:175.

26. Marx and Engels, *Collected Works*.

27. Karl Marx, *On Historical Materialism* (New York: International Publishers, 1974), 13.

28. Marx and Engels, *Collected Works*, 3:175.

29. To be fair, Christian proponents of liberation theology were not atheists or materialists. They accepted much of Marx's teachings but denied that one would have to be an atheist to embrace his critique of capitalism or to believe that the dialectic (the clash between the thesis and antithesis, producing a synthesis) was an accurate description of how history operated.

30. Marx and Engels, *Collected Works*, 3:463.

31. A more complete list of what Postmodernism is against can be found in Robert Audi, *The Cambridge Dictionary of Philosophy*, 2nd ed. (Cambridge, MA: Cambridge University Press, 2001), 725.

32. The logic of this position is very similar to the religious pluralism championed by some liberal theologians—John Hick, William Cantwell Smith, and S. Wesley Ariarajah. We must be careful not to equate these liberal theologians with outright Postmodernists. See David S. Dockery, ed., *The Challenge of Postmodernism: An Evangelical Engagement*, 2nd ed. (Grand Rapids: Baker Academic, 2001), 135, 142.

33. Kevin J. Vanhoozer, ed., *Postmodern Theology* (Cambridge, UK: Cambridge University Press, 2005), 12.

34. The British Broadcasting Corporation's (BBC) website actually lists Postmodernism as a *subset* of atheism. In addition, Charlotte Allen says that Jacques Derrida, Michel Foucault, "and their [followers] … were all militant atheists, with all the intolerance and totalitarian tendencies of that breed." Charlotte Allen, "Believe It," *National Review* 56, no. 17 (September 2004): 52.

35. Quoted in Simon Barrow, "Derrida's Enduring Legacy," *Faith in Society* (blog), October 17, 2004, http://faithinsociety.blogspot.com/2004/10/81_17.html.

36. Barrow, "Derrida's Enduring Legacy."

37. See Mark Goldblatt, "Can Humanists Talk to Poststructuralists?," *Academic Questions* 18, no. 2 (Spring, 2005): 59. "In *Dissemination* Derrida stated: 'It is thus not simply false to say that Mallarme is a Platonist or a Hegelian. But it is above all not true. And vice versa.'" As Goldblatt says, "The 'vice versa' undermines any attempt to get at what

Derrida [meant]." Derrida also regularly employed terminology that simultaneously affirmed and denied. Says Goldblatt, "The only way to read Derrida on his own terms is mentally to insert the phrase 'or not' after every one of his statements."

38. According to Millard J. Erickson, "Derrida's own statements are seldom unequivocal [having one meaning]. He either makes a statement and conjoins it with its contradictory, or makes a statement and then in another place says something very different on the subject." Millard J. Erickson, *Truth or Consequences: The Promise and Perils of Postmodernism* (Downers Grove, IL: InterVarsity, 2001), 131.

39. Robert B. Brandom, ed., *Rorty and His Critics* (Oxford: Blackwell, 2001), 344.

40. Richard Rorty and Gianni Vattimo, *The Future of Religion*, ed. Santiago Zabala (New York: Columbia University Press, 2005), 33, quoted in *Philosophia Christi* 7, no. 2 (2005): 525.

41. Quoted in Millard J. Erickson, *The Postmodern World: Discerning the Times and the Spirit of Our Age* (Wheaton, IL: Crossway Books, 2002), 49.

42. Rorty and Vattimo, *Future of Religion*, 33.

43. D. A. Carson, "Christian Witness in an Age of Pluralism," in D. A. Carson and John Woodbridge, eds., *God and Culture: Essays in Honor of Carl F. H. Henry* (Grand Rapids: Eerdmans, 1993).

44. Ian S. Markham, ed., *A World Religions Reader* (Malden, MA: Blackwell, 2000), 24.

45. Alister McGrath, *The Twilight of Atheism* (New York: Doubleday, 2004), 229.

46. Quoted in Rhonda Byrne, *The Secret* (New York: Atria Books, 2006), 158–59.

47. Matthew Fox, interview by Laura Hagar, "The Sounds of Silence," *New Age Journal* (March/April 1989): 55.

48. Etan Boritzer, *What Is God?* (Willowdale, CA: Firefly Books, 1990), 26.

49. Ralph Waldo Emerson, *Nature* (Boston: James Munroe, 1849), 8.

50. Kevin Ryerson, *Spirit Communication: The Soul's Path* (New York: Bantam Books, 1989), 106.

51. Eckhart Tolle, *A New Earth* (New York: Plume, 2005), 56–57.

52. Marilyn Ferguson, *The Aquarian Conspiracy* (Los Angeles: J. P. Tarcher, 1980), 383.

53. Abdullah Yusuf Ali, trans., *The Holy Qur'an: Text, Translation, and Commentary* (Washington, DC: American International Printing Company, 1946). We have updated punctuation and decreased the frequency of capital letters. Different versions of the Quran vary not only in translation but also in versification. Thus the chapters and verses we use, from Abdullah Yusuf Ali's translation, may differ somewhat from other versions.

54. Punishment for blasphemy is part of shariah law, which is inherently ambiguous, a matter of interpretation on the part of judges before whom the charges are brought. Muslim clerics may respond to perceived blasphemy by issuing a fatwa against the alleged offender. If convicted in a court of Muslim law, the punishment may include fines, prison, flogging, or even beheading.

55. This is different from both Judaism and Christianity. What counts as Scripture in Judaism is the Torah, the first five books of the Bible (Genesis, Exodus, Leviticus, Numbers, and Deuteronomy). The other books of what Christians call the Old Testament, along with a larger body of interpretations handed down from the time of Moses (the Talmud), comprise an expanded definition of Torah. The Muslim belief is also different from Christianity. Christians hold the Old Testament to be Scripture but also believe the New Testament is the inspired Word of God and is useful for teaching, correction, rebuke, and instruction in godliness (2 Tim. 3:16–17).

56. Select passages relating to God as Father: Malachi 2:10; Matthew 23:9; John 14:9–10; 1 Corinthians 8:6; Ephesians 1:3; 4:6; and Hebrews 1:3. Select passages relating to God as Son: John 1:1, 14; 5:18; 8:58; 10:30–33; Philippians 2:5–8; Colossians 2:9; and Hebrews 1:8. Select passages relating to God as Holy Spirit: Matthew 28:19; 2 Corinthians 3:16–18; 13:14; and Ephesians 4:4–6.

57. Jews reject the doctrine of the Trinity as well. For a fuller understanding of Judaism, we recommend the works of Michael L. Brown, *Answering Jewish Objections to Jesus: General and Historical Objections* (Grand Rapids: Baker, 2000); *Answering Jewish Objections to Jesus: Theological Objections* (Grand Rapids: Baker, 2000); and *Answering Jewish Objections to Jesus: Messianic Prophecy* (Grand Rapids: Baker, 2003).

58. Second Chronicles 36:16: "[The Israelites] kept mocking the messengers of God, despising his words and scoffing at his prophets, until the wrath of the LORD rose against his people, until there was no remedy"; Matthew 5:12: "Rejoice and be glad, for your reward is great in heaven, for so they persecuted the prophets who were before you"; Matthew 23:31: "Thus you witness against yourselves that you are sons of those who murdered the prophets"; Acts 7:52: "Which of the prophets did your fathers not persecute? And they killed those who announced beforehand the coming of the Righteous One, whom you have now betrayed and murdered."

59. Quran 4:155: "[We cursed them] for their breaking of the covenant and their disbelief in the signs of Allah and their killing of the prophets without right and their saying, 'Our hearts are wrapped.' Rather, Allah has sealed them because of their disbelief, so they believe not, except for a few."

60. First Corinthians 1:18: "The word of the cross is folly to those who are perishing, but to us who are being saved it is the power of God."

61. John 10:14–18: "I am the good shepherd. I know my own and my own know me, just as the Father knows me and I know the Father; and I lay down my life for the sheep. And I have other sheep that are not of this fold. I must bring

them also, and they will listen to my voice. So there will be one flock, one shepherd. For this reason the Father loves me, because I lay down my life that I may take it up again. No one takes it from me, but I lay it down of my own accord. I have authority to lay it down, and I have authority to take it up again. This charge I have received from my Father."

62. Isaiah 53: "Who has believed what he has heard from us? And to whom has the arm of the Lord been revealed? For he grew up before him like a young plant, and like a root out of dry ground; he had no form or majesty that we should look at him, and no beauty that we should desire him. He was despised and rejected by men; a man of sorrows, and acquainted with grief; and as one from whom men hide their faces he was despised, and we esteemed him not. Surely he has borne our griefs and carried our sorrows; yet we esteemed him stricken, smitten by God, and afflicted. But he was wounded for our transgressions; he was crushed for our iniquities; upon him was the chastisement that brought us peace, and with his stripes we are healed. All we like sheep have gone astray; we have turned—every one—to his own way; and the Lord has laid on him the iniquity of us all. He was oppressed, and he was afflicted, yet he opened not his mouth; like a lamb that is led to the slaughter, and like a sheep that before its shearers is silent, so he opened not his mouth. By oppression and judgment he was taken away; and as for his generation, who considered that he was cut off out of the land of the living, stricken for the transgression of my people? And they made his grave with the wicked and with a rich man in his death, although he had done no violence, and there was no deceit in his mouth. Yet it was the will of the Lord to crush him; he has put him to grief; when his soul makes an offering for guilt, he shall see his offspring; he shall prolong his days; the will of the Lord shall prosper in his hand. Out of the anguish of his soul he shall see and be satisfied; by his knowledge shall the righteous one, my servant, make many to be accounted righteous, and he shall bear their iniquities. Therefore I will divide him a portion with the many, and he shall divide the spoil with the strong, because he poured out his soul to death and was numbered with the transgressors; yet he bore the sin of many, and makes intercession for the transgressors"; Matthew 26:53–54: "Do you think that I cannot appeal to my Father, and he will at once send me more than twelve legions of angels? But how then should the Scriptures be fulfilled, that it must be so?"

63. Matthew 26:54: "How then should the Scriptures be fulfilled, that it must be so?"; John 10:18: "No one takes [my life] from me, but I lay it down of my own accord. I have authority to lay it down, and I have authority to take it up again. This charge I have received from my Father."

64. Romans 1:4: "[He] was declared to be the Son of God in power according to the Spirit of holiness by his resurrection from the dead, Jesus Christ our Lord."

65. First Corinthians 15:23–26: "Each in his own order: Christ the firstfruits, then at his coming those who belong to Christ. Then comes the end, when he delivers the kingdom to God the Father after destroying every rule and every authority and power. For he must reign until he has put all his enemies under his feet. The last enemy to be destroyed is death."

66. Quoted in Roy Abraham Varghese, ed., *The Intellectuals Speak Out about God* (Dallas: Lewis and Stanley, 1984), 98.

67. Psalm 19:1: "The heavens declare the glory of God, and the sky above proclaims his handiwork."

68. James Orr, *The Christian View of God and the World* (Edinburgh: Andrew Elliot, 1897), 111.

69. Clyde S. Kilby, ed., *A Mind Awake: An Anthology of C. S. Lewis* (New York: Harcourt, Brace, and World, 1968), 234.

70. A. E. Wilder-Smith, *Man's Origin, Man's Destiny* (Wheaton, IL: Harold Shaw, 1968), 55.

71. J. P. Moreland and William Lane Craig, *Philosophical Foundations for a Christian Worldview* (Downers Grove, IL: InterVarsity, 2003), 478.

72. Walter Brown, *In the Beginning* (Phoenix, AZ: Center for Scientific Creation, 2008), 30.

73. Barbara Christopher et al., *Modern Biology* (New York: Holt, Reinhart, and Winston , 1999), 281.

74. Christopher et al., *Modern Biology*.

75. Charles Darwin, *The Origin of Species by Means of Natural Selection or The Preservation of Favored Races in the Struggle for Life* (London: John Murray, 1859), Gutenberg ebook, www.gutenberg.org/files/1228/1228.txt.

76. Francis Collins, quoted in Eric Metaxas, *Socrates in the City* (New York: Dutton, 2011), 316.

77. David van Biema, "Reconciling God and Science," *Time*, July 10, 2006.

78. Antony Flew, interview by Gary Habermas, 2004, in *Philosophia Christi* (Winter 2005), www.foranswer.org /Top_Ath/Exclusive%20Interview%20with%20Former%20Atheist%20Antony%20Flew.pdf.

79. Robert Jastrow, "A Scientist Caught between Two Faiths," *Christianity Today*, August 6, 1982, quoted in Norman L. Geisler, *Systematic Theology*, 4 vols. (Minneapolis: Bethany House, 2003), 2:591.

80. Albert Einstein, *Ideas and Opinions* (New York: Crown, 1982), 40.

81. See Stephen C. Meyer, "The Origin of the Biological Information and the Higher Taxonomic Categories," Proceedings of the Biological Society of Washington, August 28, 2004; John Angus Campbell and Stephen C. Meyer, *Darwinism, Design, and Public Education* (East Lansing, MI: Michigan State University Press, 2003); Geoffrey Simmons, *What Darwin Didn't Know* (Eugene, OR: Harvest House, 2004); Michael J. Behe, *Darwin's Black Box: The Biochemical Challenge to Evolution* (New York: Free Press, 1996).

82. Colossians 2:9: "In [Christ] the whole fullness of deity dwells bodily."

83. John 6:68–69: "Simon Peter answered [Jesus], 'Lord, to whom shall we go? You have the words of eternal life, and we have believed, and have come to know, that you are the Holy One of God.'"

84. Genesis 6:6: "The LORD regretted that he had made man on the earth, and it grieved him to his heart."

85. Deuteronomy 1:37: "Even with me the LORD was angry on your account and said, 'You also shall not go in there.'"

86. Psalm 111:4: "He has caused his wondrous works to be remembered; the LORD is gracious and merciful."

87. Exodus 20:5: "You shall not bow down to them or serve them, for I the LORD your God am a jealous God, visiting the iniquity of the fathers on the children to the third and the fourth generation of those who hate me."

88. Genesis 1:4: "God saw that the light was good. And God separated the light from the darkness."

89. God revealing himself in human form is called *anthropomorphism* (*anthropos* is Greek for "human," and *morphe* is Greek for "form").

90. C. S. Lewis, *Mere Christianity* (New York: Macmillan, 1974), 45.

91. Geisler, *Systematic Theology*, 2:543, 574.

92. Leviticus 11:44: "I am the LORD your God. Consecrate yourselves therefore, and be holy, for I am holy. You shall not defile yourselves with any swarming thing that crawls on the ground."

93. *Strong's Concordance with Greek and Hebrew Lexicon*, s.v. "holy," Hebrew 6918, *qadosh*; "sacred, holy:—consecrated(1), Holy(8), holy(50), Holy One(44), holy one(3), holy ones(6), one is holy(1), saints(2)."

94. Proverbs 15:3: "The eyes of the LORD are in every place, keeping watch on the evil and the good"; Proverbs 5:21: "A man's ways are before the eyes of the LORD, and he ponders all his paths."

95. Romans 3:23: "All have sinned and fall short of the glory of God."

96. Ezekiel 33:11: "Say to them, As I live, declares the LORD God, I have no pleasure in the death of the wicked, but that the wicked turn from his way and live; turn back, turn back from your evil ways, for why will you die, O house of Israel?"

97. Jude v. 15: "[The Lord comes] to execute judgment on all and to convict all the ungodly of all their deeds of ungodliness that they have committed in such an ungodly way, and of all the harsh things that ungodly sinners have spoken against him."

98. Geisler, *Systematic Theology*, 3:398.

99. Stelman Smith and Judson Cornwall, *The Exhaustive Dictionary of Bible Names* (North Brunswick, NJ: Bridge-Logos, 1998), s.v. "Methuselah."

100. Genesis 15:16: "They shall come back here in the fourth generation, for the iniquity of the Amorites is not yet complete."

101. Exodus 32:11–14: "Moses implored the LORD his God and said, 'O LORD, why does your wrath burn hot against your people, whom you have brought out of the land of Egypt with great power and with a mighty hand? Why should the Egyptians say, "With evil intent did he bring them out, to kill them in the mountains and to consume them from the face of the earth?" Turn from your burning anger and relent from this disaster against your people. Remember Abraham, Isaac, and Israel, your servants, to whom you swore by your own self, and said to them, "I will multiply your offspring as the stars of heaven, and all this land that I have promised I will give to your offspring, and they shall inherit it forever."' And the LORD relented from the disaster that he had spoken of bringing on his people."

102. John 10:28: "I give them eternal life, and they will never perish, and no one will snatch them out of my hand."

103. Adapted from Floyd H. Barackman, *Practical Christian Theology* (Grand Rapids: Kregel, 2002), 117.

104. Jude vv.22–23: "Have mercy on those who doubt; save others by snatching them out of the fire; to others show mercy with fear, hating even the garment stained by the flesh."

105. First John 2:2: "[Christ] is the propitiation for our sins, and not for ours only but also for the sins of the whole world."

106. Colossians 1:20: "Through [Christ, God] reconcile[d] to himself all things, whether on earth or in heaven, making peace by the blood of his cross."

107. Second Corinthians 5:11–21: "Knowing the fear of the Lord, we persuade others. But what we are is known to God, and I hope it is known also to your conscience. We are not commending ourselves to you again but giving you cause to boast about us, so that you may be able to answer those who boast about outward appearance and not about what is in the heart. For if we are beside ourselves, it is for God; if we are in our right mind, it is for you. For the love of Christ controls us, because we have concluded this: that one has died for all, therefore all have died; and he died for all, that those who live might no longer live for themselves but for him who for their sake died and was raised. From now on, therefore, we regard no one according to the flesh. Even though we once regarded Christ according to the flesh, we regard him thus no longer. Therefore, if anyone is in Christ, he is a new creation. The old has passed away; behold, the new has come. All this is from God, who through Christ reconciled us to himself and gave us the ministry of reconciliation; that is, in Christ God was reconciling the world to himself, not counting their trespasses against them, and entrusting to us the message of reconciliation. Therefore, we are ambassadors for

Christ, God making his appeal through us. We implore you on behalf of Christ, be reconciled to God. For our sake he made him to be sin who knew no sin, so that in him we might become the righteousness of God."

108. John 1:12: "To all who did receive him, who believed in his name, he gave the right to become children of God."

109. John 3:3: "Jesus answered [Nicodemus], 'Truly, truly, I say to you, unless one is born again he cannot see the kingdom of God.'"

110. John 3:16: "God so loved the world, that he gave his only Son, that whoever believes in him should not perish but have eternal life."

111. Romans 8:1: "There is therefore now no condemnation for those who are in Christ Jesus."

112. Romans 6:11: "You also must consider yourselves dead to sin and alive to God in Christ Jesus."

113. Second Corinthians 5:17: "If anyone is in Christ, he is a new creation. The old has passed away; behold, the new has come."

114. Second Corinthians 5:21: "For our sake he made him to be sin who knew no sin, so that in him we might become the righteousness of God."

115. First Peter 1:18–19: "You were ransomed from the futile ways inherited from your forefathers, not with perishable things such as silver or gold, but with the precious blood of Christ."

116. Ephesians 1:7: "In [Christ] we have redemption through his blood, the forgiveness of our trespasses, according to the riches of his grace."

117. John 3:16: "God so loved the world, that he gave his only Son, that whoever believes in him should not perish but have eternal life."

118. Gene Edward Veith, *Postmodern Times: A Christian Guide to Contemporary Thought and Culture* (Wheaton, IL: Crossway Books, 1994), 193–94.

119. Mary Midgley, *Evolution as a Religion* (London: Routledge Classics, 2002), 159–60.

CHAPTER 9

PHILOSOPHY

1. PHILOSOPHY: THE LOVE OF WISDOM

Chinese philosopher Zhuangzi posed this riddle more than two thousand years ago, and philosophy students have been rolling their eyes ever since:

> Once upon a time, I, Chuang Chou, dreamt I was a butterfly, fluttering hither and thither, to all intents and purposes a butterfly. I was conscious only of my happiness as a butterfly, unaware that I was Chou. Soon I awaked, and there I was, veritably myself again. Now I do not know whether I was then a man dreaming I was a butterfly, or whether I am now a butterfly, dreaming I am a man.[1]

Some take Zhuangzi's question as a serious challenge. Most find it amusing but irrelevant, a sort of parlor trick to keep us entertained during commercials. *"If a tree falls in a forest and no one hears it, does it make a sound?"*[2]

At the end of the day, who really cares? Well, Christians should. Jesus said we should love God with our minds (Luke 10:27).[3] If we are to love God fully, we must love what God loves. God loves wisdom. And the love of wisdom forms the academic discipline of **philosophy**.

As we noted in chapter 1, philosophy comes from the Greek words *philo* ("friend") and *sophia* ("wisdom"). The philosopher seeks to be wisdom's companion in exploring the nature of reality (metaphysics) and what it means to know (epistemology). Before we launch into the chapter any further, let's take a moment to familiarize ourselves with three key questions philosophers ask and the technical terms they've devised to explain their way of thinking.

Philosophy: the study of knowledge, truth, and the nature of ultimate reality.

Metaphysics: the branch of philosophy that seeks to understand the nature of ultimate reality.

Materialism: the belief that reality is composed solely of matter.

Monism: the belief that reality is ultimately composed of one essential substance.

Dualism: the belief that reality is ultimately composed of two essential substances.

1. **"What is ultimately real?"** The study of ultimate reality is called **metaphysics**. In Greek, the word *metaphysics* means "beyond the natural things" (*meta* means "beyond"; *physics* means "natural things"). Some philosophers are *monists* (*mono* is Greek for "one") because they believe that reality consists ultimately of one sort of thing. The most common form of monism is **materialism**, which maintains that all reality is, at heart, material.[4] Other philosophers are *dualists* (*duo* is Greek for "two"), who maintain that reality consists of two sorts of things. The most common form of dualism maintains that the universe consists of both material and immaterial entities and properties. So, according to this view, the soul, an immaterial entity, is just as real as the physical body to which it is united.

Philosophers who think that everything that exists has a material explanation are called *naturalists*. All naturalists are monists (one reality) because they believe only the material world exists. On the other hand, most nonnaturalists are dualists, though some are monists because they believe only the spiritual world exists and that the physical world is an illusion.

Monism and **dualism** are both ways of approaching metaphysics. Both try to answer questions about what is real. Both grapple with questions such as

- Are we really just material objects, or do we possess a "being," an immaterial aspect to our nature, such as a soul or mind? What does it mean to "be"?
- Must all things that exist be concrete particulars, like the squirrel on the fence or the rock in my yard, or is it possible for immaterial things to exist, such as numbers, God, minds, souls, and so on?
- Can immaterial things form categories like humanness, squirrelness, kindness, or love? Can categories of meaning be universal and unchanging, describing all humans, all squirrels, all acts of kindness, and all acts of love?

2. **"What does it mean to know?"** **Epistemology** is the study of what knowledge is, how we know, what makes a belief rational to hold, and what actually constitutes knowledge (*episteme* is Greek for "knowledge").

Some philosophers think we can only know things that are discoverable by the scientific method (a view known as **scientific empiricism**). If this is so, many of our common-sense beliefs don't count as knowledge. To people who think this way, beliefs such as "It is wrong to torture children for fun," or "The *Mona Lisa* is a beautiful painting" don't really count as knowledge because they cannot be explained using the scientific method. Yet we seem to know these things, so scientific empiricism cannot be an adequate account of knowledge. There must be ways of knowing beyond those the hard sciences employ.

Epistemology: **the branch of philosophy that seeks to understand the nature of knowledge**

Scientific Empiricism: **the belief that we can know only what we discover through the scientific method.**

3. **"With what part of our being do we contemplate these questions?"** When we think about how we know and what it is to know, we are using our mental powers. But what are mental powers, exactly? Are they merely the consequence of material causes—like when a cue stick hits a billiard ball or when two parts hydrogen and one part oxygen give rise to water? Or is there something immaterial about us, a soul with the power to engage in thought and reflection? This question gives rise to what philosophers call the **mind/body problem**. Those interested in the mind/body problem study the relationship of the mind (e.g., mental events, mental functions, mental properties, and consciousness) to the physical body. Clearly, humans possess the power and ability to

Mind/Body Problem: **the study of the relationship between the mind (e.g., mental events, mental functions, mental properties, and consciousness) and the physical body.**

organize and evaluate their experiences and draw inferences from them. When we see five living things we judge to be trees and one living thing we judge to be a flower, we conclude that the first five have in common a nature called *treeness*, which is different from the sixth thing, which has a nature called *flowerness*. But what enables us to make these judgments? Is this something our brains are doing, or are our minds somehow based in our brains but rising above them as something separate and nonphysical?[5]

These three questions—what is ultimately real, what it means to know, and with what part of our being we contemplate such things—give rise to the rich and complicated field of philosophy. Based on their underlying assumptions, each of the six worldviews we are considering in this book approach these questions somewhat differently. We'll look at each worldview's metaphysics (what it says about the nature of reality and being), its epistemology (what it says about knowledge), and its approach to the mind/body problem, starting with Secularism.

2. SECULARISM

Secularists list a variety of philosophical positions that fit their worldview: **naturalism**, physicalism, materialism, organicism, and other theories "based upon science." But this range is not as broad as it sounds—each doctrine listed holds to the same core tenet: the material world is all that exists. In fact, each of the words listed is really little more than a synonym for naturalism, the philosophical belief that everything that happens can be explained in terms of natural causes (e.g., the law of gravity). If only nature exists, then the immaterial (and supernatural)—the soul, the afterlife, God—do not exist by definition.

Naturalism: the belief that all phenomena can be explained in terms of natural causes.

The commitment to naturalism causes Secularists to be skeptical of the idea of design in the universe, because if there is design, there might be a designer.[6] The naturalist cannot accept a designer or a personal first cause. Henry Miller plainly stated, "To imagine that we are going to be saved by outside intervention, whether in the shape of an analyst, a dictator, a savior, or even God, is sheer folly."[7] Susan Jacoby explains away the idea of design as nothing more than a political movement carried out by a group of "slick, media-savvy right-wingers" whose views are "almost universally rejected by respected mainstream scientists" and who survive by whipping up resentment toward a supposed "liberal establishment conspiracy to protect its Darwinist turf."[8]

Secularism is a complete philosophy. Corliss Lamont, one of the founders of the twentieth-century Secular Humanist movement, proclaimed the rejection of "all forms of supernaturalism, pantheism, and metaphysical idealism" and his belief in "man's supreme aim as working for the welfare and progress of all humanity in this one and only life, according to the methods of reason, science and democracy."[9] Let's look first at the metaphysics of Secularism and then its epistemology.

Metaphysics. Metaphysics, remember, seeks to answer questions like "What is ultimately real?" and "Of what does this reality consist?" Secularists believe the physical universe came into being without a purpose, and that nothing but the universe exists. The late Carl Sagan summed up Secularism's view: "The Cosmos is all that is or ever was or ever will be."[10] For Secularists, no personal first cause exists—only the cosmos. According to Robert G. Ingersoll, "Nature is but an endless series of efficient causes. She cannot create but she eternally transforms. There was no beginning and there can be no end."[11] Strictly speaking, then—since *physics* is all there is to account for everything—Secularism's metaphysics is reducible to physics (or at least the hard sciences). Because of this, Secularists typically avoid the question of how this material universe came to be. They often treat the universe as a given that requires no explanation outside itself. But why is there something rather than nothing? Unfortunately for Secularists, avoiding the question is not the same as answering the question.

Ironically, the most common understanding of the universe's origin, the big bang theory, seems to lead to the conclusion that the universe had a beginning. All beginnings we've observed have a cause. If the universe is caused, there must be a first cause, a being capable of bringing universes into existence, and the characteristics of this first cause must be sufficient to explain everything we see in the universe today, including value, purpose, mental lives, complexity, moral agency, drama, and design. This sounds a lot like the Christian conception of God. Secularism has a very difficult time providing a satisfying account of what common sense teaches us: the universe can't explain itself, and human beings are more than material things but are intrinsically valuable moral agents with free will and immeasurable dignity.

> Ironically, the most common understanding of the universe's origin, the big bang theory, seems to lead to the conclusion that the universe had a beginning.

Epistemology. Secularism's epistemology, or what it believes about knowledge, is straightforward: the scientific method. According to Roy Wood Sellars, "The spirit of naturalism would seem to be one with the spirit of science itself."[12] Sellars's statement is imprecise and can lead to the wrong conclusion. Strictly speaking, *science* means "the process of using the scientific method to observe and measure phenomena in the physical world, devise experiments to organize our observations, improve the accuracy of our measurements, and develop hypotheses we can test to see if our theories are actually true." What Sellars meant is not just that he liked the scientific method but that anything he couldn't figure out how to study *using* the scientific method *couldn't be known*—not by Secularists or by anyone else.

If only those things accessible to the scientific method are knowable, and if the scientific method can access only the natural world, then nothing outside of science, *including the immaterial and the supernatural*, can be known; metaphysical questions about the immaterial and the supernatural are automatically ruled out. Questions that were once answered by appealing to nonscientific concepts, usually associated with religion, such as God, the soul, or the moral law, are dismissed as "not knowable." Thus, and unsurprisingly, Carl Sagan admitted that Secularism's answers mean that "science has itself become a kind of religion."[13]

The entire worldview of Secularism hangs on the peg of epistemological naturalism: nothing outside nature can be known, so if it is not accessible using the scientific method, it cannot be an item of knowledge. Secularists not only believe this; they use it as their method to understand everything, even though the claim "Everything is natural" could never be known by using the scientific method. No matter what they study, they begin with the assumption that only nature exists. This is very important to understand: it is not that Secularists prove that only natural things can be known. It's that they *assume*—because of their method—that only natural things in the material universe can be known.

So how do we make decisions affecting the whole society? As we will see in the "Law" chapter, Secularists tend to believe in *legal positivism*, the idea that law is what those in authority have agreed to do.[14] According to Max Hocutt, "Human beings may, and do, make up their own rules."[15] But *which* human beings, and *which* rules? In great irony, Secularists end up grasping for political power to impose their view on others, something they vehemently oppose when it comes to other worldviews, particularly Christianity.

Mind/body problem. If only the natural world exists, what are human beings? They are, of course, only matter. The mind can be explained in purely physical terms, as smoke can be explained by fire. According to Corliss Lamont, "Naturalistic Humanism ... take[s] the view that the material universe came first and that mind emerged in the animal man only after some two billion years of biological evolution upon this material earth."[16] This belief is

> *Mind/Body Monism:* the belief that human beings are composed of a single substance.

a form of **mind/body monism**, since it is claiming that the universe and human beings consist of only one type of stuff—matter.

Secularism's denial of the immaterial and the supernatural as well as its reliance on science as the only source of knowledge constrains it to a very specific set of answers about mortality, mind, and the very nature of humanity. On the one hand, this means humans control their own fate. On the other hand, without God, a natural moral law, or an eternal soul, there is no purpose beyond what we can see and measure, and no hope beyond what we can accomplish in this life. E. A. Burtt said gloomily, "The ultimate accommodation necessary in a wise plan of life is acceptance of a world not made for man, owing him nothing, and in its major processes quite beyond his control."[17] Even more gloomy is the view of *Scopes* trial attorney Clarence Darrow: "The purpose of man is like the purpose of the pollywog—to wiggle along as far as he can without dying; or, to hang to life until death takes him."[18]

> **Modern science would not have arisen if not for Christianity and its worldview.**

> **When Lenin said that matter is primary, he was implying that matter is eternal and uncreated, that life spontaneously emerged from nonliving, nonconscious matter over billions of years, evolving into mind, thought, and consciousness.**

We'll get to the Christian view of philosophy in a few pages, but since Secularism seems to concentrate on Christianity, it is worth pointing out now that Christians believe science can provide real and important knowledge. The hospitals, charitable organizations, and even churches Christians founded continually make use of the advances of modern science to further the gospel and help people. In fact, as Baylor University sociologist Rodney Stark has convincingly argued, modern science would not have arisen if not for Christianity and its worldview.[19]

To Christianity, though, science is *not the only form* of knowledge. Christians believe our immortal souls can know God. We can know the natural moral law and detect design and order in the natural world. Thus Christianity, like the common sense of the vast majority of the world's citizens, rejects Secularism's narrow view of knowledge.

3. MARXISM

Only the material world exists, Marxists say—no God or gods exist. Karl Marx wrote in a letter to Friedrich Engels, "As long as we actually observe and think, we cannot possibly get away from materialism."[20] Engels said, "The materialist world outlook is simply the conception of nature as it is."[21]

Vladimir Lenin wrote, "Matter is primary nature. Sensation, thought, consciousness are the highest products of matter organized in a certain way. This is the doctrine of materialism, in general, and Marx and Engels, in particular."[22] For Lenin, matter was a philosophical category denoting objective reality—people, plants, animals, stars, and so on. "Matter is the objective reality given to us in sensation."[23] When Lenin said that matter is primary, he was implying that matter is eternal and uncreated, that life spontaneously emerged from nonliving, nonconscious matter over billions of years, evolving into mind, thought, and consciousness.[24]

Epistemology. How do we know what we know? According to the Marxist, the answer is science. Lenin said, "The fundamental characteristic of materialism arises from the objectivity of science, from the recognition of objective reality, reflected by science."[25] Marxist epistemology, like that of the Secularist, places faith in the exclusive truth of science and denies all religious truth claims. Lenin didn't just display confidence in science; he displayed unbounded optimism in his ability to understand and apply what he perceived to be true from scientific observation. According to Lenin, "Perceptions give us correct impressions of things. We directly know objects themselves."[26] The objects Lenin spoke of were strictly material—"Matter is ... the objective reality given to man in his sensations, a reality which is copied, photographed, and reflected by our sensations."[27]

According to Marxism, because anything immaterial or supernatural lacks objective, material reality, we have no means of perceiving it or of gaining knowledge about it. But this leads to a conflict: Marxism consistently speculates about what it thinks science will prove to be true, even if it is not yet proved. For example, Marxists will talk of the inevitable collapse of capitalism and the arrival of the classless society in religious—not scientific—language. Talk about a future utopia cannot be sustained using the scientific method.

Metaphysics. As previously noted, Marxist theology and philosophy deny the supernatural. The universe is all that exists and all that ever will exist. For Alexander Spirkin, a modern Marxist author, "matter is the only existing objective reality: the cause, foundation, content, and substance of all the diversity of the world."[28] Engels said we know from experience and theory "that both matter and its mode of existence, motion, are uncreatable."[29]

But answering "What is real?" merely with "The material world" misses a key aspect of how Marxists view reality. The material world has a certain quality to it that allows it to evolve to a state of perfection. This quality is the *dialectic*.

You may remember the term **dialectical materialism** from the chapter on the Marxist worldview. The dialectic is the view of history, popularized by the German philosopher Georg Wilhelm Friedrich Hegel, in which the way things are done (thesis) generates its own opposition (antithesis), and the resulting clash

> *Dialectical Materialism:* the belief that only the material world exists and that class struggles are the mechanism behind social and economic progress.

leads to a synthesis, which in turn becomes a newer, more advanced thesis.[30] The Marxist take on the dialectic goes like this: Capitalism's excesses generate resentment, which turns into rebellion. The resulting clash leads to a more enlightened economic form, which again generates its own opposition, gradually moving toward pure communism. Marxists are so convinced of the dialectic that they attribute a mystical, almost divine, status to it, even though they claim to be materialists.[31]

So what actually is real, according to the Marxist? The answer: the material universe, but with a divine, dialectic quality. This divine quality explains the order of the universe, the

> Marxists believe in order without an orderer, purpose without a purposer, and justice without any transcendent standard of Good by which to know that evil has been vanquished.

nature of being, all of history, and everything important about humanity. Marxists believe in order without an orderer, purpose without a purposer, and justice without any transcendent standard of Good by which to know that evil has been vanquished.

Mind/body problem. For the dialectical materialist, only matter actually exists. It is eternal, and everything comes from it, even societal interrelationships and what we consider to be our minds. Maurice Cornforth wrote, "Mental functions are functions of highly developed matter, namely, of the brain. Mental processes are brain processes, processes of a material, bodily organ."[32]

For the Marxist, the relationship between the body and the mind is like the relationship between you and the reflection you see when gazing into a still body of water: the reflection is not you, but it is an accurate depiction of one aspect of you—namely, your physical appearance. For Marx, "the ideal is nothing else than the material world reflected by the human mind, and translated into forms of thought."[33] Lenin echoed Marx: "The existence of the mind is shown to be dependent upon that of the body, in that the mind is declared to be secondary, a function of the brain, or a reflection of the outer world."[34] Our brains enable us to capture images of reality, which gives us the sensation of thinking and creates the impression that we have minds.

Dialectical materialism, then, is the philosophy of Marxism. Science and practical experience refine knowledge; the universe is infinite and all that will ever exist; matter is eternal and the ultimate substance; life is a product of this nonliving matter; and the mind is a reflection of this material reality. As we will see in subsequent chapters, dialectical materialism takes the Marxist well beyond philosophy. It is an entire method for viewing the world, coloring the Marxist perception of everything from ethics to history.

4. POSTMODERNISM

> *Correspondence Theory of Truth:* the view that the truth of a proposition is determined by how accurately it describes the facts of reality.

Postmodernism seems to draw a line in the sand in today's universities. Students will likely find Postmodernism playing a prominent role in humanities and social-studies courses, while Secularism still holds the line in science, engineering, and mathematics.[35] In terms of the discipline of philosophy, Postmodernism does not seem to get much traction.[36] The 2009 version of Oxford University's popular 856-page *Introduction to Philosophy* text contains not a single reference to Postmodernism in its index or glossary of terms.[37]

Nevertheless, Postmodernism, like every worldview, makes certain philosophical assumptions, some of which various philosophers have defended. For example, as we will see, Postmodernism rejects the **correspondence theory of truth** (the belief that a proposition is true if it corresponds to reality) and, relatedly, **foundationalism** (the belief that we can have a reliable foundation for knowledge). In its place Postmodernism holds to **anti-realism** (the belief that what we think we know of reality is socially constructed by human thought). Let's explore the differences between these two philosophies by looking at postmodern epistemology and metaphysics.

Foundationalism: the theory that basic beliefs exist and form the foundation for knowledge.

Epistemology. Proponents of other worldviews usually find the Postmodernist's viewpoint on knowledge disorienting. Traditionally, Truth (with a capital *T*) was understood as the relationship between the real, objective world and propositions about the world.

Anti-realism: the denial of the existence or accessibility of an objective reality.

Our statements about the world, in other words, can truly correspond to the world as it actually is. For example, according to this view, when we say that an action or person is just, we mean to say that there is an objective and transcultural standard of justice by which we can make such judgments, even though "justice" is not a material thing like a stone, a baby, or a computer.

Postmodernists, on the other hand, claim there is no universal truth, only particular, subjective truths situated in particular cultural surroundings. There is no way to reliably know "the real" or the "real world" to which truth can correspond, hence the term anti-realism. At this point you might be tempted to scream: "What? Of *course* reality exists! Let me hit you on the head and see if it *really* hurts!" But keep in mind what the Postmodernist is actually saying: our words describe only our interpretation of reality, not reality itself, and over time our words shape our understanding of reality. If you hit someone on the head, you aren't proving the existence of reality; you're proving your belief, doubtless derived from your particular social context, that it's okay to harm others to prove your point. Even if the other person says "Ouch!" you haven't proved anything about reality. "Reality" and all other concepts are expressions of how, based on our particular situations, we use language to interpret what exists.

But if words signify only other words, then words can never be used in the pursuit of Truth. Justice, the anti-realist says, is not something "out there" waiting to be perceived but a word used to describe the way people in a particular culture decide what to do when two people's preferences come into conflict. To the Postmodernist, "justice" is not universally "real"; it is situated in particular times and cultures to serve the needs of people in that local context.

A classic example of words not referring to reality is Michel Foucault's essay "This Is Not a Pipe," in which he analyzed a 1920s-era painting by Belgian artist René Magritte picturing a pipe with the phrase "*Ceci n'est pas une pipe*" ("This is not a pipe") written beneath. Neither the picture nor the phrase was a pipe, Foucault insisted, but merely a text that simulated a pipe:

To the Postmodernist, "justice" is not universally "real"; it is situated in particular times and cultures to serve the needs of people in that local context.

> [Neither words nor the visible] can be reduced to the other's terms: it is in vain that we say what we see; what

we see never resides in what we say. And it is in vain that we attempt to show, by the use of images, metaphors, or similes, what we are saying.... [The drawing] inaugurates a play of transferences that run, proliferate, propagate, and correspond within the layout of the painting, affirming and representing nothing.[38]

The primary idea behind this wordplay is the postmodern insistence that all human beings are conditioned by their cultures and languages—that is, their situations in life. We are finite creatures who are unable to gain a God's-eye view of the world. Our situations require us to interpret the world; universal, objectively true statements of fact are simply not possible.

To Postmodernists, any given statement, such as "The clouds are pink," "Water is wet," or "Let justice roll down," is true for only a small community of individuals who interpret that statement based on their own language and culture. In fact, they see it as true only as long as the community in question agrees upon this particular usage. Occasionally you'll hear someone say, "That is true for you, but not for me." Here's what he or she means: "In your interpretive community, such a claim makes sense, but not in mine. Your claim has no power over me."

> To Postmodernists, any given statement, such as "The clouds are pink," "Water is wet," or "Let justice roll down," is true for only a small community of individuals who interpret that statement based on their own language and culture.

According to Richard Rorty, truth is whatever his community of scholars allowed him to get away with. Rorty, before his death, regularly quoted the French revolutionary Denis Diderot in his speeches: "Man will never be free until the last king is strangled with the entrails of the last priest."[39] Presumably, if Rorty's community let him get away with it, and they did, then the impression that he was actually advocating such a thing would be left to stand. To Postmodernists, "reality" is not what objectively exists; it is only our *agreement* about what is. We do not discover true facts about the real world—we interpret what we see and cannot truly know reality.

Rorty and other Postmodernists aren't just being silly when they say things like this. There are, in fact, many examples of scholars in history "getting away with" theories now believed to have been mistaken. Take, for example, the theory of Claudius Ptolemy (AD 90–168) that the sun revolves around the earth (*geocentrism*). For a long time scientists thought Ptolemy was correct, not because they were stupid or afraid of the church (the common explanations we hear today), but because Ptolemy's predictions about the movement of planetary bodies actually *worked out* to their reasonable satisfaction. It wasn't until much later, when Copernicus (AD 1473–1543) and Galileo (AD 1564–1642) developed new calculations and methods of observation, that scientists changed their minds.

> To Postmodernists, "reality" is not what objectively exists; it is only our *agreement* about what is.

To Rorty's way of thinking, geocentrism was a temporary "truth" that scientists "got away with" as long as no one challenged them. It was "true" because it worked—it made sense of the evidence of the physical world, and it seemed to conveniently correspond to the teaching of Scripture, which pleased the religious people whose support made scientific exploration possible. Scientists got away with it, so according to Rorty, it was true for them at that time. The idea that truth proceeds from what works rather than what is actually *real* is called **pragmatism.**

Unsurprisingly, Christian philosophers mostly reject Rorty's argument. If **knowledge** is "justified true belief"—true when the evidence justifies it and when it corresponds to reality—the geocentric model of the universe is a "justified false belief," a theory that made sense at the time but now is not counted as knowledge because it was never true.

Rorty's argument has found wide acceptance in academic circles (except among most Christian philosophers) because of his commitment to **constructivism** (the idea that we can understand nature only by developing mental constructs to explain our sensory perceptions, and that our models of the world are all we can really know about the world). It is worth taking a moment to reflect on Rorty's point from a Christian worldview, even though we have not yet reached the Christian worldview section of the chapter. Just because something is apparently helpful or justified does not mean it is true. False beliefs, even if widely held, do not count as knowledge. Sin affects more than our motives. It affects our ability to properly understand God's truth. Anyone who has ever been embarrassingly wrong knows how important it is to remain humble, even when he thinks he's right. Philosophers call this *epistemological humility.*

Pragmatism: the belief that propositions do not mirror reality and should therefore be treated as tools and judged only by their practical consequences.

Knowledge: justified true belief.

Constructivism: the belief that scientific knowledge is merely a helpful social construct for understanding human sensory perceptions of reality but not direct and accurate knowledge of reality itself.

The search for knowledge that is "so true that we don't even need God" usually comes back to bite Christians. At the time of Ptolemy and throughout the Middle Ages, the evidence for geocentrism was so compelling that those who disagreed with it faced ridicule. Of course, Christians didn't want to be seen as "unscientific," so they went back to the Bible and "discovered" verses "proving" that the earth was the center of the universe. Ultimately, though, this strategy backfired. When the theory changed, the church was left awkwardly defending an outdated scientific doctrine. Once again today, Christians are ridiculed for being embarrassingly behind the times. However, we shouldn't panic or be too hasty to reinterpret the Bible to "prove" that Christianity is up to date with modern theories. Rather, we should be humble about ourselves, confident in God, and willing to trade in false beliefs for true ones, immature thoughts for mature ones, and weaker explanations for stronger ones.

Metaphysics. Kevin J. Vanhoozer, a shrewd observer of the postmodern scene and a somewhat sympathetic critic, traces Postmodernism's foundational ideas back to Friedrich Nietzsche.[40] Vanhoozer writes, "Nietzsche, the patron saint of postmodernity, prophesied accurately: if God is dead, then it's interpretation 'all the way down.' ... One word only points to another word and never to reality itself. No one interpretation can ever be regarded as final. As in interpretation, so in life: everything becomes undecidable."[41] Without God as our ultimate authority, we take it upon ourselves to interpret reality.

So what is really real? Certainly not essences or substances or literal identities. For the Postmodernist, these are merely words. To pursue knowledge and existence is just to play word games. Here's a baffling but revealing example: in 1991 French cultural theorist Jean Baudrillard wrote an essay, *The Gulf War Did Not Take Place*, in which he claimed that the Gulf War was not real but was merely simulated for CNN television.

> **Without God as our ultimate authority, we take it upon ourselves to interpret reality.**

Of course, Baudrillard did not say that no bombs were dropped. Rather, he argued that calling these particular military maneuvers a "war" was a question of how the parties involved defined *war*, how both Saddam Hussein and the Allied forces used words to shore up their power and get people to see things their way, and how brief clips of anti-aircraft fire were repeatedly played to give the impression that the story the Allied forces told was describing what was actually "real." In the end, the intentions of Hussein were not defeated, Baudrillard argued, so the phrase *Gulf War* refers not to a set of actions that actually took place but to a use of words—of effective rhetoric—that describe a particular viewpoint.[42] The relevance of lives being lost and property being destroyed did not seem to concern Baudrillard; he was obviously severely criticized for this. As Glenn Ward notes, Baudrillard's piece has been used "to discredit not only Baudrillard, but Postmodernism's abandonment of truth and evaluation."[43] Words make a difference. Calling an unborn human a "fetus" or "product of conception" but not a "baby" or "person" changes people's perceptions of the unborn human's value and makes abortion more permissible.

> **Words make a difference. Calling an unborn human a "fetus" or "product of conception" but not a "baby" or "person" changes people's perceptions of the unborn human's value and makes abortion more permissible.**

Fans of the cult-classic movie *The Matrix* might be interested to know that when Morpheus said to Neo, "Welcome to the desert of the real," he was quoting a phrase from Baudrillard's 1981 book *Simulacra and Simulation*. It's probably not important, but it does give you an idea of where his—and other postmodern writers'—mind-bending ideas lead.

> **The Christian worldview maintains that these categories of meaning—creation, sin, redemption, love—all exist independent of our ability to perceive them.**

Postmodern philosophy and Christian philosophy, as we've explained it, could hardly be further apart.[44] Nearly everything about Christianity is expected to be understood, not merely interpreted, and to be understood as universal in scope and application. God created the whole universe, including male and female persons, every one of whom is *universally* affected by sin. God loved the *whole world*. Christ died for the sins of the *whole world*, not just one or two particular communities. Christians are to love God with *all* their hearts and minds and their fellow human beings *around the world*. The Christian worldview maintains that these categories of meaning—creation, sin, redemption, love—all exist independent of our ability to perceive them. They come from the mind of God. Our failure to acknowledge them does not make them any less true.

Up against the postmodern insistence on the indeterminacy of words and the denial that thoughts and things have any truly understandable essence, Christianity says God chose to communicate the Truth about himself and his world by words contained in the Scriptures and the language of the heavens (Ps. 19). The meaning of God's words do not depend upon the reader's interpretation, though Scripture itself calls us to study, reflect on, and apply its words to our lives.[45] What a passage "means to me" is secondary to understanding what God intended to plainly communicate. Further, we aren't alone. We need other believers. The body of Christ has many parts (Rom. 12:4).[46] Most important, we need the Holy Spirit. As the apostle Peter said, "No prophecy of Scripture comes from someone's own interpretation. For no prophecy was ever produced by the will of man, but men spoke from God as they were carried along by the Holy Spirit" (2 Pet. 1:20–21).

> What a passage "means to me" is secondary to understanding what God intended to plainly communicate.

But what about the postmodern challenge? Do people use words in a way that leads others to see the world other than as God created it? Of course! The Bible calls it "[bearing] false witness" (Exod. 20:16). The departure from what we know to be true is, to the Christian, a demonstration of the presence of sin.

5. New Spirituality

New Spirituality looks down its nose at typical philosophical concerns, such as concerns for definitions, creating and distinguishing categories, and making logical arguments. Distinctions between ideas like is or is not, true or false, good or evil are mere human conceptions. Categories and distinctions—and other such philosophical matters—do not describe the world as it actually is. In *The Power of Myth*, one of New Spirituality's most admired books, Joseph Campbell said, "The mystery of life is beyond all human conception.... We always think in terms of opposites. But God, the ultimate, is beyond the pairs of opposites, that is all there is to it."[47] Neale Donald Walsch, a popular author who made a fortune claiming to channel God's thoughts into his books, said, "All things are One Thing. There is only One Thing, and all things are part of the One Thing That Is.[48]

The term that we think best describes this view is *spiritual monism*. Both Secularists and New Spiritualists are monists. However, while Secularists limit reality to only physical matter, New Spiritualists propose exactly the opposite—what is really real is the spiritual, not the physical. Obviously, by asserting that the essence of its subject matter is beyond human comprehension, New Spirituality creates little space for itself

> *Spiritual Monism:* the belief that reality is ultimately divine.

in today's philosophy department, where comprehending, understanding, and reasoning are pretty much the whole point of philosophizing. About the only aspect of New Spirituality of concern to philosophers is its roots in Eastern religions like Buddhism, Hinduism, and

Confucianism, traditions through which more than two billion people in the world today think about reality.

Still, there are a handful of New Spiritualist thinkers who take philosophy seriously. One of these is Ken Wilber, whose book *A Brief History of Everything* tackles many common philosophical problems from a New Spiritualist viewpoint.[49] Even if most New Spiritualists are not deeply philosophical, the widespread nature of New Spirituality in the culture justifies our examination of its views regarding reality and knowledge.

Metaphysics. From the perspective of New Spirituality, what is real? Ultimate reality is consciousness, "the essence of existence, the life force within all things."[50] Secularism and Marxism say that only *nature* exists. New Spirituality, on the other hand, says that only *spirit* exists. Robert Muller suggests this when he says, "Oh God, I know that I come from you, that I am part of you, that I will return to you, and that there will be no end to my rebirth in the eternal stream of your splendid creation."[51] What it means to "be" is entirely spiritual.

New Spiritualist metaphysics, then, begins by rejecting that "only the physical world exists." David Spangler says, "From a very early age I was aware of an extra dimension or presence to the world around me, which as I grew older I came to identify as a sacred or transcendental dimension."[52] The spiritual is very real, and if a person doesn't perceive it, then he is misperceiving. Everything has a spiritual nature, a sacred component. Recall the lyrics from "Colors of the Wind," in the Disney classic *Pocahontas*: "You think ... the Earth is just a dead thing you can claim / But I know every rock and tree and creature / Has a life, has a spirit, has a name."[53]

In singing this song the Pocahontas character implores Captain John Smith to see beyond the physical to the spiritual, because the spiritual is *all* that is actually real. This is pantheism, the idea that from a grain of sand to the Milky Way, *everything is spiritual*—whether we call it God, Gaia, or the force. According to Fritjof Capra, "The universe is no longer seen as a machine, made up of a multitude of objects, but has to be pictured as one indivisible, dynamic whole whose parts are essentially interrelated and can be understood only as patterns of a cosmic process."[54]

Christians can, of course, agree that nature is not merely a machine. Human beings have an organic nature with an intrinsic purpose and ends. Machines have only the purpose or ends imposed on them by their manufacturers. New Spirtualists, though, tend to think that all reality is immaterial (monism), whereas Christians view it as both material and immaterial (dualism).

Epistemology. To the question of what we can know and how, New Spiritualists claim that we can only really know by going beyond the mere appearances of the physical world. We need to get in touch with consciousness or even our "higher selves." Failure to do this not only leaves us without knowledge of what is real, but it also keeps us powerless in the face of other people's conceptions of reality. Shakti Gawain says, "When we consistently suppress and distrust our intuitive knowingness, looking instead for [external] authority, validation, and approval from others, we give our personal power away."[55] Ultimately, Joseph Campbell said, concern about questions of philosophy drains the "aliveness" out of life:

> What's the meaning of the universe? What's the meaning of a flea? It's just there. That's it. And your own meaning is that you're there. We're so engaged in doing things to achieve purposes of outer value that we forget that the inner value, the rapture that is associated with being alive, is what it's all about.[56]

To New Spiritualists, truth is known by feeling or experience, not by scientific knowledge. Knowledge does not contain the meaning of life. Marilyn Ferguson stated, "We need not postulate a purpose for this Ultimate Cause nor wonder who or what caused whatever Big Bang launched the visible universe. There is only the experience."[57]

Mind/body problem. New Spirituality's approach to the mind/body problem is to say that what we call our "body" is actually just a manifestation of spirituality. In terms of the quality of physical existence, there is no "there." In the words of the Dalai Lama, "Emptiness is a quality of all phenomena. As Nagarjuna states, 'There is no phenomenon that is not dependently originated; there is nothing that is not empty.'"[58]

In New Spiritualist philosophy, all is one. Therefore, only one type of ultimate reality can exist, and its essence is spiritual. Spirit is the only substance; matter is only its manifestation. The point is not *understanding* reality but *experiencing* it. Marianne Williamson, a popular New Age feminist author, says that although most people do not think this way, they should: "To say, 'God, please help me,' means, 'God, correct my thinking.' 'Deliver me from hell,' means 'Deliver me from my insane thoughts.'"[59] If you are growing in your experience of consciousness, the New Spiritualist says, you have all the philosophy you need.

6. ISLAM

During the Middle Ages the early Muslim empires established centers of learning and developed a strong philosophical tradition. Two developments were especially significant. First, a group of thinkers called the Mutazilites attempted to evaluate the doctrines of Islam from a reasoned, philosophical standpoint. This caused controversy among theologians, since the Mutazilites came to believe that a number of orthodox Muslim doctrines had major philosophical problems. Among other things, they questioned whether the Quran could be eternal and uncreated, whether its description of God was philosophically coherent, and whether God could judge with justice if everything is purely determined by his will.[60]

The second major development grew out of medieval Muslim scholars discovering the works of the Greek philosophers—especially those of Aristotle. Arab Christians had translated many of these Greek philosophical writings into Arabic, and early Muslim philosophers embarked upon a project attempting to reconcile Aristotelian thought with Islamic theology. Among those who made the greatest contributions to philosophy and became well known in the West are al-Farabi (AD 872–950); Ibn Sina (Avicenna in the West; AD 980–1037); and Ibn Rushd (Averroes; AD 1126–1198). These philosophers developed very sophisticated arguments. However, as was the case with the Mutazilites, their work raised serious questions about whether their thinking was genuinely Islamic.

Al-Ghazali (AD 1058–1111), perhaps the greatest Muslim thinker of all, argued that Islamic philosophy was not genuinely Islamic. Al-Ghazali thought philosophy was ultimately unable to lead to certain knowledge.

> *Fideism:* the belief that faith and reason are independent or at odds with one another.

As a result, he adopted an Islamic **fideism** (i.e., believing that faith and reason are independent of each other) and moved away from rational justification for beliefs and toward mysticism.

Al-Ghazali produced powerful philosophical arguments in support of this and, ironically, is thus regarded as a philosopher himself.[61]

Most scholars agree with al-Ghazali's assessment that the classical Muslim philosophical project of harmonizing Islam with Greek metaphysics was largely a failure. His arguments won the day in medieval times, but philosophy has remained diminished as a discipline within the Muslim world ever since. A few exceptions exist. Some Sufi thinkers developed philosophies in support of their mystical approach to knowing God. Strong philosophical traditions are also rising in Turkey and Iran.[62]

It remains questionable whether any Muslim thinker has articulated a distinct philosophy of Islam that obviously coheres with Islamic theology. Nevertheless, it is fair to say that traditional Islam does display a standard approach to answering the questions raised in metaphysics, epistemology, and truth.

Metaphysics. As a theistic faith, Islam generally holds a similar view of reality to Christianity. It is nonnaturalist, since it affirms the reality of both the natural and the supernatural, the material and the immaterial. Islam also affirms that God created the universe ex nihilo as an act of his will, and that while God remains separate from creation, he actively sustains it and reveals himself in it. God, in Islam, is viewed as a necessary being who could not *not* exist.[63] Muslim philosophers throughout history have offered a variety of arguments in defense of these ideas.[64] Al-Ghazali, in particular, is famous for articulating an early version of the kalam cosmological argument. It may be set out simply as follows: whatever began to exist has a cause for its coming into being; the universe began to exist; therefore, the universe has a cause for coming into being.[65] It was, however, the conviction that the universe was created ex nihilo that led to the greatest problems in reconciling Aristotle's thought to Islamic theology. Aristotle taught that the universe has always existed as a simultaneous and necessary effect of God's perfect existence. If this is so, God is not creator in the way both Christians and Muslims understand him to be.

> **Muslim metaphysics diverges from Christian metaphysics in its view of God's nature.**

Muslim metaphysics diverges from Christian metaphysics in its view of God's nature. Islam clearly rejects the concept of a personal Trinitarian God, instead viewing God as an impersonal, absolute unity. This idea of divine unity—*tawhid* in Arabic—is the preeminent concept in Islam. In Islam, one cannot have a "personal relationship" with God, since that implies some sort of change or movement in God.

Epistemology. Traditional Sunni Islam has a two-tier theory of knowledge. The top tier is the knowledge that comes through special revelation from God—primarily in the form of prophecy in the Quran and the example of Muhammad as described in the Hadith. This sort of knowledge is authoritative, providing a framework for understanding everything else. The second tier consists of all other sorts of human knowledge, such as scientific discovery, experiences through the human senses, and knowledge of other persons. These types of knowledge are regarded as fallible. They may be held to be provisionally true, but they must be understood within, and assessed by, the knowledge provided by special revelation.[66] Muslims presuppose this framework to be valid. They do not feel the need to justify it; justification is needed only for beliefs adopted through the second tier of knowledge.

Because Muslims presuppose their version of special revelation to be true and not open to questioning, they have a hard time dialoging with people who believe differently. So, for example, how do Muslims know that their belief that the Quran is the true word of God is warranted? And how can this belief not need justification when genuine alternatives exist—like the Bible? This approach to epistemology also reveals the problem for philosophy as a discipline within a Muslim worldview. The framework is essentially theological. Philosophy must take a backseat; it has no authority to challenge the assumptions and presuppositions of theology.

Not all Muslims agree with this framework. Sufism, the mystical tradition of Islam, has a radically different approach to knowledge. Sufis say God can be known through personal experience. Moreover, the Mutazilites were an example of a rationalist approach to epistemology (that is, they were looking for a way to demonstrate that Islamic presuppositions were objectively true). Some Muslim philosophers today (particularly in Turkey) are seeking to revive something of this sort of analytical approach to epistemology.

Mind/body problem. Muslim theology does not have a history of wrestling with the mind/body problem to any great degree. Muslims seem to hold a similar view to Christians, that the soul is immaterial and immortal but nevertheless properly resides in a physical body.[67] Surah 91:9–10 talks about God forming the soul and says, "The one who purifies his soul succeeds and the one who corrupts it fails." Muslim philosophy records Ibn Sina, in particular, writing at length about the human soul. Again, however, his very sophisticated (and complicated) account is a dubious attempt to reconcile Aristotle's (essentially) nondualist account of the human soul with orthodox Islamic theology.[68]

7. Christianity

Historically, Christianity and philosophy have been close friends. Francis Bacon famously said, "A little philosophy inclines man's mind to atheism, but depth in philosophy brings men's minds about to religion."[69] In the very order of creation, God made it possible for us to observe something of his revelation and to recognize our observations as meaningful. Other creatures know things, in a manner of speaking, but humans *know* that we know. We have a capacity to contemplate what our knowing Revealer shows us. Christian philosophy says that what we can know is actually there—reality actually exists for us to know, that we can train ourselves to know things because they actually exist. This is called **realism**.

> *Realism:* the belief that an objective reality exists independent of human perception or language.

Because it requires faith in special revelation through the Bible, you might assume that Christianity cannot possibly have a coherent philosophy of its own. Secularism and Marxism point to naturalism and materialism as being grounded firmly in modern scientific methodology and enlightened human experience. What kind of truth can Christians point to that is similarly well grounded? Isn't it simply a matter of reason versus faith?

Actually, the battle of ideas isn't *reason* versus faith but *faith* versus faith, and the faith of Secularism and Marxism is ailing. Even within the last few decades, the materialist explanation of existence has become untenable to many of the world's top philosophers, especially regarding the mind/body problem. Furthermore, noted atheist philosopher Thomas Nagel believes that the only solution will be a "major conceptual revolution at least as radical as [Einstein's] relativity theory."[70] Hoping for a revolution is not an appeal to reason. It is an expression of faith, a longing for a materialist or naturalist savior.

This is not to say that faith is bad. Faith precedes reason, or as W. J. Neidhardt put it, "Faith correctly viewed is that illumination by which true rationality begins."[71] In other words, every worldview begins with basic assumptions about the nature of reality, which, merely by using the scientific method or logical deduction, cannot be proved.

> **To have philosophical integrity, we must base our case on truthful assumptions and the best evidence available.**

Nor does faith replace the need for careful thinking. To have philosophical integrity, we must base our case on truthful assumptions and the best evidence available. Christian philosophers reject neither reason nor tests for truth; rather, they embrace them. The apostle Paul, for instance, when writing of Jesus's resurrection, mentioned Jesus's postresurrection appearance to an audience of five hundred men (1 Cor. 15:3–6).[72] William Lillie, the former chair of biblical studies at the University of Aberdeen said,

> What gives a special authority to the list as historical evidence is the reference to most of the five hundred brethren being still alive. St. Paul says in effect, "If you do not believe me, you can ask them." Such a statement in an admittedly genuine letter written within thirty years of the event is almost as strong evidence as one could hope to get for something that happened nearly two thousand years ago.[73]

> **Scripture offers itself up to reason to test for truth. Christians do not ask nonbelievers to blindly leap into what cannot be known but to consider historical evidence alongside spiritual claims.**

Scripture offers itself up to reason to test for truth. Christians do not ask nonbelievers to blindly leap into what cannot be known but to consider historical evidence alongside spiritual claims.

So from this view, faith precedes reason—in order to understand we must first believe.[74] Secularists and Marxists believe mind evolved out of matter. Christians believe mind existed first—the mind of God. John 1:1 says, "In the beginning was the Word." The word for "Word" is *Logos*, which, as we discussed earlier, refers to both mind and word. We might say *logos* is "a thought expressed." God thought up the universe and then expressed it into existence. Warren C. Young explained it this way:

> Christian realists are contingent dualists but not eternal dualists. They hold that there are two kinds of substance: Spirit (or God) and matter which was created by God ex nihilo as Augustine suggested. Matter is not spirit, nor is it reducible to spirit, but its existence is always dependent upon God Who created it out of nothing.[75]

Young described the Christian view as *Christian realism*.[76] More recently, some have employed the term *substance dualism*: each person has, in the words of Douglas Groothuis, "a material nature (explicable in terms of physics, chemistry and biology) and an immaterial nature (which interacts with but also transcends material states)."[77]

There are many philosophical terms we could choose for our one-phrase summary of Christian philosophy. In an effort to stress the existence of something other than the material, though, we employ the term *dualism* to describe the idea that both the material and immaterial exist.

Epistemology. Christianity says we can know things because their order has been made sensible through Jesus Christ, the incarnation of the Logos. But surely Christianity still runs into an epistemological problem: How does the Christian "know" aside from science and experience? How can the knowledge we gain through faith in biblical revelation compare to knowledge gained by careful, logical investigation?

Secularists and Marxists portray science as a superior form of knowing that trumps biblical revelation, which they regard as superstitious. But what they fail to grasp is that faith in science is still faith. Edward T. Ramsdell wrote, "The natural man is no less certainly a man of faith than the spiritual, but his faith is in the ultimacy of something other than the Word of God. The spiritual man is no less certainly a man of reason than the natural, but his reason, like that of every man, functions within the perspective of his faith."[78]

The basic problem of philosophy is not the problem of faith versus reason. "The crucial problem," said Warren C. Young, "is that some thinkers place their trust in a set of assumptions in their search for truth, while other thinkers place their trust in a quite different set of assumptions."[79] Secularists and Marxists place their trust in certain findings of science and experience, neither of which can be rationally demonstrated as the *exclusive* source of all truth. If you wish to test whether this is so, when someone says, "I only believe what I can prove using the scientific method," respond with this question: "Can you prove *that* belief using the scientific method?" The believer in scientific empiricism claims to know at least one thing science itself cannot deliver or prove.

Christians also appeal to science, history, and personal experience, but they know such avenues for discovering truth are not infallible. Scientists can make mistakes. Historians can twist the truth. Personal experience can be "reimagined" so we see only what we want to. Naturalists dismiss supernaturalism, Young pointed out, "without seeming to be at all troubled by the fact that [in so doing they are making] an emotional rather than a logical conclusion."[80]

So far, we have established two things regarding Christian philosophy: it is not irrational, and its assumptions require no more faith than any other philosophy. But this is just the beginning. As we will see, the positive case for Christian philosophy is quite strong. Let's dig in and see how.

Metaphysics. What is real? Earlier we quoted John 1:1. But let's expand a bit:

> In the beginning [of the cosmos] was the Word [Logos: mind, reason, thought, wisdom, intelligence, idea, law], and the Word was with God, and the Word was God. The same [Word] was in the beginning with God. All things were made by him; and without him was not any thing made that was made. In him was life; and the life was the light of men. (John 1:1–4 KJV)

The flow of this passage sets the parameters of a Christian metaphysics—mind before matter; God before people; plan and design before creation; life from life; and enlightenment from the Light. The orderly universe was conceived first in the mind of God. Without the

Without the Logos there would be no cosmos.

Logos there would be no cosmos. Poetry, philosophy, art, and literature describing order, design, and beauty make perfect sense to the Christian.

The Christian is not surprised to find every level of the cosmos—subatomic, atomic, organic, inorganic, subhuman, human, earth, moon, sun, stars, galaxies—manifesting a surprising order, rationality, and consistency that reflects design. The Christian view of metaphysics, the nature of reality, is an example of what C. S. Lewis termed "mere Christianity"—something about which all Christians agree. It would be an inherent contradiction for someone to claim to be a Christian and yet refuse to acknowledge the creator-God for the universe's actuality, meaning, and purpose.[81] Creation is intelligible because God is intelligent. We can understand the creation and Creator because he made us in his image with the capacity to understand him and his intelligent order.

Creation is intelligible because God is intelligent.

Mind/body problem. The nonnaturalist maintains that mind, or consciousness, is not reducible to the material (or physical) body (or brain). Christians believe the powers of the mind are a reflection of the image of God. For this reason, Christians see the nature of the mind as evidence for the existence of the nonnatural reality. As philosopher J. P. Moreland notes, naturalism cannot account for consciousness and mental events; theism can.[82] The view that the human being consists of two sorts of things—material and immaterial—is sometimes called **mind/body dualism.**

Mind/Body Dualism: **the belief that human beings are composed of immaterial minds and material bodies.**

One argument for mind/body dualism is our perception that our thinking is something different from the material world. Young said, "Man is so made that his spirit may operate upon and influence his body, and his body is so made that it may operate upon his mind or spirit."[83] The distinction between brain and mind implies a distinction about the whole order of things: matter exists (e.g., the brain), and something other than matter exists (e.g., the mind).

Minds seem to be real things that go beyond mere brain function. More than fifty years ago, James Oliver Buswell wrote, "The mind is not the brain. The 'brain track' psychology has failed.... It is a known fact that if certain parts of the brain are destroyed, and the functions corresponding to those parts impaired, the functions may be taken up by other parts of the brain. There is no exact correspondence between mind and brain."[84] New research affirms Buswell's point. Neuroscientist Mario Beauregard goes even further, claiming in *The Spiritual Brain* that what he calls "nonmaterialism" is actually a useful theory that can help solve actual medical problems, such as obsessive-compulsive disorder (OCD).[85]

A second argument for mind/body dualism is the clear distinction between mental events and physical (or material) events. Sir John Eccles has made a voluminous contribution to this discussion. His three works, *The Self and Its Brain* (with Karl Popper), *The Human Mystery*, and *The Human Psyche* are considered classics in the field. It was the position of Eccles, whose work was in medicine, not theology, that having a mind means one is conscious, and that consciousness is a mental state, not a material state. The thought *I love my mom* is not identical to the electrical impulse in my brain that occurs when I have this thought. He further contends that there are two distinct orders; that is, the brain is in the material world, and the mind is in the "world of subjective experience"[86]

We humans have a sense of mindfulness; we intuitively recognize that mental experiences are necessary to understand the physical world but yet are not part of the physical world itself.[87] Not only are we aware of our minds and those of others, but it is only *with* minds that we can understand, conceptualize, investigate, ponder, and reflect upon the deep structure of the material universe. All of this implies the existence of a God powerful enough to structure his creation with mind as an integral part. Consequently, once one grants the existence of an immaterial mind not reducible to anything in the physical universe, belief in the Ultimate Mind seems like the only rational option.

> We humans have a sense of mindfulness; we intuitively recognize that mental experiences are necessary to understand the physical world but yet are not part of the physical world itself.

We have barely scratched the surface here. There is so much exciting research and thinking going on in philosophy and science about the relationship between mind and brain, it will take a lifetime of effort to keep up with it all. Remember, though, that God is much more than an ultimate mind. The mental proof may help to establish the existence of God, but the God of *rational proofs* alone is unworthy of worship. Only the Christian God, in all his power and holiness, elicits awe and love in their proper proportion.

Christian philosophy embraces the meaningful, purposeful life shaped according to a coherent, reasonable, truthful worldview. Christians with such a worldview will not be tossed to and fro by every counterfeit worldview. Warren Young said, "It is the task of the Christian leader to understand the ideologies of his day so that he may be able to meet their challenges. The task is a never-ending one, for, although the Christian's worldview does not change, the world about him does. Thus the task ... requires eternal vigilance."[88]

The Christian worldview is consistent with the revelation of nature and the special revelation of the Bible. Materialism, naturalism, anti-realism, monism, dualism—they cannot *all* be true. To be wisdom's companion means to choose wisely, knowing the choice affects every other aspect of life. Making good choices—choices that enable us to flourish and encourage the flourishing of others—is what people think about in a field related to philosophy called *ethics*. It is such an important area that we have devoted an entire chapter to it. That's what we'll cover next.

ENDNOTES

1. Zhuangzi was a Chinese philosopher writing at about the same time as Aristotle in Greece, three hundred years before the birth of Christ.

2. This question is often attributed to the philosopher George Berkeley (1685–1753). Although he did not actually raise this question in those precise words, the philosophy he defended, idealism, requires that one believe that things exist only insofar as one perceives them. Because God perceives everything, reasoned Berkeley, the universe exists even when we don't perceive it. So, if a tree falls in a forest, and no one is there, it does make a sound because God hears it.

3. Luke 10:27: "[Jesus] answered, 'You shall love the Lord your God with all your heart and with all your soul and with all your strength and with all your mind, and your neighbor as yourself.'"

4. There are other sorts of monists, such as New Spiritualists, who believe everything is, at heart, immaterial.

5. Clinical psychiatrist Daniel Siegel says the mind is an "embodied and relational process that regulates the flow of energy and information." Two main positions have emerged on the mind/body problem. *Mind/body monism* contends that the body and mind are both purely material substances—the brain is the mind and the mind is the brain. *Mind/body dualism* says the mind is an activity, not a thing, and while the mind is somehow resident in the brain, its functions cannot be explained as purely physical. Deepak Chopra and Leonard Mlodinow, *War of the Worldviews* (New York: Three Rivers, 2011), 232–33.

6. Paul Amos Moody states, "The more I study science the more I am impressed with the thought that this world and universe have a definite design—and a design suggests a designer. It may be possible to have design without a designer, a picture without an artist, but my mind is unable to conceive of such a situation." Paul Amos Moody, *Introduction to Evolution* (New York: Harper and Row, 1970), 497; see also, William A. Dembski, *The Design Inference: Eliminating Chance through Small Probabilities* (Cambridge, UK: Cambridge University Press, 1999). High school students will enjoy observing *The Privileged Planet* documentary, distributed by Illustra Media at www .illustramedia.com. For a slightly different, though Christian, perspective, see Brad S. Gregory, "Science versus Religion? The Insights and Oversights of the 'New Atheists,'" *Logos* 12, no. 4 (2009): 17–55; Alvin Plantinga, *Where the Conflict Really Lies: Science, Religion, and Naturalism* (New York: Oxford University Press, 2012).

7. Quoted in Roger E. Greeley, ed., *The Best of Humanism* (Buffalo, NY: Prometheus Books, 1988), 149.

8. Susan Jacoby, *The Age of American Unreason* (New York: Vintage, 2008), 27.

9. Greeley, *Best of Humanism*, 149.

10. Carl Sagan, *Cosmos* (New York: Random House, 1980), 4. For an in-depth look at how Sagan fared in his confrontation with Immanuel Velikovsky, see Charles Ginenthal, *Carl Sagan and Immanuel Velikovsky* (Tempe, AZ: New Falcon, 1995).

11. Robert E. Greeley, ed., *The Best of Robert Ingersoll: Immortal Infidel* (Amherst, NY: Prometheus Books, 1983), 27.

12. Roy Wood Sellars, *Evolutionary Naturalism* (Chicago: Open Court, 1922), 5.

13. Carl Sagan, *UFO's: A Scientific Debate* (Ithaca, NY: Cornell University Press, 1972), xiv.

14. Richard Posner, *The Problem of Jurisprudence* (Cambridge, MA: Harvard University Press, 1990), 228–29.

15. Morris B. Storer, ed., *Humanist Ethics* (Buffalo, NY: Prometheus Books, 1979), 137.

16. Corliss Lamont, *Voice in the Wilderness* (Buffalo, NY: Prometheus Books, 1975), 82.

17. Edwin Arthur Burtt, *Types of Religious Philosophy* (New York: Harper and Brothers, 1939), 353. Clearly, the Humanist has no patience with the anthropic principle, which contends that the world was tailored for humankind's existence. For an excellent defense of this principle, see Roy Abraham Varghese, ed., *The Intellectuals Speak Out about God* (Dallas: Lewis and Stanley, 1984), 102.

18. Quoted in Greeley, *Best of Humanism*, 154.

19. Rodney Stark, *For the Glory of God: How Monotheism Led to Reformations, Science, Witch-hunts, and the End of Slavery* (Princeton, NJ: Princeton University Press, 2003).

20. Quoted in Greeley, *Best of Humanism*, 15.

21. Quoted in Joseph Stalin, *Dialectical and Historical Materialism* (New York: International Publishers, 1977), 15.

22. V. I. Lenin, *Materialism and Empirio-Criticism* (New York: International Publishers, 1927), 21.

23. Lenin, *Materialism and Empirio-Criticism*, 145.

24. See Delos Mckown's discussion in *The Classical Marxist Critiques of Religion: Marx, Engels, Lenin, Kautsky* (The Hague: Martinus Nijhoff, 1975), specifically the chapter on "Lenin's Critique of Religion."

25. Lenin, *Materialism and Empirio-Criticism*, 252.

26. Lenin, *Materialism and Empirio-Criticism*, 81.

27. Lenin, *Materialism and Empirio-Criticism*, 102.

28. Alexander Spirkin, *Dialectics and Materialism* (Moscow: Progress Publishers, 1983), 66.

29. Frederick Engels, *Dialectics of Nature* (New York: International Publishers, 1976), 337.

30. Gustav A. Wetter stated, "In Hegel's sense of the term, dialectic is a process in which a starting-point [a thesis, e.g., Being] is negated [the antithesis, e.g., Non-Being], thereby setting up a second position opposed to it. This second position is in turn negated, i.e., by negation of the negation, so as to reach a third position representing a synthesis [e.g., Becoming] of the two preceding, in which both are 'transcended,' i.e., abolished and at the same time preserved on a higher level of being. This third phase then figures in turn as the first step in a new dialectical process [i.e., a new thesis], leading to a new synthesis, and so on." Gustav A. Wetter, *Dialectical Materialism* (Westport, CT: Greenwood Press, 1977), 4.

31. When the dialectic is combined with materialism, which says that only the world of matter exists, you have an explanation of reality that actually has mystical attributes, according to Gustav Wetter, a Catholic priest and expert on Marxist philosophy: "In dialectical materialism ... the higher is not, as such, denied; the world is interpreted

as a process of continual ascent, which fundamentally extends into infinity. But it is supposed to be matter itself which continually attains to higher perfection under its own power, thanks to its indwelling dialectic. As Nikolai Berdyaev very rightly remarks, the dialectical materialist attribution of 'dialectic' to matter confers on it, not mental attributes only, but even divine ones." Wetter, *Dialectical Materialism*, 558.

32. Maurice Cornforth, *The Theory of Knowledge* (New York: International Publishers, 1963), 22.

33. Karl Marx, *Capital*, vol. 1, *A Critical Analysis of Capitalist Production* (London: Progress Publishers, 1889).

34. Lenin, *Materialism and Empirio-Criticism*, 66.

35. Nancy Pearcey, *Total Truth: Liberating Christianity from Its Cultural Captivity* (Wheaton, IL: Crossway Books, 2004), 107, 113.

36. Myron B. Penner, ed., *Christianity and the Postmodern Turn* (Grand Rapids: Brazos, 2005), 210.

37. John Perry, Michael Bratman, and John Martin Fischer, *Introduction to Philosophy* (New York: Oxford University Press, 2010).

38. Michel Foucault, *This Is Not a Pipe* (Berkeley, CA: University of California Press, 1983), 9, 49.

39. Ronald Hamowy, ed., *The Encyclopedia of Libertarianism* (Thousand Oaks, CA: Sage, 2008), s.v. "Diderot, Denis (1713–1784)."

40. For background material on Nietzsche, see Arthur Herman, *The Idea of Decline in Western History* (New York: Free Press, 1997); Will Durant, *The Story of Philosophy* (New York: Pocket Books, 2006); and John P. Koster, *The Atheist Syndrome* (Brentwood, TN: Wolgemuth and Hyatt, 1989).

41. Quoted in Penner, *Christianity and the Postmodern Turn*, 78.

42. See Jean Baudrillard, *The Gulf War Did Not Take Place*, trans. Paul Patton (Bloomington, IN: Indiana University Press, 1995).

43. Glenn Ward, *Teach Yourself Postmodernism*, 2nd ed. (Chicago: McGraw-Hill, 2003), 77. For a systematic analysis and critique of Postmodernism, we recommend Christopher Norris, *The Truth about Postmodernism* (Oxford, UK: Blackwell, 1996).

44. As we have acknowledged, there are Christian Postmodernists who accept God and believe many aspects of Christian doctrine. For examples of Christian Postmodernism, see Nancey Murphy, *Beyond Liberalism and Fundamentalism*, and *Anglo-American Postmodernity*; James K. A. Smith, *Who's Afraid of Postmodernism?*; Alasdair MacIntyre, *After Virtue*, and *Whose Justice? Which Rationality?*; and Stanley Grenz and John Franke, *Beyond Foundationalism*. Stanley Hauerwas is also an important figure who has written many books. For books responding to Christian Postmodernism, see Doug Groothuis, *Truth Decay*; Kevin DeYoung, *Why We're Not Emergent—By Two Guys Who Ought to Be*; R. Scott Smith, *Truth and the New Kind of Christian: The Emerging Effects of Postmodernism in the Church*, and *Naturalism and Our Knowledge of Reality: Testing Religious Truth-Claims*.

45. To correctly understand the meaning of any text of Scripture, we should heed Paul's advice to Timothy: "Do your best to present yourself to God as one approved, a workman who does not need to be ashamed and who correctly handles the word of truth" (2 Tim. 2:15). By acknowledging that God has communicated in language Truth about the real world, and by diligently studying the Bible, you can know the Truth that sets you free (John 8:32).

46. Romans 12:4: "As in one body we have many members, and the members do not all have the same function."

47. Joseph Campbell, *The Power of Myth* (New York: Doubleday, 1988), 49. One is tempted to reply, "So either God thinks in terms of opposites or he doesn't," and "That is all there is to it ... as opposed to something more?" It's hard to make any claims about reality without resorting to the claim that our propositions stand opposed to what reality might otherwise be described as being.

48. Neale Donald Walsch, *The New Revelations: A Conversation with God* (New York: Atria Books, 2002), 360.

49. See Ken Wilber, *A Brief History of Everything* (Boston: Shambhala, 2001); see also Douglas Groothuis's related review of Wilber's book *A Theory of Everything* in "A Summary Critique: Nothing Much about Everything," *Christian Research Journal* 23, no. 4 (2001) at www.equip.org/PDF/DW258.pdf.

50. Dean C. Halverson, *Crystal Clear: Understanding and Reaching New Agers* (Colorado Springs: NavPress, 1990), 91.

51. Robert Muller, *The New Genesis: Shaping a Global Spirituality* (New York: Image Books, 1984), 189.

52. David Spangler, *Emergence: The Rebirth of the Sacred* (New York: Dell, 1984), 12.

53. Stephen Schwartz, "Colors of the Wind," *Pocahontas* © 1995 Walt Disney/Mercury.

54. Fritjof Capra, *The Turning Point* (Toronto: Bantam Books, 1982), 77–78.

55. Shakti Gawain, *Living in the Light* (San Rafael: New World Library, 1986), 69.

56. Campbell, *Power of Myth*, 6.

57. Marilyn Ferguson, *The Aquarian Conspiracy* (Los Angeles: J. P. Tarcher, 1980), 383.

58. The Dalai Lama, *A Profound Mind* (New York: Three Rivers, 2011), 101.

59. Marianne Williamson, *A Return to Love: Reflections on the Principles of "A Course in Miracles"* (New York: HarperCollins, 1992), 22.

60. Oliver Leaman, *An Introduction to Classical Islamic Philosophy* (Cambridge, UK: Cambridge University Press, 2002), 13. Also see Mir Valiuddin, "Mu'tazilism: A General Mu'tazilite Position," in M. M. Sharif, ed., *A History of Muslim Philosophy* (Islamic Philosophy Online, 1961), accessed March 26, 2014, www.muslimphilosophy.com/hmp/13.htm.

61. Those interested in a fuller treatment of Islamic philosophy can consult Oliver Leaman, *An Introduction to Classical Islamic Philosophy*. The most comprehensive online resource for those wanting to go deeper, or to read the classical Muslim philosophers' writing firsthand, is Islamic Philosophy Online: Philosophia Islamica, www.muslimphilosophy.com. We also recommend Gordon H. Clark, *Thales to Dewey: A History of Philosophy* (Grand Rapids: Baker, 1980), 265.

62. According to Richard Shumack, a research fellow at the Centre for Public Christianity in Australia, with a PhD in Islamic studies (University of Melbourne), Turkish philosophers have developed their philosophy largely along analytical-rationalist lines (the idea that truths are knowable through reason). Prominent Turkish philosophers include Ioanna Kucuradi, Arda Denkel (1949–2000), and Cemal Yildirim (1925–2009). In Iran, philosophy has developed more along postmodern and anti-realist lines (philosophical approaches that begin with the assumption that ultimate reality cannot be reduced to statements we can know to be true or false). The most famous Iranian philosopher is probably Abdolkarim Soroush. Iranian philosophical journals include *Falsafeh: The Iranian Journal of Philosophy* and *Hekmat va Falsafeh*.

63. See the discussion in Fazlur Rahman, *Islam*, 2nd ed. (Chicago: University of Chicago Press, 1979), 117–27.

64. Natural theological arguments are usually seen to be of three sorts: *ontological* arguments that argue that the very concept of God is logically necessary in some way; *cosmological* arguments that argue that the existence of the universe is best explained by a divine first cause; and *teleological* arguments that argue that the intricacy and order of the universe demands a divine designer.

65. For all things al-Ghazali, including his major works, see www.ghazali.org. Note that many works are not yet translated into English.

66. An example of an influential contemporary Muslim philosopher arguing along these lines is Ismail al-Faruqi. See Ismail Raji al-Faruqi, Ismail Faruqi Online, accessed March 26, 2014, www.ismailfaruqi.com.

67. What happens to the soul upon death, in Islamic teaching, is the subject of the work of Abdulaziz Sachedina, a religion professor at the University of Virginia. In his article "Brain Death in Islamic Jurisprudence," http: //people. virginia.edu/~aas/article/article 6.htm, Sachedina says, "Death is the termination of an individual comprehensive being, capable of believing and disbelieving, and not simply a living organism. Even though later orthodox Islam came to accept the mind-body dualism, the Quran by using the term *nafs* seems to be rejecting the idea that some entity, like the soul, leaves the body at the time of death. Life does not end with death. In the same way that a person does not cease to exist in sleep, so also he does not cease to exist in death. And in the same way that a person comes back to life when walking from sleep, so also will he be revived at the great awakening on the Day of Judgment. Hence, Islam views death merely as a stage in human existence."

68. Muhammad Ali Khalidi, ed., *Medieval Islamic Philosophical Writings* (Cambridge, UK: Cambridge University Press, 2005), xix.

69. Hugh G. Dick, ed., *Select Writings of Francis Bacon* (New York: Random House, 1955), 44.

70. Thomas Nagel, *Mind and Cosmos* (New York: Oxford University Press, 2012), 42.

71. W. J. Neidhardt, "Faith, the Unrecognized Partner of Science and Religion," *Journal of the American Scientific Affiliation* 26, no. 3 (September 1974): 89–95, www.asa3.org/ASA/PSCF/1974/JASA9-74Neidhardt.html.

72. First Corinthians 15:3–6: "I delivered to you as of first importance what I also received: that Christ died for our sins in accordance with the Scriptures, that he was buried, that he was raised on the third day in accordance with the Scriptures, and that he appeared to Cephas, then to the twelve. Then he appeared to more than five hundred brothers at one time, most of whom are still alive, though some have fallen asleep."

73. See Edwin M. Yamauchi, "Easter: Myth, Hallucination, or History?," accessed March 26, 2014, http://www .leaderu.com/everystudent/easter/articles/yama.html. The quotation from William Lillie is found in "The Empty Tomb and the Resurrection," in D. E. Nineham et al., *Historicity and Chronology in the New Testament* (London: SPCK, 1965), 125.

74. "I believe, therefore I understand" is often characterized as the "Augustinian view." "I understand, therefore I believe" is, contrarily, characterized as the view of Thomas Aquinas. For a variety of reasons, we are more compelled by the Augustinian view and believe it is more consistent with biblical revelation, especially the teachings of the apostle Paul. Theologian Norman Geisler has examined both views, and his books can serve as a helpful introduction. See Norman Geisler, *Thomas Aquinas: An Evangelical Appraisal* (Eugene, OR: Wipf and Stock, 2003), and *What Augustine Says* (Eugene, OR: Wipf and Stock, 2003). If you've never read anything on Aquinas, you might want to start with G. K. Chesterton's brief study called *Saint Thomas Aquinas: The Dumb Ox* (New York: Doubleday, 1956). The term *dumb ox* is not an epithet but an ironic reference to the fact that Aquinas was called a "dumb ox" by his classmates but ended up leading a revolution in Christian thought.

75. Warren C. Young, *A Christian Approach to Philosophy* (Grand Rapids: Baker, 1975), 37.

76. Young's perspective on Christianity and philosophy is clarified in a publicly available paper he delivered in 1958 titled "Is There a Christian Philosophy?" See Warren C. Young, "Is There a Christian Philosophy?," *Bulletin of the Evangelical Theological Society* 1, no. 4 (Fall 1958): 6–14, www.biblicalstudies.org.uk/pdf/bets/vol01/philosophy _young. pdf.

77. Douglas Groothuis, *Christian Apologetics* (Downers Grove, IL: InterVarsity, 2011), 389–90.

78. Edward T. Ramsdell, *The Christian Perspective* (New York: Abingdon-Cokesbury, 1950), 42.

79. Young, *Christian Approach*, 37.

80. Young, *Christian Approach*, 182.

81. Henry, *God, Revelation, and Authority*, 5:336.

82. J. P. Moreland, "The Argument from Consciousness," in William Lane Craig and J. P. Moreland, *The Blackwell Companion to Natural Theology* (Malden, MA: Wiley-Blackwell, 2012), 296.

83. Young, *Christian Approach*, 120.

84. James Oliver Buswell Jr., *A Christian View of Being and Knowing* (Grand Rapids: Zondervan, 1960), 142.

85. See especially chapter 6 in Mario Beauregard and Denise O'Leary, *The Spiritual Brain* (New York: HarperOne, 2007).

86. John C. Eccles, *Evolution of the Brain: Creation of the Self* (New York: Routledge, 1991), 75.

87. "How can nature include mind as an integral part unless it is grounded in mind? If mind were seen as something alien or accidental, the case would be different, but the further we go in modern science the clearer it becomes that mental experience is no strange offshoot. Rather it is something which is deeply rooted in the entire structure." D. Elton Trueblood, *Philosophy of Religion* (Grand Rapids: Baker, 1957), 206.

88. Young, *Christian Approach*, 228–29. See also Ronald H. Nash, *Life's Ultimate Questions: An Introduction to Philosophy* (Grand Rapids: Zondervan, 1999); J. P. Moreland and William Lane Craig, *Philosophical Foundations for a Christian Worldview* (Downers Grove, IL: InterVarsity, 2003); and Alvin Plantinga, *Warranted Christian Belief* (Oxford, UK: Oxford University Press, 2000).

CHAPTER 10

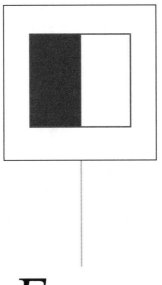

ETHICS

1. JEAN VALJEAN AND THE STUDY OF RIGHT AND WRONG

The door opened. A singular and violent group made its appearance on the threshold. Three men were holding a fourth man by the collar. The three men were gendarmes; the other was Jean Valjean.

A brigadier of gendarmes, who seemed to be in command of the group, was standing near the door. He entered and advanced to the Bishop, making a military salute.

In the meantime, Monseigneur Bienvenu had advanced as quickly as his great age permitted. "Ah! Here you are!" he exclaimed, looking at Jean Valjean.

"I am glad to see you. Well, but how is this? I gave you the candlesticks too, which are of silver like the rest, and for which you can certainly get two hundred francs. Why did you not carry them away with your forks and spoons?"

Jean Valjean opened his eyes wide, and stared at the venerable Bishop with an expression which no human tongue can render an account of.

"Monseigneur," said the brigadier of gendarmes, "so what this man said is true, then? We came across him. He was walking like a man who is running away. We stopped him to look into the matter. He had this silver—"

"And he told you," interposed the Bishop, with a smile, "that it had been given to him by a kind old fellow of a priest with whom he had passed the night? I see how the matter stands. And you have brought him back here? It is a mistake."

"In that case," replied the brigadier, "we can let him go?"

"Certainly," replied the Bishop.

Jean Valjean was trembling in every limb. He took the two candlesticks mechanically, and with a bewildered air.

"Jean Valjean, my brother, you no longer belong to evil, but to good. It is your soul that I buy from you; I withdraw it from black thoughts and the spirit of perdition, and I give it to God."[1]

The Jean Valjean character in Victor Hugo's *Les Misérables* was a broken, bitter man, a known thief who would surely rot in prison. Forgiven through an unexpected act of mercy, though, Valjean was eventually driven to repentance. Hugo's story bears witness to the universal reality of evil and injustice, and also to the possibility of hope and goodness. The popularity of *Les Misérables*—whether in book form, on stage, or in the movies—raises a hope to which all humanity clings: brutality *must* give way in the face of redemption. This is perhaps the most important thing that may be said about ethical living and, consequently, the study of ethics.

The study of right and wrong, or **ethics**—from the Greek word *ethos*, meaning "goodness"—has two functions. First, it is a guide to action. Ethics seeks to answer the question "How should we live?" That is, what does it mean to live a good life—and not just a life that *feels* good, but a life that actually *is* good? And if *everyone* lived this way, would it be good for all of us?

Second, ethics proposes a way to think through what life is about. Famed journalist Walter Lippmann said, "At the core of every moral code there is a picture of human nature, a map of the universe, and a version of history. To human nature (of the sort conceived), in a universe (of the kind imagined), after a history (so understood), the rules of the code apply."[2] Ethics is more than a guide for how to live. It has the clarifying effect of shining light on life's most important questions; indeed, many of those questions are unanswerable without it.

> **Ethics: the study of moral conduct, values, duties, and goodness.**

Christianity says all things good, true, and beautiful are based in God's character as revealed in nature and Scripture. We ought to speak truth not because we'll feel better about it or because it is reasonable to do so but because *God's nature is truth*. We ought to pursue justice not because it helps us maintain power or because the law commands it but because *God is just*. We ought to express mercy not because it will make us happy or because it is our duty but because *God is mercy*.

Because God is everywhere, Christianity says, an ethical system based on his character will reside in every soul, across all cultures, at all times. Calvin D. Linton, one-time professor at George Washington University, found that, in fact, such a basic pattern of ethical codes exists:

> There is a basic pattern of similarity among [ethical codes]. Such things as murder, lying, adultery, cowardice are, for example, almost always condemned. The universality of the ethical sense itself (the "oughtness" of conduct), and the similarities within the codes of diverse cultures indicate a common moral heritage for all mankind which materialism or naturalism cannot explain.[3]

Christians see common ethical systems among vastly different cultures as evidence of a universal law and thus a universal lawgiver. Every ethical system must either explain away such evidence or account for it. In this chapter we will seek insight into the key terms and players in the field of ethics and offer an overview of the ethical theories of the six worldviews we are studying. Hopefully by the end we'll better understand why people do what they do, and we'll better understand Christian ethics.

2. A PRIMER ON ETHICS

The difference between morality and ethics. To begin, let's clarify the difference between morality and ethics. **Morality** refers to a personal system of determining rights and wrongs based on some standard—what we prefer, what we think is good, or what we feel duty bound to do. Ethics is the "philosophical study of morality."[4] Morality is a container of right and wrong. Ethics is the study of how such a container is discovered and used. In most universities, the study of ethics is a subset of philosophy and is sometimes called *moral philosophy.*

Morality and ethics are intertwined. Personally we may proclaim our desire to "live and let live," but societies can't function very well this way. In reality, Cambridge professor Simon Blackburn says, "We prefer that our preferences are shared."[5] Sometimes Christians are criticized as intolerant busybodies who make rules about other people's business. However, intolerance works both ways. Those who become angry at restrictions on which gender of person they may marry are often delighted to support policies requiring employers to provide contraception and abortion services to their employees.

> *Morality:* **a personal standard of determining right and wrong.**

Contemplating tricky questions about moral rights and wrongs goes back, at least, to Confucius in China, Moses in the Middle East, and Socrates in Greece. Whether in monasteries, at universities, or at sidewalk cafes, the nature of right and wrong is one of humanity's most widely discussed subjects.

Two theories about ethics. In his highly respected text, *Introduction to Ethics*, University of Texas professor John Deigh places all ethical theories into one of two categories, teleological and deontological.[6] Let's define and explain these terms in light of the history of ethical studies.

Theories about ends (teleology): What is the good life? The first category of ethical theory is *teleological* (*telos* is Greek for "end" or "purpose"). Teleological theories judge actions as right or wrong by their *ends*, or purposes, those desired and intended consequences that their actions will lead to. **Teleological ethics** ask questions like "What is the good life?" "What is the purpose or end of a good life?" and "How might the good life be secured for as many people as possible?"

Teleological theories say having a good "soul" is what life is all about. Everyone wants happiness and peace. If they find it, they'll be good and then society will be good. Some philosophers who thought of ethics this way include the following:

PHILOSOPHER	NAME OF PHILOSOPHY	DESCRIPTION
Aristippus	Hedonism	Human beings should maximize their own personal pleasure.
Aristotle	Eudaimonism	The purpose of human existence is to live a life of flourishing.*
Jeremy Bentham	Utilitarianism	What is ethical is to pursue the greatest good for the greatest number of people.
Thomas Hobbes	Ethical egoism	The good life is being free to look after one's own interests.
John Stuart Mill	Ethical libertarianism	People live best when they have liberty but agree to not harm others.
Friedrich Nietzsche	Moral skepticism	Objective moral knowledge is either inaccessible or impossible.
John Dewey	Pragmatism	Since truth is whatever works, morality is whatever is useful for society.
Jean-Paul Sartre	Existentialism	Since we create our own meaning, we ought to do whatever helps us become our most authentic selves.

* We include Aristotle's teleology here for the sake of showing various views through time. But as ethicist Scott Rae points out, Aristotle's teleology is focused on the good end of a human being, whereas the other philosophies focus on the good end of human actions. Being versus doing is an important ethical distinction.

Everyone wants a meaningful life in harmony with others, right? This makes sense to philosophers and nonphilosophers alike. But one problem for this kind of ethical theory is that people can (and often do) behave against their own best interests, acting out of anger, envy, and spite, even when these reactions are irrational and produce misery. A second problem is that we are not always able to accurately predict the ends of our thoughts and actions. "Even the wisest cannot see all ends," Gandalf tells Frodo, in the Lord of the Rings trilogy, about his wish to kill Gollum. Our best intentions may not actually lead to our contentment or stability for society. A third problem is that actions (like murder or stealing or hiding the truth) might have good intentions and might even produce outcomes we find valuable but turn out to be evil. Saying "the ends justify the means" has led to some of history's greatest evils.

Theories about duty (deontology): What ought we to do? The second category of ethical theories is called *deontological* (*deon* is Greek for "duty"). Where teleological theories determine right and wrong by the desired ends of an action, deontological theories say that whether we like it or not, we "ought" to do what is right—*merely because right is right.* **Deontological ethics** rests on the belief that right and wrong actually exist independent of our situations or circumstances. The ethical question is how we might understand right and wrong and do what's right. Deontological philosophers include the following:.

PHILOSOPHER	NAME OF PHILOSOPHY	DESCRIPTION
Immanuel Kant	Transcendental idealism	*Our duty as humans is to figure out what is good without qualification and then pursue it.*
René Descartes	Rationalism	*God has made us as thinking beings, so we must use our reasoning ability to live virtuously.*

Deontological theories are very compelling to those who have a conviction that truth is absolute. But if ethical absolutes exist, why do so many people seem oblivious to them? And if absolutes are truly absolute, like the law of gravity, how can people ignore them without suffering any obvious negative consequences? Plus, what do we do when ethical absolutes come into conflict with one another?

Conflicts between ethical absolutes are more common than we might think. Most people understand the importance of telling the truth. They know human life is valuable. But if they lived in 1940s Poland and were hiding Jews in their homes, how would they resolve the potential conflict between the two? If the Nazis came to your door and asked, "Are you hiding any Jews?" what should you say? To say no would be to tell an untruth, but to say yes would be to condemn to death those under your protection. It is an ethical dilemma.

> **Deontological Ethics:** any ethical system that judges the morality of actions based upon some principle of duty.

For most people, the answer seems obvious, at least in theory: Look the Nazis in the face and mislead them. They are not owed the truth. Their laws are unjust, and the Nazis deserve to be defeated in their aims. But every aspect of this decision—what is owed, what truth is, what laws are, what constitutes justice, what it means to be deserving, whether someone should be defeated, and how to discern the proper aims of authority—must be based on some standard of right and wrong. In fact, there are instances in the Old Testament where people misled evil authorities and seem to have been commended for doing so. See, for example, Exodus 1 in which the Hebrew midwives in Egypt refused to kill male babies as instructed, and in the book of Joshua where Rahab hid the Hebrew spies and misled the authorities of Jericho who were trying to capture them, and 1 Samuel 16 when God told Samuel to use deception when he went to anoint a new king.

Ethical dilemmas like these may be infrequent, but they do happen. In World War II, Corrie ten Boom decided to defy the Nazis and hide Jews in her home. During the Cold War, Brother Andrew decided to defy the laws of communist countries and smuggle Bibles across their borders. During the civil rights movement, Martin Luther King Jr. decided to defy segregation laws and refrain from violence when attacked for doing so. Today, people rescue slaves from sex traffickers in defiance of the law. They share their Christian faith in countries where the laws specifically prohibit them from doing so.

> A true theory of ethics ought to be livable for human beings in a sinful world where right is not always obvious and not always easy to live out.

A true theory of ethics ought to be livable for human beings in a sinful world where right is not always obvious and not always easy to live out. A true theory of ethics must help us recognize that not everything legal is right and that an unjust law has no purpose if it defies the law of God. A true theory of ethics must take into account a higher law if lower laws are not to tyrannize us.

As we'll see shortly, Christianity, while not fitting neatly into either teleological or deontological categories, helps resolve these dilemmas. But first let's examine the ethical theories of each of the six worldviews in our study, starting with Secularism.

3. SECULARISM

Secularist Austin Dacey from the Center for Inquiry says, "Most of us would find it extremely difficult to do without the idea that there are objective standards of what makes a life go well, that we can be mistaken about what makes a life go well, and that it is hugely important that we not make such mistakes."[7] But even the idea of "life going well" involves an ethical judgment. On what basis can we define *well*? To the Secularist, such judgments may be made as long as the reasons for doing so are completely naturalistic. George Jacob Holyoake, in his 1846 book *English Secularism*, said, "Secularism is a code of duty pertaining to this life, founded on considerations purely human, and intended mainly for those who find theology indefinite or inadequate, unreliable or unbelievable."[8]

Simply put, Secularism binds itself to a purely naturalistic explanation of ethics. "We have not found authoritative ethical prescriptions built into the order of things," writes Simon Blackburn. "No god wrote the laws of good behavior into the cosmos. Nature has no concern for good or bad, right or wrong."[9] If nature has no concern, humans certainly do and are thus the only source of ethics according to Secularism. Max Hocutt elaborates: "The fundamental question of ethics is, who makes the rules? God or men? The theistic answer is that God makes them. The humanistic answer is that men make them. This distinction between theism and humanism is the fundamental division in moral theory."[10]

If there is no higher authority than human beings, Secularist ethics will almost always end up being seen as relativistic to one's life circumstances or cultural practices, or blanket decisions will be made about what is the greatest good for the greatest number of people. Thus, we suggest that Secularist ethics will either be *moral relativism* or *utilitarianism*.

What are the Secularists' resources for making these judgments? Must we all, as poet Ella Wheeler Wilcox phrased it, "worship at the shrine of brain"?[11] We have no choice, says Blackburn, but never fear: "If we are careful, and mature, and imaginative, and fair, and nice, and lucky, the moral mirror in which we gaze at ourselves may not show us saints. But it need not show us monsters, either."[12] But terms like *mature* and *fair* are fraught with ethical weight. What do they mean, and who gets to define them?

Secularists know we must make ethical choices based on something, but they are lost when it comes to identifying any source of how to do this without devolving into complete moral relativism. Jean-Paul Sartre expressed this poignantly in *Existentialism and Human Emotions*:

> The existentialist ... thinks it very distressing that God does not exist, because all possibility of finding values in a heaven of ideas disappears along with Him; there can no longer be an a priori Good, since there is no infinite and perfect consciousness to think it. Nowhere is it written that the Good exists, that we must be honest, that we must not lie; because the fact is we are on a plane where there are only men.[13]

The picture is of a besieged humanity desperate for guidance, who, upon finding none, chooses to bravely press on in its absence.

In practice, though, Secularists do not abandon the search for well-placed ethical anchors. Despite their various disagreements, Secularists gravitate toward explaining ethical impulses as emerging from evolutionary processes. Richard Weikart explains:

> Many argued that by providing a naturalistic account of the origin of ethics and morality, Darwinism delivered a death-blow to the prevailing Judeo-Christian ethics, as well as Kantian ethics and any other fixed moral code. If morality was built on social instincts that changed over evolutionary time, then morality must be relative to the conditions of life at any given time. Darwinism—together with other forms of historicism ascendant in the nineteenth century—thus contributed to the rise of moral relativism.[14]

Having settled on social instincts derived through evolutionary processes, many Secularists find themselves intrigued by the work of E. O. Wilson in a field called *sociobiology*. Sociobiologists seek to explain, based on evolution, why people do what they do. Mothers with a genetic impulse to protect their offspring have been more likely to have their offspring survive, for example, and this explains why human mothers will run to the aid of their crying children.

Because they are convinced of naturalism and evolution, many Secularists see supernatural explanations as not only wrong but inherently dangerous. Paul Kurtz, author of *Humanist Manifesto II*, stated, "The traditional supernaturalistic moral commandments are especially repressive of our human needs. They are immoral insofar as they foster illusions about human destiny [the afterlife] and suppress vital inclinations."[15] By Kurtz's account, then, religious ethical codes such as the Ten Commandments[16] prevent us from fulfilling our conception of the good life.

Can morality be achieved without the foundation of absolute religious beliefs? Secularists hope so, but they have difficulty agreeing on what morality means without God. The need for a consistent Secularist ethical standard was the impetus for Morris B. Storer's book *Humanist Ethics*. Storer summed up the tensions Secularists feel as they grapple with ethical issues:

> **Many Secularists see supernatural explanations as not only wrong but inherently dangerous.**

Is personal advantage the measure of right and wrong, or the advantage of all affected: Humanists differ. Is there truth in ethics? We differ. Are "right" and "wrong" expressions of heart or head? Do people have free wills? Do you measure morality by results or by principles? Do people have duties as well as rights? We have our differences on all these and more.[17]

The debate rages on, and we can understand why: it takes a lot of thinking and discussion to make up ethical systems independent of any reliable sources of revelation. In a remarkable *Time* magazine article many years ago, Henry Grunwald made a stunning observation

> **It takes a lot of thinking and discussion to make up ethical systems independent of any reliable sources of revelation.**

about Secularists' efforts to do so: "We have gradually dissolved—deconstructed—the human being into a bundle of reflexes, impulses, neuroses, nerve endings. The great religious heresy used to be making man the measure of all things; but we have come close to making man the measure of nothing."[18]

The idea that there is no absolute standard for ethics, but that our ethical stance is relative to our culture or to our individual situations, is called **moral relativism**. Many Secularists protest the term *relativism*. Their views are much more nuanced than that, they say.[19] In the in-

> **Moral Relativism: the belief that morality is relative to, or defined by, the individual or culture.**

terest of accuracy, we will not call moral relativism the ethical viewpoint of Secularism. Rather, we will describe it as a thread of thought and action weaving through the last four hundred or so years of philosophical con-

sideration. This is the case William Gairdner makes in *The Book of Absolutes*, pointing out the seeds philosophers planted that yielded the impression that God's revelation cannot be known or trusted, but that human reason and action can.[20] Here's an overview:

- René Descartes (1596–1650): By saying "I think; therefore I am," Descartes opened the door to the idea that we are each capable of arriving at the truth on our own.
- Thomas Hobbes (1588–1679): The definition of *good* is "that which is the object of any man's appetite."
- John Locke (1632–1704): To "know things" means to understand the relationships between them rather than to discern absolute qualities.
- David Hume (1711–1776): Our ideas of cause and effect are based on habit rather than certain knowledge.
- Immanuel Kant (1724–1804): There is no way of knowing, outside of the mind, what the phenomena we observe are actually like.
- Georg W. F. Hegel (1770–1831): Nothing stays the same—everything is evolving.
- John Stuart Mill (1806–1873): We are free to act as we please as long as we do not bring harm to others.

- Friedrich Nietzsche (1844–1900): Human action is guided by will, not by the false promise of a perfect world of truth that is eternal.
- William James (1842–1910): There is no universal knowledge of truth; what is good must be judged by its consequences.
- John Dewey (1859–1952): Even if there were absolute truths, we could not know them; we should focus on improving the world in the here and now.[21]

As we stated earlier, Secularists disagree about particulars, but on these two points there is no debate: when it comes to ethics, (1) God has nothing whatsoever to do with it, and (2) we're on our own. Herbert W. Schneider calls morality "an experimental art," saying it is the "basic art of living well together. Moral right and wrong must therefore be conceived in terms of moral standards generated in a particular society."[22] Paul Kurtz said that "moral principles should be treated as hypotheses," tested by their practical worth and judged by what they cause to happen.[23]

Situation ethics. The late Harvard professor Joseph Fletcher organized many Secularist ethical teachings under the heading of **situation ethics**, which says that right and wrong are determined by "the situations in which moral agents have to decide for the most beneficial course open to choice."[24] By "beneficial" Fletcher meant choosing the right course based on love. But how does this help if we have no real standard by which to recognize what love is? Based on his own understanding of love, Fletcher justified abortion and euthanasia. In the end, Fletcher's situation ethics became a prescription for doing whatever each person thinks is best in any given situation. One early sex education advocate, Arthur E. Gravatt, applied situation ethics this way: "The morality or immorality of any behavior including sexual behavior, has been put in the context of 'situation ethics.' In this approach moral behavior may differ from situation to situation. Behavior might be moral for one person and not another or moral at one time and not another."[25]

> *Situation Ethics:* the belief that the morality of an action is determined by the unique situation of that action.

Scientism. Secularists seem to view science as the primary guide for forming a workable ethical outlook. Harry Elmer Barnes, one of America's preeminent twentieth-century historians, believed that intelligent individuals would use the scientific method to determine morals, so what they conclude is by definition moral. "It should be absolutely clear to any thoughtful and informed person," wrote Barnes, "that morality, far from being divorced from intelligence, depends more thoroughly and completely upon intelligence and scientific information than any other phase of human thought."[26]

> *Scientism:* the philosophical belief that reliable knowledge is obtained solely through the scientific method.

When the scientific method becomes the basis of a belief system, it can lead to the unwarranted belief that scientific people are more intelligent and thus more moral; therefore we can trust them to do what is right. Barnes was clear: "Wide variations in capacity appear to be the most important single fact about the human race. It would seem to follow that there will be certain kinds of conduct which will not be harmful for the abler members of society; which, indeed, may be positively desirable and beneficial."[27]

There is no evidence that higher intelligence makes people more moral. While Barnes wrote this in 1925, before the Marxist purges and the Nazi gas chambers, twentieth-century history has taught clearly that scientism can take on a sinister character. And even when those events did occur, Barnes labored to explain them away, making himself an embarrassment to the academic community. By the end of his life, not even radical publishers would publish his ideas. Barnes's life is a cautionary tale for those who put too much faith in science and reason.

In the last few decades, Secularists have retooled their ethical thinking. Much of it now looks suspiciously familiar to anyone who understands the nature of Christian revelation. Secular Humanist leader Paul Kurtz, for example, insisted that Secular Humanists accept the Golden Rule and even the biblical injunction to "accept the aliens within our midst, respecting their differences."[28] Secular Humanists, Kurtz said, "ought to tell the truth, keep promises, be honest, sincere, beneficent, reliable, dependable, show fidelity, appreciation, gratitude, be fair-minded, just, tolerant, should not steal, injure, maim or harm other persons."[29] Corliss Lamont also tried to borrow Christian ethics while snubbing its foundation:

> Any humane philosophy must include such New Testament ideals as the brotherhood of man, peace on earth and the abundant life. There is much ethical wisdom, too, in the Old Testament and its Ten Commandments. Without accepting any ethical principle as a dogmatic dictum never to be questioned, the Humanist certainly adheres in general to a Biblical commandment such as, "Thou shalt not bear false witness against thy neighbor."[30]

Christians can applaud that biblical morality is being upheld, and it is to Kurtz's and Lamont's credit that they knew a good idea when they saw one. What Secularists fail to address, however, is why these values are worth defending as moral declarations. Cornelius van Til's assessment is apt: they are sitting in God's lap in order to slap him in the face. In other words, Secularists draw on truths explained only by God's existence and form them into arguments to deny his existence altogether.

Ethical debates among Secularists reveal how difficult it is to abandon an absolute standard of morality and still arrive at a coherent philosophy. Without the absolute nature of God, morality is set adrift. Will Durant admitted, "We shall find it no easy task to mold a natural ethic strong enough to maintain moral restraint and social order without the support of supernatural consolations, hopes and fears."[31] Francis Schaeffer added, "It is not just difficult, it is impossible."[32]

4. MARXISM

Unlike Secularists, Marxists have no difficulty making up their minds about ethics: everything in the universe—including society—is in a state of constant change, moving society upward toward the elimination of all social and economic class distinctions. The next social advance in history will be the move from capitalism to socialism, Marxists say, which will inevitably change society's moral ideals. Anything promoting this advance is right. Anything hindering it is wrong. This is called **proletariat morality**.

"It must be constantly borne in mind," said Howard Selsam, "that Marx and Engels denied that moral ideals, moral considerations, are central in human life and social evolution."[33] Selsam would have been more accurate to say that Marxists *have* moral ideals, but these ideals change as circumstances change. As Marx wrote in *The Communist Manifesto*, "Does it require deep intuition to comprehend that man's ideas, views and conceptions, in one word, man's consciousness, changes with every change in the conditions of his material existence, in his social relations and in his social life?"[34] We are evolving; morality must evolve too.

> *Proletariat Morality:* the belief that whatever advances the proletariat and communism is morally good, and whatever hinders the proletariat and communism is morally evil.

For Karl Marx and Friedrich Engels, "Thou shalt not steal" established a society in which some had property and some did not; such an establishment was part of the "old morality" the bourgeoisie (the owners) invented and used to oppress the property-less proletariat. G. L. Andreyev, in *What Kind of Morality Does Religion Teach?*, stated, "In the reigning morality under capitalism that act is considered moral which promotes the preservation and strengthening of the system of exploitation and the acquirement of profits. Religion merely justifies this unjust and oppressive, bloody, and inhuman system in the name of God."[35] To the Marxist, everything capitalist is immoral; everything done to oppose it, then, is moral by definition.

Marxists are grateful for any action that advances the goal of a classless society and would call it ethical. The ends justify the means. "Ethics, in short," said Selsam, "is good only as anything else is good, for what it can accomplish, for the direction in which it takes men."[36] To Andreyev, the means of revolution was justified: "From the point of view of communist morality the struggle against everything which hinders the cause of communist construction is moral and humane and for this reason we consider the struggle against the enemies of communism to be of a moral nature."[37]

> To the Marxist, everything capitalist is immoral; everything done to oppose it, then, is moral by definition.

People who are bothered by revolution, according to Marxists, fail to understand history. Evolution is painful. It involves suffering and death, and there will be blood. Nature accumulates the good and disposes of the bad. The struggle moving us toward communism is like this. The fit must survive. The unfit, along with their social institutions, must perish.

> People who are bothered by revolution, according to Marxists, fail to understand history.

The value of hatred is right and good in the Marxist ethical code as long as it is directed toward the property owners, the bourgeoisie. Hatred is needed to fuel the clash between the proletariat and the bourgeoisie. To keep their followers in a perpetual revolutionary mind-set, Marxist leaders, such as Mao Tse-tung, Joseph Stalin, Fidel Castro, and Kim Jong-Eun, decades after their respective revolutions wound down, dressed in military garb and peppered their speeches with revolutionary language. Marxism draws its *inspiration* from the hope of a more harmonious future but draws its *energy* from the rehearsal of grievances against the bourgeoisie.

Here's a powerful example, and one many in today's culture will find surprising: One Marxist who firmly believed in using any means to pursue *proletariat morality* was Ernesto ("Che") Guevara, Fidel Castro's right-hand man during the bloody Marxist revolution in Cuba. Che's diary (which has subsequently been turned into a movie, *The Motorcycle Diaries*) rationalized his radical change. Traveling across South America, Che witnessed firsthand the plight of the lower class and in response gradually embraced an ends-justify-the-means philosophy. The reality, according to columnist Paul Berman, was anything but:

> The cult of Ernesto Che Guevara is an episode in the moral callousness of our time. Che was a totalitarian. He achieved nothing but disaster.... Che presided over the Cuban Revolution's first firing squads. He founded Cuba's "labor camp" system.... The present-day cult of Che—the T-shirts, the bars, the posters—has succeeded in obscuring this dreadful reality.... He helped establish an unjust social system in Cuba and has been erected into a symbol of social justice. He stood for the ancient rigidities of Latin-American thought, in a Marxist-Leninist version, and he has been celebrated as a free-thinker and a rebel."[38]

With evolution and dialectic as the building blocks of their moral philosophy, Marxists feel free to abandon long-held moral standards in pursuit of a greater good—the creation of a classless communist society. This may court disaster, but for the Marxist, all's well that ends well; if true communism results, it will all be worth it. To paraphrase Vladimir Lenin, the only morality that communists recognize is that which furthers their interests.[39]

> **Doubtless most Marxists begin well, with a desire to shelter the poor against injustice. This is a noble concern, and righteous people ought to share it. But what means should be employed in addressing it?**

Doubtless most Marxists begin well, with a desire to shelter the poor against injustice. This is a noble concern, and righteous people ought to share it. But what means should be employed in addressing it? The biblical view is incarnation: enter into the brokenness of the oppressed. Care personally. Walk alongside. Bring change through the power of redemption. To those who reject God, the afterlife, or the soul, though, this response is met with impatience. Redemption is nice, but it is ambiguous and frustratingly slow. Revolution is laser sharp and thrillingly fast. Some, such as liberation theologians, hold out a genuine and heartfelt hope that we can have the best of both, but little in Marxist ethical theory supports such a hope.

5. NEW SPIRITUALITY

New Spirituality says everything is consciousness, or what some people refer to as "god." The good life consists in attaining higher consciousness. When each individual does this, life will be better for all. Only one ethical absolute is possible to this way of thinking: complete freedom to act in harmony with our own understanding of truth. "Free will," says Shirley

MacLaine, "is simply the enactment of the realization you are God, a realization that you are divine: free will is making everything accessible to you."[40]

To New Spiritualists, ethics is something that happens inside a person, not the result of divine commands or societal expectations. As Marilyn Ferguson wrote, "When people become autonomous, their values become internal."[41] Internalized values allow us to seek higher consciousness; external limits block our ability to get in touch with inner truth. As Vera Alder tells us, "We should search ourselves very carefully to see if we have any fixed ideas, any great shyness or self-consciousness. If we have, we must seek freedom."[42] Take "You shall not commit adultery,"[43] for example. Shakti Gawain says, "If you're setting limits on your sexual energy, it becomes distorted. If you believe it is something to be hidden, ignored, and controlled, then you learn to hold back completely or act sexually only at certain safe moments."[44]

Randall Baer, a former New Spiritualist who converted to Christianity, stated the basic New Spiritualist credo: "Create your own reality according to what feels right for you."[45] In fact, to New Spiritualists, living any other way actually hurts us. According to Eckhart Tolle, society's rules are based on ego—insisting that "we" are right and "they" are wrong. "Being right is identification with a mental position—a perspective, an opinion, a judgment, a story," he says. "For you to be right, of course, you need someone else to be wrong, and so the ego loves to make wrong in order to be right."[46]

This does not mean there are no absolute truths, Tolle insists. Indeed, there is truth. But thoughts and mental labels such as "right" and "wrong" cannot lead us to it: "The quicker you are in attaching verbal or mental labels to things, people, or situations, the more shallow and lifeless your reality becomes, and the more deadened you become to reality, the miracle of life that continuously unfolds within and around you. In this way, cleverness may be gained, but wisdom is lost, and so are joy, love, creativity, and aliveness."[47]

The truth, according to Tolle, cannot be found in "doctrines, ideologies, sets of rules, or stories."[48] He continues, "The Truth is inseparable from who you are. Yes, you *are* the Truth. If you look for it elsewhere, you will be deceived every time."[49]

Not all New Spiritualists follow such an individual path. Those who take a more Buddhist approach recognize that certain behaviors and attitudes cause suffering and diminish happiness. The Dalai Lama, the spiritual leader of Buddhism, says,

> By refraining from the ten nonvirtuous actions of killing, stealing, sexual misconduct, lying, divisive speech, harsh speech, idle gossip, covetousness, malice, and wrong view, we are restrained from causing others harm and from bringing about our own future suffering. This prepares us for a fortunate future life. If we are reborn as an animal we will have no opportunity to engage consciously in the practice of virtue. We must therefore nurture the short-term goal of a good rebirth that enables us to continue along our path toward the ultimate goal of Buddhahood.[50]

Hinduism also identifies certain traits as objectively wrong. In the Bhagavad Gita, Krishna says to Arjuna, "Hypocrisy, insolence, anger, cruelty, ignorance, conceit—these, Arjuna, are the qualities of men with demonic traits."[51] All of these traits are wrong, in the Hindu mindset, because they violate universal oneness and separate us from one another.

In the American context, though, New Spirituality seems irretrievably individualistic. The key to ethics is asserting this autonomy and freedom. Ferguson admitted as much:

New Spiritualists withhold
judgment about morality
because the truth is in
each of us.

"Autonomous human beings can create and invent. And they can change their minds, repudiating values they once held."[52] The more we exercise this freedom, the more we will "lose our dogmatic attachment to a single point of view."[53] And tolerance is the key: New Spiritualists withhold judgment about morality because the truth is in each of us. "Adam and Eve," says Marianne Williamson, "were happy until she 'ate of the knowledge of good and evil.' What that means is that everything was perfect until they began to judge—to keep their hearts open sometimes, but closed at others.... Closing our hearts destroys our peace. It's alien to our real nature."[54]

Because morality is different for each person, whatever we decide to do is right—for us. Shakti Gawain says, "I believe that every being chooses the life path and relationships that will help him or her to grow the fastest."[55] One wonders what Gawain would say about "history's horribles," such as Genghis Khan, Tomas de Torquemada, and Adolf Hitler.

Is there any accountability in New Spiritual ethics? To a certain degree. The concept of **karma** says the consequences of what we do for good or ill will eventually be visited upon us. Shirley MacLaine defines *karma* this way:

Karma: a concept found in Eastern religions, karma is the belief that good is returned to those who do good, and evil is returned to those who do evil (either in this life or the next).

Whatever action one takes will ultimately return to that person—good and bad—maybe not in this life embodiment, but sometime in the future. And no one is exempt.... For every act, for every indifference, for every misuse of life, we are finally held accountable. And it is up to us to understand what those accounts might be.[56]

However, if there is no standard by which to judge an act of "indifference" or a "misuse of life," how can we really know if we are being indifferent or misusing life? How can we distinguish the difference between cruelty and noncruelty? This is the karmic dilemma for New Spiritualists: if karma is a knowable law, then absolute ethical standards exist, and we are obligated to explain their source and obey them. Ethical relativism is false. If karmic outcomes are unknowable, though, karma can never guide our actions because we can never really know whether our actions are right or wrong.

This is the karmic
dilemma for New
Spiritualists: if karma
is a knowable law, then
absolute ethical standards
exist, and we are obligated
to explain their source and
obey them.

New Spiritualists resolve this dilemma oddly: Since everything is one, they say, any difference we perceive between good and evil and right and wrong is illusory. As Marilyn Ferguson stated, "This wholeness unites opposites.... In these spiritual traditions there is neither good nor evil. There is only light and the absence of light ... wholeness and brokenness ... flow and struggle."[57]

Good and evil work together to move us toward higher consciousness. David Spangler, one of the more bold New Spiritualist writers, said this explicitly: "Christ is the same force as Lucifer.... Lucifer prepares man for the experience of Christhood.... Lucifer works within each of us to bring us to wholeness as we move into the New Age."[58] Evil isn't really evil, then, and good isn't really good.

As confusing as this seems, the New Spiritualist believes it all works out in the end. Using a biblical example, Kevin Ryerson says,

> Criminals and murderers sometimes come back around to be murdered themselves, or perhaps to become a saint. For instance, Moses was a murderer.... He beat the fellow to death out of rage, which was not exactly the most ethical decision. But he went on to become a great intellect, a great law-giver, and is considered a saint by many people. So basically, you get many chances. Your karma is your system of judgment. There is justice.[59]

Morality, then, is nebulous. Establishing a system of ethics that works for everyone is impossible. We might be able to discern what is right for ourselves, but we cannot know whether others are doing what is right for them.

If this seems incoherent, New Spiritualists say it is because you are not sufficiently oriented to the flow of consciousness. You're too focused on how your *thoughts* will lead you to truth. Stop thinking. Get in touch with your true self. As Captain Kirk said in one of the original *Star Trek* episodes, "Sometimes a feeling is all we humans have to go on."[60] So are the laws of logic just what we *feel* to be true? Is there ever a time when we should persuade others to act differently? (And on what basis would we do this?) Is morality ever anything more than an expression of a preference? Were Hitler and Stalin just expressing a *different* morality or a *wrong* one? Is it possible for people to grow in moral understanding over time? Is there ever any moral course of action we *ought* to pursue as humans, or are all moral beliefs just expressions of cultural prejudice?[61]

6. POSTMODERNISM

Secularists and Marxists ground their ethics in atheism, materialism, and naturalism. Postmodern ethics is a bit more enigmatic. Basically, postmodern ethics looks with suspicion on both revelation and modern reason as sources of truth. The respected Polish sociologist Zygmunt Bauman frames the postmodern view as follows: "I suggest that the novelty of the postmodern approach to ethics consists first and foremost in ... the rejection of the typically modern ways of going about its moral problems (that is ... the philosophical search for absolutes, universals and foundations in theory)."[62] The British essayist Adam Phillips states bluntly, "Universal moral principles must be eradicated and reverence for individual and cultural uniqueness inculcated."[63]

The rejection of both revelation and reason is evident in the writings of the philosopher Richard Rorty. In *Achieving Our Country*, Rorty questioned God's place in the moral scheme of the universe. Referring to Walt Whitman's statement "And I call to mankind, Be not curious about God, / For I who am curious about each am not curious about God,"[64] Rorty said,

> Whitman thought there was no need to be curious about God because there is no standard, not even a divine one, against which the decisions of a free people can be

measured. Americans, [Whitman] hoped, would spend the energy that past human societies had spent on discovering God's desires on discovering one another's desires.[65]

After denying God's existence (or at least relevance), Rorty moved on to deny the existence of *any* universal moral reality "to which our moral judgments might hope to correspond, as our physical science supposedly corresponds to physical reality."[66]

So if neither revelation nor reason can act as guides, what can? To Postmodernist Jean-François Lyotard, the answer was right action. But what constitutes right action? Lyotard, for his part, was content to live with "little narratives." If philosophical truth (what we can know about reality) resides in the local community, it follows that moral truth (how we should behave) resides in the same community.[67] This was Lyotard's way of expressing **cultural relativism**, the belief that truth and morals are relative to one's culture.

> **Cultural Relativism:**
> the belief that truth and morals are relative to one's community.

Postmodernists often hesitate to use the term *cultural relativism* or *relativism*. Rorty, for example, tried to soften the word *relative*. He commented,

> This view is often referred to as "cultural relativism." But it is not relativistic, if that means saying that every moral view is as good as every other. Our moral view is, I firmly believe, much better than any competing view, even though there are a lot of people whom you will never be able to convert to it. It is one thing to say, falsely, that there is nothing to choose between us and the Nazis. It is another thing to say, correctly, that there is no neutral, common ground to argue our differences. That Nazi and I will always strike one another as begging all the crucial questions, arguing in circles.[68]

While there is no objective basis for determining what is right, Rorty insisted, his view was right when compared with, say, Nazi morality. But while making this claim, he also admitted there is no way to judge between the two views. Obviously not all Postmodernists agree with this. In fact, some would express serious disagreement. But we'll let Rorty's books speak for themselves.

> **Postmodernists say each community places moral standards on its members' actions. Every culture has its own set of moral standards and these standards evolve according to the dictates of the group.**

In the final analysis, Postmodernists say, each community places moral standards on its members' actions. Every culture has its own set of moral standards, and these standards evolve according to the dictates of the group.[69] Abortion, for example, used to be viewed with revulsion and horror. Now it is widely accepted as distasteful but necessary. The narrative has changed; what we consider to be "real" now is different from before.

But why do Postmodernists like Rorty speak and write about moral issues if morality does not actually exist independent of our minds? Rorty's revised pragmatism works backward: Christian ethics would say, "Here's what God is like, so this is how we must act," but Rorty would say, "Here's how we think we should act based on our formative story, so let's now develop a theory to accommodate it." The result is an ethical stance saying that somebody's rights are based on the fact that they were once wronged. You were once oppressed, or part of an oppressed group? Let's build a theory of ethics in order to privilege you at the expense of those whom you judge to have been your oppressors.

This reverse thinking about ethics is why Rorty considered words as merely tools of persuasion—he believed he could use words to move people who live in certain ways to see the world as he wanted it to be and then do what he wanted them to do.[70]

Not all Postmodernists agree with Rorty's willingness to tell people what to do. Postmodern psychiatrist Adam Phillips sees any ethical boundary as "a form of pontification and imperial self-aggrandizement.... No adult can know what's best for another adult; and, by the same token, no group or society can know what's best for another group or society."[71] Phillips's stance seems more in keeping with the overall postmodern mind-set, which does not allow anyone to be "right" on any particular issue, including ethics.

7. ISLAM

"There is no division of ethics and law in Islam," says the Swedish Muslim writer S. Parvez Manzoor.[72] Muslims believe Islamic law is ethical by definition, and what is ethical ought to be enshrined in every nation's laws. Because of this connection between Islamic ethics and law, we suggest you revisit the present section again after reading the "Law" chapter.

Historically, Muslims derive their ethics from the Quran and the Hadith. The Quran contains many ethical commands. The Hadith presents Muhammad as the exemplary human whom Muslims must imitate in all respects. "Muhammad was only a mortal being commissioned by God to teach the word of God and lead an exemplary life," wrote Islamic scholar Hammudah Abdalati. "He stands in history as the best model for man in piety and perfection. He is a living proof of what man can be and of what he can accomplish in the realm of excellence and virtue."[73] Because ethics is based on specific commands revealed from God, we could summarize Islamic ethics as **divine command theory**.

> *Divine Command Theory:* the belief that right and wrong are determined by God's commands.

Ram Swarup, the late Hindu thinker and author, articulated how Muslims perceive the actions and judgment of Muhammad recorded in the Hadith:

> The Prophet is caught as it were in the ordinary acts of his life—sleeping, eating, mating, praying, hating, dispensing justice, planning expeditions and revenge against his enemies. The picture that emerges is hardly flattering, and one is left wondering why in the first instance it was reported at all and whether it was done by admirers or enemies. One is also left to wonder how the believers, generation after generation, could have found this story so inspiring.
>
> The answer is that the [Muslim] believers are conditioned to look at the whole thing through the eyes of faith. An infidel in his fundamental misguidance may find the Prophet rather sensual and cruel—and certainly many of the things he did do not conform to ordinary ideas of morality—but the believers look at the whole thing differently. To them morality derives from the Prophet's actions; the moral is whatever he did. Morality does not determine the Prophet's actions, but his actions determine

and define morality. Muhammad's acts were not ordinary acts; they were Allah's own acts [i.e., acts empowered, guided and approved by Allah].

It was in this way and by this logic that Muhammad's opinions became the dogmas of Islam and his personal habits and idiosyncrasies became moral imperatives: Allah's commands for all believers in all ages and climes to follow.[74]

We might envision Muslims wearing a bracelet stamped with WWMD—What would Muhammad do? This is the only genuinely relevant ethical question in Islam.

Why is what Muhammad did so important? Because unlike the Bible, in which God reveals what he is like and what he wants us to do, the Quran presents the God of Islam as not directly knowable. If God's character cannot be known, we must content ourselves with God's decrees, which are most fully revealed in Muhammad. What Muhammad says goes.

Abdalati summarized what we can know about God and ethics through the revelation given to Muhammad:

The concept of morality in Islam centers around certain basic beliefs and principles. Among these are the following: (1) God is the Creator and Source of all goodness, truth, and beauty. (2) Man is a responsible, dignified, and honorable agent of his Creator. (3) God has put everything in the heavens and the earth in the service of mankind. (4) By His Mercy and Wisdom, God does not expect the impossible from man or hold him accountable for anything beyond his power. Nor does God forbid man to enjoy the good things of life. (5) Moderation, practicality, and balance are the guarantees of high integrity and sound morality. (6) All things are permissible in principle except what is singled out as obligatory, which must be observed, and what is singled out as forbidden, which must be avoided. (7) Man's ultimate responsibility is to God and his highest goal is the pleasure of his Creator.[75]

Required actions include the five pillars of Islam discussed in the "Islam" chapter. Ethical prohibitions include drinking wine (Quran 2:219; 4:43; 5:93–94; some Muslims apply this prohibition by analogy to all alcoholic beverages and intoxicating drugs); eating pork; animals who kill with claws, teeth, or fangs; birds of prey; rodents; reptiles; worms; and dead animals (Quran 2:172–73; 5:4–6); eating meat that has not been properly slaughtered (proper slaughter includes a prayer to Allah at the time of the slaughter); and gambling (Quran 2:219). Jihadis may also include as permissible *taqiyya* (concealment—lying for the sake of Allah to advance Islam's cause), marriage to multiple wives, and slavery.

Muslims are motivated toward ethical behavior from a desire to develop personal virtue and spirituality, to better the state of others, to strengthen relationships, and to anticipate the coming judgment. At the final judgment, all humans will have their deeds weighed in the balance. The Quran says, "Then those whose balance (of good deeds) is heavy, they will attain salvation: But those whose balance is light, will be those who have lost their souls, in Hell will they abide" (23:102–3). According to Hammudah Abdalati,

This world will come to an end someday, and the dead will rise to stand for their final and fair trial. Everything we do in this world, every intention we have, every move we make, every thought we entertain, and every word we say, all are counted and kept in accurate records. On the Day of Judgment they will be brought up. People with good records will be generously rewarded and warmly welcomed to the Heaven of God, and those with bad records will be punished and cast into Hell.... However, the Muslim believes that there definitely will be compensation and reward for the good deeds, and punishment for the evil ones. That is the Day of justice and final settlement of all accounts.[76]

Fear of an eternity in hell is a strong motivation for Muslims, especially since one cannot know with certainly what God requires of human souls.

At the end of the day, it's straightforward what constitutes ethical behavior for Muslims. Philosophical debates are rare. Standards do not change based on economic conditions. No amount of meditation will move us to higher consciousness. Whether you believe in your heart isn't as important as whether you do your duty. Perhaps, in a world of complexity and chaos, it is this straightforwardness that makes Islam attractive to so many.

8. CHRISTIANITY

Christians say God is not merely a divine rule maker or the keeper of the good; he has made us in his image to be stewards of the earth. But because we are fallen, we live with the dissonance between the way things are and the way they ought to be. Fortunately, though, this is not the end of the story: through Christ we gain a *means* of acting as God desires as well as a *desire* to act accordingly. Ethics, then, is not the exercise of our own wills but the discovery of a God who wills all and has exercised himself on our behalf.

The basis of Christian ethics is found in Jesus's instruction to love God with all our heart, soul, mind, and strength and to love our neighbor as ourselves (Luke 10:27).[77] This kind of love is derived from a peculiar Greek word, *agape* (pronounced "ah-gah-PAY").

Just as the law of gravity is apparent to anyone who jumps out of an upper-story window, the Christian worldview says that what is morally true can be seen by all whose ability to perceive is not completely distorted. Ethics is simply an expansion of a generally revealed moral order.

> *Agape:* the belief that morality is built upon two foundational moral absolutes: love of God and love of neighbor.

The idea of a moral law is not popular. Those who wish it not to exist, or who disagree about its nature, are ignoring the truth. Too often the response to the Christian claim is to attack the messenger rather than refute the message. For example, Simon Blackburn, a Cambridge professor and leader in the British Humanist Association, warns against permitting Christian involvement in the public sphere by saying, "The only reason Christians are not still burning each other is because the secular state stopped them."[78]

It is true that many evil things have been done in the name of Christ. So-called Christians have blatantly acted contrary to Christ's message. Christianity even predicts this: because of sin, people will do evil and often do it under the banner of goodness. In service of truth, they will lie. In the name of compassion, they will torture. To blame God's revelation for this, though, is to confuse the disease with the diagnosis, as one who blames the doctor for having caused the sickness he identifies, or blaming the composer when an unprepared student botches the performance of his music. When a cook ruins dinner, it might be a flaw in the recipe, but more often it is caused by mixing the wrong ingredients in the wrong order or baking them at the wrong temperature or for the wrong amount of time. To quote Robert Burns's famous poem "To a Mouse," "The best-laid schemes of mice and men oft go awry."

Muslims believe moral norms are the products of God's decree; Marxists and Secularists rely almost exclusively on their economic or naturalistic philosophy to determine ethics; Postmodernists argue for a morality based on shared "community" values; and New Spiritualists see ethical behavior as following individually determined inner truth, Christians see moral norms as proceeding from God's nature or character. Francis Schaeffer explained Christianity's uniqueness in this regard:

> One of the distinctions of the Judeo-Christian God is that not all things are the same to Him. That at first may sound rather trivial, but in reality it is one of the most profound things one can say about the Judeo-Christian God. He exists; He has a character; and not all things are the same to Him. Some things conform to His character, and some are opposed to His character.[79]

The task of Christian ethics, then, is to determine what conforms to God's character and what does not.

Seeing right and wrong as objectively absolute based on the nature and character of a personal, loving God is superior to any concept of moral relativism. Further, Christians understand human beings as free moral agents, as morally culpable, capable of observing God's character and responding—or not responding—in accordance with God's character. Acclaimed French philosopher Luc Ferry says the Christian doctrine of free will—that we have all been given natural gifts, and how we use them makes them good or bad—has "revolutionized the history of thought."[80]

> **Christians understand human beings as free moral agents, as morally culpable, capable of observing God's character and responding— or not responding— in accordance with God's character.**

To Jürgen Habermas, one of the world's top philosophers, the Judeo-Christian worldview has produced an ethic incomparable in the history of the world:

> Egalitarian universalism, from which sprang the ideas of freedom and social solidarity, of an autonomous conduct of life and emancipation, of the individual morality of conscience, human rights and democracy, is the direct heir of the Judaic ethic of justice and the Christian ethic of love. This legacy, substantially unchanged, has been the object of continual critical appropriation and reinterpretation. To this day, there is no alternative to it. And in light of the current challenges of a postnational constellation, we continue to draw on the substance of this heritage. Everything else is just idle postmodern talk.[81]

With some of the world's top philosophers pointing out its virtues, the ethical stance of Christianity is not easily intimidated. At root, though, Christianity's ethics are not complicated: "So whatever you wish that others would do to you, do also to them, for this is the Law and the Prophets" (Matt. 7:12) and "Let love be genuine. Abhor what is evil; hold fast to what is good" (Rom. 12:9).

Where, according to Christianity, do moral absolutes come from? To say that a particular moral statement can be objectively known is to say that to not know it is to commit an error. And to say that this is the case across all times and cultures is to say that the particular moral statement—such as "one ought never torture babies for fun"—ought to be universally known. The Bible does not specify these commands line by line. Rather, it gives clear guidelines for moral decision making so we can figure out what is right in the circumstances we face. The most obvious ethical principles, of course, are found in the Decalogue (the Ten Commandments),[82] which establish the basic moral law for humanity. Much of Scripture is dedicated to describing God's moral order. For example, the New Testament books of Romans and Galatians contain a number of moral directives for us to follow.

The Bible also introduces us to God incarnate, Jesus Christ, and describes his ministry and ethical teachings in an understandable way. The apex of Christ's ethical teaching is found in the Sermon on the Mount (Matt. 5–7) in which his audience realized that he was the role model for virtuous living. Irish historian and political theorist W. E. H. Lecky, who never claimed to be a Christian, admitted, "The character of Jesus has not only been the highest pattern of virtue, but the strongest incentive to its practice."[83]

In fact, the call to follow Jesus is the simplest summation of Christian ethics and at the same time the most difficult thing to do. Dietrich Bonhoeffer, a Christian who died for his faith at the hands of the Nazis during World War II, noted, "On two separate occasions Peter received the call, 'Follow me.' It was the first and last word Jesus spoke to his disciple (Mark 1:17, John 21:22)."[84] Christ asks but one thing of all Christians: "Follow me!" (Luke 9:23).[85] By following Christ we *experience* how to focus on God's glory. William Young wrote, "In declaring by word and deed the perfections, especially the moral perfections of the Most High, man finds true happiness."[86]

> By following Christ we *experience* how to focus on God's glory.

Carl F. H. Henry described the heart and soul of Christian ethics: "Hebrew-Christian ethics unequivocally defines moral obligation as man's duty to God."[87] But the use of *duty* in this sense means much more than checking obedience boxes on some cosmic list. When Jesus said, "You shall love the Lord your God with all your heart and with all your soul and with all your strength and with all your mind, and your neighbor as yourself" (Luke 10:27), he was quoting the Torah,[88] the Old Testament law, reemphasizing what God had *always* set down as the proper view of ethics.

The first part of Jesus's command—love God—shows the insufficiency of deontological (duty-based) theories of ethics. The goal is not merely to perform a duty but to

> Only seeking to reflect God's character leads to true flourishing.

love God with every aspect of our being: heart, soul, mind, and strength. Christianity involves a relationship with a person, not merely a religious responsibility. As for teleological (consequence-based) theories of ethics, we cannot sufficiently fulfill our ethical responsibilities by acting in our own best interests. Only seeking to reflect God's character leads to true flourishing.

The second part of Jesus's command applies *loving God* to *loving our neighbor as we love ourselves*. There is little room here for a self-definition of human flourishing or personal good since, at its most basic level, loving God means serving others. Carl Henry summarized this teaching:

> The Apostle John appeals to the explicit teaching of the Redeemer to show the inseparable connection between love of God and love of neighbor: "If a man says, I love God, and hateth his brother, he is a liar: for he that loveth not his brother whom he hath seen, how can he love God whom he hath not seen? And this commandment have we from him, that he who loveth God love his brother also" (1 John 4:20f). "God is love, and he that dwelleth in love dwelleth in God, and God in him" (4:16). The love of God is the service of man in love.[89]

Jesus said in Mark 10:43–45, "Whoever would be great among you must be your servant, and whoever would be first among you must be slave of all. For even the Son of Man came not to be served but to serve, and to give his life as a ransom for many." This ethical stance of servanthood is more than just serving the *spiritual* needs of others. As Norm Geisler articulates it, it has to do with serving physical needs as well:

> Man is more than a soul destined for another world; he is also a body living in this world. And as a resident of this time-space continuum man has physical and social needs which cannot be isolated from spiritual needs. Hence, in order to love man as he is—the whole man—one must exercise a concern about his social needs as well as his spiritual needs.[90]

As Christians, our faith in God does not exempt us from worldly concerns, such as feeding the hungry or caring for the sick. Jesus tells us in Matthew 25:31–46 that when we serve others, we serve him, and when we fail to serve others, we fail to serve him.

> As Christians, our faith in God does not exempt us from worldly concerns, such as feeding the hungry or caring for the sick.

These ethical guidelines go beyond what we could think up on our own. "The human mind," said C. S. Lewis, "has no more power of inventing a new value than of imagining a new primary color, or, indeed, of creating a new sun and a new sky for it to move in."[91] For the Christian, the moral order is as real as the physical order—some would say even more real. The apostle Paul said the physical order is temporary, but the order "not seen" is eternal (2 Cor. 4:18).[92] This eternal moral order reflects the character and nature of God himself.

9. The Christian Response to Relativistic Moral Systems

The greatest challenge to Christian ethics, in our judgment, comes from the ethical stance Secularism, Marxism, and Postmodernism promote. If only the natural world may be taken into account, then what is unique—and uniquely beneficial—about Christian ethics must be set aside. *No ethical standards can be known to be absolute.* Christians should think long and hard before granting this premise. As Francis Schaeffer insisted, there must be an absolute if there is to be any kind of meaningful moral order. "If there is no absolute beyond man's ideas, then there is no final appeal to judge between individuals and groups whose moral judgments conflict. We are merely left with conflicting opinions."[93] The practical Achilles' heel of relativism is this: if all we have are conflicting opinions and subjective value judgments, the most powerful will always win, regardless of their rightness. "Those who stand outside all judgments of value cannot have any ground for preferring one of their own impulses to another except the emotional strength of that impulse," wrote C. S. Lewis.[94]

> The practical Achilles' heel of relativism is this: if all we have are conflicting opinions and subjective value judgments, the most powerful will always win, regardless of their rightness.

Interestingly, there is some movement even among those of a naturalistic persuasion to extend beyond purely individualistic, personal-autonomy-driven ethical views. In *The Righteous Mind*, Jonathan Haidt, an atheistic naturalist, describes how his graduate work and several cross-cultural experiences led him to see the inadequacy of the Western idea of a person as an autonomous, individual self. Such a view, says Haidt, makes it difficult to make moral decisions and, importantly, to understand how people around the world make such decisions. In response, Haidt examined moral psychologist Richard Shweder's research and found that autonomy is only one reasonable basis for moral decision making. Community and divinity are also valid.[95]

Rather than always starting with the individual, we need to take into account the relationship between people and God's will as legitimate starting points for moral understanding.

The idea of the individual as a self-contained, autonomous unit is, according to Charles Taylor's massive and acclaimed text *A Secular Age*, a relatively recent phenomenon. It is only in the past five hundred years or so that people have gotten the sense of a "self" that is "buffered"—that a clear boundary exists between self and others. In previous times in the West, and in other nations around the world today, the boundary between the self and other people is porous—we affect one another more than we admit, for good or for ill.[96] Descartes's idea of "I think therefore I am" is insufficient not just because it is philosophically difficult to sustain but because it begins with "I" rather than with "we" or with "God."

Understanding our obligation to God is the only thing that gets us past relativism. We realize God is truth; therefore, it is always unlawful and morally wrong for a judge to take a bribe. We understand God is loving; therefore, it is universally wrong for an adult to sexually abuse a child. If ethical standards are relative to a particular culture, the best we can say is, "It is unlawful, in the present circumstances, to take a bribe or abuse a child." But strict adherence to the law does not fulfill the full duty of the ethical life. Corporations may

> If ethical standards are relative to a particular culture, the best we can say is, "It is unlawful, in the present circumstances, to take a bribe or abuse a child." But strict adherence to the law does not fulfill the full duty of the ethical life.

comply with the law and still act hurtfully. Governments may act within the proper statutes and codes and still afflict the vulnerable. "We should never forget," Martin Luther King Jr. wrote in his letter from the Birmingham jail, "that everything Adolf Hitler did in Germany was 'legal' and everything the Hungarian freedom fighters did in Hungary was 'illegal.'" Cultural relativism says what is right and wrong depends on the culture. But if this is so, culture is absolute, and those who seek to change it—as did William Wilberforce in seeking to abolish slavery—at best have no grounds for doing so, and at worst are in the wrong for imposing their views on others.

What appear to be "exceptions" to an absolute rule, such as permission to kill an intruder to protect one's family or to lie in order to help defeat an evil enemy, do not invalidate the rule but prove it. When we see a wrong done, we know it is not as it ought to be. That sense of "oughtness" tells us something of God's law having been placed in our hearts.

In conclusion, the Christian ethical system is both like and unlike any other system ever postulated. We must decide now how we will act in response. Dietrich Bonhoeffer asked,

> Who stands fast? Only the man whose final standard is not his reason, his principles, his conscience, his freedom, or his virtue, but who is ready to sacrifice all this when he is called to obedient and responsible action in faith and in exclusive allegiance to God—the responsible man, who tries to make his whole life an answer to the question and call of God. Where are these responsible people?[97]

Those willing to raise their hands in response to Bonhoeffer's question ought to be prepared to treat God's moral order with the same respect they show his physical order, to love God with all they are and have, and to treat others as they desire to be treated. Such people must be prepared for a mission to everywhere: to stand firm against tyranny and slavery in the halls of government as well as sacrifice for the sake of the gospel on the mission field. It is not the extraordinary Christians who do this but the quite ordinary ones. In putting Christian ethics into practice, believers demonstrate to a watching world that Christ's truth is worth believing and living.[98]

We have now invested three chapters studying the disciplines of theology, philosophy, and ethics, describing God as creator, redeemer, and sustainer; discussing what is real and how we know; and outlining what the good life consists of. In the next chapter we will seek to answer two questions that to many people are even more basic: what is life and where did it come from? These two questions are in the domain of biology, the study of life. And as we will shortly see, biology is much more than dissections and memorization of terms. It is in the domain of biology that many of the big worldview battles of our day are being fought.

ENDNOTES

1. Victor Hugo, *Les Misérables*, trans. Lee Fahnestock and Norman MacAfee (New York: Signet Classic, 1987), 103–6.
2. Walter Lippman, *Public Opinion* (New York: Free Press, 1965), 80, quoted in Thomas Sowell, *A Conflict of Visions* (New York: William Morrow, 1987), 18.
3. Quoted in Carl F. H. Henry, ed., *Baker's Dictionary of Christian Ethics* (Grand Rapids: Baker, 1973), 620.
4. John Deigh, *Introduction to Ethics* (Cambridge, UK: Cambridge University Press, 2010), 8.
5. Simon Blackburn, *Ethics: A Very Short Introduction* (Oxford, UK: Oxford University Press, 2001), 4.
6. Deigh, *Introduction to Ethics*, 14.
7. Austin Dacey, *The Secular Conscience* (Amherst, NY: Prometheus Books, 2008), 170–71.
8. Quoted in Dacey, *Secular Conscience*, 31.
9. Blackburn, *Ethics*, 114.
10. Quoted in Morris B. Storer, ed., *Humanist Ethics* (Buffalo, NY: Prometheus Books, 1980), 137.
11. Ella Wheeler Wilcox, "No Classes!" in *Poems of Pleasure* (New York: Belford, 1888), 115.
12. Blackburn, *Ethics*, 116.

13. Jean-Paul Sartre, *Existentialism and Human Emotions* (New York: Citadel, 1957), 22.

14. Richard Weikart, *From Darwin to Hitler: Evolutionary Ethics, Eugenics, and Racism in Germany* (New York: Palgrave-Macmillan, 2004), 230.

15. Paul Kurtz, ed., *The Humanist Alternative* (Buffalo, NY: Prometheus Books, 1973), 50.

16. See Exodus 20:1–17.

17. Storer, *Humanist Ethics*, 3.

18. Henry Grunwald, "The Year 2000," *Time*, March 30, 1992, 50–51.

19. Austin Dacey, a moral philosopher and Secularist leader, said in a *New York Times* editorial, "Perhaps a future encyclical will concentrate on the truly harmful kind of relativism. This is the misguided multiculturalism that keeps Western liberals from criticizing the oppression of women, religious minorities and apostates in Islamic societies for fear of being accused of Islamophobia. In such cases we should not shrink from the ideals of autonomy and equality but affirm them openly for what they are: objectively defensible principles of conscience." Austin Dacey, "Believing in Doubt," *New York Times*, February 3, 2006, http://www.nytimes .com/2006/02/03/opinion/03dacey.html?_r=0.

20. William D. Gairdner, *The Book of Absolutes* (Montreal: McGill-Queen's University Press, 2010).

21. Paraphrased and adapted from Gairdner, *Book of Absolutes*, 9–18.

22. Quoted in Storer, *Humanist Ethics*, 99–100.

23. Kurtz, *Humanist Alternative*, 55.

24. Joseph Fletcher, "Humanist Ethics: The Groundwork," quoted in Storer, *Humanist Ethics*, 255.

25. Arthur E. Gravatt, quoted in William H. Genne, "Our Moral Responsibility," *Journal of the American College Health Association* 15 (May 1967): 63.

26. Harry Elmer Barnes, *The New History and the Social Studies* (New York: Century, 1925), 543.

27. Barnes, *New History*, 539.

28. Paul Kurtz, *Humanist Manifesto 2000: A Call for a New Planetary Humanism* (Amherst, NY: Prometheus, 2000), 32.

29. Kurtz, *Humanist Manifesto 2000*.

30. Corliss Lamont, *A Lifetime of Dissent* (Amherst, NY: Prometheus Books, 1988), 55.

31. Quoted in Francis A. Schaeffer, *The Complete Works of Francis A. Schaeffer: A Christian View of the West*, 5 vols. (Westchester, IL: Crossway Books, 1982), 5:439.

32. Schaeffer, *Complete Works of Francis A. Schaeffer*.

33. Quoted in V. I. Lenin, *Collected Works*, 45 vols. (Moscow: Progress Publishers, 1982), 31:291.

34. Karl Marx and Frederick Engels, *Collected Works*, 40 vols. (New York: International Publishers, 1977), 6:503.

35. G. L. Andreyev, *What Kind of Morality Does Religion Teach?* (Moscow: [publisher unknown], 1959), quoted in Raymond S. Sleeper, *A Lexicon of Marxist-Leninist Semantics* (Alexandria, VA: Western Goals, 1983), 174.

36. Howard Selsam, *Socialism and Ethic* (New York: International Publishers, 1943), 98.

37. Sleeper, *Lexicon*, 175.

38. Paul Berman, "The Cult of Che: Don't Applaud *The Motorcycle Diaries*," *Slate*, September 24, 2004, http://www .slate.com/id/2107100/. See also Humberto Fontova, *The Longest Romance: The Mainstream Media and Fidel Castro* (New York: Encounter, 2013).

39. Ronald Reagan's recognition of this point was a key motivator in his stand against communism. See Paul Kengor, *The Crusader: Ronald Reagan and the Fall of Communism* (New York: Harper Perennial, 2007), 174.

40. Quoted in William Goldstein, "Life on the Astral Plane," *Publishers Weekly*, March 18, 1983, 46.

41. Marilyn Ferguson, *The Aquarian Conspiracy* (Los Angeles: J. P. Tarcher, 1980), 327.

42. Vera Alder, *When Humanity Comes of Age* (New York: Samuel Weiser, 1974), 48–49.

43. Exodus 20:14.

44. Shakti Gawain, *Living in the Light* (San Rafael, CA: New World Library, 1986), 128.

45. Randall N. Baer, *Inside the New Age Nightmare* (Lafayette, LA: Huntington House, 1989), 88.

46. Eckhart Tolle, *A New Earth* (New York: Plume, 2005), 67.

47. Tolle, *New Earth*, 26–27.

48. Tolle, *New Earth*, 70.

49. Tolle, *New Earth*, 71.

50. The Dalai Lama, *A Profound Mind* (New York: Three Rivers, 2011), 138.

51. Stephen Mitchell, trans., *Bhagavad Gita* (New York: Three Rivers, 2000), 170.

52. Ferguson, *Aquarian Conspiracy*, 331.

53. Ferguson, *Aquarian Conspiracy*, 192.

54. Marianne Williamson, *A Return to Love: Reflections on the Principles of "A Course in Miracles"* (New York: HarperCollins, 1992), 22.

55. Gawain, *Living in the Light*, 60.

56. Shirley MacLaine, *Out on a Limb* (Toronto: Bantam Books, 1984), 96, 111.

57. Ferguson, *Aquarian Conspiracy*, 381.

58. David Spangler, *Reflections of the Christ* (Forres, Scotland: Findhorn, 1977), 40–44.

59. Kevin Ryerson, *Spirit Communication: The Soul's Path* (New York: Bantam Books, 1989), 84.

60. "A Taste of Armageddon," *Star Trek*, originally aired February 23, 1967.

61. These questions form a list of arguments against what ethicist Scott Rae refers to as *subjectivism*, the notion that moral statements cannot be known to be objectively true. For more information see chapter 2, "Is There a Moral Law That We Can Know?," in Scott Rae, *Doing the Right Thing* (Grand Rapids: Zondervan, 2013). Rae's arguments are, in summary, (1) the laws of logic actually exist beyond personal preference; (2) nearly everyone practices moral persuasion—even those who claim that objective truth cannot be known; (3) morality is more than an expression of a preference—some moral reasoning can be known to be wrong; (4) people can grow in moral understanding over time, which demonstrates that there are objective standards of morality to which we can aspire; and (5) humans have an innate sense of "oughtness" that shows that we understand objectively what morality is, and that it is not merely an expression of cultural prejudice.

62. Zygmunt Bauman, *Postmodern Ethics* (Oxford, UK: Blackwell, 1993), 3–4.

63. Quoted in Algis Valiunas, "Mental Health," *Weekly Standard* 11, no. 9 (November 14, 2005): 41.

64. Walt Whitman, "Leaves of Grass," in *Selected Poems: 1855–1892*, ed. Gary Schmidgall (New York: St. Martin's Griffin, 1999), 63.

65. Richard Rorty, *Achieving Our Country: Leftist Thought in Twentieth-Century America* (Cambridge, MA: Harvard University Press, 1998), 16.

66. Robert B. Brandom, ed., *Rorty and His Critics* (Oxford, UK: Blackwell, 2001), 4–5.

67. Kevin J. Vanhoozer, *Postmodern Theology* (Cambridge, UK: Cambridge University Press, 2005), 10.

68. Richard Rorty, *Philosophy and Social Hope* (New York: Penguin Books, 1999), 15.

69. This concept of morality is explored in the essay "Ethics without Principles," quoted in Rorty, *Philosophy and Social Hope*, 72–88.

70. A theme throughout Rorty's *Philosophy and Social Hope* is the use of words, ideas, and philosophies as tools rather than true things, especially in chapters 22–26.

71. Quoted in Valiunas, "Mental Health," 41.

72. S. Parvez Manzoor, "Shari'ah: The Ethics of Action," in "Islamic Conceptual Framework," MUNA, accessed February 15, 2016, www.muslimummah.org/articles/articles.php?itemno=200&&category=Islam

73. Hammudah Abdalati, *Islam in Focus* (Indianapolis: Amana, 1978), 8.

74. Ram Swarup, *Understanding Islam through Hadis* (Delhi, India: Voice of India, 1983), xv–xvi, quoted in George W. Braswell, *Islam: Its Prophet, Peoples, Politics, and Power* (Nashville: Broadman and Holman, 1996), 83.

75. Abdalati, *Islam in Focus*, 40. The Bible grounds morality in God's essential character; the Quran teaches that God cannot ultimately be known.

76. Abdalati, *Islam in Focus*, 13.

77. Luke 10:27: "[Jesus] answered, 'You shall love the Lord your God with all your heart and with all your soul and with all your strength and with all your mind, and your neighbor as yourself.'"

78. Simon Blackburn, "Against the Grain," *Independent*, May 4, 2007, in "Professor Simon Blackburn," British Humanist Association, accessed March 19, 2014, http://humanism.org.uk/about/our-people/distinguished-supporters/professor-simon-blackburn/.

79. Francis Schaeffer, "Christian Faith and Human Rights," *Simon Greenleaf Law Review* 2 (1982/83): 5, quoted in John Montgomery, *Human Rights and Human Dignity* (Dallas: Probe Books, 1986), 113.

80. Luc Ferry, *A Brief History of Thought*, trans. Theo Cuffe (New York: Harper Perennial, 2011), 74.

81. Jürgen Habermas, *Time of Transitions* (Cambridge, UK: Polity, 2006), 151.

82. See Exodus 20:1–17.

83. W. E. H. Lecky, *History of European Morals (from Augustus to Charlemagne)*, 2 vols. (New York: George Braziller, 1955), 2:8–9.

84. Quoted in Norman L. Geisler, *Ethics: Alternatives and Issues* (Grand Rapids: Zondervan, 1979), 156.

85. Luke 9:23: "[Jesus] said to all, 'If anyone would come after me, let him deny himself and take up his cross daily and follow me.'"

86. Quoted in *Baker Dictionary of Christian Ethics*, 432–33.

87. Carl F. H. Henry, *Christian Personal Ethics* (Grand Rapids: Eerdmans, 1957), 209.

88. Leviticus 19:18: "You shall not take vengeance or bear a grudge against the sons of your own people, but you shall love your neighbor as yourself: I am the Lord"; Deuteronomy 6:5: "You shall love the Lord your God with all your heart and with all your soul and with all your might."

89. Henry, *Christian Personal Ethics*, 221–22.

90. Geisler, *Ethics*, 179. Though we like the way Geisler's point is phrased, it can give the impression that our bodies are somehow unimportant in light of our souls. This would be a wrong impression—our bodies are very important to God's design for our lives overall. See Proverbs 4:22; 1 Corinthians 6:19–20; 1 Timothy 4:7–8; and 3 John 1:2.

91. C. S. Lewis, *The Abolition of Man* (New York: Macmillan, 1973), 56–57.

92. Second Corinthians 4:18: "As we look not to the things that are seen but to the things that are unseen. For the things that are seen are transient, but the things that are unseen are eternal."

93. Francis A. Schaeffer, *How Should We Then Live?* (Old Tappan, NJ: Fleming H. Revell, 1976), 145.

94. Lewis, *Abolition of Man*, 78.

95. Jonathan Haidt, *The Righteous Mind* (New York: Pantheon, 2012), 14, 99.

96. Charles Taylor, *A Secular Age* (Cambridge, MA: Belknap, 2007), 38–39.

97. Dietrich Bonhoeffer, *Letters and Papers from Prison* (New York: Touchstone Books, 1997), 5.

98. For biblical examples of ethically responsible men and women, see Hebrews 11:32–12:3.

CHAPTER **11**

BIOLOGY

1. THE BATTLE BETWEEN FAITH AND SCIENCE

"It's all about the fabulous Monkey Trial that rocked America!" proclaimed the promotional poster for *Inherit the Wind*, a 1960 film often taken as a literal history of events surrounding the 1925 *Scopes* trial in Dayton, Tennessee.[1] As history, *Inherit the Wind* turns out to be just that—wind. Most of the details shown in the film are opposite from the actual events recorded in both the trial transcript and news reports from the time. For example, an opening scene shows an angry mob arresting Scopes for teaching evolution, throwing him in jail, and shouting for him to be lynched. In real life, Scopes was never jailed and had a friendly relationship with the people of the town throughout the trial. In the film, William Jennings Bryan is shown as a defeated, narrow-minded ignoramus. In reality, he was jovial, well informed, and articulate.[2]

Inherit the Wind's unfortunate inaccuracy has misled many people. As one of the leading evolutionary atheists Eugenie Scott acknowledges, the play is "often read and performed in high schools" and has helped promote a "negative public image" of many Christians as "foolish, unthinking, religious zealots."[3] Nonetheless, some of the themes it develops were genuinely at play in the actual *Scopes* trial and represent active sources of conflict in our society even today.

In the historical trial, one-time Democratic presidential candidate William Jennings Bryan, a Christian and creationist, agreed to be cross-examined by Clarence Darrow, an agnostic evolutionist, on the condition that Darrow would submit to a similar cross-examination by Bryan. Darrow agreed. On the stand, Bryan bantered with Darrow about the meaning of Scripture. In spite of some humorous exchanges, a thick tension was developing, as is evident from the actual trial transcript:

> Mr. Bryan: "These gentlemen have not had much chance—they did not come here to try this case. They came here to try revealed religion. I am here to defend it, and they can ask me any question they please."
>
> (Applause from the court yard.)
>
> Mr. Darrow: "Great applause from the bleachers."
>
> Mr. Bryan: "From those whom you call 'yokels.'"
>
> Mr. Darrow: "I have never called them yokels."
>
> Mr. Bryan: "That is the ignorance of Tennessee, the bigotry." [Referring to Darrow's comments to the press.]
>
> Mr. Darrow: "You mean who are applauding you?" (Applause.)
>
> Mr. Bryan: "Those are the people whom you insult."
>
> Mr. Darrow: "You insult every man of science and learning in the world because he does not believe in your fool religion."

As the cross-examination of Bryan concluded, the defense pleaded guilty, removing the chance Bryan had to cross-examine Darrow. We will never know what Bryan might have asked had he gotten his turn, but his writings reveal a deep concern with how the survival-of-the-fittest idea would be used in society. Bryan's dire predictions came true; social Darwinism became the philosophical justification for the **eugenics** movement, the sterilization of minorities, abortion, and ultimately the Nazi Holocaust.[4]

Eugenics: a social movement advocating the genetic improvement of the human race through such practices as selective breeding, compulsory sterilization, forced abortions, and genocide.

Tellingly, there is a scene at the end of *Inherit the Wind* where the Clarence Darrow character, played by Spencer Tracy, takes up a Bible and a copy of Darwin's *Origin of Species*, weighs them in his hands, and then slaps them together as if to say, "Maybe I can keep both."

This final scene sets the stage for a discussion of biology: Whom should we trust regarding important conversations about the nature of life and its origin?

In real life, Darrow gave no weight at all to the Bible. Neither does today's most famous scientist, the revered cosmologist Stephen Hawking, whose heroic struggle against the motor-neuron disease threatening to close off his brilliant mind has made him an international celebrity. To Hawking, only scientists can now answer the great questions in life:

> Humans are a curious species. We wonder, we seek answers.... How can we understand the world in which we find ourselves?... Where did all this come from? Did the universe need a creator?... Traditionally these are questions for philosophy, but philosophy is dead.... Scientists have become the bearers of the torch of discovery in our quest for knowledge.[5]

Much of the conflict between faith and science plays out on the battlefield of biology.

Much of the conflict between faith and science plays out on the battlefield of biology. Astronomers study the stars. Geologists study the earth's structure. Biologists, though, study life itself. Biology is a science in which those who are alive examine what life itself is all about.

2. BIOLOGY: A WAY OF KNOWING ABOUT LIFE

Bios means "life." **Biology** is the study of life, of thinking about the world, including what is real and how we know. Many students are fascinated by dissecting animals and learning about the complexity of life, but the central question of biology is "What *is* life?"

Not everyone thinks it is important to know what life is. Steven D. Garber's bestselling book *Biology: A Self-Teaching Guide*, for example, begins by offering the standard evolutionary arguments about how life arose but never takes up the question of how we know what life actually is.[6]

An oft-quoted source on this question is *What Is Life?* by Erwin Schrödinger, one of the founders of quantum theory:

Biology: the study of life and living organisms.

> What is the characteristic feature of life? When is a piece of matter said to be alive? When it goes on "doing something," moving, exchanging material with its environment, and so forth, and that for a much longer period than we would expect an inanimate piece of matter to "keep going" under similar circumstances. When a system that is not alive is isolated or placed in a uniform environment, all motion usually comes to a standstill very soon as a result of various kinds of friction; differences of electric or chemical potential are equalized, substances which tend to form a chemical compound do so, temperature becomes uniform by heat conduction. After that the whole system fades away into a dead, inert lump of matter. A permanent state is reached in which no observable events occur. The physicist calls this the state of thermodynamical equilibrium, or of "maximum entropy."[7]

Take a moment to study this famous passage. Note that Schrödinger didn't grapple so much with what it means to be alive as he did with what it means to be dead. This is helpful, but it still does not bring us any closer to understanding what life is.

Modern Biology, published by Holt, Rinehart, and Winston, more clearly defines Schrödinger's observations, organizing them into seven characteristics that all living things share:

1. **Organization**—high degree of order including one or more cells
2. **Response to stimuli**—adjustment when faced with physical or chemical change in the environment
3. **Homeostasis**—ability to maintain stable internal conditions
4. **Metabolism**—use of energy to power its life processes
5. **Growth and development**—growth and increase in size
6. **Reproduction**—production of new organisms like themselves
7. **Change through time**—change experienced without change in their basic genetic characteristics[8]

So far, so good. But in the minds of most people, the question immediately following "What is life?" is "How did it come into existence?" The question of how life arose very often turns people's minds to God. This is true even with scientists. The famous astrophysicist Sir Arthur Eddington, the man who explained Einstein's theory of relativity to the general public, eloquently expressed the reason:

> In the mystic sense of the creation around us, in the expression of art, in a yearning towards God, the soul grows upward and finds the fulfillment of something implanted in its nature. The sanction for this development is within us, a striving born with our consciousness or an Inner Light proceeding from a greater power than ours. Science can scarcely question this sanction, for the pursuit of science springs from a striving that the mind is impelled to follow, a questioning that will not be suppressed.[9]

Eddington acknowledged what many people suspect: We humans have a longing for God, something we know nature cannot provide. We know we are alive. We know we exist and that we direct the motions of our bodies. We know that when we say "I," we aren't thinking of ourselves as just a bundle of molecules but as actual persons. We further suspect that everything around us could not have merely come into being through random-chance processes.

The question of how life arose is vital to every worldview. It is the starting point, ground zero, for building a meaningful view of the world. A culture's understanding of the origins issue steers the values of its people: The Judeo-Christian origins perspective tells the story of morally culpable human beings made in God's image and for companionship with one another. This understanding alone leads to a particular view of free will, the intrinsic value of human life, and traditional marriage as a part of God's plan. The Darwinian origins story, on the other hand, is one of individuals in constant competition, seeking not to flourish in harmony but to survive at the expense of the other, which justifies Nietzsche's view of the world—the pursuit of unbridled power. Where you begin will determine where you end up, and this carries great consequences for everything in our lives, especially how human society should be organized. So let's dig right

> The question of how life arose is vital to every worldview. It is the starting point, ground zero, for building a meaningful view of the world.

in to see what the six worldviews we've been examining say about the study of life and how they support those views.

3. SECULARISM

"Man is the result of a purposeless and natural process that did not have him in mind. He was not planned," said George Gaylord Simpson, a respected paleontologist. "He is a state of matter, a form of life, a sort of animal, and a species of the Order Primates, akin nearly or remotely to all of life and indeed to all that is material."[10] Simpson referred to the natural processes Charles Darwin articulated in *The Origin of Species*. Some scientists are so convinced as to describe Darwin's claims as fact, not theory.[11] Evolutionary biologist Julian Huxley proclaimed, "The first point to make about Darwin's theory is that it is no longer a theory, but a fact.... Darwinism has come of age so to speak. We ... no longer [have] to bother about establishing the fact of evolution."[12]

Other scientists are a little more reserved. Even though he is committed to the idea of life arising from random-chance processes, Stephen Hawking nevertheless admits the universe has the appearance of having been designed:

> Luck in the precise form and nature of fundamental physical law is a different kind of luck from the luck we find in environmental factors. It cannot be so easily explained, and has far deeper physical and philosophical implications. Our universe and its laws appear to have a design that both is tailor-made to support us and, if we are to exist, leaves little room for alteration. That is not so easily explained, and raises the natural question of why it is that way.[13]

So is it luck or design? And if it is luck, how did we get so lucky? Secularists, for the most part, believe that Darwin's explanation of evolution is basically correct and sufficiently robust to explain the complexity of life on Earth. It is partly because of this manner of thinking that Stephen Hawking now claims to be an atheist.[14]

Before we proceed further, let's distinguish between two aspects of evolutionary theory. The idea that living things incorporate small, adaptive changes over time is termed **microevolution**. An example of microevolution would be the minor changes within a species that have, over time, produced the wide variety within a species that we now observe in the world, such as the varieties of dogs or breeds of cows. Microevolution is a well-established, observable fact of science.

Microevolution: **the belief that small, adaptive changes are capable of producing variations within the gene pool of a species.**

Macroevolution, on the other hand, is the idea that adaptive changes lead one species to become an entirely different species. Essentially, macroevolution takes the observable microevolution in our world and then extrapolates to claim it as evidence for something not observed. As a result, the term *evolution* now commonly refers to a belief system that claims the following: the first speck of

Macroevolution: **the belief that small, adaptive changes are capable of accumulating over time to produce entirely new species.**

life emerged from nonliving material and slowly evolved into one-celled organisms, some of which, through eons of genetic mutations and natural selection, turned into more complex organisms and ultimately into Homo sapiens—human beings.

Most Secularists deny the existence of design or a designer (some do not, of course; it is possible to hold to theism while embracing the Secularist belief that it should have no place in the public sphere). According to Secularist assumptions outlined in the "Theology" chapter of this volume, no life exists that cannot, from its inception, be explained by unguided natural mechanisms. The primary mechanism underlying modern Darwinian ideas about macroevolution is natural selection acting upon genetic mutations, where random changes in DNA lead to adaptations that may improve the ability of some organisms to survive and reproduce. Other oft-cited mechanisms are **genetic drift**, where some traits can be passed on (or eliminated) from one generation to another strictly by chance, and **gene flow**, in which some traits are passed along (or eliminated) when a migratory group breeds with a native group. But natural selection and random mutations are most central to the theory and are worth a closer look.

Genetic Drift: the belief that favorable traits can be passed on (or unfavorable traits eliminated) from one generation to the next strictly by chance.

Gene Flow: the belief that favorable traits can be passed on (or unfavorable eliminated) when a migratory group breeds with a native group.

Natural Selection (aka Survival of the Fittest): the process by which organisms better adapted for their environment tend to survive longer, reproduce, and pass along more favorable biological traits.

Selective Breeding: the process by which human beings selectively breed organisms with desirable traits to produce a line of offspring with the same desirable traits.

Natural selection. Through competition and other factors, such as predators, limited resources, geography, and time, Darwin proposed that only those life-forms best suited to survive and reproduce will tend to do so. Some have characterized this as "survival of the fittest" or the "struggle for existence."[15] Secularist and atheist scientist Carl Sagan insisted that "natural selection is a successful theory devised to explain the fact of evolution."[16] According to the leading evolutionary biologist Francisco Ayala, natural selection is a blind and unguided process, since "in evolution, there is no entity or person who is selecting adaptive combinations." He continues, "Natural selection does not operate according to some preordained plan. It is a purely natural process resulting from the interacting properties of physico-chemical and biological entities."[17]

Darwin felt comfortable relying on natural selection as a primary mechanism for evolution because he believed humans had already observed it through **selective breeding**. When one breeds horses to create faster offspring, one is artificially selecting a beneficial trait and, therefore, engaging in a *guided* process. This is different from Darwinian evolution, which Darwin postulated would take place in nature in a blind and unguided manner: "Natural selection is daily and hourly scrutinizing ... every variation, even the slightest; rejecting that which is bad, preserving and adding up all that is good; silently and insensibly working ... at the improvement of each organic being."[18]

Mutation and adaptation. During the 1930s, evolutionary scientists combined Darwin's idea of natural selection with the newly discovered science of genetics. Now commonly referred to as **neo-Darwinism**, this modified understanding of evolution says that new species arise from natural selection acting over vast periods of time on chance mutations in DNA. In other words, given enough time, species will experience enough genetic changes to actually change them into entirely different species.

Of course, in accepting adaptation as part of the mechanism of evolution, the Secularist must assume that adaptations that persist are somehow beneficial.[19] Explaining this often results in contortions worthy of Cirque du Soleil. For example, Julian Huxley tried to explain how even harmful diseases like schizophrenia could be viewed as beneficial:

> Genetic theory makes it plain that a clearly disadvantageous genetic character like this cannot persist in this frequency in a population unless it is balanced by some compensating advantage. In this case it appears that the advantage is that schizophrenic individuals are considerably less sensitive than normal persons to histamine, are much less prone to suffer from operative and wound shock, and do not suffer nearly so much from various allergies.[20]

Huxley's statement reveals the post-hoc nature of Darwinian argument, taking something it observes in nature and arguing backward toward its supposed cause rather than making predictions that are then observed to be true. What is the adaptive value of avoiding certain allergies? Are these allergies deadly? Do they prevent a person from reproducing? As it stands, it is hard to imagine people suffering from severe personality disorders taking comfort in their resistance to allergies.

Testing Secularist assumptions. Now we come to a very controversial question: If all life evolved through random-chance processes starting with the first speck of life, how would we know? Is it possible to test whether this assertion is true? After all, we're talking about very small changes accumulating over great periods of time—something no human could ever observe.

For this, there is one main place to turn: the fossil record. Surely, of the billions of animals that have lived and died, we would find some evidence in fossilized remains of the transition

Mutation: a change in the genetic makeup of an organism.

Adaptation: the process by which an organism or species becomes better able to survive.

Neo-Darwinism: a synthesis of Charles Darwin's and Gregor Mendel's theories, Neo-Darwinism is the belief that new species arise through the process of natural selection acting over vast periods of time on chance genetic mutations within organisms.

from one sort of animal to another, wouldn't we? After all, as Carl Sagan confidently asserted, "Evolution is a fact amply demonstrated by the fossil record."[21]

In Darwin's day, the actual evidence was missing. There was no fossil evidence that any of the major divisions of vertebrate animals (fish, amphibians, reptiles, birds, and mammals) had been crossed. He and his followers hoped further exploration would confirm the truth of their theories. Unfortunately, the fossil record has been unwilling to yield much in the way of helpful data. As the noted Harvard paleontologist Stephen Jay Gould admitted in characteristically blunt fashion,

Stasis, or nonchange, of most fossil species during their lengthy geological lifespans was tacitly acknowledged by all paleontologists, but almost never studied explicitly because prevailing theory treated stasis as uninteresting nonevidence for nonevolution. . . . The overwhelming prevalence of stasis became an embarrassing feature of the fossil record, best left ignored as a manifestation of nothing (that is, nonevolution).[22]

Gould further acknowledged, "The absence of fossil evidence for intermediary stages between major transitions in organic design ... has been a persistent and nagging problem for gradualistic accounts of evolution."[23]

Rather than give up on evolution, though, natural scientists shifted their emphasis to explaining the absence of the evidence rather than analyzing its presence. Zoologist Chris McGowan, after admitting that the fossil record does not contain evidence of macroevolution, explained this new approach: "New species probably evolve only when a segment of the population becomes isolated from the rest. Speciation occurs relatively rapidly, probably in a matter of only a few thousand years and possibly less."[24]

Punctuated equilibrium is the name given to the hypothesis that the fossil record is barren because species evolved rapidly. It was devised by paleontologists Niles Eldredge and Stephen Jay Gould. *Equilibrium* refers to the fact that species manifest a stubborn stability (stasis) in nature. *Punctuated* refers to the dramatic changes deemed necessary to explain how the gaps are bridged in the fossil record between the major types of organisms. Put the two terms together, and you arrive at this claim: science cannot discover the links between species in the fossil record because the change from one species to another occurs too rapidly, geologically speaking, to leave any fossil documentation of the transition.[25]

How does punctuated equilibrium mesh with the theory of evolution as presented by Darwin? Not as well as one might expect. In fact, it clashes directly with Darwin's ideas because it requires too much genetic change in abrupt, large steps. Darwin wrote, "If it could be demonstrated that any complex organ existed, which could not possibly have been formed by numerous, successive, slight modifications, my theory would absolutely break down."[26]

Secularists reject design but not because they have conducted research and disproven it. Rather, they assume from the beginning that the universe was not designed and that the material universe is all that exists. Harvard evolutionary biologist Richard Lewontin admits this explicitly:

> We have a prior commitment, a commitment to materialism. It is not that the methods and institutions of science somehow compel us to accept a material explanation of the phenomenal world, but, on the contrary, that we are forced by our a priori adherence to material causes to ... produce material explanations.... That materialism is absolute, for we cannot allow a Divine Foot in the door.[27]

The rejection of intelligent design, for Secularists, is a kind of self-fulfilling prophecy. They assume from the beginning that no design is possible. It's no wonder they conclude that no design took place.

In the end, here is the Secularist answer to the question of how life arose: it somehow appeared and then became more complex through a mindless process of mutation and natural selection. And if Lewontin's quote means anything, then it's not so much an "answer" but an assumption that guides their entire study of nature. Cornell University professor William Provine, a leading historian of science, wrote, "Modern science directly implies that the world is organized strictly in accordance with mechanistic principles. There are no purposive principles whatsoever in nature."[28]

> In the end, here is the Secularist answer to the question of how life arose: it somehow appeared and then became more complex through a mindless process of mutation and natural selection.

4. Marxism

Darwinism is to Marxism what adrenaline is to a bodybuilding contest, amplifying an already extreme performance. When Marx read of Darwin's theory, he immediately saw it as providing a scientific basis for his ideas about class warfare: "Darwin's [*Origin of Species*] is very important and provides me with the basis in natural science for the class struggle in history."[29] Marx wrote to his collaborator Friedrich Engels, "During ... the past four weeks I have read all sorts of things. Among others Darwin's work on Natural Selection. And though it is written in the crude English style, this is the book which contains the basis in natural science for our view."[30] Marx so admired Darwin's work that he sent him a complimentary copy of *Das Capital*.

> Marx believed Darwin's evolutionary theory justified his views of human society.

Why was Marx so impressed? First, for Marx, only matter existed, and Darwin's theory made it plausible to believe this. Second, and more important, Marx believed Darwin's evolutionary theory justified his views of human society. If biological life evolves toward greater complexity, perhaps sociological life does as well, maybe even toward his longed-for classless state:

> Darwin has interested us in the history of Nature's technology, i.e., in the formation of the organs of plants and animals, which organs serve as instruments of production for sustaining life. Does not the history of the productive organs of man, of organs that are the material basis of all social organization, deserve equal attention?[31]

Engels more straightforwardly stated the link between Darwin's and Marx's theories: "Just as Darwin discovered the law of evolution in organic nature, so Marx discovered the law of evolution in human history."[32] Douglas Futuyma's college-level textbook *Evolutionary Biology* makes this connection explicit:

> It was Darwin's theory of evolution, followed by Marx's materialistic (even if inadequate or wrong) theory of history and society and Freud's attribution of human behavior to influences over which we have little control, that provided a crucial plank to the platform of mechanism and materialism—in short, of much of science—that has since been the stage of most Western thought.[33]

The love-at-first-sight relationship between Marx and Darwinism came about because Marx wanted to believe that history is spiraling upward, not downward. Not all change is productive, of course; some societies change by self-destructing. But Darwin's theory provided a glimmer of hope: if the seemingly chaotic flow of nature produces hardier, more adaptable species of animals, Marx thought, perhaps sociological progress toward a better state is likewise inevitable.[34]

At first glance, Darwin's theory of evolutionary change appeared to be suited perfectly to the Marxist idea of dialectical materialism, the idea that only the material world exists and that history is always changing through a process of thesis, antithesis, and synthesis.[35] But the romance was not to last. V. I. Lenin seemed to sense this; in his writings he pitted Marx's and Engels's certainty against Darwin's tentativeness: "[Dialectical materialism] as formulated by Marx and Engels on the basis of Hegel's philosophy, is far more comprehensive and far richer in content than the current idea of [Darwinian] evolution is."[36]

As it turns out, Lenin was right to be concerned. Darwinian evolution—gradual change from species to species—actually works contrary to the dialectical method, which predicts the rapid development of a new synthesis. Lenin had personally observed this. In overthrowing the Russian government, the revolutionary clash between the thesis (bourgeoisie) and antithesis (proletariat) resulted in a rapid formation of a radical new government. Consequently, early twentieth-century Marxists turned their backs on the natural selection aspect of Darwin's evolutionary theory.[37]

Punctuated equilibrium allows for jumps, rapid change, and chance. It speaks the language of revolution within evolution.

In the end, punctuated equilibrium provided the model of rapid evolution suitable for Marxist theorists. It seems perfectly dialectical, "an episodic process occurring in fits and starts interspaced with long periods of stasis [i.e., lack of change]."[38] Punctuated equilibrium allows for jumps, rapid change, and chance. It speaks the language of revolution within evolution.[39] Stunningly, Stephen Jay Gould and Niles Eldredge, punctuated equilibrium's most enthusiastic cheerleaders, admitted the relationship with Hegel's dialectic, and even Marxism, to be more than coincidental:

> Alternative conceptions of change have respectable pedigrees in philosophy. Hegel's dialectical laws, translated into a materialist context, have become the official "state philosophy" of many socialist nations. These laws of change are explicitly punctuational, as befits a theory of revolutionary transformation in human society. In light of this official philosophy, it is not at all surprising that a punctuational view of speciation, much like our own, but devoid (so far as we can tell) of references to synthetic evolutionary theory and the allopatric model, has long been favored by many Russian paleontologists. It may also not be irrelevant to our personal preferences that one of us [Gould] learned his Marxism, literally, at his daddy's knee.[40]

Marxist scientists, such as Russian biophysicist Mikhail Volkenshtein, could hardly contain their enthusiasm over the "multitude of facts" supporting punctuated equilibrium.[41]

Oddly, what Volkenshtein considered to be "proofs" for punctuated equilibrium included such arguments as "no gradual transition can take place between feathers and hair, etc."[42] The absence of evidence for the old theory was seen as magically providing the missing links for the new theory.

The Marxist view of life arising through random-chance processes is similar to the Secularist view. The primary difference: Secularists look for a more gradual process, and Marxists look for a rapid, even revolutionary explanation. Secularists and Marxists would like us to think of the theory of evolution providing a rational basis for what they see as the proper structure of government and society. Christians are rightfully suspicious: What if Secularists and Marxists started with the kind of government and society they wanted and then scoured around for a scientific viewpoint to justify this sort of power grab? Sometimes what we know *shapes* what we believe; other times, what we believe shapes what we want to know about. It's a dilemma, and one Postmodernists are all too happy to exploit, as we shall see.

5. POSTMODERNISM

According to Postmodernism, which emerged from the study of literature and sociology, everything—including science and philosophy—is a story. Postmodernist Terry Eagleton says, "Science and philosophy must jettison their grandiose metaphysical claims and view themselves more modestly as just another set of narratives."[43] Postmodernists see biology as incapable of getting humanity out of the mess we're in. Psychoanalyst Jacques Lacan said gloomily, "Biology can tell us little.... Selfhood is really nothing but a fleeting, unstable, incomplete and open-ended mess of desires which cannot be fulfilled."[44]

To Postmodernists, human beings have no essence; what we think of as a "self" is socially constructed from

> Postmodernists see biology as incapable of getting humanity out of the mess we're in.

> *Anti-Essentialism:*
> the belief that entities don't possess essences (i.e., a set of necessary and defining attributes); rather, an entity's identity is thought to be the result of social construction.

all our interactions within our cultures. This view is called **anti-essentialism.**

The evolution of all of life through random-chance processes may be just another grand story to be eschewed, but a few Postmodernists have tipped their hands and embraced various aspects of evolution with enthusiasm. For example, philosopher Richard Rorty endorsed Daniel Dennett's book *Darwin's Dangerous Idea*, a book supporting the neo-Darwinian view and harshly criticizing the theory of punctuated equilibrium. Postmodern political scientist Walter Truett Anderson's *The Next Enlightenment: Integrating East and West in a New Vision of Human Evolution* approvingly cites neo-Darwinist Richard Dawkins a number of times.

Why would Postmodernists reject all metanarratives on the surface but secretly harbor an affinity for the evolution metanarrative? Maybe, as John Dewey believed and Richard Rorty approvingly cited, the evolutionary metanarrative is compelling because it gives us permission to take charge of our own evolution and go whatever direction we think best.[45] Others, such as Michel Foucault, Hayden White, Paul de Man, and Thomas Kuhn, take an *anti-teleological* stance: it is arrogant to think of human beings as the *telos* or ultimate end of evolution. As Dennett states in *Darwin's Dangerous Idea*, "The most common misunderstanding of Darwinism: the idea that Darwin showed that evolution by natural selection is a procedure for *producing* us."[46] To Dennett, evolution didn't set out to produce anything, and what it has produced has no identifiable "essence," such as humanness.

Four reasons are generally given for displacing humans as a central focus. First, Postmodernists believe, modern science has shattered the early religious myth of Adam and Eve, so we can no longer believe that God created humanity for some special purpose. Second, technological efforts at integrating people and computer technology make it meaningless to proclaim the idea of a "person." Third, our talk about "persons" is about our use of language, not any enduring essence human beings actually possess. Fourth, in terms of sheer numbers, humans are rather scarce. Stephen Jay Gould, for example, argued that "bacteria are—and always have been—the dominant form of life on Earth."[47] To Gould, it was ridiculous to think that evolution had humanity in mind, since there are so few of "us" and so many of "them."[48]

We wonder if the anti-teleological stance appeals to Postmodernists because of the tendency to want knowledge their own way or not at all. The scientific literature is replete with quotations from scientists who find their theories to be insufficient at explaining reality, lurch all the way to the opposite extreme, and say everything is the result of chance processes.[49] It seems that Postmodernists play a similar game: if we can't see the truth in any given metanarrative, then no metanarrative can be seen as true. This perhaps explains why postmodern writer Tony Jackson finds Stephen Gould's punctuated equilibrium hypothesis so compelling: it ascribes so much to chance.[50] Daniel Dennett is another example of a scientist with postmodern leanings. To Dennett, what we humans think we understand is the result of "micro-takings" performed by the brain, not indications that what we think we understand is a real entity with any objective essence.[51]

So Postmodernists seem to have given up on the search for objective knowledge. If we think we have it, they seem to say, it must be all in our heads. Chance rules. Humans have no purpose. Christians, on the other hand, in spite of science's frequent disappointments, still believe the search for true knowledge about reality is worthwhile. Philosopher J. P. Moreland explains:

> Science (at least as most scientists and philosophers understand it) assumes that the universe is intelligible and not capricious, that the mind and senses inform us about reality, that mathematics and language can be applied to the world, that knowledge is possible, that there is a uniformity in nature that justifies inductive inferences from the past to the future and from examined cases of, say, electrons, to unexamined cases, and so forth.[52]

Along the same lines, Lee Campbell, former chair of the Natural Sciences Division at Ohio Dominican College, writes, "The methods used in the sciences have produced powerful explanations about how things work and innumerable useful applications, including technology even its harshest critics would never be without."[53]

Frankly, Postmodernist discouragement with science is a little baffling. Postmodernists use all the comforts and conveniences modern science and technology can provide, yet at the same time, they deny the foundational premises on which science is established. We've all had friends who have posted Internet comments with the gist of "It is impossible to know anything for sure." But to communicate this, they are using a computer designed by engineers who actually know things about computing and how to develop usable programs, plugged into a source of electricity generated by people who know things about electricity, in climate-controlled workspaces in buildings designed by people who know things about creating safe buildings, transmitted using sophisticated technology to people they expect to know what they mean. Maybe the postmodern problem is not one of knowledge. Maybe it is a simple lack of gratitude.

6. NEW SPIRITUALITY

New Spiritualist biology is based on a belief in positive evolutionary change over time, what we refer to as **spiritual evolution**. This approach does not focus on biological change as much as humanity's upward move toward higher consciousness. Deepak Chopra says, "Spirituality can be seen as a higher form of evolution, best described as 'metabiological'—beyond biology."[54] To New Spiritualists, everything is ultimately energy that will allow people to achieve unity with others in a kind of **collective consciousness**.

New Spiritualists carefully distinguish this view from anything resembling the Christian idea of

Spiritual Evolution: the belief that humanity is continually progressing toward higher consciousness.

Collective Consciousness: the belief that everything is ultimately energy and that everyone possesses the potential to achieve divine unity with the cosmos.

creation. As Deepak Chopra phrases it, "Consciousness-directed evolution isn't the same as invoking a creator God. Instead, it introduces a property inherent in the cosmos: self-awareness."[55] Pierre Teilhard de Chardin says, "Evolution is a light illuminating all facts, a curve that all lines must follow.... Man discovers that he is nothing else than evolution become conscious of itself."[56] Evolution isn't something that happens to us; it is something we *are.*

Individually, New Spiritualists say, our thoughts evolve us either toward higher consciousness or away from it.[57] Beyond maintaining good life habits and staying positive, though, collective consciousness means that the "ultimate end of the individual is to expand into the universal oneness, which really means that the individual disappears as a separate person."[58] In other words, evolution is what will move us away from being individual selves at all to reuniting with the energy of the universe. Marilyn Ferguson wrote, "The proven plasticity of the human brain and human awareness offers the possibility that individual evolution may lead to collective evolution. When one person has unlocked a new capacity its existence is suddenly evident to others, who may then develop the same capacity."[59]

Not everyone will evolve toward higher consciousness at an even rate; rather, when enough people achieve higher consciousness, others will be absorbed (or evolved) into the enlightened collective consciousness. Thus, all people need not embrace New Spirituality before it can become a reality—dedicated New Spiritualists can simply act as the catalysts for an evolutionary leap for everyone into utopia.

While this might sound strange, let's try to understand where the New Spiritualists are coming from. They believe in biological evolution, though they are uncomfortable with Darwin's idea of gradual development through mutations and natural selection. Darwinism is too slow and its outcome too unpredictable. In fact, New Spiritualist writer Ken Wilber attempts to reclaim evolution from Darwin by arguing that much clearer (and more favorable) understandings of evolution existed long before Darwin came along.[60] In any event, New Spiritualists employ evolution to answer the "What's next?" question. David Spangler states, "In this [evolutionary] context, civilizations, like individuals, go through profound changes from time to time which represent discontinuities; that is, a jump or shift is made from one evolutionary condition to another. The new age is such a shift."[61]

Spangler is not speaking as a Secularist who views evolutionary change as a blind natural force and humanity as simply a part of the natural universe; rather, for him, evolution is a change in the flow of cosmic energy, resulting not in a more complex form of biological life but in a higher consciousness among humanity.

According to New Spiritualist writings, it also seems that a certain enlightened portion of the human race will experience an evolutionary leap of some kind into a higher consciousness, taking the rest of humanity with them. Michael Dowd believes that embracing this evolutionary process can even become a means of obtaining salvation: "Time and time again, I have watched young people experience salvation by learning about their evolutionary heritage—that they are the way they are because those drives served their ancient ancestors. Halleluiah!"[62] Marilyn Ferguson, and others, held out hope for "rapid evolution in our own time, when the equilibrium of the species is punctuated by stress. Stress in modern society is experienced at the frontiers of our psychological rather than our geographical limits."[63] Ferguson uses the terms of naturalistic punctuated equilibrium but gave these terms a New Spiritualist meaning.

Remember that instead of further human physical evolution determined by geography, environment, and natural selection, New Spiritualists emphasize that evolution is psychological. Peter Russell believes, "Evolutionary trends and patterns ... suggest a further possibility: the emergence of something beyond a single planetary consciousness or Supermind: a completely new level of evolution, as different from consciousness as consciousness is from life, and life is from matter."[64] This psychological evolution guides humanity to a higher social order—"a New One-World Order."[65]

> New Spiritualists emphasize that evolution is psychological.

In this new order, explains Armand Biteaux, "Every man is an individual Christ; this is the teaching for the New Age.... Everyone will receive the benefit of this step in human evolution."[66] New Spiritualist John White writes,

> The final appearance of the Christ will not be a man in the air before whom all must kneel. The final appearance of the Christ will be an evolutionary event. It will be the disappearance of egocentric, subhuman man and the ascension of God-centered Man. A new race, a new species, will inhabit the Earth—people who collectively have the stature of consciousness that Jesus had.[67]

Once collective higher consciousness is achieved, humanity will be at one with itself in collective godhood, consciousness, oneness, or whatever term we prefer.

Much of the basis for New Spiritualist application of evolution comes from the writings of Pierre Teilhard de Chardin, a paleontologist who started out trying to reconcile Christianity and evolution. By the end, though, he had given up Christianity and embraced "a very real 'pantheism' if you like, but an absolutely legitimate pantheism."[68] If planetary consciousness is not attainable, however, most New Spiritualists are willing to settle for achieving individual divinity.

Evolutionary biology, to the New Spiritualist, is not important in and of itself except that it provides a starting point for humanity's evolutionary leap into a higher consciousness. We don't need to long for paradise, Joseph Campbell suggested; we're already there and just aren't aware of it yet. Up against the tragic warfare and bloodshed of human history, Campbell was optimistic: "This is it, this is Eden," he said. We need to "see not the world of solid things but a world of radiance."[69]

7. Islam

Both Christians and Muslims part company with materialistic worldviews that deny the existence of God and assert a naturalistic origin and evolution of the world. As Badru D. Kateregga says, "Muslims, like Christians, do witness that God is the Creator. As Creator, he is other than creation. He is not nature; he is above and beyond his creation (transcendent). Muslims believe that God's creation is perfect."[70] The Islamic view of how things came to be is called **special creation**.

The Quran describes the universe as finely ordered, illustrating God's magnificent mind in designing it:

- "It is He who hath created for you all things that are on earth; moreover His design comprehended the heavens, for He gave order and perfection to the seven firmaments; and of all things He hath perfect knowledge" (2:29).
- "Blessed is He Who made Constellations in the skies, and placed therein a Lamp and a Moon giving light; and it is He Who made the Night and the Day to follow each other" (25:61).
- "He has created man: He has taught him speech (and Intelligence). The sun and the moon follow courses (exactly) computed; and the herbs and the trees—both (alike) bow in adoration. And the Firmament has He Raised high" (55:3–7).

For Muslims, the order of the universe provides evidence of God's existence and creative activity, and Muslim philosophers and poets have written beautifully about this manifestation of God. The Pakistani Muslim scholar Khurshid Ahmad writes,

Special Creation: the belief that the cosmos and all life were brought into existence by the creative act of God.

How can one observe the inexhaustible creativity of nature, its purposefulness, its preservation of that which is morally useful and destruction of that which is socially injurious, and yet fail to draw the conclusion that behind nature there is an All-Pervading Mind of whose incessant creative activity the processes of nature are but an outward manifestation? The stars scattered through the almost infinite space, the vast panorama of nature with its charm and beauty, the planned waxing and waning of the moon, the astonishing harmony of the seasons— all point towards one fact; there is a God, the Creator, the Governor. We witness a superb, flawless plan in the universe—can it be without a Planner? We see great enchanting beauty and harmony in its working—can it be without a Creator? We observe wonderful design in nature—can it be without a Designer? We feel a lofty purpose in physical and human existence—can it be without a Will working behind it? We find that the universe is like a superbly written fascinating novel—can it be without an Author?[71]

Divine authorship, to Muslims, is proof of a divine author. In this way, Islam and Christianity arrive at similar conclusions.

Most Muslims reject evolutionary theories on both religious and scientific grounds. As professor of Islamic studies Seyyed Hossein Nasr says, this has created a conflict in some Muslim quarters:

For a notable segment of modernized Muslims evolution remains practically like a religious article of faith whose overt contradiction of the teachings of the Quran they fail to realize. Those who think they are rendering a service to Islam by incorporating evolutionary ideas into Islamic thought are in fact falling into a most dangerous pit and are surrendering Islam to one of the most insidious pseudo-dogmas of modern man, created in the eighteenth and nineteenth centuries to enable men to forget God.[72]

Not only do Muslims wrestle with whether to accept evolution; they also are divided over whether to advocate an old or young earth. While many more traditional Muslims take the reference to "evening and morning" in Genesis 1 as twenty-four hours in duration, some contemporary Muslim spokesmen hold that the days of creation were long periods of time (though they do not normally advocate evolutionary theories). Badru Kateregga writes,

> The earth and universe were created by God through a long step-by-step process. The Quranic witness further testifies that God created the heavens and the earth and what is between them in six "periods,'" and no weariness touched him (Quran 50:38). God created the universe and the earth in an orderly step-by-step progression.[73]

> Not only do Muslims wrestle with whether to accept evolution; they also are divided over whether to advocate an old or young earth.

By and large, it seems that Muslims who have adopted evolutionary theory have done so due to the influence of secular education in the West or the importation of such theories into Muslim lands. In this regard, Muslim evolutionists have been influenced much like Christian evolutionists have been.

Because of the tension over origins in the Muslim community, the contemporary intelligent design movement has drawn the attention of some Muslims scientists and theorists. Mustafa Akyol, a Muslim writer based in Turkey, writes,

> ID [intelligent design] presents a new perspective on science, one that is based solely on scientific evidence yet is fully compatible with faith in God. That's why William Dembski, one of its leading theorists, defines ID as a bridge between science and theology. As the history of the cultural conflict between the modern West and Islam shows, ID can also be a bridge between these two civilizations. The first bricks of that bridge are now being laid in the Islamic world. In Turkey, the current debate over ID has attracted much attention in the Islamic media. Islamic newspapers are publishing translations of pieces by the leading figures of the ID movement, such as Michael J. Behe and Phillip E. Johnson. The Discovery Institute is praised in their news stories and depicted as the vanguard in the case for God.... Now, for the first time, Muslims are discovering that they share a common cause with the believers in the West.[74]

Akyol goes on to say,

> Of course, Darwinians have the right to believe in whatever they wish, but it is crucial to unveil that theirs is a subjective faith, not an objective truth, as they have been claiming for more than a century. This unveiling would mark a turning point in the history of Western civilization, by reconciling science and religion and letting people become intellectually fulfilled theists.[75]

This is good news for Christians wishing to dialogue with Muslims; there are certain places where there is common ground—and the question of biology turns out to be one of them.

Muslims affirm the existence of God and his creation of the universe. They maintain a Creator-creature distinction, as do Christians. They also believe that the design of the universe points to the existence of a designer. While some modernized Muslims have adopted evolutionary theories (as have some Christians), orthodox Muslims see such naturalistic theories as conflicting with the teachings of the Quran and Muhammad.

8. CHRISTIANITY

Much of the case for a Christian view of biology revolves around origins. How did everything come about? Some biologists say it doesn't matter—life is life, and no matter how it came about, we just seek to study it for what it is. To a certain extent, that is true: biologists who are evolutionists and creationists can work side by side and get a lot done without ever referencing the issue of origins. Still, where things came from and how they got here is an important consideration. If the story of naturalistic evolution is true, if life arose by naturalistic, random processes, then at some point in time, nonliving matter must have become alive. This affects our theories and hypotheses about how biology works and even how we categorize living organisms. Our theology affects our science, and this is true for believers and nonbelievers alike. Along with Islam, Christianity affirms special creation, that at some point and at some level, life resulted from a creative act of God.

> **Our theology affects our science, and this is true for believers and non-believers alike.**

The field of biology—and especially the origin of life—is highly relevant, even integral to our understanding of our faith. How life arose and who, if anyone, made it happen are the ground-zero questions in the battle for all other ideas. When it comes to origins, the Bible's claims seem to be at odds with much of what has been popular in science in the past 150 years. For example, while the Bible says God created our first parents (Adam and Eve) fully formed, evolutionary science says all living things evolved through random-chance processes starting with nothing. In addition, mainstream theories of cosmic evolution posit a very old universe, somewhere between 13 and 15 billion years old. A straightforward reading of Genesis 1 implies to some a more recent creation.

Disagreements between Christianity and other worldviews aside, we also face the problem of camp skirmishes among Christians: How do we interpret and respond to biological evolution's account of life's origin? In the last century, perhaps no other aspect of Christianity has troubled believers more than this.[76] Because many biologists (both Christian and non-Christian) treat evolution as a scientific fact, Christians have struggled to reconcile their faith in the Bible with the claims of science. Over time, three main views of origins have emerged among Christians:

> *Young Age Creationism:* the belief that God created the cosmos and all life in its present forms, in six literal days, around six thousand years ago.

- **Young age creationism:** As recently as six thousand years ago, God created each living organism separately (in much its present form).
- **Progressive creationism:** God created each living organism separately (in much its present form) with the capacity to change and adapt to its circumstances over time (though within

limits). God created human beings separately at a much later time.

- **Theistic evolution:** God works through the natural process of evolution.[77]

All three groups would agree that the universe, and especially life on Earth, bears the marks of a designer. But beyond that, these are major differences in the Christian community; they must not be taken lightly. Yet for the purposes of this chapter, we will attend to and defend the fact of creation itself, not its timing.[78] Specifically, we will defend the idea that God created humankind, not the other way around. As Oxford University mathematician John Lennox phrases it, "Genesis affirms that (human) life has a chemical base, but Genesis denies the reductionist addendum of the materialist—that life is nothing but chemistry."[79]

> *Progressive Creationism:* the belief that God created the cosmos and all life in its present form, in progressive stages, over a long period of time.

> *Theistic Evolution:* the belief that God created the cosmos billions of years ago and then guided the process of biological evolution to produce the diversity of life seen today.

Our approach of focusing on commonalities will, unfortunately, be dissatisfying to many readers. But in this chapter, as in others, we seek to find common ground for Christians to occupy with one another in defending the larger Christian worldview. If we fail to find common ground on the issue of how life arose, we risk yielding that ground unnecessarily to those committed to its destruction. Lennox explains:

> The question of the origin of humans—are we made in the image of God, or thrown up on the sea of the possible random permutations of matter without any ultimate significance?—is of major importance for our concept of our human identity; and it is therefore not surprising that ferocious efforts are being made to minimize the difference between humans and animals on the one hand, and the difference between humans and machines on the other. Such efforts are driven, at least in part, by the secular conviction that naturalism must in the end triumph over theism by its reductionist arguments in removing the last vestige of God from his creation. Human beings must in the end be proved to be nothing but physics and chemistry.[80]

Will naturalistic arguments triumph over theistic ones? Many Secularists, Marxists, and Postmodernists think it must necessarily be so. But before we yield any ground, let's at least consider five reasons why the Christian idea of a designer should not be dismissed out of hand.

1. Life comes only from preexisting life. If you start with nothing, you end with nothing. But the late Nobel Prize winner George Wald of Harvard University stubbornly insisted that the "reasonable" view was to believe in **spontaneous generation** because it was the only alternative to believing "in a single, primary act of supernatural creation."[81] More recently, Harvard chemist George Whitesides made a similar admission: "Most chemists believe, as do I,

> *Spontaneous Generation:* the belief that nonliving matter produced living matter through purely natural processes.

that life emerged spontaneously from mixtures of molecules in the prebiotic Earth. How? I have no idea."[82]

Ironically, Wald's and Whitesides's conclusions match atheist writer Victor Stenger's definition of *faith* as "belief in the absence of supportive evidence and even in the light of contrary evidence."[83] Stenger's definition, we think, is not a very good one; still, given his own belief in a strictly natural origin of life, this is a clear instance of science biting its own hand in the act of feeding.[84]

2. Random-chance processes do not produce intelligible information. Cambridge-trained philosopher of science Stephen Meyer posed a simple thought experiment about this. In his experiment, he left his classroom of college students for one hour picking Scrabble tiles at random and writing them on the board.

> Now imagine that upon my return they showed me a detailed message on the black-board such as Einstein's famous dictum: "God does not play dice with the universe." Would it be more reasonable for me to suppose that they had cheated (perhaps, as a gag) or that they had gotten lucky? Clearly, I should suspect (strongly) that they had cheated. I should reject the chance hypothesis. Why? I should reject chance as the best explanation not only because of the improbability of the sequence my students had generated, but also because of what I knew about the probabilistic resources available to them. If I had made a prediction before I had left the room, I would have predicted that they could not have generated a sequence of that length by chance alone in the time available.[85]

The problem is even more complex than Meyer's example, though. How would he recognize that the sentence the students presumably came up with (by way of their prank) was actually intelligible? He could do this only if he had a language—a system of words, a syntax, and other elements of a language, all created through thoughtful design—to even recognize that their sentence had meaning. What is the source of these building blocks of language? In our experience, language and information-rich systems always come from intelligence. This makes it all the more striking that life itself is built upon a language-based code in our DNA.

> In our experience, language and information-rich systems always come from intelligence.

3. The immaterial world is real. Erwin Schrödinger phrased this in a fascinating way:

> My body functions as a pure mechanism according to the Laws of Nature. Yet I know, by incontrovertible direct experience, that I am directing its motions, of which I foresee the effects, that may be fateful and all important, in which case I feel and take full responsibility for them. The only possible inference from these two facts is, I think, that I—I in the widest meaning of the word, that is to say, every conscious mind that has ever said or felt "I"—am the person, if any, who controls the "motion of the atoms" according to the Laws of Nature.[86]

As a person, Schrödinger knew his "person" was in charge of his "body," not the other way around. Mind over matter. Or perhaps mind *preceding* matter. This is very much the approach found in John 1:1 when Scripture says, "In the beginning was the Word." The Greek word for "Word," *Logos*, entails the expression of a thought. Thought preceded creation. That thoughts are real things, and yet not material things, implies the presence of an immaterial reality such as a soul.

4. Living organisms give the appearance of design. William Paley asked, if you found a watch in a field, is it more reasonable to assume it had just materialized or that it had a maker?[87] Since the nineteenth century, however, it has been widely believed that Paley's argument for a universal designer was effectively answered by the philosopher David Hume, who claimed that Paley's analogy between living things and machines was unfounded: life, it was argued, does not need an intelligent designer as machines do. Atheist Richard Dawkins followed Hume in this line of thinking, writing in *The Blind Watchmaker*, "Biology is the study of complicated things that give the appearance of having been designed for a purpose."[88] We do not need to postulate God as the designer, he says, since natural selection can perform the miracles.

In spite of Dawkins's claims, scientists can no longer ignore the idea of design. Recent discoveries reveal that life is indeed analogous to the most complex machinery, making the case for design in biology far stronger than Paley ever imagined. We now know that life is fundamentally based upon an information-rich, language-based code in our DNA that contains computer-like commands that provide instructions for building molecular machines that operate at near 100 percent energetic efficiency inside of cells. As Bruce Alberts, former president of the US National Academy of Sciences, observes,

> The entire cell can be viewed as a factory that contains an elaborate network of interlocking assembly lines, each of which is composed of a set of large protein machines.... Like machines invented by humans to deal efficiently with the macroscopic world, these protein assemblies contain highly coordinated moving parts.[89]

Biochemist Michael Behe calls these molecular machines "irreducibly complex." **Irreducible complexity** requires many parts in order to function and cannot evolve in a step-by-step Darwinian fashion.[90] If Darwinism can't do the job, then what, in our experience, can produce information, computer-like code, and factories with machines that we find in life? We know of only one cause that can produce these things: intelligence. Stephen Meyer explains this positive argument for design: "Our experience-based knowledge of information-flow confirms that systems with large amounts of specified complexity (especially codes and languages) invariably originate from an intelligent source—from a mind or personal agent."[91]

In the same spirit, Michael Denton, a molecular biologist, stated, "Paley was not only right in asserting the existence of an analogy between life and machines, but was also remarkably prophetic in guessing that the technological ingenuity realized in living systems is vastly in excess of anything yet accomplished by man."[92] At present, we think intelligent design is a fascinating explanation for the information-rich genetic codes and nanomachines that build all life.

Irreducible Complexity: **A concept that considers the complexity of integrated systems such that if any part is removed, the system ceases to function. Applied to biology, it challenges the notion that complex biological systems (e.g., the eye) could have gradually evolved through a series of intermediary steps.**

> At present, we think intelligent design is a fascinating explanation for the information-rich genetic codes and nanomachines that build all life.

5. Scientists themselves are bailing on the theory of evolution as currently constructed. A 2009 article in *Trends in Genetics* argued that breakdowns in core neo-Darwinian tenets, such as the "traditional concept of the tree of life" or the view that "natural selection is the main driving force of evolution," indicate that "the modern synthesis has crumbled, apparently, beyond repair." According to the article, "all major tenets of the modern synthesis have been, if not outright overturned, replaced by a new and incomparably more complex vision of the key aspects of evolution." It concludes, "Not to mince words, the modern synthesis is gone."[93] Likewise, a 2011 paper in *Biological Theory* concluded, "Darwinism in its current scientific incarnation has pretty much reached the end of its rope."[94]

To be fair, it is difficult to find a scientist today who thinks Darwin had it all right. There were many things Darwin did not know, and could not have known, based on the scientific discoveries known to him a century and a half ago. But even the Darwinian ideas that have been commonly accepted—such as the famous "tree of life"—are now coming under attack. A 2012 paper in the *Annual Review of Genetics* challenged universal common ancestry and concluded that "life might indeed have multiple origins."[95] Likewise, a 2009 article in *New Scientist* titled "Why Darwin Was Wrong about the Tree of Life," observed that "many biologists now argue that the tree concept is obsolete and needs to be discarded." The article quoted scientists saying things like, "We have no evidence at all that the tree of life is a reality" or "We've just annihilated the tree of life."[96]

As for the creative power of mutations, US National Academy of Sciences member biologist Lynn Margulis maintained that "new mutations don't create new species; they create offspring that are impaired."[97] She explained:

> This Darwinian claim to explain all of evolution is a popular half-truth whose lack of explicative power is compensated for only by the religious ferocity of its rhetoric.... Mutations, in summary, tend to induce sickness, death, or deficiencies. No evidence in the vast literature of heredity changes shows unambiguous evidence that random mutation itself, even with geographical isolation of populations, leads to speciation [new species]."[98]

These stunning admissions led Stephen Meyer to make an apt observation in his book *Darwin's Doubt*: "Rarely has there been such a great disparity between the popular perception of a theory and its actual standing in the relevant peer-reviewed scientific literature."[99] With so much compelling information coming to light, Christians should think twice before rejecting the idea of a creator and accepting macroevolutionary processes as a rational explanation for what life is and where it came from.

9. CONCLUSION

The information and machinery of life appears to have been designed. But that's not the whole story. Life requires many other factors to exist. As science professor Joe Francis notes,

"Water, oxygen, and light, three of the most basic necessary requirements for life, can be extremely toxic to living things. But, living organisms possess complex protection mechanisms built into each living cell, which appear to have protected life from its very first appearance on earth."[100] Intelligence is required to explain how all these coordinated parts and components were arranged to allow life to exist.

Be warned, though. Talk of a Christian view of biology is like poking a yellow-jacket nest. You are practically guaranteed that those committed to naturalism and materialism will attack. Jonathan Wells explains a common argument used to do so:

> Historian of science Gregory Radick summarizes the Darwinist's principal argument as follows: "No Designer worth His salt would have created" the features that we actually find in nature. "It would be hard to exaggerate the importance of this argument," Radick wrote, "from Darwin's day to our own, as a means of disqualifying the Designer explanation and making room for Darwinian descent with modification."[101]

Richard Dawkins offers one example of this "no Designer worth His salt would have created" argument when he says that up to 95 percent of our genetic code no longer does anything useful. No truly good designer would create so much waste, he insists. But as Wells painstakingly demonstrates, the idea that most DNA is uneaten leftovers from an evolutionary process is simply false. He concludes, "A virtual flood of recent evidence shows that they are mistaken: Much of the DNA they claim to be 'junk' actually performs important functions in living cells."[102]

It would be a mistake to just take our word for it or to draw lifelong conclusions about what we have covered in this brief chapter. But hopefully it is clear that God as designer is not an unreasonable position for either science or faith, certainly not any more unreasonable than ignoring design and believing in spontaneous generation. Don't expect naturalists and materialists, for whom the concept of a supernatural being can never be tolerated, to just change their minds. Many believe, as one scientist said, "Science must be provisionally atheistic or cease to be itself."[103] For Christian biologists, however, the world is bright and resonant in light of God's existence. As a piece of art suggests an artist, the orderly universe and complexity of life suggest a designer. This is what makes true discovery possible and makes those discoveries meaningful.

From the biblical perspective, having a sense of what life is and where it comes from is only the first of two big questions. If humans are both body and soul, we must explore the fascinating world of the soul. This is precisely what the field of psychology is designed to do, and it is to the misuses and possible redemption of psychology that we next turn our attention.

ENDNOTES

1. The *Scopes* trial took place when the newly formed American Civil Liberties Union (ACLU) challenged a Tennessee law preventing its public schools from teaching views of the origin of man that contradicted the Genesis account. Though he disagreed with the law, former Democratic presidential candidate William Jennings Bryan agreed to help defend it.

2. For a detailed account of the differences between the film and actual events, see Carol Iannone's excellent article "The Truth about *Inherit the Wind*," *First Things*, February 1997, 28–33, www.firstthings.com/article/2007/02/002-the-truth-about-inherit-the-wind--36. See also Edward J. Larson's Pulitzer Prize–winning book *Summer for the Gods: The Scopes Trial and America's Continuing Debate over Science and Religion* (New York: Basic Books, 1997).

3. Eugenie Scott, *Evolution vs. Creationism: An Introduction* (New York: Greenwood, 2004), 96–97.

4. Edward Sisson, "Debunking the Scopes 'Monkey Trial' Stereotype," in William A. Dembski and Michael R. Licona, eds., *Evidence for God* (Grand Rapids: Baker Books, 2010), 76–80.

5. Stephen Hawking and Leonard Mlodinow, *The Grand Design* (New York: Bantam Books, 2010), 5.

6. Steven D. Garber, *Biology: A Self-Teaching Guide*, 2nd ed. (Hoboken, NJ: John Wiley and Sons, 2002).

7. Erwin Schrödinger, *What Is Life?* (Cambridge, UK: Cambridge University Press, 1967), 69.

8. John H. Postlethwait and Janet L Hopson, *Modern Biology* (New York: Holt, Rinehart, and Winston, 2009), 6–9.

9. Arthur Eddington, *The Nature of the Physical World* (Cambridge, UK: Cambridge University Press, 1928), 327–28, quoted in Robert J. Spitzer, *New Proofs for the Existence of God* (Grand Rapids: Eerdmans, 2010), 286.

10. George Gaylord Simpson, *The Meaning of Evolution* (New Haven, CT: Yale University Press, 1971), 345.

11. The words *fact* and *theory* are now so often used interchangeably, it is worth pointing out the difference. A fact means something that actually exists. A theory is a set of propositions that have been tested enough to give confidence to scientists that they lead to accurate predictions about nature. A fact is a thing; a theory is an idea that works. When people say evolution is a "fact," they are misunderstanding the meaning of the word. But when people dismissively say evolution is merely a "theory," they are also making a mistake. Casey Luskin helps clear up the distinction in an online article titled "Is 'Evolution' a 'Theory' or 'Fact' or Is This Just a Trivial Game of Semantics?," Evolution News and Views, July 28, 2008, Discovery Institute, www.discovery.org/a/6401.

12. Julian Huxley, "At Random," television preview, WBBM-TV, CBS Chicago, November 21, 1959, http://www.archive.org/stream/evolutionafterda03taxs/evolutionafterda03taxs_djvu.txt. See also Sol Tax, *Evolution of Life* (Chicago: University of Chicago Press, 1960), 1.

13. Hawking and Mlodinow, *Grand Design*, 162.

14. Hawking and Mlodinow, *Grand Design*.

15. Norman Macbeth stated, "Darwin never tried to define natural selection in a rigid way.... It amounted to little more than the fact that, for various reasons, among all the individuals produced in nature some die soon and some die late. Thus natural selection for Darwin was differential mortality.... The phrase 'survival of the fittest' was not coined by Darwin. He took it over from Herbert Spencer, apparently considering it an improvement on his own natural selection. It immediately became an integral part of classical Darwinism, much to the embarrassment of modern adherents.... A species survives because it is the fittest and is the fittest because it survives, which is circular reasoning." Norman Macbeth, *Darwin Retried: An Appeal to Reason* (Boston: Gambit, 1971), 40, 62.

16. Carl Sagan, *The Dragons of Eden: Speculations on the Evolution of Human Intelligence* (New York: Random House, 1977), 6.

17. Francisco J. Ayala, "Darwin's Greatest Discovery," *Proceedings of the National Academy of Sciences USA* 104 (May 9, 2007): 8572–73.

18. Charles Darwin, *The Origin of Species by Means of Natural Selection or the Preservation of Favored Races in the Struggle for Life*, 2 vols. (New York: D. Appleton, 1898), 1:103.

19. Charles Darwin was open about the shortcomings of his theory (of course, he believed that future discoveries would rectify these shortcomings). In a particularly honest passage, Darwin admitted, "I did not formerly consider sufficiently the existence of structures which, as far as we can ... judge, are neither beneficial nor injurious, and this I believe to be one of the greatest oversights as yet detected in my work." Quoted in Macbeth, *Darwin Retried*, 73.

20. Julian Huxley, *Essays of a Humanist* (New York: Harper and Row, 1964), 67.

21. Sagan, *Dragons of Eden*, 6.

22. Stephen Jay Gould, "Cordelia's Dilemma," *Natural History* (February 1993): 15, quoted in Walter James ReMine, *The Biotic Message: Evolution versus Message Theory* (St. Paul, MN: St. Paul Science, 1993), 307.

23. Stephen Jay Gould, "Is a New and General Theory of Evolution Emerging?," *Paleobiology* 6 (1980): 127.

24. Chris McGowan, *In the Beginning* (Buffalo: Prometheus Books, 1984), 29.

25. See ReMine, *Biotic Message* for a discussion on punctuated equilibrium. ReMine says, "Punctuated equilibria is an evolutionary theory proposed in 1972 by paleontologists Stephen Jay Gould and Niles Eldredge (and soon joined by Stephen Stanley). The theory says species are typically not evolving. Rather, species are in stasis most of their existence, a state of unchanging equilibrium. The equilibrium is punctuated occasionally by short events of rapid evolution. Most evolution is said to occur speedily during these brief punctuation events" (326).

26. Darwin, *Origin of Species*, 1:229, cited in Macbeth, *Darwin Retried*, 76.

27. Richard Lewontin, "Billions and Billions of Demons," *New York Review of Books* 44 (January 1997): 28.

28. Quoted in Phillip E. Johnson, *Darwin on Trial* (Downers Grove, IL: InterVarsity, 1991), 124.

29. Karl Marx and Frederick Engels, *Selected Correspondence* (New York: International Publishers, 1942), 125.

30. Quoted in Charles J. McFadden, *The Philosophy of Communism* (Kenosha, WI: Cross, 1939), 35–36. Also see Jacques Barzun, *Darwin, Marx, and Wagner* (Chicago: University of Chicago Press, 1981) for additional material on this point.

31. Karl Marx, *Capital*, 3 vols. (London: Lawrence and Wishart, 1970), 1:341.

32. Frederick Engels, *Selected Works*, 3 vols. (New York: International Publishers, 1950), 2:153, quoted in R. N. Carew Hunt, *The Theory and Practice of Communism* (Baltimore: Penguin Books, 1966), 64. Lenin said something similar: "Just as Darwin put an end to the view of animal and plant species being unconnected, fortuitous, 'created by God' and immutable, and was the first to put biology on an absolutely scientific basis ... so Marx ... was the first to put sociology on a scientific basis." V. I. Lenin, *Collected Works*, 45 vols. (Moscow: Progress Publishers, 1977), 1:142.

33. Douglas J. Futuyma, *Evolutionary Biology*, 3rd ed. (Sunderland, MA: Sinauer Associates, 1998), 5.

34. Engels said Darwin's "new outlook on nature was complete in its main features; all rigidity was dissolved, all fixity dissipated, all particularity that had been regarded as eternal became transient, the whole of nature was shown as moving in eternal flux and cyclical course," Frederick Engels, *Dialectics of Nature* (New York: International Publishers, 1976), 13.

35. Frederick Engels, *Ludwig Feuerbach* (New York: International Publishers, 1974), 54.

36. Lenin, *Collected Works*, 24:54–55.

37. Georgi Plekhanov said, "Many people confound dialectic with the theory of evolution. Dialectic is, in fact, a theory of evolution. But it differs profoundly from the vulgar [Darwinian] theory of evolution, which is based substantially upon the principle that neither in nature nor in history do sudden changes occur, and that all changes taking place in the world occur gradually." G. Plekhanov, *Fundamental Problems of Marxism* (London: Lawrence, 1929), 145.

38. Michael Denton, *Evolution: A Theory in Crisis* (Bethesda, MD: Adler and Adler, 1985), 192–93.

39. Related to the idea of the dialectic, Richard Lewontin, one of those who worked on the theory of punctuated equilibrium, called his textbook *The Dialectical Biologist* (Harvard University Press).

40. Niles Eldredge and Stephen Jay Gould, "Punctuated Equilibria: The Tempo and Mode of Evolution Reconsidered," *Paleobiology* 3 (Spring 1977): 145–46, quoted in Luther D. Sunderland, *Darwin's Enigma* (Santee, CA: Master Book, 1988), 108.

41. Mikhail Vladimirovich Volkenshtein, *Biophysics* (Moscow: Mirv, 1983), 617.

42. Volkenshtein, *Biophysics*, 618.

43. Terry Eagleton, "Awakening from Modernity," *Times Literary Supplement*, February 20, 1987, 194, quoted in Stanley J. Grenz, *A Primer on Postmodernism* (Grand Rapids: Eerdmans, 1996), 48.

44. Quoted in Glenn Ward, *Teach Yourself Postmodernism*, 2nd ed. (Chicago: McGraw-Hill, 2003), 148–49.

45. In his quotation, Richard Rorty noted that this was John Dewey's view, but his approving reference indicates his affinity for it. See Robert B. Brandom, ed., *Rorty and His Critics* (Oxford, UK: Blackwell, 2001), 3.

46. Daniel Dennett, *Darwin's Dangerous Idea* (New York: Touchstone, 1996), 56, italics and capitalization in original.

47. Stephen Jay Gould, *Full House: The Spread of Excellence from Plato to Darwin* (Cambridge, MA: Belknap, 2011).

48. Gould's assertion runs counter to Darwin's claim that humanity "stands at the very summit of the organic scale." See Charles Darwin, *The Descent of Man and Selection in Relation to Sex* (New York: Collier, 1902), 797, quoted in Tony E. Jackson, "Charles and the Hopeful Monster: Postmodern Evolutionary Theory in 'The French Lieutenant's Woman,'" in *Twentieth Century Literature* 43, no. 2 (Summer 1997), www.questia.com/library/journal/1G1-20563363/charles-and-the-hopeful-monster-postmodern-evolutionary.

49. See Stanley Jaki's essay "Chance and Reality," in *Chance and Reality and Other Essays* (Lanham, MD: University Press of America, 1986).

50. Jackson, "Charles and the Hopeful Monster."

51. Daniel Dennett, *Brainchildren: Essays on Designing Mind* (Boston: MIT Press, 1998), 133.

52. J. P. Moreland, *Christianity and the Nature of Science: A Philosophical Investigation* (Grand Rapids: Baker, 1989), 45.

53. Lee Campbell, "Postmodern Impact: Science," in Dennis McCallum, ed., *The Death of Truth* (Minneapolis: Bethany House, 1996), 193.

54. Deepak Chopra and Leonard Mlodinow, *War of the Worldviews: Where Science and Spirituality Meet—and Do Not* (New York: Three Rivers, 2011), 154.

55. Chopra and Mlodinow, *War of the Worldviews*, 55.

56. Pierre Teilhard de Chardin, *The Phenomenon of Man* (New York: Harper and Row, 1955), 219, 221.

57. In a certain sense, we can see that our conscious thoughts *do* affect the way we live. Dean Ornish, a medical doctor who focuses on preventive medicine, points out that "more than four hundred genes change their expression in a positive way if someone practices the well-known preventive measures of diet, exercise, stress management, and good sleep" (quoted in Chopra and Mlodinow, *War of the Worldviews*, 147). This is very different from what New Spiritualists are ultimately suggesting, though.

58. Dean C. Halverson, *Crystal Clear: Understanding and Reaching New Agers* (Colorado Springs: NavPress, 1990), 77.

59. Marilyn Ferguson, *The Aquarian Conspiracy* (Los Angeles: J. P. Tarcher, 1980), 70.

60. Ken Wilber, *A Brief History of Everything* (Boston: Shambhala, 2001), 274–77.

61. David Spangler, *Emergence: The Rebirth of the Sacred* (New York: Dell, 1984), 18.

62. Michael Dowd, *Thank God for Evolution: How the Marriage of Science and Religion Will Transform Your Life and Our World* (Oakland, CA: Council Oak Books, 2007), 187.

63. Ferguson, *Aquarian Conspiracy*, 70.

64. Peter Russell, *The Global Brain* (Los Angeles: J. P. Tarcher, 1983), 99.

65. Randall N. Baer, *Inside the New Age Nightmare* (Lafayette, LA: Huntington House, 1989), 47.

66. Armand Biteaux, *The New Consciousness* (Minneapolis: Oliver Press, 1975), 128.

67. John White, "The Second Coming," *New Frontier Magazine*, December 1987, 45.

68. De Chardin, *Phenomenon of Man*, 310.

69. Joseph Campbell, *The Power of Myth* (New York: Doubleday, 1988), 230.

70. Badru D. Kateregga and David W. Shenk, *Islam and Christianity: A Muslim and a Christian in Dialogue* (Grand Rapids: Eerdmans, 1981), available on *The World of Islam: Resources for Understanding*, 2.0 (Colorado Springs: Global Mapping International, 2009), CD-ROM, 5350.

71. Khurshid Ahmad, ed., *Islam: Its Meaning and Message* (Leicester: Islamic Foundation, 1999), 29–30.

72. Quoted in Ahmad, *Islam*, 228–30.

73. Kateregga and Shenk, *Islam and Christianity*, 5273.

74. Mustafa Akyol, "Under God or Under Darwin?: Intelligent Design Could Be a Bridge between Civilizations," *National Review Online*, December 2, 2005. Akyol is a Muslim writer based in Istanbul, Turkey, and one of the expert witnesses who testified before the Kansas state education board during the hearings on evolution in 2005.

75. Akyol, "Under God or Under Darwin?"

76. David Berlinski's article "On the Origins of Life," in *Commentary* (February 2006), indicates that believing and unbelieving Jews are also extremely interested in the subject.

77. See Norman L. Geisler, *Systematic Theology*, 4 vols. (Minneapolis: Bethany House), 2:632, for a good summary of the issue. *Creation and Time* by Hugh Ross presents the case for an older universe, while *Refuting Compromise* by Jonathan Sarfati presents the case for a younger universe, along with Walter Brown, *In The Beginning* (Phoenix, AZ: Center for Scientific Creation, 2003) and Larry Vardiman, Andrew A. Snelling, and Eugene F. Chaffin, *Radioisotopes: And the Age of the Earth*, 2 vols. (El Cajon, CA: Institute for Creation Research, 2005).

78. See Geisler, *Systematic Theology*, 2:632, for a good summary of the issue. Geisler says, "There are many scientific arguments for an old universe, some of which one may find persuasive. However, none of these is foolproof, and all of them may be wrong" (649). Those advocating an older universe include Hugh Ross, *Creator and the Cosmos*; Norman Geisler, *When Skeptics Ask*; Walter Kaiser, *Hard Sayings of the Bible*; Don Stoner, *A New Look at an Old Earth*; Francis A. Schaeffer, *No Final Conflict*; and C. I. Scofield, *Rightly Dividing the Word of Truth*. Presenting a younger earth: Walt Brown, *In the Beginning*; Larry Vardiman et al., *Radioisotopes and the Age of the Earth*; Jonathan Sarfati, *Refuting Compromise*; Henry Morris, *The Long War against God*; Duane Gish, *Creation Scientists Answer Their Critics*; and Don Batten, ed., *The Revised and Expanded Answers Book*.

79. John Lennox, *Seven Days that Divide the World* (Grand Rapids: Zondervan, 2011), 69.

80. Lennox, *Seven Days*, 85.

81. George Wald, "The Origin of Life," *Scientific American* 190 (August 1954): 46, quoted in Brown, *In the Beginning*, 37.

82. George M. Whitesides, "Revolutions in Chemistry: Priestley Medalist George M. Whitesides' Address," *Chemical and Engineering News* (March 2007): 12–17.

83. Victor Stenger, *God and the Folly of Faith* (Amherst, NY: Prometheus Books, 2012), 25.

84. One proposed alternative to spontaneous generation is variously referred to as *exoevolution* or *directed panspermia*, the idea that an advanced alien civilization designed a self-replicating molecule and seeded it on the earth. While advocates say this solves the problem of how life arose on Earth, from a larger perspective, it simply pushes the question into an infinite regression: Who seeded life in *that* alien civilization? And the one previous to it? And so forth. Advocates of panspermia argue that Christianity has the same problem: Who created God? Doesn't God have to have a creator? And who created *that* creator? As we pointed out in the "Christianity," "Theology," and "Philosophy" chapters in this volume, though, the first question is whether the universe had a beginning. Either a supreme mind has always existed and, at specific points in time, created matter and the universe, or matter is eternal and formed the universe by itself. Most scientists and theologians agree that the universe had a beginning. If it did, then the argument about first cause applies. If the universe is caused, there must be a first cause, a being capable of bringing universes into existence, and the characteristics of this first cause must be sufficient to explain everything we see in the universe today, including value, purpose, mental lives, complexity, moral agency, drama, and design. This sounds a lot like the Christian conception of God.

85. Stephen C. Meyer, *Signature in the Cell* (New York: HarperOne, 2009), 221.

86. Schrödinger, *What Is Life?*, 86–87.

87. Christians need to remember that it was the psalmist who said "the heavens declare the glory of God" and his handiwork (Psalm 19:1)—a theological observation.

88. Richard Dawkins, *The Blind Watchmaker* (New York: W. W. Norton, 1996), 4. Dawkins spent more than four hundred pages in *The Blind Watchmaker* trying to show that design is only appearance, not fact.

89. Bruce Alberts, "The Cell as a Collection of Protein Machines: Preparing the Next Generation of Molecular Biologists," *Cell* (February 1998): 291–94.

90. See Michael Behe, *Darwin's Black Box: The Biochemical Challenge to Evolution* (New York: Free Press, 2006).

91. Stephen C. Meyer, "The Origin of Biological Information and the Higher Taxonomic Categories," *Proceedings of the Biological Society of Washington* 117 (2004): 213–39.

92. Denton, *Evolution*, 340.

93. Eugene V. Koonin, "The Origin at 150: Is a New Evolutionary Synthesis in Sight?," *Trends in Genetics* 25, no. 11 (2009): 473–75.

94. David J. Depew and Bruce H. Weber, "The Fate of Darwinism: Evolution after the Modern Synthesis," *Biological Theory* 6 (December 2011): 89–102.

95. Michael Syvanen, "Evolutionary Implications of Horizontal Gene Transfer," *Annual Review of Genetics* 46 (2012): 339–56.

96. Graham Lawton, "Why Darwin Was Wrong about the Tree of Life," *New Scientist*, January 21, 2009.

97. Lynn Margulis, quoted in Darry Madden, "UMass Scientist to Lead Debate on Evolutionary Theory," *Brattleboro (Vt.) Reformer*, February 3, 2006.

98. Lynn Margulis and Dorion Sagan, *Acquiring Genomes: A Theory of the Origins of the Species* (New York: Basic Books, 2003), 29.

99. Stephen C. Meyer, *Darwin's Doubt: The Explosive Origin of Animal Life and the Case for Intelligent Design* (New York: HarperOne, 2013), xii.

100. Joe Francis, "Oxygen, Water, and Light, Oh My!," in Dembski and Licona, *Evidence for God*, 63.

101. Gregory Radick, "Deviance, Darwinian-Style," *Metascience* 14, no. 3 (November 2005): 453–57, quoted in Jonathan Wells, *The Myth of Junk DNA* (Seattle: Discovery Institute, 2011), 103.

102. Wells, *Myth of Junk DNA*, 27.

103. Pennock, *Intelligent Design*, 144.

CHAPTER 12

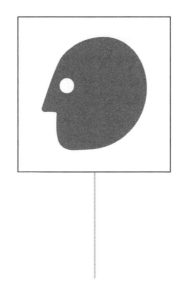

PSYCHOLOGY

1. WHAT IS WRONG WITH US AND HOW CAN WE FIX IT?

Eckhart Tolle is one of the bestselling New Spiritualist authors of all time. His two books and multiple appearances on widely viewed programs, such as *The Oprah Winfrey Show*, turned him into a spiritual phenomenon. On the Watkins list of the one hundred most popular spiritual teachers in the world, Tolle was long ranked number one.

And yet if you saw Tolle on the subway, you probably wouldn't recognize him. A small, unassuming man, Tolle seems almost unnaturally comfortable with silence. At the beginning of his speeches, he sits on a stool and stares across the audience for several minutes, not saying a word. When he does begin talking, Tolle seems hesitant, as if the selection of each word carries grave consequences. One certainly gets the impression that chatty banter is not this man's style.

None of this is by accident. Tolle calls his silent gazing at his audience, "practicing presence." By this he means contemplating his oneness with the audience and ridding himself of ego. To Tolle's way of thinking, the central problem with humanity is imagining our existence as separate individuals. Instead, we are—all together—one collective soul. The sooner we recognize this, the sooner we can begin the healing we so desperately desire.

Tolle says using the word *I* tricks people into thinking they have personalities and souls separate from all other souls. This, for Tolle, is an enormous problem:

> The word "I" embodies the greatest error and the deepest truth, depending on how it is used. In conventional usage, it is not only one of the most frequently used words in the language (together with the related words: "me," "my," "mine," and "myself") but also one of the most misleading. In normal everyday usage, "I" embodies the primordial error, a misperception of who you are, an illusory sense of identity. This is the ego.[1]

Tolle sees the ego as the source of our problems, including illness: "Amazingly but not infrequently, the ego in search of a stronger identity can and does create illnesses in order to strengthen itself through them."[2] Tolle and other spiritual teachers like him recognize a key truth: there is something wrong with us. We are unsettled. We need fixing. Whoever and whatever we are needs healing and restoration. **Psychology** is the study of who and what we are, as well as how we develop as human beings, personally and socially. Psychology follows theology: our understanding of God has massive implications for the discipline of psychology, starting with the question of whether there even is any kind of reality outside of the material world.

In fact, the word *psychology* itself implies this sort of order. The word *psyche* is Greek for "soul." *Psychology* literally means "the study of the soul." This implies that there is an immaterial, or spiritual, aspect of reality that must be understood. Theologian Wayne Grudem says,

> *Psychology*: the study of the human mind (or soul).

> Our understanding of God has massive implications for the discipline of psychology, starting with the question of whether there even is any kind of reality outside of the material world.

> Scripture is very clear that we do have a soul that is distinct from our physical bodies, which not only can function somewhat independently of our ordinary thought processes (1 Cor. 14:14; Rom. 8:16), but also, when we die, is able to go on consciously acting and relating to God apart from our physical bodies.[3]

While Christianity acknowledges the existence of the soul, three of the worldviews we are studying (Secularism, Marxism, and Postmodernism) deny it, and one, New Spirituality, denies the existence of individual souls. Because of this fundamental difference in belief, there is quite a worldview conflict in psychology.

As with the other disciplines, psychology offers a way of discovering meaning. Theology says clear thinking about God points the way. Philosophy says a precise understanding of reality and knowledge is the answer. Ethics says the pursuit of the good life is most important. Biology says understanding the nature of life will give us the answers we seek. Each discipline has its cheerleaders, those who in good nature argue that their disciplines are best. In reality, no one discipline is better than the others. All are at their best when in the pursuit of truth.

2. THE SELF IS THE NEW SOUL

We are searchers for truth. But who are the "we" doing the searching? What does it mean to be a person? What kinds of things go wrong with persons, and how might we help them heal? Psychologist Rollo May said, "Today we know a great deal about bodily chemistry and the control of physical diseases; but we know very little about why people hate, why they cannot love, why they suffer anxiety and guilt, and why they destroy each other."[4]

The psychologist knows physical health isn't the only thing. People can be physically healthy and still miserable. But what more is there? To Christianity the question of *being* is central. There are different aspects of our being—we are theological beings, philosophical beings, ethical beings, biological beings, psychological beings, and so forth. Christians see psychology, when done from a standpoint of biblical truth, as opening up and examining the idea of "being" so we can better understand ourselves and live together with others.

Psychologists see what they do as a science. They try to use the scientific method to understand people. One of psychology's heroes, Carl Rogers, said,

> [True science] will explore the private worlds of inner personal meanings, in an effort to discover lawful and orderly relationships there. In this world of inner meanings it can investigate all the issues which are meaningless for the behaviorist—purposes, goals, values, choice, perceptions of self, perceptions of others, the personal constructs with which we build our world, the responsibilities we accept or reject, the whole phenomenal world of the individual with its connective tissue of meaning.[5]

Notice Rogers's choice of the word *self* rather than *soul*. "The self," said philosopher Allan Bloom, "is the modern substitute for the soul."[6] Ironically, the idea of an immaterial soul as the seat of our personal identities does not have much of a home in the world of psychology, though the word itself means "the study of the soul."

Reflecting on how this shift came about, Bloom suggested that society's earlier preoccupation with the soul "inevitably led to neglect of this world in favor of the other world,"[7] giving the priest, as the guardian of the soul, increased influence. Machiavelli (1460) and Thomas Hobbes (1651) lashed back against the idea of the soul by talking about "a feeling self." Machiavelli and Hobbes "blazed the trail to the self, which has grown into the highway of a ubiquitous psychology without the psyche (soul)."[8]

In the 1700s the French political theorist Jean-Jacques Rousseau thought the focus on the "self" had degenerated into individual "self-interest," an insufficient base for establishing "the common good." In one sense he was right. If there is no God's-eye view of what constitutes the individual soul, it is easy to stop pursuing the good of our individual souls. The common purpose to which our souls unite becomes lost. People stop communicating. Their communities become moral ghost towns. People live aimlessly because they have no cause for which they are willing to die.[9] The cry of the populace is, "Just leave me alone." Perhaps the ultimate hell is that the wish will be granted.[10]

While it may seem merely a matter of semantics that "self" neatly replaces "soul," we believe there is an important distinction. From a Christian viewpoint, what we have now is the negative aspect of self: self-absorption, self-focus, self-interest, and just plain selfishness. We need our souls reclaimed and our selves renewed. Obviously, other worldviews disagree with both Christianity's diagnosis and proposed cure. Christianity has been a negative influence, some say; we're better off now. Professor Craig Gay from Regent College is one of a growing number of philosophers and psychologists who think only the idea of the soul—not the self—is robust enough to restore our society to health:

> **Christian psychology isn't the sanitizing of the self; it is the salvaging of the soul.**

> Indeed, unless we directly contest the distinctively modern understanding of the self, our resistance to the modern secular society will probably be construed—and may actually result—either in yet another expression of ideological manipulation, or in yet another eccentric expression of the triumph of the therapeutic.[11]

Christian psychology isn't the sanitizing of the self; it is the salvaging of the soul, which is not incidental to our humanness but fully representative of it. Only when we acknowledge spiritual reality will we gain true insight and true healing. As William Kilpatrick says, "In short, although Christianity is more than a psychology, it happens to be better psychology than psychology is."[12]

So let's begin our tour of how the worldviews under our consideration use—and abuse—psychology.

3. SECULARISM

Secular psychology is shaped by two fundamental assumptions: (1) the idea of a personal God is a myth, and (2) we are purely physical beings, highly evolved animals produced by millions of years of naturalistic causes and processes. As Leonard Mlodinow argues, we don't need an eternal and conscious universe to give our lives meaning. Our lives are as meaningful as we make them.[13]

> **Mind/Body Monism:** the belief that human beings are composed of a single substance.

Mlodinow's view expresses the guiding commitment of secular psychology: Everything must be explained by material causes. Brain functions, physical urges, and environmental stimuli explain everything, including what we conceive of as our minds, souls, and personalities. **Mind/body monism** is a term used to summarize this view: *mon* means "one." There is only one basic and fundamental reality—the material world.

> **Behaviorism:** a school of psychology that believes psychological research should be concerned with studying observable measures of behavior and not the unobservable events that take place in the mind.

Behaviorism is the branch of psychology concerned with explaining everything through material causes. Behaviorists believe all human *thought* and *personality* are merely by-products of physical interactions of the brain. For behaviorists, psychology is the task of understanding how physical stimuli encourage our physical brains and bodies to behave.

In a behaviorist approach to psychology, human beings are seen as stimulus receptors, responding in predetermined ways to their environment. If someone you like hugs you, you feel good. If someone pinches you, you reflexively pull away. Psychologist B. F. Skinner thought stimulus-response could explain just about everything: "A scientific analysis of behavior dispossesses autonomous man and turns the control he has been said to exert over to the environment. The individual ... is henceforth to be controlled by the world around him, and in large part by other men."[14]

Behaviorism is out of favor at present for two reasons: (1) human behavior is not as easy to understand and predict as animal behavior—there must be something different about us; and (2) if behaviorism is true, there really is no such thing as free will—we can only do what our natures require us to do. The idea that we are just matter in motion—that true choice is an illusion—does not sit well in our individualistic Western culture. But while sociologists and philosophers debate the merits of behaviorism, the field of **cognitive behaviorism** has advanced rapidly in psychology as researchers use neuroimaging of the brain through PET and CAT scans and MRIs to study how our mental activities are related to brain functions.[15] In fact, one of the most widely accepted definitions of *psychology* in secular textbooks today is the study and "science of behavior and mental processes."[16]

> In a behaviorist approach to psychology, human beings are seen as stimulus receptors, responding in predetermined ways to their environment.

> *Cognitive Behaviorism:* a school of psychology that reduces all behavior to cognitive functioning and seeks to explain behavior by examining underlying cognitive causes.

Today's secular psychology is often called **third force psychology**. The first force was behaviorism, and the second force was based on the theories of Sigmund Freud, perhaps the most famous psychologist to ever live. Freud thought our conscious behavior is shaped by our unconscious recollection of our past experiences. Through **psychoanalysis** he examined, among other things, dreams and slips of the tongue ("Freudian slips") in order to uncover the unconscious thoughts and motivations of his clients, as well as to discern the stage of development they were stuck in that was hindering their progress. Freud described the unconscious as a cesspool where our unwanted sexual and violent dreams, desires, and motivations reside. He called this part of our personality the *id*. The moralistic part of a person that suppresses the id is called the *superego*. While Freud's ideas are mostly discredited among scholars, his

> *Third Force Psychology:* a humanistic psychology that emerged as a reaction to the limitations of behaviorism (i.e., first force) and psychoanalysis (i.e., second force), this theory contends that human beings are innately good physical beings with personal agency who are mentally healthy when focused upon achieving self-actualization.

> *Psychoanalysis:*
> an approach to psychology developed by Sigmund Freud whereby a psychologist attempts to resolve a patient's psychological problems by uncovering and discussing the patient's unconscious, unfulfilled, or repressed desires.

idea of humans as primarily sexual beings is very much a part of popular consciousness today.[17]

Regarding our behavioral causes and our relationships with others, third force psychology tries to be a little more nuanced than Freud or his predecessors. As we will see, the assumptions of third force psychology are (1) we are good by nature and therefore can properly manage human behavior; (2) the responsibility for individual psychological illness has to do with a person's physiology, social circumstances, psychological state, mental processes, and emotions rather than with any spiritual problems; and (3) mental health can be restored when these factors are properly balanced.

Third force psychologists are suspicious of spiritual explanations because they do not believe the spirit exists. Consequently, they reject sin as a category for explaining what happens to people. Carl Rogers said, "For myself, though I am very well aware of the incredible amount of destructive, cruel, malevolent behavior in today's world—from the threats of war to the senseless violence in the streets—I do not find that this evil is inherent in human nature."[18] Erich Fromm went even further in his book *You Shall Be as Gods*, suggesting that the concept of sin is itself what keeps us sick. When we strip ourselves of society's outdated interpretation of what God wants from us, Fromm suggested we will become positive agents with virtually unlimited potential for good.[19]

Abraham Maslow, with his theory of self-actualization, expanded on Fromm's theme. To Maslow, **self-actualization** "stresses 'full-humanness,' the development of the biologically based nature of man."[20] Self-actualized people possess the following traits: an objective view of reality, acceptance of self and others, genuineness, commitment to a cause, a sense of autonomy, gratitude, peak experiences in which the self is transcended, social interest, deep and lasting relationships, tolerance of others, creativity, and self-sufficiency.[21] Self-actualization can only occur after a person's lower physiological, safety, social, and ego needs have been met. This is pure mental health: "Since this inner nature is good or neutral rather than bad, it is best to bring it out and to encourage it rather than to suppress it. If it is permitted to guide our life, we grow healthy, fruitful, and happy."[22]

> *Self-actualization:*
> the stage at which a person purportedly meets his or her full psychological potential (some characteristics include self-acceptance, genuineness, independence, gratitude, social interest, tolerance, creativity, and self-sufficiency).

Who is actually like this, though? Maslow was vague. He felt "fairly sure" that Thomas Jefferson and Abraham Lincoln "in his last days" were both self-actualized. He also singled out Albert Einstein, Eleanor Roosevelt, Jane Addams, William James, Albert Schweitzer, Aldous Huxley, and Benedict de Spinoza as "highly probable" examples of self-actualization. According to Maslow, people not yet self-actualized can learn what's right by watching those who are. Maslow said, "I propose that we explore the consequences of observing whatever our best specimens choose, and then assuming that these are the highest values for all mankind."[23]

One problem with this theory of self-actualization, though, is that the route to mental health is through self-centeredness. Carl Rogers said the philosophy of the future "will stress the value of the individual. It will, I think, center itself in the individual as the evaluating agent."[24] If this is so, "What about my needs?" could become our most urgent question. If someone else is acting in a way we think hinders our right to fulfillment, we become indignant and angry. It is his fault, not ours. Evil becomes whatever prevents a person from doing what he judges to be good for himself.

Joyce Milton's *The Road to Malpsychia: Humanistic Psychology and Our Discontents* recounts the practical failure of secular psychology by showing how it played out in the lives of some of its major proponents and leading practitioners.[25] The title is revealing—*malpsychia* means "bad psychology." Milton tells the story of Bill Coulson, Carl Rogers's coworker, who experienced firsthand the problems Rogers had putting his theory into practice. It wasn't solving anything, concluded Coulson. "In fact, it was creating new pathologies that hadn't existed before. The therapy was the disease."[26] Maslow's theories, according to Milton, suffered from his inability to account for the sin nature: "Frank Manuel, his best friend on the Brandeis faculty, had warned Maslow as early as 1960 that his inability to account for the presence of evil in the world was a potentially fatal flaw in his attempt to construct a 'religion of human nature.'"[27]

Paul C. Vitz, professor of psychology at New York University, says, "The stories of these amoral and disordered lives are not just anecdotes: They are, rather, directly relevant to the theories of these psychologists.... Psychologist, heal thyself."[28]

4. MARXISM

Marxists, as described in previous chapters, accept materialism (the idea that only matter exists) and evolution as the mechanism by which the world has reached its present level of complexity. If everything is material, how do you get people to do what you want? Marxist theorists thought psychology, especially behaviorism, could provide the answer. Through reward and punishment we can organize humans to march purposefully toward pure communism.

There's a problem, however. Marxist psychologist Joseph Nahem points out that if behaviorism is true, there really is no such thing as free will. Our brains respond to environmental stimuli. In other words, we think we are choosing our actions, but both our actions and choices are determined by factors beyond our control. Here's the rub for the Marxist: if there is no free will, how can humans engage in a conscious struggle toward communism?[29] Left to their own devices, people won't rise up; the punishing cost of revolution is too high and the potential for reward is too low.

> Here's the rub for the Marxist: if there is no free will, how can humans engage in a conscious struggle toward communism?

Reducing psychology to physiology is too mechanical; it simply cannot achieve the Marxist agenda.[30] Clearly Marxists will have to answer the free-will question, and their attempt to do so goes back to the work of B. F. Skinner. Skinner said, "The environment not only prods or lashes, it selects. Its role is similar to that in natural selection, though on a very different time scale."[31] If the environment *selects* for us, we are not free agents who make our own decisions. "The hypothesis that man is not free is essential to the application of scientific method to the study of human behavior," according to Skinner and other behaviorists.[32]

Skinner's behaviorism was not good enough for Marxism, though, because it could not explain how people might do something utterly unpredictable and risky, like start a revolution. A new approach was needed, and Ivan P. Pavlov, a Russian physiologist of the early twentieth century, came up with it. The theory is known as **classical conditioning**. Pavlov believed that mental processes were the result of purely physical causes, and that consequently such behavior could be understood and directed to perfect the human race. He arrived at this conclusion through studying the way dogs salivated in response to auditory stimuli. At first, Pavlov's dogs salivated when a bell was ringing, because they were eating at the same time. The dogs soon learned to salivate when they heard the bell even without the presence of food. These canine experiments led Pavlov to propose a theory of *conditioned reflexes*—animals can learn to respond in specific, predetermined ways when exposed to certain stimuli.

> *Classical Conditioning:* a training technique developed by Ivan Pavlov that pairs a naturally occurring stimulus and response with an unrelated stimulus, so that eventually, the unrelated stimulus is able to produce the desired response in absence of the natural stimulus.

Pavlov concluded that all animal activity could be accounted for in behaviorist terms and that "the whole complicated behavior of animals" is based on "nervous activity."[33] Since Pavlov was an evolutionist, he believed his conclusion also applied to the highest animal—human beings: "I trust that I shall not be thought rash if I express a belief that experiments on the higher nervous activities of animals will yield not a few directional indications for education and self-education in man."[34]

To this end, Pavlov believed similar conditioning could be applied to humans to educate, train, or control them to do only good. Shortly before his death, Pavlov told his lab assistants, "Now we can and must go forward.... We may use all of the experimental material for the investigation of the human being, striving to perfect the human race of the future."[35] Though Pavlov had a stormy relationship with the Marxist leadership of Russia, he continued to receive funding for his research.[36] Evidently, the Marxist leaders believed his findings would enable them to achieve their goals.

So how did Pavlov's research fit into the agenda of Marxist leaders? Remember, Marxists needed a theory for how humans—who are really nothing more than complex animals—could be induced to consciously pursue the aims of communism. The answer from Pavlov was in the relationship between thought and speech. Unlike other animals, humans have a particular ability to use speech to transcend the limits nature has set. Nahem explained: "Pavlov identified the qualitative difference between humans and animals in the possession by humans of a second signal system, i.e., speech, which was 'the latest acquisition in the process of evolution.'"[37]

Pavlov's research, conducted along with his student and colleague L. S. Vygotsky, is indeed fascinating. Here's the problem they wrestled with: Which came first, thought or speech? After all, we think with words; without them we cannot think. However, without thinking we cannot develop words. It's a paradox. To Vygotsky, thought and speech, like the hydrogen and oxygen molecules in water, could not be easily separated:

> When one approaches the problem of thinking and speech by decomposing it into its elements, one adopts the strategy of the man who resorts to the decomposition of water into hydrogen and oxygen in his search for a scientific explanation of the characteristics of water, its capacity to extinguish fire or its conformity to Archimedes law for example. This man will discover, to his chagrin, that hydrogen burns and oxygen sustains combustion. He will never succeed in explaining the characteristics of the whole by analyzing the characteristics of its elements.[38]

Vygotsky proposed thinking of words as "concealed generalizations," that is, units of verbal thinking that result from the dialectical interplay between thought and speech—all made possible by our advanced reflex, which he called our "second signal system."

Here the idea of the dialectic appears once more. Thesis and antithesis merge; the new synthesis resolves what we believed were irresolvable paradoxes. Vygotsky thought it was this way with thought and speech. The dialectical relationship between the two, thought and speech, enables humans to transcend the limits of behaviorism. Of course, though, there must be a physical cause. Pavlov and Vygotsky thought the "second signal system" in the brain accounted for the interaction of thought and speech, which refuted Skinner and made a "profound contribution to psychology."[39]

Joseph Nahem argued that all of human society can be explained by this relationship between thought and speech:

> Most decisive in its influence on our thoughts, feelings, and behavior is society and social relations.... Human beings are distinguished from animals by their social labor, their social communication, their social groupings, by their social acquisition and use of language, and by their involvement in the ideas, attitudes, morality and behavior of their society.[40]

As society grows, we internalize the speech-thought dialectic, which, according to Soviet neuropsychologist A. R. Luria, becomes a craving for more societal influence.[41] Eventually we gain the capacity to shape society as we see fit.

You can imagine how exciting this research was for Marxists: the dialectic functions everywhere! It explains the clash between property owners and workers because it explains the clash between our free will and our environmental stimuli, which in turn is explained by the interplay between thought and speech. It is the dialectic, according to Nahem, that gives free will any true meaning.[42]

Free will means we have the liberty to choose the type of society that will in turn determine our behavior. If we don't exercise the will to evolve toward communism, then we are being controlled by our situations or environments.

In the end, a communist society will expose us to proper stimuli, eliciting proper behavior and leading to mental health. But mental health wasn't really the goal of Marxist leaders. They worshipped Pavlov because he helped them see how they could both control society and make it seem as if people could exert their free will in rising up and freeing the masses.[43] The inability to rise up is what makes us sick. Because of insights gained in the field of psychology, the Marxist says, we can now see how to choose communism, and all is well.

5. POSTMODERNISM

Traditionally, we understood our personal identities as what we are born with: stable, unified souls including minds, hearts, wills, and consciences. To Postmodernism, as to Secularism, the idea of "soul" is obsolete. The idea of humans having any identifiable essence at all is obsolete. But Postmodernists go far beyond the idea of the "self" to what we refer to as the **decentered self**, that human beings are social constructions who do not have unified, objective human natures.

> *Decentered Self:* **the belief that human beings are social constructions without a singular identity, essence, or soul.**

In fact, if humans are not unified, rational individuals, we may actually have *multiple selves*.[44] The psychology of multiple selves was developed by Jacques Lacan, a French psychoanalyst, one of four French intellectuals of the 1960s whose writings forged much of postmodern thought.[45] Lacan outlined his view in an essay titled "The Mirror Stage as Formative of the Function of the I."[46] Infants look in the mirror and see their reflections as an "apperception"—a something other than the self. As we grow older we realize what this means: we are both inside ourselves and outside ourselves at the same time. There is, Michel Foucault iterated, no distinction "between public and private selves implied by the concept of human nature nor can the individual be reduced to individual consciousness; there are only practices or techniques of the self."[47]

Kenneth Gergen, a psychology professor at Swarthmore College, points out that in our technologically "saturated" society with its multiple opportunities for personal interaction, it is impossible to know which is our "real" self. The idea of "personality" (from *persona*, an actor who switches between masks on stage) is that we are all, figuratively speaking, switching between masks. Because we play so many different roles at different times and with different people, it can be disorienting to people who don't yet understand. To make more clear what life with a multiplicity of selves looks like, Gergen painted the following picture:

> Connie spent her childhood in New Jersey. After her parents were divorced, her mother moved with the children to San Diego. Connie's teen years were spent shuttling between father and mother on either coast. After she graduated from the University of Colorado, she moved to Alaska to work on a fishing boat, and then to Wyoming to become a ski instructor. Now Connie is working on a geological-survey vessel in the Antarctic, and is engaged to a man living in Portland, Oregon. Fred is a neurologist who spends many of his spare hours working to aid families from El Salvador. Although he is married to Tina, on Tuesday and Thursday nights he lives with an Asian friend with whom he has a child. On weekends he drives his BMW to Atlantic City for gambling.[48]

A theory of multiple socially constructed selves provides a way for those living in a postmodern world to see their behavior as normal, which their community considers aberrant.

Mitchell Stephens, a journalism professor at New York University, explains that "mutating lifestyles and changing intellectual currents have led a group of increasingly influential postmodern psychologists to a startling conclusion: we have no single, separate, unified self." He writes that

> a group of counselors and therapists, for example, has begun noting that we all must "create" other selves as we leave our families in search of friendship, success and love—and then move on to new friendships, new successes and new loves. Social psychologists have begun studying not only our "child selves," our "professional selves," our "friendship selves," and our "parent selves" but also what Hazel Markus labels our "possible selves," our "feared possible selves," our "ideal selves," our "fleeting selves," our "tentative selves," and our "chronically accessible selves."[49]

Glenn Ward points out the mind-bending way this changes our whole concept of who we are: the new proper response to the suggestion "Get in touch with yourself" or "Be yourself" is "Which one?"[50]

To Lacan and Foucault, the idea of a naturally whole and coherent soul, or even a stable, unified self, "has always been an illusion."[51] It is this idea that keeps us moving along with the herd rather than expressing ourselves in the ways we see fit. The truly healthy person resists society's attempts to define him and rejects any attempt to diagnosis him as insane merely for refusing to follow along.[52] Psychological health begins with recognizing that we are a flux of desires and intensities caught up in an ongoing process of change.

Hazel Rose Markus, professor of psychology at the University of Michigan, calls this "the most exciting time in psychology in decades and decades." She notes the growing realization that "there isn't just one answer to the 'Who am I?' question."

The approach of multiple selves is not without its problems. Louis Sass, a Rutgers clinical psychology professor, put it this way: "There are clearly dangers in giving up that notion of a single self. You absolve the person of responsibility for making judgments." Imagine the excuses people might make: "Hey, it wasn't my fault. One of my other selves did it."[53]

There is also the problem of identifying standards of normal and abnormal. Walter Truett Anderson says, "I have been putting words like 'abnormal' and 'deviant' in quotes, because those categorizations are under fire now, the boundary between normal and abnormal is as questionable now as all the other boundaries that once defined social reality."[54] According to Anderson, Postmodernists are not in the boundary business. Some Postmodernists intentionally broke the boundaries with deadly results. Michel Foucault, for example, was known to have promiscuously participated in the homosexual community in San Francisco, including participating in sadomasochistic rituals and using drugs, justifying his behavior with his philosophy.[55]

We might have foreseen this. The idea of the *internal* soul gave way to the idea of the *externalized* self. But how could that be defined? And how, especially in light of our very fluid culture, could it be limited to just one self? If our natures have no fundamental design and no essence, then whatever we define ourselves to be is acceptable. And if that "whatever" becomes "whatevers," who's to say it's bad? Others may think you are being inconsistent or uncooperative or rude or hurtful, but in reality, the Postmodernist says, they're braying at you from the herd, trying to get you to come back and be like everyone else. Perhaps it is true, as Japanese filmmaker Akiro Kurosawa said, "In a mad world, only the mad are sane."

6. New Spirituality

New Spiritualist psychology is closely tied to the belief that we can hasten the progress of evolution by achieving a **higher consciousness**. Ken Carey says, "Everyone anywhere who tunes into the Higher Self becomes part of the transformation. Their lives then become orchestrated from other realms."[56] When enough of us do this, society will change. For the New Spiritualist, psychology is a helpful tool because it can move us toward change. It can hasten the realization of a collective God consciousness even while it works to ensure perfect health for each of us.

> *Higher Consciousness:* the state of awareness wherein individuals realize their divinity and the divine interconnectedness of all things.

In our secular psychology section, we learned of first force psychology (behaviorism), second force psychology (Freudianism), and third force psychology (self-actualization). The psychological branch that emphasizes higher consciousness is sometimes referred to as **fourth force psychology**. According to John White, "Fourth force psychology covers a wide range of human affairs. All of them, however, are aimed at man's ultimate development—not simply a return from unhealthiness to normality—as individuals and as a species."[57]

"Ultimate development" represents the only truly healthy mind-set, said Marilyn Ferguson. "Well-being cannot be infused intravenously or ladled in by prescription. It comes from a matrix: the body mind. It reflects psychological and somatic harmony."[58]

> *Fourth Force Psychology:* a school of psychology that attempts to integrate aspects of transcendent religious teachings within the framework of modern psychology.

Whereas Secularism thinks psychological health comes from focusing on the self, Marxism says it comes from the freedom to revolt, and Postmodernism says it comes from identifying our multiple selves, the New Spiritualist view goes in the opposite direction: based on the Buddhist tradition, it denies the self altogether. According to the Dalai Lama,

> Perhaps the chief difference between Buddhism and the world's other major faith traditions lies in its presentation of our core identity. The existence of the soul or self, which is affirmed in different ways by Hinduism, Judaism, Christianity, and Islam, is not only firmly denied in Buddhism; belief in it is identified as the source of all our misery.[59]

The idea of the "self," Eckhart Tolle argues, leads to an unhealthy focus on ego. Only when we rid ourselves of this focus and tap into universal truth in the form of higher consciousness can we be set free from psychological unease.

To achieve freedom from the self, we must meditate in a way that brings us to an awareness of higher consciousness. The New Spiritualist kind of meditation is very different from the Christian tradition of meditation. New Spiritualists meditate to focus on what they view as their own God nature. Christians focus on God—who is maker, sustainer, provider, redeemer, Lord, and judge—and on his objective, external revelation of truth to us in the Bible and his presence with us through the Holy Spirit. Christian meditation involves a fully engaged

> **New Spiritualists meditate to focus on what they view as their own God nature.**

mind with a goal of understanding the truth as revealed by God. New Spiritualists believe they are part of everything; that is, part of God. People find God by emptying themselves of all but their God natures.

The children's book *What Is God?*, which teaches New Spiritualist meditation to children, clearly illustrates the difference between Christian and New Spiritualist meditation. The book says,

> And if you really want to pray to God, you can just close your eyes anywhere, and think about that feeling of God, that makes you part of everything and everybody. If you can feel that feeling of God, and everybody else can feel that feeling of God, then we can all become friends together, and we can really understand, 'What is God?' So, if you really want to feel God, you can close your eyes now, and listen to your breath go slowly in and out, and think how you are connected to everything, even if you are not touching everything.[60]

How does this relate to psychology? Higher consciousness represents purity and wellness. There is no physical, spiritual, or mental pain in higher consciousness. If you can tap into it, you will be healed.

According to Marianne Williamson, even life-threatening disease can be healed through a healthy psyche. She says, "Healing results from a transformed perception of our relationship to illness, one in which we respond to the problem with love instead of fear."[61] The healing tool Williamson recommends is **visualization**—that is, imagining events happening in the future and then willing these events to come true. This is true even with AIDS and cancer: "Imagine the AIDS virus as Darth Vader, and then unzip his suit to allow an angel to emerge. See the cancer cell or AIDS virus in all its wounded horror, and then see a golden light, or angel, or Jesus, enveloping the cell and

> *Visualization:* the act of attempting to achieve a particular outcome through concentrating and meditating upon that outcome.

transforming it from darkness into light."[62] The physical world is not really real—so if we choose the right tools, New Spiritualists believe, we can save ourselves. If we are God enough, our redemption is nigh.

New Spiritualist psychology provides the jargon and the tools for New Spirituality's relentless pursuit of higher consciousness wherein, the New Spiritualist says, true health may be found.

7. ISLAM

Islamic psychology is straightforward: we find healing and peace not by becoming more like our creator or by pursuing our own good or by meditation but by submission. The Quran

---

states, "Those who believe, and whose hearts find satisfaction in the remembrance of God: for without doubt in the remembrance of God do hearts find satisfaction. For those who believe and work righteousness, is (every) blessedness, and a beautiful place of (final) return" (13:28–29). Submission leads to psychological health.

Recall from our "Islam" chapter the basis of Islamic faith: the original religion of humanity is Islam (Quran 7:172), and every human being is born a Muslim (30:30). As stated in the Hadith, "Allah's Apostle said, 'Every child is born with a true faith of Islam [i.e., to worship none but Allah Alone]."[63] "The true Muslim believes that every person is born free from sin," wrote Hammudah Abdalati.[64] Our natural state, says Islam, is purity or *fitrah*. If we do not obey God, it is because of external influences.[65]

> *Fitrah:* the belief that all human beings have an innate predisposition toward submitting to Allah and acting morally.

As you might imagine, the doctrine of *fitrah* proceeds from a very different understanding of the doctrine of the fall. Norman Geisler and Abdul Saleeb explain:

> Despite some general similarities to the biblical version of man's fall, there are radical differences between the Christian and the Islamic interpretations of Adam's transgression. Whereas in Christian theology man's disobedience is viewed as a fundamental turning point in his relationship to God, according to the Muslim perspective this was only a single slip on Adam and Eve's part that was completely forgiven after their repentance. It had no further effect on the nature of man and the rest of creation. Neither does the fact that man was expelled from Paradise to earth (as a direct result of this transgression of divine command) play a significant role in the Islamic anthropology or soteriology.[66]

So whereas Christianity says we are inherently bound in sin and in need of a redeemer, Muslims believe we are capable of redeeming ourselves. Abdalati explains:

> Man is a responsible agent. But responsibility for sin is borne by the actual offender alone. Sin is not hereditary, transferable, or communal in nature. Every individual is responsible for his own deeds. And while man is susceptible to corruption, he is also capable of redemption and reform. This does not mean that Islam prefers the individual to the group. Individualism means little or nothing when severed from social context. What it means is that the individual has different sets of roles to play. He must play them in such a way as to guard his moral integrity, preserve his identity, observe the rights of God, and fulfill his social obligations.[67]

Christians also affirm individual responsibility and good deeds.[68] For Christians, though, faith always precedes obedience (Eph. 2:8–10).[69] We obey out of a response to salvation, our love for a God who first loved us. As we saw in the "Theology" chapter, though, Muslims do not operate from a Christian view of human fallenness. For Christians, fallenness means we are incapable of obedience without the power of the Holy Spirit; for Muslims, fallen humans are like rebellious children who could obey if they wanted to. The good deeds required of Muslims (circumcision, prayer five times a day, a pilgrimage to Mecca, avoiding pork, etc.) are possible in the flesh, and there is no excuse for anyone's failure to perform them.

According to Islam, then, we can fix ourselves. No one else can do it for us—not even a redeeming savior. According to Abdalati,

> The true Muslim believes that man must work out his salvation through the guidance of God. This means that in order to attain salvation a person must combine Faith and action, belief and practice. Faith without action is as insufficient as action without Faith. In other words, no one can attain salvation until his Faith in God becomes dynamic in his life and his beliefs are translated into reality. This is in complete harmony with other Islamic articles of Faith. It shows that God does not accept lip service, and that no true believer can be indifferent as far as practical requirements of Faith are concerned. It also shows that no one can act on behalf of another or intercede between him and God. (See, for example, Quran 10:9–10; 18:30; 103:1–3.)[70]

Those who do this will receive forgiveness from God:

- "To those who believe and do deeds of righteousness hath Allah promised forgiveness and a great reward" (Quran 5:10).
- "Establish regular prayers at the two ends of the day and at the approaches of the night; for those things that are good remove those that are evil; be that the word of remembrance to those who remember (their Lord)" (11:114).[71]

Can we ever know our deeds are enough to secure salvation, though? No. Except in one case, jihad:

> Those who have left their homes, or been driven out therefrom, or suffered harm in My Cause, or fought or been slain, verily, I will blot out from them their iniquities, and admit them into Gardens with rivers flowing beneath; a reward from the Presence of God, and from His Presence is the best of rewards. (3:195)

Jihad is the responsibility of Muslims to master the self and be dedicated to restoring others to their original state of being Muslim by the means specified in the Quran (which includes force). Many Muslims believe jihad may properly involve war against nonbelievers. The Quran seems to guarantee eternal reward to those who die in this effort.[72]

To the Muslim, what is wrong with us is a failure to submit to God in the way outlined in the Quran and the writings of the prophet Muhammad. Society is sick because of our rebellion against our true nature as Muslims. Submission to God cures us and thus cures society.

> **To the Muslim, what is wrong with us is a failure to submit to God in the way outlined in the Quran and the writings of the prophet Muhammad.**

8. CHRISTIANITY

Many see the words *Christian* and *psychology* as contradictory. Indeed, if psychology is what secular, Marxist, and postmodern psychologists say it is, there is little hope of reconciling it to Christianity. As William Kirk Kilpatrick, a professor of educational psychology, says, "If you're talking about Christianity, it is much truer to say that psychology and religion are competing faiths. If you seriously hold to one set of values, you will logically have to reject the other."[73]

What Kilpatrick says is true, but when he uses the term *psychology*, he is referring specifically to secular psychology. Our view is this: just because psychology is often done falsely does not mean it cannot be done truly. In psychology, as with the other disciplines, Christians must bring God's truth about the nature of the soul to bear in psychological considerations. Christianity says that only with full souls will we see the truth. If this is so, we think the Christian worldview contains a psychology. As Charles L. Allen aptly pointed out, "The very essence of religion is to adjust the mind and soul of man.... Healing means bringing the person into a right relationship with the physical, mental and spiritual laws of God."[74] Men and women created "in the image of God" (Gen. 1:27)[75] require a worldview that recognizes the significance of the spiritual.

> **Christian psychology begins with personhood. God is a person, Christianity says, and our personhood is somehow related to his.**

Christian psychology begins with personhood. God is a person, Christianity says, and our personhood is somehow related to his. The famed philosopher Alvin Plantinga put it this way:

> How should we think about human persons? What sorts of things, fundamentally, are they? What is it to be a human, and what is it to be a human person, and how should we think about personhood?... The first point to note is that in the Christian scheme of things, God is the premier person, the first and chief exemplar of personhood ... and the properties most important for an understanding of our personhood are properties we share with him.[76]

In other words, as J. P. Moreland and Scott Rae say, "There is something about the way God is that is like the way we are."[77] It stands to reason that God's magnificent creation required thinking, planning, artistry, and execution—all qualities God has shared with us, his image bearers. God reveals himself through creation (general revelation) and redemption (special revelation) as a person whose nature is justice, love, mercy, and grace. Our souls are the housing for our image bearing.

What is the soul, then? To answer this question we must first confront the materialism secular, Marxist, and postmodern psychologists teach. That is, we must explain how things outside the material world—like the mind—actually exist. The materialist sees the mind as an *epiphenomenon*, a shadow, so to speak, of the brain. The famous neurophysiologist Charles Sherrington described it this way: "Mind, for anything perception can compass, goes therefore in our spatial world more ghostly than a ghost. Invisible, intangible, it is a thing not even of outline; it is not a 'thing.' It remains without sensual confirmation, and remains without it forever."[78]

> *Epiphenomenalism:* the belief that mental events are completely dependent upon physical events and have no independent existence (i.e., the "mind" is a projection of the brain's activity).

Christianity denies **epiphenomenalism**—the belief that the mind is only a projection of brain activity. The mind is consciousness—supernatural, beyond natural explanation. The Bible's statements regarding body, breath of life, soul, spirit, heart, and mind suggest a dualist ontology.[79] This means our being has a twofold nature: physical (material or natural) and spiritual (supernatural). Christ's statement about fearing the one who could put "both soul and body" in hell (Matt. 10:28)[80] and the apostle Paul's statement regarding body, soul, and spirit (1 Thess. 5:23)[81] enforce the distinction.

Sir John Eccles, one of the world's most respected neurophysiologists, believed **mind/ body dualism** is the only explanation for many of the phenomena of consciousness. One of the reasons Eccles reached this conclusion is the individual's "unity of identity." Paul Weiss explains:

> Even though I know I am constantly changing—all molecules are changing, everything in me is being turned over substantially—there is nevertheless my identity, my consciousness of being essentially the same that I was 20 years ago. However much I may have changed, the continuity of my identity has remained undisrupted.[82]

Mind/Body Dualism: **the belief that human beings are composed of immaterial minds and material bodies.**

Our physical substance is changing, but our unity remains. The implication: something more than the physical brain—something spiritual or supernatural—must exist.

Human memory also supports the existence of an immaterial reality. Arthur Custance wrote more than thirty years ago, "What research has shown thus far is that there is no precise one-to-one relationship between any fragment of memory and the nerve cells in which it is supposed to be encoded."[83] Custance's work has been affirmed in more recent research.[84]

Materialists rage against this very idea. If *anything* immaterial exists, then matter is not all there is. If matter is not all there is, then materialism is false, and Secularism, Marxism, and Postmodernism will have to start over from scratch. Just in the last few years, neuroscientist Mario Beauregard has mustered an enormous amount of convincing evidence against materialism, as has philosopher Thomas Nagel. Neurosurgeon Eben Alexander even wrote a book, *Proof of Heaven*, in which he explains his conversion away from materialism after a severe disease in which his brain shut down completely for several days.[85]

If *anything* immaterial exists, then matter is not all there is. If matter is not all there is, then materialism is false, and Secularism, Marxism, and Postmodernism will have to start over from scratch.

Christian psychology says the "something else" that exists is the soul. In Genesis 2:7,[86] God breathed and humankind became living *souls*. J. P. Moreland summarizes the biblical concept of our identity when he says, "Human beings are composed of an immaterial entity—a soul, a life principle, a ground of sentience—and a body. More specifically, a human being is a unity of two distinct entities—body and soul."[87]

The Christian view of the soul is gloriously uplifting. It accounts for identity and memory.[88] It also accounts for free will as well as the sinful bent in our natures. The fall affected the soul massively. Our revolt against God caused a dramatic, reality-shattering change in our relationship to the rest of existence and even to ourselves. This change has severe ramifications for all aspects of reality, including psychology.

> If the Christian view is accurate, only Christianity offers a true, meaningful, and workable psychology.

Our sinful nature—our desire to rebel against God and our fellow beings—is the source of all psychological problems according to the Christian view. Creaturehood is too confining; we want to be God. We want to make the rules, and if we can justify it by denying God's existence, we will. In our hearts we say there is no God (Ps. 14:1).[89] Our hearts are deceitful and wicked (Jer. 17:9).[90] Only Christianity accurately identifies the problem of the heart, mind, and will in relation to God. If the Christian view is accurate, only Christianity offers a true, meaningful, and workable psychology. "The great benefit of the doctrine of sin," says Paul Vitz, "is that it reintroduces responsibility for our own behavior, responsibility for changing as well as giving meaning to our condition."[91]

It is important to understand what is meant by sin in this context, though. The various words for "sin" in both the Old Testament and the New Testament imply rebelling, deliberately engaging in wrongdoing, missing a mark, twisting something's nature, or straying down a wrong path.[92] According to Ephesians 2:1–3, there are three sources of human temptation:

> You were dead in the trespasses and sins in which you once walked, following the course of this world, following the prince of the power of the air, the spirit that is now at work in the sons of disobedience—among whom we all once lived in the passions of our flesh, carrying out the desires of the body and the mind, and were by nature children of wrath, like the rest of mankind.

First, sin arises through the world's processes ("the course of the world"). Second, Satan causes sin ("the prince of the power of the air"). Third, our desires cause us to sin ("the passions of the flesh"). Traditionally, people refer to "the world, the flesh, and the devil."

So when we say that sin is the source of all psychological problems, this includes any or all of the following:

- **Personal sin**: someone chooses to do something wrong, and this has consequences for the person's mental state (for example, a woman has sexual intercourse outside of marriage, gets pregnant, has an abortion, and then suffers from postabortive trauma).
- **Sin of others**: someone is the victim of the sinful behavior of another (for example, a person is physically attacked by another person and experiences post-traumatic stress disorder).
- **Physical fallenness**: someone has a genetic or physiological disorder due to the corruption of nature because of sin (schizophrenia or autism, for example).
- **Satanic attack**: Satan, who desires to steal, kill and destroy, can oppress or even take control of the spirit of a person, causing mental illness.

The doctrine of our two natures—physical and spiritual—combined with the doctrine of the sin nature opens up at least four therapeutic possibilities unavailable to materialism.

1. It helps free people from guilt. We experience real guilt because we are conscious of our rebellion against God. Christian psychologists acknowledge guilt and point hurting people toward deliverance through Christ's sacrificial death and resurrection. Our sins will dog us unceasingly until they are washed away by Christ's work on the cross, where God the Father declares us righteous and frees us from the penalty of sin. Only then will we have the power to live the life that God has ordained for us to live.

> We experience real guilt because we are conscious of our rebellion against God.

Secular psychology denies sin; it claims that the freedom we need is not from guilt but from the awkward posture in relation to society that creates guilty feelings. Some guilt is surely false, such as when we take on responsibility for the sins of others. But if sin is real, then at least some of our guilt is real, and we cannot merely diagnose it out of existence.[93] Some problems are physical and some are spiritual, Christianity says. To ignore the spiritual is to turn our backs on genuinely helpful solutions.

Christians believe that once Christ redeems us, we do not need to hide behind masks or switch between identities in order to gain acceptance, or feel guilty because our interactions with society have not led to the acceptance we desire. God is a heavenly Father who accepts his children unconditionally. We cannot make him love us more or less by our behavior.

2. It enables personal responsibility. The Christian psychologist stresses personal moral responsibility. It is possible for us to take this responsibility because we intuitively understand what God designed us to be, and we have a will. Secular psychologists might like to blame society for the problems individuals face, but this is a cop-out. As Karl Menninger said,

> If a group of people can be made to share the responsibility for what would be a sin if an individual did it, the load of guilt rapidly lifts from the shoulders of all concerned. Others may accuse, but the guilt shared by the many evaporates for the individual. Time passes. Memories fade. Perhaps there is a record, somewhere; but who reads it? [94]

Respected Christian counselor Larry Crabb advises therapists, "Hold your client responsible: for what? For confessing his sin, for willfully and firmly turning from it, and then for practicing the new behavior, believing that the indwelling Spirit will provide all the needed strength."[95]

To many people it seems insensitive to ask those seeking psychological health to take responsibility. After all, Scripture acknowledges sins that affect us but that we did not cause; for example, sin caused by the structures of society in which we live and generational sin. How can we take responsibility for this? The answer is to understand that moral, generational sin is something like a disease: you may have picked up a virus from a friend, but ending the friendship will not cure your cold or your friend's cold. The goal is to *heal* more than to *blame*. As Jay Adams put it, "It is important for counselors to remember that whenever clients camouflage,… sick treatment only makes them worse. To act as if they may be excused for their condition is the most unkind thing one can do. Such an approach only compounds the problem."[96]

While we live in a world of sin and are even affected by the sin of others, we can find forgiveness of sin through confession of our sins to one another (James 5:16),[97] confession of our sins to Christ (1 John 1:9),[98] reconciliation with God (2 Cor. 5:17–21),[99] and sanctification through the disciplining work of God's Spirit (1 Thess. 5:23; Heb. 12:1–11).[100]

---

3. It focuses on pursuing health rather than avoiding illness. If we truly have souls and sin is real, attempting to remove psychological pain without dealing with the underlying sin may be helping people become better sinners. When we make sinful choices, experiencing the natural and logical consequences of that pain can help drive us to repentance. The focus of Christianity is living rightly, not merely avoiding wrong behavior. The apostle Paul wrote, "Brothers, I do not consider that I have made it my own. But one thing I do: forgetting what lies behind and straining forward to what lies ahead, I press on toward the goal for the prize of the upward call of God in Christ Jesus" (Phil. 3:13–14).

> If we truly have souls and sin is real, attempting to remove psychological pain without dealing with the underlying sin may be helping people become better sinners.

More and more people are seeing the wisdom in emphasizing that one needs to do right rather than emphasizing what others have done wrong. Julia Annas from the University of Arizona once gave an address titled "Being Virtuous and Doing the Right Thing." She noted that the Virtues Project lists fifty-two virtues that have been found to be "character traits respected in seven world spiritual traditions," all of which are found in the Bible.[101]

Instead of constantly dwelling on what makes people *mentally ill*, the Christian focuses on what makes people mentally healthy, positive, joyful, and happy to be alive. Secular psychologists are catching on: "Studies show that those who believe in life after death, for example, are happier than those who do not. 'Religion provides a unifying narrative that may be difficult to come by elsewhere in society,' says sociologist Christopher Ellison of the University of Texas at Austin."[102]

Secularists, Marxists, and Postmodernists consider right and wrong to be burdensome because they hamper personal freedom. The Christian view that restrictions help rather than hurt is intriguing to a new generation of psychologists. According to Dr. Harold Koenig, a codirector of the Center for Spirituality, Theology, and Health at Duke University, the number of scholarly articles about the positive effects of religion on mental health has skyrocketed in recent years. The "thou shalt nots"—no adultery, no drugs, and so on—keep people from getting addicted or otherwise increasing their level of stress, says Koenig (that is, if they follow the rules). The strictures of religion may simplify life for adherents, and that can be a huge relief."[103]

> Instead of constantly dwelling on what makes people *mentally ill*, the Christian focuses on what makes people mentally healthy, positive, joyful, and happy to be alive.

> *Positive Psychology:* a branch of psychology that focuses on promoting mental health and happiness rather than just treating mental illness.

In psychology the emphasis on mental health rather than on mental illness is called **positive psychology** and is based on the work of Martin Seligman, former president of the American Psychological Association and professor of psychology at the University of Pennsylvania. Paul Vitz says, "What is needed to balance our understanding of the person is recognition of positive human characteristics that can both heal many of our pathologies and help to prevent psychological problems in one's future life."[104] And what are these *positive human characteristics?* Virtues that include "wisdom, courage, humanity, justice, temperance, and transcendence."[105]

4. It restores a sense of purpose in life. Paul's advice in the book of Philippians is worth many a visit to the psychologist's office: "do nothing from selfish ambition or conceit"; … "have this mind among yourselves, which [was also] in Christ Jesus"; … "do all things without grumbling or disputing"; … "rejoice in the Lord"; … "look out for … evildoers"; … "let your reasonableness be known to everyone"; … "whatever is true, … honorable, … just, … pure, … lovely, … commendable, … think about these things."[106]

Focusing on the mind of Christ restores life purpose. Francis Schaeffer outlined a simple approach to what he called "*positive psychological hygiene*": "As a Christian, instead of putting myself in practice at the center of the universe, I must do something else. This is not only right, and the failure to do so is not only sin, but it is important for me personally in this life. I must think after God, and I must will after God."[107] To "will after God" is not to think too highly of ourselves, "but in lowliness of mind let each esteem others better than [ourselves]" (Phil. 2:3).

9. Conclusion

The Christian view of human nature acknowledges the soul, spirit, mind, heart, will, consciousness, and intuition.[108] This view grants each individual moral responsibility, works to reconcile him or her with God, and gives meaning to suffering. Will this view of psychology ever recover? Paul Vitz is guardedly optimistic:

> On the horizon I see the potential for a psychology that I call "transmodern." By this term I mean a new mentality that both transcends and transforms modernity. Thus, it will leave both modern and Postmodern psychology behind. It will bring in transcendent understanding that may be idealistic and philosophical (e.g., the virtues), as well as spiritual and religious. It will transform modernity by bringing in an intelligent understanding of much of premodern wisdom…. In such a transmodern world, psychology would be the handmaid of philosophy and theology, as from the beginning it was meant to be.[109]

If psychology becomes "the handmaid of philosophy and theology," it may guide the quest for healthy souls that eludes the materialist.[110] We are offered a choice, according to William Kilpatrick, "the same choice offered to Adam and Eve: either we trust God or we take the serpent's word that we can make ourselves into gods."[111] To trust God or worship ourselves: we've seen where both will lead. Which will we choose?

And make no mistake: these choices carry massive consequences not only for our own souls but for society. What a society is, how societies become sick, and how societies might be made well is the domain of sociology. It is to the discipline of sociology that we now turn our attention.

ENDNOTES

1. Eckhart Tolle, *A New Earth* (New York: Plume, 2005), 27.

2. Tolle, *New Earth*, 51.

3. Wayne Grudem, *Systematic Theology* (Grand Rapids: Zondervan, 2009), 483.

4. Rollo May, *Psychology and the Human Dilemma* (Princeton, NJ: D. Van Nostrand, 1967), 188.

5. Quoted in Arthur Koestler and J. R. Smythies, ed., *Beyond Reductionism* (New York: Macmillan, 1970), 252.

6. Allan Bloom, *The Closing of the American Mind* (New York: Simon and Schuster, 1988), 173.

7. Bloom, *Closing of the American Mind*, 174.

8. Bloom, *Closing of the American Mind*, 175.

9. This is a reference to Dorothy L. Sayers's address "The Other Six Deadly Sins," presented to the Public Morality Council, Caxton Hall, Westminster, England, October 23, 1941. The full quote is as follows: "The sixth Deadly Sin is named by the Church *Acedia* or *Sloth*. In the world it calls itself Tolerance; but in hell it is called Despair. It is the accomplice of the other sins and their worst punishment. It is the sin which believes in nothing, cares for nothing, seeks to know nothing, interferes with nothing, enjoys nothing, loves nothing, hates nothing, finds purpose in nothing, lives for nothing, and only remains alive because there is nothing it would die for. We have known it far too well for many years. The only thing perhaps that we have not known about it is that it is mortal sin."

10. See Jeff Myers, *Secrets of Great Communicators* (Nashville: Broadman and Holman, 2006), chap. 1.

11. Craig M. Gay, *The Way of the Modern World* (Grand Rapids: Eerdmans, 1998), 262.

12. William Kirk Kilpatrick, *Psychological Seduction* (Nashville: Thomas Nelson, 1983), 15–16.

13. Deepak Chopra and Leonard Mlodinow, *War of the Worldviews: Where Science and Spirituality Meet—and Do Not* (New York: Three Rivers, 2011), 62–63.

14. B. F. Skinner, *Beyond Freedom and Dignity* (New York: Bantam Books, 1972), 96.

15. These three techniques—PET, CAT, and MRI—enable researchers to obtain vivid images of brain activity. By combining these images with behavioral stimuli, researchers can not only see what parts of the brain are stimulated by certain behaviors and what is going on inside the body, but they can even measure brain activity. *PET* stands for "positron emission tomography." In a PET scan, researchers inject a radioisotope "tracer" into the bloodstream and then use an imaging technique to create a three-dimensional image of the body. *CAT* stands for "computerized tomography." CAT scans (or CT scans) send X-rays through the body to make pictures of the body's structures. *MRI* stands for "magnetic resonance imaging." An MRI uses a powerful magnet to align the magnetic force of nuclei in the body, creating clear images of the body's tissues.

16. David G. Myers, *Exploring Psychology in Modules*, 8th ed. (New York: Worth, 2010), 3.

17. For more information on Freud, including the shortcomings of his research, see James W. Kalat, *Introduction to Psychology* (Belmont, CA: Wadsworth, 2011), 500–506.

18. Carl Rogers, "Notes on Rollo May," *Journal of Humanistic Psychology* 22, no. 3 (June 1982): 8.

19. Erich Fromm, *You Shall Be as Gods* (New York: Holt, Rinehart, and Winston, 1966), 7–8.

20. Abraham Maslow, *Toward a Psychology of Being* (New York: Van Nostrand Reinhold, 1968), vi.

21. See Duane Schultz and Sydney Ellen Schultz, *Theories of Personality*, 10th ed. (Belmont, CA: Wadsworth, 2008), 309ff.

22. Maslow, *Toward a Psychology of Being*, 149.

23. Maslow, *Toward a Psychology of Being*, 169.

24. Quoted in I. David Welch, George A. Tate, and Fred Richards, eds., *Humanistic Psychology* (Buffalo: Prometheus Books, 1978), 223.

25. Joyce Milton, *The Road to Malpsychia: Humanistic Psychology and our Discontents* (San Francisco: Encounter Books, 2002).

26. Milton, *Road to Malpsychia*, 152.

27. Milton, *Road to Malpsychia*, 171.

28. Paul C. Vitz, "The Mad Doctors," *National Review* 54, no. 16 (September 2002): 46.

29. Joseph Nahem, *Psychology and Psychiatry Today: A Marxist View* (New York: International Publishers, 1981), 48.

30. Nahem, *Psychology and Psychiatry Today*, 13.

31. Skinner, *Beyond Freedom and Dignity*, 16.

32. B.F. Skinner, *Science and Human Behavior* (New York: Macmillan, 1953), 447.

33. Ivan Pavlov, *Lectures on Conditioned Reflexes* (New York: International Publishers, 1963), 42.

34. Pavlov, *Lectures on Conditioned Reflexes*, 391.

35. Ivan Pavlov, statement to his assistants, February 21, 1936, in W. H. Gantt's introduction to Ivan P. Pavlov, *Lectures on Conditioned Reflexes*, vol. 2, *Conditioned Reflexes and Psychiatry* (New York: International Publishers, 1963), 34.

36 See Ethan Pollock, *Stalin and the Soviet Science Wars* (Princeton, NJ: Princeton University Press, 2008), chap. 6.

37. Ivan Pavlov, *Selected Works* (Moscow: Foreign Languages Publishing House, 1955), 537, in Nahem, *Psychology and Psychiatry Today*, 9.

38. L. S. Vygotsky, *The Collected Works of L. S. Vygotsky*, vol. 1, *Problems of General Psychology*, eds. Robert W. Rieber and Aaron S. Carton, Norris Minick (New York: Plenum, 1987), 45.

39. Pavlov, *Selected Works*, 537.

40. Karl Marx's third thesis on Feuerbach, cited in Nahem, *Psychology and Psychiatry Today*, 45.

41. A. R. Luria, *The Nature of Human Conflicts* (New York: Grove Press, 1960), 401–2.

42. Nahem, *Psychology and Psychiatry Today*, 46.

43. For an interesting look at the often-contentious relationship between Pavlov and Marxism, and the way Marxists sought to control Pavlov's legacy, see David Joravsky, "The Mechanical Spirit: The Stalinist Marriage of Pavlov to Marx," *Theory and Society* 4, no. 4 (Winter 1977): 457–77.

44. Mitchell Stephens, "To Thine Own Selves Be True," *Los Angeles Times Magazine*, August 23, 1992, www.nyu.edu /classes/stephens/Postmodern%20psych%20page.htm.

45. Barbara Epstein states, "The constellation of trends that I am calling Postmodernism has it origins in the writings of a group of French intellectuals of the 60s, the most preeminently Michel Foucault, Jacques Derrida, Jacques Lacan, and Jean-François Lyotard. Those who developed Postmodernism tended to be associated with the radicalism of the 60s." Barbara Epstein, "Postmodernism and the Left," *New Politics* 6, no. 2 (Winter 1997).

46. See Glenn Ward, *Teach Yourself Postmodernism*, 2nd ed. (Chicago: McGraw-Hill, 2003), 149.

47. Quoted in Ward, *Teach Yourself Postmodernism*, 141–42.

48. Kenneth Gergen, *The Saturated Self: Dilemmas of Identity in Contemporary Life* (New York: Basic Books, 2000), 171.

49. Stephens, "To Thine Own Selves."

50. Ward, *Teach Yourself Postmodernism*, 141–42.

51. Ward, *Teach Yourself Postmodernism*, 120.

52. See Gilles Deleuze and Felix Guattari, *Anti-Oedipus: Capitalism and Schizophrenia* (New York: Penguin, 2009). The authors suggest that Western civilization promotes a herd instinct that makes people fear being cut off from the group. People who cut themselves off are considered insane, but they are actually the pure ones, the true individuals.

53. Quoted in Stephens, "To Thine Own Selves."

54. Quoted in Stephens, "To Thine Own Selves."

55. Millard J. Erickson, *Truth or Consequences* (Downers Grove, IL: InterVarsity, 2005), 134.

56. Ken Carey, speech, Whole Life Expo, Los Angeles, CA, February 1987.

57. John White, *Frontiers of Consciousness* (New York: Julian Press, 1985), 7.

58. Marilyn Ferguson, *The Aquarian Conspiracy* (Los Angeles: J. P. Tarcher, 1980), 248.

59. The Dalai Lama, *A Profound Mind* (New York: Three Rivers, 2011), ix.

60. Etan Boritzer, *What Is God?* (Richmond Hill, ON: Firefly Books, 1990), 30.

61. Marianne Williamson, *A Return to Love: Reflections on the Principles of "A Course in Miracles"* (New York: HarperCollins, 1989), 208.

62. Williamson, *Return to Love*, 209.

63. Sahih al-Bukhari, vol. 2, bk. 23, hadith 441, www.quranwebsite.com/hadith/bukhari_volume_2.html.

64. Hammudah Abdalati, *Islam in Focus* (Indianapolis: Amana, 1975), 16.

65. Abdalati, *Islam in Focus*, 32.

66. Norman L. Geisler and Abdul Saleeb, *Answering Islam: The Crescent in Light of the Cross* (Grand Rapids: Baker, 1993), 44.

67. Abdalati, *Islam in Focus*, 52.

68. James 2:14: "What good is it, my brothers, if someone says he has faith but does not have works? Can that faith save him?"; James 2:20: "Do you want to be shown, you foolish person, that faith apart from works is useless?"

69. Ephesians 2:8–10: "By grace you have been saved through faith. And this is not your own doing; it is the gift of God, not a result of works, so that no one may boast. For we are his workmanship, created in Christ Jesus for good works, which God prepared beforehand, that we should walk in them."

70. Abdalati, *Islam in Focus*, 17–18. This stands in distinct contrast to biblical examples of intercession between God and sinful humans (such as Exodus 32:11–14, where Moses interceded on behalf of sinful Israel) and the biblical teaching that the eternal Holy Spirit (Romans 8:26–27) and Christ (Hebrews 7:25) intercede for us.

71. This teaching is also found in the Hadith: Sahih al-Bukhari 1:209, bk. 37, hadith 6655.

72. As the famous Arab historian Ibn Khaldun (1333–1406) said, "In the Muslim community, the holy war is a religious duty, because of the universalism of the (Muslim) mission and (the obligation to) convert everybody to Islam either by persuasion or force." Colin Chapman, *Cross and Crescent: Responding to the Challenge of Islam* (Downers Grove, IL: InterVarsity, 2003), 293.

73. William Kirk Kilpatrick, *Psychological Seduction* (Nashville: Thomas Nelson, 1983), 14.

74. Charles L. Allen, *God's Psychiatry* (Westwood, NJ: Revell, 1953), 7.

75. Genesis 1:27: "God created man in his own image, in the image of God he created him; male and female he created them."

76. Alvin Plantinga, "Advice to Christian Philosophers," *Faith and Philosophy* 1 (July 1984): 264–65, quoted in J. P. Moreland and Scott B. Rae, *Body and Soul: Human Nature and the Crisis in Ethics* (Downers Grove, IL: InterVarsity, 2000), 24.

77. Moreland and Rae, *Body and Soul*, 158.

78. Charles Sherrington, *Man on His Nature* (New York: New American Library, 1964), 256.

79. "General ontology is the most basic of metaphysics, and there are three main tasks that make up this branch of metaphysical study. First, general ontology focuses on the nature of existence itself. What is it to be or to exist? Is existence a property that something has?" J. P. Moreland and William Lane Craig, *Philosophical Foundations for a Christian Worldview* (Downers Grove, IL: InterVarsity, 2003), 175.

80. Matthew 10:28: "Do not fear those who kill the body but cannot kill the soul. Rather fear him who can destroy both soul and body in hell."

81. First Thessalonians 5:23: "May the God of peace himself sanctify you completely, and may your whole spirit and soul and body be kept blameless at the coming of our Lord Jesus Christ."

82. Quoted in Arthur Koestler and J. R. Smythies, eds., *Beyond Reductionism* (London: Hutchinson, 1969), 251–52. For an updated discussion of identity, see Moreland and Craig, *Philosophical Foundations*, 290.

83. Arthur C. Custance, *Man in Adam and in Christ* (Grand Rapids: Zondervan, 1975), 256. Also see Wilder Penfield, *The Mystery of the Mind* (Princeton, NJ: Princeton University Press, 1975).

84. Custance's work was largely based on his review of brain research by John Eccles and Wilder Penfield. But more recent research has yielded even more insights confirming Custance's thesis. See Edward F. Kelly, *Irreducible Mind* (Lanham, MD: Rowman and Littlefield, 2009), and Mario Beauregard, *Brain Wars: The Scientific Battle over the Existence of Mind and the Proof* (New York: HarperOne, 2012). See also Stewart Goetz and Mark C. Baker, *The Soul Hypothesis: Investigations into the Existence of the Soul* (New York: Bloomsbury Academic, 2010).

85. See Mario Beauregard and Denyse O'Leary, *The Spiritual Brain* (New York: HarperOne, 2007); Thomas Nagel, *Mind and Cosmos* (New York: Oxford, 2012); and Eben Alexander, *Proof of Heaven* (New York: Simon and Schuster, 2012).

86. Genesis 2:7: "The LORD God formed the man of dust from the ground and breathed into his nostrils the breath of life, and the man became a living creature."

87. Moreland and Rae, *Body and Soul*, 17.

88. One argument against mind/body dualism is that people who have suffered traumatic brain injury often emerge with different personalities. Research on this kind of thing is very difficult because we would have to know a great deal about a person's behavior, personality, and sense of identity before the injury and then try to figure out what changes can be attributed to the trauma. The research on the relationship between brain functions and psychological processes is not as advanced as those arguing against dualism would like to think. See Goetz and Baker, *Soul Hypothesis* for more information.

89. Psalm 14:1: "The fool says in his heart, 'There is no God.' They are corrupt, they do abominable deeds, there is none who does good."

90. Jeremiah 17:9: "The heart is deceitful above all things, and desperately sick; who can understand it?"

91. Paul Vitz, *Psychology as Religion* (Grand Rapids: Eerdmans, 1985), 43.

92. J. M. Milne, "Sin," in D. R. W. Wood et al., eds., *New Bible Dictionary*, 3rd ed. (Downers Grove, IL: InterVarsity, 1996), 1105–6.

93. There is a vein of psychology that argues that the vast number of possible diagnoses may actually have a hypochondriac effect, making us think of ourselves as sick. See, for example, Herb Kutchins and Stuart A. Kirk, *Making Us Crazy: DSM [Diagnostic Statistical Manual]: The Psychiatric Bible and the Creation of Mental Disorders* (New York: Free Press, 1997).

94. Karl Menninger, *Whatever Became of Sin?* (New York: Hawthorn Books, 1974), 95.

95. Lawrence Crabb Jr., *Basic Principles of Biblical Counseling* (Grand Rapids: Zondervan, 1975), 102.

96. Jay E. Adams, *Competent to Counsel* (Grand Rapids: Baker, 1970), 32–33.

97. James 5:16: "Confess your sins to one another and pray for one another, that you may be healed. The prayer of a righteous person has great power as it is working."

98. First John 1:9: "If we confess our sins, he is faithful and just to forgive us our sins and to cleanse us from all unrighteousness."

99. Second Corinthians 5:17–21: "If anyone is in Christ, he is a new creation. The old has passed away; behold, the new has come. All this is from God, who through Christ reconciled us to himself and gave us the ministry of reconciliation; that is, in Christ God was reconciling the world to himself, not counting their trespasses against them, and entrusting to us the message of reconciliation. Therefore, we are ambassadors for Christ, God making his appeal through us. We implore you on behalf of Christ, be reconciled to God. For our sake he made him to be sin who knew no sin, so that in him we might become the righteousness of God."

100. First Thessalonians 5:23: "May the God of peace himself sanctify you completely, and may your whole spirit and soul and body be kept blameless at the coming of our Lord Jesus Christ"; Hebrews 12:1–11: "Since we are surrounded

by so great a cloud of witnesses, let us also lay aside every weight, and sin which clings so closely, and let us run with endurance the race that is set before us, looking to Jesus, the founder and perfecter of our faith, who for the joy that was set before him endured the cross, despising the shame, and is seated at the right hand of the throne of God. Consider him who endured from sinners such hostility against himself, so that you may not grow weary or fainthearted. In your struggle against sin you have not yet resisted to the point of shedding your blood. And have you forgotten the exhortation that addresses you as sons? 'My son, do not regard lightly the discipline of the Lord, nor be weary when reproved by him. For the Lord disciplines the one he loves, and chastises every son whom he receives.' It is for discipline that you have to endure. God is treating you as sons. For what son is there whom his father does not discipline? If you are left without discipline, in which all have participated, then you are illegitimate children and not sons. Besides this, we have had earthly fathers who disciplined us and we respected them. Shall we not much more be subject to the Father of spirits and live? For they disciplined us for a short time as it seemed best to them, but he disciplines us for our good, that we may share his holiness. For the moment all discipline seems painful rather than pleasant, but later it yields the peaceful fruit of righteousness to those who have been trained by it."

101. See *Proceedings and Addresses of the American Philosophical Association* 78, no. 2 (November 2004). For more information on the Virtues Project, visit www.virtuesproject.com.

102. Quoted in Pamela Paul, "The Power to Uplift," *Time*, January 9, 2005, http://content.time.com/time/magazine /article/0,9171,1015870-1,00.html.

103. Paul, "Power to Uplift."

104. Paul C. Vitz, "Psychology in Recovery," *First Things*, March 2005, 19, accessed March 31, 2014, www.firstthings .com/article/2007/01/psychology-in-recovery-41.

105. Vitz, "Psychology in Recovery."

106. Selections from Philippians 2–4.

107. Francis Schaeffer, *The Complete Works of Francis Schaeffer*, 5 vols. (Westchester, IL: Crossway Books, 1982), 3:334.

108. For an accounting of soul, spirit, mind, heart, etc., see Moreland and Rae, *Body and Soul*.

109. Vitz, "Psychology in Recovery."

110. To study the different ways psychologists are attempting to reintegrate the idea of the soul into the discipline of psychology, take a look at Eric Johnson, ed., *Psychology and Christianity: The Five Views* (Downers Grove, IL: IVP Academic, 2010). The five views are (1) the levels-of-explanation view (David G. Myers), (2) the integration view (Stanton Jones), (3) the Christian psychology view (Robert C. Robers and Paul J. Watson), (4) the transformative view (John Coe and Todd Hall), and (5) the biblical counseling view (David Powlison).

111. Kilpatrick, *Psychological Seduction*, 233.

CHAPTER 13

SOCIOLOGY

1. IN THE MIDST OF A SEISMIC SHIFT

With a national population of thirteen million (roughly equivalent to present-day Illinois), America in the 1830s had a lot more elbow room. The War of Independence was still fresh in the national memory, and many of its veterans were still alive. Andrew Jackson presided over a rapidly growing economy. The country's mood, according to Thomas Low Nichols, was optimistic:

> We had no doubt that ours was the freest, most enlightened, and happiest country, in the world. We knew that where there was a will there was a way, and our teachers constantly stimulated us by the glittering prizes of wealth, honors, offices, and distinctions which were certainly within our reach.... There were a hundred avenues to wealth and fame opening fair before us, if we only chose to learn our lessons. Of course we learnt them.[1]

French sociologist Alexis de Tocqueville visited America during this time and recorded his observations in *Democracy in America*. De Tocqueville was impressed but sober: strong societies often collapse if people lose the will to maintain them. In one particularly prophetic passage, he wrote,

> Because Roman civilization perished through barbarian invasions, we are perhaps too much inclined to think that that is the only way a civilization can die. If the lights that guide us ever go out, they will fade little by little, as if of their own accord.... We therefore should not console ourselves by thinking that the barbarians are still a long way off. Some peoples may let the torch be snatched from their hands, but others stamp it out themselves.[2]

For de Tocqueville, the choice was to earn the honor of future generations by standing for truth and justice or to let history record that you lived in the greatest of times and did nothing to preserve them.

Within three decades, de Tocqueville's prophecy began coming true. America's work ethic led to an industrial boom that, in turn, reshaped society and brought to a fever pitch the tensions between the industrialized north and agrarian south. The Union was preserved and slavery abolished, and industrialization resumed at a frenzied pace with prosperity, convenience, and technological breakthroughs. But along with these benefits came child labor, pollution, and unrest—just like England fifty years prior.

> **The Industrial Revolution reshaped society and set America on a path from which, for better or worse, it could never return.**

The Industrial Revolution reshaped society and set America on a path from which, for better or worse, it could never return. How do we understand and live in a world unlike anything humankind has experienced before? Max Weber, based on his study of the Protestant tradition, thought industrialization could be rationally organized and guided. Emile Durkheim (the first person to call himself a sociologist) bemoaned the effect it had on individuals who both unleashed it and were swept along by it. But it was Karl Marx's views of the Industrial Revolution—that it was a sinister way for industrialists to enrich themselves at the expense of workers—that had an earthshaking impact.

These three individuals—Marx, Weber, and Durkheim—by analyzing and proposing solutions for the rapid changes in society that industrialization brought about, ended up forming a brand new and very influential academic discipline called **sociology**. *Socios* is the Greek word from which we get our word *society*. Whereas the psychologist studies the individual and how he or she relates to others, the sociologist studies the interactions of individuals and society.

> *Sociology:* the study of human societies and institutions.

The social situation today makes this kind of study hugely important. James Dobson and Gary Bauer argued in their book *Children at Risk*, "Nothing short of a great Civil War of Values rages today throughout North America. Two sides with vastly differing and incompatible worldviews are locked in a bitter conflict that permeates every level of society."[3] The structure, stability, and belief system of America are rapidly shifting, especially among the young:

- The percentage of students identifying themselves as liberals has reached a forty-year high: two out of three support same-sex marriage, and only one in four support military spending.[4]
- The Millennials, those born between 1980 and 2001, have the lowest level of church attendance of any generation in American history.[5]
- Among those who do attend church in high school, only 30 percent maintain a similar level of commitment in their twenties.[6]
- One out of three young people lives in a home where no biological father is present.[7] Stable families make a stable society, but instability is now the norm.
- One out of four adolescents in the United States is currently at serious risk of not achieving a productive adulthood (i.e., holding down a job, creating a stable family, and making a positive contribution to the community).[8]
- Only one in twenty families engages in any spiritual training outside of church.[9]

Societal change has the greatest effect on the most ideologically vulnerable: the young. Sociologist Christian Smith says today's young adults are "more complex, disjointed, confused, and unstable compared to the same ages in previous generations."[10] This should concern us all. Young adults may only be 15 percent of the population, but they are 100 percent of the future.

If we are to love God with all of our minds, we must gain a clear-eyed understanding of the times. This will involve the careful study of society.

2. THE STUDY OF SOCIETY IS VITAL

Beginning with the work of Marx, Weber, and Durkheim, and continuing through scholars like Charles Horton Cooley, Erving Goffman, Talcott Parsons, and George Herbert Mead, the field of sociology has had to fight for academic respect. Many in the field itself still debate whether sociology can accurately be described as a science, or whether it is even a good idea to bring the scientific method to bear on social problems.

Every academic discipline makes certain assumptions about metaphysics (what is real) and epistemology (how we know). Like psychology, modern sociology operates under assumptions that contradict the Christian worldview. For example, according to Steve Bruce, a chronicler of sociology's history, sociology hangs on three threads: "Reality is socially constructed, our behavior has hidden social causes, and much of social life is profoundly ironic."[11] These are code words. To say reality is "socially constructed" is to say that no institutions of society, such as the family, are ordained by God. To say our behavior has "hidden social causes" is to say that society causes us to do what we do; we aren't making choices but are responding to external stimuli. And if social life is "profoundly ironic" (coincidental), then there is no purpose or design in the world—only the illusion of meaning.

All three points assume materialism (only matter exists) and naturalism (all that happens can be explained by natural causes and processes); there is no supernatural reality. We have no ultimate purpose. This leads to a conflict for the Christian scholar. If sociology is truly built on these three anti-Christian assumptions, then Christian sociology is an oxymoron, like "untrue truth" or "married bachelor," which cannot exist without an unreasonable distortion of the terms employed.

And yet many sociologists have strong religious, even Christian, convictions. Pitirim Sorokin, founder of the Harvard sociology department and an ardent foe of communism, was an Orthodox Christian. Some highly regarded sociologists of our day—Peter Berger, namely, as well as James Davidson Hunter and Christian Smith—claim a Christian faith. How do we explain this?

Sociology is yet one more academic discipline where underlying assumptions conflict. As we examine the interaction between individuals and society—including origin, importance, authority, and proper structures—should we regard certain philosophical assumptions, such as "only nature exists," to be absolutely true? Secular, Marxist, and postmodern sociologists say yes; New Spiritualists, Muslims, and Christians say no. Which perspective will lead to the best work in sociology? To answer this question, we will explore each worldview's approach as it seeks to understand individuals and society. We will focus mostly on family, marriage, and child rearing, since political, legal, and economic structures will be considered in later chapters.

3. SECULARISM

Perhaps, Victor thinks, a hike in the mountains will help. He hopes to relieve his heavy agony—brought on by the destruction wrought by Victor's own creation. But he is sadly mistaken. There on the icy slopes, Dr. Victor Frankenstein comes face-to-face with the superhuman monster he brought to life and which has in turn killed those dearest to him.

Victor's revulsion is complete: "Abhorred monster," he cries out, "fiend that thou art! The tortures of hell are too mild a vengeance for thy crimes."[12]

Frankenstein's monster will have none of it. "I was benevolent and good; misery made me a fiend. Make me happy, and again I shall be virtuous."[13]

Mary Shelley's story helps us understand the starting point of secular sociology: individual selves who are free to do what makes them happy. This is called **personal autonomy**. Unfortunately, to secular sociologists, society conspires against our yearning to be free to do what we want, and this hurts both individuals and society. "Essentially man is internally motivated toward positive personal and social ends," say Robert Tannenbaum and Sheldon A. Davis. "The extent to which he is not motivated results from a process of demotivation generated by his relationships and/or environment."[14] According to the secular sociologist, society constrains us—and society must set us free.[15]

Personal Autonomy: the belief that individuals should have the freedom to decide what is right for their own lies and live in whatever manner brings them the most happiness.

When secular sociologists think of societal constraints against personal autonomy, their thoughts almost always turn to the political realm. Those who enroll in sociology classes are often caught off guard by their professors' advocacy of society-wide, and specifically governmental, solutions to human problems. The nature of the discipline is, says Patricia Hill Collins, "highly political."[16] It is common to see "science" deployed as a veneer to give credibility to the preordained, politically correct solutions at which sociologists aim.[17] As Secular Humanist historian Vern Bullough admitted in reference to sexual politics, "Politics and science go hand in hand. In the end it is gay activism which determines what researchers say about gay people."[18]

Secularists often use sociology as a forward operating base from which they can take political ground and simultaneously sally forth against ideas they find distasteful. According to Christian Smith, sociology was conceived with two goals: to do away with religious influence and to advance progressivism. Referring to two of its founders, Auguste Comte and Herbert Spencer, Smith says, "Both provided what proved to be key intellectual tools utilized by rising academic elites seeking to displace religious authority in order to make room for themselves as new, secular cultural authorities."[19] Secular assumptions "provide the positive knowledge for a secular basis of a new and progressive social order."[20]

> Sociology was conceived with two goals: to do away with religious influence and to advance progressivism.

While Smith indicts sociology as being inherently anti-religious, others, like Christopher Dawson, say that the dismissal of religious concerns was inevitable based on the way the specialized disciplines are organized.[21] But in sociology's case, this is too charitable. If Smith is correct, sociology is a pillow carefully embroidered to suffocate religious impulses while they doze. According to Hunter Baker, Secularists view religion as properly irrelevant to public life:

> Although the U.S. is one of the most religious of the developed nations, there is still an expectation among those who define public reality in the media, academy, and government that appeals to God should be saved for one's private life.... To swim against the tide of secular modernity indicates one may be uncivil, unbalanced, and possibly even dangerous.[22]

In this view, religion is quaint and a little bit crazy, but essentially it's harmless until people smuggle it into public life—at which time it becomes alarming.

Organizing sociology around secular principles does lead to some philosophical problems. For example, if only matter exists, then human "choices" aren't really choices at all—we can do only what our genes and our environment make us do. This is called *determinism*. One popular sociology textbook, written by Anthony Giddens and his colleagues, though, positions sociology as a *response* to determinism:

> There is a basic flaw in human reasoning that goes something like this: the things that we see before us are inevitable. They are natural and cannot be changed. What sociology teaches us is that in many ways we are freer than we think—that the things that we think are natural are actually created by human beings.[23]

One purpose of sociology, the authors say, is "to disentangle what is biological from what is socially constructed."[24] While Giddens and his colleagues express suspicion toward **biological determinism**, they acknowledge a sort of **sociological determinism** in which human actions are "quite determined by our social roles, gender, race, and class."[25] This makes it hard to tell whether they are responding to determinism or expanding their definition of it in order to explain the complexities of human behavior.[26]

Biological Determinism: the belief that our actions are ultimately the result of our genetic makeup.

Sociological Determinism: the belief that our actions are ultimately the result of social conditions.

Deviance: behavior or actions that violate consensual social norms.

Determinism, whether biological or sociological, leads to another philosophical dilemma on the ethical nature of human behavior. If human behavior is determined, people cannot choose their actions. Thus, nothing they do is either good or bad, nor is it done out of an ethical impulse. There is no sin nature; people merely do what they do. But this does not square with our experience; we *know* certain things are wrong even before any courts of law weigh in. Sociologists acknowledge that some people do things most of us do not like. But instead of calling it *sin*, they use the term **deviance**, which is defined as "nonconformity to a set of norms that are accepted by a significant number of people in a community or society."[27]

So there is no sin—just nonconformity. And yet sociologists constantly express concern about things in society they don't like, such as inequality between the sexes and races. On what basis would they say these things are wrong? Telling a society to stop providing unequal access to societal rewards[28] is to tell them to do something sociology declares impossible—to right a wrong by making an actual, conscious free choice. In a purely materialistic and naturalistic world, people could no more choose to stand against inequality than they could choose to run as fast as cheetahs or breathe through gill slits. They just don't have the equipment, and that's all there is to it.

How, one might ask, can society be made up of sinless people and yet be filled with so much sin? The sociologist's response is to say that, once formed, society takes on a life of its own and then forces us into living in certain ways that hurt us. Psychologist Erich Fromm spoke of "the social process which creates man"[29] and said, "Just as primitive man was helpless before natural forces, modern man is helpless before the social and economic forces created by himself."[30] Sane people create society, which goes insane and then drives everybody crazy.

What kinds of bad structures do good people create? Secular sociologists point mostly to government and religion. With good intentions, people invent rules they cannot live by, which in turn suffocate their freedom to grow as they naturally would. Walda Katz-Fishman and George Benello declare that secular sociology "seeks the concrete betterment of humankind and is opposed to theories that seek either to glorify the status quo or to march human beings lockstep into history in the interests of a vision imposed from above."[31]

"Religious institutions are the enemy." Where have you heard this before? In the secular approach to every discipline we have examined so far, of course. If, Secularists say, society tries to line up with the expectations of a nonexistent deity, then it will eventually disappoint everyone. Deluded people driving a vehicle of fantasy will never arrive at the destination of reality. This is a charge Christians and others might lay against Secularism as well, but we'll get to that soon enough.

Secular sociologists are particularly critical of the biblical view of the family. Marriage, they say, is exhibit number one of Christianity's failure to provide for human potential and growth. To Lawrence Casler, a psychology professor whose academic study included observing and interviewing nudists, "Marriage and family life have been largely responsible … for today's prevailing neurotic climate, with its pervasive insecurity, and it is precisely this climate that makes so difficult the acceptance of a different, healthier way of life."[32] The idea of a man and woman faithful to each other for life isn't all it is cracked up to be, Secularists hold. Women trade freedom for security, and what they get is slavery. As Syracuse "sexologist" Sol Gordon maintained, "The traditional family, with all its supposed attributes, enslaved woman; it reduced her to a breeder and caretaker of children, a servant to her spouse, a cleaning lady, and at times a victim of the labor market as well."[33]

> Secular sociologists are particularly critical of the biblical view of the family.

Secular sociologists have suggested numerous alternative lifestyles to replace the traditional family. Robert N. Whitehurst, the late professor of sociology at the University of Windsor in Ontario, Canada, advocated open marriage (i.e., open to adultery), triads, cooperatives, collectives, urban communes, extended intimates, swinging and group marriage, and part-time marriage.[34] In *A New Bill of Sexual Rights and Responsibilities*, sex educator Lester Kirkendall advocated all of the above but also included something in his list called "genital associations," though no one is quite sure what this means.[35]

Most people get suspicious at this point; it's one thing to tolerate aberrant sexuality but quite another to make it appear to be normal or even good. In making the case for normalizing what used to be seen as deviant, secular sociology has been considerably helped by popular-culture presentations of likable characters who embrace alternative lifestyles. For example, the Gay and Lesbian Alliance Against Defamation (GLAAD) offers a series of awards to TV shows that, in part, "[impact] society in a significant way." When choosing nominees, they ask question like, "Does this project dramatically increase the cultural dialogue about LGBT (lesbian, gay, bisexual, and transgender) issues? Or, does this project reach an audience that is not regularly exposed to LGBT images and issues?"[36]

As we stated earlier, social experimentation ends up being most harmful for the most vulnerable. In this case, the ones hurt are children. A raft of research demonstrates that sexual experimentation on the part of parents is strongly correlated to negative outcomes for the children, such as crime and substance abuse, whereas the children most likely to succeed as adults are those who grow up with a mother and father.[37] In spite of this, Casler envisioned a society where children will be better off because everyone in the family will be free from the norms that make some people unhappy: "It is supposed that the principles of ethical, productive, and happy living will be learned more readily when children are free of the insecurities, engendered chiefly by parents, that ordinarily obstruct the internalization of these modes of thought."[38]

> A raft of research demonstrates that sexual experimentation on the part of parents is strongly correlated to negative outcomes for the children, such as crime and substance abuse, whereas the children most likely to succeed as adults are those who grow up with a mother and father.

Casler may truly believe this, but it's not because of evidence. When confronted with overwhelming documentation to the contrary, secular sociologists become defensive. Advocating for traditional families is, in effect, a condemnation of all other families, which is harmful to children who live in those families. This is an odd way of arguing. Would these professors tell their students not to pay attention in class because serious study is, in effect, a condemnation of less-studious students? We doubt it. They instead would encourage less-studious students to study. So why don't these same scholars encourage people to enter traditional marriages, maintain them, and raise good kids? As John Stonestreet points out, every worldview is willing to sacrifice something on the altar of its convictions. If we are primarily animals, and if the sexual impulse is the strongest impulse we have, then Secularism is willing to sacrifice *everything* on the altar of sexual freedom: innocence, the safety of children, protection of the unborn human; indeed, what it means to be human altogether.[39]

For Secularists, tradition is pathological; to return to the way society used to be makes things worse, not better. Give us power to reorient society according to our ideology, Secularists say, and we'll fix things right up. Erich Fromm, for example, quite openly bid for such power. He defined the "sane society" as "that which corresponds to the needs of man—not necessarily to what he feels to be his needs, because even the most pathological aims can be felt subjectively as that which the person wants most; but to what his needs are objectively, as they can be ascertained by the study of man."[40] We might be forgiven for reading this statement as "*We*, the experts, will tell you what you need." If, based on materialism and naturalism, secular sociologists were to do the telling, would things get better or worse? Secular sociologists think they'd be better, and so they press ahead in that assumption.

4. MARXISM

According to the Marxist theoretician G. V. Plekhanov, Marxists ground their sociology in what they consider to be the scientific foundation of "Darwinism in its application to social science."[41] Humanity is evolving both biologically and socially; as humanity improves, so does society. Marxists fervently believe humanity's evolution will move them beyond the misery-inducing capitalist structures of society. As we saw in the chapter on Marxism, V. I. Lenin believed this evolution would even eliminate the need for government: "Only in Communist society when the resistance of the capitalists has been completely broken, when the capitalists have disappeared, when there are no classes ... only then the State ceases to exist."[42]

Proletariat Society: a socialist society shaped by Communist Party officials to promote the values of the working class over the bourgeoisie

To the Marxists, a good society is a **proletariat society** in which society becomes healthy by abandoning capitalism and embracing the values of the workers, which the Marxists see as more pure.

As mentioned earlier, Marx is widely considered to be one of the founders of sociology. The other two founders, Max Weber and Emile Durkheim, began their work after Marx's death. Marx would probably have been suspicious of Weber and Durkheim because they seemed to focus on making the best of industrialism's negative side effects. Marx didn't want to *improve* present conditions within the existing framework; he wanted instead to *overthrow* the framework.

As you recall from our summary of the worldview, Marxists believe that economic realities are at the root of everything. A time of economic revolution is inevitable, Marx believed, and this transforms everything else:

> [At a certain stage of society] the material productive forces of society come into conflict with the existing relations of production.... From forms of development of the productive forces these relations turn into their fetters. Then begins an era of social revolution. The changes in the economic foundation lead sooner or later to the transformation of the whole immense superstructure.[43]

In spite of some Marxists' suspicions of secular sociology, Marx did believe, as Secularists do, that human beings are nothing more than what their societies make them: "The mode of production of material life conditions the general process of social, political, and intellectual life. It is not the consciousness of men that determines their existence but their social existence that determines their consciousness."[44] Our material conditions, not our aspirations, will determine what we become.[45]

Marxists see religion as a stumbling block hampering the development of the classless society. In the quest for this utopian existence, the church makes things worse, not better. Clemens Dutt summarizes the Marxist view:

> The influence of the church promotes the schism of the [workers'] movement. Reactionary churchmen everywhere try to isolate religious workers from their class brothers by attracting them into separate organizations of a clerical nature ... and thus diverting them from the struggle against capitalism.[46]

This explains why, in the former Soviet Union, Marxists aggressively sought to eliminate the influence of the church. In the early days following the October Revolution, in an effort to discourage anyone from joining the clergy, Marxists discriminated against priests. When this failed to wipe out religion, Marxists tried to further restrict the church through state controls. On April 8, 1929, for example, the USSR enacted a law forbidding religious organizations from carrying out charitable activities or meeting at any time other than for religious services. In effect, Marxist sociologists declared war against the church, a conflict that continues to the present day wherever communists are in power.[47] When the final Soviet leader, Mikhail Gorbachev, said that the communists had launched a "war on religion," he correctly described the sentiments of not only Karl Marx but Marxist sociologists and a long line of communists worldwide even today.[48]

Marxists also consider the traditional idea of the family to hinder progress because it is seen as illicitly hoarding capital and wealth. According to Marxist revolutionary and novelist Alexandra Kollontai, "The family deprives the worker of revolutionary consciousness" and must, therefore, be shunned.[49] In *The Communist Manifesto* Marx wrote, "The bourgeois family will vanish as a matter of course when its complement vanishes, and both will vanish with the vanishing of capital." Furthermore, "The bourgeois sees his wife [as] a mere instrument of production. He hears that the instruments of production are to be

> **Marxists also consider the traditional idea of the family to hinder progress because it is seen as illicitly hoarding capital and wealth.**

---

exploited in common, and, naturally, can come to no other conclusion that the lot of being common to all will likewise fall to the women."[50]

Once the proletariat is in power, Marxists believe, a new utopian society will develop a higher form of family. No one is really sure what this higher form will look like, except for one thing: there will be few sexual boundaries in it. Friedrich Engels seemed almost giddy about this:

> With the transfer of the means of production into common ownership, the single family ceases to be the economic unit of society. Private housekeeping is transformed into a social industry. The care and education of the children becomes a public affair; society looks after all children alike, whether they are legitimate or not. This removes all the anxiety about the consequences [of sex] which today is the most essential social-moral as well as economic factor that prevents a girl from giving herself completely to the man she loves. Will not that suffice to bring about the gradual growth of unconstrained sexual intercourse and with it a more tolerant public opinion in regard to a maiden's honor and a woman's shame?[51]

In this brave new world, men and women become sexually free because the abolition of private property is supposed to free people from so-called moral restrictions that many believe to actually be a form of economic oppression. Everyone belongs to everyone, and that solves everything.

When asked, "What influence will the communist order of society have on the family?" Engels answered,

> It will make the relation between the sexes a purely private relation which concerns only the persons involved, and in which society has no call to interfere. It is able to do this because it abolishes private property and educates children communally, thus destroying the twin foundations of hitherto existing marriage—the dependence through private property of the wife upon the husband and of the children upon the parents.[52]

The care of children also becomes a public affair in Marxist society. The "school becomes literally a home."[53] Alienating children from their parents keeps them from picking up their parents' lingering attachment to the old ways of living.

While the USSR no longer exists as such, the bloodshed it produced convinced most of the world to view Marx's utopian schemes as tragedy rather than triumph. Some Marxist evangelists, such as literature professor Terry Eagleton, shrug off this tragedy by blaming it on bad Marxists rather than on Marxism itself.[54] Marxism failed, Eagleton says, because it did not have the opportunity to take over the entire world and impose its system universally.[55] For obvious reasons, most nations have considered and rejected this "I know you think I am a totalitarian, but give me complete control of the world and I will show you I am not" argument. When someone says, "I'm no thief, but I offer you a choice: your money or your life," you should assume, despite whatever he claims to be, that he is prepared to take both. For the record, Marx himself insisted that communism must be imposed worldwide. The final words of *The Communist Manifesto* call upon the workers of the world to "unite"—they have "a world to win."[56]

Contrary to popular sentiment that Marxism is a good idea on paper that just never worked in practice, the frightening implications of a Marxist sociology show that Marxism was a bad idea right from the start. Its underlying assumptions simply do not match up with reality. Some years ago a movie called *Enemy at the Gates* captured this sentiment with poetic precision. As the ace Russian sniper Vassili waits patiently for his target, his friend Danilov says,

> For the record, Marx himself insisted that communism must be imposed worldwide. The final words of *The Communist Manifesto* call upon the workers of the world to "unite"—they have "a world to win."

> I've been such a fool, Vassili. Man will always be man. There is no new man. We tried so hard to create a society that was equal, where there would be nothing to envy your neighbor. But there is always something to envy. A smile, a friendship, something you don't have and want to appropriate. In this world, even a Soviet one, there will always be rich and poor—rich in gifts, poor in gifts; rich in love, poor in love.

Overlooking this simple truth, Marxism pushed the domino of envy, setting in motion a cascade of consequences affecting billions of people to this day. Short of a miraculous change of heart and mind at the societal level, the suffering is almost sure to continue.

5. POSTMODERNISM

The Postmodernist agrees with the Secularist and the Marxist: humans are nothing more than the sum total of the economic, legal, and personal relationships developed in a given society. Michel Foucault said,

> The most crucial subject to our existence [is] the society in which we live, the economic relations within which it functions, and the system of power which defines the regular forms and the regular permissions and prohibitions of our conduct. The essence of our life consists, after all, of the political functioning of the society in which we find ourselves.[57]

Living within this order is "the essence of our life." Our culture determines who we are. To Fredric Jameson, a Marxist professor who regularly comments on Postmodernism, not even space and time are "natural"; they are "projected afterimages" of structures of making and acquiring things.[58]

Postmodernism in sociology, then, can be described as **social constructionism**, the belief that human beings and society do not have essences that exist in and of themselves, but are constructed through many layers of conversations and experiences.

Social Constructionism: the belief that human beings and society are social constructions shaped by language and subjective experiences.

If society is the sum total of our relationships, then what glue holds those relationships together? Jacques Derrida said the one thing that universally signifies the relationship between our physical existence and our minds is spoken language.[59] Spoken language (and our writing down what we say) is at the heart of the Postmodernists' concern. If no metanarratives (unifying stories about the world that aspire to explain everything as if from a God's-eye viewpoint) are true, all we can do is talk about our preferences, and these preferences are all valid, no matter how ridiculous or incoherent they appear.[60] Ironically, Postmodernists end up building a metanarrative of *talk*, and those who chat away under the illusion that their talk is worth listening to, or whose nonverbal behavior situates them powerfully, become the new cultural elite.

When it comes to deconstructing society's institutions, Postmodernists are particularly critical of religion, especially Roman Catholicism. In *The Future of Religion*, Richard Rorty described his view as "anticlericalism" rather than "atheism." He didn't object to congregations of "the faithful" but targeted "ecclesiastical institutions" as dangerous to a society's health. "Religion is unobjectionable," he said, "as long as it is privatized."[61] You can be crazy on your own time—but when religious people start getting together, they form ideas about society, and such ideas must be firmly rejected. In his speeches, Rorty often quoted Denis Diderot: "Man will never be free until the last king is strangled with the entrails of the last priest."[62]

Postmodernists, those of a Secularist bent anyway, show their contempt for Christian concepts of love, sex, and marriage. Postmodernist psychiatrist Adam Phillips is particularly harsh: "The only sane foregone conclusion about any relationship is that it is an experiment; and that exactly what it is an experiment in will never be clear to the participants. For the sane, so-called relationships could never be subject to contract."[63] To this way of thinking, it is insane to desire marriage. The very concept of a father, mother, and children forms a "heterosexist norm," which enables society "to marginalize some sexual practices as 'against nature,' and thereby [attempt] to prove the naturalness of the heterosexual monogamy and family values upon which mainstream society bases itself."[64]

So how should we rid ourselves of this "heterosexist norm?" By pushing the boundaries so far that people forget what used to be normal. This means talking about sex all the time, and the more deviant, the better. According to Foucault,

> [Talk about sex reveals] an ever expanding encyclopedia of preferences, gratifications and perversions. It creates a realm of perversion by discovering, commenting on and exploring it. It brings it into being as an object of study and in doing so serves to categorize and objectify those who occupy what has been made into the secret underworld of "deviance."[65]

To Foucault, the problem was not the perversion of sex but feeling guilty for having done so: "We must ... ask why we burden ourselves today with so much guilt for having once made sex a sin."[66]

Speaking for himself, Foucault admitted to being "a disciple of the Marquis de Sade."[67] This is, or ought to be, troubling to civilized people. De Sade was a French aristocrat who sexually mistreated everyone around him and gleefully recorded his violent and criminal acts in books. The term *sadism*, the enjoyment of inflicting pain on others, is derived from his name.

For Postmodernists, there is something wrong with people who are uncomfortable with endless talk about aberrant sexuality. Some universities, Yale University, the University of Southern California, and the University of Tennessee among them, host "sex weeks" in which pornographic films are screened, porn stars are featured on campus (as speakers, presumably), and safe-sex kits are handed out. Many universities have approved courses that focus on issues related to sex and gender conflicts. For example, Stanford University's 2013–2014 course listing included FEMGEN 140A—Destroying Dichotomies: Exploring Multiple Sex, Gender, and Sexual Identities:

> For Postmodernists, there is something wrong with people who are uncomfortable with endless talk about aberrant sexuality.

> This course is designed to broaden the student's awareness of the human experience by introducing scholarly debates about sex, gender and sexual identities and expressions. We will consider the socially constructed nature of sex, gender and sexuality and examine the history and community of those who identify as intersexual, transgender, homosexual, bisexual, asexual, pansexual and/or queer through texts, discussion, films, and class presentations.[68]

Why, one might ask, do Postmodernists insist on being so "in your face" about sex? As you will recall from our chapter on Postmodernism, Postmodernists view all metanarratives with suspicion. To Jean-François Lyotard, openly talking about things that make people uncomfortable was a way to "gnaw away at the great institutionalized narrative apparatuses … by increasing the number of skirmishes that take place on the sidelines."[69]

For Lyotard, this "gnawing away" included picking quarrels with people who disagree, turning vices into virtues. He went so far as to defend the actions of the North American Man/Boy Love Association (NAMBLA), whose motto was once "Eight is too late," meaning that men should be allowed to engage in consensual sex with boys under the age of eight.[70] Glenn Ward says, "None of these activities might strike you as particularly radical—they are perhaps not going to bring about a revolution—but from Lyotard's point of view they can be valued as disruptive skirmishes in the social system."[71]

It is unclear what Postmodernists think these actions will accomplish, if anything, in building a healthy society. This much is clear, though: Postmodernists, those who react so strongly against the idea that we have any direct access to reality, act as if they have direct access when it comes to trying to break the "heterosexist norm" so that everything possible becomes permissible, everything permissible becomes desirable, and everything desirable becomes normal. If you don't like it, don't be surprised if Postmodernists accuse you of being a bigot who wants to mandate your intolerant point of view.

6. New Spirituality

Because social institutions imply structure and limits, New Spiritualists tend to view them as outdated. The only limit is this: be responsible. "Your decision to evolve consciously through responsible choice," says Gary Zukav, "contributes not only to your own evolution, but also to the evolution of all of those aspects of humanity in which you participate. It is not just you that is evolving through your decisions, but the entirety of humanity."[72]

As we discussed in the "Psychology" chapter, the New Spiritualist says there is no such thing as an individual person, or "self." There is only consciousness, and we are all an inseparable part of it. Psychology, the study of the person, and sociology, the study of society, are

> **Collective Consciousness:** the belief that everything is ultimately energy and that everyone possesses the potential to achieve divine unity with the cosmos.

really the same thing. In sociology, New Spirituality can be described by the term **collective consciousness**, the belief that together we can pursue higher consciousness and arrive at a healthy, happy society.

New Spiritualists express concern when they perceive society's structures as limiting people's ability or inclination to pursue higher consciousness. According to Marilyn Ferguson, "Every society, by offering its automatic judgments, limits the vision of its members. From our earliest years we are seduced into a system of beliefs that becomes so inextricably braided into our experience that we cannot tell culture from nature."[73]

Social institutions, according to the New Spiritualist, should be structured to encourage the search for inner truth. David Spangler suggests looking at the objects, people, and events in our lives and saying, "You are sacred. In you and with you I can find the sacramental passages that reconnect me to the wholeness of creation." With this perspective it will presumably become clear what kind of political, economic, artistic, educational, or scientific institutions we need.[74]

New Spiritualists who have meditated on these "sacramental passages" have apparently concluded one thing, at least: marriage is a sacramental dead end. Shakti Gawain enthuses, "People who divorce almost inevitably feel that they have failed, because they assume all marriages should last forever. In most such cases, however, the marriage has actually been a total success—it's helped each person to grow to the point where they no longer need its old form."[75]

What of those who may be hurt by the divorce, the children or a spouse who wants to stay married? Their pain simply shows how unenlightened they are. To Gawain, attempting to maintain traditional marriage and family is counterevolutionary:

> Relationships and families as we've known them seem to be falling apart at a rapid rate. Many people are panicky about this; some try to re-establish the old traditions and value systems in order to cling to a feeling of order and stability in their lives. It's useless to try to go backward, however, because our consciousness has already evolved beyond the level where we were willing to make the sacrifices necessary to live that way.[76]

Limits hamper growth; let us do away with them. According to Kevin Ryerson, "An individual's sexual preference should be viewed as neither good nor evil—such preferences are but the functioning of the body's dialogue to and with another."[77]

The heart of society's problem, New Spiritualists say, is ignorance of higher consciousness. Education is needed. In an essay titled "A Religion for the New Age," author and poet John Dunphy implores educators to view themselves as evangelists:

> I am convinced that the battle for humankind's future must be waged and won in the public school classrooms by teachers who correctly perceive their role as proselytizers of a new faith: a religion of humanity that recognizes and respects the spark of what theologians call the Divinity in every human being. These teachers must embody the same selfless dedication as the most rabid fundamentalist preachers.[78]

Many New Spiritualists have taken up the challenge of educating the rising generation to their way of thinking. When Marilyn Ferguson interviewed New Spiritualist professionals for her book *The Aquarian Conspiracy*, "more were involved in education than in any other single category of work."[79] By teaching children the proper attitudes toward themselves and consciousness, New Spiritualist educators hope to usher in higher consciousness.

> Many New Spiritualists have taken up the challenge of educating the rising generation to their way of thinking.

According to the New Spiritualist, modern society's traditional views hinder our evolution. If we transcend those limits and become truly aware of our God nature, we gain the power to change society. Society can help by changing whatever institutions inhibit our individual evolution to higher consciousness.

7. ISLAM

Whereas Secularism, Marxism, Postmodernism, and New Spirituality minimize the sociological significance of the family, Islam enshrines it. In fact, many people perceive that boundaries between the family, church, and state do not exist in Islam. Islam is a totalizing worldview that accounts for and dictates the structure of everything. Muslims often describe this vision as *ummah*, which refers to a shared sense of identity among Muslims all over the world that extends to community, religious belief, and even political structures. Muslims believe Islam provides a perfect harmony between the individual and society, holding both in concert with each other. According to Khurshid Ahmad,

> Islam ... establishes a balance between individualism and collectivism. It believes in the individual personality of man and holds everyone personally accountable to God. It guarantees the fundamental rights of the individual and does not permit anyone to tamper with them. It makes the proper development of the personality of man one of the prime objectives of its educational policy. It does not subscribe to the view that man must lose his individuality in society or in the state.... On the other hand, it also awakens a sense of social responsibility in man, organizes human beings in a society and a state and enjoins the individual to subscribe to the social good.[80]

"Equality for all" may be Ahmad's ideal vision of Islam, but one would be wise to read the fine print. On the surface, the Quran sets men and women on equal spiritual footing before Allah, but other Islamic writings view women as destined for eternal punishment unless strictly controlled. A passage in the *Sunnah*, a respected source about Muhammad's teachings, says, "I looked at Paradise and found poor people forming the majority of its inhabitants; and I looked at Hell and saw that the majority of its inhabitants were women."[81]

> On the surface, the Quran sets men and women on equal spiritual footing before Allah, but other Islamic writings view women as destined for eternal punishment unless strictly controlled.

The Muslim view of marriage has traditionally been a business contract that reflects a deep distrust of women. The following are the primary features of marriage found in the Quran:

- A Muslim man may marry up to four wives, granted that he treat them equally and provide for each of them (4:3).

- A Muslim man is allowed to have sex with women he has captured during war (23:1–6; 33:50; 70:22–30).

- A Muslim man may marry a woman *temporarily*, a marriage lasting a relatively short time (4:24).

- Muslim men may marry Jewish or Christian wives (5:5)—though not women from other religions (2:221), and yet, Muslim women may never marry non-Muslims (2:221).[82]

- Unsubmissive women may be beaten (4:34).

- "Your wives are as a tilth unto you; so approach your tilth when or how ye will" (2:223), meaning that women are to be plowed like a field—men may have sexual access to their wives whenever and however they please, except when the wife is menstruating (2:222).

- Adultery is severely punished (4:15–18; 17:32; 24:20), but in common practice, the application of punishment often falls much harder on women than men, since the value of a woman's testimony is discounted.

- Men may divorce their wives (60:1–2; 65:1–2; 226:242), though reconciliation is to be sought (4:35). The Quran makes no allowance for a woman to divorce her husband, although some Muslim countries have permitted it.

Patriarchal (from the Latin word for "father," *patri*), the word we use to refer to a society dominated by men, accurately describes most Muslim societies. In a **patriarchal society**, the primary duty of women is to have children, especially male children. Vivienne Stacey paints a troubling picture:

> *Patriarchal Society:* a society dominated by men.

How often a wife is in distress because she has not produced a child! The wife who produces only girls will also seek religious help as well as perhaps medical help. If she has a son she will want more sons in case the child dies, as it may easily do. So a woman's importance in society in general is estimated by her ability to produce sons. This is an inequality between the sexes which the laws of a country and the efforts of family planning associations can do little about.[83]

Muslims educated in Western universities have tried to move past the conflict between these traditions and genetics or other physical concerns. Nevertheless, men expect their wives to bear male children, and women's fear of failing to fulfill these expectations persists in the Muslim world.

When it comes to the actual organization of society, Islam does not distinguish between social institutions and the state. Islam is a comprehensive reality, a form of government as well as a religion. Today, the Muslim world is divided between those who favor nation-states (with laws, constitutions, and boundaries distinct from other nations) and those who favor **pan-Islam** (the vision that the Muslim community should be united, with diminished or nonexistent national boundaries). Those who favor nation-states sometimes produce Muslim nations where the population is predominantly Muslim but shariah is not the law of the land, or not purely so. For example, Turkey is a Muslim nation whose constitution is not based on shariah law. Although most of its population is Muslim, Turkey (as of this writing) is a secular nation.

However, even within these more moderate countries, Muslims who favor a pan-Islamic community are seeking the establishment of shariah through reform, denouncement, protest, and even terrorism. Much of the international instability in the early twenty-first century in nations like Egypt is due to those Islamists who want to dethrone the dominant Secularism and create a state more faithful to Islamic teachings.

> *Pan-Islam:* the belief that all Muslims should be united under a single Islamic state or that the world should be united under a global Islamic state.

8. CHRISTIANITY

Let's return to a dilemma we faced at the beginning of this chapter. If the underlying assumptions of sociology are inherently anti-Christian, is Christian sociology actually possible? The answer to this question is straightforward: yes, provided that sociology is properly defined by its object of study—individuals and society—rather than by Secularist assumptions that mandate certain methods. We need more tools in the toolbox.

We also need to understand where these tools come from. Pitirim Sorokin, the founder of Harvard's sociology department, attempted to offer an understanding in *Social and Cultural Dynamics*. Sorokin proposed that sociology needs to distinguish between "first culture and second culture societies."[84] First cultures assume truth exists, which leads to certain methods of inquiry. Second cultures assume truth does not exist, which changes how they see the world. Trying to understand first cultures with second-culture assumptions is like trying to explain why people are attracted to the *Mona Lisa* painting by weighing it or using a computer to analyze its coloring. Scales and computers are not bad; they are just limited in assessing aesthetic value.

Sorokin irritated sociologists because he was, in effect, proposing a sociology of sociology. He examined how many sociologists arrived at their viewpoints and why. This digging around in sociology's toolbox made sociologists appear to have a political or social, rather than scholarly, agenda. It didn't matter to them if Sorokin was correct. They didn't like it. Once the sociological community embraced a limited Secularist toolbox, Sorokin's name and significant contribution to the field were all but erased from contemporary sociological study.[85]

We think Sorokin's point was valid and helpful. We can better understand individuals and society if, rather than forcing them to submit to unsuitable methods of analysis, we approach them on their own terms. When we look at individuals and society on their own terms, the Christian sociological claim becomes simple: society functions best when organized around the family (father, mother, and children) and the institutions naturally flowing from it. We see the foundations of culture in Genesis 1 when God said to the man and woman, "Be fruitful and multiply; fill the earth." We see family in Genesis 2 when the man and woman became "one flesh" in order to accomplish the command to be fruitful and multiply. We see the initiations of worship, government, urbanization, agriculture, animal domestication,

> The Christian sociological claim becomes simple: society functions best when organized around the family (father, mother, and children) and the institutions naturally flowing from it.

music, metallurgy, and the development of weapons in Genesis 4. Civil government with the power to punish those who stray is assumed as well. The basic institutions of society were there from the start.

Those who view God, Adam and Eve, the garden of Eden, the fall, and the divine institution (and hence the sanctity) of the family as nothing more than prescientific myths risk ending up with a very different sociology than those who see those events as legitimate history. Christians say that ignorance of and rebellion against God's design is the best explanation for the failures we see in contemporary society, such as drug and alcohol abuse, crime, abortion, sexual perversion, human trafficking, disease, and poverty.

For Christians, the family (as opposed to individuals, economic structures, spoken language, higher consciousness, or the Quran) is the glue of society. Societies can survive the miseries of corruption, violence, and crime, but if the family falls apart, societal collapse is inevitable.[86] Such unraveling is now a statistical reality: poverty is epidemic among families headed by single women; young men and women between seventeen and twenty-four years of age are far more likely to abuse drugs or commit crimes if they come from fatherless homes; legalized abortion has led to a devaluing of children; and child-abuse rates have risen in tandem with abortion rates. Being raised by parents who have been involved in same-sex relationships is correlated with several negative social outcomes, including crime, substance abuse, and forced sexual encounters.[87]

According to the biblical view, the correction for these ills is a disciplined commitment to marriage between one man and one woman, for life. This, not bigotry, explains why Christians call for a return to traditional marriage and traditional values, such as love, fidelity, and respect.

How does the family fit with the church and the government in the Christian view? It starts with this: God owns everything. Abraham Kuyper, a deeply respected theologian who eventually became the prime minister of the Netherlands, famously summarized the authority of Christ over all things: "There is not one square inch of the entire creation about which Jesus Christ does not cry out, 'This is mine! This belongs to me!' "[88]

As God's image bearers, we are caretakers. We are to watch over creation, reflecting and expressing God's truth. In what areas of society are we to do this? Christian theologians have contemplated this question for a long time. The Puritan theologian and Cambridge professor William Perkins studied biblical texts and concluded that God had ordained three distinct spheres of society:

> Now all societies of men are bodies, a family is a body, and so is every particular Church a body, and the Commonwealth also; and in these bodies there are several members, which are men walking in several callings and offices, the execution whereof must tend to the happy and good estate of the rest, yea of all men everywhere, as much as possible is.[89]

Perkins's emphasis on three spheres of society—family, church, and state—became the basis for a lecture series Kuyper gave at Princeton University at the end of the nineteenth century.[90] Kuyper called for a view of **sphere sovereignty** in which each sphere has a proper domain. When the spheres are balanced and each institution is properly managing its own areas of responsibility, peace and prosperity result. When they are imbalanced because an institution abandons its responsibility or oversteps into another domain, society begins to unravel and head toward oppression and misery.

Think of sphere sovereignty as three balloons in a box just big enough to fit them all. If one balloon is blown up bigger, the other two get squeezed. Sphere sovereignty says the balance between the institutions in society is like that. If the church sphere gets too big, as often happened in the Middle Ages, families and the government will get squeezed. If the family sphere gets too big, as happened in Italy in the 1400s when a handful of powerful families, such as the Medici, controlled everything, the church and the government will find it difficult to operate properly. Today, the rapid expansion of government can be expected to hurt families and churches.

> *Sphere Sovereignty:* the belief that God ordained certain spheres of society, such as family, church, and state, and that society functions best when each sphere is properly managing its own area of responsibility.

How do we decide wisely about the proper balance between the spheres? When faced with a decision, such as who should take care of the poor, we need to grapple with three questions:

1. Is this the proper domain of this sphere?
2. What is the effect on the other spheres?
3. Could this problem be better solved another way?

Let's say a city government has to make decisions about caring for children who are without families. The city could decide to take matters into its own hands and house the children in city-run orphanages. Is this wise? The government taking on the responsibility of raising children could risk damaging the family sphere and allowing the church to forgo its responsibility to the fatherless. Also, the government is not equipped like the family or the church to offer the sort of precise solutions required when dealing with individual lives.

If, on the other hand, the city government asks churches for help, the churches can recruit and support families willing to take in foster children. The government can exercise its proper role as a clearinghouse for identifying children in need of help. Families can expand their borders and give unwanted children a loving environment in which to grow and flourish.

Thinking properly about the role of each sphere of society not only relieves the government of improperly bearing too many responsibilities but also mobilizes communities of people to seek solutions at the level closest to the problem. This principle of selecting the solution closest to the level of the problem is called **subsidiarity**.

> The government is not equipped like the family or the church to offer the sort of precise solutions required when dealing with individual lives.

Applying sphere sovereignty takes practice, but it avoids idolizing civil government—or churches and families, for that matter—and it points the way to using the assets of our communities in the way God designed. It pries away the illicit allure of government as a place to gain power and prestige, putting it back in the hands of people who truly want to serve rather than be served. This, as we will see in our chapter on politics, is a major step toward integrity in political involvement.

Subsidiarity: **the belief that decisions are best handled at the organizational or societal level closest to the issues or persons affected.**

In addition to promoting a balanced approach to society's institutions, a Christian approach to sociology accounts for individual free will and responsibility better than a sociological approach based on materialism and naturalism: because we are made in God's image, we can each bear responsibility for our actions. If right and wrong and good and evil actually exist, if there is more than the natural, material world, more than atoms swirling through space, and if we are free to choose right over wrong and good over evil, then taking responsibility can actually make society better.

Responsibility is the passport to the world of society-shaping opportunity. William Stanmeyer explains:

> If man's behavior were somehow conditioned by genetic code or social externals then no just judge could blame him for the evil he commits. But the scripture teaches unequivocally that God blamed Adam and Eve for succumbing to the temptation to disobedience and punished them accordingly.[91]

Adam and Eve's failure to obey God in the garden of Eden resulted not only in their expulsion from the garden paradise but also in a cycle of paranoia, blame, and harmful actions toward others.

Adam and Eve were, in the words of Saint Augustine, "free but not freed"—able to choose but incapable of fully choosing the good. We suffer from the same malady today. We lose the ability to create a flourishing society and are bled of the motivation to do so. Human persistence in choosing the wrong course has left the scar tissue of alienation, imperfection, and sin everywhere. Choosing to step away from our responsibility takes a little fire out of our souls, so to speak. It diminishes who we are as persons and deprives us of purpose.

Here are some tragic examples: The philosopher Jean-Jacques Rousseau proclaimed a love of childhood innocence, but he abandoned all five of his children to orphanages, where their chances of survival were remote. Karl Marx destroyed his relationship with his loving wife by impregnating their housekeeper. Friedrich Engels nervously shuffled between two homes so he could live with both his wife and his lover.[92] However, it's not just atheists who provide these examples. King David impregnated a woman and then had her husband killed, which led to a civil war within his own family. Noted Christians have fallen morally. Scripture says, "The heart is deceitful above all things and desperately sick" (Jer. 17:9). None of us are immune.

Adam and Eve's failure to obey God in the garden of Eden resulted not only in their expulsion from the garden paradise but also in a cycle of paranoia, blame, and harmful actions toward others.

9. Implications Unique to a Christian View of Sociology

The human condition is a sordid tale of degeneration and devolution rather than evolution. Alienation pervades our relationships with God, with others, and even within ourselves. It almost goes without saying that sociologists who have this humble understanding will interpret data differently from those who believe we are inherently good but have been corrupted by our society and environment.

The Christian worldview promotes involvement in making society better, but it does so based on actual truths and a call to responsible choices. Christian sociology sees each person as valuable and able to contribute to society. Thus we are not helpless in the face of societal and environmental pressures. We are mighty as image bearers of God. C. S. Lewis explained that atheists may think that "nations, classes, civilizations must be more important than individuals," because "individuals live only seventy odd years each and the group may last for centuries. But to the Christian, individuals are more important, for they live eternally; and races, civilizations and the like are in comparison the creatures of a day."[93]

Here are some of the implications unique to a Christian view of sociology:

The importance of the individual as a social being. We were created as social beings (Gen. 2:20)[94] and recognize the role society plays in history as well as in our relationships with God. Society exists because we are relational. S. D. Gaede says, "God designed the human being to be a relational creature. Note this point well. Humankind was created to relate to other beings. It was not an accident. It was not the result of sin. It was an intentional, creational given."[95] Nevertheless, because of the fall we continue to experience alienation, which Gaede refers to as the "relational dilemma." Because Christians understand the cause of this dilemma, we can point the way to solutions.

The embrace of human value. Greece and Rome were haughty, elite-driven cultures with no respect for ordinary people.[96] And yet Jesus taught that the "last will be first and the first will be last" (Matt. 20:16; Mark 10:43; Luke 22:27).[97] In Christ's economy, image bearers of God succeed by serving other image bearers of God. This leads to dramatic change: *followers* become *constituents* and *subjects* become *customers*. It was Christians who elevated the status of women, built hospitals and schools, and instituted ministries to the poor. According to Rodney Stark, effective moral opposition to slavery arose only because of Christian theology.[98] Various cultures have opposed slavery in certain circumstances or for themselves, but opposing slavery in all its forms because it was sinful was a Christian impulse unique in the world to this very day.

> It was Christians who elevated the status of women, built hospitals and schools, and instituted ministries to the poor.

The recognition of both the individual and society. Some worldviews have a radical focus on the individual. Others ignore individuals and focus only on society. From a Christian perspective, both must be valued. This perspective ensures, as one Christian sociology text memorably phrased it, that we "can never be reduced to either a mere atomistic individual or a mere integer in some social whole."[99] Both the individual and societal groups are accountable to God (Acts 17:31),[100] and if each person acts responsibly, then each societal institution can focus on governing its realm of interest properly and allowing other institutions the same freedom.

A proper balance between the institutions of family, church, and state. In Christian sociology, the family, the church, and the state are God-ordained institutions. Dietrich Bonhoeffer and some others rightly included labor as a fourth God-ordained institution. Realizing that God ordained these societal institutions demonstrates the relevance of Christianity to every aspect of reality. Bonhoeffer explained, "It is God's will that there shall be labor, marriage, government, and church in the world; and it is His will that all these, each in its own way, shall be through Christ, directed towards Christ, and in Christ.... This means that there can be no retreating from a 'secular' into a 'spiritual' sphere."[101] Nothing lies outside the realm of Christianity's influence. All society, indeed all of life, is bound inextricably with God and his plan for the world. In Bonhoeffer's view, "the world is relative to Christ."[102]

An ennobling perspective on government. Even though governmental leaders often make poor decisions, Christian sociology does not take a pessimistic view of government. Instead, Christian sociology is optimistic because our freedom and responsibility before God grant us dignity and significance, which empowers us to structure governments properly, protect the innocent, and maintain justice. Francis Schaeffer explained that we are "not a cog in a machine, ... not a piece of theater; [we] really can influence history. From the biblical viewpoint, [we are] lost, but great."[103] Christians like William Carey and William Wilberforce, for example, were able to work through both the church and government to change society—and history—by bringing an end to the slave trade.[104] Because of our understanding of the sin nature, though, it is wise to keep government's powers in perspective. Government is not God. It secures rights but does not invent them. It acknowledges human value but does not grant it. Government is not the source of all of our problems, nor is it the solution to them.

> Government is not the source of all of our problems, nor is it the solution to them.

A love for the family. From a Christian worldview, God ordained the family (Gen. 2:23–25)[105] and is a fundamental social institution. Scripture teaches in Ephesians 5:25 that husbands should love their wives just as "Christ loved the church." In ancient Greece and Rome, sexual perversion, especially homosexual pedophilia, was common. Only in Christianity, said Will Durant, did sexual fidelity become a virtue.[106] If marriage and the family are in trouble, society will be in trouble. Christians should give serious consideration to promoting marriage—not just in the abstract but in concrete ways—by helping husbands and wives stay together and encouraging them to be moral and spiritual examples to their children. All of society benefits.

A proper role for the church. God ordained the church to serve specific functions. One principal role of the church is to proclaim the truth regarding sin, repentance, and salvation. Another role is to form individuals into communities working together to nurture one another and serve the larger society. The church can model true community by demonstrating what it means to "love your neighbor as yourself."[107] Francis Schaeffer was adamant about the need for community in the Christian church: "I am convinced that in the 20th century people all over the world will not listen if we have the right doctrine, the right polity, but are not exhibiting community."[108] This timeless call to serve others in love is grounded in Ephesians 4:11–16, which says,

> [God] gave the apostles, the prophets, the evangelists, the shepherds and teachers, to equip the saints for the work of ministry, for building up the body of Christ.... We are to grow up in every way into him who is the head, into Christ, from whom the whole body, joined and held together by every joint with which it is equipped, when each part is working properly, makes the body grow so that it builds itself up in love.

The church is not merely a place for people to listen to sermons. It is a place where laborers, bankers, medical practitioners, missionaries, craftsmen, elected officials, mechanics, scientists, restauranteurs, clerks, students, entrepreneurs, geologists, pastors, teachers, dishwashers, equipment operators, childcare providers, government bureaucrats, moms, dads, children, and singles all learn to obey God in every area where Christ has authority.

Jesus made clear the significance of the church in the Christian worldview. At a place called Caesarea Philippi, Jesus asked his disciples, "Who do you say that I am?" Peter replied, "You are the Christ, the Son of the living God." Upon hearing Peter's reply, Jesus said, "I tell you, you are Peter, and on this rock I will build my church, and the gates of hell shall not prevail against it."[109] This reference to Peter (*petros*, or "stone") and "rock" (*petra*, or "large rock") combine poetically with the reference to the gates of Hades—both features of Caesarea Philippi, which was a center of religious and political worship. Jesus was giving an object lesson: wherever people gather is where the church is to be built.

Furthermore, in using the word *church* (*ekklēsia*), Jesus was framing the civic purpose of the church. The word *ekklēsia*, according to pastor Tony Evans, essentially refers to a group of people who have been "called out from the general population to serve in the parliament, congress, or counsel of the community in order to establish the governance, guidelines, rules, and regulations for the broader citizenry." Evans continues, "To be a part of the church of Jesus Christ, as Jesus defined it, is to be a part of a spiritual legislative body tasked to enact heaven's viewpoint in hell's society."[110]

Jesus taught that the church is more than a place to worship at the edges of culture; it belongs at the very center of culture and society in order to teach and model who God is and how the human race might be redeemed. The church is a feast, a forever family. More than that, in a world where evil tries to ensnare us, the church is a unifying force. It stands against evil and reminds society of what is true and just. The church is not just a way of living for those who like it; it is the very model of what the good life is all about.

> Jesus taught that the church is more than a place to worship at the edges of culture; it belongs at the very center of culture and society in order to teach and model who God is and how the human race might be redeemed.

10. CONCLUSION

Worldviews committed to materialism and naturalism discount the ability of individual human beings to make a difference in society. Their followers also tend persistently to attack the traditional family.[111] The Christian worldview is constantly criticized for its call to self-restraint, responsibility, work, and caring for others even when it is not convenient. But the evidence of history speaks more loudly. We are not free to wreak mayhem in the social order, but we are free to serve others in love and to serve and love God.

What difference does it make? Christianity's impact was aptly summarized by the nineteenth-century poet James Russell Lowell:

> I challenge any skeptic to find a ten-square-mile spot on this planet where they can live their lives in peace and safety and decency, where womanhood is honored, where infancy and old age are revered, where they can educate their children, where the Gospel of Jesus Christ has not gone first to prepare the way. If they find such a place, then I would encourage them to emigrate thither and there proclaim their unbelief.[112]

Those who hold to Christian values of society need not apologize or timidly defer to those who scorn them, but neither should they have a haughty attitude. Our first response, the Christian worldview says, is gratitude to God—for creating us to flourish and for making it possible to do so. Our second response, immediately following, is to act on that gratefulness as stewards made in God's image.

In order to live together in peace and harmony, though, we need a firm basis for how society ought to establish order and secure justice. This gets into the field of law, in which the collision between worldviews threatens to become a winner-takes-all approach to society. Simultaneously fascinating, complicated, and disturbing, the study of law is the topic to which we next turn our attention.

ENDNOTES

1. Thomas Low Nichols, *Forty Years of American Life* (Portland: Angell Press, 2007), 20. See an excerpt at "A Portrait of America, 1830," EyeWitness to History, 2008, accessed April 3, 2014, www.eyewitnesstohistory.com/america1830.htm.

2. Alexis de Tocqueville, *Democracy in America,* trans. George Lawrence (New York: Harper Perennial, 1988), 464–65.

3. James C. Dobson and Gary L. Bauer, *Children at Risk: The Battle for the Hearts and Minds of Our Kids* (Dallas: Word, 1990), 19.

4. UCLA annual survey, 2008, cited in Kathy Wyer, "Political Engagement among College Freshmen Hits 40-Year High," January 22, 2009, UCLA Newsroom, http://newsroom.ucla.edu/releases/political-engagement-of-college-78404.

5. "Twentysomethings Struggle to Find Their Place in Christian Churches," Barna Research Online, September 24, 2003, www.barna.org/component/content/article/5-barna-update/45-barna-update-sp-657/127-twenty somethings-struggle-to-find-their-place-in-christian-churches#.VszmhFj2bIU.

6. Ken Ham and Britt Beemer, *Already Gone: Why Your Kids Will Quit Church and What You Can Do to Stop It* (Green Forest, AR: Master Books, 2009), 24.

7. "America's Families and Living Arrangements: 2011," US Census Bureau, accessed March 27, 2014, www.census.gov /hhes/families/data/cps2011.html.

8. See Kathleen A. Kovner Kline, *Hardwired to Connect: The New Scientific Case for Authoritative Communities* (New York: Broadway, 2003), 8. This crucial report was produced jointly by the YMCA of the USA, the Commission on Children at Risk, Dartmouth Medical School, and the Institute for American Values.

9. George Barna, *Transforming Children into Spiritual Champions* (Ventura, CA: Regal Books, 2003), 125.

10. Quoted in James Tonkowich, "When Scripture Becomes an A-La-Carte Menu," *By Faith,* June 17, 2010, http://byfaithonline.com/when-scripture-becomes-an-a-la-carte-menu/.

11. Steve Bruce, *Sociology: A Very Short Introduction* (Oxford, UK: Oxford University Press, 1999), 18.

12. Mary Wollstonecraft Shelley, *Frankenstein, or the Modern Prometheus* (Rockville, MD: TARK Classic Fiction, 2008), 76.

13. Shelley, *Frankenstein.* J. F. Baldwin Jr.'s *Deadliest Monster* (New Braunfels, TX: Fishermen Press, 2005) is an excellent book exploring the view of human nature in Shelley's *Frankenstein* and Robert Louis Stevenson's *The Strange Case of Dr. Jekyll and Mr. Hyde.*

14. Quoted in John F. Glass and John R. Staude, eds., *Humanistic Society* (Pacific Palisades, CA: Goodyear, 1972), 352.

15. According to Maurice R. Stein, "Humanist sociology views society as a historically evolving enterprise that can only be understood through the struggle to liberate human potentialities." Quoted in Glass and Staude, *Humanistic Society,* 165.

16. Patricia Hill Collins, "Perceptivity and the Activist Potential of the Sociology Classroom," *Humanity and Society* (August 1986): 341.

17. This use of science is sometimes called *postnormal science.*

18. Quoted in Mark Schoofs, "International Forum Debates Treatment of Homosexuality," *Washington Blade,* December 18, 1987, 19.

19. Christian Smith, "Secularizing American Higher Education," in Christian Smith, ed. *The Secular Revolution: Power, Interests, and Conflict in the Secularization of American Public Life* (Berkeley, CA: University of California Press, 2003), 101.

20. Smith, *Secular Revolution.*

21. See the introduction to Christopher Dawson, *Religion and the Rise of Western Culture* (New York: Doubleday, 1950). Dawson was a highly regarded historian whose remarks on the subject were part of his Gifford Lectures, a historical lecture series given at universities in Scotland.

22. Hunter Baker, *The End of Secularism* (Wheaton, IL: Crossway Books, 2009), 25.

23. Anthony Giddens et al., *Introduction to Sociology* (New York: W. W. Norton, 2012), 5.

24. Giddens, *Introduction to Sociology,* 5–6.

25. Giddens, *Introduction to Sociology,* 8.

26. Giddens et al. say, "A long-standing debate in the social sciences revolves around questions of free will and determinism. For example, a deterministic framework would predict that where an individual ends up in life is significantly if not entirely influenced by the position into which he or she is born. The sociological imagination can be quite deterministic in that it pushes us to see that in many ways the lives of individuals are quite determined by our social roles, gender, race, and class. Yet we would not want you to take away the lesson that individuals are trapped or controlled like puppets." The authors go on to explain that sociologists are not looking for hard-and-fast rules but probabilities in which human behavior can be predicted based on factors sociologists can isolate and study. Giddens, *Introduction to Sociology.*

27. Giddens, *Introduction to Sociology,* 186.

28. This is the definition of *inequality* given in Giddens, *Introduction to Sociology,* 224.

29. Erich Fromm, *Escape from Freedom* (New York: Holt, Rinehart, and Winston, 1969), 12.

30. Erich Fromm, *The Sane Society* (New York: Holt, Rinehart, and Winston, 1955), 362.

31. Walda Katz-Fishman and C. George Benello, *Readings in Humanist Sociology* (Bayside, NY: General Hall, 1986), 3.

32. Lawrence Casler, in Robert Rimmer, "An Interview with Robert Rimmer on Premarital Communes and Group Marriages," *Humanist* (March/April 1974): 14.

33. Sol Gordon, "The Egalitarian Family Is Alive and Well," *Humanist* (May/June 1975): 18.

34. Robert N. Whitehurst, "Alternative Life-styles," *Humanist* (May/June 1975): 24.

35. Lester Kirkendall, *A New Bill of Sexual Rights and Responsibilities* (Buffalo, NY: Prometheus Books, 1976), 9.

36. "GLAAD Media Awards Selection Process," GLAAD Media Awards, accessed April 3, 2014, www.glaad.org/media awards/22/selections.

37. See, for example, Mark Regnerus, "How Different Are the Adult Children of Parents Who Have Same-Sex Relationships?," *Social Science Research* 41 (2012): 752–70.

38. Lawrence Casler, "Permissive Matrimony: Proposals for the Future," *Humanist* (March/April 1974): 6–7.

39. A particularly horrifying example of this way of thinking is Mary Elizabeth Williams's article at Salon.com. Williams concludes the article with this line: "I would put the life of a mother over the life of a fetus every single time—even if I still need to acknowledge my conviction that the fetus is indeed a life. A life worth sacrificing." Mary Elizabeth Williams, "So What If Abortion Ends Life?," *Salon*, January 23, 2013, www.salon.com/2013/01/23/so_what_if_abortion_ends_life/.

40. Fromm, *Sane Society*, 20.

41. G. V. Plekhanov, *The Role of the Individual in History* (New York: International Publishers, 1940), 200.

42. V. I. Lenin, *The State and Revolution* (New York: International Publishers, 1932), 73.

43. Karl Marx and Friedrich Engels, *The Individual and Society* (Moscow: Progress Publishers, 1984), 193.

44. Marx and Engels, *Individual and Society*, 162.

45. Joseph Stalin said we must rely "on the concrete conditions of the material life of society, as the determining force of social development; not on the good wishes of great men." Joseph Stalin, *Problems of Leninism* (Moscow: Progress Publishers, 1947), 579, quoted in Gustav A. Wetter, *Dialectical Materialism* (Westport, CT: Greenwood, 1977), 217.

46. Clemens Dutt, ed., *Fundamentals of Marxism-Leninism* (Moscow: Progress Publishers, 1959), 310, cited in Raymond S. Sleeper, ed., *A Lexicon of Marxist-Leninist Semantics* (Alexandria, VA: Western Goals, 1983), 36.

47. Anne Applebaum documents the way this happened in Eastern Europe as well. The Communist Parties identified popular priests, developed charges against them, and had them arrested as a matter of course. See Anne Applebaum, *Iron Curtain* (New York: Doubleday, 2012).

48. Mikhail Gorbachev, *Memoirs* (New York: Doubleday, 1996), 328.

49. Alexandra M. Kollontai, *Communism and the Family* (New York: Andrade's Bookshop, 1920), 10, quoted in H. Kent Geiger, *The Family in Soviet Russia* (Cambridge, MA: Harvard University Press, 1970), 51.

50. Karl Marx and Friedrich Engels, *The Communist Manifesto* (New York: Penguin Books, 2002), 240.

51. Frederick Engels, *The Origin of the Family, Private Property, and the State* (New York: International Publishers, 1942), 67.

52. Karl Marx and Frederick Engels, *Collected Works*, 40 vols. (New York: International Publishers, 1976), 6:354.

53. V. Yazykova, *Socialist Life Style and the Family* (Moscow: Progress Publishers, 1984), 7.

54. Terry Eagleton, *Why Marx Was Right* (New Haven, CT: Yale University Press, 2011), 15.

55. Eagleton, *Why Marx Was Right*, 17.

56. Marx and Engels, *Communist Manifesto*, 258.

57. Noam Chomsky and Michel Foucault, *Human Nature: Justice vs. Power* (New York: New Press, 2006), 37.

58. Fredric Jameson, *Postmodernism: Or, the Cultural Logic of Late Capitalism* (Durham, NC: Duke University Press, 1991), 367.

59. Jacques Derrida, *Of Grammatology*, trans. Gayatri Chakravorty Spivak (Baltimore: Johns Hopkins University Press, 1997), 11.

60. Theodore Dalrymple warns, "Grammatical latitudinarianism [the elimination of any rules or purpose of language] is the natural ideological ally of moral and cultural relativism." Theodore Dalrymple, *Not with a Bang but a Whimper* (Chatham, UK: Monday Books, 2009), 47.

61. Richard Rorty and Gianni Vattimo, *The Future of Religion* (New York: Columbia University Press, 2005), 33.

62. Ronald Hamowy, ed., *The Encyclopedia of Libertarianism* (Thousand Oaks, CA: Sage, 2008), s.v. "Diderot, Denis (1713–1784)."

63. Quoted in Algis Valiunas, "Mental Health," *Weekly Standard* 11, no. 9 (November 2005): 41.

64. Glenn Ward, *Teach Yourself Postmodernism*, 2nd ed. (Chicago: McGraw-Hill, 2003), 145.

65. Quoted in Ward, *Teach Yourself Postmodernism*, 146.

66. Michel Foucault, *The Foucault Reader*, ed. Paul Rabinow (New York: Pantheon Books, 1984), 29.

67. Mark Lilla, *The Reckless Mind: Intellectuals in Politics* (New York: New York Review Books, 2001), 142. See the "Postmodern Politics" section for more on the Marquis de Sade.

68. For more course listings, visit Stanford University's Program in Feminist, Gender, and Sexuality Studies at https://feminist.stanford.edu/courses.

69. Ward, *Teach Yourself Postmodernism*, 176.

70. See Anne Henderschott, *The Politics of Deviance* (San Francisco: Encounter Books, 2002).

71. Ward, *Teach Yourself Postmodernism*, 176–77.

72. Gary Zukav, *The Seat of the Soul* (New York: Simon and Schuster, 1989), 164.

73. Marilyn Ferguson, *The Aquarian Conspiracy* (Los Angeles: J. P. Tarcher, 1980), 104.

74. David Spangler, *Emergence: The Rebirth of the Sacred* (New York: Dell, 1984), 82.

75. Shakti Gawain, *Living in the Light* (San Rafael, CA: New World Library, 1986), 110.

76. Gawain, *Living in the Light*, 3.

77. Kevin Ryerson, *Spirit Communication: The Soul's Path* (New York: Bantam Books, 1989), 172.

78. John J. Dunphy, "A Religion for a New Age," *Humanist* (January/February 1983): 26.

79. Ferguson, *Aquarian Conspiracy*, 280.

80. Khurshid Ahmad, *Islam: Its Meaning and Message*, 3rd ed. (Leicester, UK: Islamic Foundation, 1999), 38–39.

81. Sahih al-Bukhari, vol. 4, bk. 54, hadith 464, http://sahih-bukhari.com/Pages/Bukhari_4_54.php.

82. Non-Muslim women who marry Muslim men are portrayed in the movie *Not without My Daughter* (MGM, 1991). This true-to-life story portrays a Muslim man living in the United States who is caught up the fervor of the Iranian revolution led by Ayatollah Khomeini in 1979. He returns to Iran, ostensibly for "a visit," taking his American wife and daughter with him. When he refuses to leave, his wife battles Islamic law and tradition in her fight to escape with her daughter and return to the States.

83. Vivienne Stacey, *The Life of Muslim Women* (Toronto: Fellowship of Faith for Muslims, 1980), 34–35.

84. Pitirim Sorokin, *Social and Cultural Dynamics* (Boston: Porter Sargent, 1957), 15.

85. In the Giddens sociology text we referenced earlier, Sorokin merits only one reference in 705 pages of text, and that on a point of paltry significance.

86. For a helpful essay on this subject, see Kerby Anderson, "The Decline of a Nation," Probe Ministries, May 27, 1991, accessed March 27, 2014, www.probe.org/the-decline-of-a-nation/.

87. See, for example, Regnerus, "How Different Are the Adult Children?"

88. Abraham Kuyper, *Near unto God: Daily Meditations Adapted for Contemporary Christians*, ed. James C. Schaap (Grand Rapids: CRC Publications, 1997), 7.

89. Quoted in William Carl Placher, *Callings: Twenty Centuries of Christian Wisdom on Vocation* (Grand Rapids: Eerdmans, 2005), 264.

90. Abraham Kuyper, *Calvinism: Six Stone-Lectures* (Princeton, NJ: Princeton Theological Seminary, 1898).

91. William A. Stanmeyer, *Clear and Present Danger* (Ann Arbor: Servant Books, 1983), 161.

92. These and more examples may be found in Paul Johnson, *Intellectuals* (New York: Harper and Row, 1988).

93. C. S. Lewis, *God in the Dock* (Grand Rapids: Eerdmans, 1972), 109–10.

94. Genesis 2:20: "The man gave names to all livestock and to the birds of the heavens and to every beast of the field. But for Adam there was not found a helper fit for him."

95. S. D. Gaede, *Where Gods May Dwell* (Grand Rapids: Zondervan, 1985), 75–76.

96. For more information, see "What If Jesus Had Never Been Born?," *Summit Journal* 11, no. 12 (December 2011), www .summit.org/media/journal/2011-12-Summit-Journal.pdf.

97. Matthew 20:16: "The last will be first, and the first last"; Mark 10:43: "It shall not be so among you. But whoever would be great among you must be your servant"; Luke 22:27: "Who is the greater, one who reclines at table or one who serves? Is it not the one who reclines at table? But I am among you as the one who serves."

98. Rodney Stark, *For the Glory of God* (Princeton, NJ: Princeton University Press, 2003), 291. All Christians should carefully study the entirety of Stark's chapter 4, "God's Justice: The Sin of Slavery."

99. Rockne McCarthy et al., *Society, State, and Schools* (Grand Rapids: Eerdmans, 1982), 151.

100. Acts 17:31: "[God] has fixed a day on which he will judge the world in righteousness by a man whom he has appointed; and of this he has given assurance to all by raising him from the dead."

101. Dietrich Bonhoeffer, *Ethics* (New York: Macmillan 1959), 207.

102. Bonhoeffer, *Ethics*.

103. Francis A. Schaeffer, *Death in the City* (Downers Grove, IL: InterVarsity, 1976), 21.

104. Hugh Thomas, *The Slave Trade: The Story of the Atlantic Slave Trade: 1440–1870* (New York: Simon and Schuster, 1999). Bringing the slave trade to an end was one of the great feats of human history. It was accomplished primarily by evangelical Christians. "Moreover, within Western civilization, the principal impetus for the abolition of slavery came first from very conservative religious activists—people who would today be called 'the religious right.' Clearly, this story is not 'politically correct' in today's terms. Hence it is ignored, as if it never happened." Thomas Sowell, *Black Rednecks and White Liberals* (San Francisco: Encounter Books, 2005), 116.

105. Genesis 2:23–25: "The man said, 'This at last is bone of my bones and flesh of my flesh; she shall be called Woman, because she was taken out of Man.' Therefore a man shall leave his father and his mother and hold fast to his wife, and they shall become one flesh. And the man and his wife were both naked and were not ashamed."

106. Will Durant, *The Story of Civilization*, vol. 3, *Caesar and Christ* (New York: Simon and Schuster, 1944), 598.

107. Matthew 22:39–40: "A second [command] is like [the first]: You shall love your neighbor as yourself. On these two commandments depend all the Law and the Prophets."

108. Francis A. Schaeffer, *The Church at the End of the 20th Century* (Downers Grove, IL: InterVarsity, 1974), 73.

109. Matthew 16:18: "I [Jesus] tell you, you are Peter, and on this rock I will build my church, and the gates of hell shall not prevail against it."

110. Tony Evans, *Oneness Embraced* (Chicago: Moody, 2011), 251.

111. A spate of books written in the 1990s made this argument initially. Today, academic research has caught up with what these authors intuitively understood to be true. For the latest research, see FamilyFacts.org, www .familyfacts. org. For an in-depth look at the pioneers who raised the alarm, we recommend Dobson and Bauer, *Children at Risk*; Phyllis Schlafly, *Child Abuse in the Classroom* (Alton, IL: Marquette, 1985); Judith A. Reisman and Edward W. Eichel, *Kinsey, Sex, and Fraud* (Lafayette, LA: Huntington House, 1990); B. K. Eakman, *Cloning of the American Mind: Eradicating Morality through Education* (Lafayette, LA: Huntington House, 1998); Allan Bloom, *The Closing of the American Mind* (New York: Simon and Schuster, 1987); and Thomas Sowell, *Inside American Education: The Decline, the Deception, the Dogmas* (New York: Free Press, 1993).

112. Quoted in D. James Kennedy and Jerry Newcombe, *What If Jesus Had Never Been Born?* (Nashville: Thomas Nelson, 1994), 238.

CHAPTER 14

LAW

1. ANIMAL FARM

It was just after the sheep had returned, on a pleasant evening when the animals had finished work and were making their way back to the farm buildings, that the terrified neighing of a horse sounded from the yard. Startled, the animals stopped in their tracks. It was Clover's voice. She neighed again, and all the animals broke into a gallop and rushed into the yard. Then they saw what Clover had seen.

It was a pig walking on his hind legs.

Yes, it was Squealer. A little awkwardly, as though not quite used to supporting his considerable bulk in that position. But with perfect balance, he was strolling across the yard.

And a moment later, out from the door of the farmhouse came a long file of pigs, all walking on their hind legs. Some did it better than others, one or two were even a trifle unsteady and looked as though they would have liked the support of a stick, but every one of them made his way right round the yard successfully. And finally there was a tremendous baying of dogs and a shrill crowing from the black cockerel, and out came Napoleon himself, majestically upright, casting haughty glances from side to side, and with his dogs gamboling round him.

He carried a whip in his trotter.

There was a deadly silence. Amazed, terrified, huddling together, the animals watched the long line of pigs march slowly round the yard. It was as though the world had turned upside down. Then there came a moment when the first shock had worn off and when, in spite of everything—in spite of their terror of the dogs, and of the habit, developed through long years, of never complaining, never criticizing, no matter what happened—they might have uttered some word of protest. But just at that moment, as though at a signal, all the sheep burst out into a tremendous bleating of—

"Four legs good, two legs better! Four legs good, two legs better! Four legs good, two legs better!"

It went on for five minutes without stopping. And by the time the sheep had quieted down, the chance to utter any protest had passed, for the pigs had marched back into the farmhouse.

Benjamin felt a nose nuzzling at his shoulder. He looked round. It was Clover. Her old eyes looked dimmer than ever. Without saying anything, she tugged gently at his mane and led him round to the end of the big barn, where the Seven Commandments were written. For a minute or two they stood gazing at the tatted wall with its white lettering.

"My sight is failing," she said finally. "Even when I was young I could not have read what was written there. But it appears to me that that wall looks different. Are the Seven Commandments the same as they used to be, Benjamin?"

For once Benjamin consented to break his rule, and he read out to her what was written on the wall. There was nothing there now except a single Commandment. It ran,

ALL ANIMALS ARE EQUAL,

BUT SOME ANIMALS ARE MORE EQUAL THAN OTHERS.[1]

So goes the stunning conclusion of George Orwell's *Animal Farm*, a political satire in which the prize boar Old Major describes his dream of liberation from the drunken Mr. Jones, inspiring the animals to revolt. When the dust settles, the pigs—having taught themselves to read and write—take charge and gradually change the rules to benefit themselves. They lie, manipulate, and exploit the other animals until misery proves the revolution a farce and the new laws meaningless. In the end, the pigs make peace with humans. Too late, the rest of the creatures realized the truth that life after the revolution was better for the pigs but worse for the rest of them.

2. Slavery and Freedom

As the Roman statesman Cicero claimed, "*Legum servi sumus ut liberi esse possimus*" ("We are slaves of the law so that we may be free").[2] The Latin word for **law** Cicero used, *legum*, is the word from which we get our words *legislate* and *legislature*. The study of law revolves around the question, "What constitutes *orderly* and *just* governance?"

It is a human paradox that to be free we must abide by laws that constrain our freedom. Either we must discipline ourselves to submit to an orderly way of life, or we will be forced to submit to tyranny. As Edmund Burke said, "Society cannot exist unless a controlling power upon will and appetite be placed somewhere, and the less of it there is within, the more there must be without. It is ordained in the eternal constitution of things, that men of intemperate minds cannot be free. Their passions forge their fetters."[3]

A society's measured pursuit of just laws is one of the primary factors that determine its level of thriving.

> *Law:* the study of ordinances designed to help citizens coexist peacefully.

> It is a human paradox that to be free we must abide by laws that constrain our freedom.

Lawmakers and legal scholars must consider whether the law sufficiently punishes evildoing while, at the same time, avoids harming the initiative of hardworking law abiders. Liberty and justice for all.

America's founders wondered whether such a system was truly possible and whether the people genuinely had the will to sustain it. As Benjamin Franklin emerged from the constitutional convention, a bystander, Mrs. Powel, asked, "Well, Doctor, what have we got? A republic or a monarchy?" "A republic," replied Franklin, "if you can keep it."[4] Franklin understood what was at stake. Whether the people were prepared for self-government was far from certain.

Closer to our own time, Judge Learned Hand said,

> I often wonder whether we do not rest our hopes too much upon constitutions, upon laws and upon courts. These are false hopes; believe me, these are false hopes. Liberty lies in the hearts of men and women; when it dies there, no constitution, no law, no court can even do much to help it. While it lies there it needs no constitution, no law, no court to save it.[5]

The message is clear: if there is no love of liberty in the heart, there will be no law of liberty in the land.

There is reason for similar uncertainty today. Harold J. Berman, former professor of law at Harvard Law School, believed law was rooted in religion and transcendent qualities.[6] These foundational beliefs, he said, are giving way to laws "geared more to expediency and less to morality.... As a result," he concluded, "the historical soil of the Western legal tradition is being washed away ... and the tradition itself is threatened with collapse"[7]

What set this collapse in motion? Berman believed the dam broke in the aftermath of World War I (1914–1918). How could the most enlightened, best educated, most scientifically astute nations in the world mow one another down in frightening numbers? Berman was less concerned with who was at fault than with the realization that all of the West's legal structures could not prevent the near destruction of civilization.[8]

The question now comes to us. Will we be able to maintain a lawful society amid the challenges of our own time? Many people do not believe Christians are capable of doing anything with law except using it to make people miserable. Are they right? Let's seek an answer by digging into a bit of the history and purpose of law. Along the way we'll examine each of the six worldviews we're considering and conclude with an examination of the Christian worldview, which makes what most people will doubtless think is a radical claim: the structure of law derives from God, who is simultaneously beyond us (transcendent) and with us (immanent). Because he is beyond us, his character forms the enduring definition of all that is good. Because he is with us, his law applies to all people in all places at all times.

3. Overview of Law

What constitutes orderly and just governance? To answer this question, let's look separately at both *order* and *justice*.

Order. Nothing happens in our communities without laws establishing order. Most of us, if we're thirsty, think nothing of going to the kitchen sink to get a drink of water. For this to

> *Order:* the administrative aspect of the law that focuses on ensuring safety and efficiency.

happen, predictability and safety must be a function of law. Water comes into your dwelling courtesy of a water district governing the acquisition, testing, delivery, and proper disposal of water. This includes regulations about which kinds of pipes will be used, how those pipes will be installed, how agreements will be made for laying pipe across private-property boundaries, who should fix broken pipes, how taxes are to be collected to pay for this maintenance, how the water is to be acquired in the first place, what price people will be charged for it, how they will pay, and what happens when they do not.

All of these are administrative regulations. They are a part of our law but are focused more on order than justice. If a water pipe breaks, people may be irked at the inconvenience. It would be stretching it if they complained of an injustice having been committed against them in the same way if someone had intentionally broken the pipes or was hoarding all the water for himself.

One of the earliest sources of administrative regulations is actually recorded in what Jewish people call the Torah, which contains the Mosaic law. Reading these laws today can be confusing, especially since laws about crime are mixed in with laws about personal hygiene, diet, disease prevention, and even compensation for personal injury.

It's important to keep in mind, however, that the idea of a written law was almost unheard of in the world at that time, and these were former slaves who should have had little, if any, idea of how to govern themselves. Much was at stake. In a desert land surrounded by hostile, wicked forces and with no natural sources of food and water, even small mistakes could doom the community.

Much of the law God revealed to Moses still forms the basis for law today, especially in the West. Take, for example, Exodus 21:33: "When a man opens a pit, or when a man digs a pit and does not cover it, and an ox or a donkey falls into it, the owner of the pit shall make restoration. He shall give money to its owner, and the dead beast shall be his." This law established relationships between neighbors. In reference to a case about a conflict between two neighbors, Lord Atkin said in the nineteenth century,

> The rule that you are to love your neighbour becomes in law: You must not injure your neighbour, and the lawyer's question: Who is my neighbour? receives a restricted reply. You must take reasonable care to avoid acts or omissions which you can reasonably foresee would be likely to injure your neighbour. Who, then, in law, is my neighbour? The answer seems to be persons who are so closely and directly affected by my act that I ought reasonably to have them in contemplation as being so affected when I am directing my mind to the acts or omissions which are called into question.[9]

The biblical principles regarding neighbors' obligations to one another became the basis of **tort law** (from the Latin word *torquere*, meaning "twisted out of its natural shape"). Tort law governs harms that can come as people live and work together. It includes remedies for things like negligence, which is when a person harms another person through carelessness when that person was obligated to have been more careful. In securing order, though, it is possible to hurt people in violation of the law. This leads to the second function of law, securing justice.

Tort Law: the area of law governing remedies for those wronged by others, such as through negligence.

Justice. In defining *justice*, Yale University's Nicholas Wolterstorff said, "A society is just insofar as its members enjoy the goods to which they have a right."[10] This assumes, of course, that there is a higher law that has been revealed. The founders of America referred to *securing* liberty, not *granting* it. The Constitution of the United States is formed around this premise, as is evident in its preamble:

> We the People of the United States, in Order to form a more perfect Union, establish Justice, insure domestic Tranquility, provide for the common defence, promote the general Welfare, and secure the Blessings of Liberty to ourselves and our Posterity, do ordain and establish this Constitution for the United States of America.

By securing liberty, the Constitution assumes that laws are discovered, not developed; found, not created. Most of the founders believed this is so because everyone can observe God's revelation in nature if they have not suppressed their ability to observe it by other commitments. On this basis, it is possible to establish a body of laws to remove barriers to economic arrangements, create a framework for resolving disputes, establish accountability that restrains evil, and provide a better environment in which everyone is allowed to flourish if they choose to do so.

Of course, some philosophers have tried to develop a basis for justice apart from referencing God's nature and character. Many law textbooks, for example, go back to the philosophy of utilitarianism, as Jeremy Bentham (1748–1832) articulated it: "Nature has placed mankind under the governance of two sovereign masters, pain and pleasure," he said.[11] Bentham believed justice could be secured through a "felicific calculus"—the greatest happiness for the greatest number of people.

Wolterstorff strongly disagrees with Bentham. The pursuit of happiness (*eudaimonia*, the Greek word for "a life well lived") is problematic because our idea of happiness today has little to do with creating space for living virtuously. Trying to make everybody happy would only result in using government coercion to give people what they want.[12] It would be legal, but it might not be right.

In order to secure justice, we have to get to the root of the question "What is legal?" versus "What is right?" In the twentieth century this came to a head in the Nuremberg trials of the major war criminals after World War II. Were these trials legitimate? After all, Germany had a body of laws and a court system. If the highest law is the law of the state, then everything the Nazis did was *legal*. Clearly these monsters needed to be punished, but on what *basis*?

If law is based on morality known by everyone at all times in all cultures, the answer is straightforward. Nazi law was a perversion of clear standards that were obvious to anyone and should thus, by its nature, have been deemed illegal. Secularists, though, cannot rationally take this perspective. From their viewpoint, there is no revealed morality. Because we are evolving as human beings, our morality changes to meet our new circumstances.

This question was not resolved. In Nuremberg the international community proceeded even though the laws the Nazis were accused of breaking did not exist when they were in power. What gave the Allied forces the right to try the Nazis? Because they assumed power by winning the war? If power is a sufficient basis for law, did the Nazis have the right to do what they wanted as long as they were in power? Would they have been justified to continue their atrocities had they won the war? If not, why not?

The fiercest debate on this issue was carried out between two legal scholars, H. L. A. Hart and Lon Fuller. Hart argued for **legal positivism**, which says that law is what those who have the authority agree to do. Fuller, on the other hand, took a **natural law** view: law should be based on an internal morality that all people possess.[13] In his book on the subject, Fuller, a law professor at Harvard, said just laws are based on eight rules:

1. The rules must be spelled out so people will know what to do and what not to do.
2. The rules must be publicized so people will know about them.
3. The rules must not be used to judge actions taken before the rules were adopted.
4. The rules must be clear and understandable.
5. The rules must not contradict one another.
6. It must be within the power of the people affected to follow the rules.

7. The rules must not be changed frequently, or the people who are to follow them will be unable to decide what to do.
8. Those in charge of enforcing the rules must actually do so.[14]

These common sense principles, constantly referred to in debates about whether certain laws are appropriate, provide the basis for legal standards to this day.

Since the time of Fuller, though, the focus has moved to "justice as fairness," or using the law to redistribute society's goods in order to compensate for unfair advantages some are said to have received. In *A Theory of Justice*, widely considered the most important work of legal philosophy of our time, the late Harvard professor John Rawls proposed a new kind of justice called *distributive justice*. "These principles are the principles of social justice," he wrote. "They provide a way of assigning rights and duties in the basic institutions of society and they define the appropriate distribution of the benefits and burdens of social cooperation."[15] There are obviously many controversies surrounding this view, and we will examine them in a little more detail in the upcoming chapter on politics.

As with each discipline we have examined, we'll now look at the radically different views of law that each of the six different worldviews hold.

4. SECULARISM

As we have seen, Secularists believe morality to be both constructed by humans and subject to change. If there is no such thing as an objective standard of right and wrong, however, then laws designed to ensure fairness and justice might actually create unfairness and injustice. After all, Secularist theology says God does not exist or is irrelevant, and that only matter exists (materialism). Secularist biology and sociology, on the assumption that only matter exists, assume that everything around us can be explained through natural processes (naturalism). These two assumptions form the secular view of society, according to Julian Huxley: "Our present knowledge indeed forces us to the view that the world of reality is evolution—a single process of self-transformation."[16] Natural processes, Secularists assume, have selected humans as the most advanced species. Secularists trust themselves to create a just legal system because, as Malachi Martin pointed out, "we ourselves are the authors of our destiny. Man is exalted. The God-Man is repudiated; and with him, the idea of man's fallenness is rejected."[17]

The key understanding of Secularist law is that it must be created to respond to where we think we are in our evolutionary process. This is far different from the Western tradition of **common law**, which is the basis of law in the United States. In common law, there are few written laws. From the law's perspective (we are not talking about a moral perspective here), it is assumed that an action is legal unless it is specifically prohibited. If a dispute arises, a judge hears the case, examines previous similar cases, and finally makes a ruling. This form of ruling is called *stare decisis*, which is Latin for "it stands decided." The judge then explains his or her ruling in writing.

> *Common Law:* a legal system in which courts reach legal decisions based upon prior judicial precedent reached through common sense and reason.

In the Western tradition, legal writings form a body of what is called *case law*. Lawyers study these cases and compose briefs to persuade judges to see the cases the way they think gives their clients an advantage. Is a certain tax deduction legal? To know the answer, you have to delve into court cases where people challenged the law to see what the judge decided. If the Internal Revenue Service challenges your deduction, and you decide to take the case to court, you can assume a judge will look at previous cases to determine your case.

Common law assumes that what people did in the past was based on common sense and reason, and that it should set a precedent for what to do now. Attorneys get paid to scan history and pluck out cases they think are relevant and try to persuade judges to see it their way. Juries of citizens are often involved and are trusted to determine whether an injustice has occurred. A verdict of guilty or not guilty is then rendered.

> Common law assumes that what people did in the past was based on common sense and reason, and that it should set a precedent for what to do now.

Here's the problem from the Secularist viewpoint: If you believe humanity is evolving and that people in the past were ignorant and unenlightened, why would you care about precedent? You wouldn't. Newer is better. For example, when Ruth Bader Ginsburg, as of this writing a member of the United States Supreme Court, appeared on Egyptian television, she publicly lamented having "a rather old constitution." She recommended Egyptians look to newer, "better" constitutions than the US Constitution.[18]

As you might imagine, Darwin's evolutionary theory profoundly influenced the Secularist conception of law. Oliver Wendell Holmes Jr., a famous twentieth-century Supreme Court justice, said, "I see no reason for attributing to man a significance different in kind from that which belongs to a baboon or a grain of sand."[19] Holmes thought our own time demanded something more than common sense or reason: "The felt necessities of the time, the prevalent moral and political theories, intuitions of public policy, avowed or unconscious, even the prejudices which judges share with their fellow-men, have a good deal more to do than the syllogism in determining the rules by which men should be governed."[20]

If we are really no different from baboons in need only of laws that fit the necessities of our time, Secularists assume that we'll have a better society when we set aside the archaic laws of the past and explore new legal ground. Political scientist Bradley C. S. Watson describes Secularists as follows:

> Whatever the theoretical roots or disciplinary orientations of the realists, all saw the Constitution as a fundamentally flawed document and decried any efforts to interpret it on its own terms. Statutory law, and even more the Constitution, was seen as an epiphenomenon of deep class biases and social forces unrelated to principles of right or justice. At the same time, it was assumed the best and brightest could extract themselves from the influence of these social phenomena that swept others along like tiny corks on a great river. Given a clear-eyed view of what law "really" is, along with sympathetic legislatures, the right kinds of sociological arguments, and, eventually, a less conservative judiciary, they could put themselves in the vanguard of history.[21]

Obviously, this kind of thinking does not lead to confidence in a natural law that is true for all times in all cultures. Secularist philosopher Delos McKown asks sarcastically, "When, one wonders, in evolutionary history did hominids first acquire natural rights?"[22] For Paul Kurtz, "Most ... rights have evolved out of the cultural, economic, political, and social structures that have prevailed."[23] This denial of natural rights leads to a denial of natural law: "How are these principles [of equality, freedom, etc.] to be justified?" asked Kurtz. "They are not derived from a divine or natural law, nor do they have any special metaphysical status. They are rules offered to govern how we shall behave. They can be justified only by reference to their results."[24]

> **This denial of natural rights leads to a denial of natural law.**

If laws and rights are not—as the signers of the Declaration of Independence thought—derived from the "Laws of Nature and Nature's God," where *do* they come from? The answer is legal positivism, which says that law is not tied to morality. Rather, it is whatever the order of things declares it to be. Les Greene, professor of philosophy at Oxford University, offers a thorough and clear definition of legal positivism:

> **If laws and rights are not—as the signers of the Declaration of Independence thought— derived from the "Laws of Nature and Nature's God," where *do* they come from?**

> What laws are in force in that system depends on what social standards its officials recognize as authoritative; for example, legislative enactments, judicial decisions, or social customs.... According to positivism, law is a matter of what has been posited (ordered, decided, practiced, tolerated, etc.); as we might say in a more modern idiom, positivism is the view that law is a social construction.[25]

Legal positivism says that law is what those in power choose to do. To put it plainly, "might makes right." Morality and law are not related, except by coincidence. According to Max Hocutt, "Human beings may, and do, make up their own rules. All existing moralities and all existing laws are human artifacts, products of human society, social conventions."[26]

So where did we ever get the idea that laws were based in objective standards? To Roscoe Pound, one of the twentieth century's most cited legal authorities, governments gave that impression in their efforts to convince the governed that law was a fixed thing:

> From the time when lawgivers gave over the attempt to maintain the general security by belief that particular bodies of human law had been divinely dictated or divinely revealed or divinely sanctioned, they have had to wrestle with the problem of proving to mankind that the law was something fixed and settled, whose authority was beyond question, while at the same time enabling it to make constant readjustments and occasional radical changes under the pressure of infinite and variable human desires.[27]

As judges make these decisions, the idea of representative democracy gives way to what Robert Bork called "Olympianism," the belief that activist judges are an intellectual elite ordained to shape a nation's destiny from the bench.[28]

Matter is all there is. We are evolving. God is irrelevant. The founders were naive. The ideas that truth is self-evident; that all are created equal by a creator who gives unalienable rights to life, liberty, and the pursuit of happiness; and that just power is derived from the consent of the governed, to the Secularist, are nothing more than relics of past thinking.

5. MARXISM

To the Marxist, the idea of law based on God's revelation is nothing more than a means of controlling the workers and preventing society's evolution toward communism. Lenin said, "In what sense do we repudiate ethics and morality?... In the sense in which it was preached by the bourgeoisie, who derived ethics from God's commandments. We, of course, say that we do not believe in God." Since Marx did not believe in God,[29] it was inconceivable that laws would be based on his will. Rather, they were based on the will of the bourgeoisie: "Your very ideas are but the outgrowth of the conditions of your bourgeoisie production and bourgeoisie property, just as your jurisprudence is but the will of your class made into a law for all."[30]

L. S. Jawitsch, a modern-day Marxist legal theorist, maintained Lenin's denial of anything supernatural, saying, "There are no eternal, immutable principles of law."[31] But Marxists go further: law is only necessary because economic classes exist and come into conflict with one another. Engels said,

> In order that these ... classes with conflicting economic interests, may not annihilate themselves and society in a useless struggle, a power becomes necessary that stands apparently above society and has the function of keeping down the conflicts and maintaining "order." And this power, the outgrowth of society, but assuming supremacy over it and becoming more and more divorced from it, is the State.[32]

Lenin affirmed this thinking: "The State is an organ of class domination, an organ of oppression of one class by another."[33] Laws are thus imposed by the state to quell these disturbances.

The Marxist reasons that if economic classes cease to exist because the proletariat (working class) has triumphed over the bourgeoisie (the property owners), then no law or government will really be necessary. In the short run, new socialist laws will need to be devised to remove the exploitation built into bourgeois law, but this will pass away. According to Jawitsch, "An anti-exploiter tendency is what characterizes the special features of all the principles of the law of socialist society in [its] most concentrated form."[34]

> **The Marxist reasons that if economic classes cease to exist because the proletariat (working class) has triumphed over the bourgeoisie (the property owners), then no law or government will really be necessary.**

This new system of law, it is supposed, will be built around the needs of the workers and farmers. Howard Selsam explained:

Marxism, which has been so often accused of seeking to eliminate moral considerations from human life and history emphasizes rather the moral issues involved in every situation. It does so, however, not by standing on a false platform of absolute right, but by identifying itself with the real needs and interests of the workers and farmers.[35]

Such a system of law must be flexible because the needs of the workers and farmers may change through time. E. B. Pashukanis wrote, "We require that our legislation possess maximum elasticity. We cannot fetter ourselves by any sort of system."[36]

The courts must be structured with the same goals. Jawitsch described law in a Marxist society this way: "As a component of the legal superstructure law is closely linked with the political superstructure and with the state."[37] Lenin agreed, saying, "A court is an organ of state power. Liberals sometimes forget that. It is a sin for a Marxist to forget it."[38] Courts must be reoriented to remove the vestiges of bourgeoisie law by any means, including authorizing violence. Lenin said boldly, "The revolutionary dictatorship of the proletariat is won and maintained by the use of violence by the proletariat against the bourgeoisie, rule that is unrestricted by any laws."[39] No restrictions on this power will be tolerated. Given these assumptions, it is easy to see why Marxists are not interested in Western ideas about human rights.[40]

According to **proletariat law**, only the working class is capable of deciding the laws because only they have the necessary "class-consciousness." Of course, not every person in the working class can make these decisions, so the Communist Party takes on that responsibility on their behalf. Andrey Vyshinsky explained: "There might be collisions and discrepancies between the formal commands of laws and those of the proletarian revolution.... This collision must be solved only by the subordination of the formal commands of law to those of party policy."[41] This is a fancy way of saying, as the pigs said in *Animal Farm*, "All animals are equal, but animals some are more equal than others."[42]

> *Proletariat Law:*
> a system of laws shaped by Communist Party officials that are intended to promote the interests of the working class over the bourgeoisie.

Of course, Marxist theorists insist, this kind of brute force is made necessary only because of capitalism. Once society has been thoroughly disinfected, all people will create and live in an environment that promotes harmony, and the need for law will dissolve. Criminal activity will be practically nonexistent, Marxists claim, and the causes of anti-social activity, injustice, and inequality will cease to exist. John Plamenatz said that in a communist society, crime will be "virtually unknown" because "motives will be less urgent and frequent, and the offender will be more easily brought to his senses by the need to regain the good opinion of his neighbors."[43]

The fact that no such society has ever materialized fails to discourage Marxists, even today. Their faith in their underlying assumptions is so complete, they think it must be true. If we haven't seen it yet, it is because of the ongoing power of capitalism and the refusal of current legislatures and courts to destroy it.

But ideas have consequences: a view that fails to acknowledge the dignity of humans as God's image bearers or the source of law as God's nature and character will have a devastating impact on society. If the ideas of Lenin, Stalin, Mao Tse-tung, Pol Pot, and other Marxist dictators are any indication, the consequence is one of body count. Marxist governments have managed to kill, on purpose, more human beings than any other worldview in history.[44]

6. POSTMODERNISM

When Sonia Sotomayor was nominated as a United States Supreme Court justice, a line from a speech she had given at the University of California, Berkley, became the target of scrutiny. "I would hope," she said, "that a wise Latina woman with the richness of her experiences would more often than not reach a better conclusion than a white male who hasn't lived that life."[45] Why would a different race entail different understandings of wisdom? It sounds like a denial of absolute truth. President Obama, who had nominated her, took to the television cameras to allay people's concerns. She was quickly confirmed, and she joined the court. However, a closer look at the entire speech, called "A Latino Judge's Voice," reveals that critics of her judicial philosophy had not taken the quote "out of context," as the American people were told. In her speech Sotomayor approvingly quoted Harvard Law School professor Martha Minnow, who said, "There is no objective stance but only a series of perspectives—no neutrality, no escape from choice in judging."[46]

If Justice Sotomayor thinks law cannot be neutral, that there is no basis for how one applies the law, then what foundation is there for any true understanding of law and justice? A graduate of one of Summit Ministries' twelve-day leadership schools was able to pose this precise question as a US Senate staffer attending a lecture by Justice Sotomayor: "Justice Sotomayor, what should be the foundation for understanding and applying justice in America?" After an extended moment of silence, Sotomayor replied, "I don't think I've ever considered that question in that form before." After another moment of silence, she concluded, "I suppose for me it would be the inherent dignity of all people, but I'm not sure what it would be for anyone else."[47]

Setting aside the question of how a Supreme Court justice of the United States might have never considered the foundations of justice, Sotomayor's answer betrays something of the Postmodern view of law. What might be a foundation for one person might not be a foundation "for anyone else." If law has no essential nature, if there is no essential moral truth, what does it mean to speak of people's "inherent" value? Are empirical data, objective knowledge, objective facts, and claims of "justice" nothing more than tricks people in power perform to make everyone else see them as right?

> It's not that Postmodernists don't want justice. It's that they view anything resulting from the power structures of Christianity and the Enlightenment as unjust.

It's not that Postmodernists don't want justice. It's that they view anything resulting from the power structures of Christianity and the Enlightenment as unjust. Therefore the postmodern understanding of justice in relation to the law is not actually connected to any objective standards. Rather, it is the process of uncovering the various forms of oppression. As Daniel Farber and Suzanna Sherry argue,

Postmodernists attack the concepts of reason and objective truth, condemning them as components of white male domination. They prefer the more subjective "ways of knowing" supposedly favored by women and minorities, such as storytelling. As to the rule of law, it is an article of [postmodern] faith that legal rules are indeterminate and serve only to disguise the law's white male bias.[48]

For this reason, Postmodernists are bent on sniffing out and destroying religious roots and transcendent qualities from Western law. They *embrace* the fragmentation and subjectivity of law because it puts the spotlight on social justice and helps create left-wing political change. But if there is no such thing as true justice, what merit is there to Postmodernist complaints about injustice? Figuring out the Postmodernist answer to that question requires us to consider ideas well outside the normal bounds of legal thought.

Postmodernism in law forms a frontal assault on traditional Western law. Leading the attack is the **critical legal studies** (CLS) movement, which for thirty years or so has focused on publishing "critiques of law focused on progressive—even radical—political change rather than on efficient government."[49] In fact, the CLS slogan is "Critique is all there is." As we saw in the chapter on Postmodernism, this way of thinking is based on the work of Jacques Derrida, who tried to show how texts of all kinds could be "deconstructed" to reveal their hidden meanings. Legal scholars use Derrida's techniques to dissect laws to discover how they create or contribute to "unequal power relations."[50]

Critical Legal Studies (CLS): the practice of deconstructing laws in order to discover their subjective meaning and biased intent.

Postmodernists take **social constructionism**, the Secularist view of sociology, a step further: if reality is socially constructed, and if we feel oppressed, then those who did the constructing have probably constructed reality to secure their own power ("hegemony"). Just as Foucault saw all relationships between people as power relationships, Postmodernists assert that objective knowledge is, as Farber and Sherry describe, "a power relation, one category of people benefiting at the expense of another category of people."[51] Farber and Sherry quote one feminist as saying, "Feminist analysis begins with the principle that objective reality is a myth."[52] Universal standards of legal judgment, common to all, do not exist. Therefore, any view of law a feminist thinks enshrines patriarchy is invalid on its face.

Social Constructionism: the belief that human beings and society are social constructions shaped by law and subjective experience.

So what do you do if you think the law is being used improperly to enshrine a metanarrative with which you disagree? If others have used the law to illegitimately gain power, Postmodernists don't feel bad about using the law to get it back. There is no objective means of knowing truth, no objective concept of justice—only politics. As Stanley Fish, professor of law and English, admits, "The name of the game has always been politics."[53] In the same speech cited earlier, Sotomayor said, "I accept the proposition that, as Judge Resnick describes it, 'to judge is an exercise of power.'"[54]

If others have used the law to illegitimately gain power, Postmodernists don't feel bad about using the law to get it back.

So let's see if we've got this: objective reasoning is bad, and law is not about justice but about political power. If these statements are accurate, why should we listen to Postmodernists? They're just as biased as anyone else. Recognizing this problem, some Postmodernists have decided to stop trying to make logical arguments to appeal to the mind and start telling stories that appeal to the heart. Farber and Sherry explain:

> Because the scholarship of women and people of color reflects their distinctive knowledge [gained from listening to and telling stories], the radical multiculturalists argue, it cannot be judged or tested by traditional standards. Instead, they imply, it should be judged according to its political effect: it should be judged "in terms of its ability to advance the interests of the outsider community," because "outsider scholarship is often aimed not at understanding the law, but at changing it."[55]

If this idea of *changing* the law rather than *understanding* it sounds familiar, it's because it is. This is how Marx viewed the academic disciplines; we should harness them to change the world in our image. The change Postmodernists pursue is not aimed toward any stable sense of justice; rather, it is driven by a sense of inevitable injustice. As a case in point, here is Justice Sotomayor's questionable quotation in its full context:

> Justice O'Connor has often been cited as saying that a wise old man and wise old woman will reach the same conclusion in deciding cases. I am not so sure Justice O'Connor is the author of that line.... I am also not so sure that I agree with the statement. First, as Professor Martha Minnow has noted, there can never be a universal definition of wise. Second, I would hope that a wise Latina woman with the richness of her experiences would more often than not reach a better conclusion than a white male who hasn't lived that life.[56]

To Postmodernists, this makes perfect sense. "Law" isn't based on any objective truth. It's just the perspective a person brings to a situation. Justice Sotomayor thinks this would lead to better decisions. But couldn't it just as well lead to worse ones?

In 2006 a part-time stripper named Crystal Gail Mangum accused three members of the Duke University lacrosse team of rape. After a thorough and very public examination of the evidence, all charges were dropped and the students were proclaimed innocent. Prosecuting attorney Mike Nifong lost his law license because of several ethical violations. During the process, a group of eighty-eight Duke University professors signed an advertisement in a Duke newspaper implying that the charges were true. Forsaking the principle of "innocent until proven guilty," one of the professors behind the advertisement, Wahneema Lubiano, called the lacrosse players "almost perfect offenders" and "exemplars of the upper end of the class hierarchy, the politically dominant race and ethnicity, the dominant gender, the dominant sexuality, and the dominant social group on campus" and promised to pursue the issue "regardless of the 'truth' established ... and 'whatever happens with the court case.' "[57]

In the mind of Lubiano, the story Magnum told was true even though it didn't accord with the facts, because it nonetheless fit Lubiano's conception of how the world is. Lubiano's actions, along with the other eighty-seven professors who joined her crusade, created an emotional backlash against the lacrosse players (one professor even flunked two of the players without justification, a decision she reversed only when a court decision forced her to do so). The lives of many people were upended, and many reputations were besmirched. Much injustice was done in the service of a story that rang true for people who could imagine, as has happened in history, a powerless, young black woman being mistreated by powerful white men.

Farber and Sherry illustrate how this shift influences legal theory: "Rather than relying solely on legal or interdisciplinary authorities, empirical data, or rigorous analysis, legal scholars have begun to offer stories, often about their own real or imagined experiences."[58] If logic and dispassionate reasoning are tools of white male bias, then stories confirming this must be true, whether they are factual or not.

Trial lawyer Gary Saalman predicts the results of a postmodern focus on racial, gender, and cultural politics becoming an integral part of the legal system:

> Postmodern legal theory trickles down to breed cynicism toward all government and the entire criminal justice system. This, then, is the real issue. No one questions the fact that law requires interpretation, or that judges or juries may have acted unfairly, sometimes based on race or gender bias. The question is this: How do we view such unfairness? Do we accept that all people must inevitably be unfair and subjective, as postmodernists claim? Or do we recognize such unfairness as the evil it is and resist it? When we accept what postmodernism preaches, we lose all basis for calling the system to fairness. We instead challenge minority populations to pursue power so they can take their turn.[59]

Saalman's point is worth taking seriously. Yes, injustice exists, but which response is the better remedy: to search for true justice or to cynically abandon the idea of justice altogether?

Postmodernists say they speak for the dispossessed, but by their own admission, they are merely trying to grab the reins of power from the hands of others. If what they say about the powerlessness of minorities and women is true, though, this is a risky strategy. It is precarious to advocate the use of raw power when you are not the one who possesses it. In the end, Postmodernism depends for its success on whether people who actually believe in justice are touched by its stories of injustice. We are not aware of any other worldview like this, which depends for its success on the goodwill of those whose sensibilities have been refined by their thoroughgoing rejection of its underlying assumptions.

> **Postmodernists say they speak for the dispossessed, but by their own admission, they are merely trying to grab the reins of power from the hands of others.**

7. NEW SPIRITUALITY

New Spiritualists do not spend much energy discussing law, justice, and judgment. They prefer instead to concentrate on personal inner development, getting in touch with the God within. As Marianne Williamson says, "As extensions of God, we are ourselves the spirit of compassion, and in our right minds, we don't seek to judge but to heal."[60]

The unwillingness of New Spiritualists to develop a coherent theory of law, though, carries great implications for all of society. If each of us is a god, we can decide the legality of an action only by getting in touch with our inner gods. Each of us is his or her own legal authority, and any manifestation of outside authority hinders our communication with our godhood. Shakti Gawain explains:

The real problem with commitment to an external form is that it doesn't allow room for the inevitable changes and growth of people and relationships. If you promise to feel or behave by a certain set of rules, eventually you are going to have to choose between being true to yourself and being true to those rules.[61]

If we choose to honor a set of rules other than inner truth, we sacrifice our godhood. Gawain reiterates what happens when we look to authority outside ourselves: "When we consistently suppress and distrust our intuitive knowingness, looking instead for [external] authority, validation, and approval from others, we give our personal power away."[62]

New Spiritualists, then, focus on their own power, authority, and rules as they pursue higher consciousness. Gawain explains: "As each of us connects with our inner spiritual awareness, we learn that the creative power of the universe is within us. We also learn that we can create our own reality and take responsibility for doing so."[63]

We struggle with what to call this, because it is more of a form of personal empowerment than a concept of law. Perhaps we should call it **self-law**. It does not say that the law is in our hearts but that there is no law *except* that which is in our hearts. Anything hindering our search for higher consciousness is bad. David Spangler, through the voice of what he claimed was a channeled spirit, said, "Their world (of darkness) is under the law and shall disappear"[64]

> *Self-law:* the legal perspective that maintains actions are lawful only if honorable to the god within and unlawful if imposed by an outside authority.

Having an inadequate concept of law makes it difficult for New Spiritualists to grapple with difficult realities like crime. According to Kevin Ryerson, "Mankind, and all life, is basically good."[65] People who commit crimes are guilty not of violating a standard of justice but of succumbing to the pain experienced by falling short in their quest for higher consciousness. Eckhart Tolle seems to even relish this kind of legal defense: "To my knowledge so far, no defense lawyer has said to the judge—although the day may not be far off—'This is a case of diminished responsibility. My client's pain-body was activated, and he did not know what he was doing. In fact, he didn't do it. His pain-body did.' "[66]

> In the New Spiritualist worldview, achieving higher consciousness is the most important thing.

In the New Spiritualist worldview, achieving higher consciousness is the most important thing. Mark Satin says, "Getting in touch with our selves would appear to be, not just fun (though it can be that), and not self-indulgence at all, but an imperative for survival that's built right in to the structure of the universe. (Maybe even an evolutionary imperative.)"[67] Joseph Campbell agreed, saying, "I always tell my students [to] go where your body and soul want to go. When you have the feeling, then stay with it, and don't let anyone throw you off."[68] People should follow their bliss, according to Campbell.[69] What implications follow the application of this to law and justice? New Spiritualists aren't worried—the search for higher consciousness goes on.

8. Islam

Freedom House, a nonprofit organization cataloging the state of freedom in the world's nations, rejoiced in its 2013 report that despite an overall decrease in freedom in the world, at least one Muslim-dominated nation, Egypt, was freer after its revolution than before.[70] The researchers at Freedom House, though, have missed one of the most significant aspects of this revolution. The president of Egypt at the time of their report, Mohamed Morsi, is a member of the Muslim Brotherhood, a group deeply committed to Islamizing the world. In a presidential address, Morsi led the crowd in a call and response:

Mohamed Morsi: The Koran is our constitution.

Crowd: The Koran is our constitution.

Mohamed Morsi: The Prophet Muhammad is our leader.

Crowd: The Prophet Muhammad is our leader.

Mohamed Morsi: Jihad is our path.

Crowd: Jihad is our path.

Mohamed Morsi: And death for the sake of Allah is our most lofty aspiration.

Crowd: And death for the sake of Allah is our most lofty aspiration.

Mohamed Morsi: Above all—Allah is our goal.

Morsi followed this chant with a pledge to aggressively implement shariah law: "The shari'a, then the shari'a,[71] and finally, the shari'a. This nation will enjoy blessing and revival only through the Islamic shari'a." At the time of this writing, Morsi has been deposed in a military coup. But that someone with Morsi's beliefs could take over such an influential nation is unsettling, to say the least.

Western observers cannot understand the incredible implications of this speech without an understanding of Islam's highly developed and detailed legal traditions. Unlike the Christian worldview, Islam teaches that God reveals only his law, not himself.[72] The body of laws based on this revelation, shariah, is seen as divine law, coeternal with God.[73] Indeed, "the *Shari'ah* itself is considered to be a timeless manifestation of the will of God, subject neither to history nor circumstance."[74] The goal of Muslim jurists, according to journalist and Islam expert Malise Ruthven, "is not law making, but *fiqh*—understanding or knowledge of a law deemed to exist already."[75] Understanding **shariah law** involves a thorough study of four sources: the Quran, the *Sunnah* (the practice of Muhammad), the *ima'* (consensus of the Islamic community), and *qiyas* (analogical reasoning). It specifies five categories of laws: acts that are commanded, forbidden, disapproved, recommended, and indifferent.[76]

> *Shariah Law:* Derived primarily from the Quran and *Sunnah*, shariah law is the moral and legal code that governs the lives of Muslims. Shariah addresses a wide variety of subjects, such as diet, hygiene, prayer, contracts, business, crime, and punishment.

For legal scholar Havva G. Guney-Ruebenacker, shariah law is primarily for the purpose of protecting "human life, human reason, offspring, right to property and freedom of speech."[77] But when the provisions of shariah are taken together, most Westerners would be horrified: killing of homosexuals, adulterers, apostates (people who leave Islam), and blasphemers (anyone who says anything negative about Allah or the prophet Muhammad). Marital rape is condoned, amputation of limbs for theft is commanded, and whipping, selling into slavery, and oppressing nonconverts is demanded, as is the nonnegotiable duty of war against infidels.[78]

What impact does this have on America? Journalist Paul Williams, an unabashed Secularist, is deeply alarmed:

> If Islam continues to grow at its present rate, critical mass will be achieved by 2020 and the eventual Muslim transformation of America will become a statistical possibility. This is not to say that sharia will be the law of the land, but it is to affirm that the religion of the prophet will be a force that cannot be denied by our elected officials. Demands will be met; concessions granted.[79]

A Muslim Brotherhood strategy document discovered, translated, and entered into the transcript of a 2007 trial of leaders of the Holy Land Foundation for supporting a foreign terrorist organization supported Williams's concern. This document read, in part,

> The process of settlement is a "Civilization-Jihadist Process" with all the word means. The *Ikhwan* [Islamic religious militia] must understand that their work in America is a kind of grand Jihad in eliminating and destroying the Western civilization from within and "sabotaging" its miserable house by their hands and the hands of the believers so that it is eliminated and God's religion is made victorious over all other religions.[80]

Whether the Muslim Brotherhood has the resources to carry out this mission, and whether the American people have the political will to resist it remains to be seen.

The greatest concern shariah-law critics express is the inevitability of human rights violations, the destruction of due process, and the corruption of those nations following it. Lord Acton coined the now-famous phrase, "Power tends to corrupt; absolute power corrupts absolutely."[81] Humans should not be trusted with too much power. In the United States, this has led to a distribution of power among the branches of government, the executive, the legislative, and the judicial. This division balances power and checks its abuse.

> The greatest concern shariah-law critics express is the inevitability of human rights violations, the destruction of due process, and the corruption of those nations following it.

Islam, as we have seen earlier in this volume, does not share the sin-nature view. Ruthven says,

> Because the Islamist model is predicated on the belief in government by morally impeccable individuals who can be counted on to resist temptation, it does not generate institutions capable of functioning autonomously by means of structural checks and balances. Political institutions function only as a result of the virtue of those who run them, but virtue can become widespread only if society is already Islamic.[82]

Muslims do not share the view that leaders inherently tend toward corruption, and thus they are much more willing to abide authoritarian government. No wonder nations with a predominately Muslim population tend toward dictatorship or monarchy. In its report *Freedom in the World 2013*, Freedom House listed forty-seven nations that received a rating of "not free." Of the countries in the Middle East and North Africa, most of which have Muslim governments and largely Muslim populations, only 22 percent were free, and 66 percent were not free.[83]

In Saudi Arabia, churches are prohibited from being built. Christians must worship in the privacy of their own homes and refrain from even praying out loud so that faithful Muslims can remain untainted by Christianity. In Algeria, a law passed in 2005 pronounced as criminal any means of enticing a Muslim to another religion, including even producing, storing, or distributing "printed documents or audio-visual formats or any other format or means which seeks to shake the faith of a Muslim."[84]

So far, opposition to Islamic law's growth is limited. Shariah law is spreading rapidly, and people seem incapable of speaking up against it. This may be changing. In 2011, a group of reform-minded Muslims issued a statement that read, in part,

> Like all totalitarianisms, Islamism is nurtured by fears and frustrations. The preachers of hate bet on these feelings in order to form battalions destined to impose a world of inequality. But we clearly and firmly state: nothing, not even despair, justifies the choice of obscurantism, totalitarianism and hatred.[85]

Whether this call to action will be heeded, or whether it is too little, too late, cannot be known at the present time. Much depends on how proponents of democratic freedom respond.

Even a casual look at Freedom House's "Map of Freedom" reveals an undeniable link between freedom and worldview.[86] Against the Muslim tendency toward totalitarianism, the nations with the highest regard for basic human rights and the rule of law are those influenced most by Christianity. Law cannot be discussed in isolation from other aspects of a worldview. In order to retain personal freedoms within a society, a legal system must have a sustainable foundation. Ideas have consequences.

Law cannot be discussed in isolation from other aspects of a worldview.

9. CHRISTIANITY

Christians believe that God gave us divine laws and the means of discovering them. Carl F. H. Henry says, "God is the only Legislator. Earthly rulers and legislative bodies are alike accountable to Him from whom stems all obligation—religious, ethical and civil"[87] (2 Chron. 20:6; Acts 17:24–31).[88]

You may be thinking, *Now wait a minute. You just criticized Islamic law by saying that its supposed "divine inspiration" from God is what makes it so scary. Now you're saying that Christian law is divinely inspired. What's the difference?*

The issue is not one of divine inspiration but of the nature and character of that divinity and the revelation proceeding from it. As Russell Kirk said, "To cut off Law from its ethical sources is to strike a terrible blow at the rule of law."[89] Our premise in this section of the chapter will be as follows: Christians, in acknowledging humans as image bearers of God but also taking into account human fallenness, have created a system of justice that, while imperfect, has provided for greater order and justice than any other system. We will examine this claim by discussing the basic precepts of Christian law, a Christian view of natural law, and the implications of applying a biblical view to society.

Christian law consists of six basic precepts:

1. The source of all divine law is the character and nature of God. Francis Schaeffer said, "God has a character, and His character is the law of the universe."[90] Not all things are the same to God. Some things conform to his character, and some do not.
2. The moral order proceeds from and reflects the character of God—his holiness, justice, truth, love, and mercy. God's moral order is as real as the physical order.
3. We are created in God's image and thus are significant. Our lives are not afterthoughts or accidents. God established human government to protect human life, rights, and dignity (Gen. 9:6; Rom. 13).[91]
4. We humans possess a nature that is in rebellion against God, and thus we need to turn from our vain ways (Acts 14: 8–18; James 5:1–6).[92] Because of this aspect of our nature, we must have restraint and accountability.
5. God the creator became God the redeemer by taking on the very human form he had created (John 1:14).[93]
6. God will judge the whole human race through Christ according to his standard of good and evil (Acts 17:31; Rom. 2:16; 2 Cor. 5:10).[94]

To the Christian, these precepts form a moral law that is as true as the law of gravity. People who ignore or deny the law of gravity by jumping off a tall building don't violate the law; they prove it. In the same way, ignoring or denying the prohibition against murder or theft has severe consequences for a citizenry. People become discouraged, afraid, and unmotivated when justice is thrown off kilter and not set right again. To quote John Whitehead, when fundamental principles of law are undermined, "public confidence in law and public willingness to abide by law are also sapped."[95]

So where should we turn to understand law? Once again, the concepts of general and special revelation come into play not only as the basis for our understanding of God but also for our understanding of human law.[96] The bankruptcy of the world's legal and ethical codes demonstrates the need for a legal system based outside human interests. John Warwick Montgomery wrote, "The horrors of our recent history [have] forced us to recognize the puerile inadequacy of tying ultimate legal standards to the mores of a particular society, even if that society is our own."[97]

General Revelation:
God's universal revelation about himself and morality that can be obtained through nature.

General revelation and natural law. Let's begin with general revelation. God's **general revelation** to us is of both a physical and a moral character. We know this revelation through our consciences, which provide an innate sense of right and wrong. The apostle Paul said,

"When Gentiles, who do not have the law, by nature do what the law requires, they are a law to themselves, even though they do not have the law" (Rom. 2:14).

Romans 1–2 implies that all humans know a higher law exists even if they fail to obey it. In our fallen, sinful nature, we reveal that we have an understanding of what is right. Though we "see through a glass darkly" (1 Cor. 13:12 KJV), still we see. We know intuitively that certain things cut against the moral order (Rom. 1:26–32): sexual brokenness, rebellion, spitefulness, pride, boasting, disobedience, covenant breaking, and brutality.[98]

William Blackstone, one of the most influential figures in the history of law, described the Christian view of natural law this way:

> Man, considered as a creature, must necessarily be subject to the laws of his creator, for he is an entirely dependent being.... And consequently as man depends absolutely upon his maker for everything, it is necessary that he should in all points conform to his maker's will. This will of his maker is called the law of nature.[99]

Blackstone's view is consistent with the biblical account of creation, moral order, and divine law.

Special revelation and divine law. In addition to natural law, Christian legal theory must take into account God's **special revelation** of his moral order and divine law, the Bible. Natural law gives us a general concept of right and wrong. The Bible fleshes out that skeletal framework, telling us what God considers moral and lawful. In the biblical account, when God brought the nation of Israel out of Egypt, he clearly told them not to follow the legal structures either of Egypt, where they had been, or of Canaan, where they were going. Instead he set Israel apart with its own set of laws.

> *Special Revelation:* God's unique revelation about himself through the Scriptures, miraculous events (e.g. dreams, visions, prophets, prophecy, etc.), and Jesus Christ.

There seem to have been three kinds of laws in ancient Israel. Some were moral laws (prohibitions against incest, adultery, sodomy, and bestiality), ceremonial laws (laws prohibiting eating certain kinds of foods or wearing certain kinds of clothes), and judicial laws (laws against theft or lying in economic transactions). Some of these laws seem to have been specific to their particular situation, and the reasons for them are lost to us today. (As an example, imagine archaeologists two thousand years in the future puzzling over why our society considered it illegal to drive on the left side of the road.) Other laws, though, were based on realities about human design, the nature of the world, and what it takes to establish and sustain honorable homes and communities.

Throughout history Christians have seen the Bible as the only true source for discovering the nature of rights and justice, without which we will have misery. Noah Webster put it this way:

> The moral principles and precepts contained in the scriptures ought to form the basis of all our civil constitutions and laws.... All the miseries and evils which men suffer from vice, crime, ambition, injustice, oppression, slavery, and war, proceed from their despising or neglecting the precepts contained in the Bible.[100]

For Webster, if we fail to heed divine law, nothing else we do will matter:

> As there is a God in heaven, who exercises a moral government over the affairs of this world, so certainly will the neglect of the divine command, in the choice of rulers, be followed by bad laws and a bad administration; by laws unjust or partial, by corruption, tyranny, impunity of crimes, waste of public money, and a thousand other evils. Men may devise and adopt new forms of government; they may amend old forms, repair breaches, and punish violators of the constitution; there is, there can be, no effectual remedy, but obedience to the divine law.[101]

America's Declaration of Independence was crafted on the understanding that Webster articulated. Thomas Jefferson said,

> God who gave us life gave us liberty. And can the liberties of a nation be thought secure when we have removed their only firm basis, a conviction in the minds of the people that these liberties are the gift of God? That they are not to be violated but with His wrath? Indeed, I tremble for my country when I reflect that God is just; that His justice cannot sleep forever.[102]

Though Jefferson denied much of biblical revelation, he grasped enough of God's nature to recognize that if liberty is something humans give, then humans can take it away. It is either inalienable or impotent.

Because of the importance of self-government to just laws, the Christian tradition not only weighs in on what we have the right to do to others and to expect from them but also what we have the right to do to ourselves. Gary Amos says, "Men have rights, such as the right to life. But because a man has a duty to live his life for God, the right is unalienable. He can defend his life against all others, but not destroy it himself. No man has the right to do harm to himself, to commit suicide, or to waste his life."[103]

Other worldviews, such as Marxism, are utopian in that they insist on the absolute elimination of the Marxist view of sin (capitalism) before society will function properly. As long as any vestige of capitalism remains, Marxists will refuse to take any responsibility for the consequences of their actions.

> **It should also be said that the goal of Christian law is not to force people to convert to Christianity but to stabilize society by ensuring that the innocent are protected and the guilty are punished.**

From a Christian viewpoint, utopian visions are nothing more than mere fantasies, because the law cannot make everything turn out the way we want. We are made in God's image, but we are fallen. Our natures are corrupted by sin; no legal system can cause every person to always act morally. The best we can do is develop systems of accountability that make order and justice more likely than not.

It should also be said that the goal of Christian law is not to force people to convert to Christianity but to stabilize society by ensuring that the innocent are protected and the guilty are punished. This is what God requires of us: "to act justly and to love mercy and to walk humbly with [our] God" (Mic. 6:8 NIV). As justice rises, however, the law can shine light on God's law and how our longing for mercy and grace might be fulfilled

(Eph. 2). When society is just, people have a big view of God. When society is unjust, people have a small view of God.

10. Conclusion

We've hinted throughout this chapter at something most people find patently obvious but that must be carefully explored: Good laws don't just happen. They're the result of careful deliberation on the part of people who have society's best interests at heart. How this happens is something people in the domain of politics have studied for centuries. In the next chapter we'll turn our attention toward the political realm to see if we can get beyond the stereotypes of politicians to discern how to best use power to organize community.

ENDNOTES

1. Adapted from George Orwell, *Animal Farm* (Boston: Harcourt, 1949).

2. M. Tulli Ciceronis, *Orationes*, eds. George Long and A. J. Macleane (London: Whitaker, 1855), 2:353.

3. Edmund Burke, "Letter to Francois Louis Thibault de Menonville," published as "Letter to a Member of the National Assembly, 1791," in *Reflections on the Revolution in France* (Oxford, UK: Oxford University Press, 1999), 289.

4. Comments of James McHenry, in Max Farrand, ed., *The Records of the Federal Convention of 1787* (New Haven, CT: Yale University Press), 3:85.

5. Judge Learned Hand, "The Spirit of Liberty Speech," 1944, Providence Forum, www.providenceforum.org /spiritoflibertyspeech.

6. Harold Berman, *Law and Revolution: The Formation of the Western Legal Tradition* (Cambridge, MA: Harvard University Press, 1983), 39. See also the quotation and surrounding analysis in Daniel A. Farber and Suzanna Sherry, *Beyond All Reason: The Radical Assault on Truth in American Law* (Oxford, UK: Oxford University Press, 1997), 39.

7. Berman, *Law and Revolution*, 39.

8. Berman, *Law and Revolution*, 40.

9. James Richard Atkin, *Donoghue v. Stevenson*, 1932, quoted in Carol Harlow, *Understanding Tort Law*, 3rd ed. (London: Sweet and Maxwell, 2005), 47–48.

10. Nicholas Wolterstorff, *Justice: Rights and Wrongs* (Princeton, NJ: Princeton University Press, 2008), 35.

11. Quoted in Raymond Wacks, *Law: A Very Short Introduction* (Oxford, UK: Oxford University Press, 2008), 23.

12. See "Why Eudaimonism Cannot Serve as a Framework for a Theory of Rights," in Wolterstorff, *Justice*, chap. 7.

13. Richard Posner, *The Problem of Jurisprudence* (Cambridge, MA: Harvard University Press, 1990), 228–29.

14. Summarized from Lon Luvois Fuller, *The Morality of Law* (New Haven, CT: Yale University Press, 1964), 33–38.

15. John Rawls, *A Theory of Justice* (Cambridge, MA: Belknap, 2005), 4.

16. Quoted in J. R. Newman, ed., *What Is Science?* (New York: Simon and Schuster, 1955), 278.

17. Malachi Martin, *The Keys of This Blood* (New York: Simon and Schuster, 1990), 656.

18. Quoted in John Tabin, "Justice Ginsburg to Egypt: Don't Look to the US Constitution as a Model," *Spectacle Blog*, February 2, 2012, http://spectator.org/blog/2012/02/02/justice-ginsburg-to-egypt-dont.

19. Quoted in Richard Hertz, *Chance and Symbol* (Chicago: University of Chicago Press, 1948), 107. See also Albert W. Alschuler, *Law without Values: The Life, Work, and Legacy of Justice Holmes* (Chicago: University of Chicago Press, 2000). Holmes admitted his decisions were based on the fact that humanity is an evolving animal and that the concept of survival of the fittest was important to him. To some, this justifies a legal focus on animal rights. Morris B. Storer says, "What is there that's different about a human being that dictates the right to life for all humans (unarguably in most circumstances) where most people acknowledge no such right in other animals? That justifies equal right to liberty where we fence the others in, equal justice under law where the other animals are not granted any trial at all." Morris B. Storer, ed., *Humanist Ethics* (Buffalo, NY: Prometheus Books, 1980), 291.

20. Quoted in Raymond Wacks, *Law*, 24.

21. Bradley C. S. Watson, "Republics of Conscience," *National Review* 64, no. 21 (October 29, 2012): 37.

22. Delos McKown, "Demythologizing Natural Human Rights," *Humanist* (November/December 1989): 22.

23. Paul Kurtz, *Forbidden Fruit* (Buffalo, NY: Prometheus Books, 1988), 196.

24. Paul Kurtz, *The Fullness of Life* (Buffalo, NY: Prometheus Books, 1988), 162.

25. Leslie Green, *Stanford Encyclopedia of Philosophy*, January 3, 2003, s.v. "Legal Positivism," http://plato.stanford.edu/entries/legal-positivism/.

26. Quoted in Storer, ed., *Humanist Ethics*, 137.

27. Roscoe Pound, *An Introduction to the Philosophy of Law* (New Haven, CT: Yale University Press, 1969), 3.

28. Robert Bork, speech to the Council on National Policy (Washington, DC, May 13, 2006).

29. V. I. Lenin, *On Socialist Ideology and Culture* (Moscow: Foreign Languages Publishing House, 1981), 51–52, quoted in James D. Bales, *Communism and the Reality of Moral Law* (Nutley, NJ: Craig Press, 1969), 2.

30. Karl Marx and Friedrich Engels, *Manifesto of the Communist Party* (Chicago: Charles H. Kerr, 1906), 39.

31. L. S. Jawitsch, *The General Theory of Law* (Moscow: Progress Publishers, 1981), 160.

32. Friedrich Engels, *The Origin of the Family, Private Property, and the State* (Chicago: Kerr, 1902), 206.

33. V. I. Lenin, *The State and Revolution* (New York: International Publishers, 1932), 9.

34. Jawitsch, *General Theory of Law*, 160.

35. Howard Selsam, *Socialism and Ethics* (New York: International Publishers, 1943), 13.

36. E. B. Pashukanis in a speech regarding the Soviet state and the revolution of law (Moscow, 1930).

37. Jawitsch, *General Theory of Law*, 290.

38. Lenin, *Collected Works* (Moscow: Progress Publishers, 1981), 25:155, quoted in John Hazard, *Settling Disputes in Soviet Society* (New York: Columbia University Press, 1960), 3.

39. V. I. Lenin, *Collected Works*, 28:236.

40. Wacks says, "Marxists, for example, have long rejected the very idea that the law can be a neutral body of rules which guarantees liberty and legality. They spurn, in short, the ideal of the rule of law." Wacks, *Law*, 150.

41. Andrey Y. Vyshinsky, *Judiciary of the USSR*, 2nd ed. (Moscow: Progress Publishers, 1935), 32, quoted in Berman, *Justice in the USSR: An Interpretation of Soviet Law* (New York: Vintage, 1963), 42–43.

42. Orwell, *Animal Farm*, 80.

43. John Plamenatz, *Man and Society*, 2 vols. (London: Longmans, 1963), 2:374, quoted in R. W. Makepeace, *Marxist Ideology and Soviet Criminal Law* (Totowa, NJ: Barnes and Noble, 1980), 35.

44. As we noted earlier in this volume, R. J. Rummel demonstrates that more human beings in the twentieth-century died at the hands of their governments, committed to Marxist or fascist ideology, than in all previous centuries combined. See *Death by Government* (New Brunswick, NJ: Transaction, 1994).

45. See full text of Sonya Sotomayor's 2001 lecture at "Lecture: A Latina Judge's Voice," *New York Times*, May 14, 2009, www.nytimes.com/2009/05/15/us/politics/15judge.text.html?pagewanted=all&_r=0.

46. "Lecture: A Latina Judge's Voice."

47. For a compelling narrative of this example, see John Stonestreet's November 17, 2009, lecture on Postmodernism at www.summit.org/resources/summit-lecture-series/postmodernism-1/.

48. Farber and Sherry, *Beyond All Reason*, 5.

49. Farber and Sherry, *Beyond All Reason*, 19.

50. Farber and Sherry, *Beyond All Reason*, 21.

51. Farber and Sherry, *Beyond All Reason*, 24.

52. Quoted in Farber and Sherry, *Beyond All Reason*, 23.

53. Quoted in Dennis McCallum, ed., *The Death of Truth* (Minneapolis: Bethany House, 1996), 170. See Stanley Fish, *There's No Such Thing as Free Speech: And It's a Good Thing, Too* (Oxford, UK: Oxford University Press, 1993).

54. "Lecture: A Latina Judge's Voice."

55. Farber and Sherry, *Beyond All Reason*, 30.

56. "Lecture: A Latina Judge's Voice."

57. Quoted in Stuart Taylor Jr. and K. C. Johnson, *Until Proven Innocent* (New York: St. Martin's, 2008), 145–46.

58. Farber and Sherry, *Beyond All Reason*, 39.

59. Quoted in McCallum, *Death of Truth*, 175.

60. Marianne Williamson, *A Return to Love* (New York: HarperCollins, 1989), 37.

61. Shakti Gawain, *Living in the Light* (San Rafael, CA: New World Library, 1986), 110.

62. Gawain, *Living in the Light*, 37.

63. Gawain, *Living in the Light*, 3.

64. David Spangler, *Revelation: The Birth of a New Age* (Middleton, WI: Lorain Press, 1976), 65.

65. Quoted in Shirley MacLaine, *Out on a Limb* (New York: Bantam Books, 1989), 204.

66. Eckhart Tolle, *A New Earth* (New York: Plume, 2005), 163.

67. Mark Satin, *New Age Politics* (New York: Dell, 1978), 103.

68. Joseph Campbell, *The Power of Myth* (New York: Doubleday, 1988), 118.

69. Campbell, *The Power of Myth*.

70. Arch Puddington, *Freedom in the World 2013: Democratic Breakthroughs in the Balance* (Washington, DC: Freedom House, 2013), www.freedomhouse.org/sites/default/files/FIW%202013%20Booklet%20-%20for%20Web_0.pdf.

71. Quoted in Andrew Bostom, *Sharia versus Freedom* (Amherst, NY: Prometheus Books, 2012), 44.

72. Bostom, *Sharia versus Freedom*, 73.

73. Malise Ruthven, *Islam: A Very Short Introduction* (Oxford, UK: Oxford University Press, 1997), 86.

74. Additionally, Ruthven observes, "by defining correct behavior or orthopraxy at the social level, the Shari'ah has left its distinctive imprint on a way of living that has evolved over time and varies from one country to another in accordance with local custom." Ruthven, *Islam*, 86.

75. Ruthven, *Islam*.

76. (1) Commanded (such as the five pillars and jihad—disobedience is punished in this life and the next, and obedience is rewarded in the next life); (2) forbidden (such as thievery and drinking wine—engaging in them is worthy of punishment in this life and the next, and avoiding them is worthy of reward in paradise); (3) disapproved (such as divorce—acts that are discouraged, the avoidance of which may be worthy of reward in paradise); (4) recommended (such as extra charitable acts—acts that are commended on Earth and rewarded in paradise); (5) indifferent (without positive or negative consequences).

77. Havva G. Guney-Ruebenacker, "Islamic Law: An Ever-Evolving Science under the Light of Divine Revelation and Human Reason," www.averroes-foundation.org/articles/islamic_law_evolving.html.

78. In his more than seven-hundred-page book *Sharia versus Freedom*, Andrew Bostom documents these facts from hundreds of Islamic sources and demonstrates conclusively the overwhelming acceptance and support of these provisions—and more—among the world's Muslims.

79. Paul L. Williams, *Crescent Moon Rising* (Amherst, NY: Prometheus Books, 2013), 25–26.

80. Mohamed Akram, "An Explanatory Memorandum on the General Strategic Goal for the Group in North America," May 22, 1991, 7. This memorandum was found in 2004 during a search of the home of Ismael Elbarasse, one of the Muslim Brotherhood's representatives in the United States. It was entered into evidence in the July 2007 trial of seven leaders of the Holy Land Foundation for Relief and Development (HLF). The defendants stood accused of providing material support and resources to a foreign terrorist organization (Hamas). The trial ended in a mistrial. A subsequent 2008 trial obtained convictions and life sentences against HLF founders Ghassan Elashi, former CEO Shukri Abu-Baker, Mufid Abdulqader, Abdulrahman Odeh, and Mohammad El-Mezain.

81. Lord Acton, letter to Bishop Mandell Creighton (1887). See John Bartlett, *Familiar Quotations*, 13th and centennial ed. (Boston: Little, Brown 1955), 335.

82. Ruthven, *Islam*, 90.

83. Puddington, *Freedom in the World 2013*.

84. Samuel Shahid, "Rights of Non-Muslims in an Islamic State," Answering Islam, accessed March 27, 2014, www.answering-islam.org/NonMuslims/rights.htm.

85. The full statement reads, "After having overcome fascism, Nazism, and Stalinism, the world now faces a new global totalitarian threat: Islamism. We—writers, journalists and public intellectuals—call for resistance to religious totalitarianism. (1) Instead, we call for the promotion of freedom, equal opportunity and secular values worldwide. (2) The necessity of these universal values has been revealed by events since the publication of the Muhammad drawings in European newspapers. This struggle will not be won by arms, but in the arena of ideas. What we are witnessing is not a clash of civilizations, nor an antagonism of West versus East, but a global struggle between democrats and theocrats. (3) Like all totalitarianisms, Islamism is nurtured by fears and frustrations. The preachers of hate bet on these feelings in order to form battalions destined to impose a world of inequality. But we clearly and firmly state: nothing, not even despair, justifies the choice of obscurantism, totalitarianism and hatred. (4) Islamism is a reactionary ideology which kills equality, freedom and secularism wherever it is present. Its success can only lead to a world of greater power imbalances: man's domination of woman, the Islamists' domination of all others. (5) To counter this, we must assure universal rights to oppressed people. For that reason, we reject 'cultural relativism' which consists of accepting that Muslim men and women should be deprived of their right to equality and freedom in the name of their cultural traditions. (6) We refuse to renounce our critical spirit out of fear of being accused of 'Islamophobia,' an unfortunate concept that confuses criticism of Islamic practices with the stigmatization of Muslims themselves. (7) We plead for the universality of free expression, so that a critical spirit may be exercised on every continent, against every abuse and dogma. (8) We appeal to democrats and free spirits of all countries that our century should be one of enlightenment, not of obscurantism." Signed by Ayaan Hirsi Ali, Chahla Chafiq, Caroline Fourest, Bernard-Henri Levy, Irshad Manji, Mehdi Mozaffari, Maryam Namazie, Taslima Nasreen, Salman Rushdie, Antoine Sfeir, Philippe Val, and Ibn Warraq; quoted in Irshad Manji, *Allah, Liberty, and Love* (New York: Free Press, 2011), 144–45.

86. To view Freedom House's "Map of Freedom" for the current year, go to www.freedomhouse.org/reports.

87. Carl F. H. Henry, *Twilight of a Great Civilization* (Westchester, IL: Crossway Books, 1988), 147.

88. Second Chronicles 20:6: "[Jehoshaphat] said, O LORD, the God of our ancestors, are you not God in heaven? Do you not rule over all the kingdoms of the nations? In your hand are power and might, so that none is able to withstand you"; Acts 17:24–31 (KJV): "God that made the world and all things therein, seeing that he is Lord of

heaven and earth, dwelleth not in temples made with hands; neither is worshipped with men's hands, as though he needed any thing, seeing he giveth to all life, and breath, and all things; and hath made of one blood all nations of men to dwell on all the face of the earth, and hath determined the times before appointed, and the bounds of their habitation; that they should seek the Lord, if haply they might feel after him, and find him, though he be not far from every one of us: for in him we live, and move, and have our being; as certain also of your own poets have said, For we are also his offspring. Forasmuch then as we are the offspring of God, we ought not to think that the Godhead is like unto gold, or silver, or stone, graven by art and man's device. And the times of this ignorance God winked at; but now commandeth all men every where to repent: because he hath appointed a day, in the which he will judge the world in righteousness by that man whom he hath ordained; whereof he hath given assurance unto all men, in that he hath raised him from the dead."

89. Russell Kirk, "The Christian Postulates of English and American Law," *Journal of Christian Jurisprudence* (1980): 66.

90. Francis Schaeffer, *The Complete Works of Francis A. Schaeffer: A Christian Worldview*, 5 vols. (Westchester, IL: Crossway Books, 1982), 2:249.

91. Genesis 9:6: "Whoever sheds the blood of man, by man shall his blood be shed, for God made man in his own image"; Romans 13: "Let every person be subject to the governing authorities. For there is no authority except from God, and those that exist have been instituted by God. Therefore whoever resists the authorities resists what God has appointed, and those who resist will incur judgment. For rulers are not a terror to good conduct, but to bad. Would you have no fear of the one who is in authority? Then do what is good, and you will receive his approval, for he is God's servant for your good. But if you do wrong, be afraid, for he does not bear the sword in vain. For he is the servant of God, an avenger who carries out God's wrath on the wrongdoer. Therefore one must be in subjection, not only to avoid God's wrath but also for the sake of conscience. For because of this you also pay taxes, for the authorities are ministers of God, attending to this very thing. Pay to all what is owed to them: taxes to whom taxes are owed, revenue to whom revenue is owed, respect to whom respect is owed, honor to whom honor is owed. Owe no one anything, except to love each other, for the one who loves another has fulfilled the law. For the commandments, 'You shall not commit adultery, You shall not murder, You shall not steal, You shall not covet,' and any other commandment, are summed up in this word: 'You shall love your neighbor as yourself.' Love does no wrong to a neighbor; therefore love is the fulfilling of the law. Besides this you know the time, that the hour has come for you to wake from sleep. For salvation is nearer to us now than when we first believed. The night is far gone; the day is at hand. So then let us cast off the works of darkness and put on the armor of light. Let us walk properly as in the daytime, not in orgies and drunkenness, not in sexual immorality and sensuality, not in quarreling and jealousy. But put on the Lord Jesus Christ, and make no provision for the flesh, to gratify its desires."

92. Acts 14:8–18: "Now at Lystra there was a man sitting who could not use his feet. He was crippled from birth and had never walked. He listened to Paul speaking. And Paul, looking intently at him and seeing that he had faith to be made well, said in a loud voice, 'Stand upright on your feet.' And he sprang up and began walking. And when the crowds saw what Paul had done, they lifted up their voices, saying in Lycaonian, 'The gods have come down to us in the likeness of men!' Barnabas they called Zeus, and Paul, Hermes, because he was the chief speaker. And the priest of Zeus, whose temple was at the entrance to the city, brought oxen and garlands to the gates and wanted to offer sacrifice with the crowds. But when the apostles Barnabas and Paul heard of it, they tore their garments and rushed out into the crowd, crying out, 'Men, why are you doing these things? We also are men, of like nature with you, and we bring you good news, that you should turn from these vain things to a living God, who made the heaven and the earth and the sea and all that is in them. In past generations he allowed all the nations to walk in their own ways. Yet he did not leave himself without witness, for he did good by giving you rains from heaven and fruitful seasons, satisfying your hearts with food and gladness.' Even with these words they scarcely restrained the people from offering sacrifice to them"; James 5:1–6: "Come now, you rich, weep and howl for the miseries that are coming upon you. Your riches have rotted and your garments are moth-eaten. Your gold and silver have corroded, and their corrosion will be evidence against you and will eat your flesh like fire. You have laid up treasure in the last days. Behold, the wages of the laborers who mowed your fields, which you kept back by fraud, are crying out against you, and the cries of the harvesters have reached the ears of the Lord of hosts. You have lived on the earth in luxury and in self-indulgence. You have fattened your hearts in a day of slaughter. You have condemned and murdered the righteous person. He does not resist you."

93. John 1:14: "The Word became flesh and dwelt among us, and we have seen his glory, glory as of the only Son from the Father, full of grace and truth."

94. Acts 17:31: "[God] has fixed a day on which he will judge the world in righteousness by a man whom he has appointed; and of this he has given assurance to all by raising him from the dead"; Romans 2:16: "On that day ..., according to my gospel, God [will] judge the secrets of men by Christ Jesus"; 2 Corinthians 5:10: "We must all appear before the judgment seat of Christ, so that each one may receive what is due for what he has done in the body, whether good or evil."

95. John W. Whitehead, *The Second American Revolution* (Westchester, IL: Crossway Books, 1988), 80.

96. John Eidsmoe says of general and special revelation, "Upon these two foundations, the law of nature and the law of revelation [the Bible], depend all human laws." John Eidsmoe, *Christianity and the Constitution* (Grand Rapids: Baker, 1987), 58.

97. John Warwick Montgomery, *The Law above the Law* (Minneapolis: Dimension Books, 1975), 26.

98. Romans 1:26–32: "For this reason God gave them up to dishonorable passions. For their women exchanged natural relations for those that are contrary to nature; and the men likewise gave up natural relations with women and were consumed with passion for one another, men committing shameless acts with men and receiving in themselves the due penalty for their error. And since they did not see fit to acknowledge God, God gave them up to a debased mind to do what ought not to be done. They were filled with all manner of unrighteousness, evil, covetousness, malice. They are full of envy, murder, strife, deceit, maliciousness. They are gossips, slanderers, haters of God, insolent, haughty, boastful, inventors of evil, disobedient to parents, foolish, faithless, heartless, ruthless. Though they know God's decree that those who practice such things deserve to die, they not only do them but give approval to those who practice them."

99. William Blackstone, *Commentaries on the Laws of England*, in *Commentaries with Notes of Reference to the Constitution and Laws of the Federal Government of the United States and of the Commonwealth of Virginia*, 5 vols., ed. St. George Tucker (Philadelphia: William Young Birch and Abraham Small, 1803; repr., South Hackensack, NJ: Rothman Reprints, 1969), 1:38–39.

100. Noah Webster, *History of the United States: To Which Is Prefixed a Brief Historical Account of Our English Ancestors, from the Dispersion at Babel, to Their Migration to America, and of the Conquest of South America, by the Spaniards* (New Haven: Durrie and Peck, 1832), 339.

101. Noah Webster, *Value of the Bible and Excellence of the Christian Religion for Use of Families and Schools* (New Haven: Durrie and Peck, 1834), 175–76.

102. Thomas Jefferson, *The Works of Thomas Jefferson*, comp. and ed. Paul L. Ford (New York: G. P. Putnam's Sons, 1894), 3:267.

103. Gary T. Amos, *Defending the Declaration* (Brentwood, TN: Wolgemuth and Hyatt, 1989), 117.

CHAPTER 15

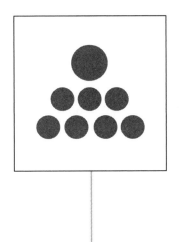

POLITICS

1. THE LORD OF THE RINGS

The key to power over the world was in his grasp, literally. And it horrified the young Hobbit.

"Take it, Gandalf," Frodo pleaded.

Gandalf replied, "Don't tempt me, Frodo. I dare not take it. Not even to keep it safe. Understand me, Frodo. I would use this ring from a desire to do good, but through me, it would wield a power too great and terrible to imagine."

Would you take the ring? Generations of readers of J. R. R. Tolkien's Lord of the Rings trilogy have asked themselves this question. Tolkien presented it as a devil's bargain, best articulated by Lord Acton: "Power tends to corrupt; absolute power corrupts absolutely."[1] The ring represented absolute power; its possession portended absolute corruption.

Power tempts everyone. Those who have felt helpless and oppressed, those who do not feel sufficiently respected, those who shudder at the immense power of evil have all heard the voice of power quietly urging, "Take the ring."

Power, simply, is the ability to do something or act in a particular way.[2] People talk about power all the time—a powerful serve in tennis, a powerful engine in a race car, or even consumer products such as power drinks. The power to influence society is an altogether different consideration, entailing the authority to do good in tension with the temptation to accomplish that good through evil means. This is nowhere truer than in politics. *Polis* is the Greek word for "city" (or "community"), and *politikos* is "of, or relating to, the citizens within a community." **Politics**, then, seeks to answer the question, "What is the best way to use power in order to organize community for the citizens?"

> *Power:* the ability to do something or act in a particular way.

> *Politics:* the study of community governance.

> Properly conceived, politics offers a platform from which to encourage virtue, and virtue is at the heart of good government.

Politics often calls to mind political commercials or people with fake smiles wearing suits and kissing babies. Though politicians are often portrayed as silly and pompous, the study of politics matters. Everyone lives in multiple political jurisdictions: neighborhoods, cities, counties, states, nations. Where you live implies a set of personally applicable rules. But who makes those rules? Who picks the rule makers?

Properly conceived, politics offers a platform from which to encourage virtue, and virtue is at the heart of good government. To those who think liberty alone is necessary, the great British statesman Edmund Burke said, "What is liberty without wisdom and without virtue? It is the greatest of all possible evils; for it is folly, vice, and madness, without tuition or restraint."[3]

With this backdrop, let us take a brief tour through political thought, often called *political philosophy*. We'll then examine each of the six worldviews to see how they understand this endeavor so critical to human flourishing.

2. HISTORY AND PHILOSOPHY OF POLITICS

If you think politics is pristine, you've never seen a political campaign. In America, nasty accusations have been part of political campaigning from the beginning. In its opposition to Abraham Lincoln, for example, the Albany *Atlas and Argus* newspaper claimed that he was "the ugliest man in the Union." Of course, Lincoln handled the accusations with his characteristic dry wit. When accused of being two-faced, Lincoln replied, "I leave it to my audience. If I had another face, do you think I'd wear this one?"[4]

Campaign chicanery aside, questions about good governance are deadly serious. People have different interests and concerns. Conflict is inevitable. Aristotle said that because we are thinking creatures living in community, we are by our very nature political animals. Harvard political science professor Harvey Mansfield elaborates on the analogy in this way:

Other animals are gregarious, bees for example, but they are not political because they do not speak or reason about what is advantageous and harmful, just and unjust, good and bad; they are confined to feeling pain and pleasure. Human beings have to reason about these matters, as they are not perfectly clear.[5]

To the degree that we have the power of reason and live in community with one another, political engagement is necessary for a healthy human society.

More than just about anything else, political ideas carry the greatest consequences for greater numbers of people. Billions can be affected. Decisions that promoted freedom have brought blessing to nations all over the world, while decisions that squelched freedom have led to bloodshed and misery. Once again, ideas have consequences.

What you believe about how to rule in the best interests of the citizens depends on what you believe about human nature. Two views have emerged in history, the sin nature view and the pure nature view. Obviously there are many intermediate positions, but for the sake of introduction, we'll focus on the sin nature and pure nature views in particular.

Let's look at the **sin nature view of politics** first. The idea of sin goes back to Scripture; both the Old and New Testament words for *sin* imply losing one's way, straying from a path, or cracking one's relationship with God.[6] In political terms, the sin nature is the idea that humans are violent and government is necessary to secure peace via social contract. The term **social contract** refers to the agreement citizens enter into with a government to secure protection from those who would harm them. Without this social contract, English political philosopher Thomas Hobbes (1588–1679) famously said that human life is "solitary, poore, nasty, brutish, and short."[7] John Locke (1632–1704), another famous English political philosopher, suggested that the social contract secures our natural rights to life, health, liberty, and possessions.

So what political power should government have, then? According to Locke, no more than the people give it:

> Political power, then, I take to be a right of making laws, with penalties of death, and consequently all less penalties for the regulating and preserving of property, and of employing the force of the community in the execution of such laws, and in the defense of the commonwealth from foreign injury, and all of this only for the public good.[8]

Locke's philosophy had a dramatic influence on America's founding fathers.[9] Thomas Jefferson, for example, considered him to be one of the three greatest men who ever lived, along with Isaac Newton and Francis Bacon.

Samuel Rutherford was also influential. A Scottish Presbyterian pastor and theology professor at the University of St. Andrews, Rutherford published a book in 1644 called *Lex*

> *Sin Nature View of Politics:* the belief that human beings are inherently sinful, and government is necessary to secure peace.

> *Social Contract:* the belief that individuals want a society for either an implicit or explicit agreement with their government whereby citizens forfeit some freedoms in exchange for safety.

Rex, which means, "the law is the king." It was a direct confrontation of the idea that kings rule by divine right, and whatever they do is right because God put them into that position.[10] In other words, kings were above the law and the common morality expected of citizens. Rutherford was condemned to burn at the stake for proposing this idea, but he died before the sentence could be carried out.

A contrasting view might be called the **pure nature view of politics**. As articulated by the French philosopher Jean-Jacques Rousseau, this political view says people may not know what goodness is, but this does not necessarily make them bad. Under the right conditions, Rousseau argued, human beings are perfectible. If individuals are corrupt, it is society that corrupts them.

> *Pure Nature View of Politics:* the belief that human beings are inherently good and can be perfected under the right political conditions.

Rousseau inspired those who sparked the French Revolution. Many Americans (including Jefferson) thought France's bid for freedom was a promising echo of the American Revolution, but their hopes dissolved as the revolutionaries took a hard turn toward revenge. Apparently, these revolutionaries believed not in reforming society but in destroying it and rebuilding an altogether new society. When the dust settled, the revolutionaries had executed more than forty thousand people.

One of the leading revolutionaries, Maximilien Robespierre, forthrightly justified his vengeful spirit in an address on Christmas Day 1793:

> The revolutionary government owes to the good citizen all the protection of the nation; it owes nothing to the Enemies of the People but death.... If the revolutionary government must be more active in its march and more free in [its] movements than an ordinary government, is it for that less fair and legitimate? No; it is supported by the most holy of all laws: the Salvation of the People.

It's ironic that Robespierre's belief in his own purity led him to unflinchingly send his enemies to a horrifying death. Even more ironic was that just a few months after his Christmas Day address, the revolutionaries he had inspired and trained guillotined Robespierre without trial. As with Haman of old (in the book of Esther), Robespierre found himself facing the gallows he had built for others.

Most of the American founders distrusted the pure nature view. They knew that human nature tended toward corruption. Even those with "unassailable character" would bring disaster if they ruled without accountability. Just as the French Revolution confirmed this thesis for the founders, the bloodshed of the twentieth century confirms it for us today. "No half-century ever witnessed slaughter on such a scale," said Nuremberg judge and future Supreme Court justice Robert Jackson, "such cruelties and inhumanities, such wholesale deportations of peoples into slavery, such annihilations of minorities."[11] As we have said many times, ideas have consequences. Bad ideas have bad consequences, and the consequences of a belief in the inherent goodness of human beings are tragic.

Both the sin nature and pure nature views are social-contract views. Today a new social-contract view has emerged owing to the work of Harvard philosopher John Rawls and asks a procedural question: How should society's resources be distributed? Rawls's view is thus called **distributive justice**, and it is seen as an important advance in philosophy and politics. Even Rawls's primary opponent, fellow Harvard philosopher Robert Nozick, said, "Political philosophers now must either work within Rawls's theory or explain why not."[12]

> *Distributive Justice:* the belief that a just society should seek to redistribute its citizens' resources equally among everyone.

Theoretically, distributive justice is a question of law, but since it bears on how political structures should be set up (and since students will most likely run into it in political-science courses), we think it is worth examining in a little more detail. Society exists, Rawls thought, because individuals surrender some of their rights in exchange for protection. But prejudice has led to an unequal distribution of resources, making it difficult for some people to succeed. Distributive-justice advocates favor "spreading the wealth" through redistribution.

By the equal distribution of social goods, Rawls meant not only income and wealth but also liberty, opportunity, and self-respect. All of these must be distributed equally, he said, unless it is to everyone's advantage to have them not so distributed.[13] This could be done, Rawls believed, in an unbiased fashion.[14]

A generation of political-science students studied John Rawls's ideas. One of them, Barack Obama, while running for office actually told a potential voter, "I think when you spread the wealth around, it's good for everybody."[15] This is a Rawlsian idea, and many people think it sounds compassionate. But remember what redistribution means: the government is coercing some people to give up their resources—by threat of punishment—so they may be given to others.

Distributive justice makes several controversial assumptions about the world and humanity, including the following:

1. Social goods can be quantified. We know how to count money and assess the value of wealth, but how do we quantify liberty, opportunity, or self-respect?
2. Redistribution accomplishes fairness, which assumes that the current distribution arose through unfairness.
3. Resources are best in the hands of people who want them rather than those most capable of stewarding them.
4. Redistribution is the morally right thing to do.
5. People are basically good—if disadvantages were removed, they would be able to succeed.
6. People actually *want* to succeed. Yet even in fairly well-ordered societies, there are those who want to fail and sabotage their own success through addictions, risk taking, or self-destructive behavior.
7. Only persons who are able to *claim* their rights actually have them. The unborn, the feeble, and the elderly do not factor into these considerations.

Having briefly toured the history of political philosophy, we are now ready to look at how each of the six worldviews we are studying deals with political questions. Each begins

---

Political Conservatism: a system of government based on respect for historical precedent, limited government, a strict interpretation of the US Constitution, and adherence to traditional moral principles based on natural law.

Political Liberalism: a system of government based upon the belief that individual and social ills are best ameliorated through direct government intervention.

Progressivism: the belief in human progress; the belief that political systems can be used to create economic prosperity, minimize risk, and advance society.

with different assumptions and therefore arrives at different conclusions. As thoughtful citizens, we need to understand this if we are to articulately defend the truth.

3. SECULARISM

Liberalism is a term often associated with a Secularist approach to politics.[16] Historically, liberalism referred to a political philosophy based on individual freedom and democratic rule (often called **political conservatism** in the United States today), but today **political liberalism** refers to a set of political positions, such as guaranteeing a woman unrestricted access to abortion, promotion of same-sex marriage, redistribution of wealth, heavy regulation of business, and affirmative action.[17] Another term encompassing much of the secular view of politics is *progressivism*, which is the belief that political systems can be used to help people progress toward economic prosperity, social safety, and an advanced society. Often liberalism and progressivism merge under the presumed belief that liberal political positions are the means by which progress will occur. Obviously, many Secularists disagree with one or more of these positions, but there is a very close relationship between atheism, materialism, and naturalism and those who embrace liberal political views.[18]

Remember, a secular worldview assumes we are evolving animals who are now capable of seeking our own perfection as a species. Julian Huxley, who believed that "all reality is a single process of evolution,"[19] wrote, "The evolutionary process is at last becoming conscious of itself and is beginning to study itself with a view to directing its future course."[20]

In order for humanity to evolve in this way, Francis Williams said, we must "stop thinking politically as Capitalists, or communists, Christians, Muslims, Hindus or Buddhists, and think as Secularists.... A world in which men have both hydrogen bombs and closed minds is altogether too dangerous."[21] Clearly, Williams thought Secularists are the open-minded ones.

Is it ever possible to have a stable political foundation if there is no moral truth based on God's nature and character? Secularists affirm that it is. Secularist philosopher Sidney Hook said we have rights because of our ability to participate in society: "The rights of man depend upon his nature, needs, capacities, and aspirations, not upon his origins. Children have rights not because they are our creatures but because of what they are and will become. It is not God but the human community that endows its members with rights."[22]

Hook would have been uncomfortable with the "there are no moral truths" mantra. For him, morality was whatever a society agrees is right: "The democratic open society must be neutral to all religious overbeliefs; but no matter how secular it conceives itself to be, it cannot be neutral to moral issues. It seeks to draw these issues into the area of public discussion in the hope that a reasonable consensus may be achieved."[23]

Based on its framework of rights, Secularism seems to favor the principles of distributive justice because only people who are equal economically can participate equally in the political realm. V. M. Tarkunde said, "A genuine political democracy is not possible in the absence of economic democracy."[24] To political scientist Walter Truett Anderson, this lack of "economic democracy" hinders society's progress: "When people are deprived of the fundamental necessities, as are millions of Americans and even more millions of human beings in other countries, their capacity for development is frustrated at the most basic level."[25]

> Based on its framework of rights, Secularism seems to favor the principles of distributive justice because only people who are equal economically can participate equally in the political realm.

We can all agree that there is injustice and poverty in the world. But what is the solution? To political liberals like Tarkunde and Anderson, the answer is "economic democracy," which political theorists recognize to be code for socialism.[26] Not all Secularists support such a thing. Milton Friedman wrote, "The use of force to achieve equality will destroy freedom, and the force, introduced for good purposes, will end up in the hands of people who use it to promote their own interests."[27] As a Secularist and an agnostic, Friedman embraced—indeed championed—a free market approach to economics.[28] The drive toward equality of outcome, he thought, would destroy the freedom to prosper. We'd all be worse off. But Friedman wasn't alone among Secularists in this way of thinking. A fast-emerging philosophy of economics today is **libertarianism**, which holds up complete individual liberty as the highest good. Libertarianism in its modern form has a significant history in the thought of 1964 Republican presidential candidate Barry Goldwater, economist Murray Rothbard, and more recently in the writing of John Rawls's opponent quoted earlier, Robert Nozick. Another figure in the movement, Ayn Rand, wrote a series of novels to outline her philosophy of objectivism. These novels, including *Fountainhead* and *Atlas Shrugged*, have gained a new popularity in our own time. Each year, Rand's books still sell more than a million copies, promoting the ideas of libertarianism, radical individualism, and an unflinching promotion of self-interest. While many Christians find themselves compelled by libertarian arguments, their interest is often rebuffed when it comes to certain social issues such as marriage and abortion.

> *Libertarianism:* a political philosophy that upholds individual liberty as that highest good based upon the principle that people should be allowed to do whatever they want as along as they do not infringe upon the rights of others.

Since it is believed that our knowledge of truth is always evolving, Secularism is always on the lookout for new ideas—"new" is almost always assumed to be superior. Julian

Huxley admitted this tendency: "Major steps in the human phase of evolution are achieved by breakthroughs to new dominant patterns of mental organization, of knowledge, ideas and beliefs—ideological instead of physiological or biological organization."[29] The fixation on breakthroughs leading to further evolution underscores the utopian nature of the secular worldview. It is a progressive view; our genes have figured out how to push us toward survival, our ethics have evolved as a survival mechanism, and those whose ethics do not lead to survivability do not survive. Perfectibility is an expectation; over time, perfectible people should be able to create a nearly perfect government, right?

Utopian visions have one thing in common: everyone in the world must go along for them to work.[30] A nation or group of nations could derail the plan by a lack of cooperation, and this must not be allowed. This is why Secularists commonly speak in the language of "global consciousness" or even "world government." An example from Paul Kurtz: "Today there are powerful forces moving us toward a new ethical global consciousness."[31] Kurtz was a Secular Humanist evangelist. It's no surprise to hear him advocate his view as the answer: "Humanism, we believe, can play a significant role in helping to foster the development of a genuine world community."[32]

> Utopian visions have one thing in common: everyone in the world must go along for them to work.

At present, global consciousness doesn't seem to be working out too well for Secularists, especially those in America. Global political strategist Ian Bremmer says the percentage of people in the world who think the United States should "mind its own business" is at an all-time high.[33] At the same time, other nations do not seem interested in stepping forward and becoming the organizing force for international cooperation. Particularly in today's economic climate, it's "every nation for itself," pursuing its own aims of advancement.[34] Gathering nations together to agree on anything important, Bremmer says, is like "herding cats ... together with animals that don't like cats."[35]

Leading Secularists are baffled by the resistance of the world's nations to the idea of world government, which they believe must be put in charge by force, if necessary. At least this seems to have been the mind-set of Lucile W. Green, a long-time secular activist promoting world government, who said ominously in a 1968 article, "All those who share the vision of the human community as part of one world should be willing to take any measures that will awaken world opinion to bring it about."[36]

C. S. Lewis was prophetic in this regard. In his book *The Abolition of Man*, he referred to "the Conditioners" who have a utopian vision for recreating society: "But the man-moulders of the new age will be armed with the powers of an omnicompetent state and an irresistible scientific technique: we shall get at last a race of conditioners who really can cut out all posterity in what shape they please."[37] The path of the conditioners is based on the idea that people, some of them at least, are inherently intelligent and good. They are worthy to be conditioners and to make decisions on our behalf. They believe their motives are pure and that they can be trusted with complete power to transform society.

As we will see, the Christian view does not, as Secularism does, dispense with the idea of human fallenness. Christianity admits that we are inherently corrupt and in need of accountability, and that we are not, and cannot be, smart enough to manipulate our way to a better life for everyone. The best we can do is try to secure justice and freedom so people can do what they think best for themselves, their families, and their communities.

4. MARXISM

In classical Marxism, all politics is really about economic power. Classical Marxists defined *political power* as "controlling the means of production." Contemporary Marxists, discussed later, see the world as structured between the haves ("core") and the have-nots ("periphery"). Karl Marx called economic structures "the real foundation on which rise moral, legal and political superstructures and to which definite forms of social consciousness correspond."[38] To use a Lord of the Rings allusion, economics is the "one ring to rule them all." Once a nation's economic structure is rightly ordered, Marxists believe politics will fall in line behind it. We'll cover economics in detail in the next chapter, but for now let's review the key terms from the earlier chapter devoted to Marxism:

- *Communism:* the Marxist ideal of classless utopian society in which all property is commonly owned.
- *Capitalism:* an economic system in which private citizens own the means of production rather than the government, and in which prices are determined by competition.
- *Socialism:* the abolition of private property. A communist society will be based on socialism— the claim that the banning of private property will lead to everyone "owning" everything.

Marxists see a democratic state or republic, especially in a capitalist economic system, as undesirable. According to Friedrich Engels, "The modern state, no matter what its form, is essentially a capitalist machine."[39] For V. I. Lenin, "democracy" was nothing more than a power play to make oppressed people think they weren't oppressed, a "subordination of the minority to the majority, i.e., an organization for the systematic use of force by one class against another, by one section of the population against another."[40] Cuba's dictator, Fidel Castro, said, "I find capitalism repugnant. It is filthy, it is gross, it is alienating ... because it causes war, hypocrisy and

> **Christianity admits that we are inherently corrupt and in need of accountability, and that we are not, and cannot be, smart enough to manipulate our way to a better life for everyone.**

> *Communism:* the Marxist ideal of a classless and stateless utopian society in which all property is commonly owned and each person is paid according to his or her abilities and needs.

> *Capitalism:* an economic system in which capital assets are privately owned, and the prices, production, and distribution of goods and services are determined by competition within a free market.

> *Socialism:* an economic system based upon governmental or communal ownership of the means of production and distribution of goods and services.

competition."[41] Perhaps the late Venezuelan socialist leader Hugo Chavez framed it most starkly: "Capitalism leads us straight to hell."[42]

What capitalists call *democracy* is not democracy at all, Marxists say. If it were a genuine democracy, they say, it would focus more on the proletariat. If the history of Marxist states is any indication, though, the Marxist idea of democracy is anything but the rule of the people.

Remember, Marxists see communism as a state of perfection in which government will not be necessary. The ideal state for the Marxist is no state at all.[43] Any remaining government is a sign that class antagonism has not yet been cleansed away. Lenin said, referencing Marx, "The State could neither arise nor maintain itself if a reconciliation of classes were possible."[44] In the transition from capitalism to communism, however, the state remains a necessary evil. Marx wrote, "Between capitalist and communist society lies the period of the revolutionary transformation of the one into the other. Corresponding to this is also a political transition period in which the state can be nothing but the revolutionary dictatorship of the proletariat."[45]

There are three steps in the transition from capitalism to communism:

1. Instituting statism. Using the government to seize the means of production, and indeed all sectors of the economy, from private businesses.

> *Statism:* a political system in which a highly centralized government holds the concentration of economic controls and planning.

2. Suppressing capitalism. Capitalists must be prevented from rising again. Lenin said, "We must crush [the bourgeoisie] in order to free humanity from wage-slavery; their resistance must be broken by force."[46] In addition, the dictatorship of the proletariat will require confiscation of property. All of this will be accomplished through the guidance and governance of the Marxist Party.

3. Dissolving the state. Marxists say the state evolved at a point in history when it was necessary, and it will cease to exist when it is no longer so.[47] Eliminate the bourgeoisie and you can eliminate the state: "Only in communist society, when the resistance of the capitalists has been completely crushed, when the capitalists have disappeared, when there are no classes ... only then 'the state ... ceases to exist,' and 'it becomes possible to speak of freedom.'"[48] Freedom, in the Marxist sense, means no government at all.

Lenin continued, "So long as the state exists, there is no freedom. When there is freedom, there will be no state."[49]

> The political history of Marxism from the October Revolution of 1917 in Russia to the Tiananmen Square student uprising of 1989 in China and more recent crackdowns in Cuba, Venezuela, and elsewhere showcases Marxism's ruthless, efficient killing machine.

Some Marxists are uncomfortable with Marx's and Lenin's talk about "crushing" their enemies. They say it was exaggeration for the purpose of making a point, or they point to examples of capitalists crushing their own enemies. However, the political history of Marxism from the October Revolution of 1917 in Russia to the Tiananmen Square student uprising of 1989 in China and more recent crackdowns in Cuba, Venezuela, and elsewhere showcases Marxism's ruthless, efficient killing machine. Talk about "crushing" is not hyperbole to Marxists. The death toll of Marxism stands at more than one hundred million people, as devastating as a modern-day black plague.[50]

Marx and Engels do have contemporary intellectual and political disciples. The most common critical approach in universities is a neo-Marxism focused on the key concept of dependency. The idea is that a "core" group of capitalist countries (e.g. the United States, Japan, and Western Europe) have structured international relations so that "periphery" societies remain exploited, underdeveloped sources of cheap labor and raw materials. The core does this by encouraging a local capitalist core in national capitals (e.g. Brasilia, Nairobi, New Delhi), which runs the capitalist machine to great profit on the backs of their fellow citizens. The periphery remains dependent on the core for its very survival.[51]

This type of argument is precisely that made by contemporary political Marxists, particularly in Latin America, such as the Castro brothers (Cuba), the late Hugo Chavez (Venezuela), Evo Morales (Bolivia), Rafael Correa (Ecuador), and Daniel Ortega (Nicaragua). These political Marxists have used the core-periphery distinction to justify statism and suppression just as their forebears Stalin and Mao did. The result: the "nationalizing" (takeover) of key industries and the suppression of individual freedoms.[52]

5. POSTMODERNISM

The old saying "Everybody talks about the weather, but no one does anything about it" is perhaps an appropriate aphorism for postmodern politics. Remember from our "Postmodernism" chapter, Postmodernists believe reality is not directly accessible to us. We operate based on our interpretations of reality, which are in turn based on our cultural and personal situations.

In the end, though, we must all be governed. Unfortunately, Postmodernism is primarily a *critical theory* that presumably points out problems but avoids proposing concrete solutions because, for Postmodernists, politics is only and always a tool of oppression. Critiquing the abuse *is* the solution; there is nothing more to be done. This view of politics sounds like **anarchism**—and, in a way, it *is* advocating **anarchy**. Jean-François Lyotard explained: "With the destruction of the grand narratives, there is no longer any unifying identity for the subject or society. Instead, individuals are the sites where ranges of conflicting moral and political codes intersect, and the social bond is fragmented."[53]

> *Anarchism:* the belief that government is inherently oppressive and should therefore be abolished, giving individuals the opportunity to govern themselves.

> *Anarchy:* a society that exists without government control.

Barbara Epstein observes, "One reason that Postmodernism has taken hold so widely is that it is much easier to be critical than to present a positive vision."[54] In some ways, then, Postmodernism has become a form of carrying on about the problems rather than proposing workable solutions. Some people might call this whining, but Postmodernism is resolute: If modern metanarratives fail to account for reality, political visions will only make things worse. We can't solve problems; we can only manage them.[55]

We call this view **political pessimism** to draw attention to the gloominess Postmodernists feel about the whole realm of politics. Postmodernists suffer from what French cultural theorist Jean Baudrillard called a "cynical, despairing rejection of ... belief."[56] Why the despair? Anthony Thomson says it is "fueled by the failure of Marxian-inspired State socialism."[57] Apparently, Postmodernists had a crush on Marxism; when it broke their hearts, they despaired of ever falling in love again.[58]

Michel Foucault exemplified political pessimism. He believed there was no ultimate purpose (*telos*) to life, no "deep teleology of a primeval destination."[59] Foucault contented himself with developing what he called a "genealogy of morals"—a means of exploring how people deviously secure their influence.[60] People in power develop systems of marking, classifying, record keeping, and evaluating to make their despotism seem matter-of-fact. Once in power, politicians don't violently dismember their opponents—they suck their blood through bureaucracy.[61] All governments do this, whether democracies or dictatorships, according to Foucault: "Do you imagine the mechanisms of power that operate between technicians, foremen and workers are that much different here and in the Soviet Union?"[62]

Not all Postmodernists are pessimistic about politics. The writings of Jean-François Lyotard, Richard Rorty, and to some extent Foucault hinted at a politics that can be used, at the local level, to "enhance individual freedom" and bring about "progressive change."[63] The solutions are almost always liberal, though. Stephen R. C. Hicks agrees, writing, "Of the major names in the Postmodernist movement there is not a single figure who is not leftwing in a serious way."[64]

Rorty, for example, embraced a straight-line progressivism with an anti-Christian bias: "I see the 'orthodox' (the people who think that hounding gays out of the military promotes traditional family values) as the same honest, decent, blinkered, disastrous people who voted for Hitler in 1933. I see the 'progressives' as defining the only America I care about."[65]

Though Foucault often just played with words and ideas as if they were a game, the political positions he did stake out were radical. When asked about Marxist revolution, for example, he said, "When the proletariat takes power, it may be quite possible that the proletariat will exert toward the classes over which it has triumphed a violent, dictatorial, and even bloody power. I can't see what objection could possibly be made to this."[66] When a group of people gains power and immediately turns toward exacting vengeance against its enemies rather than implementing a positive agenda, it tells you everything you need to know about what that group truly values. Foucault's nonchalant response to Marxists' off-with-their-heads mentality challenges everything he taught about justice and oppression.

Postmodernists, while typically content to point fingers, have among them those who have observed political oppression and decided to act. Out of this impulse to fix things has emerged something called **identity politics**. Identity politics refers to the ways certain groups of people are oppressed because of who they are—women, minorities, and homosexuals, for example.

The goal of identity politics is not truth, though, but revolt against oppressive structures. Alan Sokal quotes feminist Kelly Oliver: "In order to be revolutionary ... feminist theories should be political tools, strategies for overcoming oppression in specific concrete situations. The goal, then, of feminist theory should be to develop strategic theories—not true theories, not false theories, but strategic theories."[67] Whether it truly represents reality is not as important as whether it works.

Today universities are the battleground for intense conflict between people demanding power. What some call **political correctness** includes speech codes and sensitivity training for people considered to be unenlightened. For example, a woman who opposes abortion is cast as one trying to strip other women of power and dignity and masking her power grab in the language of "protecting babies." To the forces of political correctness, this person needs to undergo reeducation to adjust her antiquated views. Similarly, people who think homosexual practice is wrong are said to be using the language of morality to strip homosexuals of their humanity, and this must be corrected at the earliest age before bigotry takes hold.[68]

> *Political Correctness:* the censoring of language, ideas, acts, or policies that are perceived to discriminate or alienate minority social groups.

Postmodernism often originates in despair over what Postmodernists see as a failure of political leadership. But instead of lifting people to hope for—and work for—a genuinely good political force capable of ruling well on behalf of its citizens, it tends toward destruction. If politics is about power and power is about oppression, people who possess power must be assumed to be guilty and stripped of their influence. Of course, with no standard by which guilt or innocence can be measured, we have nothing to trust but the word of postmodern critics. This is the Postmodernist path to power: deplore it and then seize it. Will Postmodernists be able to use this power to seek true justice, or will they use their influence to turn the tables and claw out the eyes of those they believe have blinded them?

6. NEW SPIRITUALITY

New Spirituality, remember, is a Western version of Eastern religions, a New Age philosophy, religion, and lifestyle. New Spiritualists are concerned about the failure of political institutions not just because they despise quarreling and corruption but because their growth has taken over the personal responsibility individuals used to take. Marilyn Ferguson said,

> The failure of other social institutions has caused us to heap even more responsibility on government, the most unwieldy institution of all. We have relinquished more and more autonomy to the state, forcing government to assume functions once performed by communities, families, churches—people. Many social tasks have reverted to government by default, and the end result has been creeping paralysis—unreality.[69]

"The political system needs to be transformed, not reformed," said Ferguson.[70] This won't happen unless individual people get their acts together: "Social transformation follows a

> *Autarchy:* the rule of oneself; self-government.

chain reaction of personal change."[71] If we want good government, we must first of all govern ourselves; Ferguson called this approach to governance **autarchy**, which means the governing self.[72]

Though personal transformation is important to other worldviews, such as Christianity, no other worldview—not even Christianity—puts as much emphasis as New Spirituality on personal transformation as the key to political transformation. New Spiritualists talk about increasing people's personal power—not to foment revolution but to clear away life's debris. The stream of consciousness, then, may flow pure and clean. This, to Ferguson, was power used "not as a battering ram or to glorify the ego but in service to life. *Appropriate* power."[73]

To New Spiritualists, personal power could lead to transformation on a global scale, transcending all material and individual boundaries—including national and political ones. According to Donald Keys, humanity is "on the verge of something entirely new, a further evolutionary step unlike any other: the emergence of the first global civilization."[74]

> **To New Spiritualists, personal power could lead to transformation on a global scale, transcending all material and individual boundaries—including national and political ones.**

How exactly does personal transformation lead to political transformation? New Spiritualists believe collective consciousness is perfection: if we change to align ourselves with it, the world changes too. Ferguson explained: "The new collective is the new politics. As soon as we begin to work for a different kind of a world, the world changes for us."[75]

Ferguson was a clear and compelling writer whose infectious vision for the future made her a trusted sage to several liberal leaders, including Al Gore and Dennis Kucinich. But it was a quantum physicist named John Hagelin who really laid New Spirituality's political cards on the table by forming a political philosophy and even a political party. The story of how this happened is fascinating.

In the 1960s the Maharishi Mahesh Yogi invented Transcendental Meditation (TM) and gained fame as the guru to the Beatles. His forty thousand trained teachers spread the word, building training centers and even a college, the Maharishi University of Management in tiny Fairfield, Iowa. Approximately one thousand students attend the university, learning how to use Transcendental Meditation to study more effectively and advance their careers.

Hagelin, a professor at the university, articulated the Maharishi's political ideas in *Manual for a Perfect Government*, subtitled *How to Harness the Laws of Nature to Bring Maximum Success to Governmental Administration*. In the early 1990s, Hagelin formed a new political party, the Natural Law Party (NLP), which included a military policy calling for a "coherence-creating group" of five thousand to ten thousand troops to rush into trouble spots to meditate.[76] This "prevention wing," Hagelin claimed, "is fully capable of preventing the outbreak of war."[77]

While probably not all New Spiritualists agree with the principles of the Natural Law Party, all do seem to agree that personal transformation will bring about political transformation, which results in less crime, better treatment of workers, greater health, and increasing prosperity. Advocates think these results may even bring the various political parties together, since all of their concerns will be addressed: people will be better taken care of, taxes will go

---

down, the environment will be cleaner, and government will shrink. In the end, believes Mark Satin, these changes will spread around the entire globe, leading to "much more planetary cooperation."[78]

New Spiritualists are careful to maintain that their idea of planetary cooperation is different from a politically oriented world government, as in Secularism, Marxism, and Islam. David Spangler explains: "Unlike many historical expressions of the one-world idea, which focus in particular upon the establishment of a world government, the vision of the New Age qua planetary civilization arises less out of politics than out of what is called the holistic vision."[79]

So, to New Spiritualists, change starts with the person. "Power to the people," said Marilyn Ferguson. "One by one by one."[80] Satin says, "In New Age society we would learn to make our own decisions and not to hang on others. But that wouldn't isolate us from others; ... it would make us more attractive to others and more confident about being in community with them."[81]

The idea of autarchy (self-government) assumes a lot of the planet's seven billion inhabitants, who may not want to go along with the program or who may be suspicious of it. Never fear, says Satin. If enough people get on board, humanity's evolution toward a new world order "can be speeded up."[82]

> The idea of autarchy (self-government) assumes a lot of the planet's seven billion inhabitants, who may not want to go along with the program or who may be suspicious of it.

This approach is not without its problems. The move toward a planetary order will require people to release strong convictions. Former United Nations assistant secretary general Robert Muller said, "Religions must actively cooperate to bring to unprecedented heights a better understanding of the mysteries of life and of our place in the universe. 'My religion, right or wrong,' ... must be abandoned forever in the Planetary Age."[83] Of course, New Spiritualists argue that what they're doing is not religious but scientific. Consciousness is what it is—aligning with it is really the only long-term option. It's physics, not religion, they say.

The New Spiritualist worldview of politics is a strange brew made by mixing together "God is energy, not a person" with "people are basically good and perfectible," while adding a touch of godlikeness and sifting out our sin nature. It's a utopian plan. But the true definition of the word *utopia* means "no place," and that's exactly where its critics are afraid it will lead.

7. ISLAM

While there are obviously some exceptions, such as the nation of Turkey, which at this writing is a secular state with a predominant Muslim population, the overarching goal of Islamic politics seems to be the establishment of a global Islamic state ruled by religious leaders (Islamic theocracy) according to the principles of shariah law.[84] The mechanism is, according to prominent Muslim authors, jihad, though their use of the term does not always entail terrorizing unbelievers. Rather, jihad calls for warfare against anything hindering the advance of Islam, whether the temptations of the flesh or the reticence of nonbelievers. All Muslims must participate, Khurshid Ahmad says. "Jihad has been made obligatory, which means that the individual should, when the occasion arises, offer even his life for the defense and protection of Islam and the Islamic state."[85]

Remember from our chapter on Islam that a Muslim is one who performs the five pillars of Islam and believes the Quran to be the complete and final revelation of God. Commitment to God involves sacrifice of one's time, energy, and wealth to promote the cause. Jihad implies a readiness to give whatever one has, including his or her life, for the sake of Allah.[86]

Jesus taught his disciples not to take up arms against his detractors, but Muhammad taught his disciples to conquer anyone who opposed them or who refused to become Muslims. Afif A. Tabbarah recounts an example of Muhammad's teachings in action:

> Muhammad sent his delegates to eight neighboring rulers with messages calling them to embrace Islam. The appeal was rejected. Some of them even killed the Prophet's delegates, and some tore the message and threatened the delegates who had brought it. In that case, Moslems found no other alternative but fighting, after being certain that those rulers had slain the Prophet's delegates, misled their people, and ruled them in oppression and tyranny.[87]

The message these delegates carried was, essentially, *"You see our power and what happens to those who resist. Convert to Islam now and secure peace for yourselves."* In Islam, *peace* means "the state of submission experienced after everyone either adopts Islam or submits to its rule."

Contemporary Muslim apologists attempt to soften the concept of jihad, emphasizing its call to self-discipline or arguing that the early conquests of Muhammad and his companions were purely defensive. It makes sense, in our age of tension between Muslims and non-Muslims, that Muslims would emphasize jihad as the internal spiritual struggle of Muslims. Downplaying the role of jihadi aggression helps alleviate their neighbors' and friends' fears. But what is often not said, publicly at least, is that many jihadis see the personal-discipline aspect of jihad as a Muslim's war against his own flesh *so that* he may be disciplined in the fight against non-Muslim forces. It is inaccurate and misleading to say that jihad has nothing to do with the war for Islamic supremacy.

The assertion that Muslims see jihad as purely defensive simply does not fit the historical facts. Fazlur Rahman writes, "The most unacceptable [explanation] on historical grounds, however, is the stand of those modern Muslim apologists who have tried to explain the jihad of the early Community in purely defensive terms."[88] Early jihad, and jihad ever since, has never been purely defensive but rather characteristically offensive, as the history of Islam clearly reveals.[89] Indeed, the only way that one can understand the Crusades—with their many excesses—is to realize that they were a response to two centuries of aggression when Islamic armies poured across North Africa, the Iberian Peninsula, and today's Middle East.

What consequences would follow successful jihad? Primarily, we could expect that Muslims would insist on developing a separate form of law by which they would be governed. As we saw in the "Law" chapter, this is called *shariah*. Components of shariah are increasingly being implemented in Europe and even in the United States. The late Kirsten Heisig, a

German judge, said, "The law is slipping out of our hands. It's moving to the streets, or into a parallel system where an imam or another representative of the Koran determines what must be done."[90]

Muslims are allowed to practice shariah in limited circumstances in countries like Canada, Australia, and Great Britain, but it is coming to America as well. Ali Khan, a Muslim man who serves as a professor of law at Washburn University in Topeka, Kansas, has defended even some of the most radical provisions of shariah, including the practice of killing Muslims who leave the faith.[91] Harvard's Muslim chaplain Taha Abdul-Basser has proclaimed that such killing may make people uncomfortable, but there is "great wisdom" in it, and it should not be dismissed out of hand."[92] In *Crescent Moon Rising*, Paul Williams documents the growth of radical Islam in America, including a growing number of wife-beating and honor-killing cases.[93]

As Muslims take the first place in a given society, they become the leaders, and nonbelievers are made to submit. In Muslim-dominated countries, Christians and Jews ("people of the Book") are called *dhimmis* and are expected to express submission to their Muslim rulers by paying a tax called *jizya*. The Quran says, "Fight those who believe not in God nor the Last Day, nor hold that forbidden which hath been forbidden by God and His Apostle, nor acknowledge the Religion of Truth, (even if they are) of the People of the Book, until they pay the *jizya* with willing submission, and feel themselves subdued" (9:29). Paying the tax is a tribute to Muslim authority and a tacit agreement that their personal views, what Abdullah Yusuf Ali called their "personal liberty of conscience" are to be kept to themselves.[94]

> *Dhimmis:* non-Muslims living in Islamic states.

> *Jizyah:* a tax imposed on *dhimmis* living in Islamic states.

A few Muslim leaders, *very* few, publicly criticize this program of takeover. An Indian Muslim leader Akbar Ladak revealed the true aims of the Islamists bent on takeover and called on his Muslim brothers and sisters to resist them:

> Today, our relatively free, increasingly multicultural societies are under threat, first and foremost by Muslim extremists who have declared their intent to bring about a global caliphate. Theirs is a hateful and misogynist philosophy, financed by oil-rich dictators. That it twists my beloved faith to justify a simplistic ideology gives it a powerful allure for Muslims who haven't had the exposure to varied ideas and strains within Islam.
>
> We, Muslims living in free societies, need to be in the forefront of this fight. We fight not only for the security and integrity of the societies we live in, but also for the soul of our faith. Only we can present an alternative interpretation of Islam which promotes the vision of peace, progress and equality.[95]

Reading between the lines of Ladak's statement, one can see the true agenda and immense power of the Islamist leaders as they move forcefully toward a global Islamic state. If Ladak is worried, maybe we should be worried too. But there is hope: perhaps it is possible to form a coalition of reform-minded Muslims and non-Muslims to halt the abuses of radical Islamists.

8. CHRISTIANITY

The essential Christian political worldview is this: citizens of the kingdom of heaven should be the best citizens in the kingdom of the world because their allegiance is to something higher than the state. God insists his people do justice, love mercy, and walk in humility with him (Mic. 6:8).[96] If they do, it is a hopeful antidote to the hopelessness of legal positivism—the idea that law is what those in authority have agreed to do, with no particular tie to morality. If there is nothing higher than the state, then the state is God and right in all it does. Hitler's perverse medical experiments performed on children without anesthesia, leading to their deaths, were *legal* because Hitler was the law. Indeed, opposing those acts was, by the reasoning of legal positives, *illegal* because the state is supreme, and whoever controls it is right.[97]

In a fallen world, government's primary mission is to preserve justice and punish evil so that humans may flourish. This sometimes calls for the protection of human life by the taking of human life (as in capital punishment and just war). In Genesis 9:6 we see the development of civil government when cities were formed around the principle of preventing human bloodshed.[98] But would government have been necessary if humans were not fallen? Not for punishing evil, of course, but punishing evil is not all that governments do. Governments establish order, set up structures to deliver goods and services, such as roads and utilities; keep records; ensure a smooth flow of traffic; and so forth. Interestingly, government seems to be part of God's perfect plan of redemption. Among the names given Jesus Christ throughout the Bible is a political title, King of Kings and Lord of Lords.[99]

The Christian worldview sees government as an institution God established to promote security and justice (order), protect the innocent, and secure the rights God has granted so people can flourish. This is a position articulated at length by Saint Augustine and later affirmed by many Christian thinkers, including John Calvin and Martin Luther. It is a position rooted in Scripture: because God ordained government, it is a sacred institution whose rulers are ministers of God for good (Rom. 13). The apostle Peter instructed Christians to "submit ... for the Lord's sake to every authority instituted among men, whether to the king, as the supreme authority, or to governors, who are sent by him to punish those who do wrong and to commend those who do right" (1 Pet. 2:13–14 NIV 1984).

Through time, at least half a dozen views of politics have emerged in the church. We will first take a look at five of these that have philosophical problems and then consider an orthodox Christian view. It is critical that you answer this question yourself: Would Jesus even want his followers to be involved in politics?

9. FIVE CHRISTIAN POSITIONS ON POLITICAL INVOLVEMENT

1. "Christians shouldn't be involved." In response to intellectual attacks on Christianity in the 1800s, some Christian leaders tried to make peace by insisting that religion and the intellect occupy different domains, answer different questions, and therefore pose no threat to one another. Henry Ward Beecher, the famous nineteenth-century preacher (and brother of Harriet Beecher

Stowe, author of *Uncle Tom's Cabin*), said, "While we are taught by the scientists in truths that belong to the sensual nature, while we are taught by the economists of things that belong to the social nature, we need the Christian ministry to teach us those things which are invisible."

Though we respect Beecher's work as an abolitionist, we think his compromise gives away too much. Saying that Christianity deals only with the invisible is to create a "secular-sacred divide" in which we are not permitted to bring biblically informed solutions to bear on our nation's problems.

2. **"Society isn't worth redeeming."** Joel Carpenter summarizes a common view among Christian leaders in the late 1800s and through the 1900s about societal change:

> What were the prospects for the "true church," then, in these times of decline and apostasy? Fundamentalists believed that God would continue to use his "faithful remnant" to witness to the truth and gather out of the world a "people for His name" (Acts 15:14). Until Jesus came for them at the Rapture, Bible-believing Christians were to win the lost, heed the signs of the times, keep themselves pure from error, and expose and condemn false religion.[100]

For example, nineteenth-century evangelist Dwight L. Moody said, "I look upon this world as a wrecked vessel. God has given me a lifeboat and said to me, 'Moody, save all you can.'"[101] While well intentioned, Moody's statement pulled Christians' attention away from making society better, and many churches prided themselves on this anti-cultural perspective. Life was hard, and church was a place to go to find temporary relief by reminding oneself of the heavenly delights that awaited the faithful. But this perspective assumes that what happens on this earth is ultimately unimportant to God, a theology that cannot be sustained scripturally.

3. **"Political structures can't change the human heart."** When Shane Claiborne walks on stage, what the audience sees is a skinny, white guy with dreadlocks. What they hear, though, is a hard-hitting social-justice message delivered with winsomeness and humor. Part of Claiborne's message is to encourage Christians to stay out of politics. "Jesus taught that his followers ... should not attempt to 'run the world,'" he says.[102] For Claiborne, Christians are citizens of heaven only. We should have no allegiance to an earthly kingdom. The best we can do is form an alternate community so attractive to people in the world that they want to join it.

> **Without a doubt, politics can become an idol, and we must resist any program encouraging people to turn to politics rather than to Christ for salvation.**

Without a doubt, politics can become an idol, and we must resist any program encouraging people to turn to politics rather than to Christ for salvation. But just because something doesn't change hearts does not mean it is unimportant. Police don't change the human heart, but we still think law enforcement has value. Food doesn't change our spiritual condition, but we still eat. Politics can't bring heaven to Earth, but it can bring heavenly values to bear on earthly problems. As Thomas Aquinas put it, "Grace does not destroy nature, but completes it."[103]

4. **"Christianity is only about the institution of the church and is not relevant to civil government."** *Two-kingdoms theology* hails from a small group of Reformed theologians who teach that Martin Luther's distinction between the kingdom of heaven and the kingdom of

man actually represents the kingdom of the church and the kingdom of the world. The Bible, they say, is only relevant to the life of the church, not to civil government.

One advocate of the two-kingdoms theology, Michael Horton, phrases it straightforwardly: "The central message of Christianity is not a worldview, a way of life, or a program for personal and societal change; it is a gospel."[104] Of course, it's debatable whether these theologians have properly interpreted Luther, and whether it's a good idea even if they have. The fact is, people always make decisions based on some system of ethics. If this system isn't biblically informed, it will be informed by something else.

5. "Christians *should* be involved, and they should try to take over." Some Christians don't run *away* from politics; they run toward it. Their enthusiasm is admirable, but it is all too easy to just become appendages of one of the political parties, serving its interests instead of God's. Christians on both the right and the left can suffer from the political illusion. Some believe that liberals of ill intent have hijacked America, and they think their job is "to reclaim America for Christ, whatever the cost." Others see a spiritual dimension in government itself and are not above shaming conservatives as unspiritual, even mean spirited and unchristian.

The French thinker Jacques Ellul warned of what he called "the political illusion," which assumes that all problems are, at root, political. Consequently, it is also assumed that all solutions are political.

Is there a common ground between these various factions? Probably not. People hold their views for very deep reasons—their upbringing, their sense of moral rightness, the people who have influenced their lives, or the applause of those whose admiration they crave. Instead of looking for a middle ground, let's see if we can find something of an original position in the Bible about the structures of society and the gospel's influence therein. At the very least, such a study will help us live with greater integrity in grappling with the difficult political issues of our day.

10. JESUS AND POLITICS

"Jesus didn't talk politics" some Christians claim, usually because they dislike the brand of involvement churchgoers are choosing. Even if it were the case that Jesus didn't talk politics, this approach is difficult to sustain biblically: Jesus did not work for a corporation, go to war, get married, or have children. "What did Jesus do?" is inadequate for discerning how Christ's teachings should be applied to today's problems. Jesus lived consistently with a biblical understanding of how human beings are designed to bear God's image. The whole counsel of the Bible shows us how we might do the same.

But to the particular question of whether Jesus was involved in politics during his ministry, we have several pieces of evidence that he was. First, the Gospels mention Jesus's frequent presence in the synagogue. In those days, according to Jewish scholar Lee I. Levine, the synagogue was not only a place of worship but also "a courtroom, school, hostel, a place for political meetings, social gatherings," and a center for community functions. Levine says the synagogue served the same purposes in the time of Jesus as the "city gates" served in Old Testament times—a gathering place for civic discourse and at times adjudication of rival legal claims.[105] It is difficult to imagine Jesus as presented in the Gospels being on the fringes of rather than involved in community affairs.

Second, in Jesus's time, politics and religion were tightly intertwined. Jesus interacted with many different groups, all of which had distinct religious and political views.[106] Throughout Jesus's ministry, people from various sects tried to humiliate him; it backfired every time. On one occasion some of the leaders tried to get Jesus to side either with the pro-Roman or anti-Roman forces by asking whether it was right to pay taxes to Caesar. Jesus replied, "Render to Caesar the things that are Caesar's, and to God the things that are God's" (Matt. 22:21). This statement carries both political and religious significance.

Third, Jesus himself never spoke explicitly against government. He never told his followers to eschew society and hide in the desert (like the Essenes), tear down government (like the revolutionary Zealots), or join those in power (like the Herodians). He did not tell the centurion or any official of influence to quit his position, and he commonly used leaders of various sorts in his parables. Indeed, no New Testament writer told law-enforcement, military, or government officials to quit their jobs if they came to Christ. In contrast, they were told to act honestly and justly in their respective vocations (see, for example, Luke 3:14 and Acts 10).

> Even if Jesus's words and actions do not form an *ideology of politics*, they clearly do form a *theology of engagement*.

Even if Jesus's words and actions do not form an *ideology of politics*, they clearly do form a *theology of engagement*. God has something to say to a lost and dying world, and he has chosen us to be the mouthpieces. In Matthew 28:18–20, Jesus told the disciples to go out and make more disciples by teaching everyone everywhere to obey God in every area in which Jesus Christ has authority (which is all areas).[107] It isn't just "how to get to heaven" but "how to obey God in all you do."

Based on these considerations, here are some answers to common questions Christians ask about politics:

Why is political involvement necessary? James Madison said, "If men were angels, no government would be necessary. If angels were to govern men, neither external nor internal controls on government would be necessary."[108] But we are *not* angels, and government *is* necessary. Our evil inclinations must be kept in check by laws and a government capable of enforcing them. In America, the founding fathers grappled with the problem of protecting ordinary citizens from the sin natures of those in authority. They devised a system of checks and balances among the branches of government to prevent power from collecting in the hands of a few. By broadly distributing power and responsibility, the American system of government minimizes the abuse of power.

What is the purpose of government? According to the Christian worldview, God instituted human government to protect the rights he gave us. This protection, or security, both from overt violence and more generally in structuring communities, is called *political order*. Human nature is capable of both vice and virtue. Protecting the human rights of life, liberty, property, work, rest, worship, and a free press from those who would diminish them means promoting order and justice. E. Calvin Beisner says justice and truth are interrelated, for justice is the practice of truth in human relationships. He concludes, "Justice is rendering to each his due according to a right standard."[109] The right standard is God's moral order, which is based on the very character of God. This standard insists that the innocent citizens of society be protected from those intent on marring God's image by depriving people of life, liberty, or the pursuit of happiness.

What is the government's responsibility? In the "Sociology" chapter we talked about two principles that apply in politics as well. The first was **sphere sovereignty**, Abraham Kuyper's idea that there are three primary spheres in society: government, church, and family. Each sphere, or institution, must be balanced with the others.[110] The second principle was **subsidiarity**, which is the principle of mobilized communities of people seeking solutions at the level closest to the problem.

- Government's purpose is to secure justice and freedom. It possesses the power of prosecution and coercion to punish people for not doing what is right and to require of them the necessary support for securing justice and freedom. The *church's* purpose is to manifest God's love and grace on Earth. Its powers are persuasion and compassion—getting people to see their need for God and tangibly helping lift them out of dire circumstances, restoring them to their image-bearing capacity. The family's purpose is to manifest God's community and creativity, including procreativity. It has the powers of procreation and community—influencing the world by raising children who will make a positive contribution to society.

- Given the delegated powers of government, it is unreasonable to ask government to exercise true compassion. It can only coerce people to help one another according to its own definition of help and prosecute them if they fail to do so. A government that attempts to regulate procreation, community, persuasion, and compassion inevitably smothers and oppresses its citizens. History tells us that government services and controls come at a high price—diminishing other institutions and establishing a base of power from which government grows in its forcefulness.

What happens when government oversteps its bounds? Today, many political leaders do not understand their place in God's universe, and so they attempt to usurp God's sovereignty, which covers everyone and everything, everywhere, for all time (Ps. 103:19).[111] Government can never take the place of the church. Charles Colson, a high-level political official who served a prison sentence for abuse of power and ultimately came to faith in Christ, gave a foresighted warning: "Excise belief in God and you are left with only two principles: the individual and the State. In this situation, however, there is no mediating structure to generate moral values and, therefore, no counterbalance to the inevitable ambitions of the State."[112]

Sphere Sovereignty: the belief that God ordained certain spheres of society, such as family, church, and state, and that society functions best when each sphere is properly managing its own area of responsibility.

Subsidiarity: the belief that decisions are best handled at the organizational or societal level closest to the issues or persons affected.

Theocracy: a state ruled by religious leaders or one particular religion.

William Penn concluded, "If we are not governed by God, then we will be ruled by tyrants."[113] Sadly, thousands of years of human experience prove this. And through time the coercive activity of government has become even more brutal.[114]

Doesn't Christian involvement lead to theocracy? The term *theocracy* means "rule by religious leaders." As outlined in this chapter, we think Christian involvement is one of the few things that save a nation *from* theocracy. Islam assumes its leaders should be given greater power in order to create the perfect society. Secularism's belief that humans are perfectible and Marxism's some-are-more-equal-than-others view share the same assumption. Christians, on the other hand, who believe in God's ultimate authority and a biblical view of human nature, are suspicious of claims about society's perfectibility. They distrust leaders who demand more power than is absolutely necessary to secure justice and freedom.[115]

> **Christians do not believe the state is the means to salvation.**

Christianity is not utopian. Christians do not believe the state is the means to salvation. Chuck Colson wrote, "While Christian teaching emphasizes that each person has worth and responsibility before God, utopianism argues that salvation can only be achieved collectively."[116] The Christian worldview is based on transcendent law applied impartially to all. It prizes accountability above efficiency and human flourishing above the accumulation of power.

Is there ever a time when Christians should disobey the government? The Christian view of politics begins with the sovereignty of God, not the sovereignty of the state. The Bible clearly tells Christians to respect, obey, and participate in governance because the state exists to do God's will (Rom. 13:1–7). If the state structures itself in a way that denies justice or freedom rather than securing it, it must be opposed. Christians must be willing to say to governing authorities, as did Peter and the apostles, "We must obey God rather than men" (Acts 5:29). We should be respectful but firm, as Shadrach, Meshach, and Abednego were when facing Nebuchadnezzar's demand for worship:

> O Nebuchadnezzar, we have no need to answer you in this matter. If this be so, our God whom we serve is able to deliver us from the burning fiery furnace, and he will deliver us out of your hand, O king. But if not, be it known to you, O king, that we will not serve your gods or worship the golden image that you have set up. (Dan. 3:16–18)

Francis Schaeffer said, "The bottom line is that at a certain point there is not only the right, but the duty, to disobey the State."[117] Resisting the laws of an unjust government is called **civil disobedience**. Our disobedience to the state may even result in imprisonment or death, but in such instances, it is for the sake of our conscience that we act in the hope that the consciences of our neighbors and leaders will be moved to restore justice.

In a democratic form of government, citizens' duty to promote justice and freedom requires that they not blindly follow leaders who deny their responsibility to God. Rather, citizens hold them accountable by voting, persuading, petitioning, running for political office, or serving in nonelected positions where we may be able to influence those in power.[118]

> *Civil Disobedience:* the practice of resisting a government's unjust laws.

11. CONCLUSION

God ordains governments to secure justice and freedom. When government authority rests within the bounds of this ordination, we submit willingly to the state's authority. When the state abuses its authority or claims to be sovereign over God, Christians must acknowledge God's transcendent law first. Contrary to people who say Christians are unpatriotic because they do not support the government in every instance, Christians should be able to say with a clear conscience that politics will be better when people always bring rightness to government rather than assume the government is always right.

> Christians should be able to say with a clear conscience that politics will be better when people always bring rightness to government rather than assume the government is always right.

Our ongoing struggle to create and maintain just government may or may not be effective. We must, however, remain obedient to God in all circumstances. As Chuck Colson said, "Christians are to do their duty as best they can. But even when they feel that they are making no difference, that they are failing to bring Christian values to the public arena, success is not the criteria. Faithfulness is."[119]

A society with just laws and orderly governance is certainly a better place to live than a society without them. And if such a society has a reasonable means of ensuring the proper use of power to secure the good of the citizenry, it will be even better still. But how does this affect the way people make a living? How does it relate to how people provide goods and services to one another to secure a means of provision for their families? What role do law and politics play in these decisions? All of these questions revolve around the study of economics, and exploring how a Christian worldview answers them will be our goal in the next chapter.

ENDNOTES

1. Lord Acton, letter to Bishop Mandell Creighton (1887), in John Bartlett, *Familiar Quotations*, 13th and centennial ed. (Boston: Little, Brown, 1955), 335. Lord Acton's English name was Sir John Dalberg-Acton (John Emerich Edward Dalberg-Acton, first Baron Acton, KCVO, DL.

2. *Merriam-Webster's Collegiate Dictionary* defines *power* as "the ability to act or produce an effect."

3. Edmund Burke, *Reflections on the Revolution in France* (New York: Library of Liberal Arts, 1955), 288.

4. Quoted in Kathleen Hall Jamieson, *Dirty Politics* (New York: Oxford University Press, 1992), 46.

5. Harvey Mansfield, *A Student's Guide to Political Philosophy* (Wilmington: Intercollegiate Studies Institute, 2001), 17–18.

6. See C. N. Jeffords, "Sin," in David Noel Freedman, A. C. Myers, and A. B. Beck, eds., *Eerdmans Dictionary of the Bible* (Grand Rapids: Eerdmans, 2000), 1124. See also Joel F. Williams, "Way," in Freedman, Myers, and Beck, *Eerdmans Dictionary of the Bible*, 1370–71. Williams says, "In the concrete sense, a road (Deut. 1:2; Ruth 1:7) or a movement along a particular path, i.e., a journey (Exod. 13:21; 1 Kgs. 19:4). However, Heb. *derek* was also employed more broadly. To walk in the ways of God meant to live according to his will and commandments (Deut. 10:12–13; 1 Kgs. 3:14). In Isaiah 'the way of the Lord' can refer to God's provision of deliverance from enslavement or exile (Isa. 40:3; 43:16–19). The word was often used to identify the overall direction of a person's life, whether righteous or wicked (Judg. 2:17–19; Ps. 1:6; cf. Matt 7:13–14), wise or foolish (Prov. 4:11; 12:15). In the NT Gk. *hodos* has a similar range of meanings. In Mark's Gospel it is used repeatedly to present Jesus as 'on the way,' i.e., on his journey to Jerusalem (Mark 8:27; 9:33–34; 10:32). The broader context adds a deeper significance to these more literal references, since Jesus's willingness to go the way of suffering provides an example for his followers who must also prepare to suffer (Mark 8:31–34). In John 14:6 Jesus claims to be 'the way,' i.e., the only means of access to God (cf. Heb. 9:8; 10:19–20). In Acts 'the Way' functions as a title for the Christian message (Acts 19:9, 23; 22:4; 24:22) or the Christian community (9:2; 24:14)."

7. Thomas Hobbes, *Leviathan* (New York: Penguin Classics, 1985), 186.

8. John Locke, *Of Civil Government* (London: Dent, 1924), 118.

9. In his *Two Treatises on Government*, Locke made his case by arguing from the book of Genesis that Adam was the king of creation, and that his rightful heir was not the king but all of us. The monarchy, it is safe to say, was not impressed.

10. The title may be just two words, but the subtitle of Rutherford's book ran to 136 words, making clear that it was an argument against the monarchy: "Or the Law and the Prince; A Dispute for The Just Prerogative of King and People: Containing the Reasons and Causes of the Most Necessary Defensive Wars of the Kingdom of Scotland, and of Their Expedition for the Aid and Help of Their Dear Brethren of England; in Which Their Innocency Is Asserted, and a Full Answer Is Given to a Seditious Pamphlet, Entitled, 'SACRO-SANCTA REGUM MAJESTAS,' or the Sacred and Royal Prerogative of Christian Kings; under the name of J. A., but Penned by John Maxwell, the Excommunicate Popish Prelate; with a Scriptural Confutation of the Ruinous Grounds of W. Barclay, H. Grotius, H. Arnisæus, Ant. de Domi. Popish Bishop of Spilato, and of Other Late Anti-Magitratical Royalists, as the Author of Ossorianum, Dr. Ferne, E. Symmons, the Doctors of Aberdeen, etc. In Forty-four Questions."

11. Quoted in John Montgomery, *Human Rights and Human Dignity* (Calgary: Canadian Institute for Law, Theology, and Public Policy, 2005), 107.

12. Robert Nozick, *Anarchy, State, and Utopia* (New York: Basic Books, 1977), 183.

13. John Rawls, *A Theory of Justice* (Cambridge, MA: Belknap, 2005), 62.

14. In a concession to those who say people cannot be completely free from judgment in the real world, Rawls called for a "reflective equilibrium" between the principles that are ideal and people's considered judgments—those in which their moral capacities are most likely to be displayed without distortion.

15. Quoted in Susan Jones, "'Spread the Wealth Around' Comment Comes Back to Haunt Obama," *CNS News*, October 15, 2008, http://cnsnews.com/news/article/spread-wealth-around-comment-comes-back-haunt-obama.

16. *Liberalism* as we are using it in this text refers to how the term is used in the United States. In other Western nations, the term carries different connotations.

17. *Affirmative action* means giving certain preferences to "under-represented" groups, such as when a government building project is required to hire a certain number of minority-owned subcontractors, or when a university policy requires a certain percentage of minority students to be accepted each year, regardless of the students' ability to perform at a college level.

18. A thorough article explaining this trend from an atheist, Secularist point of view can be found at Adam Brown, "Why Atheists Align with Democrats," Atheism Resource, accessed March 27, 2014, www.atheismresource .com/2012/why-atheists-align-with-democrats.

19. Julian Huxley, *The Humanist Frame* (New York: Harper and Brothers, 1961), 15.

20. Huxley, *The Humanist Frame*, 7.

21. Quoted in Huxley, *The Humanist Frame*, 107.

22. Sidney Hook, "Solzhenitsyn and Secular Humanism: A Response," *Humanist* (November/December 1978): 6.

23. Sidney Hook, *Religion in a Free Society* (Lincoln, NE: University of Nebraska Press, 1967), 36.

24. V. M. Tarkunde, "An Outline of Radical Humanism," *Humanist* (July/August 1988): 13.

25. Walter Truett Anderson, *Politics and the New Humanism* (Pacific Palisades, CA: Goodyear, 1973), 141.

26. See especially chapter 5 in David Schweickart, *After Capitalism*, 2nd ed. (Lanham, MD: Rowman and Littlefield, 2011).

27. Quoted in Thomas Sowell, *The Quest for Cosmic Justice* (New York: Free Press, 1999), 6–7.

28. James A. Nuechterlein, "Milton Friedman by Lanny Ebenstein," *Commentary*, May 1, 2007, 286.

29. Huxley, *Humanist Frame*, 16.

30. The characteristics of utopian schemes were the subject of Thomas Molnar's book *Utopia: The Perennial Heresy* (London: Sheed and Ward, 1967).

31. Paul Kurtz, *Forbidden Fruit* (Buffalo, NY: Prometheus Books, 1988), 146. Among these forces are Marxism, Postmodernism, New Spirituality, Secularism, and various internationalist and transnationalist organizations, including the Council on Foreign Relations, Club of Rome, the Bilderberg Group, Trilateral Commission, and the United Nations. Biblical Christianity constitutes one major opposition to one-world government; Revelation 13 declares that the head of a man-made world government will be the Beast or Antichrist. For a fairly complete list of organizations and movements striving for a world order, see Malachi Martin, *The Keys of This Blood* (New York: Simon and Schuster, 1990), 275.

32. Paul Kurtz, "A Declaration of Interdependence: A New Global Ethics," *Free Inquiry* (Fall 1988): 6.

33. Ian Bremmer, *Every Nation for Itself* (New York: Portfolio, 2012), 13.

34. Bremmer, *Every Nation for Itself*, 21.

35. Bremmer, *Every Nation for Itself*, 26.

36. Lucile W. Green, "The Call for a World Constitutional Convention," *Humanist* (July/August 1968): 13.

37. C. S. Lewis, *The Abolition of Man* (New York: Macmillan, 1952), 73.

38. Karl Marx, *A Contribution to the Critique of Political Economy* (Chicago: C. H. Kerr, 1911), 11.

39. Karl Marx, Friedrich Engels, and V. I. Lenin, *On the Dictatorship of the Proletariat* (Moscow: Progress Publishers, 1984), 124.

40. Marx, Engels, and Lenin, *On the Dictatorship*, 243.

41. Fidel Castro, January 1994, quoted in Sebastian Balfour, *Castro* (London: Longman, 2009), 1553.

42. Hugo Chavez, "Hugo Chavez on Climate Change and Capitalism," *Climate and Capitalism*, March 6, 2013, http://climateandcapitalism.com/2013/03/06/hugo-chavez-on-climate-change-and-capitalism/.

43. According to Marx, "political power is merely the organized power of one class for oppressing another." Marx, Engels, and Lenin, *On the Dictatorship*, 59.

44. V. I. Lenin, *The State and Revolution* (New York: International Publishers, 1932), 9.

45. Marx, Engels, and Lenin, *On the Dictatorship*, 122.

46. V. I. Lenin, *Selected Works*, 38 vols. (New York: International Publishers, 1938), 7:81.

47. Friedrich Engels, *The Origin of the Family, Private Property, and the State* (Chicago: Kerr, 1902), 206.

48. Marx, Engels, and Lenin, *On the Dictatorship*, 249–50.

49. Marx, Engels, and Lenin, *On the Dictatorship*, 256.

50. This allusion comes from R. J. Rummel, *Death by Government* (New Brunswick, NJ: Transaction Publishers, 1994), 9.

51. Immanuel Wallerstein, *The Politics of the World-Economy: The States, the Movements, and the Civilizations* (Cambridge, UK: Cambridge University Press, 1984); Wil Hout, *Capitalism and the Third World: Development, Dependence, and the World System* (Hants, England: Edward Elgar, 1993).

52. Fernando H. Cardoso and Enzo Faletto, *Dependency and Development in Latin America* (Berkeley, CA: University of California Press, 1979).

53. Quoted in Mark Lilla, *The Reckless Mind: Intellectuals in Politics* (New York: New York Review Books, 2001), 29.

54. Barbara Epstein, "Postmodernism and the Left," *New Politics*, n.s., 6, no. 2, (Winter 1997), http://nova.wpunj.edu/newpolitics/issue22/epstei22.htm.

55. Foucault "does not seem to have felt it necessary to have a fully worked-out political position, since in some ways it was precisely this sense of having to hold to a party line which he was reacting against." Lilla, *Reckless Mind*, 15.

56. Quoted in Steven Best and Douglas Kellner, "Postmodern Politics and the Battle for the Future," Illuminations, accessed March 19, 2014, http://uta.edu/huma/illuminations/kell28.htm.

57. Anthony Thomson, "Post-Modernism and Social Justice," paper presented at annual meeting of the Society of Socialist Studies, St. John's, Newfoundland, June 7, 1997, http://ace.acadiau.ca/soci/agt/constitutivecrim.htm. He references Stuart Henry and Dragan Milovanovic, *Constitutive Criminology: Beyond Postmodernism* (London: Sage, 1996), 4.

58. Most of the early French Postmodernists emerged from the Marxist tradition—some grew up in families supportive of leftist causes, and others were former Stalinists. Foucault initially joined the Maoist Gauche Prolétarienne and the French Communist Party but left once he discovered the Marxist stance toward homosexuality. As time went on, Foucault moved further away from Marxism, particularly the "state-centered focus" of classic Marxism. Foucault would later write, "Marxism exists in nineteenth century thought as a fish exists in water; that is, it ceases to breathe anywhere else." See Michel Foucault, *The Order of Things: An Archaeology of the Human Sciences* (New York: Vintage, 1994), 262.

59. Michel Foucault, *Discipline and Punish* (New York: Vintage, 1991), 64–65.

60. Michel Foucault, *Power/Knowledge: Selected Interviews and Other Writings, 1972–1977* (New York: Vintage, 1977), 51.

61. Foucault, *Power/Knowledge*, 71.

62. Foucault, *Power/Knowledge*.

63. Best and Kellner, "Postmodern Politics."

64. Stephen R. C. Hicks, *Explaining Postmodernism: Skepticism and Socialism from Rousseau to Foucault* (Tempe, AZ: Scholargy, 2004), 85.

65. Richard Rorty, *Philosophy and Social Hope* (New York: Penguin, 1999), 17.

66. Quoted in Lilla, *Reckless Mind*, 150.

67. Kelly Oliver, "Keller's Gender/Science System: Is the Philosophy of Science to Science as Science Is to Nature?" *Hypatia* 3, no. 3 (Winter 1989): 146, quoted in Alan D. Sokal, "Transgressing the Boundaries: Towards a Transformative Hermaneutics of Quantum Gravity," *Social Text* 46/47 (Spring/Summer 1996): 217–252.

68. See, for example, the following books written for children and taught in many school districts across America: *Heather Has Two Mommies*; *Daddy's Roommate*; *Gay Pride Parade*; *The King and King*; and others.

69. Marilyn Ferguson, *The Aquarian Conspiracy* (New York: Tarcher/Penguin, 1980), 200–201.

70. Ferguson, *Aquarian Conspiracy*, 197.

71. Ferguson, *Aquarian Conspiracy*, 195.

72. Ferguson, *Aquarian Conspiracy*, 197

73. Ferguson, *Aquarian Conspiracy*, 195.

74. Donald Keys, *Earth at Omega: Passage to Planetization* (Boston: Branden, 1982), iii.

75. Ferguson, *Aquarian Conspiracy*, 214.

76. John Hagelin, *Manual for a Perfect Government* (Fairfield, IA: Maharishi University of Management, 1998), 143.

77. Hagelin, *Manual for a Perfect Government*, 144.

78. Mark Satin, *New Age Politics* (New York: Dell, 1978), 22.

79. David Spangler, *Emergence: The Rebirth of the Sacred* (New York: Dell, 1984), 42.

80. Ferguson, *Aquarian Conspiracy*, 256.

81. Satin, *New Age Politics*, 106.

82. Satin, *New Age Politics*, 20–21.

83. Robert Muller, *The New Genesis: Shaping a Global Spirituality* (New York: Image Books, 1984), 164.

84. Colin Chapman quotes Zaki Badawi about the inability of Islam to develop a theology or political system that doesn't involve being in control: "As we know, the history of Islam as a faith is also the history of a state and a community of believers living by Divine law. The Muslims, jurists and theologians, have always expounded Islam as both a Government and a faith. This reflects the historical fact that Muslims, from the start, lived under their own law. Muslim theologians naturally produced a theology with this in view—it is a theology of the majority. Being a minority was not seriously considered or even contemplated. The theologians were divided in their attitude to the question of minority status. Some declared that it should not take place; that is to say that a Muslim is forbidden to live for any lengthy period of time under non-Muslim rule. Others suggested that a Muslim living under non-Muslim rule is under no obligation to follow the law of Islam in matters of public law. Neither of these two extremes is satisfactory. Throughout the history of Islam some pockets of Muslims lived under the sway of non-Muslim rulers, often without an alternative. They nonetheless felt sufficiently committed to their faith to attempt to regulate their lives in accordance with its rules and regulations in so far as their circumstances permitted. In other words, the practice of the community rather than the theories of the theologians provided a solution. Nevertheless Muslim theology offers, up to the present, no systematic formulation of the status of being a minority. The question is being examined. It is hoped that the matter will be brought to focus and that Muslim theologians from all over the Muslim world will delve into this thorny subject and allay the conscience of the many Muslims living in the West and also to chart a course for Islamic survival, even revival, in a secular society." Colin Chapman, *Cross and Crescent: Responding to the Challenge of Islam* (Downers Grove, IL: InterVarsity, 2003), 149–50.

85. Chapman, *Cross and Crescent*, 39.

86. Chapman, *Cross and Crescent*, 23.

87. Afif A. Tabbarah, *The Spirit of Islam: Doctrine and Teachings* (Beirut: Dar El-llm Lilmalayin, 1978), 384.

88. Fazlur Rahman, *Islam*, 2nd ed. (Chicago: University of Chicago Press, 1991), 37.

89. An extensive discussion of the theory and history of jihad is presented in Serge Trifkovic, *The Sword of the Prophet: Islam; History, Theology, Impact on the World* (Boston: Regina Orthodox Press, 2002).

90. Quoted in Andrew Bostom, *Sharia versus Freedom* (Amherst, NY: Prometheus Books, 2012), 158.

91. Bostom, *Sharia versus Freedom*, 148.

92. Bostom, *Sharia versus Freedom*.

93. See Paul L. Williams, *Crescent Moon Rising* (Amherst, NY: Prometheus Books, 2013).

94. Abdullah Yusuf Ali, *The Holy Qur'an: Text, Translation, and Commentary* (Washington, DC: American International Printing, 1946), 447.

95. Attributed to Akbar Ladak in Irshad Manji, *Allah, Liberty, and Love* (New York: Free Press, 2011), 60–61.

96. Micah 6:8: "He has told you, O man, what is good; and what does the LORD require of you but to do justice, and to love kindness, and to walk humbly with your God?"

97. For more information on legal positivism, consult the "Law" chapter of this volume. The fiercest debate on this issue was carried out between two legal scholars, H. L. A. Hart and Lon Fuller. Hart, arguing for *legal positivism*, said that law is what those who have the authority agree to do. The answer is legal positivism. As we saw earlier, legal positivism says that law is not tied to morality but is whatever the order of things declares it to be. Les Greene, professor of philosophy at Oxford University, offers a thorough and clear definition of *legal positivism*: "Whether a society has a legal system depends on the presence of certain structures of governance, not on the extent to which it satisfies ideals of justice, democracy, or the rule of law. What laws are in force in that system depends on what social standards its officials recognize as authoritative; for example, legislative enactments, judicial decisions, or social customs. The fact that a policy would be just, wise, efficient, or prudent is never sufficient reason for thinking that it is actually the law, and the fact that it is unjust, unwise, inefficient or imprudent is never sufficient reason for doubting it. According to positivism, law is a matter of what has been posited (ordered, decided, practiced, tolerated, etc.); as we might say in a more modern idiom, positivism is the view that law is a social construction." From Leslie Green, "Legal Positivism," *Stanford Encyclopedia of Philosophy*, 2003, http://plato.

stanford.edu/entries/legal-positivism. Legal positivism, strictly speaking, says that the powerful make the rules: "might makes right." Morality and law are not related, except by coincidence. According to Max Hocutt, "Human beings may, and do, make up their own rules. All existing moralities and all existing laws are human artifacts, products of human society, social conventions." Quoted in Morris B. Storer, ed., *Humanist Ethics* (Buffalo, NY: Prometheus Books, 1980), 137.

98. Genesis 9:6: "Whoever sheds the blood of man, by man shall his blood be shed, for God made man in his own image."

99. Revelation 19:16: "On his robe and on his thigh he has a name written, King of kings and Lord of lords"; see also Isaiah 9:6: "To us a child is born, to us a son is given; and the government shall be upon his shoulder, and his name shall be called Wonderful Counselor, Mighty God, Everlasting Father, Prince of Peace"; Luke 1:33: "[Christ] will reign over the house of Jacob forever, and of his kingdom there will be no end"; 1 Timothy 6:15: "[God] will display [Christ's appearance] at the proper time—he who is the blessed and only Sovereign, the King of kings and Lord of lords."

100. Joel Carpenter, *Revive Us Again: The Reawakening of American Fundamentalism* (New York: Oxford University Press, 1997), 111.

101. Quoted in Carpenter, *Revive Us Again*, 117.

102. Quoted in James Davidson Hunter, *To Change the World* (New York: Oxford University Press, 2010), 160.

103. Thomas Aquinas, pt. 928, in Thomas Gilby, *St. Thomas Aquinas: Philosophical Texts* (Whitefish, MT: Kessinger, 2003), 320.

104. Michael Horton, *Christless Christianity: The Alternative Gospel of the American Church* (Grand Rapids: Baker, 2008), 105.

105. Lee I. Levine, *The Ancient Synagogue: The First Thousand Years* (New Haven: Yale University Press, 2005), 29–30.

106. The five groups operating in Jesus's day are discussed in detail in Jeff Myers's video course *Political Animal*, available at www.summit.org. (1) Herodians: These were the people from King Herod's court. The Bible gives us many accounts of Herodian moral corruption even as they outwardly portrayed themselves as the gatekeepers who allowed Rome to maintain its power but not at the expense of the Jewish religion. (2) Sadducees: Sadducees were the spiritual leaders—the priestly class. In a devout society, such people were widely admired; they were the rock stars of their day. Typically coming from wealthy families, they prized the status and wealth they gained as the spiritual elite. (3) Essenes: Essenes were the "throw them all out" crowd. Disgusted with hypocrisy, they moved into the desert to isolate themselves from the "sons of darkness." They were the "God's people shouldn't be involved in politics or anything else" group of Jesus's day. (4) Zealots: Zealots insisted on a radical overthrow of all secular rule. They looked back in history to the Jewish hero Judas Maccabees, who routed the Seleucid Empire that dated back to the conquest of Alexander the Great. The Zealots sought to incite rebellion against Rome. (5) Pharisees: The Pharisees looked back on their ancestors' disobedience to God as the primary cause of their misery. If they could only obey God exactly, they reasoned, he would have no reason to be displeased with them and would thus restore them to their rightful dominion.

107. Matthew 28:18–20: "Jesus came and said to [his disciples], 'All authority in heaven and on earth has been given to me. Go therefore and make disciples of all nations, baptizing them in the name of the Father and of the Son and of the Holy Spirit, teaching them to observe all that I have commanded you. And behold, I am with you always, to the end of the age.'"

108. See no. 51 in Alexander Hamilton et al., *The Federalist Papers* (New York: Pocket Books, 1964), 122.

109. E. Calvin Beisner, *Prosperity and Poverty: The Compassionate Use of Resources in a World of Scarcity* (Westchester, IL: Crossway Books, 1988), 45.

110. Abraham Kuyper, *Calvinism: Six Stone-Lectures* (New York: Revell, 1899), 98–142.

111. Psalm 103:19: "The LORD has established his throne in the heavens, and his kingdom rules over all."

112. Charles Colson, *Kingdoms in Conflict* (Grand Rapids: Zondervan, 1987), 226.

113. Quoted in Francis A. Schaeffer, *A Christian Manifesto* (Westchester, IL: Crossway Books, 1982), 34.

114. As an example, the thousands of years of experiments with socialist economic systems have resulted in nothing but failure and tragedy—fascism, Nazism, and communism rely on the faulty ideas of socialism and Darwinian evolution. Their catastrophic failings are documented in Igor Shafarevich's *The Socialist Phenomenon* (New York: Harper and Row, 1980). See also Ludwig von Mises, *Socialism* (Indianapolis: Liberty Fund Classics, 1981), and Joshua Muravchik, *Heaven on Earth: The Rise and Fall of Socialism* (San Francisco: Encounter Books, 2002).

115. Charles Colson called the belief in human perfectibility "the most subtle and dangerous delusion of our times." See *Who Speaks for God?* (Westchester, IL: Crossway Books, 1988), 144.

116. Colson, *Kingdoms in Conflict*, 77. For an understanding of the ideas presently in the mix of modern-day utopianism, consult Stewart Justman, *Fool's Paradise: The Unreal World of Pop Psychology* (Chicago: Ivan R. Dee, 2005). Justman says, "The German expatriate who served as perhaps the foremost intellectual patron of the student revolt of the 1960s, Herbert Marcuse, wrote in 1970 that "the new theory of man ... implies the genesis of a new morality as the heir and the negation of the Judeo-Christian morality which up to now has characterized the history of Western

civilization." Marcuse, a Marxist and fellow of the Frankfurt School, contended that Christian morality is repressive, self-defeating, and obsolete (133).

117. Schaeffer, *Christian Manifesto*, 93. An example of the proper time for disobedience recently arose when the American government (through its public-health services) advised churches to amend their attitude toward homosexuality. Churches must be allowed to speak to the biblical teachings on the subject without fear of censure or sanction.

118. Proverbs 29:2: "When the righteous increase, the people rejoice, but when the wicked rule, the people groan."

119. Colson, *Kingdoms in Conflict*, 291.

CHAPTER 16

ECONOMICS

1. ECONOMICS AND *THE DARK KNIGHT RISES*

Dr. Jonathan Crane, aka "The Scarecrow," is a psychopath who lives to create fear. In *The Dark Knight Rises*, Crane relishes sentencing Gotham's leaders to death or exile by crossing a partially frozen river, where they will fall through and drown. Exile means death. Just before Batman rides to the rescue, Commissioner Gordon is brought before the court:

Gordon: *No lawyer, no witnesses? What sort of due process is this?*

Crane: *Your guilt has been determined. This is merely a sentencing hearing. Now, what will it be? Death or Exile?*

Gordon: *Crane, if you think we're going to walk out on that ice willingly, you got another thing coming!*

Crane: *So it's death then?*

Gordon: *Looks that way.*

Crane: *Very well. Death!* [Smashes gavel] *By exile!*

The Dark Knight Rises is a modern-day retelling of Charles Dickens's novel *A Tale of Two Cities*, set during the French Revolution. Commissioner Gordon even quotes Dickens's sacrificial hero, Sydney Carton, in his eulogy for Batman: "It is a far, far better thing that I do, than I have ever done; it is a far, far better rest that I go to, than I have ever known."[1]

At first, the film seems to endorse revolution. It pictures the elite enjoying frivolous parties while the poor suffer miserably in the sewers. Selina Kyle (aka Catwoman), a jewel thief with a Robin Hood flair, expresses the resentment: "There's a storm coming, Mr. Wayne. You and your friends better batten down the hatches, because when it hits, you're all gonna wonder how you ever thought you could live so large and leave so little for the rest of us."

When the storm does come, Kyle—along with everyone else—realizes she has believed lies about how to fix society. It takes more than resentment, revenge, and revolution to improve life. This isn't just a story about Batman; it's a story about economics.

Today we live in an era of greater and more widespread prosperity than ever before in history. It didn't happen by accident. Is it possible to maintain this prosperity? Is it possible to expand it to free even more people to become the kinds of stewards of creation God designed them to be? To answer these questions, we must understand the fascinating and often complicated discipline of economics.

2. WHY ECONOMICS MATTERS

In Latin, the word for "**economics**" comes from the Greek word *oikonomos*, which means "the art of running a household."[2] Economists don't run households per se, but they do study institutions and human beings, especially how they compete, cooperate, and distribute goods, services, and information. From the sale of groceries to the capitalization of multi-billion-dollar building projects, economists try to figure out why some economies produce wealth and others are impoverished. They look at the role society's institutions play, especially government, businesses, voluntary associations, and human institutions like families. Beyond investigating the nature of such things, economists are often called upon to give their opinions about what policies *ought* to be pursued.[3] US presidents, for instance, have a small army of "economic advisors."

Economics: the study of the management of resources.

At its most basic level, economics is about scarcity: resources (time, materials, money) are limited, so we must make choices. If there were no scarcity, there would be no need for the study of economics. How families and businesses and governments make choices in the midst of scarcity determines their own economic situations, and it affects their country's economic situation as well. One of the most profound biblical truths for economics appears at the very beginning, in Genesis 1, when God told human beings to be "fruitful and multiply," "fill the earth," and rule over creation (Gen. 1:28).[4] It is as if God looked at his creation and proclaimed, "Be abundant!" God enjoys a world teeming with life, purpose, and creativity. Because of sin, though, we have death, aimlessness, and plodding predictability instead.

One of sin's most painful consequences is poverty. In the time of Christ and throughout most of human history, everyone was poor, certainly by modern standards. In fact, even the wealthy were poor by today's standards. According to economist Angus Maddison, the average person two thousand years ago, in today's dollars, made about a dollar a day, the World Bank's definition of extreme poverty.[5] Poverty exacts a heavy emotional and spiritual toll, but its most costly effect is hopelessness. As Compassion International's Scott Todd says, the voice of poverty whispers, "It won't get any better. Just give up."[6] Poverty sweeps away the desire to change and thereby the ability to effect it.

> One of the most profound biblical truths for economics appears at the very beginning.

Widespread poverty reigned well into the eighteenth century. In the world depicted in Jane Austen's books and their movie adaptations, society settled into a state of haves and have-nots. As Sylvia Nasar says, "Everybody knew his or her place, and no one questioned it."[7] Working conditions were deplorable. Starvation was common. Then something changed, and quickly. Nasar reports,

> A mere fifty years after [Austen's] death, that world was altered beyond recognition. It was not only the "extraordinary advance in wealth, luxury and refinement of taste" or the unprecedented improvement in the circumstances of those whose condition was assumed to be irremediable.... It was the sense that the changes were not accidental or a matter of luck, but the result of human intention, will, and knowledge.[8]

For millennia it was always winter and never Christmas, but then springtime arrived almost overnight.[9] Today's US economy is thirty times as big as it was two hundred years ago.[10] Prosperity is spreading, and people around the world are being rapidly lifted out of poverty. According to Todd, extreme poverty has dropped in half just in the last generation, from 52 percent of the world's population to 26 percent.[11]

How all this happened forms a remarkable story. If we understand it, we may live to see continued growth in the health and well-being of people all over the world. If we don't, we put everything at risk. Even today, with growing prosperity, many countries are where they were two hundred years ago, or even worse. What are they missing? Is there hope for them? To answer these questions, let's take a quick look at what economists know and how they know it.

> Extreme poverty has dropped in half just in the last generation, from 52 percent of the world's population to 26 percent.

3. Economics at a Glance

Earlier we defined *economics* as "the management of a household." But economists actually look at two things: *households*, the basic units where economic consumption takes place, and *firms*, groups of individuals organized to produce goods and services. Economists study households and firms on two levels: **microeconomics**, or how households and firms decide

Microeconomics: the branch of economics that studies how households and firms buy, sell, and allocate resources.

Macroeconomics: the branch of economics that studies how large economies function as a whole, focusing on such things as gross domestic product (GDP), unemployment, tax rates, and inflation.

Free Market Economy: an economy in which economic decisions are freely made by households and firms.

Capital: goods used to produce other goods and services.

to buy and sell goods and services, and **macroeconomics**, or how the economy as a whole functions: growth, money, taxation, and so on.

Most nations have something like a **free market economy**, in which economic decisions are made by millions of households and firms rather than by a central planning authority.[12] Even communist countries—perhaps with the exception of North Korea—allow households and firms to buy and sell goods and services to an extent. It simply would not be possible to exist otherwise.[13]

Today economists often articulate the concept of a market in terms devised by a Scottish philosopher named Adam Smith. Smith thought people should be free to accumulate as much **capital** (goods used to produce other goods) as they wanted as long as it was acquired through legal means. Because they would have to serve other people to get what they wanted for themselves, the free exchange of goods and services served as a "guiding hand" in forming a mature, prosperous economy. As George Gilder points out, Smith's theory sounds selfish, but it gave economists a way of understanding economic activity:

It seems preposterous to most people to say that the way to create a good and bountiful society is to give maximum freedom to a group of predatory philistines [but] ... economists could find in Smith's theory of self-interest an apparently safe and orderly, even mechanically predictable, core of calculation as the source of economic growth.[14]

Jean-Baptiste Say was another early scholar whose economic ideas gained traction. Say thought if people could be free to produce and trade their goods and services, their willingness to supply what people wanted would create a demand, and the economy would

Say's Law: formulated by Jean-Baptiste Say, Say's law is the belief that the availability of a good or service creates a demand equal to its value (i.e., product value is a function of supply and demand).

grow. **Say's law** claims that the availability of something on the market creates a demand equal to its value. In short, "supply creates demand."[15] A person who makes a product is motivated to sell it as quickly as possible and use his or her earnings to purchase something else. This basic process, repeated millions of times, creates economic growth.

But economists don't just study the world as it *is*. They also make claims about how it *ought to be*.[16] Studying the world as it is, ideally, is a descriptive and empirical task. Studying the world as we think it ought to be is normative and aspirational. There's nothing wrong with doing both of these things as long as we are clear about what is happening. Unfortunately, some economists are captive to utopian visions based on wrong assumptions about God, humans, and the world. As the experiences of communism have taught us, or should have taught us, the misguided desire to create a heaven on earth will more than likely create a hell on earth. That's why it's important to ask, "What assumptions are you making about nature, society, religion, and ethics?"

> **Our good intentions cannot wish away economic reality. As always, ideas have consequences: we need to be sure our ideas are based on truth, or else the consequences could be devastating.**

But even if there is general agreement on how the world ought to be, the best way to move toward it is to first discover what the world is really like. Wishing for there to be less poverty in the world does not automatically mean that our actions will fulfill that goal. Some policies might help. Some might have no effect. Some might harm. To determine which actions and policies in the economy are most likely to help, we have to return to the known facts and theoretical insights about economic reality. Our good intentions cannot wish away economic reality. As always, ideas have consequences: we need to be sure our ideas are based on truth, or else the consequences could be devastating.

Experience has taught economists that several building blocks are necessary for a well-functioning economy. Let's take a look at five of the most vital and see how our own country's policies stack up.

4. FIVE BUILDING BLOCKS OF ECONOMIC SUCCESS

Most people around the world would rather have an income than not have one. They would rather have food than go hungry. They would rather have security than uncertainty. All of these things, though, require a thriving economy, and desire alone cannot make that happen. A well-functioning economy is based on time-tested building blocks of success. Here are five of the most important:

1. The rule of law. If a person thinks his investment could be swept away by chaos or by the whims of a dictator, he is unlikely to take the risk. Economic growth requires predictability and stability. When it comes to economics, a poorly functioning government is like a prison guard keeping people locked up so they can't do bad things. A well-functioning government is like a traffic cop helping the economy flow smoothly.

According to the United States Constitution, one function of the federal government is to promote the "general welfare" (well-being) of American citizens. People disagree about how to do this. To some it means ensuring economic efficiency or creating wealth. To others it means enforcing economic equity. N. Gregory Mankiw, an economics professor at Harvard, explains the difference:

> The question of efficiency is whether the pie is as big as possible. The question of equity is whether the pie is divided fairly. Evaluating the equity of a market outcome is more

difficult than evaluating the efficiency. Whereas efficiency is an objective goal that can be judged on strictly positive grounds, equity involves normative judgments that go beyond economics and enter into the realm of political philosophy.[17]

Again, there's nothing wrong with bringing normative or ethical concerns to economic questions. But when a government tries to divide the pie "fairly," it is presuming to have knowledge it doesn't have. Its actions run the risk of violating people's rights, stealing their property, and making things worse, not better. Experience says it may not be desirable or even possible to use governmental authority to shape or transform society in an economic sense.

For free exchange and economic prosperity, however, one thing government must do is protect the right to private property, including personal possessions, land, and means of production. Government must secure the right to intellectual property, including copyrights, patents, and so forth. This takes a lot of thoughtfulness in today's technological society. How do you help protect people's ideas, not just their work or physical property?

Take computers, for example. Computers require software, which, at root, is code—a list of instructions. What does it mean to own such a thing? This is especially difficult because software is not bought or sold like groceries. Developers sell *permission* to *use* the code. When you install a new app or program and click the "Agree" box, you agree to borrow or rent the code but not keep it for yourself. A government without a stable rule of law based on absolute truth will find it impossible to deal with economic innovations such as these. And without predictability, innovation grinds to a halt.

> **Without predictability, innovation grinds to a halt.**

2. A strictly limited role of government in the marketplace. Government's proper role is maintaining the rule of law, which is needed to set up the conditions for free exchanges in the economy. But government intervention in the economy often goes far beyond that basic and legitimate role. Government that oversteps its proper bounds can actually violate the rule of law. Government should be powerful enough to enforce the rule of law but not so unlimited in its scope that it violates the rule of law with impunity.

Imagine stepping up to a church bake-sale table to purchase a cupcake and having a government agent block your way. "I'm sorry, you can't buy your cupcake because this bake sale does not possess a business license, and our agents have not certified that its foods were prepared in a properly inspected commercial kitchen." This agent thinks he is *protecting* you from possible harm even if you're willing to take the risk. The effect, however, is to destroy the bake sale.

Wise governments try to anticipate the consequences of intervening in an otherwise free exchange. That's because the cost of such coercive intervention in market exchanges often vastly exceeds the *benefits*. By scrambling the basic signals of communication in a market, such intervention can create uncertainty, steal motivation, and slow the economy to a crawl. For instance, a city government may impose price controls on rental housing in order to keep housing within reach of its poorer citizens. But the effect of such controls will be to create a shortage in housing—just the opposite of their noble intentions.

In the past, another form of government intervention has been the attempt to equalize people economically through confiscating wealth and redistributing it.[18] In the 1960s, president

Lyndon Johnson declared a "war on poverty" and committed billions of tax dollars to develop welfare programs, build housing, and buy food for poor people. Most Americans like the idea of a social safety net and agree we should help people get back on their feet. But how much did the kind of intervention represented by the War on Poverty actually help? In the six years before the War on Poverty began, poverty had dropped to 15 percent. After the federal government spent trillions of dollars, the poverty rate today remains between 12 percent and 15 percent. Jay Richards says somberly, "The statistics hide the full cost: not only did the War on Poverty fail; it created economic and social problems worse than those it was meant to solve."[19]

> Wise governments try to anticipate the consequences of intervening in an otherwise free exchange. That's because the cost of such coercive intervention in market exchanges often vastly exceeds the benefits.

Sometimes intervention on behalf of those needing help can actually hurt them. For example, the federal government gives several billion dollars in aid to countries in Africa. It also gives several billion dollars a year to American cotton farmers so they can sell their cotton at about 25 percent below the price on the world market. This subsidy makes it hard for African countries to sell their cotton profitably.[20] Martin Meredith says, "The trade losses associated with U.S. farm subsidies that West Africa's eight main cotton exporters suffered outweighed the benefits they received from U.S. aid."[21] These interventions cost taxpayers billions of dollars and simultaneously hurt the world's poor. It is a legitimate question to ask how this can possibly be justified.

Creating a social safety net for the poor, widows, and orphans is a laudable goal, but it does not follow that the federal government should create or maintain the net.

3. Freedom to pursue ideas. As Cambridge economist Partha Dasgupta says, "Many economists ... regard the production of new ideas as the prime factor behind

> Sometimes intervention on behalf of those needing help can actually hurt them.

economic progress."[22] Good ideas are not inevitable; they arise as people have freedom to trade and acquire what they want. Jay Richards tells a story of his sixth-grade teacher using a simple game to demonstrate this. She handed a small gift to each student—a pack of gum, a doll, a superball—and broke the class into five groups of five. She asked them to rate their satisfaction with their gift on a scale of one to ten and then compiled the scores. Next she allowed students to trade their gifts with others in their group. The satisfaction score went up. Finally the teacher allowed students to trade with anyone in the class. Students' satisfaction scores went way up, and not one person's score went down.

What changed? It wasn't the number of gifts or their cost. It was the freedom to trade for gifts matching their *ideas* about what they wanted. At root, economics is about *mind*, not *matter*. Dasgupta notes that economies grow "when people acquire knowledge and make use of it, or when people make better use of what they know."[23] According to economist Michael Novak, the American founders' understanding of this principle is why they guaranteed *in the Constitution* the right to own ideas through copyrights and patents.[24] No wonder most technological breakthroughs since then have taken place in the United States.

Humans are ruled not merely by instinct but by intellect. Freeing people to think and dream and create is integral to a strong society. Bernard Lonergan expresses this whimsically:

> Deep within us all, emergent when the noise of other appetites is stilled, there is a drive to know, to understand, to see why, to discover the reason, to find the cause, to explain.... It can absorb a man. It can keep him for hours, day after day, year after year, in the narrow prison of his study or his laboratory. It can send him on dangerous voyages of exploration. It can withdraw him from other interests, other pursuits, other pleasures, other achievements. It can fill his waking thoughts, hide from him the world of ordinary affairs, invade the very fabric of his dreams. It can demand endless sacrifices that are made without regret though there is only the hope, never a certain promise, of success. What better symbol could one find for this obscure, exigent, imperious drive, than a man [Archimedes], naked, running, excitedly crying, "I've got it"?[25]

An economy grows best when it accounts for the natural creativity flowing from what the Bible describes as humans' capacity to bear God's image.

4. Participation. Jim Clifton, chairman and CEO of Gallup, argues that people make ten thousand to twenty thousand small decisions a day. Multiply this by three hundred million people and 365 days, and you have one quadrillion (a one followed by fifteen zeroes) decisions being made every year in America alone.[26] No central planning agency, even a smart one, could ever manage or control these decisions.

As we saw earlier, the knowledge to make an economy work is in people's minds, dispersed across hundreds of millions of people, not in a computer. They pick up cues and make minute adjustments without even realizing they are doing so, and the sum total of this mental activity is greater than any one person can account for. George Gilder explains:

> When one moves from this multifarious mass of information to rely on written or documented learning alone, one reduces total knowledge by a factor of millions, which is to say, incalculably. But [as economist Jay] Forrester pointed out, when one moves on from written knowledge to mathematical data—the kind of information that can be programmed onto a computer—one reduces total knowledge by another factor of millions, by another astronomical swath. Yet every socialist plan normally begins with just such a draconian reduction, just such a holocaust of human learning and skills, leaving only a pile of statistical ashes, a dry and sterile residue of numbers, from which to reconstruct the edifice of economic activity.[27]

Any economic system attempting to control this process, then, must ignore the fact that humans are more than physical. We have spirits. We have ideas. We interact with one another spiritually and on the level of ideas. When an economy is relatively free, people's ideas generate economic stability and prosperity. Much of *this* activity isn't even in large corporations but in what Daniel Pink calls *microenterprises*—businesses with no employees. There are more than twenty-one million of them in the United States.[28]

5. Sustainability. Some policies, such as wealth redistribution, may be popular in the short term but can bankrupt the government and devastate society in the long run. Government programs are costly. When costs exceed revenue—which is true with nearly every program in the United States federal government at the present time—it sets in motion a vicious cycle in which the government consumes more and more resources than would otherwise be used to create economic growth. Unless we have significant— even exuberant—economic growth, we will never be able to generate enough tax revenue even to pay the federal government's enormous debt, which, at this writing,

> **When an economy is relatively free, people's ideas generate economic stability and prosperity.**

totals about eighteen trillion dollars. (This doesn't include the much larger "unfunded liabilities" in such programs as Social Security and Medicare.) As George Gilder says, "The fatal problem of a system without accumulations of personal income and without the possibility of large profits is not the lack of incentives but the lack of dynamism and flexibility."[29] We need dynamism and flexibility now more than ever to sustain our way of life.

It's wrong to steal. So why do politicians think borrowing money that someone else must repay in the future is a moral thing to do? Isn't it a form of theft from future generations? As Dasgupta frames it,

> In this reckoning, sustainable development requires that relative to their populations each generation should bequeath to its successor at least as large a productive base as it had itself inherited. Notice that the requirement is derived from a relatively weak notion of intergenerational justice. Sustainable development demands that future generations have no less of the means to meet their needs that we do ourselves; it demands nothing more.[30]

If Dasgupta is right, we not only have a moral obligation to steward our natural resources; we also have a moral obligation to stand against any economic program that will hurt those who come after us. "Debt," says Richard Lamm from the Institute for Public Policy Studies at the University of Denver and the former Democratic governor of Colorado, "is an intergenerational transfer from our children to the current generation, and they are too young to complain. There are no lobbyists for the future."[31]

Eighteen *trillion* dollars in government debt is a staggering sum. At an income of about forty million dollars a year, it would take basketball star LeBron James four hundred thousand seasons to earn that much money. Even the world's richest man would need more than three hundred lifetimes to earn enough to pay it all. The story of how we got in this mess is simultaneously embarrassing and enraging. In the early part of the twentieth century, a British economist named John Maynard Keynes noticed the boom-and-bust cycle in the free market and thought government could smooth it out by borrowing money to stimulate demand. This would kick-start the economy, he believed.[32] Keynes went beyond using the government to help poor people. He thought we should spend money on anything likely to stimulate demand. The ensuing growth would result in more earnings and thus higher tax revenue. The government could use this revenue to repay its debt. With government's help, we could literally spend ourselves into prosperity.

At first it worked. Government stimulated the economy, and the economy came to life. But each subsequent stimulus was less and less effective. Short-term gain, long-term pain. Now, although every dollar of government debt produces only about eight cents of economic value (which means that ninety-two cents has been wasted), the whole amount still must be paid back with interest.[33] The level of government debt has grown so large it *cannot be paid back with the tax revenue the economy generates.* Today's leaders will die, but the debt they incurred will live on and grow larger every year. It is a toxic burden to future generations that makes a mockery of the idea of sustainability. Here's a chart showing each individual's share of the national debt in inflation-adjusted dollars:

- 1915—$667
- 1945—$8,767
- 1975—$17,617
- 2005—$30,154
- 2011—$47,093

If these trends continue, the share of government debt each of us will be responsible for will be far greater than we will ever realistically be able to pay. When the bill comes due, the government will either default on its obligations, setting off a panic and plunging the world into an economic nightmare, or it will try to print enough dollars to pay its bills. Adding more printed money into the economy decreases the value of all other dollars. Something similar happened to Germany in the 1930s, when money lost its value so rapidly that a wheelbarrow full of money—which once could have helped one live comfortably for years—was no longer even enough to buy a loaf of bread. The desperation of Germany helps explain why they so eagerly embraced Adolf Hitler, thus lighting the spark to ignite World War II and the deaths of tens of millions.

> Adding more printed money into the economy decreases the value of all other dollars.

Five fundamentals of economics: the rule of law, limited government, freedom of ideas, participation, and sustainability. Without these five factors, economies function poorly and hurt people in the process. With this backdrop, let's examine each of our six worldviews to see how they meet the tests of economic truth.

5. SECULARISM

Karl Marx defined *capitalism* as "a market-directed economy based on the private ownership of goods and resources." It's a term with an odd lineage, and using it as Marx did limits its meaning. (In fact, *no one* defends capitalism as Marx defined it.) **Capitalism**, however, also means the freedom to exchange goods and services as people see fit. In this sense, it is a synonym for a free market economy or free enterprise. On the other hand, **socialism** refers to an economic system in which citizens forfeit property rights in exchange for a central planning authority that attempts to provide economic stability. The state owns property and the "means of production." In practice, most economies are a mixture

> *Capitalism:* an economic system in which capital assets are privately owned, and the prices, production, and distribution of goods and services are determined by competition within a free market.

of both—they allow free exchange but also require of citizens the support of central planning in many areas.

> *Socialism:* an economic system based on governmental or communal ownership of the means of production and distribution of goods and services.

Historically, Secularists have embraced socialism, and for three reasons:

1. Secularists believed socialism was the key to future human development. Early Secularists were not bothered by the idea of government coercion being used to accomplish socialist goals, because big problems needed a big solution. Erich Fromm once again: "The aim of socialism is an association in which the full development of each is the condition for the full development of all."[34]

2. Secularists believed socialism was more democratic. Secularists chose socialism because of the evils they saw as inherent in capitalism. Fromm explained: "The giant corporations which control the economic—and to a large degree the political—destiny of the country, constitute the very opposite of the democratic process; they represent power without control by those submitted to it."[35]

3. Secularists believed socialism stopped exploitation. Corliss Lamont embraced socialism because of the "tremendous waste inherent in the capitalist system and its wanton exploitation of men and natural resources."[36] To Lamont's way of thinking, those who think otherwise are not freedom lovers but fascists: "Since fascism is simply capitalism stripped of all democratic pretenses and other unessentials—capitalism in the nude, as it were—the danger of fascism remains as long as the capitalist system is with us."[37]

> The most influential people who shaped Secularist thought in the last century were socialists.

The most influential people who shaped Secularist thought in the last century were socialists. Given Secularism's assumptions, we can see why. Socialism makes sense to those who believe humans are inherently good and smart enough to develop a good society without divine guidance. Erich Fromm was typical in his sentiment: "We socialists are not ashamed to confess that we have a deep faith in man and in a vision of a new, human form of society."[38]

Today, though, many Secularists shy away from identifying themselves as socialists. For some it is because of the glaring inefficiencies and oppressions they saw in socialist regimes. It is hard to see the havoc socialism wreaked in the former Soviet Union, China, Cuba, North Korea, and a host of other Asian, Latin American, South American, and African countries and still be a cheerleader for it. Socialism has failed in every case to cure human fallenness—to create the "new socialist man"—and to lift people out of poverty.

Today many Secularists remain socialist, but others are more nuanced. Some Secularists insist that they cannot be labeled in "old" categories, such as capitalism or socialism. They prefer new expressions, such as the "politics of meaning," which, according to Jonah Goldberg, refers to orienting all of society's institutions, including economics, around the state. Such an "intelligently plural economy," according to John Kenneth Galbraith, would of course involve the public ownership of certain industries.[39]

We refer to this new-and-improved kind of socialism as *economic interventionism*, a belief that a strong program of government intervention is necessary to curb the free market and make a better society. Why the criticism of the free market? If people have the freedom to choose, they sometimes choose badly. They might even start seeing their value in purely economic terms, devaluing themselves and others. Erich Fromm said, "What is modern man's relationship to his fellow man? It is one between two abstractions, two living machines, who use each other."[40] To Fromm, the only way to avoid this is through a "fundamental reorganization of our economic and social system.[41]

As you will recall, Secularists believe only matter exists. Every problem and every solution is materialistic. Equality, whatever it is, must be some material quantity, such as income or purchasing power. Thus, Secularists who embrace economic interventionism consider financial poverty—not spiritual poverty, relational poverty, or a poverty of ideas—to be the best measure of equality. As we saw in the "Secularism" chapter, Secularists believe people are basically good but have been made bad by society. Poor people are poor because rich people have taken away their resources. If this can be equalized, poor people will become productive and society will improve. Crime and other anti-social behavior will decrease.

So what is the solution? Interventionists believe smart, pure leaders will be able to discern what is best and make decisions for the good of all. Such leaders may restrict freedom, yes, but Secularists believe it is okay because they only have everyone's best interests at heart. To John Dewey, this is a very moral thing to do: "Social control of economic forces is ... necessary if anything approaching economic equality and liberty is to be realized."[42]

To Jonah Goldberg, the idea that the state is the answer is "ultimately a theocratic doctrine because it seeks to answer the fundamental questions about existence, argues that they can only be answered collectively, and insists that the state put those answers into practice."[43] If no God exists, the state is the most powerful thing and ought to be worshipped.

A minority of Secularists, though, go in precisely the opposite direction of economic interventionism. A few, like the twentieth-century Ayn Rand, defended capitalism as the only just economic system. She thought the only proper end for individuals was to pursue their self-interests. She even referred to selfishness as a virtue. Much of her thought is popular today among a group of people who refer to themselves as *libertarians*.

Libertarianism is in many ways the exact opposite of interventionism. Interventionism says the state can produce a good society. Libertarianism believes that only individuals with complete liberty from state interference can do so. Both are utopian of a sort—one trusts the state to be "god"; the other gives that responsibility to individuals. If Secularism's underlying assumptions about God, the world, and the moral state of human beings are true, then utopian solutions are very attractive, whether they involve elites making decisions for everyone else or believing that society will be better if everyone pursues their own interests.

6. MARXISM

Just as a piranha can't help biting, capitalism (that is, a market-oriented economy) can't help exploiting. Karl Marx thought this for two reasons. First, he thought the bourgeoisie—the business owners—could make their profits only by paying workers less than what they were worth and getting them to work harder than necessary to produce a good or service the business owners could sell for more than it was worth (what it cost to produce). Only in this way could the owner become wealthy. The more capitalism succeeds, Marx believed, the worse the problem gets: "Accumulation of wealth at one pole is, therefore, at the same time accumulation of misery, agony of toil, slavery, ignorance, brutality, mental degradation, at the opposite pole."[44] Marx's view is called the **surplus value theory of labor**. He referred to profit, then, as **surplus value**.

The second flaw inherent in capitalism, Marx thought, is its chaotic nature. With socialism, the state controls everything in a rational and orderly way, from production to distribution. In a capitalistic system, economic decisions are made by every producer and consumer, such as store owners, farmers, and moms with shopping lists. This purportedly makes capitalism spontaneous, erratic, freewheeling, uncontrollable, and, to Marx, dangerous. In fact, he believed capitalists keep the economy unstable *on purpose* to give the bourgeoisie more power. This could be solved, Marx thought, by having the state take over all decisions related to production and distribution.

> *Surplus Value Theory of Labor:* According to Karl Marx, the value of a good or service should be equal to the average number of labor hours required to produce the good or service. This implies that setting prices above this cost leads to a situation in which the bourgeoisie amass wealth at the expense of the proletariat.

> *Surplus Value:* according to Karl Marx, surplus value is the value of a commodity or service that exceeds the cost of labor; i.e., profit.

Most economists now believe Marx was wrong, and tragically so. He had a profound worldview problem. As a materialist and naturalist, Marx did not believe that human beings were made in the image of the creative God, or that, as a result, human beings could create new wealth by their economic activity. He didn't believe humanity possessed a "God-given" *anything*; humans were just "matter in motion." As George Gilder phrased it, "Marx ... erroneously located the means of production in the material arrangements of the society rather than in the metaphysical capital of human freedom and creativity."[45] Creativity, hard work, innovation, problem-solving ability, team-building skills, successful cooperation, efficiency, persuasion, service, opportunity, entrepreneurial risk, and ventures—all of these are economic resources as well. They're like a healthy lifestyle of nutrition and exercise that creates opportunities for growth and generates hopefulness and initiative. Because of Marx's stunted view of what it means to be human, though, his economic philosophy was destined to remain puny and Eeyore-like.

Part of the capitalist critique of Marxism is its hostile attitude toward private property. But if people can't control their property—their possessions, their ideas, their skills—they will have no incentive to produce; governmental coercion carries a very high cost and very few benefits. But Marxists shoot back that doing nothing is worse. Capitalism is a ticking time bomb that will bring about its own destruction. Engels said,

> Whilst the capitalist mode of production more and more completely transforms the great majority of the population into proletarians, it creates the power which, under

---

ECONOMICS

- 407 -

penalty of its own destruction, is forced to accomplish this revolution. [Eventually] the proletariat seizes political power and turns the means of production into state property.[46]

Sooner or later the proletariat will be fed up with their treatment and demand the destruction of the system that demeaned them. According to Raymond Sleeper, "The system of exploitations does not disappear of itself. It is destroyed only as the result of the revolutionary struggle and the victory of the proletariat."[47]

Of course, this transition would not happen all at once. Capitalism does at least produce things, and Marxists wanted to wait to destroy it until, according to Engels, "the necessary quantity of the means of production has been created."[48] This is ironic. Marx and Engels recognized that capitalist societies created wealth even as their theory denied it in the relation between business owners and workers. In the end, they believed, they could do better. Under communism, "Private ownership will automatically have ceased to exist, money will have become superfluous, and production will have so increased and men will be so much changed that the last forms of the old social relations will also be able to fall away."[49]

> Whereas many Secularists see socialism as a middle ground between capitalism and communism, Marxists see socialism as the gateway to communism.

Whereas many Secularists see socialism as a middle ground between capitalism and communism, Marxists see socialism as the gateway to communism. Lenin said, "Theoretically, there can be no doubt that between capitalism and communism there lies a definite transition period which must combine the features and properties of both these forms of social economy."[50] This is why Secularists who advocate socialism are sometimes suspected of being Marxists hiding their true intentions.

As we noted earlier, the goal of Marxism is to move toward worldwide communism, which leads in turn to communist utopia. The text *Political Economy* explains:

> Once the exploiting classes with their parasitic consumption have been abolished, the national income becomes wholly at the disposal of the people. Working conditions are radically altered, housing conditions in town and country substantially improved and all the achievements of modern culture made accessible to the working people.[51]

This is the Marxist version of paradise. The evils of capitalism will have been removed, humanity will have achieved perfection, and government will have ceased to exist. In short, Marxists believe communism is the ideal economic system and the foundation for utopia in all aspects of society. Kenneth Neill Cameron explained: "Marx and Engels expected that communist society would be the last form of human society, for once the world's productive forces were communally owned no other form could arise."[52]

What if something goes wrong? It mustn't! Perfection is part of the plan. Scarcity somehow ceases to exist. Everyone will have a job, Sleeper enthuses, because it will be written into the constitution:

> Can capitalist society with its chronic unemployment ensure each citizen the opportunity to work, let alone to choose the work he likes? Clearly, it cannot. But the socialist

system makes the right to work a constitutional right of a citizen, delivering him from the oppressive anxiety and uncertainty over the morrow.[53]

It *will* be this way because communists *want* it to be. Lenin said, "Outside of socialism, there is no salvation for mankind from war, hunger and the further destruction of millions and millions of human beings."[54] War. Hunger. Destruction of millions. But which economic system, historically, is most guilty of producing those results? Clearly socialism. And which worldview has most frequently underwritten socialism?

7. POSTMODERNISM

It is hard to tell what Postmodernists think about economics. They avoid using terms with which all economists are familiar, such as wages, pensions, interest rates, inflation, Social Security, and retirement. Instead, they use words most people find obscure, like fragmentation, differentiation, chronology, pastiche, anti-foundationalism, and pluralism. If those aren't enough, David Ruccio and Jack Amariglio, two professors fascinated with Marxism and Postmodernism, also add to their list "the undecidability of meaning, the textuality of discursivity of knowledge, the inconceivability of pure 'presence,' the irrelevance of intention, the insuperability of authenticity, the impossibility of representation, the celebration of play, difference, plurality, chance, inconsequence, and marginality."[55]

In addition to these arcane ideas, one concept seems to be at the heart of postmodern economics: the decentered self.[56] *Decentering* usually refers to a person who stops seeing him- or herself as the center of reality. To Postmodernists, though, the **decentered self** is a self with no core. Humans are social constructions, fictional stories we tell ourselves or have heard from others—or worse, fictions we have come to believe. There is no unified, rational being underlying who we are. Of course, these stories do not correspond to anything objective or eternal. If they are true in any sense, it is because we find them persuasive, not because they are ultimately and finally

> *Decentered Self:* the belief that human beings are social constructions without any singular identifiable essence, nature, or soul.

true. The decentered self is at odds with the notion of a person who has inherent value and is capable of stewarding economic resources. Thus the Postmodernist tools for explaining and reproducing economic success are severely limited.

Further, Postmodernists find the very idea of humans having an actual nature given to them by God as *the* source of the injustice in the world. Gender is just one example. The idea of a difference between men and women has been "inculcated by an oppressive patriarchal society."[57] Only when we recognize the fictions created by our gender constructions can we overcome the economic oppression those fictions reinforce.

In some ways Postmodernism began as a response to Marxism's failure.[58] Michel Foucault, for example, reacted against "the purely economic and State-centered focus [of socialism and nationalism] ... stressing that power

> In some ways Postmodernism began as a response to Marxism's failure.

needs to be reconceptualized and the role of the State, and the function of the economic, need a radical revisioning."[59] Toward the end of his life, Foucault even began encouraging his students to read Friedrich A. Hayek and Ludwig von Mises, two economists suspicious of anything hampering free markets.[60] Perhaps his vision was more libertarian (radical freedom from government intervention) than anything else. Richard Rorty also saw socialism as a failure: "Just about the only constructive suggestion Marx made, the abolition of private property, has been tried. It did not work."[61] Rorty criticized socialism and offered an alternative, writing,

> Most people on my side of this … cultural war have given up on socialism in light of the history of nationalization [of] enterprises and central planning in Central and Eastern Europe. We are willing to grant that welfare-state capitalism is the best we can hope for. Most of us who were brought up Trotskyite now feel forced to admit that Lenin and Trotsky did more harm than good.[62]

In place of Marxism, Rorty suggested a form of intervention that is neither a totally state-planned economy nor a completely free market economy but a combination of the two. The state would redistribute wealth created in a partially or mostly free market environment. He called it "welfare-state capitalism."

Rorty was not as shy as other Postmodernists about proposing a direction he thought society should go and in suggesting universal ethical norms that he elsewhere claimed did not exist. Economics, he said, should have as its "transcultural imperative" the alleviating of human suffering.[63] **Economic interventionism** will accomplish this, he thought. As he told a college audience in 1999,

> The non-West has a lot of justified complaints to make about the West, but it does owe a lot to Western ingenuity. The West is good at coming up with devices for lessening human suffering.… These devices are used to prevent the strong from having their way with the weak and, thereby, to prevent the weak from suffering as much as they would have otherwise.[64]

Economic Interventionism: an economic system in which the government influences aspects of a market economy in an attempt to improve the public good.

Other Postmodernists, however, believe Rorty is too optimistic and that all economic systems are a disappointment. Iain Grant writes, "If the tools of the past— Marxism, the Enlightenment project, market liberalism and so on—have been tried and found wanting, then [as Jean-Francois Lyotard suggested] experiment is demanded."[65] If everything we have tried has failed, what is the harm in experimenting? Maybe, by chance, we will invent some new economic idea that will better serve people.

Even Ruccio and Amariglio try to limit their readers' expectations: "We don't envision (or for that matter, seek to promote) a separate Postmodern economic theory."[66] In fact, they are "hesitant to argue that Postmodernism shows the way forward" and are content with conversations and encounters "rather than a new [economic] home."[67] When one starts with the denial of the truth of human nature, even of the self, as Postmodernism does, it is hard to arrive at anything approximating an economic viewpoint (or any other type of viewpoint, for that matter). And without any true access to reality, developing a system of economic exchange based on trust is simply impossible.

> Without any true access to reality, developing a system of economic exchange based on trust is simply impossible.

8. NEW SPIRITUALITY

New Spirituality focuses on tapping into the higher consciousness. Consciousness, New Spiritualists believe, is what is really real. It makes the universe operate efficiently and effectively. If we can tap into it, then we can transform human society. Michael Bernard Beckwith says,

> There is a lie that acts like a virus within the mind of humanity. And that lie is, "There's not enough good to go around." There's lack and there's limitation and there's just not enough. And that lie has people living in fear, greed, stinginess. And those thoughts of fear, greed, stinginess, and lack become their experience. So the world has taken a nightmare pill. The truth is that there's more than enough good to go around. There's more than enough creative ideas. There's more than enough power. There's more than enough love. There's more than enough joy. All of this begins to come through a mind that is aware of its own infinite nature.[68]

The universe wants life and abundance, New Spiritualists say. It wants to evolve. And since abundance is immaterial (of the spirit), the way to make it come to you is to act as if you have it. Eckhart Tolle puts it this way: "You don't have it? Just act as if you had it, and it will come. Then, soon after you start giving, you will start receiving. You cannot receive what you don't give. Outflow determines inflow."[69]

This may sound like an odd way to approach economics, but to New Spiritualists, what actually exists is the immaterial world, not the material, and any economic system failing to take this into account will be inadequate. Marilyn Ferguson claimed, "Both capitalism and socialism, as we know them, pivot on material values. They are inadequate philosophies for a transformed society."[70] Economic problems are a symptom of a greater spiritual problem. Shirley MacLaine believes that greed, envy, slander, theft, and covetousness are only "a manifestation of the need for human love."[71]

All concern with the marketplace will be moot in the coming transformed New Age. People of the future will not be concerned with meeting financial needs but with pursuing their inner truth. New Spiritualists believe if we all follow our inner voice, society will lack for nothing. Shakti Gawain says,

> We make a contribution to the world just by being ourselves in every moment. There are no more rigid categories in our lives—this is work, this is play. It all blends into the flow of following the universe and money flows in as a result of the open channel that's created. You no longer work in order to make money. Work is no longer something you have to do in order to sustain life. Instead, the delight that comes from expressing yourself becomes the greatest reward.[72]

Gawain also says, "The more you are willing to trust yourself, and take the risks to follow your inner guidance, the more money you will have. The universe will pay you to be yourself and do what you really love!"[73]

In New Spiritualist economics, "The more attuned a person is to higher consciousness the more the universe will demonstrate this level of enlightenment by mirroring more 'god-money in action.' The more enlightened a person is, the more money and success will naturally occur in life."[74] It is based on this insight that we call the New Spiritualist view of economics **universal enlightened production**.

As Marianne Williamson says, "Our purpose on this earth is to be happy."[75] Personal prosperity is at the heart of New Spiritualist economics. In many ways, this seems selfish but can sound almost biblical to the nondiscerning. As Kevin Ryerson says, "God does not work for you; God works through you."[76]

Universal Enlightened Production: the belief that an individual's financial success is directly proportional to his or her level of enlightenment; the belief that positive thought creates wealth.

As we saw in our chapter on politics, some New Spiritualists think more meditation would lead to greater health and productivity. Big government wouldn't be as necessary. Others desire something more invasive. Vera Alder, for example, described the monetary system of the future: "As ... individual needs would largely be supplied on the ration-card system, the need for handling of money would dwindle. There would, of course, be a universal currency the world over. There would be a central bank."[77]

Few New Spiritualists concern themselves with economics because they assume that economics is a matter for the unenlightened. There is no need to study economic systems to discover the nature of the economic realm. When people achieve higher consciousness, they will make wise economic choices. They will achieve material success. Poverty will disappear. Economic theorizing will be irrelevant.

9. ISLAM

Khurshid Ahmad says, "Islamic economics is rooted in Islam's particular worldview and derives its value-premises from the ethico-social teachings of the Quran and *Sunnah*."[78] At this point, Islam's economic program is not evident because, according to Syed Nawab Haider Naqvi, the national professor of economics in Pakistan, it is still "an evolving discipline."[79] Naqvi says, "The Muslim society of today is not yet a society on its own. It is still under the shadow of the Western system: and, as such, it is doubtful how 'representative' of the Islamic ethos its current behavior can be."[80]

Still, it's not hard to look at Islamic beliefs about God, human nature, and the world and figure out what a consistent Islamic economic viewpoint would be.

- Islam does not have a concept of original sin that taints everything and everyone.
- Everyone in the world was born a Muslim—if they are not now Muslim, it is because they are in rebellion and must be brought back in line.
- There is an afterlife and there will be a final judgment. No action is hidden from God (Quran 9:105).

- God exists and is just, and his will as revealed in the Quran instructs Muslims to feed the poor, give alms, help orphans, provide loans without interest (to Muslims), not hoard food, and not gamble.

Islamic economics does not just involve a series of prohibitions. Muslims are to work hard and share their wealth with fellow Muslims in need. They can earn income, amass wealth, and enjoy all good things.

The principles of shariah law do have an economic component, however limited. We call this **shariah economics**. According to Naqvi, the Islamic economic vision is based on four foundational principles for the Islamic approach to economics: unity, equilibrium, free will, and responsibility. Let's look at each in turn.

1. Unity. In Islamic theology, God is a stark unity, a single divine person without partners. This concept is called *tawhid* (sometimes spelled *tawheed* or *tauhid*). He is the creator of all things, the one to whom all humans will give account. As such, all humans should submit to God. They must become Muslim. *Islam* means "submission," as we have seen, and this entails aligning all desires, ambitions, and actions with God's will, a will expressed in his commands. "My service and sacrifice, my life and my death, are all of them for God, the creator and Lord of all the worlds" (Quran 6:162). Corresponding to the unity of God is the unity of humanity, which requires political unity. Muslims do not believe in human fallenness in the same way Christians do, so they tend to be less suspicious than Christians of concentrated political power. We must all be united in a global Islamic state, Muslims believe. National boundaries, war, and religious divisions may make this seem impossible, but economic resources must be used to fulfill this vision of universal unity of the *ummah*, the Muslim community.

> **Shariah Economics:** derived primarily from the Quran and *Sunnah*, shariah economics is the economic requirements that govern the lives of Muslims.

> **Ummah:** from the Arabic word for "nation," *ummah* is the collective community of Muslims around the world.

2. Equilibrium. "Verily God has enjoined justice and kindness" (Quran 16:90). Muslims must reflect justice and kindness in all social institutions, not just economic transactions, and also in the care of the poor. As such, "the needs of all the least-fortunate members in Muslim society constitute the first charge on the real resources of the society," observes Naqvi.[81] Islam affirms the value of private property and recognizes the reality of economic disparity. But Islam also affirms that there is a basic standard of living (e.g., food, clothing, shelter) due to all. Regular warnings are given to the wealthy (59:7; 70:24–25).

3. Free will. Muslims believe we are responsible for our beliefs and actions. We can choose to do right or wrong; we are capable of both virtue and vice. Greed, selfishness, gluttony, exaggerated materialism, and the like are expressions of our nature gone astray. Naqvi says,

> In the final analysis, we can say that, notwithstanding the differences of emphasis, there has been a tacit agreement among theologians that man is responsible for his acts,

and that God, by His very nature, is just in deciding man's fate according to his deeds. Concomitantly, therefore, man must have freedom of will in shaping his destiny.[82]

4. Responsibility. Corresponding to free will is responsibility. Not only are we responsible to God; we are also responsible to our fellow humans. Almsgiving is central to being responsible in our economic activities and "mostly takes the form of giving to the poor and the needy."[83] Hoarding wealth at the expense of the well-being of other Muslims is prohibited. "You will never come to piety unless you spend of things you love" (Quran 3:92). Muslims believe that by giving we become better people and fulfill our moral responsibility to God, ourselves, and our fellow human beings. Some even believe that generosity can atone for sins.

Muslim law has economic implications in four areas.

1. Almsgiving. The Arabic word for almsgiving is *zakat*. It is one of the pillars of Islam. Every Muslim is required to give 2.5 percent (one-fortieth) of his or her annual net income (income after expenses, taxes, etc.) to the poor, either directly or through charities.[84]

2. Inheritance. While Islam respects the individual's right to own property, that right terminates on the owner's death, and the property is distributed according to a complex formula.[85] A Muslim's estate is to be divided up among relatives (Quran 2:180). Upon the death of a wife, the husband is to receive one-half of her estate, while upon the death of a husband, the wife is to receive one-quarter of his estate (4:7–12). Such practices, unequal though they are, are understood as a divine wealth-redistribution plan.

> *Zakat:* the fourth pillar of Islam, *zakat* is the donation of 2.5 percent of a Muslim's annual income.

> *Riba:* an Arabic word meaning either interest or excessive interest.

> *Usury:* the practice of lending money at an exorbitant rate of interest.

> *Jizya:* a tax imposed on *dhimmis* (i.e., non-Muslims) living in Islamic states.

3. *Riba*. Islamic economics prohibits interest on loans (Quran 2:274–76, 278–79; 3:130–31; 30:39; 83:1–6). This is commonly understood to mean that when lending money to fellow Muslims, interest on that loan is forbidden. But some Muslims wonder whether the prohibition pertains to any interest at all, or to *usury*, a word that means "excessive or unfair interest," not simple interest. "Nearly all English translations of the Quran translate *riba* as usury," Naqvi observes.[86] Nevertheless, Naqvi says, some Muslims seek to replace all forms of interest with something they refer to as profit-and-loss sharing (PLS). Unfortunately, as a financial instrument, PLS is not doing well and may not be able to sustain Islamic economics in the long term.[87]

4. *Jizya*. Unbelievers in Muslim communities are called *dhimmis*. While Jews and Christians are "people of the Book," they are not Muslim and do not enjoy the same privileges as Muslims. As we have noted in previous chapters, they are taxed at much higher rates—rates unspecified in the Quran (9:29). Usually this extra tax, called the *jizya*, is supposed to be in return for protection and provision as non-Muslim citizens within these communities. However, historically this has often led to various forms of abuse, including destruction of churches, slavery, seizure of property, dismemberment, torture, and death.[88]

While the principles of Islamic economics are set forth by Muslim scholars, such as Hammudah Abdalati and Syed Naqvi, current economic practices in Muslim nations don't look anything like the ideal. "A small wealthy class rules many Muslim nations while the masses are extremely poor," observes George Braswell Jr. "In some countries the government collects zakat; many people resent the zakat and question how the money is used. Islam prohibits usury, yet this prohibition is seldom followed either on an individual or national level." But even if these conditions were fully met, oppression, alienation, terror, expulsion of non-Muslims, and death remains characteristic in almost all Muslim nations.[89]

10. CHRISTIANITY

Different Christians hold different views about which economic system most reflects biblical teaching. Some believe the Bible encourages a system of private property and individual responsibility (Isa. 65:21–25; Jer. 32:43–44; Acts 5:1–4; Eph. 4:28).[90] Others support a socialist economy.[91] Still others, called *liberation theologians*, believe the Bible teaches a form of Marxism they believe will usher in the kingdom of God. All seem to agree on one thing: Ultimately, God owns it all and expects us to take care of it and increase its value. This is called **biblical stewardship**.

> **Biblical Stewardship:** the act of managing and caring for resources that ultimately belong to God.

No economic system can save us or usher in the kingdom of God. Still, the Bible presents many clear principles that have specific economic implications: "Better a little [wealth] with righteousness than great revenues with injustice" (Prov. 16:8), and "Let the thief no longer steal, but rather let him labor, doing honest work with his own hands, so that he may have something to share with anyone in need" (Eph. 4:28).[92] And two of the Ten Commandments ("Do not steal" and "Do not covet")[93] imply the legitimacy of private property. Applying biblical principles like these leads to economic policies under which humans can flourish.

Today, the realistic choice is between some form of socialism (centralized control) or some form of capitalism (free enterprise or open markets). Neither economic system exists in its purest form. All capitalist systems contain some elements of socialism and vice versa. Some Christians see television evangelists traveling on private jets and living in mansions while poor people struggle, and they view socialism as the antidote to such hypocrisy. Others look at the principles of stewardship and hard work and prefer capitalism.

We must be clear: this is not a decision about whether or not to be just and compassionate but rather about how to best be just and compassionate. Is it through freedom, rule of law, initiative, ingenuity, and hard work or through centralized government planning? Ronald Nash was a Christian philosopher and economist who put the distinction in perspective:

> One dominant feature of capitalism is economic freedom, the right of people to exchange things voluntarily, free from force, fraud, and theft. Capitalism is more than this, of course, but its concern with free exchange is obvious. Socialism, on the other

hand, seeks to replace the freedom of the market with a group of central planners who exercise control over essential market functions.[94]

As we have seen in the preceding chapters, socialism has produced miserable results, even if we set aside the moral problem of such massive and widespread coercion. Robert Sheaffer says, "No intellectually honest person today can deny that the history of socialism is a sorry tale of economic failure and crimes against humanity."[95]

> **When viewed through the lenses of justice and compassion, the evidence demonstrates the advantage of capitalism over socialism.**

Additionally, when viewed through the lenses of justice and compassion, the evidence demonstrates the advantage of capitalism over socialism. In terms of justice, socialism violates all five of the generally agreed-upon principles outlined earlier. In terms of compassion, even Secularists like Marvin Zimmerman admit, "I contend that the evidence supports the view that democratic capitalism is more productive of human good than democratic socialism."[96]

Christians who believe socialism (or even communism) is more desirable than capitalism must trust that centralized planning will more justly distribute scarce resources despite all the evidence against that proposition. It's the Christian thing to do, they say. After all, the early Christians sold their belongings and held all things in common (Acts 2:44–45).[97] However, Christian socialists fail to consider that Acts 2:46–47[98] describes Christians eating with others in their homes, and Acts 5:1–4[99] assumes that Christians are free to own and sell property. The Bible respects private property and at the same time promotes the virtues of sharing and giving.[100]

Of course, we must have a proper definition of *capitalism*—a word with a problematic history—to make sense of all this. We think Rodney Stark's definition is sound:

> Capitalism is an economic system wherein privately owned, relatively well-organized, and stable firms pursue complex commercial activities within a relatively free (unregulated) market, taking a systematic, long-term approach to investing and reinvesting wealth (directly or indirectly) in productive activities involving a hired workforce, and guided by anticipated and actual returns.[101]

Stark argues that capitalism centers around property rights, free markets, free labor, cash-credit, management, and an ethic that looks upon work as a virtue, not a vice. He maintains that these virtues can be traced directly to Christian influence.[102]

> **Every person is accountable to God for the use of whatever he has.**

With this background, let's look at how biblical principles and a proper understanding of capitalism converge.

Biblical stewardship. We are accountable to God for how we use property and how we steward it. E. Calvin Beisner says, "Biblical stewardship views God as Owner of all things (Ps. 24:1) and man—individually and collectively—as His steward. Every person is accountable to God for the use of whatever he has (Gen. 1:26–30, 2:15). Every person's responsibility as a steward is to maximize the Owner's return on His investment by using it to serve others (Matt. 25:14–30)."[103]

Private property. Those Christians who believe socialism is more just and compassionate than capitalism say public ownership of property does away with greed and envy. This way of thinking, though, is incompatible with biblical teachings. Irving E. Howard says, "The commandment 'Thou shalt not steal' is the clearest declaration of the right to private property in the Old Testament."[104] Both the Old and New Testaments teach about private property and good stewardship of property.[105] Beisner asks the pointed question, "Why does Scripture require restitution, including multiple restitution, in cases of theft, even if paying the restitution requires selling oneself into slavery (Exodus 22:1ff.)?"[106] Ownership of property is a God-given right, and stewardship is a God-given responsibility.

Work. Our right to own property stems from our duty to work. After God sent Adam and Eve away from the garden of Eden, he decreed a lifetime of hard work (Gen. 3:17–19).[107] However, work was a part of God's commands *before* the fall, and God still mercifully allows the acquiring of property and ideas as a reward of hard work. The very existence of private property encourages diligence and fruitfulness: "Lazy hands make a man poor, but diligent hands bring wealth" (Prov. 10:4). The apostle Paul taught the relationship between work and property when he said, "Even when we were with you, we gave you this rule: 'If a man will not work, he shall not eat'" (2 Thess. 3:10). Hard work is the difference between those who are talented and those whose talents produce high performance.[108]

Trust. Scripture puts a high priority on truth: don't lie, don't cheat, and do unto others as you would have them do to you. When people live by these principles, they trust one another more; this sort of trust leads to a thriving nation and drastically lowers what economists call *transaction costs*. Using data from the World Values Survey, researchers found a strong correlation between a nation's level of trust and their economic growth, civic participation, quality of government service, infant survival rate, educational achievement, tax compliance, and efficient administration of laws. Corruption was significantly lower in these countries as well.[109] It's the responsibility of each one of us to generate trust. According to Michael Lewis's account of the financial crisis in the early twenty-first century, the country of Greece suffers from a high rate of people who cheat on their taxes and try to take a large share of government benefits. This systemic corruption has had a contagious effect on people, incentivizing them to not follow the rules.[110]

Competition. The Bible instructs employers to pay well those who work hard.[111] Because the lazy tend to become or remain poor (Prov. 10:4; 14:23; 21:25),[112] workers have an incentive to produce at a high level, which is the basis of what we call *economic competition*. Although it sounds paradoxical, competition in the context of the rule of law leads to cooperation in a well-functioning capitalist society. This phenomenon is called the *principle of comparative advantage*, which says that individuals in a free market economy can produce valuable goods or services by specializing in an area where there is the least absolute disadvantage. In other words, focusing on producing goods or services through cooperation

> Although it sounds paradoxical, competition in the context of rule of law leads to cooperation in a well-functioning capitalist society.

benefits society as a whole. This in turn creates more goods and services that can benefit the poor and also reinforces our worth and dignity in the sense that our work and diligence contribute to the welfare of society.

Social justice. Christian socialists believe our obligations to the poor demand an equal sharing of limited resources. The Bible, however, stresses not showing special favor to the rich or to the poor (Lev. 19:15).[113] E. Calvin Beisner counters the socialist interpretation of social justice when he says, "God is not 'on the side of the poor,' despite protests to the contrary. Any law, therefore, that gives an advantage in the economic sphere to anyone, rich or poor, violates Biblical justice."[114] Justice requires equality before the law rather than equality of income or ability. Impartiality, not equality, is the key to a biblical understanding. Beisner continues, "The Bible demands impartiality, which—because people differ in interests, gifts, capacities, and stations in life—must invariably result in conditional inequality."[115]

11. CONCLUSION

When we examine the biblical principles of economics in light of the other competing worldviews we are considering, several conclusions spring readily to mind.

- We should all work hard to produce abundance. Work is a virtue, not a vice.[116]
- We should support the rule of law so people can have freedom to come up with ideas and turn them into economic benefit for themselves and others.
- We should focus on impartial administration of justice rather than equal distribution of goods.
- Equality is important, but the focus should be equal treatment before the law rather than on equal economic outcome.[117]
- The Bible does not teach socialism or communism.[118]
- We must take into consideration the rising generation—have we left them a sufficient productive base so they too can thrive? Have we operated government in such a way that it will help rather than hinder?

The Christian worldview embraces the peaceful and free exchange of goods and services without fraud, theft, or breach of contract. Private property and stewardship are necessary and good. While not everyone possesses the same skills, interests, or connections, every human being does bear God's image and is capable of working hard to come up with good ideas to make life better for themselves and others. If we all take responsibility to do this, we will see abundance continue to grow and truth and rightness continue to spread throughout the world.

> The Christian worldview embraces the peaceful and free exchange of goods and services without fraud, theft, or breach of contract.

But there is still a problem. In our fallenness, we humans too often forget the lessons learned from past societies about how to establish good laws and encourage productive economic activity. The study of history is necessary to help us grasp how people in the past thought and lived, and how we might learn from their successes and failures to help humans flourish in our own time. As we will see in the next chapter, though, the study of history isn't straightforward. Each worldview approaches it differently, and this affects what course of action its adherents suggest for the future.

ENDNOTES

1. *The Dark Knight Rises*, directed by Christopher Nolan (Warner Brothers, 2012); see also Jerry Bowyer, "Why Batman's 'The Dark Knight' is an Instant Conservative Classic," *Forbes*, July 26, 2012, www.forbes.com /sites/jerrybowyer/2012/07/26/why-batmans-the-dark-knight-rises-is-an-instant-conservative-classic/.

2. N. Gregory Mankiw, *Principles of Economics*, 4th ed. (Mason, OH: South-Western, 2007), 3.

3. Mankiw, *Principles of Economics*.

4. Genesis 1:28: "God blessed [Adam and Eve]. And God said to them, 'Be fruitful and multiply and fill the earth and subdue it, and have dominion over the fish of the sea and over the birds of the heavens and over every living thing that moves on the earth.'"

5. Cited in Partha Dasgupta, *Economics: A Very Short Introduction* (Oxford, UK: Oxford University Press, 2007), 16.

6. Scott Todd, *Fast Living: How the Church Will End Extreme Poverty* (Colorado Springs: Compassion International, 2011), 71.

7. Sylvia Nasar, *The Grand Pursuit* (New York: Simon and Schuster, 2011), xiii.

8. Nasar, *The Grand Pursuit*.

9. Economist Cleon Skousen called this the "five thousand year leap." For more information, see his book *The Five Thousand Year Leap: 28 Great Ideas That Changed the World* (Provo, UT: PowerThink, 2009).

10. Growth in this sense is measured by "per capita GDP," which means the gross domestic product—the total of all goods and services produced, divided by the number of people, and adjusted for inflation. Dasgupta, *Economics*, 17.

11. Todd, *Fast Living*, 37.

12. Mankiw, *Principles of Economics*, 9.

13. Estimates are that up to 10 percent of the North Korean population may have starved to death as a result of the actions of the totalitarian, communist North Korean government.

14. George Gilder, *Wealth and Poverty* (Washington, DC: Regnery, 2012), 42.

15. Gilder, *Wealth and Poverty*, 56.

16. Mankiw, *Principles of Economics*, 28–29.

17. Mankiw, *Principles of Economics*, 148.

18. The classic example of government interference in the economy was Franklin D. Roosevelt's New Deal. Says Clarence Carson, "The New Deal gave the impression that much was going on and something was being done, especially in the early months. It was the responsibility of government to set things right, so its programs said, to rescue the banks, manage the money, organize and rehabilitate industry, put people to work, provide emergency relief, save the farmers, and put everything on an even keel. The New Deal was part bread and part circus; it was scurry, experiment, legislate, create agencies, and spend money. The motif of the New Deal was to do something even if it was wrong, but do something." Clarence B. Carson, *The Welfare State, 1929–1985* (Wadley, AL: American Textbook Committee, 1985), 50.

19. Jay Richards, *Money, Greed, and God* (New York: HarperOne, 2009), 47.

20. Martin Meredith, *The Fate of Africa: A History of Fifty Years of Independence* (New York: Public Affairs, 2005), 684.

21. Meredith, *The Fate of Africa*.

22. Dasgupta, *Economics*, 20.

23. Dasgupta, *Economics*, 24.

24. Michael Novak, *The Fire of Invention* (Lanham, MD: Rowman and Littlefield, 1997), 53.

25. Bernard Lonergan, *Insight: A Study of Human Understanding* (New York: Longmans, 1957), 4, quoted in Novak, *Fire of Invention*, 77.

26. Jim Clifton, *The Coming Jobs War* (New York: Gallup, 2011), 51.

27. Gilder, *Wealth and Poverty*, 45.

28. Daniel Pink, *To Sell Is Human* (New York: Riverhead Books, 2012), 29.

29. Gilder, *Wealth and Poverty*, 37.

30. Dasgupta, *Economics*, 126–127.

31. Richard D. Lamm, "I Have a Plan to Destroy America," *Centennial Review* 5, no. 5 (May 2013): 1.

32. Keynes argued that because the level of output and employment chiefly respond to the rate of consumer demand, we should use fiscal or monetary policies to stimulate demand. In Gilder, *Wealth and Poverty*, 55.

33. This figure is derived from a presentation titled "A Borrowed Prosperity," delivered by Toby Neugebauer, cofounder of Quantum Energy Partners, available at Summit Ministries, http://vimeo.com/29115347. Neugebauer shows that in the last decade, every incremental dollar of debt added only eight cents of real economic value to the gross domestic product (GDP). If you invested a dollar and wanted an 8 percent return, the return would need to be $1.08. If the return is only $0.08, it means you have lost $0.92.

34. Erich Fromm, *On Disobedience and Other Essays* (New York: Seabury, 1981), 75–76.

35. Fromm, *On Disobedience and Other Essays*, 62.

36. Corliss Lamont, *Voice in the Wilderness* (Buffalo: Prometheus Books, 1975), 166.

37. Lamont, *Voice in the Wilderness*. Lamont was clearly confused about economic theories. In reality, fascism is more closely akin to socialism than to capitalism, for while fascism leaves titular ownership of productive property in private hands, it insists that only the central government should control productive property. Capitalist philosophy has always held that control is an essential element of ownership. The only difference between fascism and socialism, therefore, is that the former allows people to hold legal title to capital, but neither allows them to control it.

38. Fromm, *On Disobedience and Other Essays*, 90.

39. John Kenneth Galbraith, *Economics, Peace, and Laughter* (Boston: Houghton Mifflin, 1971), 101.

40. Erich Fromm, *Beyond the Chains of Illusion* (New York: Simon and Schuster, 1962), quoted in Ross Ellenhorn, "Toward a Humanistic Social Work: Social Work for Conviviality," *Humanity and Society* (May 1988): 166.

41. Erich Fromm, *The Sane Society* (New York: Holt, 1990), 277.

42. John Dewey, *Liberalism and Social Action* (New York: G. P. Putnam's Sons, 1935), 356–57.

43. Jonah Goldberg, *Liberal Fascism: The Secret History of the American Left from Mussolini to the Politics of Meaning* (New York: Doubleday, 2007), 336.

44. Karl Marx, *Capital* (London: Sonnenschein, 1982), 660–61, quoted in Harry W. Laidler, *History of Socialism* (New York: Thomas Y. Crowell, 1968), 152–53.

45. Gilder, *Wealth and Poverty*, 51.

46. Frederick Engels, *Socialism: Utopian and Scientific* (New York: International Publishers, 1935), 69.

47. Raymond Sleeper, ed., *A Lexicon of Marxist-Leninist Semantics* (Alexandria, VA: Western Goals, 1983), 30.

48. Karl Marx and Frederick Engels, *Collected Works*, 40 vols. (New York: International Publishers, 1976), 6:350.

49. Marx and Engels, *Collected Works*, 6:351.

50. V. I. Lenin, *Collected Works*, 45 vols. (Moscow: Progress Publishers, 1980), 30:107.

51. G. A. Kozlov, ed., *Political Economy: Socialism* (Moscow: Progress Publishers, 1977), 55.

52. Kenneth N. Cameron, *Marxism: The Science of Society* (Boston: Bergin and Garvey, 1985), 85.

53. Sleeper, *Lexicon of Marxist-Leninist Semantics*, 302.

54. Quoted in John Strachey, *The Theory and Practice of Socialism* (New York: Random House, 1936), title page.

55. David F. Ruccio and Jack Amariglio, *Postmodern Moments in Modern Economics* (Princeton, NJ: Princeton University Press, 2003), 17–18.

56. Ruccio and Amariglio, *Postmodern Moments*, 14.

57. Stanley Kurtz, "Can We Make Boys and Girls Alike?," *City Journal*, 2005, www.city-journal.org/html/15_2_boys_girls.html.

58. Anthony Thomson, "Post-Modernism and Social Justice," paper presented at annual meeting of the Society of Socialist Studies, St. John's, Newfoundland, June 7, 1997, http://ace.acadiau.ca/soci/agt/constitutivecrim.htm, citing Stuart Henry and Dragan Milovanovic, *Constitutive Criminology: Beyond Postmodernism* (London: Sage, 1996), 4.

59. Robert Eaglestone, ed., *Routledge Critical Thinkers* (New York: Routledge, 2003), 15.

60. Mark Lilla, *The Reckless Mind: Intellectuals in Politics* (New York: New York Review Books, 2001), 153. Foucault's biographer, Didier Eribon, wrote, Foucault "had been seen with an iron rod in his hands, ready to do battle with militant communists; he had been seen throwing rocks at the police." Didier Eribon, *Michel Foucault* (Cambridge, MA: Harvard University Press, 1992), 209.

61. Richard Rorty, *Philosophy and Social Hope* (New York: Penguin, 2000), 214.

62. Richard Rorty, "Trotsky and Wild Orchids," in *Wild Orchids and Trotsky: Messages from American Universities*, ed., Mark Edmundson (New York: Penguin Books, 1993), 47.

63. Rorty, "Trotsky and Wild Orchids."

64. Richard Rorty, "The Communitarian Impulse," speech at Colorado College, Colorado Springs, Colorado, February 5, 1999, www2.coloradocollege.edu/academics/anniversary/Transcripts/RortyTXT.htm.

65. Quoted in Stuart Sim, ed., *The Routledge Companion to Postmodernism* (London: Routledge, 2004), 40.

66. Ruccio and Amariglio, *Postmodern Moments*, 295.

67. Ruccio and Amariglio, *Postmodern Moments*, 299.

68. Quoted in Rhonda Byrne, *The Secret* (New York: Atria Books, 2006), 147.

69. Eckhart Tolle, *A New Earth* (New York: Plume, 2005), 191.

70. Marilyn Ferguson, *The Aquarian Conspiracy* (Los Angeles: J. P. Tarcher, 1980), 326–27.

71. Shirley MacLaine, *Out on a Limb* (New York: Bantam Books, 1989), 291.

72. Shakti Gawain, *Living in the Light* (San Rafael, CA: New World Library, 1986), 110.

73. Gawain, *Living in the Light*, 142.

74. Randall N. Baer, *Inside the New Age Nightmare* (Lafayette, LA: Huntington House, 1989), 140.

75. Quoted in Baer, *Inside the New Age Nightmare*, 171.

76. Kevin Ryerson, *Spirit Communication: The Soul's Path* (New York: Bantam Books, 1989), 160.

77. Vera Alder, *When Humanity Comes of Age* (New York: Samuel Weiser, 1974), 48–49.

78. Quoted in Syed Nawab Haider Naqvi, *Islam, Economics, and Society* (London: Kegan Paul International, 1994), xiii.

79. Naqvi, *Islam, Economics, and Society*, xiv.

80. Naqvi, *Islam, Economics, and Society*.

81. Naqvi, *Islam, Economics, and Society*, 27–28.

82. Naqvi, *Islam, Economics, and Society*, 35.

83. Naqvi, *Islam, Economics, and Society*, 32.

84. "[A man's] personal expenses, his family allowances, his necessary expenditures, his due credits—all are paid first, and Zakat is for the net balance." Hammudah Abdalati, *Islam in Focus* (Indianapolis: American Trust, 1975), 97.

85. This wasn't the case when Abraham purchased a piece of property to bury his wife Sarah (Gen. 23:12–20). Abraham certainly expected "deeded property" would last more than two generations!

86. Naqvi, *Islam, Economics, and Society*, 117.

87. A profit-and-loss-sharing arrangement avoids charging interest by purchasing an item (e.g., house, equipment, etc.) on behalf of the person who wants it and then reselling it to him or her at a profit, usually accepting installment payments. Such contracts can be grouped together and sold like shares of stock that can go up or down in value depending on their performance. For more see Naqvi, *Islam, Economics, and Society*, 141–43.

88. See the discussion in Stuart Robinson, *Mosques and Miracles: Revealing Islam and God's Grace*, 2nd ed. (Upper Mt. Gravatt, Australia: City Harvest, 2004), 202. Robinson records that even as recent as 1997, almost fifty Christians were killed, several in a Sunday school class, apparently because they failed to pay *jizya*.

89. The Voice of the Martyrs illustrates this observation with impressive regularity (www.persecution.com).

90. Isaiah 65:21–25: "'They shall build houses and inhabit them; they shall plant vineyards and eat their fruit. They shall not build and another inhabit; they shall not plant and another eat; for like the days of a tree shall the days of my people be, and my chosen shall long enjoy the work of their hands. They shall not labor in vain or bear children for calamity, for they shall be the offspring of the blessed of the LORD, and their descendants with them. Before they call I will answer; while they are yet speaking I will hear. The wolf and the lamb shall graze together; the lion shall eat straw like the ox, and dust shall be the serpent's food. They shall not hurt or destroy in all my holy mountain,' says the LORD"; Jeremiah 32:43–44: "Fields shall be bought in this land of which you are saying, 'It is a desolation, without man or beast; it is given into the hand of the Chaldeans.' Fields shall be bought for money, and deeds shall be signed and sealed and witnessed, in the land of Benjamin, in the places about Jerusalem, and in the cities of Judah, in the cities of the hill country, in the cities of the Shephelah, and in the cities of the Negeb; for I will restore their fortunes, declares the LORD"; Acts 5:1–4: "A man named Ananias, with his wife Sapphira, sold a piece of property, and with his wife's knowledge he kept back for himself some of the proceeds and brought only a part of it and laid it at the apostles' feet. But Peter said, 'Ananias, why has Satan filled your heart to lie to the Holy Spirit and to keep back for yourself part of the proceeds of the land? While it remained unsold, did it not remain your own? And after it was sold, was it not at your disposal? Why is it that you have contrived this deed in your heart? You have not lied to men but to God'"; Ephesians 4:28: "Let the thief no longer steal, but rather let him labor, doing honest work with his own hands, so that he may have something to share with anyone in need."

91. As we discussed earlier, *socialism* basically means "the absence of private property." More specifically, the means of production are owned in common, by the force of law. To gain biblical support for this, socialists often cite Acts 2:44–45, in which the believers held their goods in common. This is a problematic interpretation for two reasons. First, in the early church people gave up their goods willingly, not by government edict. Second, the ownership of private property is assumed: people couldn't have sold their goods if they did not own them in the first place.

92. See also 1 Timothy 6:17–19: "As for the rich in this present age, charge them not to be haughty, nor to set their hopes on the uncertainty of riches, but on God, who richly provides us with everything to enjoy. They are to do good, to be rich in good works, to be generous and ready to share, thus storing up treasure for themselves as a good foundation for the future, so that they may take hold of that which is truly life"; 2 Thessalonians 3:7–13: "You yourselves know how you ought to imitate us, because we were not idle when we were with you, nor did we eat anyone's bread without paying for it, but with toil and labor we worked night and day, that we might not be a burden to any of you. It was not because we do not have that right, but to give you in ourselves an example to imitate. For even when we were with you, we would give you this command: If anyone is not willing to work, let him not eat. For we hear that some among you walk in idleness, not busy at work, but busybodies. Now such persons we command

and encourage in the Lord Jesus Christ to do their work quietly and to earn their own living. As for you, brothers, do not grow weary in doing good."

93. See Exodus 20:15–17.

94. Ronald H. Nash, *Poverty and Wealth: The Christian Debate over Capitalism* (Westchester, IL: Crossway Books, 1987), 63.

95. Robert Sheaffer, "Socialism Is Incompatible with Humanism," *Free Inquiry* (Fall 1989): 19.

96. Quoted in Paul Kurtz, ed., *Sidney Hook: Philosopher of Democracy and Humanism* (Buffalo: Prometheus Books, 1983), 80.

97. Acts 2:44–45: "All who believed were together and had all things in common. And they were selling their possessions and belongings and distributing the proceeds to all, as any had need."

98. Acts 2:46–47: "Day by day, attending the temple together and breaking bread in their homes, they received their food with glad and generous hearts, praising God and having favor with all the people. And the Lord added to their number day by day those who were being saved."

99. Acts 5:1–4: "A man named Ananias, with his wife Sapphira, sold a piece of property, and with his wife's knowledge he kept back for himself some of the proceeds and brought only a part of it and laid it at the apostles' feet. But Peter said, 'Ananias, why has Satan filled your heart to lie to the Holy Spirit and to keep back for yourself part of the proceeds of the land? While it remained unsold, did it not remain your own? And after it was sold, was it not at your disposal? Why is it that you have contrived this deed in your heart? You have not lied to man but to God.'"

100. See especially Proverbs 31; Isaiah 65:21–22; Jeremiah 32:43–44; Acts 5:1–4; and Ephesians 4:28.

101. Rodney Stark, *The Victory of Reason: How Christianity Led to Freedom, Capitalism, and Western Success* (New York: Random House, 2005), 56.

102. Stark, *Victory of Reason*, 55.

103. E. Calvin Beisner, *Prosperity and Poverty: The Compassionate Use of Resources in a World of Scarcity* (Westchester, IL: Crossway Books, 1988), xi–xii.

104. Irving E. Howard, *The Christian Alternative to Socialism* (Arlington, VA: Better Books, 1966), 4.

105. See Genesis 23:13–20; Deuteronomy 8; Ruth 2; Isaiah 65:21–22; Jeremiah 32:42–44; Psalm 112; Proverbs 31; Micah 4:1–4; Luke 12:13–15; Acts 5:1–4; Ephesians 4:28.

106. Beisner, *Prosperity and Poverty*, 66.

107. Genesis 3:17–19: "To Adam [God] said, 'Because you have listened to the voice of your wife and have eaten of the tree of which I commanded you, you shall not eat of it, cursed is the ground because of you; in pain you shall eat of it all the days of your life; thorns and thistles it shall bring forth for you; and you shall eat the plants of the field. By the sweat of your face you shall eat bread, till you return to the ground, for out of it you were taken; for you are dust, and to dust you shall return.'"

108. An excellent book on this topic is Geoffrey Colvin, *Talent Is Overrated* (New York: Portfolio, 2008).

109. World Values Survey, cited in Dasgupta, *Economics*, 58.

110. Michael Lewis, *Boomerang* (New York: W. W. Norton, 2011), 54.

111. Leviticus 19:13: "You shall not oppress your neighbor or rob him. The wages of a hired worker shall not remain with you all night until the morning"; Deuteronomy 24:14–15: "You shall not oppress a hired worker who is poor and needy, whether he is one of your brothers or one of the sojourners who are in your land within your towns. You shall give him his wages on the same day, before the sun sets (for he is poor and counts on it), lest he cry against you to the LORD, and you be guilty of sin"; Deuteronomy 25:4: "You shall not muzzle an ox when it is treading out the grain"; 1 Timothy 5:18: "The Scripture says, 'You shall not muzzle an ox when it treads out the grain,' and, 'The laborer deserves his wages.'"

112. Proverbs 10:4: "A slack hand causes poverty, but the hand of the diligent makes rich"; Proverbs 14:23: "In all toil there is profit, but mere talk tends only to poverty"; Proverbs 21:25: "The desire of the sluggard kills him, for his hands refuse to labor."

113. Leviticus 19:15: "You shall do no injustice in court. You shall not be partial to the poor or defer to the great, but in righteousness shall you judge your neighbor."

114. Beisner, *Prosperity and Poverty*, 52.

115. Beisner, *Prosperity and Poverty*.

116. The Greeks and Romans, in contrast, grounded their case for slavery in the idea that work is a vice, a view both Aristotle and Plato endorsed. Stark, *Victory of Reason*, 26–27.

117. Michael Novak explains: "Given the diversity and liberty of human life, no fair and free system can possibly guarantee equal outcomes. A democratic system depends for its legitimacy, therefore, not upon equal results but upon a sense of equal opportunity." Michael Novak, *The Spirit of Democratic Capitalism* (New York: Simon and Schuster, 1982), 15.

118. This was evident even to Engels, who wrote, "If some few passages of the Bible may be favourable to Communism, the general spirit of its doctrines is, nevertheless, totally opposed to it." Marx and Engels, *Collected Works*, 3:399.

CHAPTER **17**

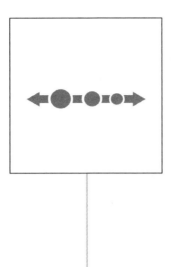

HISTORY

1. WHAT MAKES GREAT HISTORY?

London, England. The soaring dome of Saint Paul's Cathedral defines the skyline of the north bank of the Thames River. If you visit, be sure to explore the crypt. It's not as creepy and dark as it sounds. It is the final resting place of many interesting people, including naval hero Admiral Lord Nelson and Sir Christopher Wren, the architect of Saint Paul's. Above Wren's tomb is an inscription in Latin that reads, "Reader, if you seek his monument, look about you." Saint Paul's extravagance bears witness to Wren's greatnesss.

Orange, Virginia. Montpelier is a plantation home not far from Thomas Jefferson's Monticello. A short hike from the main house is a gravesite where James Madison is buried. Madison was the father of the Constitution, negotiator of the Louisiana Purchase, and our fourth president. Madison's monument is honorable but plain. In fact, for more than twenty years after his death, there was no grave marker at all. According to biographer Richard Brookhiser, Madison needed no extravagant monument. Brookhiser wrote, "If you seek his monument, look about you. Madison's circumambient monument is American constitutionalism."[1] Some great men achieve greatness through works of art or architecture; James Madison achieved greatness through his ideas.

Why do most historians treat Madison as great? Yes, he was president, but many other presidents are all but ignored by historians today. Yes, he was present at the constitutional convention, but so were fifty-four others, and few would be able to name more than two or three of them. Historians study people and events from the past, examining how they thought and lived. In this chapter we'll look at how **history** has been studied in the past and how it ought to be studied today. Along the way, we'll look at the approach to history of each of the six worldviews we have been studying throughout this volume.

> *History:* the study of past events.

2. A Primer on History

The sun rises and sets, but our organization of days, months, seasons, and years—the fact that we seek to make the most of our time on this planet—is unique to how humans think. People are born and people die, but that certain human events are worth remembering—that these are worth pause, consideration, and reflection—is unique to how humans think.

What people believe about the cause, nature, and purpose of the universe determines how they understand and use time. Time, then, is inherently religious.[2] Many ancient Greek philosophers thought everyday events were relatively meaningless. The universe just is—it has no goal. Some Eastern religions hold this view as well. As G. K. Chesterton once observed, "It is fitting that the Buddha be pictured with his eyes closed; there is nothing important to see."[3]

A few ancient Greeks, though, went against the grain. For example, Herodotus is known as the father of history because of the way he gathered evidence, tested it for accuracy, and wrote about it. Even though some of what he wrote sounds crazy—Arion riding on the tail of a dolphin, for instance—he nevertheless inquired into what happened and devised a way to describe it. His work, then, is considered among the earliest attempts to compose history.[4]

> Herodotus is known as the father of history because of the way he gathered evidence, tested it for accuracy, and wrote about it.

Whereas Herodotus focused on people and places and faithfully recorded what he heard, even if it was mythical, the historian Thucydides was a bit more scientific. Thucydides omitted from his accounts interference from the gods or anything that did not meet the test of cause and effect. He focused instead on the larger picture of why, in light of the political situation, things happened as they did. Both Herodotus and Thucydides were celebrated by early leaders who thought the examples of history, especially how great men gained and maintained power, helped them rule more effectively.

Later, in the medieval and Renaissance periods, history was often recorded in story, song, poems, and speeches rather than comprehensive narratives. The purpose was different too; namely, situating people's problems in the larger context of past events to give them a sense of identity.[5]

Another group of careful historians was the ancient Hebrews. University of Liverpool's Kenneth Anderson Kitchen describes their accurate record keeping: "In terms of general reliability … the Old Testament comes out remarkably well, so long as its writings and writers are treated fairly and evenhandedly, in line with independent data, open to all."[6] Oddly, secular scholars seem to discount these narratives. Rhetoric scholar Kenneth Burke, a non-Christian, thought they were wrong to do so. He laid the blame at the feet of "parochial-minded persons" who "dismiss all thought before a certain date as 'ignorance' and 'superstition.'"[7] Because we think too much of our current knowledge, Burke thought, as a way of self-correcting, we should cherish the lore of history, even that which modern people think was in error.

Today, the study of history is in trouble for two reasons. First, there are massive disagreements about what makes historical people and events important. Why, for example, should we focus on presidents? With one exception, they were all white men. What about women? What about people of color? Aren't they also important? And who is to say that only our leaders are important? Sometimes everyday people do something to affect the course of history. If we're looking only at elected officials, wealthy people, or "winners," we'll miss those other stories.

Furthermore, choosing what to study from history is complicated because it is impossible to take into account *all* the facts. A **fact** is something known to exist in reality. Past events are known to us through facts. For example, the Continental Congress adopted the Declaration of Independence on July 4, 1776. Abraham Lincoln died on April 15, 1865. The Japanese attacked Pearl Harbor on December 7, 1941.

Historians, however, can't take into account every single fact. They have to discern carefully which facts had a shaping influence. And who decides which facts had a shaping influence? Historian and Marxist sympathizer E. Hallet Carr thought it was impossible to say:

> *Fact:* something that is indisputably known to be true.

> It used to be said that facts speak for themselves. This is, of course, untrue. The facts speak only when the historian calls on them: it is he who decides to which facts to give the floor, and in what order or context…. It is the historian who has decided for his own reasons that Caesar's crossing of that petty stream, the Rubicon, is a fact of history, whereas the crossing of the Rubicon by millions of other people before or since interests nobody at all.[8]

The way Carr used the word *fact* is confusing. The historian who pays attention to Julius Caesar's crossing of the Rubicon is not merely making a "petty stream" seem more important than it was; rather, he's responding to a reality from history that Roman armies were expected to disband before crossing the Rubicon on their way home. Caesar's failure to disband was immediately seen as a declaration of civil war, exactly as he intended. The crossing of the Rubicon was a point of no return. Today it enters the discussion in many meaningful ways, including whether America should forsake its tradition of not using its national army as a police force.[9]

History is not relative; it is rigorous. As Nancy Isenberg says, "History is not a bedtime story. It is a comprehensive engagement with often obscure documents and books no longer read—books shelved in old archives, and fragile pamphlets contemporaneous with the subject under study—all of which reflect a world view not ours."[10] Some find this kind of study fascinating. Others are bored by it or don't see the point. The industrialist Henry Ford said, "I don't know much about history, and I wouldn't give a nickel for all the history in the world." We may not enjoy everything about the study of history, but we ought to try. Knowing history is part of understanding the times so we can know what we ought to do.

> The call goes out to smart Christians to make history their vocation not for fame or riches but to vividly tell the story of what God is doing through flawed people in order to accomplish his grand purposes.

Today, history is being hijacked in the service of anti-Christian worldviews. The call goes out to smart Christians to make history their vocation not for fame or riches but to vividly tell the story of what God is doing through flawed people in order to accomplish his grand purposes. It is a call to battle to advance truth and also to guard against the flanking maneuvers of error.

The second reason the study of history is in trouble is because people use it to achieve their own agendas rather than as part of the search for truth. The writers of Scripture seemed to do their best to "tell" on themselves, to reveal unflattering details about themselves. This is uncharacteristic of people who are trying to amass personal power. One example is Peter in the Gospels, who, in the account he sourced for the gospel of Mark, told of his missteps and follies, including how women often understood the truth when men did not (this in an age when women were not even considered to be reliable witnesses in court). Like those writers, historians should be prepared to make accurate arguments and offer genuine proof for them.

Christianity is based in history. The biblical authors were saying, "Here are the facts about what actually happened as God worked and continues to work in the lives of people from the beginning of time to the present and on into the future." The past matters. What people did *then* shows us what to do and what not to do now. Often the hero and villain in biblical narratives are the same person, honoring God in one season of life and dishonoring him in another. Taken as a whole, the Christian narrative of history has profoundly shaped all of Western civilization.[11]

3. WHAT DO HISTORIANS DO?

In *Philosophy of History,* Georg F. W. Hegel wrote, "What experience and history teach is this—that people and governments never have learned anything from history, or acted on principles deduced from it."[12] For Hegel, to study history was to interpret the past in order to establish a story of how life is, which then justifies our vision of the future.

Using history to justify our course may sound reasonable, but it can be dangerous. Historians can't know every fact about the past. Even if they could, their accounts of those facts would be incomprehensibly difficult to read. So historians select facts they think are relevant and discard those they deem irrelevant. All of this is affected by their worldview. John H. Arnold, former professor of history at the University of East Anglia, admits, "As historians, we are caught up in our own bundles of interests, morals, ethics, philosophies, ideas on how the world works, and why people do the things they do."[13]

The Marxist historian E. Hallet Carr took it even further. We do history, he said, "to increase man's understanding of, and *mastery over*, his environment."[14] By this way of thinking, historical facts not fitting the narrative we want to establish are seen as defective and thus useless. Even the conservative Oxford professor Michael Oakeshott questioned whether objectivity was possible. "History is the historian's experience," he said. "It is 'made' by nobody save the historian: to write history is the only way of making it."[15]

Historians all have biases, but does this mean all accounts of history are therefore false? Not necessarily. "History," said the respected Hungarian historian John Lukacs, "is the remembered past, meaning all that we remember of the past, in every possible way, the corollary of this being that the entire past of mankind is history, at least potentially so."[16] He's right. The historian should only say "how it really was," as Leopold von Ranke phrased it.[17] The reader of the historian's work must be discerning about whether the historian is remembering what really happened or

> **Historians all have biases, but does this mean all accounts of history are therefore false?**

merely what he wants to have happened. Historians should be prepared to reveal their underlying assumptions to readers, and readers should be prepared to see how the historians' treatment of the facts stacks up to what else is known. Only when readers engage in this way with the historians can history be properly grasped.

The writing of history is called **historiography**. Historiography is what historians do. They look at past events and reconstruct what happened in their minds so as to communicate it to their audiences. Historians have ten tools to work with, according to Hans Meyerhoff: subject matter, facts, primary aim, language, fact/theory/interpretation, methods, explanations, freedom, values, and meaning. Using these tools, Carr claimed, creates "an unending dialogue between the past and present."[18]

There is one more key term you need to know: **historicism**. Historicism is when historians go beyond the writing of history and project an interpretation of history onto the future. Karl Popper defined *historicism* as "an approach to the social sciences which assumes that *historical prediction* is their only aim, and which assumes that this aim is attainable by discovering the 'rhythms' or the 'patterns,' the 'laws' or the 'trends' that underlie the evolution of history."[19]

> *Historiography:* the writing of history or the study of the methodology historians use to reconstruct historical events.

According to Popper's definition, seeing history as progress from lower to higher states is historicism because it makes further progress appear inevitable (usually in the direction the historian himself thinks we should go). To see history only as class warfare also counts as historicism because it makes class warfare seem inevitable. Not everyone, of course, finds Popper's

> *Historicism:* the writing of history for the purpose of making certain future states appear to be inevitable, thus projecting an interpretation of history onto the future.

definition of *historicism* so clear cut. Carr criticized Popper for using historicism "as a catch-all for any opinion about history which he dislikes."[20] Whether Carr said this as a historian or as a Marxist is unclear.

Still, most historians find historicism suspicious. Dutch philosopher Herman Dooyeweerd thought historicism dangerous because it promotes relativism in the sense that what we count as "true" depends on what we want to be true. It also promotes **determinism**, the idea that we are ruled by an inescapable fate.[21] Herbert Schlossberg concurs. Today, he says, we are captive to a way of thinking that "dismisses history as a subject of study [and] exalt[s] it as a principle of inevitability. You do not control your life … but are subject to fate or to the inexorable powers that control the universe."[22]

Determinism: the belief that all events, including human actions, are the inevitable and necessary results of previous actions.

Historicism is a powerful tool in the hands of those who crave power and is usually employed for unjust purposes. Using history to argue that your view is inevitable and that opponents should just step aside is deeply immoral. It's like trying to win the debate for truth by canceling the debate altogether, or like preposting the score on the scoreboard and then claiming to have won the basketball game.

So there are proper and improper ways to study history. This means understanding a worldview's *philosophy* of history is just as important as understanding its interpretation of historical events. We'll focus on both but with greater emphasis on how each worldview's underlying assumptions cause it to look at history in a particular way and thus demand that the world fall in line with its conclusions.

4. SECULARISM

The basic Secularist assumption regarding history can be summed up in one phrase: **social progress**. Most Westerners sense things getting better over time. We might not like the direction our political leaders are moving, but we do expect the next generation of smartphones to be an improvement on the last. We observe urban areas decaying, but we also expect medical treatments to advance through time. If we take the long view of history, there are many periods of progression toward greater wealth and better technology. How to sustain these trends is one reason we study history. As Herbert Butterfield said in *The Whig Interpretation of History*, our study can reveal how historical events morally and/or substantively contributed to or detracted from our present state.[23] History can guide us to learn from our mistakes, act rightly in our current circumstances, and get better over time.

Social Progress: the belief that society will continually improve through human initiative.

But Secularism is dedicated to human progress for entirely different reasons. The Secularists we've studied believe history to be the evolution of both organisms and human society—from the simple to the complex, from weaker to stronger. Progress is inevitable. Charles S. Peirce thought the "laws of nature are themselves evolved as the universe moves from a chaotic spontaneity toward perfect order."[24] Bertrand Russell, the atheist British philosopher, said that technology will guide us in harnessing these laws to our own purposes: "Science used to be valued as a means of getting to *know* the world; now, owing to the triumph of technique, it is conceived as showing how to *change* the world."[25] As we progress, our ideas also evolve. Julian Huxley said, "Major steps in the human phase of evolution are achieved by breakthroughs to new dominant patterns of mental organization, of knowledge, ideas and beliefs—ideological instead of physiological or biological organization."[26] For Huxley, holding progressive ideas is a sign of a person's advanced evolutionary state.

The idea of progress built into the laws of nature—or perhaps the idea of progress as a law of nature—can be traced back to Herbert Spencer, a contemporary of Charles Darwin. Spencer enthusiastically embraced evolution because he thought it explained why certain races are more advanced than others and why certain classes within those races were superior. History, Spencer thought, reveals a necessary progression from homogeneity (sameness) to heterogeneity (variety), from lower and simpler states of organization to higher and more complex states of organization. Progress is "not an accident, not a thing within human control, but a beneficent necessity."[27]

Although most people today recoil at Spencer's patently racist and elitist arguments,[28] he was not alone in holding such views. Darwin claimed to not apply his theories to human society but still put the subtitle of *Origin of Species* as *The Preservation of Favored Races in the Struggle for Life*. While frowning on Spencer's and Darwin's racism, Secularists still enthusiastically embrace the underlying argument that society will "evolve" in the direction smart people think it should go. This unbounded optimism underlies the original defining document of Secularism, the *Humanist Manifesto I* (1933).

Nazism and Marxism temporarily frustrated Secularists' infatuation with progress. How could leaders like Hitler and Stalin, who also enthusiastically embraced the inevitability of human progress, act so inhumanely? Their brutality made a farce of optimism. The tone of the *Humanist Manifesto II* (published in 1973) is noticeably more subdued than its predecessor: "Nazism has shown the depths of brutality of which humanity is capable. Other totalitarian regimes have suppressed human rights without ending poverty. Science has sometimes brought evil as well as good."[29]

As they entered the 1960s, Secularists seemed to suffer from a collective sense of depression. P. W. Atkins, an Oxford chemist, phrased it well: "We are the children of chaos, and the deep structure of change is decay. At root, there is only corruption, and the unstemmable tide of chaos. Gone is purpose; all that is left is direction."[30] Bertrand Russell moaned, "The universe is vast and men are but tiny specks on an insignificant planet."[31]

But where some saw only bleakness, others saw dignity. Chaos may reign, but the brave mock fate and press on. The playwright Albert Camus imagined humans in the place of Sisyphus, the man in Greek mythology condemned to forever roll a boulder up a hill, only to have it roll down again. Camus cast Sisyphus not merely as the victim of absurdity but as a tragic hero who accepted his fate with scorning determination. Of course, his task was absurd, but he mocked the gods by remaining happy. Camus said, "Happiness and the absurd are two sons of the same earth" that "drive out of this world a god who had come into it with dissatisfaction and a preference for futile sufferings. It makes of fate a human matter, which must be settled among men."[32]

If life is an accident, then let's smile and make the best of it, Secularists say. As Athos proclaimed in Alexander Dumas's *Three Musketeers*, "Eh, gentlemen, let us reckon upon accidents! Life is a chaplet of little miseries, which the philosopher unstrings with a smile." Out of chaos we form our own meaning. "No deity will save us; we must save ourselves," says the *Humanist Manifesto II*.[33] Corliss Lamont went even further: "Humanism assigns to man nothing less than the task of being his own savior and redeemer."[34]

> If life is an accident, then let's smile and make the best of it, Secularists say.

We are messiahs, Erich Fromm thought, on the cusp of a new stage in history: "The messianic time is the next step in history, not its abolition. The messianic time is the time when man will have been fully born. When man was expelled from Paradise he lost his home; in the messianic time he will be at home again—in the world."[35] As messiahs, the *Humanist Manifesto II* hints, we can even perform acts bordering on the miraculous: "Using technology wisely, we can control our environment, conquer poverty, markedly reduce disease, extend our life-span, significantly modify our behavior, alter the course of human evolution and cultural development, unlock vast new powers, and provide humankind with unparalleled opportunity for achieving an abundant and meaningful life."[36]

If you sense a contradiction between *believing our course to be determined and claiming freedom to shape our course as we see fit*, you're not alone. The esteemed historian Sir Isaiah Berlin said, "If the determinist hypothesis were true and adequately accounted for the actual world ... the notion of human responsibility, as ordinarily understood, would no longer apply to any actual, but only to imaginary or conceivable, states of affairs."[37] And yet we are responsible. Corliss Lamont attempted to explain the contradiction by saying, "Within certain limits prescribed by our earthly circumstances and by scientific law, individual human beings, entire nations, and mankind in general are free to choose the paths that they truly wish to follow. To a significant degree they are the molders of their own fate and hold in their own hands the shape of things to come."[38]

Bertrand Russell was quite defensive when confronted with this contradiction between determinism and **free will**. It is actually the idea of supernatural truth that is to blame for our predicament, he thought, because it makes Secularists feel "robbed of personality, futile, unimportant, the slaves of circumstance, unable to vary in the slightest degree the part assigned to them by nature from the very beginning."[39] This defensiveness, combined with a messiah complex, may explain why Secularists are so intent on discounting the Bible as historically inaccurate—especially its historical account of Christ's resurrection and ascension.[40]

> *Free Will:* the belief that human beings have the capacity to voluntarily choose a course of action from among various alternatives.

What comes next, according to Secularists? Victor J. Stenger thought technology will enable the continued evolution of humans to even higher states of being. This new evolution will not come about "by the painfully slow and largely random process of biological evolution," he said, but through the rapid and guided advances of technology. "This new form of 'life' I will call, for historical reasons, the computer."[41] Stenger believed that computers will eventually prove more capable than humans in every meaningful realm of life, saying, "If there is anything we do that computers cannot, be patient. In time they will do it better, if it is worth doing at all."[42]

Richard Carrier actually ends his book *Sense and Goodness without God* with a chapter titled "The Secular Humanist's Heaven." He says that one of the first orders of business will be to abolish death or, as he puts it, "We might even make immortality possible. It may even happen that, in the fullness of time, we will be able to transfer our minds, by transferring the patterns of our brains, into computer-simulated worlds that are in even more perfect regulation than the physical world, a true paradise.... It is possible it will never die."[43]

As we can see, history is not only about the past for the Secularist. It aims for a future heaven on earth. We are our own saviors, and we are redeeming ourselves. In spite of some setbacks—the plague, global wars, and so on—we are moving ever closer to perfection.

When Secularists speak of human beings controlling their own evolution, they aren't talking about all humans. They're talking about people they believe "get it." These elites will embrace Secularist assumptions about God, nature, and humans. They are what C. S. Lewis called "the Conditioners." If nothing supernatural exists, then humans "are mere nature to be kneaded and cut into new shapes for the pleasures of masters who must, by hypothesis, have no motive but their own 'natural' impulses.... It is not that they are bad men. They are not men at all[;] ... they have stepped into the void."[44]

5. MARXISM

Recall the idea of dialectical materialism: Marxists borrowing Hegel's dialectic, which frames all of history in terms of thesis, antithesis, and synthesis. Unlike Hegel's dialectic, though, the Marxist idea is *materialistic*, which means it assumes that matter is all that exists. According to this theory, nature guides society through certain economic phases in a constant upward spiral: from primitive communism to slavery to feudalism to capitalism to socialism and then to communism. The continued clash of the bourgeoisie (the present thesis) with the proletariat (the present antithesis) will lead society through a transitional phase of socialism and finally—when the clash is resolved—communism will be achieved. This theory is called **historical materialism**.

History, for the Marxist, is the account of matter in motion. God has nothing to do with it. Matter obeys specific laws in the universe, particularly the laws of the dialectic, which declare that economic structures will eventually evolve into communism. And from communism, the perfect societal superstructure will arise. This alone is the source of progress in the world.

The laws of the dialectic, according to Maurice Cornforth, are economic in nature: "Historical development is not determined by the personal decisions of public men, but by the movement of classes."[45] V. I. Lenin put it this way: "According to the theory of socialism, i.e., of Marxism ... the real driving force of history is the revolutionary class struggle."[46] The dialectic, according to Marxists, carries the force of natural law just as does the law of gravity. It is the only thing that matters. Joseph Stalin asserted, "The practical activity of the party

> **Historical Materialism:** the belief that society is guided by nature through progressive socioeconomic phases: tribalism, slavery, feudalism, capitalism, socialism, and ultimately communism.

of the proletariat must not be based on the good wishes of 'outstanding individuals,' not on the dictates of 'reason,' 'universal morals,' etc., but on the laws of development of society and on the study of these laws."[47]

Marxists are absolutely convinced the dialectical laws will lead to a perfect communist society. As with Secularism, the specter of historical inevitability rises in Marxism too, according to Lenin: "Communists should know that the future belongs to them.… In all cases and in all countries communism is becoming steeled and is spreading[;] its roots are so deep that persecution does not weaken it, does not debilitate it, but strengthens it."[48]

If everything is completely determined, then it wouldn't really matter what humans do, since they can't "choose" to do anything. Because Marxists need action that leads to revolution, they developed a limited version of free will, distinguishing between being totally free and being free within the constraints of history. Karl Marx wrote, "Men make their own history, but they do not make it just as they please; they do not make it under circumstances chosen by themselves, but under circumstances directly encountered, given and transmitted from the past."[49]

The freedom to pursue not their own wills but the laws of the proletariat is important to Marxists for a simple reason: if people are free to do what they want, they are free to *resist* revolution as well as to *foment* it. Marxists' firm conviction is that no amount of human will can stop the collapse of capitalism, the rise of socialism, and the steady transition from socialism to communism. Maurice Cornforth declared, "From the point of view of the capitalist class, Marx's theory is certainly 'fatalistic.' It says: You cannot contrive a managed capitalism, you cannot do away with the class struggle, and you cannot keep the system going indefinitely."[50]

> Marxists' firm conviction is that no amount of human will can stop the collapse of capitalism, the rise of socialism, and the steady transition from socialism to communism.

How does the Marxist view of the laws of the dialectic affect the way it studies history? First, Marxists call into question the objectivity of all other views of history. Howard Zinn, a Marxist historian, was even more blunt: "Objectivity is impossible and it is also undesirable ... because if you have any kind of a social aim ... then it requires that you make your selection on the basis of what you think will advance causes of humanity."[51]

Zinn certainly had a social aim, and it is worth examining closely because his book *A People's History of the United States* is a popular history textbook in universities today. Zinn reinterpreted the events of America's founding from a class-warfare perspective in an intentionally controversial way. For example, Zinn portrayed the founding of the United States as a "diabolically creative way to ensure oppression."[52] Zinn seemed fairly uninterested in whether his telling of history was consistent with previous historical work. His book contains not a single footnote to source or add credibility to his arguments.

Second, having called into question the objectivity of other views, Marxists insist on considering their own views to be objectively true. To the Marxist, writing history is a form of what Kenneth Burke called "secular prayer," or interpreting events in order to highlight certain words and feelings, coaching the reader into seeing and believing what the Marxist sees and believes. This, of course, includes class struggle and driving the audience into a corner by eliminating all other possible explanations for this but the Marxist one.[53]

Marxists view history from the standpoint of atheism, dialectical materialism, and naturalism. The dialectic is a law of nature guaranteeing the movement away from capitalism toward a communist utopia. Human beings cannot stop this process, but they can catalyze it

> Having called into question the objectivity of other views, Marxists insist on considering their own views to be objectively true.

through revolutionary activity. Only people who act in concert with the laws of the dialectic will have impact. The task of the historian is to organize facts about the past to show the futility of prolonging capitalism. History is fixed, like a rigged boxing match. We can cheer all we want, but the boxer paid to "take a dive" is going to lose. We might as well clap and stomp for the predetermined winner—communism—encouraging him to win the bout more decisively. Capitalism will die. The bourgeoisie will collapse. Marxism will win. As Karl Marx himself phrased it, "History is the judge—its executioner, the proletarian."[54]

6. POSTMODERNISM

Traditional historians sift through the evidence at hand to reconstruct as accurate a view of past events as they can. They may differ in their interpretations, but they discipline themselves to be as truthful as possible. When new information comes to light, they take it into account by revising or supplementing their narratives to reflect truth more accurately. Objectivity is a genuine goal.

Postmodernists not only think objectivity is impossible, but they even call into question the idea of "facts." Alasdair MacIntyre even says "facts," as a means of directly knowing about reality itself, "like telescopes and wigs for gentlemen, were a seventeenth-century invention."[55]

All historical accounts are fiction, many Postmodernists say.[56] Less radical Postmodernists take a soft view of history as fiction, saying history is what we make of it. Historical facts are inaccessible, so historians reconstruct the past based on their ideological bent. Some more radical Postmodernists see no ultimate purpose in history, advocating nihilism instead (*nihil* is Latin for "nothing"—**nihilism** means "a belief in nothing").

As you will remember from previous chapters, Postmodernists deny that universal truth can be known. Thus they believe historians are fooling themselves and their readers by striving for objectivity. Each culture and each historical period has its own social system through which it generates its own norms. External truth does not exist. No one outside of a particular culture or historical period can really understand it. Umberto Eco's novel *The Name of the Rose* sums up the postmodern point of view nicely. After a long, logical search for truth, the detective character concludes, "There was no plot ... and I discovered it by mistake."[57]

> Postmodernists not only think objectivity is impossible, but they even call into question the idea of "facts."

> *Nihilism:* the view that the world and human existence are without meaning, purpose, comprehensible truth, or essential value.

But Postmodernists say we can use **deconstruction** to show that the work of historians is not objective and how they are unwittingly operating in the service of so-called universal truths that secure power for the elite and oppress everyone else. Hayden White, in his book *Metahistory* (*meta* meaning "beyond") purports to show how we can deconstruct historians' motives by analyzing the literary structures they use in their craft.[58] The "metacode" historians use, White argues, will reveal how historians get us to believe in "a human universal on the basis of which trans-cultural messages about the shared reality can be transmitted."[59]

> *Deconstruction:* a method of literary analysis that questions the ability of language to represent reality adequately and seeks to discern and expose the purported underlying ideologies of a text.

At the end of the day, scholars like White aren't showing how to do history. They're trying to show how to undo it. Michel Foucault took a similar approach. Mark Poster observes, "Foucault offers a new way of thinking about history, writing history and deploying history in current political struggles. Foucault is an anti-historian, one who in writing history, threatens every canon of the craft."[60]

For Foucault, "truth" and "knowledge" were tools of power. If we accept others' claims to know the truth, we're just giving them power over us. This is why Foucault thought history was a fiction—it is a way to organize arguments we cannot know to be true that lead the reader to conclusions we wish them to reach. Foucault didn't even exempt himself from this criticism:

> For Foucault, "truth" and "knowledge" were tools of power. If we accept others' claims to know the truth, we're just giving them power over us.

> I am well aware that I have never written anything but fictions. I do not mean to say, however, that truth is therefore absent. It seems to me that the possibility exists for fiction to function in truth, for a fictional discourse to induce effects of truth, and for bringing it about that a true discourse engenders or "manufactures" something that does not as yet exist, that it "fictions" it. One "fictions" history on the basis of a political reality that makes it true, one "fictions" a politics not yet in existence on the basis of a historical truth.[61]

This wordplay shows what Foucault actually meant when he used the word *truth*. Truth is not an inherent quality of historical arguments; it's only an impression people get when they hear those arguments.

If objective truth and knowledge are not possible, then what should historians do? On this point Foucault was explicitly clear: the historian is to look back into the past to see how those in power have used historical arguments to secure their power:

> The intellectual no longer has to play the role of an advisor. The project, tactics and goals to be adopted are a matter for those who do the fighting. What the intellectual can do is to provide instruments of analysis, and at present this is the historian's essential role. What's effectively needed is a ramified, penetrative perception of the present, one that makes it possible to locate lines of weakness, strong points, positions where the

instances of power have secured and implanted themselves by a system of organization dating back over 150 years.[62]

If the Postmodernist is so suspicious about the way historical arguments have "secured and implanted" power, one would think Postmodernists would attack Marxists and Secularists with a frenzy. The reality, though, is that Postmodernism is a sort of grandchild of Marxism. As Jacques Derrida admitted, his deconstruction was a radicalization "within the tradition of a certain Marxism, in a certain spirit of Marxism."[63] Postmodernists are likely to protect their Marxist grandparent, or even incorporate some of his assumptions, in turning the guns on other worldviews, such as Christianity.

Marxism's parenthood of Postmodernism is clearest in the trend toward **historical revisionism**. Analyzing history in order to see how some unjustly wrest power from others doesn't just happen in economics. It happens in race relations, gender relations, and in every other area where the powerful oppress the weak, the different, the alienated. Gene Veith explains:

> Post-Marxist radicalism constructs new revolutionary ideologies by replacing Marx's concern for the oppressed working class with other oppressed groups (blacks, women, gays). Status and moral legitimacy come from being "excluded from power." The victim has the favored role.... To be black, female or gay is to enjoy a sort of secular sainthood. But even these categories are segmenting into ever-smaller sects of victimhood.[64]

> *Historical Revisionism:*
> **the act of reinterpreting the past to serve an ideological purpose.**

Postmodernists have blown up the idea of objective historical study and from its rubble have instead assigned to oppressed social minorities the responsibility of building new historical methods. Some feminist historians, for example, think men cannot write histories of women because men simply cannot understand women—that is, masculine ideologies would oppress feminine ideologies. Feminist histories are needed, feminists say, to attempt to expose a male-dominated, patriarchal past and point the way for empowering women. Every repressed group, including minorities, ethnicities, nationalities, and sexualities, has an injustice that must be exposed, and this calls for revolution against the established order.

Tom Dixon writes, "Social historians are often driven by activist goals. Historical research becomes not an attempt to understand the past but a propaganda tool for use in modern political and social power struggles."[65] Dixon also notes, "Postmodern cultural historians consider bias unavoidable in whole or even in part. As a result we see a growing willingness to arrange and edit facts in a way that supports the message of particular historians."[66]

As you can imagine, the postmodern approach to history is controversial. No one doubts whether powerful people abuse their power, but does this really mean objective history is impossible to ascertain? Without any sort of standard for what counts as truth and knowledge, stories of abuse are just tales told by some culture about itself and thus meaningless for everyone else. If it didn't happen to us or in our culture, we are not even really capable of understanding it or caring about it. Rewriting history to highlight the stories of the oppressed not only fails to help the oppressed, but it blurs the line between remembering the past and revising it. Further, the revisionist approach does little to draw society together toward harmonious civility. It engenders a new tribalism, pitting every group against the other in a game of one-upmanship: Whose claim to victimhood is greater?

So, Secularists look for evolutionary progress, Marxists anticipate the inevitable move toward pure communism, and the Postmodernist view of history is distinctly *ateleological* (i.e., without a purpose).[67] For most Postmodernists, there are no "facts." There are only various degrees of fiction.

7. New Spirituality

The New Spiritualist trusts spiritual evolution to guide humanity unswervingly toward perfection. In a very real sense, members of the New Spiritualist movement place their faith in evolution as humanity's savior. Marilyn Ferguson said, "For the first time in history, humankind has come upon the control panel of change—an understanding of how transformation occurs. We are living in the change of change, the time in which we can intentionally align ourselves with nature for rapid remaking of ourselves and our collapsing institutions."[68]

To the New Spiritualist, all that really exists is consciousness. This is no magical or mystical realm; rather, this is what the real universe is. For the New Spiritualist, tapping into this reality is a scientific undertaking. The Maharishi Mahesh Yogi, inventor of Transcendental Meditation (TM), put it this way:

> History does not record a time when man was free from suffering, and so life was declared a struggle. "Life is a struggle"—it's a very common axiom in English. But now a new time has come for the world, and it is a scientific phenomenon we are witnessing. It's not impractical idealism we are talking about, high-sounding moral values with no basis. This is something that has been verified subjectively by millions of people, something that has been verified objectively by ... hundreds of experiments. It is a technology, like the use of a lever, to do something previously found impossible.[69]

The Maharishi believed if enough people would learn Transcendental Meditation and practice it together, we could move to a time and place where suffering will be a thing of the past.

How is it possible for lots of people tapping into their higher consciousness to change the world? Shakti Gawain explains: "Every individual's consciousness is connected to, and is a part of, the mass consciousness. When a small but significant number of individuals have moved into a new level of awareness and significantly changed their behavior, that change is felt in the entire mass consciousness."[70] According to New Spiritualists, we need to realize our true power to accelerate evolution. David Spangler describes this as the "individual's sense of being a co-creator with history, of being involved in a process of conscious and participatory evolution."[71]

Evolutionary Godhood: the belief that we are progressing through history toward the ultimate goal of realizing our own divinity.

We use the term *evolutionary godhood* to describe the view that as we arise from darkness through our growing understanding of consciousness, we begin to see our true potential as gods. As Marianne Williamson states, "When love reaches a critical mass, when enough people become miracle-minded, the world will experience a radical shift."[72]

History, then, from a New Spiritualist view, is sort of like the Secularist idea of evolutionary progress, but on hyperdrive. New Spiritualist evolution moves from being material and natural to being spiritual. Benjamin Ferencz and Ken Keyes explain: "We have seen that humankind is not simply moving in a vicious killing circle; it is on an upward climb toward completing the governmental structure of the world. We are inspired by our great progress toward planethood."[73]

Ferencz, Keyes, and other New Spiritualist writers take pains to note that this is not science fiction. Their optimism is "justified by the facts."[74] Indeed, physicist Paul Davies shared this optimism: "Far from sliding towards a featureless state, the Universe is progressing from featurelessness to states of greater organization and complexity. This cosmic progress defines a global arrow of time that points in the opposite way to the thermodynamic arrow."[75]

If new, higher states of being can solve our problems as humans, then there really is no point in understanding history except to name the dogmas we have outgrown. New Spiritualists claim that Christianity, for example, was helpful at a certain time in the past, but we have outgrown it. Joseph Campbell said, "The old-time religion belongs to another age, another people, another set of human values, another universe. By going back you throw yourself out of sync with history."[76] The theistic religions in particular—Judaism, Christianity, and Islam—"have disqualified themselves for the future," according to Campbell.[77] Religion is part of the baggage we must leave behind to speed our way to the mountaintop of human potential.

Christianity is no longer relevant, let alone true, say New Spiritualists in advocating their viewpoint as the only appropriate religion for our modern age, and it alone can foster our evolutionary leap into higher consciousness. To make matters worse, Christianity is sexist too. Eckhart Tolle's philosophy of history is the story of the male form dominating the female form, which is what led to the Inquisition and witch burning. "Males who denied the feminine even within themselves were now running the world, a world that was totally out of balance. The rest is history, or rather a case history of insanity."[78]

In his book *The Road Less Traveled*, bestselling author M. Scott Peck said, "God wants us to become Himself (or Herself or Itself). We are growing toward godhood. God is the goal of evolution. It is God who is the source of the evolutionary force and God who is the destination. This is what we mean when we say that He is the Alpha and the Omega, the beginning and the end."[79] According to *A Course in Miracles*, every person will eventually be absorbed into a "Divine Abstract" where there are "no distinctions, where no words are communicated, and where there are no events—only a static, eternal now."[80]

Some members of the New Spiritualist movement, unsatisfied with the concept of evolution as the redemptive force in history, look for an actual savior to guide humanity to higher consciousness. Donald H. Yott suggests that a "Savior appears every two thousand years (more or less) for the different ages. Each Savior brings the tone or key-note for the age."[81] A spirit channeled by Levi H. Dowling proclaimed, "In the ages to come, man will attain to greater heights. And then, at last, a mighty Master Soul will come to earth to light the way up to the throne of perfect man."[82]

Biological evolution has given us our present state, according to New Spiritualists, but only spiritual evolution will get us to the next state. Lest we become apathetic and lazy, they say, we must see how our own actions could speed the process along if we would leave behind our beliefs about what is true, good, and beautiful and work harder at tapping into the higher consciousness.

8. ISLAM

Islam is going to win the war of ideas, said Islamic scholar Muhammad Qutb: "Islam is the only future hope of humanity, and its victorious emergence out of the present ideological warfare is the only guarantee of man's salvation."[83] If this sounds familiar, it is because Islam, like most of the other worldviews we have considered, carries with it a sense of historical inevitability. But unlike Secularism, Marxism, or New Spirituality, this view is not held based on what the Islamic worldview hopes to have happen in the future but on what has happened in the past. Hammudah Abdalati explained: "The world is a becoming entity, created by the will of a Designer and sustained by Him for meaningful purposes. Historical currents take place in accordance with His will and follow established laws. They are not directed by blind chance, nor are they random and disorderly incidents."[84]

> Biological evolution has given us our present state, according to New Spiritualists, but only spiritual evolution will get us to the next state.

The term **pan-Islam** best captures the essence of the Islamic approach to history. The global Islamic state is the destination of all people. Jihad, the Muslim equivalent of evangelism, is the vehicle.[85] Historical arguments are fuel in the tank, providing the combustion Islamists need to fire the imaginations of Muslims around the world and inspire them to work together for this great cause. As we have seen in this volume, most Muslims express a moderate view, in which the aggressive nature of Islamic teaching and practice has been curbed by such realities as the Western value of civic tolerance and pluralism. Yet there are still a significant number of Muslims, perhaps hundreds of millions, whom we would call *Islamists*. They believe all humanity will one day bow to Allah freely or by force.[86]

> *Pan-Islam:* the belief that all Muslims should be united under a single Islamic state or that the world should be united under a global Islamic state.

As we have seen in previous chapters, Islamic countries are among the most vociferous persecutors of Christians, presenting probably the greatest missionary challenge to the church and exhibiting the most prominent external threat to the biblical values of freedom, justice, and order. Most Christians are not aware of this or of Islam's plans for dramatic expansion. When they do become aware, they feel helpless to respond. There is an urgent need for Christians to thoughtfully and prayerfully study Islam, explore how to respond in grace and love, and be prepared to vigilantly defend the truth.[87]

We can see the aims of Islam, but what exactly is the view of history it holds to justify its aggressive movement toward a global Islamic state? There are two answers to this question, both requiring insight into some subtle aspects of Muslim theology. First, because of its understanding of Allah's nature and character, Islam freely pursues its aims without fear of social sanction or regard to what other worldviews deem possible. Unlike Marxism, which sees the dialectic as a law of nature inevitably bringing about communism, Islam places natural laws in the character of Allah himself, not as part of his creation.[88]

Second, because Allah does not follow natural laws, Muslims are not obligated to understand the world or to use their minds to have dominion over it. According to Muslim and historian Caesar E. Farah, Muslim philosophy is similar to Greek philosophy, which, as we saw earlier, did not think much of history or science, because what is really *real* is the ideal. Islam, Farah wrote, sought to "*assimilate* rather than *to generate*, with the conscious striving to adapt the results of Greek thinking to Muslim philosophical conceptions."[89] The Muslim view of history, then, is quite different from the others we have studied. It does not ask its followers to imagine a fanciful utopia to come. It demands obedience to God, who is working his will in the world. To some, this may sound very similar to the Christian worldview. But the Christian view of incarnation sets Christianity apart in what we think is a very compelling way.

9. CHRISTIANITY

From the Christian perspective, history is an epic unfolding of God's ultimate plan for all humanity. Knowing that God has been active throughout history helps us understand our own roles in the day-to-day history of our lives. "It is always a 'Now,'" wrote Herbert Butterfield, "that is in direct relation to eternity—not a far future."[90]

For the Christian, history is not wrapped around certain philosophies of the past, the present plans of humans, or the future utopia that self-appointed messiahs desire. It is the unfolding of God's story in real time, the tangible manifestation of an eternal and omnipresent creator who not only set the universe in motion but is present in it. God was in the garden with Adam and Eve. He was in the burning bush, speaking to Moses. He was in the pillar of cloud by day and the pillar of fire by night, guiding the Israelites to the Promised Land. The child in the manger. The suffering Savior on the cross. The linen-wrapped body in the tomb. The victorious risen Christ. All God, every one of them, and even now God is present with us through the Holy Spirit.

The Christian story of history—beginning, middle, and end—is not of a God who must be chased after or an ethereal presence who must be dreamed about but of a person who *has* come, and *is* come, and *will* come, as real as anything is real, living in us and among us. It is the story that explains all the other stories, a narrative of redemption in which God buys back those who are made in his image. Thus we call the Christian view of history a **redemptive narrative**.

In his speech to the religiously inclined philosophers of Athens, the apostle Paul spoke of God being with us in such a way that our hearts would be tuned to his presence:

> [God] made from one man every nation of mankind to live on all the face of the earth, having determined allotted periods and the boundaries of their dwelling place, that they should seek God, and perhaps feel their way toward him and find him. Yet he is actually not far from each one of us, for "In him we live and move and have our being." As even some of your own poets have said, "For we are indeed his offspring." (Acts 17:26–28)

Redemptive Narrative: the Christian metanarrative that describes the course of history unfolding according to the biblical chronicle of God's creative act, humanity's rebellion, Christ's redemptive sacrifice, and God's eventual restoration of his creation.

This is far different from the Muslim view of history, in which God is free to intervene but is unknown to us and therefore unpredictable. In the Christian view, God makes himself known—not exhaustively but sufficiently. We see as though through a dark glass, but we see. His presence guides us, but his mystery raises our curiosity so we will seek to know him more completely. History is moving in a direction!

Christians are not blissfully ignorant of the tragedy encompassing much of our lives but place it in the context of God's fullest expression of himself: Jesus Christ. Galatians 4:4 says, "When the fullness of time had come, God sent forth his Son, born of woman, born under the law." The language is that of a pregnancy and a birth. God planted the seed of his plan, it grew, and through suffering it was born, promising redemption from pain and sorrow. Because of this, Christians hold no unreasonable expectations of perfection in our lifetimes. Rather, we anticipate persecution and trials while expecting the triumph of righteousness, peace, and joy in the end because of Jesus Christ.

> God planted the seed of his plan, it grew, and through suffering it was born, promising redemption from pain and sorrow. Because of this, Christians hold no unreasonable expectations of perfection in our lifetime.

Christians often speak of the unfolding of God's plan as a sequence of creation, fall, and redemption: even though God created the world very good, humans rebelled against him; still, God has revealed in Jesus Christ his ultimate plan for divine intervention, redemption, and restoration. Christianity is more than a mere set of ideas; it is entirely embedded in the real world of human history. Creation is sacred and stands under the blessing, judging, and redeeming purposes of God.

The idea of purpose—of the redeeming purposes of God—implies God's constant supervision, a direction for the course of human events, and an ultimate end or goal. The basis for the Christian worldview appeared in human history more than two thousand years ago in the person of Jesus Christ. While "Christ died for our sins" is solid orthodox Christian theology, "Christ died" is history. And "Christ dying so we may live" is both a guide to the present and a promise for the future. Let's take a look at each in turn—the past, present, and future—in light of Christ's sacrifice.

Making sense of the past in light of Christ's sacrifice. Christianity is rooted in history. It makes specific claims about past events and ties its very claims to truth to the validity of those claims. The Bible practically invites scrutiny with its specific claims—historical claims—about what happened when and where. It is possible to find evidence to prove or disprove them. In fact, the Bible itself claims that either Christ is a historical figure and the Bible is a historical document that describes God's communications with humanity and records real events in the life of Christ, or the Christian faith is bankrupt and our so-called faith is described as pathetic (1 Cor. 15:14).[91]

> Everyone places faith in something, hopefully something true.

Everyone places faith in something, hopefully something true. Is the Christian faith anchored in historical truth? If biblical scholarship is any indication, it is well placed indeed. This is not to say that Christianity is without its critics. Most of the negative criticism of the Bible, though, Norman L. Geisler points out, "is pre-archaeological based on unproven philosophical presuppositions that have subsequently been antiquated by archaeology."[92] The Bible was authored accurately. It tells of a Christ we know to have been an actual historical figure, and who—based on the weight of evidence—actually did die on the cross and rise again from the dead.

Making sense of the present in light of Christ's sacrifice. Clearly belief in history as the story of creation, fall, redemption, and restoration carries enormous implications for humanity. If the Christian philosophy of history is correct, the big picture of God's story invests every moment of our lives with purpose. C. S. Lewis explained: "Where a God who is totally purposive and totally foreseeing acts upon a Nature which is totally interlocked, there can be no accidents or loose ends, nothing whatever of which we can safely use the word 'merely.' Nothing is 'merely a by-product' of anything else. All results are intended from the first."[93]

This belief about the direction of history is known as a **linear conception of history**. That is, Christians believe that human history had a specific beginning (creation) and is being directed by God toward a specific end (restoration). This framework implies that historic events follow a cause-and-effect course toward that end.

The Christian idea that history is linear has influenced all of Western civilization. Prior to Christianity's influence, pagans held to a **cyclical conception of history**, believing events in consecutive societies repeated over and over. That history was directional created a unique conception of the movement of humanity through time. John Warwick Montgomery says, "The importance of the Biblical conception cannot be overstressed. Here for the first time Western man was presented with a purposive, goal-directed interpretation of history. The classical doctrine of recurrence had been able to give a 'substantiality' to history, but it had not given it any aim or direction."[94]

> *Linear Conception of History:* the belief that history follows a chronological pattern of cause and effect.

> *Cyclical Conception of History:* the belief that history follows a repeating pattern of recurring ages.

Direction implies a starting point and an ending point as well as a route. These, in turn, require revelation. Just as viewing the earth from a satellite gives a larger perspective about events on the ground, Christianity enables humanity to look at itself from above, from God's perspective. This infuses it with meaning far beyond the passing of one day into the next or the passing of one cultural system into the next.

Indeed, living as if every minute in our day is charged with meaning enables us to see our place in the entire scope of history. Butterfield explained: "There are some people who bring their sins home to themselves and say that this is a chastisement from God; or they say that God is testing them, trying them in the fire, fitting them for some more important work that he has for them to do. Those who adopt this view in their individual lives will easily see that it enlarges and projects itself onto the scale of all history."[95]

> Indeed, living as if every minute in our day is charged with meaning enables us to see our place in the entire scope of history.

Because we can see the larger view of history and our place in it through God's revelation in nature and in Scripture, we can understand the times and know what we ought to do. God works through our actions to direct history toward his ultimate end: a day of judgment, the restoration of the heavens and the earth (2 Pet. 3:13),[96] and the age to come, with Jesus Christ as King of Kings and Lord of Lords. This is a present hope as well as a future hope. Wise men still seek him, and for good reason; he is the only source of meaning in history and in life. Indeed, if what the Bible says about Christ is true, it is the very hinge on which all else in history swings. C. S. Lewis said, "The central miracle asserted by the Christian is the incarnation. They say that God became man.... If the thing happened, it was the greatest event in the history of the earth, the very thing the whole story has been about."[97]

Making sense of the future in light of Christ's sacrifice. The Bible's promise of a future kingdom ushered in by Jesus Christ is far more hopeful than any utopian scheme that sinful, mortal humans have dreamed up. Genesis 3:15 describes an ongoing battle between good and evil that involves every human being, a battle that would be resolved when the offspring of the woman (often thought of as the coming Messiah) crushed the work of the Evil One.[98] Correspondingly, Jesus is described as the "the Alpha and the Omega," the beginning and the end of history (Rev. 1:8).[99]

D. W. Bebbington says that since Jesus won the battle against evil on the cross, "the outcome of world history is therefore already assured. God will continue to direct the course of events up to their end when the outcome will be made plain."[100] At the end of all things, the day of judgment (Acts 17:31; Rom. 2:12–16)[101] will make Christ's victory over sin apparent to all. Though no Christian through the ages secured this victory, all will share in the triumph. To put it in World War II terms, we live between D-day (invasion) and V-day (victory). Redemption is on the march. It is only a matter of time. And yet the Bible doesn't tell Christians to sit back and let God do the work. Christians are to engage in exercising stewardship over creation and, when it comes to history, studying the world God created and telling the truth about the past—even when it is uncomfortable.

> Christians are to engage in exercising stewardship over creation and, when it comes to history, studying the world God created and telling the truth about the past—even when it is uncomfortable.

10. CONCLUSION

In God's plan, the difficulties we face in a fallen world have meaning. As the apostle Paul said, "I consider that our present sufferings are not worth comparing with the glory that will be revealed in us" (Rom. 8:18; 2 Cor. 4:11–18).[102] This is supremely good news. Everything else becomes meaningful in its telling. This is the true meaning of history.

With this examination of the study of history, we are nearing the completion of our text. We've looked at six dominant evangelistic worldviews and how they operate not only in the study of history but in other disciplines all college students will find familiar, including theology, philosophy, ethics, biology, psychology, sociology, law, politics, and economics. It's been a long time since we embarked on this study, though, so let's invest one more chapter in reviewing key lessons and understanding the Christian worldview in the light of everything we've looked at so far.

ENDNOTES

1. Richard Brookhiser, *James Madison* (New York: Basic Books, 2011), 249.

2. Herbert Schlossberg, *Idols for Destruction* (Nashville: Thomas Nelson, 1983), 12.

3. Quoted in Schlossberg, *Idols for Destruction*, 12–13.

4. John H. Arnold, *History: A Very Short Introduction* (Oxford, UK: Oxford University Press, 2000), 18.

5. Arnold, *History*, 33. An early example of this was Saint Augustine, who used historical arguments to support his theological arguments. See, for example, his book *City of God against the Pagans*.

6. K. A. Kitchen, *On the Reliability of the Old Testament* (Grand Rapids: Eerdmans, 2003), 500.

7. Kenneth Burke, *Attitudes toward History*, 2nd ed. (Berkeley, CA: University of California Press, 1959), 172.

8. Edward Hallet Carr, *What Is History?* (New York: Vintage Books, 1961), 5–10.

9. The doctrine of *posse comitatus* (Latin for "force of the county") has been a federal statute since 1878. It became law in response to the presence of federal troops in the former Confederate states after the Civil War. The law specifies that federal troops may not exercise the power to keep law and order outside of federal property except in very limited circumstances. This law prevents the president from using the army to increase his power over the states.

10. Nancy Isenberg, *Fallen Founder: The Life of Aaron Burr* (New York: Viking, 2007), ix.

11. Schlossberg, *Idols for Destruction*, 13.

12. G. W. F. Hegel, introduction to *Philosophy of History*, trans. J. Sibree, rev. ed. (New York: Wiley, 1944).

13. Arnold, *History*, 12.

14. Carr, *What Is History?*, 111, emphasis added.

15. Quoted in John Lukacs, *Historical Consciousness: The Remembered Past* (New Brunswick, NJ: Transaction, 1994), 152.

16. Lukacs, *Historical Consciousness*, 152–53.

17. Quoted in Arnold, *History*, 36.

18. Carr, *What Is History?*, 34.

19. Karl R. Popper, *The Poverty of Historicism* (Boston: Beacon, 1957), 3.

20. Carr, *What Is History?*, 120.

21. Schlossberg, *Idols for Destruction*, 14–15.

22. Herbert Schlossberg spends several pages grappling with an argument made by David Donald, the late Harvard professor and Pulitzer Prize–winning historian whose essay in the *New York Times*, "Our Irrelevant History," makes a particular interpretation of history seem inevitable. See the discussion in Schlossberg, *Idols for Destruction*, 22–25.

23. Herbert Butterfield, *The Whig Interpretation of History* (London: G. Bell and Sons, 1963), 12.

24. John C. Greene, "The Concept of Order in Darwinism," in Paul G. Kuntz, ed., *The Concept of Order* (Seattle: University of Washington Press, 1968), 99.

25. Emphasis is in the original. Bertrand Russell, *The Impact of Science on Society* (New York: Columbia University Press, 1951), 45.

26. Julian Huxley, *Essays of a Humanist* (New York: Harper and Row, 1964), 76.

27. Paraphrase of Spencer's ideas, Greene, "The Concept of Order in Darwinism," in Kuntz, *Concept of Order*, 94.

28. In the essay Spencer was clear that he did not hold these conclusions as tentative. They were absolute, observable, and incontrovertible. Here's an extended quotation: "The advance from the simple to the complex, through a process of successive differentiations, is seen alike in the earliest changes of the Universe to which we can reason our way back; and in the earliest changes which we can inductively establish; it is seen in the geologic and climatic evolution of the Earth, and of every single organism on its surface; it is seen in the evolution of Humanity, whether contemplated in the civilized individual, or in the aggregation of races; it is seen in the evolution of Society in respect alike of its political, its religious, and its economical organization; and it is seen in the evolution of all those endless concrete and abstract products of human activity which constitute the environment of our daily life. From the remotest past which Science can fathom, up to the novelties of yesterday, that in which Progress essentially consists, is the transformation of the homogeneous into the heterogeneous. Herbert Spencer, "Progress: Its Law and Cause," *Westminster Review* 67 (April 1857): 445–47, 451, 454–56, 464–65.

29. Paul Kurtz, ed., *Humanist Manifesto II* (Buffalo, NY: Prometheus Books, 1980), 13.

30. P. W. Atkins, *The Second Law* (New York: W. H. Freeman, 1984), 189.

31. Bertrand Russell, *The Basic Writings of Bertrand Russell*, eds. Robert E. Egner and Lester E. Denonn (New York: Simon and Schuster, 1961), 685.

32. Albert Camus, "The Myth of Sisyphus," in Walter Kaufmann, ed. and trans., *Existentialism from Dostoevsky to Sarte* (Cleveland: Meridian Books, 1956), 315.

33. Kurtz, *Humanist Manifesto II*, 16.

34. Corliss Lamont, *The Philosophy of Humanism* (New York: Frederick Ungar, 1982), 283.

35. Erich Fromm, *You Shall Be as Gods* (New York: Rinehart and Winston, 1966), 123.

36. Kurtz, *Humanist Manifesto II*, 14.

37. Isaiah Berlin, "Historical Inevitability," in Hans Meyerhoff, ed., *The Philosophy of History in Our Time* (Garden City, NY: Doubleday Anchor, 1959), 252.

38. Lamont, *Philosophy of Humanism*, 282.

39. Bertrand Russell, *Religion and Science* (Oxford, UK: Oxford University Press, 1961), 169.

40. Harry Elmer Barnes said the following about the accuracy of the Bible: "Biblical criticism, applied to the New Testament, has removed the element of supernaturalism from the biographies of its founders as thoroughly as Old Testament criticism has from those of its heroes." Harry Elmer Barnes, *The New History and the Social Studies* (New York: Century, 1925), 21. For a thoughtful and powerful response, see vol. 1 of Norman Geisler, *Systematic Theology*, 4 vols. (Minneapolis: Bethany House, 2002), chaps. 25–26.

41. Victor J. Stenger, *Not by Design* (Buffalo, NY: Prometheus Books, 1988), 186.

42. Stenger, *Not by Design*, 188.

43. Richard Carrier, *Sense and Goodness without God: A Defense of Metaphysical Naturalism* (Bloomington, IN: Author-House, 2005), 406.

44. C. S. Lewis, *The Abolition of Man* (New York: Macmillan, 1952), chap. 3.

45. Maurice Cornforth, *Historical Materialism* (New York: International Publishers, 1972), 68.

46. V. I. Lenin, *Collected Works*, 45 vols. (Moscow: Progress Publishers, 1980), 11:71.

47. Joseph Stalin, *Dialectical and Historical Materialism* (New York: International Publishers, 1977), 19.

48. Lenin, *Collected Works*, 2:57.

49. Karl Marx, Frederick Engels, and V. I. Lenin, *On Historical Materialism* (New York: International Publishers, 1974), 120. In another place Marx wrote, "Are men free to choose this or that form of society for themselves? By no means.... Assume particular stages of development in production, commerce and consumption and you will have a corresponding social structure, a corresponding organization of the family, of orders or of classes, in a word, a corresponding civil society.... It is superfluous to add that men are not free to choose their productive forces—which are the basis of all their history." Karl Marx, *The Poverty of Philosophy* (New York: International Publishers, 1936), 152–53.

50. Maurice Cornforth, *The Open Philosophy and the Open Society* (New York: International Publishers, 1976), 159.

51. Howard Zinn, *A People's History of the United States: 1492–Present* (New York: HarperCollins, 2005), 646.

52. Dan Flynn, "Master of Deceit," *Front Page Magazine*, June 3, 2003, http://archive.frontpagemag.com/readArticle .aspx?ARTID=17914.

53. Kenneth Burke, *Attitudes toward History*, 2nd ed. (Berkeley, CA: University of California Press, 1959), 322.

54. Marx, Engels, and Lenin, *On Historical Materialism*, 135.

55. Alasdair MacIntyre, *Whose Justice? Which Rationality?* (Notre Dame: University of Notre Dame Press, 1989), 357.

56. Christopher Butler, *Postmodernism: A Very Short Introduction* (Oxford, UK: Oxford University Press, 2002), 32–36.

57. Umberto Eco, *The Name of the Rose* (Boston: Mariner, 1983), 527.

58. Hayden White, *Metahistory* (Baltimore: Johns Hopkins University Press, 1973), ix.

59. Hayden White, quoted in E. Culpepper Clark, "Argument and Historical Analysis," in J. Robert Cox and Charles A. Willard, eds., *Advances in Argumentation Theory and Research* (Carbondale, IL: Southern Illinois University Press, 1982), 314.

60. Mark Poster, *Foucault, Marxismn and History: Mode of Production versus Mode of Information* (Cambridge, MA: Polity Press, 1984), quoted in Keith Windschuttle, *The Killing of History: How Literary Critics and Social Theories Are Murdering Our Past* (San Francisco: Encounter Books, 1996), 132.

61. Michel Foucault, *Power/Knowledge: Selected Interviews and Other Writings 1972–1977*, ed. Colin Gordon (New York: Pantheon Books, 1980), 193, quoted in Windschuttle, *Killing of History*, 151.

62. Foucault, *Power/Knowledge*, 62.

63. Jacques Derrida, *Moscou aller-retour* (Saint Etienne: De l'Aube, 1995), quoted in Stephen R. C. Hicks, *Explaining Postmodernism: Skepticism and Socialism from Rousseau to Foucault* (Tempe, AZ: Scholargy, 2004), 186.

64. Gene Edward Veith, *Postmodern Times: A Christian Guide to Contemporary Thought and Culture* (Wheaton, IL: Crossway Books, 1994), 161.

65. Quoted in Dennis McCallum, ed., *The Death of Truth* (Minneapolis: Bethany House, 1996), 133.

66. Quoted in McCallum, *Death of Truth*, 138–39.

67. See Mark Goldblatt's article, "Can Humanists Talk to Poststructuralists?," in *Academic Questions* 18, no. 2 (Spring 2005). Goldblatt's answer: "This is why humanists, in the end, cannot talk to poststructuralists." Goldblatt levels at

Derrida the following charge: "For Derrida winds up his analysis with another logical throw-away: 'Neither/nor, that is, simultaneously either/or.' In other words, whatever Derrida is affirming, he is also simultaneously denying. From a humanist perspective, the only way to read Derrida on his own terms is mentally to insert the phrase 'or not' after every one of his statements" (59).

68. Marilyn Ferguson, *The Aquarian Conspiracy* (Los Angeles: J. P. Tarcher, 1980), 71.

69. Quoted in Robert M. Oates, *Permanent Peace* (Fairfield, IA: Institute of Science, Technology, and Public Policy, 2002), 190.

70. Shakti Gawain, *Living in the Light* (San Rafael, CA: New World Library, 1986), 179.

71. David Spangler, *Emergence: The Rebirth of the Sacred* (New York: Dell, 1984), 12.

72. Marianne Williamson, *A Return to Love: Reflections on the Principles of "A Course in Miracles"* (New York: HarperCollins, 1989), 71.

73. Benjamin B. Ferencz and Ken Keyes Jr., *Planethood* (Coos Bay, OR: Vision Books, 1988), 141.

74. Ferencz and Keyes, *Planethood*, 33.

75. Paul Davies, "Great Balls of Fire," *New Scientist* 24, vol. 31 (December 1987): 64.

76. Joseph Campbell, *The Power of Myth* (New York: Doubleday, 1988), 18.

77. Campbell, *Power of Myth*, 30.

78. Eckhart Tolle, *A New Earth* (New York: Plume, 2005), 156.

79. M. Scott Peck, *The Road Less Traveled* (New York: Simon and Schuster, 1978), 269–70. Peck apparently converted late in life to Christianity, but his statement in this particular book underscores the way New Spiritualists often appropriate biblical language to reach distinctly unbiblical conclusions.

80. Quoted in Dean C. Halverson, *Crystal Clear: Understanding and Reaching New Agers* (Colorado Springs: NavPress, 1990), 77.

81. Donald H. Yott, *Man and Metaphysics* (New York: Weiser, 1980), 74.

82. Levi H. Dowling and Eva H. Dowling, *The Aquarian Gospel of Jesus the Christ* (Los Angeles: DeVorss, 1972), 24.

83. Quoted in Khurshid Ahmad, ed., *Islam: Its Meaning and Message* (Leicester: Islamic Foundation, 1999), 253.

84. Hammudah Abdalati, *Islam in Focus* (Indianapolis: American Trust, 1975), 51.

85. One sobering analysis of Islam's inherent militancy is Serge Trifkovic, *The Sword of the Prophet: Islam, History, Theology, and Impact on the World* (Boston: Regina Orthodox Press, 2002). See also the Bat Ye'or, *Islam and Dhimmitude: Where Civilizations Collide*, trans. Miriam Kochan and David Littman (Madison, NJ: Fairleigh Dickinson University Press, 2002); and Cyril Glasse, *The Concise Encyclopedia of Islam* (New York: HarperCollins, 1991), 209, cited in Alvin J. Schmidt, *The Great Divide: The Failure of Islam and the Triumph of the West* (Boston: Regina Orthodox Press, 2004), 222.

86. According to Mark Steyn, Islam is "the fastest-growing religion in Europe and North America: in the United Kingdom, more Muslims than Christians attend religious services each week. Meanwhile, in areas of traditionally moderate Islam, from the Balkans to Indonesia, Muslims are becoming radicalized and fiercer in their faith." One of the radicalized groups serving Islam today, the infamous al-Qaeda founded by Osama bin Laden, has an English counterpart called Tablighi Jamaat. According to Steyn, "Tablighi Jamaat is an openly Islamist organization of global reach and, according to the FBI, an al Qaeda recruiting front for terrorists." The organization currently has a mosque capable of hosting six thousand worshippers and is actively seeking to build what will be, according to Steyn, "the biggest house of worship in the United Kingdom: it will hold 70,000 people—only 10,000 fewer than the Olympic stadium, and 67,000 more than the largest Christian facility (Liverpool's Anglican cathedral)." Mark Steyn, *America Alone: The End of the World as We Know It* (Washington, DC: Regnery, 2006), 95.

87. One of the many sources available for these purposes is Stuart Robinson, *Mosque and Miracles: Revealing Islam and God's Grace* (Queensland, Australia: City Harvest, 2004).

88. Sociologist Rodney Stark writes, "Allah is not presented as a lawful creator but has been conceived of as an extremely active God who intrudes on the world as he deems it appropriate. Consequently, there soon arose a major theological bloc within Islam that condemned all efforts to formulate natural laws as blasphemy insofar as they denied Allah's freedom to act." Rodney Stark, *For the Glory of God* (Princeton, NJ: Princeton University Press, 2003), 154.

89. Quoted in Stark, *For the Glory of God*, 155. According to Stark, the focus on assimilating rather than generating explains why the Muslims—and the Greeks before them—had "a theoretical collection of facts, and isolated crafts and technologies," but "they never broke through to real science" (152).

90. Herbert Butterfield, *Christianity and History* (New York: Charles Scribner's Sons, 1950), 66.

91. First Corinthians 15:14: "If Christ has not been raised, then our preaching is in vain and your faith is in vain."

92. Geisler, *Systematic Theology*, 1:461.

93. C. S. Lewis, *Miracles: A Preliminary Study* (London: Geoffrey Bles, 1952), 149. Norman Geisler says of Lewis's work on miracles, "The best overall apologetic for miracles written in this century." Norman Geisler, *Miracles and Modern Thought* (Dallas: Probe Ministries International, 1982), 167. Geisler's work is part of the Christian Free University curriculum and is self-published.

94. John Warwick Montgomery, *The Shape of the Past* (Minneapolis: Bethany Fellowship, 1975), 42.

95. Quoted in C. T. McIntire, ed., *God, History, and Historians: An Anthology of Modern Christian Views of History* (Oxford, UK: Oxford University Press, 1977), 201. Creation, fall, redemption—the progression of events in God's creation: that all was created good, but humanity rebelled against God and requires divine redemption. Thus, all of creation is sacred and stands under the blessing, judging, and redeeming purposes of God.

96. Second Peter 3:13: "According to [God's] promise we are waiting for new heavens and a new earth in which righteousness dwells."

97. Lewis, *Miracles*, 173–74.

98. Genesis 3:15: "'I will put enmity between you and the woman, and between your offspring and her offspring; he shall bruise your head, and you shall bruise his heel.'"

99. Revelation 1:8: "'I am the Alpha and the Omega,' says the Lord God, 'who is and who was and who is to come, the Almighty.'"

100. D. W. Bebbington, *Patterns in History* (Downers Grove, IL: InterVarsity, 1979), 169.

101. Acts 17:31: "[God] has fixed a day on which he will judge the world in righteousness by a man whom he has appointed; and of this he has given assurance to all by raising him from the dead"; Romans 2:12–16: "All who have sinned without the law will also perish without the law, and all who have sinned under the law will be judged by the law. For it is not the hearers of the law who are righteous before God, but the doers of the law who will be justified. For when Gentiles, who do not have the law, by nature do what the law requires, they are a law to themselves, even though they do not have the law. They show that the work of the law is written on their hearts, while their conscience also bears witness, and their conflicting thoughts accuse or even excuse them on that day when, according to my gospel, God judges the secrets of men by Christ Jesus."

102. Romans 8:18: "I consider that the sufferings of this present time are not worth comparing with the glory that is to be revealed to us"; 1 Corinthians 4:11–18: "We who live are always being given over to death for Jesus' sake, so that the life of Jesus also may be manifested in our mortal flesh. So death is at work in us, but life in you. Since we have the same spirit of faith according to what has been written, 'I believed, and so I spoke,' we also believe, and so we also speak, knowing that he who raised the Lord Jesus will raise us also with Jesus and bring us with you into his presence. For it is all for your sake, so that as grace extends to more and more people it may increase thanksgiving, to the glory of God. So we do not lose heart. Though our outer self is wasting away, our inner self is being renewed day by day. For this light momentary affliction is preparing for us an eternal weight of glory beyond all comparison, as we look not to the things that are seen but to the things that are unseen. For the things that are seen are transient, but the things that are unseen are eternal."

CHAPTER **18**

18

CONCLUSION

1. THE WORLD IS NO LONGER FLAT

Once Square met Sphere, he would never be the same. Having lived in a two-dimensional world all his life, Square could not even conceive of a third dimension. When the messianic Sphere selected him to experience space and then proclaim freedom from flatness to his two-dimensional world, Square returned from Spaceland filled with joy. But he was promptly imprisoned and his message of freedom stifled. The rest of Flatland just couldn't handle the truth.

Edwin A. Abbott's story *Flatland* has been put to many uses, including as an anti-Christian diatribe. But the central question asked in the story is an important one. What would happen if we suddenly discovered that there was more to reality than we had previously experienced? Would this be seen as a revolutionary breakthrough or as a threat?

In this book we have explored an intriguing possibility: rather than *preventing* us from grasping reality, Christianity sets us free to truly experience the fullness of reality. Perhaps, as J. R. R. Tolkien persuaded C. S. Lewis, Christianity is the great myth that has come true. It brings reality into focus in a new way—not only the outer world of society with its laws and structures but also the inner world where we long for healing and wholeness. In Christianity we find something to believe in that is worthy of our faith. We find a proclamation of hope that reaches across all times and all cultures. Suddenly a dimension of aliveness has been added to our existence.

But proclaiming the truth of Christianity is threatening to many, just as spheres, cones, and cylinders were a threat to a world that had known only circles, triangles, and squares. Will we continue to proclaim it anyway? This concluding chapter is our opportunity to review what we've learned so far, discern what difference it makes in our lives, and determine how we should share it with others.

2. Ideas Flow in Patterns

As we saw in chapter 1, people find success in any endeavor—whether tennis or chess or philosophy—by recognizing the rules and patterns that exist. If we can understand them, we will know what to do. Do these patterns and rules extend to life itself? Can we find answers to life's big questions? It's taken quite a number of pages to arrive at a conclusion, but the answer is yes.

We reached this conclusion by exploring six major worldviews. A worldview, as you remember, is "a pattern of ideas, beliefs, convictions, and habits *that help us make sense of God, the world, and our relationship to God and the world.*" A worldview provides a map to help us know where we need to go in life, the distance between where we are and where we need to go, and how best to get from where we are to where we need to be. Let's review what we've learned about each of these six worldviews.

3. Islam

As we have seen, Islam is a major world religion, boasting a membership of nearly one-fourth of the world's population. The largest Muslim populations in the world reside not in Arab countries but in Indonesia, Pakistan, India, and Bangladesh. Founded by Muhammad, Islam teaches that God, *Allah* in Arabic, created everything and set the universe in order.[1] Islam's distinctives include the following:

***Islam* means "submission."** A Muslim is "one who submits" to Allah and the principles of Islam as embodied in the *ummah*, the worldwide community of Muslims. For Muslims, the *ummah* binds together religious commands, ideology, and cultural practices, providing both a comforting sense of belonging and a reassuring hierarchy. To be separated from it is to be alienated and lost.

Muslims believe the Quran to be the only authoritative and uncorrupted scripture preserved without error. Muslims believe the words of the Quran are the literal words of God, which were dictated word for word to the prophet Muhammad through the angel Jibril (Gabriel). Muslims believe the Bible was corrupted over time and is an unreliable source of truth. The Quran, however, Muslims believe, is preserved in heaven itself (85:21–22).[2]

Muslims believe every human being is born a Muslim. Those who are not currently committed to Islam are in rebellion against their nature, Muslims say. God sent prophets to speak to the nations and correct these errors of belief and practice. In the end, everyone will submit to Allah.

Muhammad is, to Muslims, the final and best prophet. Of all the prophets Allah has sent, Muhammad and his message seal the truth of Islam. His message even supersedes the message of Jesus, and therefore Islam supersedes Christianity, in the mind of Muslims, and indeed is the *fulfillment* of it.

> Those who are not currently committed to Islam are in rebellion against their nature, Muslims say.

Islam has a conception of humanity and fallenness that is very different from that of Christianity. Muslims see humans as slaves of God, not sons and daughters made in his image. The idea of humanity falling irretrievably into sin is also foreign to Islam. To become a Muslim does not require redemption in the sense of being "made new" but adherence to the five pillars of Islam.[3] Having no concept of human fallenness, Muslims see political authority not as inherently prone to corruption but as capable of advancing God's agenda.

In this volume we have used the term *Muslim* to describe those who have grown up in Islam and try to follow its practices. *Islamists* is used for a separate group that embraces the full application of shariah law, the moral code of Islam outlined in the Quran and other teachings and rulings Muslims consider authoritative.[4]

> By committing themselves to physical violence, jihadis have made themselves into a sort of army dedicated to destroying the West.

Finally, jihadis are those willing to use force to bring about a global Islamic state. By committing themselves to physical violence, jihadis have made themselves into a sort of army dedicated to destroying the West.[5]

4. SECULARISM

The main concern for Secularists is the here and now (as opposed to eternity) and human beings (as opposed to God). Secularists close themselves off to spiritual experience, at least as it relates to public concerns, such as education and government. In the 1930s a group of atheist and agnostic professors wrote and signed a document called the *Humanist Manifesto* outlining an inspirational "faith" to replace the dogmatic "old attitudes" promoted by theistic religions. David Niose, president of the American Humanist Association, believes 12 to 18 percent of Americans are Secularists.[6] Secularism's key beliefs include the following:

Materialism: only matter exists. As Georgetown professor Jacques Berlinerblau says, "The secularish are here-and-now people. They live for this world, not for the next."[7] If

---

materialism is true, concerns about nonmaterial things like God, spirituality, or an afterlife are misguided or even dangerous.

Naturalism: everything that exists can be explained through natural processes. There is no God who created the world; our present state is best explained by the evolution of all of life, beginning with the first self-replicating molecule.

Atheism: the irrelevance of God to public life. Secularists are functionally atheistic in that they see belief in God as irrelevant and probably dangerous. Belief in God, Secularists say, keeps people unenlightened and slows human progress. Belief in a world beyond this one is an especially dire threat.[8]

Secularists are people of faith: they have deep faith in the scientific method, the theory of naturalistic evolution, and materialism. They have faith in what they consider to be reasoned arguments for their views. They have faith in human ability to solve the world's problem and create a perfect society. Above all, they have faith in their own capacity to do battle with those of a religious persuasion, until public life is swept clean of what they regard as primitive superstition.

5. MARXISM

A Marxist is one who embraces the philosophy of Karl Marx that capitalism must be overthrown. Marxism begins with socialism: heavy taxation, government control of businesses, and the elimination of laws protecting private property. Eventually the means of production will be owned in common, and government itself, Marxists say, will be unnecessary. This state of existence is called *communism*, which means "working in common."[9] One in five people in the world live under Marxist regimes, and at any major university, you'll find professors overtly evangelistic about Marxism or at least sympathetic to its aims. Marxism's key beliefs include the following:

Dialectical materialism. *Dialectic* is a view of history that says the way people view the world and act on it at any given time in history (the thesis) spawns a reaction whose goal is the negation of the way things are done (the *antithesis*).

> One in five people in the world live under Marxist regimes, and at any major university, you'll find professors overtly evangelistic about Marxism or at least sympathetic to its aims.

Materialism says that only the world of matter exists. No God or gods exist. "In our evolutionary conception of the universe," Friedrich Engels said, "there is absolutely no room for either a Creator or a Ruler."[10] To Karl Marx, the combination of the dialectic process and materialistic philosophy created the combustible materials with which those who find themselves chilled by the status quo may spark the fire of revolution.[11] Out of the ashes of the ensuing blaze, a society will rise that is more advanced, and more communist, than before (the *synthesis*).

Economic determinism. To the Marxist, everything in history can be explained by the economic struggle between the bourgeoisie (property owners) and the proletariat (property-less workers). It explains everything—politics, religion, law, and culture. Today, Marxists apply this analysis by looking at all kinds of conflicts—between the haves and have-nots, religious and nonreligious, blacks and whites, men and women, heterosexuals and homosexuals—as evidence of the dialectic process at work. Such conflicts are proxies for the true struggle. Scratch any conflict and it will bleed economics. Economic determinism says that economics, not politics, is at the root of society.

In *The Communist Manifesto*, Marx said, "The Communists disdain to conceal their views and aims. They openly declare that their ends can be attained only by the forcible overthrow of all existing social conditions."[12] Tens of millions of unmarked graves testify to the fact that the lighting of the fires of revolution, contrary to Marx's hope, led not to a glorious utopia but to something else altogether.

> Tens of millions of unmarked graves testify to the fact that the lighting of the fires of revolution, contrary to Marx's hope, led not to a glorious utopia but to something else altogether.

6. New Spirituality

What we call "New Spirituality" is often referred to as the New Age movement, neopaganism, new consciousness, or just "spirituality." Despite its frequent positive references to God and Jesus Christ, New Spirituality is committed to a radically un-Christian view of the world, the nature of God, and the purpose of human beings in this world and the next.[13] New Spirituality's influences range from Hinduism and Buddhism to the personal introspection of Ralph Waldo Emerson and Henry David Thoreau, with a good dose of pop psychology thrown in. New Spirituality's key beliefs include the following:

> New Spirituality's influences range from Hinduism and Buddhism to the personal introspection of Ralph Waldo Emerson and Henry David Thoreau, with a good dose of pop psychology thrown in.

Everything is consciousness. "The whole is made up of existence and Being, the manifested and the unmanifested, the whole and God," says Eckhart Tolle. "So when you become aligned with the whole, you become a conscious part of the interconnectedness of the whole and its purpose: the emergence of consciousness into this world."[14] For New Spiritualists, everything is energy, even thoughts.[15] Good thoughts produce good energy, and bad thoughts inhibit it.

Every person is God. If all is consciousness, and we call this consciousness "god," then god is not a separate person with identifiable attributes, as Christianity claims. Rather, New Spiritualists say, god is energy, an impersonal force of which we are a part. Every person is god. Theologians use the word *pantheism* to describe this belief. (*Pan* means "all" and *theos* means "God.")

The purpose of life is overcoming "self." New Spiritualists use the term *self* in a different way than Secularists and Postmodernists, for whom "self" is a nonreligious stand-in for the "soul." To New Spiritualists, success in life comes from being *free* from the self, from any conception of ego, from an identification as "I" or "mine." People gain temporary freedom from the self through such practices as yoga and meditation. Final freedom from self comes, New Spiritualists believe, through *reincarnation*: a series of rebirths through which they hope to become more enlightened.

What would stop us from achieving this vision? According to the Dalai Lama, an ignorant "grasping at a sense of self" is what gets in our way.[16] Forgoing the self and tapping into higher consciousness leads to true goodness. Eckhart Tolle says, "You do not become good by trying to be good, but by finding the goodness that is already within you, and allowing that goodness to emerge. But it can only emerge if something fundamental changes in your state of consciousness."[17]

7. POSTMODERNISM

Most worldviews state and defend their basic assumptions about reality. Postmodernists, though, try to position their thinking as a way to see *through* other worldviews, not as a worldview itself. *Postmodernism* is the term given to the reaction against modernism, the period of time from the 1700s through the 1900s in which biblical belief and practice gave way to scientific investigation and empiricism (the idea that we can know only what our senses can perceive). Postmodernists think any claims to objective understanding, whether scientific or religious, are arrogant and oppressive. Since worldviews are always held by people situated in particular cultures at particular times, none can achieve a pristine, God's-eye view of reality. Postmodernism's key beliefs include the following:

> Since worldviews are always held by people situated in particular cultures at particular times, none can achieve a pristine, God's-eye view of reality.

Poststructuralism. Up against the early twentieth-century emphasis on structuralism, which focused on how language functions to create and sustain culture, Postmodernism is regarded as "poststructuralist" because it focuses not on how language functions but on how it structures our relationships and interpretations of reality. To Postmodernists, when we think we are describing reality, we are only describing our particular ways of seeing the world. We are trapped in our perspectives.

Deconstruction. According to Jacques Derrida, texts of all kinds should be "deconstructed" to reveal their underlying assumptions and ideologies. Because no one's unique cultural interpretation has power over anyone else's, readers should focus on their own thoughts and feelings rather than on the meaning the author intended to communicate.[18] An author who insists on being taken literally will hear from the Postmodernist, "That's just *your* interpretation."

> Understanding the persuasive power of metanarratives, Postmodernists say, is the key to uncovering their secret power and freeing ourselves from their grip.

Subjectivity. Postmodernists think language functions as a tool of power by establishing "metanarratives," unifying stories about the world that aspire to totally explain everything as if from a God's-eye viewpoint. Metanarratives become so powerful that people who embrace them literally cannot imagine the world being any other way. Understanding the persuasive power of metanarratives, Postmodernists say, is the key to uncovering their secret power and freeing ourselves from their grip.

Social construction. We are products of our cultures. Not only are our thoughts and statements about reality constructed through our experiences with language and culture, but we ourselves are socially constructed. We don't exist as persons. We are not souls. Rather, we are "a collage of social constructs."[19]

Postmodernism claims that because we cannot know reality *exhaustively*, we cannot know it *truly*. Thoughtful philosophers, such as Edmund Husserl, have responded to this way of thinking by pointing out that thoughts are not just random; they are *about* things, and they are *intended* to be about things. Thoughts have properties as do the objects of our thoughts, and they present themselves consistently no matter who is thinking about them. If someone says A and you hear B, it is not because A has no essence but because either their speaking or your hearing is messed up. Postmodernism's attacks on language are a serious attack on meaning itself. As Michael Bauman has noted, the slaughter of hundreds of millions of innocents in the twentieth century amply demonstrates that when words lose their meaning, people lose their lives.[20]

8. CHRISTIANITY

Christianity posits the existence of God as a personal, relational, creative being who has made himself known through nature and through Scripture. God is not a force to be used but a person to be known. Relationship is not something God *does* but something he *is*. God is trinity, one God made manifest in three persons: God the Father, God the Son, and God the Holy Spirit.[21] This relationship in the Godhead is closely tied to who we are and what God would have us do. Matthew 28:19 says, "Go therefore and make disciples of all nations, baptizing them in the name of the *Father* and of the *Son* and of the *Holy Spirit*." All three are critical to our mission in the world. Christianity's key concepts include the following:

God is the designer. Though the universe is full of energy, pure energy does not create. Only persons create. As the English astronomer and mathematician Fred Hoyle pointed out, there is a better chance of producing a Boeing 747 via a junkyard explosion than there is of arriving at life by accident.[22] The undirected flow of energy can never explain the complexity of even the simplest living systems, not to mention the complex living systems we see every day.[23] Christianity says a creator-God, not a sequence of random cosmic accidents, is responsible for an orderly, beautiful, meaningful cosmos.

Humans are made in God's image and yet are fallen. Only in the Bible do we find an adequate basis for our personhood, with a soul composed of will, intellect, and emotions. The Bible's description of humanity's fall into sin further explains why there is hate in our hearts (Jer. 17:9),[24] and indeed, why the entire universe "groans" (Rom. 8:20–22).[25] Disobedience broke all of the key relationships in our lives. We were made to walk in God's straight way; in sin we veer toward the abyss.

Humans may experience redemption. Some worldviews say there is no purpose to our existence beyond the physical. Other worldviews say there is no purpose to physical existence beyond the spiritual. In Christianity, Jesus Christ, being fully God and fully man, became flesh and dwelled among his people, offering humanity a way out of its sinful state of rebellion and brokenness (Rom. 5:6–8).[26] By acknowledging that Jesus is Lord (Rom. 10:9),[27] we can trade the exhausting belief in a cycle of rebirths into a one-time rebirth as a child of God (1 Pet. 1:23).[28]

Humans have purpose. Once spiritual rebirth takes place, our growth in understanding God develops as we love him with our hearts, souls, minds, and strength (Mark 12:30).[29] In regard to our minds, the apostle Paul told believers in Rome to "renew their minds" so they

> We can trade the exhausting belief in a cycle of rebirths into a one-time rebirth as a child of God.

could understand God's will (Rom. 12:1–2).[30] To Timothy, Paul said, "Do your best to present yourself to God as one approved, a worker who has no need to be ashamed, rightly handling the word of truth" (2 Tim. 2:15).

Reality is knowable. Christianity says God's revelation of himself in nature and Scripture enables us to know him not only as creator and redeemer but also as a moral lawgiver. We can discern from God's revelation a system of ethics by which we can know the difference between right and wrong, live accordingly, and encourage others to do so as well. This knowledge is in the hearts of all (Rom. 2:15).[31] Professor J. Budziszewski frames it succinctly when he says there are some things "we can't not know."[32]

9. So Which Worldview Is Best?

Everyone likes to win. Everyone wants to think their worldview is the most reasonable and intelligent and that it answers the questions about what is wrong with the world, how it might be fixed, and why others ought to adopt that particular worldview.

But the collision of worldviews is not like a tournament in which worldview "teams" battle with one another for bragging rights. It is rather more like a rescue operation. Humanity is adrift and flailing, and each "rescue team" brings equipment to the scene in hopes of being helpful, whether that equipment is logic, livability, internal peace, or evidence of success.

Sometimes worldviews bring the wrong equipment to the scene of the rescue. Other times they simply do not possess what is needed for a successful rescue. For example, if we are *spiritually* in peril, then worldviews that deny the existence of anything spiritual won't have a rope long enough to reach us in the depths of our drowning. If our spiritual peril has implications for the physical world, a worldview that denies the existence of the physical world won't be able to tell that someone is actually drowning in the first place. And a worldview that believes we have no direct access to reality will just chat about humanity's dilemma even as it slips beneath the waves.

So while worldviews may get certain things correct, it's imperative that they get enough correct. There is more than just one test for worldviews. There are at least four that should be considered:

1. **The test of reason**: Is it reasonable? Can it be logically stated and defended?
2. **The test of the outer world**: Is there some external, corroborating evidence to support it?
3. **The test of the inner world**: Does it adequately address the "victories, disappointments, blessings, crises, and relationships of our everyday world"?
4. **The test of the real world**: Are its consequences good or bad when applied in any given cultural context?[33]

Christianity claims to meet not just one or two of these tests but all four. Acknowledging this does not make Christians any better than anyone else. It just shows that Christianity best describes the contours of reality as it actually exists, can be logically defended as true, enables us to live in harmony with our creator and our fellow humans, and carries with it positive consequences when applied to society. Christianity is the worldview best able to resolve humanity's plight both spiritually and physically.

We have seen throughout this book that Christianity's doctrine of humans having inherent value as God's image bearers led to the development of science, education, modern medicine, and many other things we find valuable and good. When Christianity came on the scene, the most advanced cultures in the world were haughty and aristocratic, with no respect for ordinary people.[34] And yet Jesus taught that the "last will be first and the first will be last" (Matt. 20:16; Mark 10:43; Luke 22:27). Christians elevated the status of women, built hospitals and schools, and instituted ministries to the poor. It was because of Christianity that a sustained opposition to slavery arose.[35]

> Christians elevated the status of women, built hospitals and schools, and instituted ministries to the poor. It was because of Christianity that a sustained opposition to slavery arose.

Some worldviews are almost unthinkingly optimistic about the human condition. Christianity is not among them. The Christian doctrine of the fall identifies the root problem that is the source of all evil and corruption in the world. Is it not ironic that the worldview proclaiming the corruption of humankind has led to so much good, while worldviews proclaiming the goodness of humankind have led to so much corruption? Marxism is the clearest example, having staked its credibility in direct opposition to biblical truth. It led to the slaughter of more than one hundred million people, more than twice the combined dead from World Wars I and II.[36] Ideas have consequences. Good ideas have good consequences, and bad ideas have bad ones.

What about faith? As we have seen, all worldviews involve faith. A valid faith is not just one a person can sustain but one whose object is *worthy* of that faith. Is Christianity worthy? Through our study we have come to see that Christianity is more than a set of commands and inspirational sayings. It is a story of a personal, relational God who created optimal conditions for human flourishing against which humanity has rebelled and continues to rebel. It's also the story of the Creator buying back the rebels in order to set things right again. It is the one story that makes sense of all the others.

As we draw to a close, let's review what each worldview says about the ten academic disciplines we've studied, with a specific emphasis on the reasonableness of the Christian worldview.

10. Theology

Theology is the study of God and seeks to answer the questions, "Is there a God" and "How does God relate to the world?" Thomas Aquinas described theology as the queen of the sciences and philosophy as merely its handmaiden, because our understanding of God enables us to understand everything else. Like Christianity, **Islam** posits belief in one God who exists, who created the

> Thomas Aquinas described theology as the queen of the sciences and philosophy as merely its handmaiden, because our understanding of God enables us to understand everything else.

world, and who will one day hold humans to account. Unlike Christianity, Muslims reject the doctrine of the Trinity and therefore the idea that Jesus Christ was God in the flesh.

Secularism is, as the American philosopher Harold H. Titus says, a "religion without God"[37] that has "abandoned all conceptions of a supernatural and all forms of cosmic support."[38] Secularism holds that God is either nonexistent or irrelevant.

> **Secularism holds that God is either nonexistent or irrelevant.**

Both views put humanity in God's place. **Marxism** does not follow Secularism in attempting to soften atheism's image. From the days of Marx to the present, Marxism has consistently presented itself as atheistic: God does not, cannot, and must not exist.[39] God is an impediment to Marxism's aims.[40]

Postmodernism holds that no religious truth claims can be known to accurately describe reality.[41] Secularists and Marxists are atheist by conviction; classic Postmodernism, on the other hand, is atheistic by *consequence*. True knowledge about God is impossible, and any knowledge we claim to have about him is socially constructed. To **New Spirituality**, though, God definitely exists, but not as a person. God is the spiritual energy of which the universe is composed. For New Spiritualists, there is no difference in essence between the Creator and the creation. We are, as Ralph Waldo Emerson put it, "part or particle of God."[42]

Up against these other worldviews, **Christianity** boldly proclaims the existence of a personal, triune God who desires to be in relationship with those who bear his image. From the very first verse of the Bible, "In the beginning God created the heavens and the earth" (Gen. 1:1), Christianity proclaims God as designer. This comports with our observations.

> **God's orderly nature led to modern science.**

If the universe were disorderly or chaotic, we couldn't expect it to behave in meaningful ways under controlled conditions. God's orderly nature led to modern science, according to C. S. Lewis; people "expected Law in Nature because they believed in a Legislator."[43]

But God is not a detached designer. The Bible presents him as all-powerful, self-determining, holy, patient, and loving. If such a God exists, Secularism and Marxism fall short; they fail to explain the "why" behind the "what" of life. New Spirituality would also fall short because its conception of God as an "it" fails to describe God as he actually exists. If God is triune; if he is truly three coexistent, coeternal persons in one, equal in purpose and in essence but different in function, then Islam cannot account for God's love or his sacrifice for our sins. There is no security, just severity. And if God exists and is personal and triune, Postmodernism's understanding of reality as socially constructed fails to explain the world as it is.[44]

> **From the Christian viewpoint, it is not that the truth about God is *unknowable* or that we are confused; it is that truth is *knowable* and we have *rebelled*.**

From the Christian viewpoint, it is not that the truth about God is *unknowable* or that we are confused; it is that truth is *knowable* and we have *rebelled*. Because of God's offer of redemption, we can live as if the universe is as purposeful as it appears to be.

11. PHILOSOPHY

Philosophy means the "love of wisdom." Our study of philosophy focused on three questions: (1) "What is ultimately real?" (metaphysics); (2) "What does it mean to know?" (epistemology); and (3) "With what part of our being do we contemplate these questions?" (mind/body problem). **Islam** affirms the reality of both the natural and the supernatural, the material and the immaterial. Islam also affirms that God created the universe ex nihilo, and that while he remains separate from creation, he actively sustains it and reveals himself in it.[45] To Muslims, the only way to know reality is to study the Quran and the example of Muhammad, because only they are authoritative.

The core tenets of **Secularism** in philosophy are materialism and naturalism. To Secularists, the material world is all that exists, and all phenomena have a natural explanation. If only nature exists, then the immaterial (and supernatural)—the soul, the afterlife, God—do not exist by definition. Nothing but the universe exists, and the only way to reliably understand reality is the scientific method. **Marxism** agrees with Secularism in its denial of the supernatural. The universe is all that exists and all that ever will exist. How do we know what we know? According to the Marxist, the answer is science. For the dialectical materialist, only matter actually exists. It is eternal and everything comes from it, even societal interrelationships and what we consider to be our minds.

To **New Spirituality**, ultimate reality is consciousness, "the essence of existence, the life force within all things."[46] Secularism and Marxism say that only *nature exists*; New Spirituality says only *spirit* exists, and we can know it by getting in touch with our "higher selves." When it comes to knowing reality, **Postmodernism** says we have no capacity as humans to transcend our cultural and personal experiences to obtain a God's-eye view. Our explanations of reality aren't really explanations; they're interpretations based on our situations in life. Essences, substances, and literal identities are not real. They're just words.

Christian philosophy is regaining ground these days as many top philosophers see materialist explanations as untenable.[47] The work of Christian philosophers is demonstrating that the battle of ideas isn't *reason* versus faith but *faith* versus faith, and that Christian faith is well placed. **Christianity** says we can know things because their order has been made sensible through Jesus Christ, the incarnation of the Logos.

> The work of Christian philosophers is demonstrating that the battle of ideas isn't *reason* versus faith but *faith* versus faith, and that Christian faith is well placed.

In metaphysics, Christianity posits mind before matter; God before people; plan and design before creation; life from life; and enlightenment from *the* Light. The orderly universe was conceived first in the mind of God. Without Logos there would be no cosmos. Because of this, Christians are not surprised to find every level of the cosmos—subatomic, atomic, organic, inorganic, subhuman, human, earth, moon, sun, stars, galaxies—manifesting order, rationality, and consistency that reflects design. Thoughtful Christians ought to see beyond the cold rationality of scientific observation, though. Design in nature is something that may be joyfully explored through poetry, art, and literature, as well as through science.

The Christian view of the mind/body problem is also gaining influence because of its claim that mind, or consciousness, is not reducible to the material (or physical) body (or brain). Christians believe the powers of the mind to be a reflection of the image of God. For this reason, Christians see the nature of the mind as evidence for the existence of the nonnatural reality. As philosopher J. P. Moreland notes, naturalism cannot account for consciousness and mental events; theism can.[48]

12. ETHICS

The study of right and wrong, or *ethics*—from the Greek word *ethos*, meaning "character"—has two functions. First, it is a guide to action, answering the question, "How should we live?" That is, what does it mean to pursue a life that not merely *feels* good but actually *is* good? And if *everyone* lived this way, would it be good for all of us? Second, ethics proposes a way to think through what life is about. It has the clarifying effect of shining light on life's most important questions; indeed, many of those questions are unanswerable without it.

> **Muslims believe Islamic law is by definition ethical, and what is ethical ought to be enshrined in every nation's laws.**

"There is no division of ethics and law" in **Islam**, says the Swedish Muslim writer S. Parvez Manzoor.[49] Muslims believe Islamic law is by definition ethical, and what is ethical ought to be enshrined in every nation's laws. Historically, Muslims derive their ethics from the Quran and the Hadith, which describes the actions of Muhammad that Muslims consider to be exemplary.[50]

Simply put, **Secularism** binds itself to a purely naturalistic explanation for ethics. "We have not found authoritative ethical prescriptions built into the order of things," writes Simon Blackburn. "No god wrote the laws of good behavior into the cosmos. Nature has no concern for good or bad, right or wrong."[51]

In **Marxism**, everything in the universe—including society—is in a state of constant change, moving society upward toward the elimination of all social and economic class

> **In Marxism, everything in the universe—including society—is in a state of constant change, moving society upward toward the elimination of all social and economic class distinctions.**

distinctions. Anything promoting this advance is right. Anything hindering it is wrong. This is called *proletariat morality*.

In **New Spirituality**, ethics is seen as something that happens inside a person, not the result of divine commands or societal expectations. Internalized values allow us to seek higher consciousness; external limits block our ability to get in touch with inner truth. And yet we are held accountable through the law of karma: your actions will ultimately return to you, good or bad.[52]

Postmodernism looks with suspicion on both revelation and modern reason as sources of morality. The British essayist Adam Phillips states bluntly, "Universal moral principles must be eradicated and reverence for individual and cultural uniqueness inculcated."[53]

Christianity says that just as the law of gravity is apparent to anyone who jumps out of an upper-story window, what is morally true can be seen by those with an undistorted ability to perceive. Ethics is simply an expansion of a generally revealed moral order. All things good, true, and beautiful are based in God's character as revealed in nature and Scripture. We ought to speak truth not because we'll feel better about it or because it is reasonable to do so but because *God is truth*. We ought to pursue justice not because it helps us maintain power or because the law commands it but because *God is just*. We ought to express mercy not because it will make us happy or because it is our duty but because *God is mercy*.

God is everywhere, Christianity says, so an ethical system based on his character will reside in every soul across all cultures at all times. Calvin D. Linton, one-time professor at George Washington University, found this to be so in actual fact. Even among the diversity of the world's cultures there seems to be a common moral law that materialism or naturalism are at a loss to explain.[54] Christians see this as evidence of a universal law, and thus a universal lawgiver. Every ethical system must either explain away such evidence or account for it.

13. BIOLOGY

Bios means "life." Biology is the study of life. The most basic question of biology is "How did life come into existence?" The question of first origin requires contemplation of God, even for scientists.

Islam, along with Christianity, parts company with materialistic worldviews that deny the existence of God and assert a naturalistic origin and evolution of the world. As Badru D. Kateregga says, "Muslims, like Christians, do witness that God is the Creator. As Creator, he is other than creation. He is not nature; he is above and beyond his creation (transcendent). Muslims believe that God's creation is perfect."[55]

The respected paleontologist George Gaylord Simpson summarized **Secularism** in biology when he said, "Man is the result of a purposeless and natural process that did not have him in mind. He was not planned."[56] As for all the rest of life, Cornell University professor William Provine, a leading historian of science, wrote, "Modern science directly implies that the world is organized strictly in accordance with mechanistic principles. There are no purposive principles whatsoever in nature."[57]

For **Marxism**, only matter exists, and Charles Darwin's theory made it plausible to believe this. Second, and more important, Marx believed Darwin's evolutionary theory justified his views of human society. If biological life evolves toward greater complexity, perhaps sociological life does as well, maybe even toward Marx's longed-for classless state.

New Spiritualist biology is based on a belief in positive evolutionary change over time. This approach does not focus on biological change as much as humanity's upward move toward higher consciousness. Deepak Chopra says, "Spirituality can be seen as a higher form of evolution, best described as 'metabiological'—beyond biology."[58] To New Spiritualists, everything is ultimately energy that will allow people to achieve unity with others in a kind of *collective consciousness*.

By contrast, in **Postmodernism**, everything—including science and philosophy—is experienced within the context of culturally bound stories. Postmodernist Terry Eagleton says, "Science and philosophy must jettison their grandiose metaphysical claims and view themselves more modestly as just another set of narratives."[59] Evolution did not have us in

---

mind. Even when we say "us," we're using words to interpret what we see, not describing an actual essence such as humanness.

The field of biology—and especially the origin of life—is highly relevant to **Christianity**. From a Christian perspective, God created humankind, not the other way around. As Oxford University mathematician John Lennox phrases it, "Genesis affirms that (human) life has a chemical base, but Genesis denies the reductionist addendum of the materialist—that life is nothing but chemistry."[60]

> From a Christian perspective, God created humankind, not the other way around.

The evidence for a strictly material explanation for life is not nearly as strong as materialists would like it to be. Life only comes from preexisting life. If you start with nothing, you end with nothing. But the late Nobel Prize–winner George Wald of Harvard University stubbornly insisted that the "reasonable" view was to believe in spontaneous generation because it was the only alternative to believing "in a single, primary act of supernatural creation."[61] More recently, Harvard chemist George Whitesides made a similar admission: "Most chemists believe, as do I, that life emerged spontaneously from mixtures of molecules in the prebiotic Earth. How? I have no idea."[62]

Further, it is unlikely that random-chance processes could produce anything recognizable as intelligent. In our experience, language and information-rich systems always come from intelligence. This makes it all the more striking that life itself is built upon a language-based code in our DNA. DNA contains computer-like commands that provide instructions for building molecular machines that operate at near 100 percent energetic efficiency inside of cells. For Christian biologists, the world is bright and resonant in light of God's existence. As a piece of art suggests an artist, our orderly and complex universe suggests a designer. This insight makes true discovery possible and meaningful.

14. PSYCHOLOGY

Psychology is the study of who and what we are, as well as how we develop as human beings, personally and socially. Psychology follows theology: our understanding of God has massive implications for the discipline of psychology starting with the question of whether there even is any kind of reality outside of the material world, and followed closely by the question of whether we are responsible to anything higher than our own sense of self. The word *psyche* is Greek for "soul." *Psychology* literally means "the study of the soul." This implies that there is an immaterial or spiritual aspect of reality that must be understood. Not every worldview, however, acknowledges that.

Psychology in **Islam** is straightforward: we find healing and peace not by becoming more like our creator or by pursuing our own good or by meditation but by submission to God. The Quran states, "Those who believe, and whose hearts find satisfaction in the remembrance of God: for without doubt in the remembrance of God do hearts find satisfaction. For those who believe and work righteousness, is (every) blessedness, and a beautiful place of (final) return" (13:28–29).

Secular psychology is shaped by two fundamental assumptions: (1) the idea of a personal God is a myth, and (2) we are purely physical beings, highly evolved animals produced by millions of years of naturalistic causes and processes. It is a person's physical circumstances and physical processes rather than spiritual problems that lead to psychological illness. Self-actualization will allow a person to become healthy and happy.[63] The founder of **Marxist** psychology, Ivan P. Pavlov, concluded that all animal activity could be accounted for in behaviorist terms.[64] Humans could be conditioned to do good, and researchers who understood how to control their development could strive for the perfection of the human race.[65]

The **New Spiritualist** view goes in the opposite direction; based on the Buddhist tradition, it denies the self altogether. The idea of the "self," Eckhart Tolle argues, leads to an unhealthy focus on ego. Only when we rid ourselves of this focus and tap into universal truth in the form of higher consciousness can we be set free from psychological unease.

In **Postmodernism** the ideas of "self" or "soul" are obsolete. Humans have no identifiable essence. Our sense of self is a social construct and is constantly being reconstructed based on the cultures in which we live. We have, therefore, a multiplicity of "selves."[66] All talk of souls and egos are just stories told by our various selves.

Christian psychology begins with personhood. God is a person, Christianity says, and our personhood is somehow related to his. As J. P. Moreland and Scott Rae say, "There is something about the way God is that is like the way we are."[67] It stands to reason that God's magnificent creation required thinking, planning, artistry, and execution—all qualities God has shared with us, his image bearers. God reveals himself through creation (general revelation) and Scripture (special revelation) as a person whose nature is justice, love, mercy, and grace. Our souls are the housing for our image bearing.

> Christian psychology begins with personhood.

Christians see psychology, when done from a standpoint of biblical truth, as opening up and examining the idea of what it means to be a soul. Thus, we can better understand ourselves and live together. Christian psychology helps in this process by acknowledging all aspects of reality—the physical, spiritual, social, and relational—that offer true insight and healing.

Christians take the Bible's statements regarding body, breath of life, soul, spirit, heart, and mind to mean that we have an immaterial as well as a material reality.[68] Scientists have begun to amass corroborating evidence for this view, to the point where it is now respectable to think that materialism fails to account for all of reality, and that something more must exist.[69] This is a good thing, because the Christian view of the soul is gloriously uplifting. It accounts for identity and memory.[70] It helps free people from guilt. It enables personal responsibility. It focuses on pursuing health rather than avoiding illness. It keeps people away from harmful behaviors. It restores purpose in life.

15. SOCIOLOGY

Socios is the Greek word from which we get our word *society*. Whereas psychology studies the individual and how he or she relates to others, sociology studies the interactions of individuals and society. When it comes to the actual organization of society, **Islam** does not distinguish between social institutions and the state. Islam is a comprehensive reality, a form of government as well as a religion. The goal of Islam is to gain such power and make itself so attractive that a global Islamic state, ruled by shariah law, will emerge to solve the problems caused by people's rebellion against Allah.

Secular sociology hangs on three threads: (1) No institutions of society, such as the family, are ordained by God; (2) society causes us to do what we do: we aren't making choices but are responding to external stimuli; and (3) social life is profoundly ironic (coincidental), without purpose or design. Therefore, there is only the illusion of meaning.[71]

Marxists fervently believe humanity's evolution will move them beyond the misery-inducing capitalist structures of society. Society will heal itself when the resistance of capitalism has been broken and economic classes have ceased to exist. Even the state will not be necessary then.[72]

As we discussed in the "Psychology" chapter, the **New Spiritualist** says there is no such thing as an individual person or "self." There is only consciousness, and we are all an inseparable part of it. Psychology, the study of the person, and sociology, the study of society, are really the same thing. Social institutions, according to the New Spiritualist, should be structured to encourage the search for inner truth.

> The New Spiritualist says there is no such thing as an individual person or "self." There is only consciousness, and we are all an inseparable part of it.

Postmodernism, on the other hand, agrees with the Secularist and the Marxist: humans are nothing more than the sum total of the economic, legal, and personal relationships developed in a given society. Michel Foucault said our culture determines who we are. If we don't like it, our best option is to deconstruct those institutions, reveal the way they manipulate others, and strip them of their power.

For **Christianity**, God has ordained multiple institutions to play roles in the collective caretaking of his creation. The family (as opposed to individuals, economic structures, governments, spoken language, higher consciousness, or the Quran) is the central institution of society. Societies can survive tragedy and economic disaster, but if the family falls apart, societal collapse is inevitable.[73] Such unraveling is now a statistical reality.[74] At its most basic level, the Christian sociological claim is that society functions best when organized around the natural family (father, mother, and children).

Other institutions naturally flow from the family, most notably the church and the state. Each institution has what theologian Abraham Kuyper called "sphere sovereignty," or a proper domain in which the institution best exerts authority. When one institution takes over another sphere, there is disorder and imbalance. The Christian conception of sociology recognizes the value of persons as well as the balance between persons and society and the valuable roles of the family, government, and church.

> The Christian conception of sociology recognizes the value of persons as well as the balance between persons and society and the valuable roles of the family, government, and church.

Worldviews committed to materialism and naturalism discount the ability of individual human beings to make a difference in society, the value of the traditional family, and the place of the church in the public square.[75] The Christian worldview is constantly criticized for its call to self-restraint, responsibility, work, and caring for others even when it is not convenient. But the evidence of history speaks more loudly. We are not free to wreak mayhem in the social order, but we are free to serve others in love and to serve and love God.

16. LAW

The Latin word for "law," *legum*, is the word from which we get our words *legislate* and *legislature*. The study of law revolves around the question "What constitutes *orderly* and *just* governance?" A society's measured pursuit of just laws is a primary factor in its thriving. Lawmakers and legal scholars must consider whether the law is sufficiently punishing evil-doing while at the same time not harming the initiative of hardworking law abiders. There are two aspects to law:

- **Order**: nothing happens in our communities without laws establishing order. We can't even get a drink from the tap without laws governing the safe and predictable delivery of water.
- **Justice**: society must have laws to protect rights and punish wrongs. In the American context, such rights are seen as coming from God. Government does not grant them but merely secures them.

Islam teaches that God reveals only his law, not himself.[76] The body of laws based on this revelation, shariah, is seen as divine law, coeternal with God.[77] Indeed, "the shariah itself is considered to be a timeless manifestation of the will of God, subject neither to history nor circumstance."[78] Muslims understand that the implementation of shariah requires tough measures. They are thus more likely to construct authoritarian governments than those who believe government's primary role is to ensure freedom.

> **Muslims understand that the implementation of shariah requires tough measures. They are thus more likely to construct authoritarian governments than those who believe government's primary role is to ensure freedom.**

Secularist theology says God does not exist or is irrelevant, and that only matter exists (materialism). Secularist biology and sociology, on the assumption that only matter exists, say that everything around us can be explained through natural processes (natural-ism). These two assumptions form the secular view of society. Secularists trust themselves to create a just legal system because they reject the idea of fallenness.[79] As we saw in the chapter on law, this legal structure is called *legal positivism*, which says that the "law" is whatever those in authority have agreed to do. It does not have an anchor in transcendent truth.

Marxism denies God's very existence, so it is inconceivable for Marxists to see laws as based on divine will. Rather laws were based on the will of the bourgeoisie: "Your very ideas are but the outgrowth of the conditions of your bourgeoisie production and bourgeoisie property, just as your jurisprudence is but the will of your class made into a law for all."[80] The proletariat must overthrow such laws by any means necessary, including violent ones.

New Spiritualists do not spend much energy discussing law, justice, and judgment, preferring instead to concentrate on personal inner development, getting in touch with the God within. It does not say that the law is in our hearts but that no law *exists* except that which is in our hearts. Anything hindering our search for higher consciousness is bad.

Postmodernists focus on structures of society rather than the heart. They view as unjust anything resulting from traditional power structures, such as Christianity, the Enlightenment, heterosexism, or patriarchy. Therefore, the postmodern understanding of justice in relation to the law is not actually connected to any objective standards. Rather, it is the process of uncovering the various forms of oppression. This way of thinking continues to creep into judicial decisions, most recently—and notably—through the decision of Supreme Court justice Anthony Kennedy to overthrow the Defense of Marriage Act (DOMA) because he viewed it as oppressive to people experiencing same-sex attraction. In a similar vein, New Mexico Supreme Court justice Richard Bosson recently wrote an opinion reflecting the view of the court that the refusal of a New Mexico photography studio to photograph a gay wedding violated the human rights of a gay couple. In these cases, the battle against "heterosexism" was seen to trump religious and economic freedom.

Christianity says God gave us divine laws and the means of discovering them. Carl F. H. Henry says, "God is the only Legislator. Earthly rulers and legislative bodies are alike accountable to Him from whom stems all obligation—religious, ethical and civil."[81] As Russell Kirk said, "To cut off Law from its ethical sources is to strike a terrible blow at the rule of law."[82] Christians, in acknowledging humans as image bearers of God but also taking into account human fallenness, have created a system of justice that, while imperfect, has provided for greater order and justice than any other system.

Christianity focuses on two aspects of law. First is general revelation and natural law. God's general revelation to us is of both a physical and a moral character. We know this revelation through our consciences, which provide an innate sense of right and wrong. Second is special revelation and divine law. In addition to natural law, Christian legal theory must take into account God's special revelation of his moral order and divine law, the Bible. Natural law gives us a general concept of right and wrong, while the Bible fleshes out that skeletal framework, telling us what God considers moral and lawful.

> Natural law gives us a general concept of right and wrong, while the Bible fleshes out that skeletal framework, telling us what God considers moral and lawful.

> The goal of Christian law is not to force people to convert to Christianity but to stabilize society by ensuring that the innocent are protected and the guilty are punished.

Other worldviews, such as Marxism, are utopian in that they insist that law may be used to eliminate capitalism. As long as any vestige of capitalism remains, if Marxist writings are to be believed, Marxists will refuse to view any of their actions as a violation of law.

From a Christian view, utopian visions are pure fantasy. The law cannot make everything turn out the way we want because, even though we are made in God's image, our natures are corrupted by sin; no legal system can cause every person to always act morally. The best we can do is develop systems of accountability that make order and justice more likely than not.

The goal of Christian law is not to force people to convert to Christianity but to stabilize society by ensuring that the innocent are protected and the guilty are punished. This is what God requires of us, "to act justly and to love mercy and to walk humbly with [our] God" (Mic. 6:8). As justice rises, however, the law can shine light on God's law and how our hearts' longing for mercy and grace might be fulfilled (Eph. 2). When society is just, people have a big view of God. When society is unjust, people have a small view of God.

17. POLITICS

Polis is the Greek word for "city" (or community), and *politikos* is "of, or relating to, the citizens within a community." Politics, then, seeks to answer the question "What is the best way to use power in order to organize community for the citizens?" **Islam** is probably the boldest worldview in this regard. The goal of Islam in politics is to establish a global Islamic state ruled by religious leaders (theocracy) according to the principles of shariah law. The vision, explains Khurshid Ahmad, is to "unite the entire human race under one banner."[83] The mechanism is jihad. All Muslims are obligated to participate.[84]

> A Secularist worldview assumes we are evolving animals who are now capable of seeking our own perfection as a species.

A **Secularist** worldview assumes we are evolving animals who are now capable of seeking our own perfection as a species. Julian Huxley, who believed that "all reality is a single process of evolution,"[85] wrote, "the evolutionary process is at last becoming conscious of itself and is beginning to study itself with a view to directing its future course."[86] In this view, politics can be used to move society more quickly and forcefully toward the course secular elites believe it should be pursuing.

In classical **Marxism**, all politics is really about economics. Marx called economic structures "the real foundation on which rise moral, legal and political superstructures and to which definite forms of social consciousness correspond."[87] Once a nation's economic structure is rightly ordered, Marxists believe politics will fall in line behind it.

No other worldview—not even Christianity—puts as much emphasis as **New Spirituality** on personal transformation as *the* key to political transformation. New Spiritualists talk about increasing people's personal power because this will lead to collective consciousness and ultimately "planetary cooperation."[88]

In response to all other worldviews, **Postmodernism** is primarily a "critical theory" that points out problems but avoids proposing concrete solutions because, for Postmodernists, politics is only and always a tool of oppression. Critiquing the abuse *is* the solution. So a postmodern approach to politics looks to unseat power structures in a society.

The essential **Christian** worldview of politics is this: citizens of the kingdom of heaven will be the best citizens in the kingdom of earth because their allegiance is to something higher than the state. God insists his people do justice, love mercy, and walk in humility with him (Mic. 6:8). If they do, it is a hopeful antidote to the hopelessness of legal positivism—the idea

---

that law is what those in authority have agreed to do, with no particular tie to morality. If there is nothing higher than the state, then the state is God and is right in all it does.

In a fallen world, government's primary mission is to preserve justice and punish evil so that humans may flourish. Governments establish order; set up structures to deliver goods and services , such as roads and utilities; keep records; ensure a smooth flow of traffic; offer protection; and so forth. The Christian worldview sees government as an institution God established to promote security and justice (order), protect the innocent, and secure the rights God has granted so people can flourish. Government does have a role to play.

Many people think Christians want to establish a theocracy, rule by religious leaders. We think Christian involvement is one of the few things that *save* a nation *from* theocracy. Islam assumes its leaders have no sin and should be given greater power in order to create the perfect society. Secularism's belief that humans are perfectible and Marxism's view that "some are more equal than others" share the same assumption. As we have demonstrated, these are all religious worldviews. If they established themselves in power, without the kind of accountability called for only with a view of human fallenness, they would be truly theocratic. Christianity, on the other hand, based on a belief in God's ultimate authority and a biblical view of human nature, is suspicious of claims about society's perfectibility. Christians distrust leaders who demand more power than is absolutely necessary to secure justice and freedom.[89]

> The Christian worldview is based on transcendent law applied impartially to all. It prizes accountability above efficiency and human flourishing above the accumulation of power.

Christianity is not utopian. Christians do not believe the state is the means to salvation. Chuck Colson wrote, "While Christian teaching emphasizes that each person has worth and responsibility before God, utopianism argues that salvation can only be achieved collectively."[90] The Christian worldview is based on transcendent law applied impartially to all. It prizes accountability above efficiency and human flourishing above the accumulation of power.

18. ECONOMICS

In Latin, the word for "economics" comes from the Greek word *oikonomos*, meaning "the art of running a household."[91] Economists study institutions and human beings, especially how they compete, cooperate, and distribute goods, services, and information. But economists don't just study the world as it *is*. They also make claims about how it *ought to be*.[92] Unfortunately, some economists are captive to utopian visions based on wrong assumptions about God, humans, and the world. This is why the answers to life's ultimate questions matter so much in making economic decisions.

In **Islam** people are seen as being responsible for their beliefs and actions. We can choose to do right or wrong. Since we are responsible to God, Muslims say, we are responsible to take care of our fellow human beings. Almsgiving is central to being responsible in economic activities and "mostly takes the form of giving to the poor and the needy."[93] Hoarding wealth at the expense of the well-being of other Muslims is prohibited.

A minority of **Secularists** express a libertarian impulse that the government's only role is to secure freedom so people can pursue their own self-interests. But Secularists are much more likely to be represented on the socialist side of the spectrum.[94] Socialism makes sense to those who believe humans are inherently good and smart enough to develop a good society without divine guidance.

As a materialist and naturalist worldview, **Marxism** cannot easily conceive of human beings, made in the image of a creative God, using creativity, hard work, innovation, problem-solving ability, team-building skills, successful cooperation, efficiency, persuasion, service, opportunity, entrepreneurial risk, and ventures instead of revolution to solve economic problems. All of these are immaterial solutions, and Marxism is firmly committed to the idea that humans are merely "matter in motion."

The universe wants life and abundance, **New Spiritualists** say. It wants to evolve. And since abundance is immaterial (of the spirit), the way to make it come to you is to act as if you have it. Eckhart Tolle put it this way: "You don't have it? Just act as if you had it, and it will come. Then, soon after you start giving, you will start receiving. You cannot receive what you don't give. Outflow determines inflow."[95]

Postmodernists are suspicious of all authoritative claims about economic realities. When one starts with the denial of truth, of human nature, even of the self, as Postmodernism does, it is hard to arrive at anything approximating an economic viewpoint (or any other type of viewpoint, for that matter). And without any true access to reality, developing a system of economic exchange based on trust is simply impossible. The focus for Postmodernists is instead on redistributing wealth based on their perceptions of how various groups have been denied power in the past.

Christianity begins with the assumption that no economic system can save us or usher in the kingdom of God. Still, the Bible presents many clear principles that have specific economic implications: "Better a little [wealth] with righteousness than great revenues with injustice" (Prov. 16:8), and "Let the thief no longer steal, but rather let him labor, doing honest work with his own hands, so that he may have something to share with anyone in need" (Eph. 4:28). And two of the Ten Commandments ("Do not steal" and "Do not covet")[96] imply the legitimacy of private property. Applying biblical principles like these leads to economic policies under which humans can flourish.

How can Christians use economics to inspire human flourishing? In this text, we have considered the following: (1) We should all work hard to produce abundance. Work is a virtue, not a vice;[97] (2) we should support the rule of law so people can have freedom to come up with ideas and turn them into economic benefit for themselves and others; (3) we should focus on impartial administration of justice rather than equal distribution of goods; (4) equality is important, but the focus should be equal treatment before the law rather than on equal economic *outcomes*;[98] (5) we ought to be wary of those who teach destructive and disproven theories, such as socialism or communism;[99] and (6) we must take into consideration the rising generation. Have we left them a sufficient productive base so they too can thrive? Have we operated our government in such a way that it will help rather than hinder?

19. HISTORY

What people believe about the cause, nature, and purpose of the universe determines how they understand and use time. Time, then, is inherently religious.[100] History is the study of the way people, based on various religious worldviews, act through time to accomplish their goals. The study of history is vital because by looking back at the past, we can see how people's decisions affected their fellow humans' ability to flourish. As George Santayana famously admonished, "Those who cannot remember the past are condemned to repeat it."[101] We thus need an accurate view of the past if we are to sustain trends toward greater wealth, justice, and sustainability. History can guide us to learn from our mistakes, act rightly in our current circumstances, and get better over time.[102]

> The study of history is vital because by looking back at the past, we can see how people's decisions affected their fellow humans' ability to flourish.

To Muhammad Qutb, "**Islam** is the only future hope of humanity, and its victorious emergence out of the present ideological warfare is the only guarantee of man's salvation."[103] Islam, like the other worldviews, carries with it a sense of historical inevitability. But unlike Secularism, Marxism, or New Spirituality, this view is not held based on what the Islamic worldview hopes to have happen in the future but on what has happened in the past. Allah is pleased not when we come up with new ways of doing things but when we carefully study and replicate Muhammad's way of life as much as possible.

Secularists believe history to be the evolution of both organisms and human society—from the simple to the complex, from weaker to stronger. Progress is inevitable.[104] As we progress, our ideas also evolve. Julian Huxley said, "Major steps in the human phase of evolution are achieved by breakthroughs to new dominant patterns of mental organization, of knowledge, ideas and beliefs—ideological instead of physiological or biological organization."[105]

> Secularists believe history to be the evolution of both organisms and human society—from the simple to the complex, from weaker to stronger. Progress is inevitable.

To **Marxists**, society is guided by nature through certain economic phases in a constant upward spiral: from tribalism to slavery to feudalism to capitalism and then to socialism. The continued clash of the bourgeoisie (the present thesis) with the proletariat (the present antithesis) will lead society through a transitional phase of socialism and finally—when the clash is resolved due to the abolition of classes (synthesis)—toward communism.

The **New Spiritualist** trusts spiritual evolution to guide humanity unswervingly toward perfection. In a very real sense, members of the New Spiritualist movement place their faith in the inevitable evolution toward oneness as humanity's savior. History, then, from a New Spiritualist view, is sort of like the Secularist idea of evolutionary progress, but on hyperdrive. Benjamin Ferencz and Ken Keyes explain: "We are inspired by our great progress toward planethood."[106]

Postmodernists will have none of this. To them, all historical accounts are fiction.[107] Less radical Postmodernists take a soft view of history as fiction, saying history is what we make of it. Historical facts are inaccessible, so historians reconstruct the past based on their ideological bent. Some more radical Postmodernists see no ultimate purpose in history, advocating nihilism instead (*nihil* is Latin for "nothing"—so *nihilism* means "a belief in nothing").

From the **Christian** perspective, history is an epic unfolding of God's ultimate plan for all humanity. Knowing that God has been active throughout history helps us understand our own roles in the day-to-day history of our lives. "It is always a 'Now,'" wrote Herbert Butterfield, "that is in direct relation to eternity—not a far future."[108]

For the Christian, history is not wrapped around certain philosophies of the past, the present plans of humans, or the future utopia self-appointed messiahs desire. As we saw in the "History" chapter, history is the unfolding of God's story in real time, the tangible manifestation of an eternal and omnipresent creator who not only set the universe in motion but is also present in it. The Christian story of history—beginning, middle, and end—is not of a God who must be chased after or an ethereal presence who must be dreamed about but a person who *has* come, *is* come, and *will* come, as real as anything is real, living in us and among us.

20. OTHER AREAS OF POSSIBLE STUDY

We recognize that our ten disciplines are not the sum total of what ought to be covered. There surely is a Christian view of mathematics, chemistry, engineering, athletics, agriculture, medicine, and so many others as well. Many more books could be written.

Art is one area we're very concerned about. Especially in a postmodern age, there has been an aggressive attempt to hijack the arts to "disrupt bourgeois fantasies about art," as Glenn Ward phrases it.[109] The most famous example of this disruptiveness—dare we say destruction—of art was Marcel Duchamp's display of a urinal, titled *Fountain*, in 1917. As Stephen Hicks elaborates, "Duchamp's urinal was the fitting symbol. Everything is waste to be flushed away."[110] We encourage readers interested in a Christian worldview of art to begin with Nancy Pearcey's *Saving Leonardo*.[111]

Another area needing the touch of a Christian worldview is the field of education. Unfortunately, education has become its own area of study focused on the delivery and measurement of educational experiences rather than the content of education itself. On college campuses, education is seen as a "safehaven for the religious," in that religious people are more likely to become education majors and become more religious throughout their courses of study.[112] Concerned at losing influence over the next generation, other worldviews are trying to get in the game too. From a Marxist perspective, Madan Sarup says, the education system is one of capitalism's tools to ensure oppression, especially of women.[113] Changing this, according to Walter Truett Anderson, means indoctrinating children with language that will "create a human being sensitive to its racial, sexual, and class identity."[114]

Woe to those who tread on this politically correct agenda. Richard Zeller, a former sociology professor at Bowling Green State University in Ohio, attempted to introduce a new course examining the effects of political correctness on the educational process. The university's director of women's studies, Kathleen Dixon, said without any hint of intended irony, "We forbid any course that says we restrict free speech."[115] The course was voted down, and Zeller resigned his long-time post in protest.

21. How Then Should We Live?

As Christians we need to take seriously the cultural commission God gave our first parents in the garden of Eden (Gen. 1:28).[116] The clear direction of this commission goes beyond tending the garden and naming animals. God commanded Adam and Eve to "multiply" and fill the earth with people (which implies taking charge of a growing social order). Jesus echoed this theme when he told his disciples they were "salt and light" (Matt. 5:13–14).[117] If our society is tasteless and dark, it is because we have failed to preserve and enlighten. Furthermore, Jesus's Great Commission (Matt. 28:18–20)[118] speaks of spreading the good news of Jesus's authority. Nowhere does Scripture rescind God's cultural commission—it is still our responsibility.

Christians should be involved in every area of society: as educators, elected officials, bureaucrats, artists, musicians, authors, movie producers, business leaders, reporters, and moms and dads committed to raising children who will secure their legacy of godly, courageous leadership. Properly understood, Christianity doesn't just make sense of itself; it makes sense of everything in society. As C. S. Lewis phrased it, "I believe in Christianity as I believe that the sun has risen, not only because I see it, but because by it I see everything else."[119]

> Christians should be involved in every area of society: as educators, elected officials, bureaucrats, artists, musicians, authors, movie producers, business leaders, and moms and dads committed to raising children who will secure their legacy of godly, courageous leadership.

Probably one of the clearest places to see the positive influence of Christianity today is in the area of ethics. As image bearers of God, all people have an innate sense of right and wrong, an *oughtness* associated with behavior that accounts for goodness, kindness, and generosity. We know instinctively that it is wrong to murder fellow human beings, to steal their spouses, or to covet their possessions. It is wrong to steal from a blind man's cup and torture children. On the other hand, we know it is morally right to love our neighbor as ourselves and to be the Good Samaritan instead of the thief or Pharisee. It is right to love our creator, who gave us a rational mind and a moral conscience.

It is hard to over emphasize how different this is from the other worldviews we've considered. Islam has a strong sense of what is right and wrong, but when it comes to living in loving community with those who do not embrace its faith, Islam becomes harsh, unforgiving, and even cruel. Secularism is discovering that science alone is unable to lead us to a common understanding of right or wrong.[120] Marxism actually views cruel treatment of people with whom it disagrees as *necessary* and not morally questionable.[121] To New Spirituality, *indifference* to suffering is actually the basis of a good life. Love and compassion make the problem worse, binding us to pain and suffering and prolonging negativity.

In contrast, Christianity says we are obligated to help people in need. Proverbs 24:11–12 says, "Rescue those who are being taken away to death; hold back those who are stumbling to the slaughter. If you say, 'Behold, we did not know this,' does not he who weighs the heart perceive it? Does not he who keeps watch over your soul know it, and will he not repay man according to his work?" As we saw earlier in this text, biblical teachings like this pricked the conscience of the revered Mahatma Gandhi, who said it was Christian missionaries—not fellow Hindus—who "awakened in him a revulsion for the caste system and for the maltreatment of outcastes."[122]

22. Conclusion

In the end, we can be confident that the Christian worldview provides the best way to understand the contours of the world as it actually is. This is not a cause for gloating but a call to pray (2 Chron. 7:14; Col. 1:9–14),[123] study (2 Tim. 2:15),[124] and understand the times (1 Chron. 12:32)[125] so as to rebuild the foundations (Luke 6:47–49)[126] of a broken world.

At Summit Ministries we see our students doing this in many areas of life. One notable area is opposing abortion, which more and more young people today see as a social-justice issue. Three decades ago Peter Singer, a professor of ethics, prophesied, "Whatever the future holds, it is likely to prove impossible to restore in full the sanctity-of-life view.... Why should we believe that the mere fact that a being is a member of the species Homo Sapiens endows its life with some unique, almost infinite value?"[127]

Lila Rose and Joe Baker apparently didn't believe Singer. Maybe they didn't even read his prophesy. After all, they weren't even born when he made it. As a teenager, Lila became convinced of a prolife position and began an organized effort to send undercover investigators into Planned Parenthood offices and abortion clinics to see what actually took place there. Her YouTube videos garnered millions of views and helped cement a prolife view among those in the rising generation.[128] For his part, Joe started a ministry called Save the Storks, which parks a mobile clinic and counseling center outside abortion clinics. Stork vans offer free ultrasounds to pregnant women considering abortion. When these women see their "fetuses" as living, breathing human beings, three out of five cancel their abortion appointments.[129]

> In the end, we can be confident that the Christian worldview provides the best way to understand the contours of the world as it actually is.

Without question, *Roe v. Wade* represented a major legal setback for protecting the sanctity of human life in the United States. It signaled that the most vulnerable among us are disposable. But as it turns out, Singer could not have been more wrong: the public debate is far from over. According to the Pew Research Center, 47 percent of Americans think abortion is morally wrong, compared to 13 percent who say it's morally acceptable and 27 percent who say it's not a moral issue.[130] In the first quarter of 2013, nearly seven hundred bills were introduced in state legislatures across the country to make abortion less frequent; 47 percent of all health-related bills have focused on abortion.[131]

Opportunities to stand for truth and fight against evil and injustice on the basis of a Christian worldview continue to grow. People may not be interested in the Christian worldview at first, but nearly all people—even most college professors—are on a quest for meaning and purpose.[132]

And purpose is what God's plan gives us. As we embrace it, God sweeps aside the curtain of history, which enables us to glimpse his making all things new. Our lives are purposeful not because we are smart enough to save ourselves, or because we are energetic enough to revolt against the powers that be, or because we are part of a higher consciousness, or because we are bold enough to assert our rights, or even because we are faithful enough to obey. In his grace and mercy God runs to us, wraps us in his arms, cleans us up, dresses us in robes of righteousness, places the rings of image-bearing purpose back on our hands, and prepares a feast to welcome us home. Nothing we possess and nothing we can do merits this. Christ's sacrifice enables salvation, salvation secures sanctification, and sanctification restores significance. This is the true, the good, and the beautiful. Those who grasp it and live it will truly have understood the times.

ENDNOTES

1. Khurshid Ahmad, *Islam: Its Meaning and Message*, 3rd ed. (Leicester, UK: Islamic Foundation, 1999), 29.

2. The other major source for Islamic theology today is the Hadith. The Hadith are traditions of the teachings, rulings, and actions of Muhammad and his early and chief companions. These traditions include the *Sunnah*, descriptions of Muhammad's exemplary actions. Faslur Rahman states, "The difference between the two is that whereas a Hadith as such is a mere report ... the Sunna is the very same report when it acquires a normative quality and becomes a practical principle for the Muslim"; "this authority of Muhammad refers to the verbal and performative behavior of the Prophet outside the Qur'an"; and "to his Companions his life was a religious paradigm and as such normative." Faslur Rahman, *Islam*, 2nd ed. (Chicago: University of Chicago Press, 1979).

3. For more information, see chapter 3 in this edition on the worldview of Islam.

4. Quotes from the Quran in this book primarily came from the translation of Abdullah Yusuf Ali. It is an older translation (sounding much like the King James Version of the Bible), but one that is well respected and widely known. See Abdullah Yusuf Ali, *The Holy Qur'an: Text, Translation, and Commentary* (Washington, DC: American International Printing Company, 1946). In some quotations from Ali's translation, we have taken the liberty of smoothing out the text, removing unnecessary punctuation and poetic capitalization of letters.

5. From personal conversations with Nabeel Qureshi, May 2013.

6. Cited in David Niose, *Nonbeliever Nation: The Rise of Secular America* (New York: Palgrave Macmillan, 2012), 14.

7. Jacques Berlinerblau, *How to Be Secular: A Call to Arms for Religious Freedom* (New York: Houghton Mifflin Harcourt, 2012), 180.

8. Georgetown professor Jacques Berlinerblau says, "Secularism cannot tolerate religious groups that are *otherworldly* in radical ways," by which he means concerned with life after death. Berlinerblau, *How to Be Secular*, 183.

9. V. I. Lenin, *Selected Works*, 38 vols. (New York: International Publishers, 1938), 9:479.

10. Frederick Engels, *Socialism: Utopian and Scientific* (New York: International Publishers, 1935), 21.

11. V. I. Lenin, *Collected Works*, 45 vols. (Moscow: Progress Publishers, 1977), 7:409. Lenin wrote of the "great Hegelian dialectics which Marxism made its own, having first turned it right side up."

12. Karl Marx and Frederick Engels, *Collected Works*, 40 vols. (New York: International Publishers, 1976), 6:519.

13. As we have seen earlier in this text, New Spiritualist writers often refer to Jesus in a very positive but unbiblical way. Most see Jesus as a good man who managed to transcend ego and thus serves as an example worth following. Others refer to "Christ consciousness" as what made Jesus unique, and we may also attain this consciousness through various New Spiritualist practices. For more information, see Douglas Groothuis, *Jesus in an Age of Controversy* (Eugene, OR: Wipf and Stock, 2002).

14. Eckhart Tolle, *A New Earth* (New York: Plume, 2005), 277.

15. Quoted in Rhonda Byrne, *The Secret* (New York: Atria Books, 2006), 155.

16. The Dalai Lama, *A Profound Mind* (New York: Three Rivers, 2011), 22.

17. Tolle, *New Earth*, 13.

18. Kevin J. Vanhoozer, *Is There a Meaning in This Text?* (Grand Rapids: Zondervan, 1998), 158.

19. Walter Truett Anderson, *Reality Isn't What It Used to Be: Theatrical Politics, Ready-to-Wear Religion, Global Myths, Primitive Chic, and Other Wonders of the Postmodern World* (San Francisco: Harper and Row, 1990), 3.

20. Michael Bauman makes this statement in a lecture titled "The Meaning of Meaning" given frequently at Summit Ministries' twelve-day conferences. To view the lecture, go to www.summit.org/resources/summit-lecture-series/the-meaning-of-meaning/.

21. See the extended discussion and footnotes in chapter 2 of this edition on the Christian worldview.

22. Fred Hoyle, *The Intelligent Universe* (London: Michael Joseph, 1983), 18–19.

23. Charles Thaxton, Walter Bradley, and Roger Olsen, *The Mystery of Life's Origin: Reassessing Current Theories* (New York: Philosophical Library, 1984), 186. Students particularly interested in biological origins should also read Percival Davis and Dean Kenyon, *Of Pandas and People*, 2nd ed. (Richardson, TX: Foundation for Thought and Ethics, 1993).

24. Jeremiah 17:9: "The heart is deceitful above all things, and desperately sick; who can understand it?"

25. Romans 8:20–22: "The creation was subjected to futility, not willingly, but because of him who subjected it, in hope that the creation itself will be set free from its bondage to corruption and obtain the freedom of the glory of the children of God. For we know that the whole creation has been groaning together in the pains of childbirth until now."

26. Romans 5:6–8: "While we were still weak, at the right time Christ died for the ungodly. For one will scarcely die for a righteous person—though perhaps for a good person one would dare even to die— but God shows his love for us in that while we were still sinners, Christ died for us."

27. Romans 10:9: "If you confess with your mouth that Jesus is Lord and believe in your heart that God raised him from the dead, you will be saved."

28. First Peter 1:23: "You have been born again, not of perishable seed but of imperishable, through the living and abiding word of God."

29. Mark 12:30: "You shall love the Lord your God with all your heart and with all your soul and with all your mind and with all your strength."

30. Romans 12:1–2: "I appeal to you therefore, brothers, by the mercies of God, to present your bodies as a living sacrifice, holy and acceptable to God, which is your spiritual worship. Do not be conformed to this world, but be transformed by the renewal of your mind, that by testing you may discern what is the will of God, what is good and acceptable and perfect."

31. Romans 2:15: "[People] show that the work of the law is written on their hearts, while their conscience also bears witness, and their conflicting thoughts accuse or even excuse them."

32. J. Budziszewski, *The Revenge of Conscience: Politics and the Fall of Man* (Dallas: Spence, 1999), xv.

33. See chapter 3, "Putting Worldviews to the Test," in W. Gary Phillips, William E. Brown, and John Stonestreet, *Making Sense of Your World: A Biblical Worldview* (Salem, WI: Sheffield, 2008), 61–90.

34. For more information, see "What If Jesus Had Never Been Born?," *Summit Journal* 11, no. 12 (December 2011), www .summit.org/media/journal/2011-12-Summit-Journal.pdf.

35. Rodney Stark, *For the Glory of God* (Princeton: Princeton University Press, 2003), 291. All Christians should carefully study the entirety of chapter 4, "God's Justice: The Sin of Slavery."

36. Political scientist R. J. Rummel estimates that communism killed about 110 million people in the twentieth century (R. J. Rummel, "How Many Did Communist Regimes Murder?," November 1993, posted at University of Hawaii, accessed April 2, 2014, www.hawaii.edu/powerkills/COM.ART.HTM.), while *The Black Book of Communism: Crimes, Terror, Repression* (Cambridge, MA: Harvard University Press, 1999), estimates nearly 100 million. The total may never really be known. Alexander Yakovlev, in his important 2002 work *A Century of Violence in Soviet Russia* (New Haven, CT: Yale University Press, 2004), estimated that Stalin alone killed more than 60 million; the latest figures of 70-million–plus killed under China's Mao Tse-tung are recorded by Jung Chang and Jon Halliday in their seminal work *Mao: The Unknown Story* (New York: Anchor, 2006).

37. Harold H. Titus, "Humanistic Naturalism," *Humanist*, no. 1 (1954): 33.

38. Titus, "Humanistic Naturalism," 30.

39. See David B. T. Aikman, "The Role of Atheism in the Marxist tradition" (PhD dissertation, UMI Dissertation Services, 1979). Aikman covers all aspects of Marxist atheism in his five-hundred-plus-page dissertation.

40. V. I. Lenin, *Complete Collected Works*, 45 vols. (Moscow: Progress Publishers, 1978), 10:83.

41. The logic of this position is very similar to the religious pluralism championed by some liberal theologians—John Hick, William Cantwell Smith, and S. Wesley Ariarajah. We must be careful not to equate these liberal theologians with outright Postmodernists. David S. Dockery, ed., *The Challenge of Postmodernism: An Evangelical Engagement*, 2nd ed. (Grand Rapids: Baker Academic, 2001), 135, 142.

42. Ralph Waldo Emerson, *Nature* (Boston: James Munroe, 1849), 8.

43. Clyde S. Kilby, ed., *A Mind Awake: An Anthology of C. S. Lewis* (New York: Harcourt, Brace, and World, 1968), 234.

44. Gene Edward Veith, *Postmodern Times: A Christian Guide to Contemporary Thought and Culture* (Wheaton, IL: Crossway Books, 1994), 193–94.

45. See the discussion in Rahman, *Islam*, 117–27.

46. Dean C. Halverson, *Crystal Clear: Understanding and Reaching New Agers* (Colorado Springs: NavPress, 1990), 91.

47. As noted atheist philosopher Thomas Nagel says, the only solution will be a "major conceptual revolution at least as radical as relativity theory." Thomas Nagel, *Mind and Cosmos* (New York: Oxford University Press, 2012), 42.

48. J. P. Moreland, "The Argument from Consciousness," in William Lane Craig and J. P. Moreland, *The Blackwell Companion to Natural Theology* (Malden, MA: Wiley-Blackwell, 2012), 296.

49. S. Parvez Manzoor, "Shari'ah: The Ethics of Action," in "Islamic Conceptual Framework," MUNA, accessed February 15, 2016, www.muslimummah.org/articles/articles.php?itemno=200&&category=Islam.

50. Hammudah Abdalati, *Islam in Focus* (Indianapolis: Amana, 1978), 8.

51. Simon Blackburn, *Ethics: A Very Short Introduction* (Oxford, UK: Oxford University Press, 2001), 114.

52. Shirley MacLaine, *Out on a Limb* (Toronto: Bantam Books, 1984), 96, 111.

53. Quoted in Algis Valiunas, "Mental Health: In the Post-Freudian World, It's a Matter of Opinion," *Weekly Standard* 11, no. 9 (November 2005).

54. Carl F. H. Henry, ed., *Baker's Dictionary of Christian Ethics* (Grand Rapids: Baker, 1973), 620.

55. Badru D. Kateregga and David W. Shenk, *Islam and Christianity: A Muslim and a Christian in Dialogue* (Grand Rapids: Eerdmans, 1981), available on *The World of Islam: Resources for Understanding*, 2.0 (Colorado Springs: Global Mapping International, 2009), CD-ROM, 5350.

56. George Gaylord Simpson, *The Meaning of Evolution* (New Haven, CT: Yale University Press, 1971), 345.

57. Quoted in Phillip E. Johnson, *Darwin on Trial* (Downers Grove, IL: InterVarsity, 1991), 124.

58. Deepak Chopra and Leonard Mlodinow, *War of the Worldviews* (New York: Three Rivers, 2011), 154.

59. Terry Eagleton, "Awakening from Modernity," *Times Literary Supplement*, February 20, 1987, 194, quoted in Stanley J. Grenz, *A Primer on Postmodernism* (Grand Rapids: Eerdmans, 1996), 48.

60. John Lennox, *Seven Days That Divide the World* (Grand Rapids: Zondervan, 2011), 69.

61. George Wald, "The Origin of Life," *Scientific American* 190 (August 1954): 46, quoted in Walter Brown, *In the Beginning* (Phoenix: Center for Scientific Creation, 2003), 37.

62. George M. Whitesides, "Revolutions in Chemistry: Priestley Medalist George M. Whitesides' Address," *Chemical and Engineering News* 85 (March 2007): 12–17.

63. Abraham Maslow, *Toward a Psychology of Being* (New York: Van Nostrand Reinhold, 1968), 149.

64. Ivan P. Pavlov, *Lectures on Conditioned Reflexes* (New York: International Publishers, 1963), 42.

65. Ivan P. Pavlov, statement to his assistants, February 21, 1936, in W. H. Gantt's introduction to Ivan P. Pavlov, *Lectures on Conditioned Reflexes*, vol. 2, *Conditioned Reflexes and Psychiatry* (New York: International Publishers, 1963), 34.

66. Mitchell Stephens, "To Thine Own Selves Be True," *Los Angeles Times Magazine*, August 23, 1992. Online article accessed April 2, 2014, www.nyu.edu/classes/stephens/Postmodern%20psych%20page.htm.

67. J. P. Moreland and Scott B. Rae, *Body and Soul: Human Nature and the Crisis in Ethics* (Downers Grove, IL: InterVarsity, 2000), 158.

68. "General ontology is the most basic of metaphysics, and there are three main tasks that make up this branch of metaphysical study. First, general ontology focuses on the nature of existence itself. What is it to be or to exist? Is existence a property that something has? Etc." J. P. Moreland and William Lane Craig, *Philosophical Foundations for a Christian Worldview* (Downers Grove, IL: InterVarsity, 2003), 175.

69. See Mario Beauregard and Denyse O'Leary, *The Spiritual Brain* (New York: HarperOne, 2007); Thomas Nagel, *Mind and Cosmos* (New York: Oxford University Press, 2012); Eben Alexander, *Proof of Heaven* (New York: Simon and Schuster, 2012).

70. As we discussed in the "Psychology" chapter of this edition, one argument against mind/brain dualism is that people who have suffered traumatic brain injury often emerge with a different personality. Research on this kind of thing is very difficult because we would have to know a great deal about the person's behavior, personality, and sense of identity before the injury and then try to figure out what changes can be attributed to the trauma. The research on the relationship between brain functions and psychological processes is not as advanced as those arguing against dualism would like to think. For more information, see Stewart Goetz and Mark C. Baker, *The Soul Hypothesis: Investigations into the Existence of the Soul* (New York: Bloomsbury Academic, 2010).

71. Steve Bruce, *Sociology: A Very Short Introduction* (Oxford, UK: Oxford University Press, 1999), 18.

72. V. I. Lenin, *The State and Revolution* (New York: International Publishers, 1932), 73.

73. For a helpful essay on this subject, see Kerby Anderson, "The Decline of a Nation," Probe Ministries, May 27, 1991, accessed April 2, 2014, www.probe.org/the-decline-of-a-nation/.

74. See, for example, Mark Regnerus, "How Different Are the Adult Children of Parents Who Have Same-Sex Relationships? Findings from the New Family Structures Study," *Social Science Research* 41 (2012): 752–70.

75. For the latest research, see FamilyFacts.org, www.familyfacts.org.

76. Andrew Bostom, *Sharia versus Freedom* (Amherst, NY: Prometheus Books, 2012), 73.

77. Malise Ruthven, *Islam: A Very Short Introduction* (Oxford, UK: Oxford University Press, 1997), 86.

78. Additionally, Ruthven observes, "By defining correct behavior or orthopraxy at the social level, the Shariah has left its distinctive imprint on a way of living that has evolved over time and varies from one country to another in accordance with custom." Ruthven, *Islam*, 86.

79. Malachi Martin, *The Keys of This Blood* (New York: Simon and Schuster, 1990), 656.

CONCLUSION

80. Karl Marx and Friedrich Engels, *Manifesto of the Communist Party* (Chicago: Charles H. Kerr, 1906), 39.

81. Carl F. H. Henry, *Twilight of a Great Civilization* (Westchester, IL: Crossway Books, 1988), 147.

82. Russell Kirk, "The Christian Postulates of English and American Law," *Journal of Christian Jurisprudence* (1980): 66.

83. Khurshid Ahmad, *Islam: Its Meaning and Message*, 3rd ed. (Leicester: Islamic Foundation, 1999), 40–41.

84. Ahmad, *Islam*, 39.

85. Julian Huxley, *The Humanist Frame* (New York: Harper and Brothers, 1961), 15.

86. Huxley, *Humanist Frame*, 7.

87. Karl Marx, *A Contribution to the Critique of Political Economy* (Chicago: C. H. Kerr, 1911), 11.

88. Mark Satin, *New Age Politics* (New York: Dell, 1978), 22.

89. Charles Colson called the belief in human perfectibility "the most subtle and dangerous delusion of our times." See *Who Speaks for God?* (Westchester, IL: Crossway Books, 1988), 144.

90. Charles Colson, *Kingdoms in Conflict* (Grand Rapids: Zondervan, 1987), 77. For an understanding of the ideas presently in the mix of modern-day utopianism, consult Stewart Justman, *Fool's Paradise: The Unreal World of Pop Psychology* (Chicago: Ivan R. Dee, 2005). Says Justman, "The German expatriate who served as perhaps the foremost intellectual patron of the student revolt of the 1960s, Herbert Marcuse, wrote in 1970 that 'the new theory of man ... implies the genesis of a new morality as the heir and the negation of the Judeo-Christian morality which up to now has characterized the history of Western civilization.'" Marcuse, a Marxist and fellow of the Frankfurt School, contended that Christian morality is repressive, self-defeating, and obsolete (133).

91. N. Gregory Mankiw, *Principles of Economics*, 4th ed. (Mason, OH: South-Western, 2007), 3.

92. Mankiw, *Principles of Economics*, 28–29.

93. Syed Nawab Haider Naqvi, *Islam, Economics, and Society* (London: Kegan Paul, 1994), 32.

94. For more information, see Hunter Baker, "Social Leveling: Socialism and Secularism," Acton Institute, accessed April 2, 2014, www.acton.org/pub/religion-liberty/volume-21-number-1/social-leveling-socialism-secularism.

95. Tolle, *New Earth*, 191.

96. See Exodus 20:1–17.

97. The Greeks and Romans, in contrast, grounded their case for slavery in the idea that work is a vice, a view both Aristotle and Plato endorsed. Rodney Stark, *The Victory of Reason: How Christianity Led to Freedom, Capitalism, and Western Success* (New York: Random House, 2005), 26–27.

98. Michael Novak explains: "Given the diversity and liberty of human life, no fair and free system can possibly guarantee equal outcomes. A democratic system depends for its legitimacy, therefore, not upon equal results but upon a sense of equal opportunity." Michael Novak, *The Spirit of Democratic Capitalism* (New York: Simon and Schuster, 1982), 15.

99. This was evident even to Engels, who wrote, "If some few passages of the Bible may be favourable to Communism, the general spirit of its doctrines is, nevertheless, totally opposed to it." Marx and Engels, *Collected Works*, 3:399.

100. Herbert Schlossberg, *Idols for Destruction* (Nashville: Thomas Nelson, 1983), 12.

101. George Santayana, *The Life of Reason* (Middlesex, UK: Echo Library, 2006), 131.

102. Herbert Butterfield noted that our study can reveal how historical events morally and/or substantively contributed to or detracted from our present state. See Herbert Butterfield, *The Whig Interpretation of History* (London: G. Bell and Sons, 1963), 12.

103. Quoted in Ahmad, *Islam: Its Meaning and Message*, 253.

104. Philosopher Charles S. Peirce thought the "laws of nature are themselves evolved as the universe moves from a chaotic spontaneity toward perfect order." See John C. Greene, "The Concept of Order in Darwinism," in Paul G. Kuntz, ed., *The Concept of Order* (Seattle: University of Washington Press, 1968), 99.

105. Julian Huxley, *Essays of a Humanist* (New York: Harper and Row, 1964), 76.

106. Benjamin B. Ferencz and Ken Keyes Jr., *Planethood* (Coos Bay, OR: Vision Books, 1988), 141.

107. Christopher Butler, *Postmodernism: A Very Short Introduction* (Oxford, UK: Oxford University Press, 2002), 32–36.

108. Herbert Butterfield, *Christianity and History* (New York: Charles Scribner's Sons, 1950), 66.

109. Glenn Ward, *Teach Yourself Postmodernism*, 2nd ed. (Chicago: McGraw-Hill, 2003), 51.

110. Stephen R. C. Hicks, *Exploring Postmodernism: Skepticism and Socialism from Rousseau to Foucault* (Tempe, AZ: Scholargy, 2004), 196.

111. Nancy Pearcey, *Saving Leonardo: A Call to Resist the Secular Assault on Mind, Morals, and Meaning* (Nashville: B&H, 2010). See also H. R. Rookmaaker, *Modern Art and the Death of Culture* (Wheaton, IL: Crossway Books, 1994).

112. Miles S. Kimball et al., "Empirics on the Origins of Preferences: The Case of College Major and Religiosity," working paper no. 15182 (National Bureau of Economic Research, July 2009), 22.

113. Madan Sarup, *Education, State, and Crisis* (London: Routledge and Kegan, 1982), 91.

114. Walter Truett Anderson, *The Future of the Self: Exploring the Post-Identity Society* (New York: Tarcher, 1997), 17.

115. Quoted in Larry Elder, "Campus Gulag," *Front Page Magazine*, October 2, 2000, www.frontpagemag.com/Articles/Printable.asp?ID=2711.

116. Genesis 1:28: "God blessed [Adam and Eve]. And God said to them, 'Be fruitful and multiply and fill the earth and subdue it, and have dominion over the fish of the sea and over the birds of the heavens and over every living thing that moves on the earth.'"

117. Matthew 5:13–14: "You are the salt of the earth, but if salt has lost its taste, how shall its saltiness be restored? It is no longer good for anything except to be thrown out and trampled under people's feet. You are the light of the world. A city set on a hill cannot be hidden."

118. Matthew 28:18–20: "Jesus came and said to [his disciples], 'All authority in heaven and on earth has been given to me. Go therefore and make disciples of all nations, baptizing them in the name of the Father and of the Son and of the Holy Spirit, teaching them to observe all that I have commanded you. And behold, I am with you always, to the end of the age.'"

119. C. S. Lewis, *The Weight of Glory* (New York: Macmillan, 1980), 91–92.

120. John Lennox, *God and Stephen Hawking* (Oxford: Lion Hudson, 2011), 76.

121. Marx, Lenin, Stalin, and a host of other Marxist heroes saw it as a moral duty to overthrow the exploiters by any means necessary. It was well worth the price paid, said Lenin: "Even if for every hundred correct things we committed 10,000 mistakes, our revolution would still be—and it will be in the judgment of history—great and invincible." Lenin, *Collected Works*, 28:72.

122. John Warwick Montgomery, *Human Rights and Human Dignity* (Grand Rapids: Zondervan, 1986), 113.

123. Second Chronicles 7:14: "If my people who are called by my name humble themselves, and pray and seek my face and turn from their wicked ways, then I will hear from heaven and will forgive their sin and heal their land"; Colossians 1:9–14: "From the day we heard, we have not ceased to pray for you, asking that you may be filled with the knowledge of his will in all spiritual wisdom and understanding, so as to walk in a manner worthy of the Lord, fully pleasing to him, bearing fruit in every good work and increasing in the knowledge of God. May you be strengthened with all power, according to his glorious might, for all endurance and patience with joy, giving thanks to the Father, who has qualified you to share in the inheritance of the saints in light. He has delivered us from the domain of darkness and transferred us to the kingdom of his beloved Son, in whom we have redemption, the forgiveness of sins."

124. Second Timothy 2:15: "Do your best to present yourself to God as one approved, a worker who has no need to be ashamed, rightly handling the word of truth."

125. First Chronicles 12:32: "Of Issachar, men who had understanding of the times, to know what Israel ought to do, 200 chiefs, and all their kinsmen under their command."

126. Luke 6:47–49: "Everyone who comes to me and hears my words and does them, I will show you what he is like: he is like a man building a house, who dug deep and laid the foundation on the rock. And when a flood arose, the stream broke against that house and could not shake it, because it had been well built. But the one who hears and does not do them is like a man who built a house on the ground without a foundation. When the stream broke against it, immediately it fell, and the ruin of that house was great."

127. Peter Singer, "Sanctity of Life or Quality of Life?," *Pediactrics* 71, no. 1 (1983): 128–29, quoted in Lennox, *Seven Days*, 68.

128. For more information, see Lila Rose's organization Live Action at www.liveaction.org/.

129. For more information, see Save the Storks at http://savethestorks.com/.

130. "Public Opinion on Abortion and Roe v. Wade," Pew Forum, January 22, 2013, www.pewforum.org/2013/01/22/public-opinion-on-abortion-and-roe-v-wade/.

131. The Guttmacher Institute is one of the leading proabortion organizations and tracks various abortion-related statistics. To see their publication bemoaning legislation is a good thing. "State Policy Trends 2013: Abortion Moves to the Fore," Guttmacher Institute, April 11, 2013, www.guttmacher.org/media/inthenews/2013/04/11/index.html.

132. Even 81 percent of college professors considered themselves to be spiritual, according to a UCLA study. Alexander W. Astin et al., *Spirituality and the Professoriate: A National Study of Faculty Beliefs, Attitudes, and Behaviors* (Los Angeles: Higher Education Research Institute, 2005).

GLOSSARY

Adaptation: the process by which an organism or species becomes better able to survive.

Agape: the belief that morality is built upon two foundational moral absolutes: love of God and love of neighbor.

Anarchism: the belief that government is inherently oppressive and should therefore be abolished, giving individuals the opportunity to govern themselves.

Anarchy: a society that exists without government control.

Animism: the belief that various spirits inhabit plants, animals, and physical objects.

Anthropic Principle: the theory that the universe contains all the necessary properties that make the existence of intelligent life inevitable.

Anti-Essentialism: the belief that entities don't possess essences (i.e., a set of necessary and defining attributes); rather, an entity's identity is thought to be the result of social construction.

Anti-Realism: the denial of the existence or accessibility of an objective reality.

Atheism: the belief that God does not exist.

Autarchy: the rule of oneself; self-government.

Behaviorism: a school of psychology that believes psychological research should be concerned with studying observable measures of behavior and not the unobservable events that take place in the mind.

Biblical Stewardship: the act of managing and caring for resources that ultimately belong to God.

Big Bang Theory: the theory that the universe arose around fourteen billion years ago from an extremely dense state that rapidly expanded and continues to expand today.

Biological Determinism: the belief that our actions are ultimately the result of our genetic makeup.

Biology: the study of life and living organisms.

Bourgeoisie: a term used in Marxist theory to describe those who own the means of production.

Capital: goods used to produce other goods and services.

Capitalism: an economic system in which capital assets are privately owned, and the prices, production, and distribution of goods and services are determined by competition within a free market.

Case Law: a legal system in which lawyers compose briefs and present arguments in order to persuade judges.

Channeling: the practice of communicating with disembodied spirits through a medium.

Christian Left: an array of left-wing Christian political groups that tend to embrace socialist theories to combat poverty and economic injustices.

Christian Postmodernism: a hybrid worldview that incorporates elements of postmodern philosophy and Christian theology.

Christianity: a theistic worldview centered on the person of Jesus Christ that derives its understanding of the world through the teachings of the Holy Bible.

Civil Disobedience: the practice of resisting a government's unjust laws.

Class Consciousness: the belief that the working class is becoming increasingly aware of its position in society and its oppression by the bourgeoisie.

Classical Conditioning: a training technique developed by Ivan Pavlov that pairs a naturally occurring stimulus and response with an unrelated stimulus, so that eventually, the unrelated stimulus is able to produce the desired response in absence of the natural stimulus.

Cognitive Behaviorism: a school of psychology that reduces all behavior to cognitive functioning and seeks to explain behavior by examining underlying cognitive causes.

Collective Consciousness: the belief that everything is ultimately energy and that everyone possesses the potential to achieve divine unity with the cosmos.

Common Law: a legal system in which courts reach legal decisions based upon prior judicial precedent reached through common sense and reason.

Communism: the Marxist ideal of a classless and stateless utopian society in which all property is commonly owned and each person is paid according to his or her abilities and needs.

Communist Manifesto: commissioned by the Communist League and written by Karl Marx and Friedrich Engels, *The Communist Manifesto* is the 1848 political tract outlining the league's goal and means for eliminating capitalism and achieving a communist society through a proletariat revolution.

Conditioned Reflex: an automatic response engrained within an animal through the repeated introduction of certain stimuli.

Consciousness: the belief in a divine interconnected essence of reality.

Constructivism: the belief that scientific knowledge is merely a helpful social construct for understanding human sensory perceptions of reality but not direct and accurate knowledge of reality itself.

Correspondence Theory of Truth: the view that the truth of a proposition is determined by how accurately it describes the facts of reality.

Cosmological Argument: an argument for God's existence that begins with the premise that something caused the universe to exist and ends with the conclusion that God is the best explanation for the existence of the universe.

Cosmology: the study of the structure, origin, and design of the universe.

Critical Legal Studies (CLS): the practice of deconstructing laws in order to discover their subjective meaning and biased intent.

Cultural Relativism: the belief that truth and morals are relative to one's community.

Cyclical Conception of History: the belief that history follows a repeating pattern of recurring ages.

Decentered Self: the belief that human beings are social constructions without any singular identifiable essence, nature, or soul.

Deconstruction: a method of literary analysis that questions the ability of language to represent reality adequately and seeks to discern and expose the purported underlying ideologies of a text.

Deep Ecology: an environmental philosophy based on the idea that all living beings form a spiritual and ecologically interconnected system, which is presently threatened by the harmful impact of human beings; a philosophy that advocates a radical restructuring of society toward environmental preservation, simple living, legal rights for all living creatures, and a reduction in the human population.

Deism: the belief that God exists and that he created the world, but that he currently stands completely aloof from his creation; the belief that reason and nature sufficiently reveal the existence of God, but that God has not revealed himself through any type of special revelation.

Deontological Ethics: any ethical system that judges the morality of actions based upon some principle of duty.

Descriptive Pluralism: the belief that we should be tolerant of competing religions in order to get along with one another.

Determinism: the belief that all events, including human actions, are the inevitable and necessary results of previous actions.

Deviance: behavior or actions that violate consensual social norms.

Dhimmis: non-Muslims living in Islamic states.

Dhimmitude: a provision in shariah law that allows *dhimmis* (i.e., non-Muslims) to live in Islamic states in exchange for paying the *jizya* (i.e., tax).

Dialectical Materialism: the belief that only the material world exists and that class struggles are the mechanism behind social and economic progress (e.g., the current economic clash between the proletariat and bourgeoisie will eventually give way to socialism and the end of capitalism).

Distributive Justice: the belief that a just society should seek to redistribute its citizens' resources equally among everyone.

Divine Command Theory: the belief that right and wrong are determined by God's commands.

Dualism: the belief that reality is ultimately composed of two essential substances.

Ecofeminism: a political philosophy that links the oppression of women and the exploitation of the environment with the values inherent in what advocates refer to as Western patriarchal society.

Economic Competition: rivalry between two or more companies to offer the best products at the best prices and at the highest profit margins.

Economic Determinism: the belief that economics determines the entire course of human history, ultimately and inevitability leading to a communist future.

Economic Interventionism: an economic system in which the government influences aspects of a market economy in an attempt to improve the public good.

Economics: the study of the management of resources.

Epiphenomenalism: the belief that mental events are completely dependent upon physical events and have no independent existence (i.e., the "mind" is a projection of the brain's activity).

Epiphenomenon: secondary phenomenon that supervenes from a primary phenomenon but cannot be reduced to the primary phenomenon.

Epistemological Humility: a humble attitude toward the beliefs we hold realizing that our beliefs might be incomplete or mistaken.

Epistemology: the branch of philosophy that seeks to understand the nature of knowledge.

Ethical Egoism: the belief that we ought to do whatever is in our own best interest.

Ethical Libertarianism: the belief that human beings should be free to act however they want as long as they don't infringe on anyone else's liberty.

Ethics: the study of moral conduct, values, duties, and goodness.

Eudaimonism: the belief that the purpose of human existence is to live a life of flourishing.

Eugenics: a social movement advocating the genetic improvement of the human race through such practices as selective breeding, compulsory sterilization, forced abortions, and genocide.

Evolutionary Godhood: the belief that we are progressing through history toward the ultimate goal of realizing our own divinity.

Existentialism: the belief that there is no inherent purpose in the universe; therefore, it is up to human beings to create meaning for themselves.

Fact: something that is indisputably known to be true.

Fascism: a political system usually headed by a charismatic leader and based upon a strong sense of pride, superiority, and veneration of one's state that asserts the right of stronger nations and people to displace or eradicate the weaker states.

Fatalism: the belief that all events are predetermined and inevitable.

Fideism: the belief that faith and reason are independent or at odds with one another.

Fitrah: the belief that all human beings have an innate predisposition toward submitting to Allah and acting morally.

Foundationalism: the theory that basic beliefs exist and form the foundation for knowledge.

Fourth Force Psychology: a school of psychology that attempts to integrate aspects of transcendental religious teachings within the framework of modern psychology.

Free Market Economy: an economy in which economic decisions are freely made by households and firms.

Free Will: the belief that human beings have the capacity to voluntarily choose a course of action from among various alternatives.

Gaia Hypothesis: postulated by James Lovelock, the Gaia hypothesis is the theory that all living organisms form a collective, self-regulating living entity.

Gene Flow: the belief that favorable traits can be passed on (or unfavorable eliminated) when a migratory group breeds with a native group.

General Revelation: God's universal revelation about himself (Ps. 19:1–6; Rom. 1:18–20) and morality (Rom. 2:14–15) that can be obtained through nature.

Genetic Drift: the belief that favorable traits can be passed on (or unfavorable traits eliminated) from one generation to the next strictly by chance.

Genetic Information Theory: the theory that the complexity and information within DNA molecules reveal evidence for design.

Hadith: The oral history of Muhammad's teachings, rulings, and the actions of his early companions.

Hajj: the fifth pillar of Islam, *hajj* is the mandatory pilgrimage to Mecca for all Muslims with the ability and means to make the journey.

Hedonism: the belief that we ought to do whatever maximizes our own personal pleasure.

Hegelian Dialectic: an aspect of Hegel's idealism that purports that humanity's philosophical theories are constantly evolving through the conflict and resolution of competing beliefs—as conflicting ideas are proposed and assessed, the collective of humanity keeps what is true and progresses forward toward absolute knowledge. The dialectic works through stages or cycles: a thesis (i.e., a dominant theory) and an antithesis (i.e., any viable and conflicting theory) will inevitably clash, resulting in some type of synthesis of the two opposing ideas. The resulting synthesis then becomes the new thesis, which competes with its own antithesis and produces a new synthesis.

Hierarchy of Needs: a psychological theory proposed by Abraham Maslow that contends that after individuals meet their basic needs, they will seek to satisfy successively higher needs until they reach their full human potential.

Higher Consciousness: the state of awareness wherein individuals realize their divinity and the divine interconnectedness of all things.

Historical Materialism: the belief that society is guided by nature through progressive socioeconomic phases: tribalism, slavery, feudalism, capitalism, socialism, and ultimately communism.

Historical Revisionism: the act of reinterpreting the past to serve an ideological purpose.

Historicism: the writing of history for the purpose of making certain future states appear to be inevitable, thus projecting an interpretation of history onto the future.

Historiography: the writing of history or the study of the methodology historians use to reconstruct historical events.

Humanist Manifesto: the title of three manifestos laying out a Secular Humanist worldview. They are *Humanist Manifesto I* (1933), *Humanist Manifesto II* (1973), and *Humanist Manifesto 2000*. The central theme of all three is the elaboration of a philosophy and value system that do not include belief in God.

Identity Politics: a political ideology that seeks to advance the interests of particular social groups who are the purported victims of social injustices because of their particular identities (e.g., women, minorities, and homosexuals).

Intelligent Design Movement: a scientific movement that studies the information, design, and complexity found within the cosmos and concludes that an intelligent designer is the most plausible explanation for life and the universe.

Intelligent Design: the study of information, complexity, and design in life and the cosmos; the theory that life could not have arisen by chance and random natural processes but was designed by an intelligent being.

Irreducible Complexity: A concept that considers the complexity of integrated systems such that if any part is removed, the system ceases to function. Applied to biology, it challenges the notion that complex biological systems (e.g., the eye) could have gradually evolved through a series of intermediary steps.

Islam: a theistic worldview centered on the life of the prophet Muhammad that derives its understanding of the world through the teachings of the Quran, Hadith, and *Sunnah*.

Islamic Theocracy: a state ruled by Islam and Islamic religious leaders.

Islamist: a Muslim who embraces the full application of shariah law and who views jihad as a call to conquer nonbelieving nations.

Jihad: from the Arabic word translated as "struggle," jihad is both the inner spiritual battle of every Muslim to fulfill his or her religious duties and the outer, physical struggle against the enemies of Islam.

Jihadi: an Islamist who embraces the use of terrorism in pursuit of jihad.

Jizya: a tax imposed on *dhimmis* (i.e., non-Muslims) living in Islamic states.

Justice: the enforcement aspect of the law that focuses on reasonable, proper, fair, and equal rules.

Kalam Cosmological Argument: an argument for God's existence that begins with the premise that something caused the universe to exist and ends with the conclusion that God is the best explanation for that cause.

Karma: a concept found in Eastern religions, karma is the belief that good is returned to those who do good, and evil is returned to those who do evil (either in this life or the next).

Knowledge: justified true belief.

Law: the study of ordinances designed to help citizens coexist peacefully.

Legal Positivism: the belief that laws are rules created by human authorities and that there is no inherent or necessary connection between law and morality.

Liberation Theology: a political movement that interprets the teachings of Jesus Christ as a call to liberate the poor from the materialistic conditions of social, economic, and political oppression.

Libertarianism: a political philosophy that upholds individual liberty as that highest good based upon the principle that people should be allowed to do whatever they want as along as they do not infringe upon the rights of others.

Linear Conception of History: the belief that history follows a chronological pattern of cause and effect.

Macroeconomics: the branch of economics that studies how large economies function as a whole, focusing on such things as gross domestic product (GDP), unemployment, tax rates, inflation, and the like.

Macroevolution: the belief that small, adaptive changes are capable of accumulating over time to produce entirely new species.

Maharishi Effect: the belief that positive improvement in the quality of life within a community can be brought about by a large group of people collectively engaged in the practice of Transcendental Mediation (TM), first described by Maharishi Mahesh Yogi.

Marxism: an atheistic and materialistic worldview based on the ideas of Karl Marx that promotes the abolition of private property, the public ownership of the means of production (i.e., socialism), and the utopian dream of a future communistic state.

Materialism: the belief that reality is composed solely of matter.

Meditation: the art of focusing one's mind to induce a higher state of consciousness.

Metanarrative: a single, overarching interpretation, or grand story, of reality.

Metaphysics: the branch of philosophy that seeks to understand the nature of ultimate reality.

Microeconomics: the branch of economics that studies how households and firms buy, sell, and allocate resources.

Microenterprises: businesses with no employees.

Microevolution: the belief that small, adaptive changes are capable of producing variations within the gene pool of a species.

Mind/Body Dualism: the belief that human beings are composed of immaterial minds and material bodies.

Mind/Body Monism: the belief that human beings are composed of a single substance.

Mind/Body Problem: the study of the relationship between the mind (e.g., mental events, mental functions, mental properties, and consciousness) and the physical body.

Modernism: A broad term used to describe a range of arts, attitudes, philosophies, and cultural moods that emerged following the eighteenth-century Enlightenment. It is characterized by a strong belief in rationalism, empiricism, science, and technological progress, as well as skepticism toward the supernatural, special revelation, and the authority of religion.

Monism: the belief that reality is ultimately composed of one essential substance.

Monomyth: popularized by Joseph Campbell, a monomyth is the theory that cultures throughout time have shared a common theme within their popular stories—the "hero's journey," which unfolds in three distinct acts: the hero's departure, initiation, and triumphant return.

Monotheism: the belief in a single deity.

Moral Relativism: the belief that morality is relative to, or defined by, the individual or culture.

Moral Skepticism: the belief that moral knowledge is either unknowable or does not exist.

Morality: a personal standard of determining right and wrong.

Mutation: a change in the genetic makeup of an organism.

Natural Law: the belief that laws are rules based upon on an internal code of morality possessed by all people.

Natural Selection (aka Survival of the Fittest): the process by which organisms better adapted for their environment tend to survive longer, reproduce, and pass along more favorable biological traits.

Naturalism: the belief that all phenomena can be explained in terms of natural causes.

Nazism (aka National Socialism): the totalitarian, fascist, and socialist political system of World War II Germany that sought to establish its perceived racial superiority by eliminating all non-Aryan people and nations.

Neo-Darwinism: a synthesis of Charles Darwin's and Gregor Mendel's theories, neo-Darwinism is the belief that new species arise through the process of natural selection acting over vast periods of time on chance genetic mutations within organisms.

New Atheism: a contemporary form of atheism that not only denies the existence of God but also contends that religion should be vehemently criticized, condemned, and opposed.

New Spirituality: a pantheistic worldview that teaches everything and everyone are connected through divine consciousness.

Nihilism: the view that the world and human existence are without meaning, purpose, comprehensible truth, or essential value.

Nirvana: a concept found in Indian religions, nirvana is the transcendent state of ultimate peace and highest happiness achieved through one's release from the bondages of karma, suffering, worldly desire, and individual consciousness.

Objectivism: a worldview developed by Ayn Rand based on metaphysical realism, ethical egoism, laissez-faire economics, and political libertarianism.

Occult: Various spiritual or supernatural practices including alchemy, astrology, divination, and magic that can be found in religious groups observing Gnosticism, neo-paganism, Satanism, Wicca, and the like.

Ontology: a subcategory of metaphysics, ontology is the study of existence and being.

Order: the administrative aspect of the law that focuses on ensuring safety and efficiency.

Pan-Islam: the belief that all Muslims should be united under a single Islamic state or that the world should be united under a global Islamic state.

Panspermia: the belief that life exists throughout the universe and has been dispersed by interstellar bodies, such as asteroids, meteoroids, and comets.

Pantheism: the belief that everything in the universe is ultimately divine.

Patriarchal Society: a society dominated by men.

Personal Autonomy: the belief that individuals should have the freedom to decide what is right for their own lives and live in whatever manner brings them the most happiness.

Philosophy: the study of knowledge, truth, and the nature of ultimate reality.

Physics: the study of matter and its motion through time and space.

Political Conservatism: a system of government based on respect for historical precedent, limited government, a strict interpretation of the US Constitution, and adherence to traditional moral principles based on natural law.

Political Correctness: the censoring of language, ideas, acts, or policies that are perceived to discriminate or alienate minority social groups.

Political Liberalism: a system of government based upon the belief that individual and social ills are best ameliorated through direct government intervention.

Political Pessimism: a general distrust for any political system's ability to alleviate social problems.

Politics: the study of community governance.

Polytheism: the belief in a multitude of deities.

Positive Psychology: a branch of psychology that focuses on promoting mental health and happiness rather than just treating mental illness.

Postmodernism: a skeptical worldview, founded as a reaction to modernism, that is suspicious of metanarratives and teaches that ultimate reality is inaccessible, knowledge is a social construct, and truth claims are political power plays.

Poststructuralism: an intellectual movement that agrees with structuralism—it is more important to study language and relationship because it is impossible to have knowledge of objective reality—but progresses further by contending that human communication is not really about things but about the views and motivations of those involved in the conversation.

Power: the ability to do something or act in a particular way.

Pragmatism: the belief that propositions do not mirror reality and should therefore be treated as tools and judged only by their practical consequences.

Prescriptive Pluralism: the belief that we should be tolerant of other religions because no single religion can be universally true for everyone.

Principle of Comparative Advantage: an economic principal that states a company or nation that focuses on producing goods and services at the lowest opportunity cost can maximize its profits and create an economy with the best prices for consumers. (E.g., if Nation A can produce one hundred shirts at ten dollars per hour or fifty shoes at ten dollars per hour, and Nation B can produce one hundred shoes at ten dollars per hour or fifty shirts at ten dollars per hour, then it is best for Nation A to produce shirts, Nation B to produce shoes, and for both nations to trade with each other.)

Progressive Creationism: the belief that God created the cosmos and all life in its present form, in progressive stages, over a long period of time.

Progressivism: the belief in human progress; the belief that political systems can be used to create economic prosperity, minimize risk, and advance society.

Proletariat: a term used in Marxist theory to describe the working-class wage earners who do not own the means of production.

Proletariat Law: a system of laws shaped by Communist Party officials that are intended to promote the interests of the working class over the bourgeoisie.

Proletariat Morality: the belief that whatever advances the proletariat and communism is morally good, and whatever hinders the proletariat and communism is morally evil.

Proletariat Society: a socialist society shaped by Communist Party officials to promote the values of the working class over the bourgeoisie.

Propaganda: biased, selective, misleading, and/or manipulating information circulated with the goal of changing opinions and influencing action toward a particular position or cause.

Psychoanalysis: an approach to psychology developed by Sigmund Freud whereby a psychologist attempts to resolve a patient's psychological problems by uncovering and discussing the patient's unconscious, unfulfilled, or repressed desires.

Psychology: the study of the human mind (or soul).

Punctuated Equilibrium: the belief that evolutionary changes occur over relatively quick periods of time, followed by periods of time with little or no evolutionary change.

Pure Nature View of Politics: the belief that human beings are inherently good and can be perfected under the right political conditions.

Quantum Physics: the branch of physics dealing with physical phenomena on the subatomic level, where particles behave in a fashion difficult to quantify and understand using the scientific method.

Quran: the central holy book of Islam that Muslims believe to be the literal word of God, recited verbatim from God to Muhammad through the angel Gabriel.

Realism: the belief that an objective reality exists independent of human perception or language.

Redemptive Narrative: the Christian metanarrative that describes the course of history unfolding according to the biblical chronicle of God's creative act, humanity's rebellion, Christ's redemptive sacrifice, and God's eventual restoration of his creation.

Reincarnation: the belief that after biological death, the soul is reborn in a new body—either animal, human, or spirit—to continue its quest for enlightenment.

Relativism: the belief that truth, knowledge, or morality is relative to the individual, society, or historical context.

Religion: a system of belief that attempts to define the nature of God and how human beings can understand and interact with the divine; any system of belief that prescribes certain responses to the existence (or non existence) of the divine.

Religious Pluralism: the acknowledgment that many different religions exist in today's diverse society.

Riba: an Arabic word meaning either interest or excessive interest.

Sadism: named after Marquis de Sade, the practice of obtaining gratification by inflicting pain (especially sexual pain) on others.

Salat: the second pillar of Islam, *salat* is praying five times per day facing Mecca.

Sawm: the fourth pillar of Islam, *sawm* is a special time set aside for fasting during the month of Ramadan.

Say's Law: formulated by Jean-Baptiste Say, Say's law is the belief that the availability of a good or service creates a demand equal to its value (i.e., product value is a function of supply and demand).

Scientific Empiricism: the belief that we can know only what we discover through the scientific method.

Scientific Method: a process of empirical inquiry that seeks to understand the phenomena of the physical world through hypothesizing, observing, measuring, experimenting, predicting, and testing.

Scientism: the philosophical belief that reliable knowledge is obtained solely through the scientific method.

Second Law of Thermodynamics: a scientific law that states that the amount of usable energy in a closed system will decrease over time.

Secular Humanism: a religious and philosophical worldview that makes humankind the ultimate norm by which truth and values are to be determined; a worldview that reveres human reason, evolution, naturalism, and secular theories of ethics while rejecting every form of supernatural religion.

Secularism: an atheistic and materialistic worldview that advocates a public society free from the influence of religion.

Selective Breeding: the process by which human beings selectively breed organisms with desirable traits to produce a line of offspring with the same desirable traits.

Self-actualization: the stage at which a person purportedly meets his or her full psychological potential (some characteristics include self-acceptance, genuineness, independence, gratitude, social interest, tolerance, creativity, and self-sufficiency).

Self-law: the legal perspective that maintains actions are lawful only if honorable to the god within and unlawful if imposed by an outside authority.

Shahada: the first pillar of Islam, *shahada* is the confession of faith: "There is no God but Allah, and Muhammad is his prophet."

Shariah Economics: derived primarily from the Quran and Sunnah, shariah economics is the economic requirements that govern the lives of Muslims.

Shariah Law: Derived primarily from the Quran and *Sunnah*, shariah law is the moral and legal code that governs the lives of Muslims. Shariah addresses a wide variety of subjects, such as diet, hygiene, prayer, contracts, business, crime, and punishment.

Shiite Islam: (aka Shia Islam): the second largest branch of Islam, this faction believes that Muhammad's successor should be someone from his bloodline.

Shirk: the unforgivable sin of idolatry or polytheism in Islam; in Arabic it means to "partner" another with God; i.e., worship anyone or anything besides Allah.

Sin Nature View of Politics: the belief that human beings are inherently sinful, and government is necessary to secure peace.

Situation Ethics: the belief that the morality of an action is determined by the unique situation of that action.

Social Constructionism: the belief that human beings and society are social constructions shaped by language and subjective experiences.

Social Contract: the belief that individuals within a society form either an implicit or explicit agreement with their government, whereby citizens forfeit some freedoms in exchange for safety.

Social Darwinism: the application of the Darwinian theory of natural selection to the disciplines of sociology, economics, and politics.

Social Progress: the belief that society will continually improve through human initiative.

Socialism: an economic system based upon governmental or communal ownership of the means of production and distribution of goods and services.

Sociological Determinism: the belief that our actions are ultimately the result of social conditions.

Sociology: the study of human societies and institutions.

Sophism: a pre-Socratic school of philosophy that taught the art of rhetoric and held skeptical views of truth, knowledge, and morality; a derogatory term used to describe a specious argument intended to manipulate, trick, or deceive.

Special Creation: the belief that the cosmos and all life were brought into existence by the creative act of God.

Special Revelation: God's unique revelation about himself through the Scriptures (Ps. 19:7–11; 2 Tim. 3:14–17), miraculous events (e.g., dreams, visions, prophets, prophecy, etc.), and Jesus Christ (John 1:1–18).

Sphere Sovereignty: the belief that God ordained certain spheres of society, such as family, church, and state, and that society functions best when each sphere is properly managing its own area of responsibility.

Spiritual Evolution: the belief that humanity is continually progressing toward higher consciousness.

Spiritual Monism: the belief that reality is ultimately divine.

Spontaneous Generation: the belief that nonliving matter produced living matter through purely natural processes.

State Capitalism: the practice of federal governments taking ownership and management control of private businesses.

Statism: a political system in which a highly centralized government holds the concentration of economic controls and planning.

Structuralism: an intellectual movement that believes human knowledge is not based on an accurate understanding of reality but is the product of linguistically constructed forms or grammars that societies have developed over time.

Subsidiarity: the belief that decisions are best handled at the organizational or societal level closest to the issues or persons affected.

Sufi Islam: a branch of Islam that arose as a protest to the worldliness invading the Muslim faith, this faction believes that Allah has a personal and mystical nature.

Sunnah: part of the Hadith describing Muhammad's exemplary actions.

Sunni Islam: the largest branch of Islam, this faction believes that Muhammad's successor should be chosen by a consensus of Muslims.

Surplus Value Theory of Labor: According to Karl Marx, the value of a good or service should be equal to the average number of labor hours required to produce the good or service. This implies that setting prices above this cost leads to a situation in which the bourgeoisie amass wealth at the expense of the proletariat.

Surplus Value: according to Karl Marx, surplus value is the value of a commodity or service that exceeds the cost of labor; that is, profit.

Tawhid: the Islamic belief that God is a single divine person without partners.

Teleological Ethics: any ethical system that judges the morality of actions based upon their consequences.

Teleology: the study of design and purpose in nature.

Theism: the belief in the existence of a God or gods.

Theistic Evolution: the belief that God created the cosmos billions of years ago and then guided the process of biological evolution to produce the diversity of life seen today.

Theocracy: a state ruled by religious leaders or one particular religion.

Theological Suspicion: a general distrust toward any religion claiming to know absolute truth about reality.

Theology: the study of God.

Third Force Psychology: a humanistic psychology that emerged as a reaction to the limitations of behaviorism (i.e., first force) and psychoanalysis (i.e., second force), this theory contends that human beings are innately good physical beings with personal agency who are mentally healthy when focused upon achieving self-actualization.

Tolerance: the willingness to recognize and respect the dignity of those with whom one disagrees.

Tort Law: the area of law governing remedies for those wronged by others, such as through negligence.

Transaction Costs: the expenses incurred when making an economic exchange (e.g., legal fees, contract fees, communication charges, warranty options, etc.).

Transcendentalism: a religious and philosophical movement that arose in the early 1800s as a reaction against rationalism and organized religion, it teaches that human beings are inherently good and that nature is fundamentally divine.

Transhumanism: a humanistic movement that hopes to advance humanity beyond its physical and mental limitations through the application and integration of biotechnology.

Trinitarian Monotheism: the belief in one God recognized as three separate and distinct persons: Father, Son, and Spirit.

Ummah: from the Arabic word for "nation," *ummah* is the collective community of Muslims around the world.

Universal Enlightened Production: the belief that an individual's financial success is directly proportional to his or her level of enlightenment; the belief that positive thought creates wealth.

Usury: the practice of lending money at an exorbitant rate of interest.

Utilitarianism: the belief that we ought to do whatever maximizes happiness and reduces suffering for the greatest number of people.

Visualization: the act of attempting to achieve a particular outcome through concentrating and meditating upon that outcome.

Welfare-State Capitalism: a combined capitalistic and socialistic economy in which the state redistributes wealth created in a free market environment.

Worldview: a pattern of ideas, beliefs, convictions, and habits that help us make sense of God, the world, and our relationship to God and the world.

Young Age Creationism: the belief that God created the cosmos and all life in its present forms, in six literal days, around six thousand years ago.

Zakat: the third pillar of Islam, *zakat* is the donation of 2.5 percent of a Muslim's annual income.

INDEX

capitalism, 13, 100, 103, 105, 107, 109, 110, 113, 114, 115, 117, 120, 124, 178, 192, 205, 234, 235, 303, 314, 315, 332, 347, 358, 373–74, 389, 390, 404, 405, 406, 407, 408, 410, 411, 415, 416, 417, 420, 422, 423, 433, 434, 435, 454, 466, 468, 472, 473, 479, 482, 484, 487, 496, 498

Capra, Fritjof, 212, 221

Carey, Ken, 292, 303

Carey, William, 328

Carpenter, Joel, 383, 392

Carrier, Richard, 433, 446

Casanova, Jose, 77, 94

Casler, Lawrence, 313–14, 332

Castro, Fidel, 102, 235, 236, 249, 373, 374, 375, 390

Chambers, Whittaker, 118

Chavez, Hugo, 374, 375, 390

Chopra, Deepak, 12, 92, 125, 126, 127, 128–30, 137, 140, 142, 144, 220, 265, 266, 277, 302, 463, 478

Christian Left, 14, 112, 482

Christian Postmodernism 165, 221, 482

Christian Postmodernists, 165, 171, 221

Claiborne, Shane, 383

Clifton, Jim, 402, 419

Cold War, 94, 230

Collins, Francis, 46, 186, 194

Colson, Charles, 386–387, 388, 392, 393, 470, 479

Common Faith, 23, 192

Communist League, 109, 482

Communist Manifesto, 13, 100, 103, 109, 113, 114, 115, 117, 118, 119, 177, 316, 317, 332, 482

Communist Party, 109, 116, 166, 314, 347, 360, 390, 479, 492

Confucianism, 7, 212

Confucius, 136, 168, 227

Cornforth, Maurice, 206, 221, 433, 434, 446

correspondence theory of truth, 149, 169, 206, 207, 483

Cosmic Humanism, 22–23, 125

Courtois, Stephane, 39, 48, 117, 119

Craig, William Lane, 194, 223, 304, 478

Crick, Francis, 79, 186

critical legal studies (CLS), 349, 483

Crusades, 380

Cuba, 101, 102, 236, 374, 375, 405

- D -

Dalai Lama, 92, 128, 129, 131, 132, 133, 142, 143, 166, 171, 213, 222, 237, 250, 292, 303, 455, 476

Darrow, Clarence, 204, 254, 255

Darwin, Charles, 39, 47, 84, 85, 86, 95, 108, 180, 186, 194, 202, 249, 255, 257, 258, 259, 261, 262, 266, 274, 276, 277, 278, 279, 344, 431, 463, 478, 490

Darwinism, 194, 231, 254, 257, 258, 259, 261, 262, 264, 266, 269, 273, 274, 275, 276, 277, 279, 314, 392, 445, 479, 490, 495

Davies, Paul, 439, 447

Dawkins, Richard, 87, 90, 95, 175, 192, 264, 273, 275, 279

Dawson, Christopher, 311, 331

de Chardin, Pierre Teilhard, 266, 267, 277, 278

decentered self, 290, 409, 483

deconstruction, 14, 157, 164, 165, 168, 436, 437, 456, 483

Deigh, John, 228, 249

Deleuze, Gilles, 179, 303

Dembski, William A., 220, 269, 276, 279

Dennett, Daniel, 87, 154, 160, 164, 170, 175, 264, 265, 277

Federer, William J., 70, 103, 117

Ferencz, Benjamin, 144, 439, 447, 472, 479

Ferguson, Marilyn, 12, 126, 133, 134, 142, 143, 182, 193, 213, 222, 237, 238, 249, 250, 266, 267, 278, 292, 303, 320, 321, 333, 377–79, 391, 411, 421, 438, 447

Ferry, Luc, 12, 23, 244, 250

Feuerbach, Ludwig, 118, 153, 177, 277, 303

Feyerabend, Paul, 160, 161, 170

fideism, 214, 485

first cause, 29, 63, 133, 185, 202, 222, 278

First Law of Thermodynamics, 185

Fish, Stanley, 162, 349, 360

Fletcher, Joseph, 233, 249

Flew, Antony, 186, 194

Folsom, Burton, 103, 118

Foster, William Z., 109, 111, 119

Foucault, Michel, 14, 153–54, 157, 162, 166, 169, 179, 192, 200, 207, 221, 264, 290, 291, 303, 317, 318, 332, 333, 349, 376, 390, 410, 420, 436–37, 446–47, 466, 479

foundationalism, 207, 221, 485

Francis, Joe, 275, 279

Franklin, Benjamin, 78, 339

Freud, Sigmund, 86, 181, 262, 285–286, 302, 492

Freudianism, 292

Friedman, Milton, 371, 389

Fromm, Erich, 286, 302, 312, 314, 332, 405, 406, 420, 432, 446

Fuller, Lon, 342, 343, 359, 391

Fuller, Robert C., 127, 142

fundamentalism, 221, 392

- G -

Gaia hypothesis, 13, 134–35, 143, 212, 486

Gairdner, William, 232, 249

Galbraith, John Kenneth, 406, 420

Gandhi, Mahatma, 139, 475

Garber, Steven D., 255, 276

Gawain, Shakti, 12, 212, 222, 237, 249, 250, 320, 333, 352, 360, 411–12, 421, 420, 438, 447

Gay, Craig, 81, 95, 284, 302

GDP (gross domestic product), 398, 419, 420, 488

Geisler, Norman, 23, 63, 71, 194, 195, 222–23, 246, 251, 278, 294, 303, 443, 446, 448

genetic information theory, 186, 486

general revelation, 34, 35, 36, 45, 62, 84, 86, 108, 133, 160, 162, 182, 183, 184, 296, 356, 465, 468, 486

Gergen, Kenneth, 163, 171, 290, 303

Gettysburg Address, 189

Giddens, Anthony, 311–12, 331–2, 333

Gilder, George, 398, 402, 403, 407, 419, 420

Gimenez, Martha, 104, 118

GLAAD (Gay and Lesbian Alliance Against Defamation), 313, 332

Gladwell, Malcolm, 3, 22

Goldberg, Jonah, 406, 420

Goldblatt, Mark, 179, 192–3, 447

Golden Rule, 234

Gorbachev, Mikhail, 315, 332

Gorgias, 151–52, 157, 163

Gould, Stephen Jay, 260, 263, 264, 276, 277

Graham, Billy, 92

Gramsci, Antonio, 109

Grenz, Stanley, 221, 277, 478

Groothuis, Douglas, 5, 142, 143, 217, 221, 223, 476

Grudem, Wayne, 282, 302

Grunwald, Henry, 232, 249

Guatemala, 148, 169

Guevara, Ernesto Che, 100, 102, 117, 236

- *H* -

Habermas, Gary, 44, 194

Habermas, Jürgen, 168, 244, 250

Hagelin, John, 378, 391

Halliday, Jon, 39, 47, 117, 477

Hamas, 70, 361

Harris, Sam, 87, 175

Hawking, Stephen, 255, 257, 276, 480

hedonism, 228, 486

Hegel, Georg Wilhelm Friedrich, 35, 105, 106, 113, 118, 119, 177, 191, 205, 220, 232, 262, 263, 428, 433, 445, 486

Heidegger, Martin, 14, 156, 157, 162, 170

Henry, Carl F. H., 38, 40, 47, 48, 191, 192, 193, 223, 245, 246, 249, 251,355, 361, 468, 478, 479

Herodians, 385, 392

Herodotus, 426

Herskovits, Melville, 166, 171

Hick, John, 192, 477

Hicks, Stephen, 376, 390, 446, 473, 479

higher consciousness, 22, 23, 89, 113, 135, 136, 137, 236, 237, 238, 243, 265, 266, 267, 292, 293, 320, 321, 324, 352, 411, 412, 438, 439, 440, 456, 462, 463, 465, 466, 468, 476, 486, 496

Hinduism, 7, 23, 56, 83, 131, 142, 192, 212, 237, 292, 455

historical materialism, 118, 192, 220, 433, 446, 487

historical revisionism, 437, 487

historicism, 231, 429–30, 445, 487

historiography, 429, 487

Hitchens, Christopher, 37, 87, 175

Hitler, Adolf, 8, 40, 90, 94, 95, 96, 101, 102, 167, 238, 239, 248, 249, 376, 382, 404, 431

Hobbes, Thomas, 228, 232, 283, 367, 389

Hocutt, Max, 203, 230, 345, 392

Hofstadter, Douglas R., 161, 170

Holmes, Oliver Wendell, 344, 359

Hook, Sidney, 370, 371, 389, 422

hooks, bell, 104

Horton, Michael, 384, 392

Hoyle, Fred, 35, 47, 457, 477

Hugo, Victor, 226, 248

Human Genome Project, 186

Humanism, Christian, 175

Humanist Manifesto, 79–80, 87, 94, 95, 96, 166, 171, 187, 231, 249, 431, 432, 446, 453, 487

Hume, David, 35, 232, 273

Hunter, James Davidson, 310, 392

Husserl, Edmund, 155, 170, 457

Huxley, Aldous, 286

Huxley, Julian, 13, 43, 48, 85, 88, 90, 95, 96, 175, 176, 192, 257, 259, 276, 343, 370, 372, 389, 431, 445, 469, 479

- *I* -

I, Rigoberta Menchu, 148, 169

identity politics, 376–77, 487

intelligent design, 9, 23, 95, 134, 187, 261, 269, 274, 278, 279, 487

irreducible complexity, 273, 487

Isenberg, Nancy, 428, 445

Islam, pillars of, 66–67, 242, 361, 380, 414, 453, 486, 493, 494, 498

Islamic states, 52, 53, 56, 66, 72, 323, 361, 379, 380, 381, 382, 413, 414, 440, 453, 466, 469, 484, 488, 490

Islamic theocracy, 379, 487

Islamists, 51, 54, 55, 65, 67, 323, 354, 361, 381, 382, 440, 447, 453, 487–88

Islamophobia, 249, 361

- J -

Jackson, Maggie, 78, 94

Jacoby, Susan, 78, 81, 94, 202, 220

Jainism, 7

James, William, 233, 286

Jameson, Fredric, 104, 114, 120, 317, 332

Jefferson, Thomas, 78, 286, 358, 363, 368, 426

jihad, 54, 55, 62, 65, 67, 70, 71, 295, 353, 354, 361, 380, 381, 391, 440, 469, 487, 488

jihadis, 55, 65, 242, 380, 453, 488

jizya, 66, 69, 72, 114, 381, 414, 415, 421, 484, 488

Johnson, Phillip E., 269, 277, 478

Judaism, 11, 56, 59, 183, 193, 292, 439

Juergensmeyer, Mark, 84, 94, 95

- K -

Kaaba, 56, 57

kalam cosmological argument, 63, 214, 488

Kant, Immanuel, 35, 191, 229, 231, 232

Kateregga, Badru D., 61, 64, 71, 267, 269, 278, 463, 478

Kennedy, Anthony, 468

Kennedy, D. James, 40, 48, 334

Keyes, Ken, Jr., 144, 439, 447, 472, 479

Keynes, John Maynard, 403, 420

Khrushchev, Nikita, 110, 111, 115, 119, 120

Kilby, Clyde, 95, 194, 477

Kilpatrick, William Kirk, 284, 295, 296, 301, 302, 303, 305

Kim Jong-Eun, 235

King, Martin Luther, Jr, 230, 247

Kirk, Russell, 355, 362, 468, 479

Kollontai, Alexandra, 315, 332

Krishna, 123, 124, 131, 237

Kuhn, Thomas, 161, 170, 264

Kurtz, Paul, 13, 78, 87, 91, 93, 95, 96, 166, 171, 174–5, 192, 231, 233, 234, 249, 345, 359, 372, 389, 390, 422, 446

Kuyper, Abraham, 324, 325, 333, 385, 386, 392, 466

- L -

Lacan, Jacques, 162, 179, 263, 264, 290, 291, 303

Lamm, Richard, 403, 420

Lamont, Corliss, 13, 88, 95, 113, 202, 203, 220, 234, 249, 405, 420, 432, 446

legal positivism, 203, 342, 345, 360, 382, 391–92, 467, 470, 488

Leibniz, Gottfried, 35

Lenin, Vladimir, 101, 107, 108, 110, 112, 115, 116, 118, 119, 120, 177, 192, 204, 205, 206, 220, 221, 236, 249, 262, 277, 314, 332, 346, 347, 360, 373, 374, 390, 408, 410, 420, 433–34, 446, 476, 477, 478, 480

Lennox, John, 271, 278, 464, 478, 480

libertarianism, 221, 332, 371, 406, 488, 490

Lincoln, Abraham, 189, 286, 366, 427

Linton, Calvin D., 227, 463

Locke, John, 35, 232, 367–68, 388–89

Loken, Kristanna, 174, 192

London, Herbert, 104, 118

Lonergan, Bernard, 402, 419

Lovelock, James, 134–35, 486

Lucas, George, 22, 25, 128, 142

Luther, Martin, 32, 47, 382, 384

Lyotard, Jean-François, 14, 158, 159, 162, 170, 179, 240, 303, 319, 375, 376, 410

- M -

MacIntyre, Alasdair, 165, 170, 171, 221, 435, 446

MacLaine, Shirley, 130, 131, 132, 236–37, 238, 250, 360, 411, 421, 478

macroevolution, 18, 257–58, 260, 274, 488

Madison, James, 385, 426, 445

Maharishi Effect, 138, 488

Maharishi Mahesh Yogi, 138, 378, 438, 488

Mankiw, N. Gregory, 400, 419, 479

Mansfield, Harvey, 367, 388

Mao Tse-tung, 13, 14, 39, 101, 117, 235, 347, 477

Martin, David, 93

Martin, Malachi, 343, 359, 389, 479

Marx, Karl, 8, 13, 14, 22, 39, 100, 104–20, 166, 177–8, 192, 204, 206, 220, 221, 235, 249, 261, 262, 277, 303, 308, 309, 315, 316, 317, 327, 332, 346, 350, 360, 373, 374, 375, 390, 404, 407, 408, 410, 420, 423, 434, 435, 437, 446, 454, 455, 460, 463, 469, 476, 479, 480, 482, 488, 496

Maslow, Abraham, 86, 286–7, 302, 478, 486

materialism, 77, 79, 84, 88, 92, 93, 106, 140, 200, 202, 204, 205, 219, 220, 221, 227, 239, 261, 262, 275, 287, 296, 297, 298, 310, 314, 326, 330, 343, 370, 414, 453–54, 461, 463, 465, 466, 467, 489

May, Rollo, 283, 302

McDowell, Josh, 44, 49

McGrath, Alister, 164, 171, 193

McKown, Delos, 220, 345, 359

Mecca, 12, 56, 57, 66, 67, 71, 294, 486, 493

Medina, 12, 57

Mendel, Gregor, 259, 490

Menninger, Karl, 299, 304

Meredith, Martin, 401, 419

metanarrative, 14, 21, 125, 148, 158–9, 160, 164, 166, 178, 264, 318, 319, 349, 376, 456, 489, 491, 493

metaphysics, 46, 200, 201, 202, 205, 207, 210, 212, 214, 217, 218, 304, 309, 447, 461, 478, 489, 490

Meyer, Stephen, 9, 95, 194, 272, 273, 274, 279

microevolution, 257, 258, 489

Midgley, Mary, 169, 191, 196

Mill, John Stuart, 228, 233

Milton, Joyce, 287, 302

mind/body dualism, 218, 219, 220, 297, 304, 489

mind/body monism, 88, 204, 220, 284, 489

mind/body problem, 201, 203, 206, 213, 215, 216, 218, 220, 461, 462, 489

Minnow, Martha, 348, 350

Mlodinow, Leonard, 142, 144, 220, 276, 277, 284, 302, 478

modernism, 14, 148, 149, 153, 154, 158, 171, 456, 489, 491

Mogahed, Dalia, 53, 70

Montgomery, John Warwick, 144, 250, 356, 363, 389, 443, 448, 480

Montgomery, Ruth, 130, 142

Moody, Paul Amos, 35, 47, 220

moral skepticism, 228, 489

Moreland, J. P., 47, 95, 170, 194, 218, 223, 265, 277, 296, 297, 303, 304, 305, 462, 465, 478

Motorcycle Diaries, 102, 236, 249

Moyers, Bill, 22, 25, 142

Muller, Robert, 138, 212, 221, 379, 391

Murphy, Nancey, 165, 171, 221

Muslim Brotherhood, 353, 354, 361

Myers, Jeff, 4, 22, 302, 392

- N -

Nagel, Ernest, 31, 46, 177

Nagel, Thomas, 93, 96, 216, 222, 297, 304, 478

Nahem, Joseph, 288, 289, 302, 303

NAMBLA (North American Man/Boy Love Association), 319

Naqvi, Syed Nawab Haider, 113–14, 119, 412, 413, 414, 415, 421, 479

Nasar, Sylvia, 397, 419

Nash, Ronald, 223, 416, 422

Nation of Islam, 58, 69, 72

natural rights, 344, 345, 367

natural selection, 93, 185, 194, 258–9, 261, 263, 264, 266, 267, 273, 274, 276, 288, 490, 495

Nazism, 7, 102, 165, 361, 392, 431, 490

Nebuchadnezzar, 188, 387

Negri, Antonio, 109–10, 119

neo-Darwinian, 259, 264, 274, 490

neo-Marxism, 375

neo-orthodox theology, 191

neuropsychology, 143, 289

New Age movement, 12, 23, 125, 136, 143, 181, 193, 213, 221, 239, 250, 266, 267, 278, 320, 333, 360, 372, 377, 379, 391, 411, 421, 447, 455, 477, 479

New Atheism, 87, 175–76, 490

New Atheists, 89, 175, 176, 220

Newspeak, 157

Newton, Isaac, 133, 185, 368

Nichols, Thomas Low, 307, 331

Nietzsche, Friedrich, 14, 86, 152–3, 154, 163, 169, 179, 210, 221, 228, 233, 257

Niose, David, 77, 81, 90, 91, 94, 95, 96, 453, 476

NLP (Natural Law Party), 378–9

Noebel, David A., 3–4

Novak, Michael, 402, 419, 422–3, 479

Nozick, Robert, 369, 371, 389

Nuremberg trials, 342, 368

- O -

Obama, Barack, 76, 94, 119, 348, 369, 389

objective reality, 129, 156, 159, 164, 204, 205, 207, 215, 349, 481, 491, 493

objective truth, 43, 93, 119, 120, 152, 158, 164, 165, 166, 250, 269, 348, 350, 436

occult, 136, 490

October Revolution, 315, 374

Origin of Species, 86, 95, 108, 194, 255, 257, 261, 276, 277, 431

Orr, James, 184, 194

Orwell, George, 157, 170, 338, 359, 360

- P -

Paine, Thomas, 86

Paley, William, 273

pan-Islam, 323, 440, 490

Pasteur, Louis, 108, 185

patriarchal society, 104, 135, 322, 410, 437, 484, 491

Pavlov, Ivan, 288–9, 302, 465, 478, 482

Pearcey, Nancy, 170, 221, 473, 479

Peck, M. Scott, 439, 447

Peirce, Charles S., 430–31, 479

Penner, Myron B., 149, 151, 169, 221

personal autonomy, 237, 247, 249, 286, 310–11, 377, 491

Phillips, Adam, 239, 241, 318, 462

Pink, Daniel, 403, 420

Planned Parenthood, 475

Plantinga, Alvin, 220, 223, 296, 303

Plantinga, Cornelius, 32, 47

Plato, 34, 152, 277, 422, 479

PLS (profit-and-loss sharing), 414–15, 421

Polanyi, Michael, 161, 170

political correctness, 377, 473, 491

Popper, Karl, 219, 429, 430, 445

Poster, Mark, 436, 446

Pot, Pol, 101, 102, 347

Pound, Roscoe, 345, 360

Price, John Randolph, 136, 143

private property, 13, 19, 100, 102, 105, 112, 114, 115, 207, 316, 332, 340, 360, 373, 390, 400, 408, 410, 413, 415, 416, 417, 418, 421, 454, 471, 488

progressive creationism, 271, 492

proletariat, 105, 106, 107, 110, 112, 116, 177, 205, 235, 236, 262, 316, 346, 347, 374, 376, 390, 407, 408, 433, 434, 454, 468, 472, 482, 484, 492, 496

proletariat morality, 110, 235–36, 462, 492

proletariat society, 314, 492

Provine, William, 261, 463

Ptolemy, Claudius, 208, 209

punctuated equilibrium, 260, 262–63, 264, 267, 276, 277, 492

- Q -

Qureshi, Nabeel, 55, 70, 476

- R -

Rae, Scott, 228, 250, 296, 303, 304, 305, 465, 478

Ramsdell, Edward T., 217, 223

Rand, Ayn, 371, 406, 490

Rawls, John, 343, 359, 369, 371, 389

Reagan, Ronald, 249

realism, 170, 215, 217, 490, 493

Red Brigades, 109

reincarnation, 13, 131, 132, 182, 455, 493

religious pluralism, 179, 180, 192, 477, 493

Religious Right, 90, 334

Richards, Jay, 401, 419

Rogers, Carl, 283, 286, 287, 302

Roosevelt, Eleanor, 286

Roosevelt, Franklin D., 419

Roosevelt, Theodore, 57, 71

Rorty, Richard, 8, 9, 14, 23, 148–49, 164, 169, 171, 179, 180, 193, 208, 209, 239–41, 250, 264, 277, 318, 332, 376, 390, 410, 420

Rose, Lila, 475, 480

Rousseau, Jean-Jacques, 176, 192, 283, 327, 368, 390, 447, 479

Ruccio, David, 163, 171, 283, 409, 410, 420, 421

Rummel, R. J., 23, 39, 48, 117, 171, 360, 390, 477

Ruse, Michael, 85, 95

Rushdie, Salman, 55, 361

Russell, Bertrand, 12, 23, 86, 169, 175, 176, 192, 431, 432, 445, 446

Ruthven, Malise, 67–68, 72, 353, 354, 361, 478–9

Ryerson, Kevin, 182, 193, 239, 250, 320, 333, 352, 412, 421

- S -

Sagan, Carl, 34, 47, 84, 95, 194, 202, 203, 220, 258, 260, 276

Santayana, George, 117, 472, 479

Satanism, 490

Satin, Mark, 352, 360, 379, 391, 479

Sartre, Jean-Paul, 228, 231, 249

Say, Jean-Baptiste, 398, 493

Sayers, Dorothy, 31, 47, 302

Schaeffer, Francis, 129, 142, 234, 244, 246, 249, 250, 251, 278, 301, 305, 328, 329, 333, 334, 356, 362, 387, 392, 393

Schlafly, Phyllis, 334

Schlossberg, Herbert, 430, 445, 479

Schrödinger, Erwin, 255–56, 272, 276, 279

scientific empiricism, 201, 217, 494

scientific method, 43, 85, 93, 124, 133, 176, 201, 203, 205, 216, 217, 233, 283, 288, 309, 454, 461, 493, 494

scientism, 43, 233, 234, 494

Secular Humanism, 13, 23, 80, 113, 389, 494

self-actualization, 285, 286, 287, 292, 465, 494, 497

self-government, 339, 358, 378, 379, 481

Sellars, Roy Wood, 79, 203, 220

Selsam, Howard, 235, 249, 346, 360

Shahid, Samuel, 68, 72, 361

shariah economics, 413, 494

shariah law, 54, 55, 65, 66, 68, 193, 323, 353–55, 379, 413, 453, 466, 469, 484, 487, 494

Shelley, Mary, 310, 331

Sherrington, Charles, 296, 304

Shia Islam, 57, 494

Shiite Islam, 57, 494

Shintoism, 7

Simpson, George Gaylord, 23, 257, 276, 463, 478

Singer, Peter, 475, 480

Sleeper, Raymond S., 118, 119, 249, 315, 332, 408, 409, 420

Smith, Christian, 79, 94, 309–11, 331

Smith, R. Scott, 150, 169, 170, 171, 221

social contract, 192, 367, 369, 495

socialism, 96, 100, 102, 104, 105, 106–7, 112, 113, 114, 115, 116, 117, 118, 119, 120, 165, 167, 171, 205, 234, 249, 360, 371, 373, 376, 390, 392, 393, 405–11, 415–16, 417, 418, 420, 421, 422, 433–34, 447, 454, 471, 472, 476, 479, 484, 487, 488, 490, 495

Socrates, 152, 194, 227

sophism, 152, 169, 495

Sorokin, Pitirim, 310, 323, 333

Sotomayor, Sonia, 348, 349, 350, 360

Soviet Union, 42, 101, 104, 111, 113, 315, 376, 405

Sowell, Thomas, 248, 334, 389

Spangler, David, 136, 143, 212, 221, 238, 250, 278, 320, 333, 352, 360, 379, 391, 438, 447

special creation, 12, 85, 86, 185, 268, 270, 495

special revelation, 34, 35, 36, 37, 38, 45, 62, 63, 84, 86, 108, 109, 133, 135, 149, 153, 162, 182, 183, 184, 187, 214–15, 219, 356, 357, 363, 465, 468, 483, 489, 495

Spencer, Herbert, 276, 311, 431, 445–46

Spinoza, Benedict de, 286

Spirkin, Alexander, 205, 220

spontaneous generation, 18, 95, 108, 119, 185–86, 271–2, 275, 278, 464, 496

Stacey, Vivienne, 322, 333

Stalin, Joseph, 39, 101, 102, 110, 111, 113, 116, 117, 120, 220, 235, 239, 302, 332, 347, 375, 431, 434, 446, 477, 480

Stanmeyer, William, 326, 333

Stark, Rodney, 94, 204, 220, 328, 333, 416, 422, 447, 477, 479

Star Wars, 25, 30, 128

state capitalism, 103, 117, 118, 496

Stenger, Victor J., 89, 95, 272, 278, 432, 433, 446

Stephens, Mitchell, 163, 171, 291, 303, 478

Stonestreet, John, 5, 24, 314, 360, 477

Storer, Morris B., 96, 220, 232, 249, 359, 360, 392

Stowe, Harriet Beecher, 383

Sufi Islam, 58, 496

Sufism, 58, 141, 215

Sunni Islam, 57, 214, 496